Motif®
Debugging and Performance Tuning

Douglas A. Young

Silicon Graphics, Inc.
Mountain View, CA

P T R Prentice Hall
Englewood Cliffs, New Jersey 07632

Library of Congress Cataloging-in-Publication Data

Young, Douglas A.

Motif debugging and performance tuning / Douglas A. Young.

p. cm.

Includes bibliographical references and index.

ISBN 0-13-147984-9 (alk. paper)

1. X Window System (Computer system) 2. Motif (Computer file)

I. Title.

QA76.76.W56Y65 1995

005.1'4--dc20 94-18449

CIP

Editorial/production supervision: *Jane Bonnell*
Cover design: *Jeannette Jacobs*
Cover art: *Stockworks © Rob Colvin*
Manufacturing manager: *Alexis R. Heydt*
Acquisitions editor: *Gregory G. Doench*

Prentice-Hall, Inc.
A Paramount Communications Company
Englewood Cliffs, New Jersey 07632

The publisher offers discounts on this book when ordered in bulk quantities.
For more information, contact: Corporate Sales Department, P T R Prentice Hall,
113 Sylvan Ave., Englewood Cliffs, NJ 07632.
Phone (201) 592-2863 Fax (201) 592-2249

Text printed on recycled paper.

Printed in the United States of America

10 9 8 7 6 5 4 3 2 1

ISBN 0-13-147984-9

Prentice-Hall International (UK) Limited, *London*
Prentice-Hall of Australia Pty. Limited, *Sydney*
Prentice-Hall Canada Inc., *Toronto*
Prentice-Hall Hispanoamericana, S.A., *Mexico*
Prentice-Hall of India Private Limited, *New Delhi*
Prentice-Hall of Japan, Inc., *Tokyo*
Simon & Schuster Asia Pte. Ltd., *Singapore*
Editora Prentice-Hall do Brasil, Ltda., *Rio de Janeiro*

Contents

Preface

Not long ago, X and Motif applications were mostly distributed among other X programmers, who were usually forgiving about the quality of these programs. Much of the X community was in a learning mode, and many programmers were happy if they could produce an application that worked, more or less. Today, X applications are being written for the commercial marketplace, and standards of excellence have been raised considerably. Users expect applications to be sophisticated, visually appealing, easy-to-use, and most of all, to exhibit no obvious defects. However, the complexity of X and Motif applications can make this quality hard to achieve. Debugging interactive graphics programs can be particularly difficult.

The increasing complexity and sophistication of graphical interfaces also provides other challenges. Each new feature has a cost, and programs with graphical interfaces seem to have grown larger and slower over time. It is often difficult to provide the features users demand without sacrificing performance.

Although information about how to write Motif and X applications is readily available, techniques for developing robust programs that have good performance are less widely known. The primary goal of this book is to describe and demonstrate *techniques* that you can apply to find bugs or improve performance. This book also contains many examples of specific types of bugs that commonly occur in Motif applications, and examines specific types of performance problems. This book also describes some of the readily-available tools that can help programmers understand and improve Motif programs.

This book is meant for readers who are somewhat familiar with Motif, or are in the process of learning Motif, and is not an introduction to X or Motif programming. You should either be familiar with basic X/Xt/Motif programming techniques or be ready to refer to other sources for any background information you may need.

This book consists of two logical sections. Chapters 1 through 6 discuss tools and techniques for debugging X and Motif applications. Chapters 7 through 12 discuss ways to improve the performance of Motif applications. Each topic in this book has been chosen because it relates directly to Motif and X programming. General debugging and performance tuning techniques are intentionally neglected because this information is available elsewhere. Therefore, this book contains no examples of bugs caused by off-by-one errors, unterminated while loops, or other common programming errors. There are also no examples of improving performance by unwinding loops or traversing multi-dimensional arrays in the most efficient order. Instead, the material focuses on bugs and performance issues that relate to the unique characteristics of Motif applications.

The examples in this book come from several sources. Some are contrived examples written specifically to illustrate a point, although these examples are almost always inspired by some real-life program. Other examples demonstrate problems that Motif programmers seem to encounter frequently. Still other examples were suggested by problems discussed on the various X news groups.

Several of the examples are taken from my earlier book, *The X Window System: Programming and Applications with Xt, Second Motif Edition*. All debugging and performance discussions stand on their own, and there is no assumption that you have read the earlier book. However, the examples from *The X Window System* are useful for several reasons. In particular, I wanted to avoid creating programs that were deliberately contrived to have bugs or performance problems which I could then "fix." The examples in this earlier book were written to provide good examples that were bug-free and reasonably efficient. The challenge is to show how these programs could be made more efficient and more robust.

All examples in this book are written in ANSI C, using Motif 1.2 and X11R5. The programs were tested on Silicon Graphics, Hewlett-Packard, and Sun workstations and should be reasonably applicable to any X/Motif environment. The source code for all examples is available for those who would like to experiment further with the ideas in this book. See the appendix on page 563 for details.

Acknowledgments

Many people helped make this book better by reviewing early drafts of the material, providing ideas and inspiration, and also by creating and finding bugs and performance problems in all sorts of programs. Steve Mikes originally started me thinking about debugging when he asked me to write an article about the subject for the *X Journal*. Some of the discussions in this book are expansions on the ideas presented in the resulting article, which appeared in the March 1993 "Testing & Debugging" issue. Donna Converse, Oliver Jones, and Ken Lee also influenced my thoughts about debugging when we participated in a debugging panel session at Xhibition '93.

Dave Bouvier, Kirk Erickson, Marty Itzowitz, Oliver Jones, Ken Lee, Michael Portuesi, Kim Rachmeler, Jerry Smith, Pete Sullivan, and Joel Tessler all offered comments that helped improve this material. I owe a special thanks to Roger Chickering, who allowed me to steal his idea for the `maptime` program described in Chapter 8. This program is a simplified version of Roger's original `stime`.

And of course, I must thank the many people who contributed unknowingly, directly or indirectly, to the examples in this book. Some contributed by asking for help with buggy or poorly performing programs, which ultimately provided inspiration for some of the examples in this book. Because these problems were real, the examples derived from them should be valuable to everyone. Others helped by pointing out bugs and performance problems in my own code. I hope I have partially returned the favor by sharing my own mistakes and the corresponding solutions with others.

Douglas A. Young

1

Introduction to Debugging Motif Applications

In an ideal world, a program would be designed, the code would be written, and the resulting application would run exactly as intended with no further effort. Unfortunately, in the real world, few programs run correctly the first time. It is almost inevitable that a program of any reasonable size will exhibit defects, called *bugs*, of one type or another. Most programs contain some number of bugs even when they are released as products.

The first part of this book discusses bugs that commonly occur in Motif programs and explores techniques for preventing and fixing them. Although Motif applications have much in common with other C-based programs, Motif programs also have unique characteristics that present interesting challenges to programmers. Instead of focusing on common algorithmic bugs, typos, and other errors that might be found in any program, this book concentrates on those aspects of debugging that are unique, or particularly troublesome, in X and Motif applications. The goal is to show how these bugs might occur so they can be anticipated and avoided, and to show how they can be identified and fixed, if necessary.

This chapter introduces Motif debugging by exploring some reasons why bugs occur within the context of a Motif application.

1.1 What are Bugs and What Causes Them?

A bug is any defect that keeps a program from performing the user's intended task. According to legend, the term "bug" was coined when an early computer suffered a breakdown. The problem was traced to a moth caught in the hardware.[1] Programmers still talk about bugs as if they were living organisms: "a bug got into my program," or "I ran into three bugs", or the ever-popular "there was a bug in the last release, but it seems to have gone away now". Of course, bugs do not just randomly "get into" programs, and they don't just go away. They are the result of some type of error made by the engineers developing the software. The tendency to think of bugs as living things is a consequence of the complexity of many contemporary software systems, and the inability of an individual programmer to comprehend an entire system.

One book that addresses debugging [Thielen92] tries to strip away the mystique that sometimes surrounds bugs by pointing out that bugs appear in code, not through any magic, but because some programmer types in faulty code, plain and simple. It is certainly true that bugs are simply errors introduced by programmers. Anyone who has spent any time programming will be thoroughly familiar with the arithmetic and logic errors, oversights, and typos that everyone makes when writing code.

However, the picture of a single programmer typing errors into a program is only part of the story, particularly with respect to the complex software systems common today. A programmer developing a small stand-alone program that implements a sorting algorithm (perhaps as a homework assignment) has little doubt about the ultimate source of any errors that appear in the program. But few contemporary programs are written entirely by one programmer. Even the simplest program relies heavily on underlying software, from the compilers, linkers, and assemblers used to create the executable, to the operating system on which the program runs. And of course, most programs use at least one, and possibly dozens, of libraries that usually are written and maintained by someone else.

In many software systems, programs are more like glue that holds together libraries and other pre-existing software modules than the kind of programs

[1] While this is an interesting and amusing story, there is evidence that the term "bug" was used to refer to errors or failure conditions even before computers were invented.

demonstrated in books on algorithms. The programmer's job is to tie together existing functions and modules to create new large-scale systems. X and Motif provide a perfect example. With just a few lines of code, a programmer can create a program that provides a graphical user interface and supports complex features such as inter-application communication, internationalization, and user customization. A seemingly simple, 100 line Motif program controls hundreds of thousands of lines of code in the libraries beneath it.

When writing such programs, a programmer is largely at the mercy of the lower level libraries and software systems on which the program depends. Because these libraries and other parts of the system tend to be extremely large and complex, few programmers can possibly understand all the software they control in a program. Often, the underlying platform is constantly shifting as new versions of libraries, operating systems, and so on, are released. Bugs are fixed and new features added to compilers, libraries, and even the underlying hardware, creating an ever-shifting base on which contemporary programs are built.

X adds some interesting wrinkles to this picture. Once an X-based program has been delivered, a user can easily run the software in environments in which the software has never been tested. X makes it possible to display a program on completely different hardware, using a different implementation of the X server from that with which the program was tested. As a practical matter, few programmers are able to test a program on all the systems that support X.

X also allows users to switch window managers at will, even while a program is running. Even on a targeted system, end-users can radically alter the environment in which the program operates. Particularly with Motif applications, users can customize programs by changing resources. Colors, fonts, window sizes, and even the language of the character set used to display text can be changed easily by any end-user. In such a shifting environment, bugs sometimes do just *seem* to appear. They don't, of course, and one of the goals of this book is to suggest ways to keep bugs from catching us by surprise.

A Real-life Example

Consider an example of a bug that "just appeared." A project I worked on encountered a strange problem with a large Motif-based software system we had developed. A customer reported that the system consistently died after reporting an X error. The X error indicated that the program was calling `XClearArea()` with a value of `0xfffffe` as a width parameter. The customer rightfully stated that this was an illegal value for a `ClearArea` request and asked us to fix our software. As we looked into the problem, we found that our system was indeed issuing the erroneous request. However, the program did not exit, or even report an error, in our environment.

With further investigation, we discovered that the error only occurred when the program was displayed on a specific system from another vendor. Although the X protocol specifies that this value is out of range, our server did not reject the value, but simply ignored it. Our server was based on the MIT sample server, which allows this value to pass without generating an error. Because most X implementations are based on the MIT sample server, every server we tried worked fine, except the server on the system the customer was trying to use. The server that detected the error took the protocol specification more literally and generated an error. To further complicate the issue, the source of the erroneous value turned out to be deep in the version of the Motif library on which our product was built. A simple logic error using unsigned arithmetic converted what should have been a negative number (which would have been ignored) to the large value used as an argument to `XClearArea()`. By the time we encountered the problem, the bug had already been found and fixed in a more recent release of Motif.

So, we had a situation in which the code we wrote ourselves did not contain an error (not this one, anyway!). One release of Motif did indeed contain a bug, the result of a simple programmer error. However, this Motif error was not detected, by us or the OSF, because of another (rather benign) error in almost everyone's X server. To us, this bug clearly seemed to just appear out of nowhere. No reasonable amount of testing would have caught this error in our product before it occurred, because it is unlikely that we would have tested the specific vendor's hardware that revealed the problem. We could have inspected the X protocol traffic by hand, of course. However, from a practical standpoint, trying to out-guess the X server's treatment of the values in each of thousands of requests would be infeasible.

The complexity and interconnectivity of layers of software present in today's systems virtually ensure that bugs will appear in even the most carefully written code. It is possible for even the most innocuous change or "improvement" made to one part of a large program to break another part of the application. Bug fixes, improvements in efficiency, and new features all change the way the software behaves, and unexpected problems are almost certain to occur, even if your code is written perfectly.

A Hypothetical Example

Changing requirements, miscommunication between members of a team, poor documentation, or incomplete specifications can also be sources of many bugs. Because software often evolves over time, it is common for functions and modules to be used for purposes they were not originally designed to support. For example, suppose one programmer, who we will call Programmer A, writes a callback function that can be installed in an XmTextField widget to perform file name completion. The function allows the user to enter a file name by typing a partial file name followed by a special completion character. The completion character can be specified as client data when the callback is registered. Such a function could be written like this, assuming the existence of an external function that returns a completed file name when given an incomplete name:

```
/***************************************************
 * CompleteFileCallback.c: Complete a file name.
 ***************************************************/
#include <Xm/Xm.h>
#include <Xm/TextF.h>

/*
 * Replace the contents of the text field with the
 * complete name of a file that matches the current text.
 */

extern char *GetCompleteFileName ( char * );

void CompleteFileCallback ( Widget    w,
                            XtPointer clientData,
                            XtPointer callData )
{
    XmTextVerifyCallbackStruct *cbs =
                ( XmTextVerifyCallbackStruct * ) callData;
    char completionChar = ( char ) clientData;

    if ( cbs->text->ptr &&
         cbs->text->ptr[0] == completionChar )
    {
       char *str = XmTextFieldGetString ( w );
       XmTextFieldSetString ( w, GetCompleteFileName ( str ) );
    }
}
```

Because `CompleteFileCallback()` seems like a useful function, Programmer A might put it in a library, to allow others to use it. He might also provide a header file that declares the function, along with a brief explanation of its purpose. The header file might look like this:

```
/**********************************************
 * Utilities.h: Declarations for useful
 *              project-wide functions.
 **********************************************/

/*
 * Callback to complete the partial file name in a text
 * field. Specify completion character as client data.
 */

extern void CompleteFileCallback ( Widget, XtPointer, XtPointer );
```

So far, everything seems fine. We will assume the callback function has been tested and exhibits no obvious bugs. It is also good that the function has been identified as a useful utility that might be reused elsewhere. Maintaining a collection of reusable, well-tested functions is one way to reduce bugs.

However, consider what could go wrong if another programmer, Programmer B, happens to browse through the code and discovers the function description and declaration in a header file at some later time. Programmer B knows that there have been many requests to enhance the system to allow a partial file name to be completed and accepted automatically when the user hits the <RETURN> key. (The current implementation requires the user to type a space to complete the name, and the <RETURN> key to enter it.) Although Programmer B isn't sure where to look to find the source to the function, the comment seems clear enough. A quick check shows that this function is already being used successfully elsewhere in the system to complete file names when a space is entered. So, Programmer B quickly modifies the program by installing `CompleteFileCallback()` as the `XmNactivateCallback` function for all text fields in the system. Based, on the comment in the header file, all she believes she needs to do is call `XtAddCallback()`, specifying a newline character as client data, like this:

```
/* Other code ... */
XtAddCallback ( fileTextWidget, XmNactivateCallback,
                CompleteFileCallback, '\n' );
```

Hopefully, Programmer B tests this new feature, because there are several problems. The first will become evident the first time a user types a <RETURN> key. The program is quite likely to crash with a core dump! The reason is simple. The callback function was originally designed to be used as an `XmNmodifyVerify` callback, but is registered in this example as an `XmNactivateCallback` callback function. The XmTextField widget's `XmNmodifyVerify` callbacks receive a call data structure of type `XmTextVerifyCallbackStruct`, as expected by the `CompleteFile-Callback()` function. However, `XmNactivateCallback` functions are passed a structure of type `XmAnyCallbackStruct`, which does not have the fields referenced in the `CompleteFileCallback()` function. Although the programmer might get lucky, the odds are high that attempting to dereference these pointers in the function will cause the program to crash.

Given this situation, Programmer B is likely to file a bug report with Programmer A, claiming that Programmer A's function causes a core dump. Programmer A, on the other hand, will probably reply that this function has been functioning perfectly for several years, has had heavy use, and cannot possibly be the source of the problem.

On the premise that bugs don't "just happen" and are directly caused by a programmer's error, who caused this bug? The bug was caused by both, and arguably neither. Programmer B is perhaps the most guilty because she called a function that she did not completely understand. Programmer A, on the other hand was not entirely clear in the comments provided as documentation. The limitations of the function were not clearly spelled out. In addition, the function, which was made available for general use, did not guard against misuse in any way. From another perspective, neither wrote any bad code. Programmer A wrote a function that worked correctly when used as intended. Programmer B's code would have worked fine, if only the function really did what she expected it to do. The bug occurred because of a lack of communication and understanding.

Consider another problem that could occur with this function. Suppose that this time Programmer B uses the function to add file name completion to all uses of the Motif XmFileSelectionBox dialog. She properly adds the function as an `XmNmodifyVerifyCallback` with the XmFileSelectionBox widget's text widget, tests the results and everything works correctly.

However, one day, long after the project has been completed, users begin to experience crashes when using the file selection dialogs. The only clue is that a new release of Motif has recently been installed on the system. Because shared libraries allow existing applications to bind dynamically with new libraries, the program is using a new Motif library rather than the one it was tested against. The potential problem in this hypothetical case is that the Motif XmFileSelectionBox widget has a conditional preprocessor statement (an `ifdef`) that controls whether the widget creates an XmTextField widget or an XmText widget. If the new library was configured to use the XmText widget, the `CompleteFileCallback()` function could fail because it calls functions that assume they are being passed an XmTextField widget.

Who is responsible for this bug? Programmer B clearly isn't because she used the function correctly, as it was designed to be used. It could be argued that Programmer A is again somewhat guilty for not guarding his function against possible runtime errors, but this situation is not one that could be reasonably anticipated. The programmer who created and released the new version of Motif could be at fault, but he or she probably had a good reason for changing the default behavior of the XmFileSelectionBox widget. Even if a warning had been issued about the change to Motif, what are the chances that anyone would remember that a particular callback in a long completed project had an implicit assumption about the type of the text widget used in an XmFile-SelectionBox widget? Perhaps the user could be blamed for installing a new version of Motif on his or her system?

Purists may argue that such problems arise because of poor software engineering discipline, and that such scenarios should never occur. Ideally, all software interfaces and behavior should be fully specified, changes and evolution carefully controlled, and so on. Unfortunately, that is not how things work in reality, in spite of best efforts. This book is written to address the practical aspects of software development, not theoretical goals. We all call functions that we have not written ourselves with little confirmation of what the function really does. It would be impossible to meet schedule demands if we explored every line of code, and chased down every possible hidden assumption buried in every system call and library function used in our code. How many programmers are certain they understand exactly what `printf()` does in all cases? `realloc()`? `execve()`?

The point of this discussion is not to relieve developers from responsibility for errors that appear in their programs, of course. In fact, the opposite is true. Besides being responsible for the bugs we all enter directly into our code, programmers who leverage large software systems and libraries like X and Motif must continually broaden their scope and increase their understanding of all the software involved. It is not enough to prevent, or at least find and eliminate, logic and other bugs that we ourselves type into our programs. We must be able to anticipate and fix, or at least work around, problems that occur or could possibly occur in the system as a whole.

1.2 Debugging: Art, Craft, or Science?

Debugging, like software development and many other engineering disciplines, is a craft that involves aspects of both art and science. Debugging can be considered a science in that there are some known steps and techniques that can be applied. Like many sciences, the primary activity in any successful debugging effort involves the systematic gathering of data.

However, most software systems are so complex that most programmers who are particularly good at debugging find many opportunities to demonstrate a degree of creativity normally associated with more artistic endeavors. Without creative approaches, leaps of logic, and other unquantifiable techniques, many debugging efforts would collapse under the weight of the information that must be gathered. In this respect, debugging is like solving a mystery. The programmer acts as a detective who must sift through complex and sometimes conflicting evidence to pursue the areas most likely to yield a solution.

As in any mystery, isolating a bug requires a programmer to gather as many relevant facts as possible. Programmers who have knowledge in the subject to which the bug is related have a definite advantage when it comes to debugging. Often, what seems like a leap of logic is simply a process of drawing on experience and specific domain knowledge to zero in on relevant details quickly. Therefore, when working with bugs in Motif applications, time spent learning about X, Xt, and Motif is time well spent. Several books on these topics are recommended later in this chapter, although practical experience cannot be replaced.

There are several basic techniques that can be applied to the process of finding any bug. The basis of any strategy should be the scientific method, which, adapted somewhat for debugging, might be stated as:

1. Identify a bug.

2. Gather data about the bug.

3. Form a theory about the cause of the bug.

4. Devise an experiment to test the theory.

5. If the theory is correct, move on to fixing the bug, otherwise go back to step 2 or 3, as needed, to form a new theory.

6. Form a theory about how the bug should be fixed.

7. Fix the bug.

8. Test that the bug fix works correctly. If not, go back to step 6, or even step 2, as needed.

The step of identifying a bug may come as the result of testing during the development stage, the formal testing that is often done before releasing a piece of software to others, or because of a problem reported by a user. Testing is, of course, worthy of an entire discussion in its own right, but is beyond the scope of this book.

The steps of forming and testing a theory is where both creativity and knowledge come into play. One of the first steps is to try to reproduce the bug, and to narrow the problem as much as possible. For most programs, the true cause of any given bug may not be at all clear at first. A bug may require a long sequence of specific user actions to duplicate. In the worst case, the user may not even remember exactly what steps lead up to the bug. Until a bug can be reproduced at will, it is extremely difficult to determine the cause of the bug.

Once a bug can be reproduced reliably, the next step is prune the observed data until the range of possibilities has been reduced to a manageable size. For example, imagine a user who reports "I was using your program while logged into my workstation from home, using my X terminal. I brought up the Open File dialog and opened a file, modified some data, and saved the file. Then I clicked on the Update button and the program crashed." Although this report is very specific about the steps that led up to the error, it is necessary to isolate the causes of the bug further before trying to fix the bug.

For example, does the bug occur every time the user clicks on the Update button, or only after the sequence described in the report? Does it matter that the file was saved, or only that a new file was loaded? Does the problem occur every time a file is read, or only if the described actions are performed immediately after starting the program? Perhaps the problem only occurs after the program has been running for a few hours. And what exactly does the report mean by "modified some data?" In an X environment, there are endless other questions that could be asked. For example, does the error occur only when running on a remote X terminal, or is that information irrelevant? Does the error occur when the user's .Xdefaults file is present, only when the `RESOURCE_MANAGER` property is set by xrdb, only when a certain font is used? The answers to these questions could all potentially affect the program's behavior in some way. Fortunately, it is usually possible to narrow the range of possibilities quickly.

Often, particularly when receiving bug reports from informal testing, such as actual use, the bug reports contain only a small amount of useful information. For example, consider the original `CompleteFileCallback()` problem discussed in the previous section. If Programmer B files a bug report that is like many I (and probably you) have seen, the bug report is likely to say something like "`CompleteFileCallback()` core dumps when trying to complete file name." Before Programmer A can begin to form a hypothesis, more information is needed. When does the bug happen? Only in Programmer B's program? Only when a specific character is typed?

What the bug report does not say may also be important. For example, sometimes it is equally useful to know when the bug does *not* occur. There may be other missing information that the report overlooked. For example, was the program running in the French locale? Was the file being loaded on an NFS-mounted file system? Was the system out of disk space?

One technique that is useful when trying to fix bugs is to try to reproduce the problem in a small, easily understood program. All too often, bugs in a large program are too difficult to understand because of the large number of variables involved.

There are two advantages to trying to reproduce a bug with a small program. First, it is a good way to be sure you understand the exact nature of the bug. If you can write a program that does nothing but demonstrate the bug easily and reproducibly, then steps 1 though 5, as listed above, are completed. The simple example can also serve as a test case for any proposed fixes.

Second, if you have large program, and you believe your bug is caused by someone else's code (a library, like X or Motif), your case will be more believable if you can demonstrate the bug with a simple example. Few people will be willing to look through 100,000 lines of code to understand the cause of the bug. It can also be very hard to prove that the bug isn't caused by your program. As we will see, it is easy to introduce bugs in an application that appear, on the surface, to be bugs in underlying libraries like Motif. The simpler the test case, the more likely the bug will be accepted and fixed by whoever is responsible.

1.3 General C Programming and Bugs

Although X and Motif have a major impact on the design, structure, and implementation of any application, real applications consist of more than just user interface. Furthermore, because Motif programs are generally written in C or C++, they are susceptible to the same programmer errors that appear in any program. When writing in C, memory-related problems, pointer misuse, and array overruns are common. In addition, programmers inevitably make logic and algorithmic errors that must be identified and fixed before a program can run correctly, no matter what language or libraries they use.

In spite of the focus of this book, most of the errors programmers encounter while developing Motif applications have little to do with X or Motif. General debugging skills are an important part of programming with Motif, just as they are with any type of programming. There are several good sources of information for those who would like to learn more about general techniques for debugging and guarding against bugs. The following books may be useful starting places:

Books that discuss basic debugging

Maguire, Steve, *Writing Solid Code*, Microsoft Press, 1993.

McConnell, Steve, *Code Complete*, Microsoft Press, 1993.

Stitt, Martin, *Debugging: Creative Techniques and Tools for Software Repair*, John Wiley, 1992.

Ward, Robert, *A Programmer's Introduction to Debugging C, R & D Publications, 1989.*

1.4 The Challenge of Debugging Motif Programs

Although the books listed in the previous section contain information that all programmers should find useful, they focus mainly on general C programming, errors commonly made when writing loops, dereferencing pointers, assigning values, and so on. While all programs have these characteristics, Motif programs have many unique aspects. The following sections explore a few of the architectural characteristics of Motif applications that make debugging particularly challenging.

Multi-Process Event-Driven Systems

Every Motif application is part of a multi-process system, consisting of at least the X server and the client application. Usually, a window manager process is also involved. Therefore, the process we think of as the "application" is really just one small part of the complete system. The application both controls and is controlled by the other processes by initiating and reacting to interprocess communication. Figure 1.1 shows how these different processes fit together.

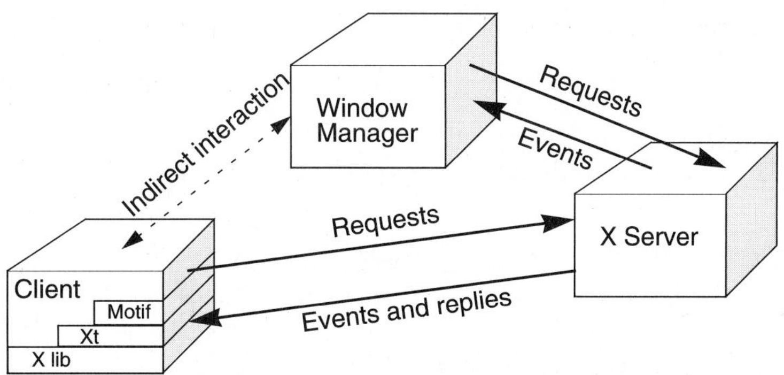

Figure 1.1 Multi-process architecture of an X application.

All Motif applications send requests to, and receive events from, the X server. Some window manipulation requests are not handled directly by the X server, but are instead forwarded to the window manager. Although the window manager relies on the X server to perform all operations, it actively participates in the program's user interface. The window manager indirectly controls the size and position of an application's windows and even determines whether each window is visible on the screen.

Of course, introducing additional clients may produce a much more complex architecture than the scenario shown in Figure 1.1. All processes, including the X server and the window manager run asynchronously with respect to each other. Besides sharing the X server and the window manager, multiple clients may share files or other data, and compete for operating system and other system resources.

The Complexity of Interactive Graphical Interfaces

Motif programs, like all interactive programs with graphical user interfaces, are inherently more complex than similar non-interactive programs even if we ignore the multi-process environment. Consider, for example, a simple function whose purpose is to obtain a user's name and address. In a non-windowing environment, this function might be written like this:

```
void GetNameAndAddress ( char *nameReturn, char *addrReturn )
{
    printf ( "Enter your name: " );
    scanf ( "%s", nameReturn );
    printf ( "Enter your address: " );
    scanf ( "%s", addrReturn );
}
```

The function is simple, straightforward, and gets the job done. Once, this function would have even been considered "interactive", because it requires the user to enter input while the program is running. However, character-based interfaces are not "user friendly", nor really interactive by current standards. There is no room for error in entering the information. The user cannot edit the text, make corrections once the data has been entered, or request help or additional information about what is required. The user does not "interact" with the system so much as "respond" to questions posed by the application.

Figure 1.2 shows an example of how a contemporary program with a graphical user interface might provide this same basic functionality. This component doesn't exist, but we can imagine how a user might expect such a dialog to behave in a contemporary application.

It is obvious that this implementation is more visual than the function `GetNameAndAdress()`, but there is much more here than is immediately obvious. Programmers who expect the task of creating a graphical interface to add only a small amount of complexity to that of a pre-GUI equivalent will be shocked at the burden placed on the implementor of this hypothetical dialog. This dialog allows the user to enter a name and an address, as before. However, the user can now edit the name and address as often as needed. The information can be cut from another window and pasted into the dialog text fields. Alternately, the information can be entered by dragging and dropping one of several data representations into the dialog. For example, the user could drag an icon that represents the user in another application and drop it on the dialog, using Motif's drag and drop protocol.

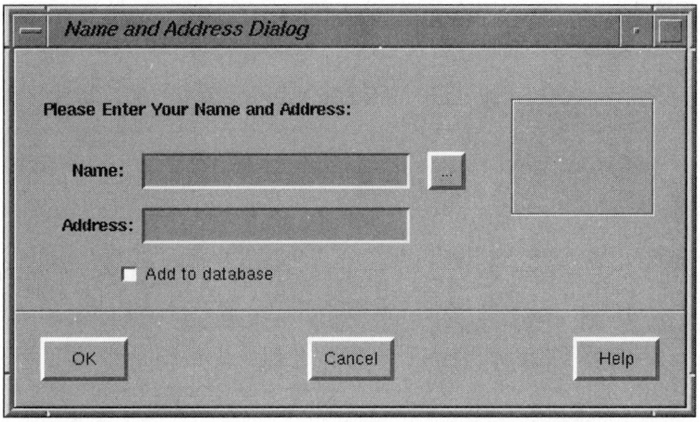

Figure 1.2 A hypothetical name and address dialog.

Motif provides some of this functionality automatically, but other features of this hypothetical dialog are the responsibility of the program. For example, the user can decide to cancel the entire operation, which was not something supported at all by the non-GUI version. The user should be able to click on the Help button to learn how to use the dialog, what information needs to be entered, and so on. The button labeled with an ellipsis, to the right of the Name field can be clicked to bring up a scrolling list of known names and addresses, which presumably are stored in a database somewhere. Selecting the "Add to database" button indicates that a newly entered name should be added to this database for future use. Of course, the Name field also supports automatic completion of names already in the database, and once a recognized name has been entered, the dialog updates the address field automatically. The box in the upper right corner displays an image (a photograph) associated with a name, once the user enters a recognized name. Double clicking on the image area brings up an import tool that allows the user to provide an image for newly entered names. Alternately, a new image can be added by dropping an existing image on the image area.

The dialog described here is a completely hypothetical design. Although quite powerful, this imaginary dialog is not unlike those provided by many existing applications today. Consider the demands the complexity of this functionality compared to the pre-GUI implementation shown earlier. And of course, we are discussing one dialog – a small portion of a complete program! It is no wonder that designing and implementing a modern application with a graphical user interface is extremely challenging, requires more time and effort, and produces many bugs.

It is also easy to see how debugging such a program could be a considerable challenge. The original non-GUI function had only seven lines of code. The dialog described above involves multiple processes, drag and drop protocols, help systems, databases, image manipulation and so on.

Other Issues

Besides the complexity of modern applications, there are some pragmatic issues that arise when working with Motif. When writing a Motif application, a programmer is working with at least three libraries, each of which has its own rules, interfaces, and idiosyncracies. As discussed earlier, programmers can easily introduce bugs because of misunderstandings about how one or more of these libraries work.

Obviously, it is important to pass the correct number and type of arguments to all X, Xt and Motif functions, and also to understand what each function does and when each should and should not be used. It is also necessary to know what values each function returns and how return values should be handled. Some functions have no return value, but others return status information that should be checked. Some functions return pointers to dynamically allocated memory that should be freed when the memory is no longer needed. Still other functions return pointers to private data that should not be freed.

It is also important to understand the underlying architecture of all three libraries. Often, programmers make errors because of mistaken assumptions about how the system works. It is important to understand the large-scale architecture of the X environment, as described on page 13, but there are smaller details of equal importance. For example, Xt destroys widgets in two phases. The first marks the widget as destroyed, while the second phase actually frees the memory associated with a widget. The second phase can take place at a later time, possibly after additional callbacks and event handlers have been called. It is easy for programs to contain very subtle bugs, based on a misunderstanding or ignorance of such features.

Without a solid understanding of how these characteristics affect the way an application must be written, a programmer may develop an unsound architecture that may result in an inherently buggy program.

1.5 A Classic Beginner's Bug

Consider, for example, the following program, which has a simple, classic bug that will be obvious to most programmers with some experience with X, but that may be baffling to someone unacquainted with X's architecture. This program is supposed to display a window that contains a line drawn between each top and bottom corner to display a crude "X". The program initializes Xt and creates a Motif XmDrawingArea widget in which to display the "X". After realizing the widgets to place the window on the screen, the program determines the size of the window and calls some Xlib drawing functions to draw the figure in the XmDrawingArea widget's window.

```
/**********************************************
 * xlogobug.c: A buggy program
 **********************************************/
#include <Xm/Xm.h>
#include <Xm/DrawingA.h>

void main ( int argc, char **argv )
{
    Widget       shell, canvas;
    XtAppContext app;
    int          width, height;
    XGCValues    values;
    GC           gc;

   /*
    * Initialize Xt and create a shell widget.
    */

    shell = XtAppInitialize ( &app, "Xlogobug", NULL, 0,
                              &argc, argv, NULL, NULL, 0 );

   /*
    * Create a drawing area widget in which to
    * display a pair of lines that form an X.
    */

    canvas = XtCreateManagedWidget ( "canvas",
                                     xmDrawingAreaWidgetClass,
                                     shell,
                                     NULL, 0 );

```

```
    /*
     * Realize all widgets so the drawing area widget's
     * window will exist and be displayed on the screen.
     */

     XtRealizeWidget ( shell );

    /*
     * Determine the size of the canvas widget to allow
     * the lines to be drawn. Also get the widget's
     * foreground color to use when creating a graphics
     * context, which is needed to draw the lines.
     */

     XtVaGetValues ( canvas,
                     XmNwidth,      &width,
                     XmNheight,     &height,
                     XmNforeground, &values.foreground,
                     NULL );

    /*
     * Create a GC using the widget's foreground color.
     */

     gc = XtGetGC ( canvas, GCForeground, &values );

    /*
     * Draw an X into the canvas widget's window, using the
     * widget's size to draw a line diagonally between
     * each corner.
     */

Bug! XDrawLine ( XtDisplay ( canvas ), XtWindow ( canvas ),
                 gc, 0, 0, width, height );

     XDrawLine ( XtDisplay ( canvas ), XtWindow ( canvas ),
                 gc, width, 0, 0, height );

    /*
     * Start handling events.
     */

     XtAppMainLoop ( app );
}
```

This program contains several bugs, but the most obvious one will quickly be discovered the first time the program is run. The lines drawn on the window simply do not appear because, at the time the calls to `XDrawLine()` are made, the window is almost certainly not displayed on the screen.

To make a window appear (by realizing the `shell` widget) a program sends a request to the X server, which eventually processes the request. If a window manager is running, X does not display the window, but instead sends a notification to the window manager that an application has requested a window to be mapped. Most window managers reparent the application's window in another window that adds various window manager decorations, and then eventually maps the window.

The communication between the application, the X server, and the window manager takes time, and the program will almost certainly have executed the remaining lines of code, which request the X server to draw lines in the window, before the window manager has had time to display the window. Figure 1.3 shows a greatly simplified timeline of the events and requests that flow between the application, the X server, and the window manager.

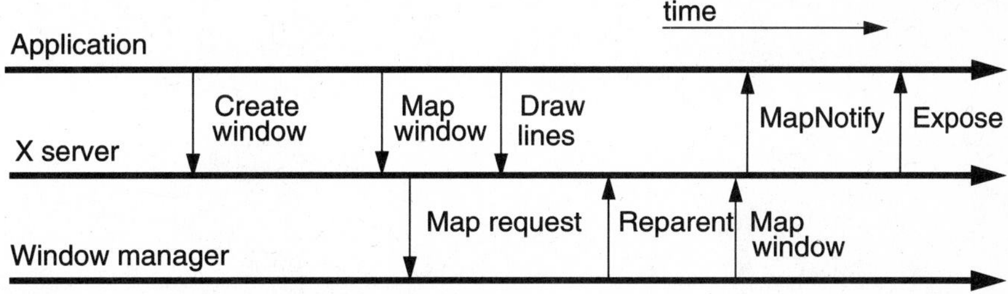

Figure 1.3 A timeline of application, server, and window manager traffic.

Because of the asynchronous interaction between the various processes, the window in this example will appear empty. (The lines will appear if this program is run with no window manager.)

For this example to have any chance of working, the program must be redesigned to use a callback function that is called when the window is exposed. `XDrawLine()` must be called in this callback to display the crossing lines.

Modifying the program in this way also fixes a second bug, which would show up the first time the original program is covered and then uncovered (if it worked at all, of course.) Because the program does not respond to `Expose` events by redrawing any damaged portions of the canvas window, the lines would not continue to be redisplayed, even if they did appear initially.

A version of `xlogobug` that fixes the problems described above is shown below. Notice that many parts of the program have been moved. Additions to the previous version are shown in a bold font. Although this version of `xlogobug` is more architecturally correct, there are still several bugs in this program, to be discussed later.

```
/**********************************************************
 * xlogobug.c: A buggy program, version 2 (Still buggy)
 **********************************************************/
#include <Xm/Xm.h>
#include <Xm/DrawingA.h>

GC  gc;

void ExposeCallback ( Widget     w,
                      XtPointer clientData,
                      XtPointer callData )
{
    int width, height;

   /*
    * Determine the size of the canvas widget to allow
    * the lines to be drawn.
    */

    XtVaGetValues ( w,
                    XmNwidth,  &width,
                    XmNheight, &height,
                    NULL );

   /*
    * Draw an X in the canvas widget's window, using the
    * widget's size to draw lines diagonally between corners.
    */

    XDrawLine ( XtDisplay ( w ), XtWindow ( w ), gc,
                0, 0, width, height);

    XDrawLine ( XtDisplay ( w ), XtWindow ( w ), gc,
                width, 0, 0, height);
}

void main ( int argc, char **argv )
{
    Widget       shell, canvas;
    XtAppContext app;
    XGCValues    values;
```

```
    /*
     * Initialize Xt and create a shell widget.
     */

     shell = XtAppInitialize ( &app, "Xlogohbug", NULL, 0,
                               &argc, argv, NULL, NULL, 0 );

    /*
     * Create a drawing area widget in which to
     * display a pair of lines that form an X.
     */

     canvas = XtCreateManagedWidget ( "canvas",
                                      xmDrawingAreaWidgetClass,
                                      shell, NULL, 0 );
    /*
     * Add a callback to be invoked when the contents of
     * the canvas widget should be drawn.
     */

     XtAddCallback ( canvas, XmNexposeCallback,
                     ExposeCallback, NULL );
    /*
     * Get the widget's foreground color to use when creating
     * a graphics context, which is needed to draw the lines.
     */

     XtVaGetValues ( canvas,
                     XmNforeground, &values.foreground,
                     NULL );
    /*
     * Create a GC using the widget's foreground color.
     */

     gc = XtGetGC ( canvas, GCForeground, &values );

    /*
     * Realize all widgets so the drawing area widget's
     * window will exist.
     */

     XtRealizeWidget ( shell );

    /*
     * Start handling events.
     */

     XtAppMainLoop ( app );
}
```

This program now responds to `Expose` events, which the X server sends any time the `canvas` widget's window needs to be redrawn. One `Expose` event will be sent after the window is initially mapped by the window manager, and the lines should appear. Unfortunately, there is still another bug in this program that prevents it from working correctly, and the lines do not appear where they should be drawn. Chapter 3 discusses the `xlogobug` program again and describes how to isolate and fix this bug.

The problem demonstrated by the `xlogobug` program is so fundamental that there is very little that can be done to debug it, although there are some tools and techniques that could be used to gather information that might lead to its solution. For example, `xscope`, discussed in the following chapter, could produce a trace of the traffic between the application, X server, and window manager. An experienced X programmer could use this information to deduce the sequence of events shown in Figure 1.3. However, most beginners, who are most likely to make this type of fundamental error, may have difficulty understanding the `xscope` output.

This example demonstrates a problem that is most easily avoided by developing a good understanding of the X Window System and the proper architectural model for Motif applications. Fortunately, there is no shortage of books, classes and educational materials that can help a beginner develop an approach that reduces the chances of making fundamental errors. Programmers should be sure that they have a thorough understanding of how to write Motif applications. Consulting a more experienced programmer can also be helpful when a program exhibits puzzling behavior. Additional time spent learning will more than pay off later in reduced time debugging and maintaining programs.

1.6 Learning More About X and Motif

Programmers who are just starting with Motif and X will find many useful introductory texts that can help explain the models presented by X and Motif. Experienced Motif programmers can benefit from reading tutorials as well, because debugging is easier if you have a wide range of experience. Reading about various techniques and looking at examples written by different programmers provides exposure to the many ways X and Motif can be used, and therefore provides information that can be used when debugging. The following are just a few suggestions:

X and Motif Tutorials

Jones, Oliver, *Introduction to the X Window System*, Prentice Hall, 1989.

George, Alistair, and Mark Riches, *Advanced Motif Programming*, Prentice Hall, 1994.

McMinds, Donald, *Mastering OSF/Motif Widgets*, Addison Wesley, 1993.

Young, Douglas, *The X Window System, Programming and Applications with Xt, Second OSF/Motif Edition*, Prentice Hall, 1994.

Young, Douglas, *Object-Oriented Programming with C++ and OSF/Motif*, Prentice Hall, 1992.

The books listed above, as well as many others, can help programmers understand the programming model X and Motif programs should follow, which is important when debugging applications. For serious debugging, programmers also need concise and authoritative reference materials. A great deal of information is available in on-line man pages. Each X, Xt, and Motif function and widget has a man page. Man pages are often the most convenient way to get precise, up-to-date information about function parameters, return values, error conditions, resources and resource types, related functions, and other details that programmers need.

In addition, the following reference books provide information that can be invaluable when developing and debugging applications. These books are updated with each new release of the corresponding library, so be sure to get the editions that match your X development environment.

X and Motif Reference Books

Scheifler, Robert, *X Window System*, DEC Press, 1992.

Asente, Paul, and Ralph Swick, *The X Window System Toolkit*, DEC Press, 1992.

Open Software Foundation, *OSF/Motif Programmers Reference*, Prentice Hall, 1994.

Open Software Foundation, *OSF/Motif Style Guide*, Prentice Hall, 1994.

There are also several publications dedicated to X that contain timely and supplemental material. These include:

The X Journal, SIGS Publications

The X Resource, O'Reilly and Associates

There is an active X community of programmers who interact using the Internet, which can also be an excellent source of information and assistance. There are news groups dedicated to X, Motif, Xt, as well as other toolkits. Programmers frequently use these bulletin boards to discuss bugs and other problems they may be facing. Lists of frequently asked questions (FAQ) are posted periodically on these groups. These lists are invaluable (and free) sources of commonly encountered bugs and solutions.

The news groups that relate to Motif include:

comp.windows.x

comp.windows.x.intrinsics

comp.windows.x.motif

1.7 Conclusion

This chapter provides some general background and explores a few of the reasons bugs occur, particularly in Motif and X applications. Some bugs are simply typos, logic errors, and so on, but others are more subtle and challenging. Like most modern, interactive programs, Motif applications tend to be complex. Many bugs occur because one or more features of X, Xt, or Motif are misunderstood. In addition to the normal problems caused by misusing or misunderstanding specific features, the architecture presented by X and Motif creates a challenge. Because all Motif applications are part of an asynchronous, multi-process, event-driven environment, a sound architectural design is a prerequisite for managing software quality.

Even when programs are correctly architected, bugs still occur. Fortunately, there are some specific techniques that have proven effective when working with X and Motif. It is also possible to list specific errors that are frequently made when working with the X libraries. It is useful to know about these common errors and to be able to employ some basic tools and techniques when finding and fixing bugs.

The first part of this book, Chapters 1 through 6, discusses some areas in which bugs commonly occur in Motif programs. Chapter 2 begins by discussing techniques and coding styles that can help prevent Motif-related bugs from occurring, or at least make bugs easier to find when they do occur. Chapter 3 describes some tools that can useful for isolating and identifying Motif and X-related bugs. Some of these tools are unique to Motif or X applications, while others may be useful when debugging any program.

Chapter 4 discusses the difficulties a programmer may face when trying to identify the source of various types of bugs and describes typical errors that may be encountered using Motif, Xlib, and Xt. Chapter 5 discusses issues related to dynamic memory allocation, which can cause significant problems for all Motif programs. Finally, Chapter 6 demonstrates ways to handle visual problems that can occur when creating a program's widget layout.

2

Avoiding Bugs

It is almost inevitable that any significant software system will have bugs. Programmers make mistakes, and even with the most careful testing, the best that can be achieved is to have no *known* bugs. Even if you write completely bug-free code, the odds are high that your software will exhibit problems at some point. Bugs may appear when you port the program to different hardware platforms, when you upgrade to newer libraries, compilers, or operating systems, or when displaying the program on a different X server. However, even if bugs cannot be eliminated completely, programmers can try to anticipate certain commonly-encountered types of bugs and plan to avoid them. Programmers can also write programs in a way that makes bugs easier to find and fix when they do occur.

One rule of thumb is that bugs discovered later in the lifecycle of a software product are more expensive, and often more difficult to fix than those caught earlier. As the size and complexity of a software system grows, bugs become harder to find, just due to the amount of code that must be examined. Once a bug is found, any change will require a great deal of testing, which takes time and effort. Of course, a bug discovered after you deliver a product to a customer can be extremely costly when you consider time spent investigating and understanding the bug, understanding the customer's environment, shipping fixes and updates, and so on.

Therefore, the best way to deal with bugs is to invest extra time during the early stages of a project to prevent bugs and to make it easier to find them when they do occur. Although this approach requires extra effort just at the point in a project where everyone is anxious to get something working quickly, the investment will pay off in time saved later.

This chapter discusses some ways to avoid and detect certain types of bugs that commonly occur in Motif applications.

2.1 Programming Defensively

One of the examples discussed in Chapter 1 involved a bug that could occur in a callback function that performs file name completion. The original function works fine when used as intended. However, software has a way of being used in unexpected situations. Other programmers, who may not fully understand what a function was designed to do, may stretch the function beyond its intended limits. Even if you are using code that you wrote yourself, you may not remember all the assumptions you made in the implementation.

One way to deal with such situations is to design the code to guard against misuse. There are several ways to program defensively, but the basic idea is to assume that any given piece of code will be misused at some point. Taking this viewpoint, we need to think about what could possibly go wrong, instead of considering only how a function should work when used correctly.

For example, the discussion of the `CompleteFileCallback()` function in Chapter 1 identifies several possible ways that misusing that function could introduce hard-to-identify bugs. However, most of the problems could have been avoided by programming defensively. One way to make the `CompleteFileCallback()` callback function more robust is to make sure it can handle all the situations in which the function is likely to be used. Another is to make sure the function doesn't cause a fatal error when it is used incorrectly. Still another approach is to help a programmer who misuses the function discover the error early.

Let's start by looking at how the `CompleteFileCallback()` function could be written to not dump core when used improperly. The following implementation takes advantage of the fact that all Motif callback functions are passed a call data structure whose first member reports the reason the callback was invoked. This implementation simply returns if the `reason` field of the call data structure is set to any value except `XmCR_MODIFYING_TEXT_VALUE`. This version of `CompleteFileCallback()` also uses a Motif convenience function, `XmIsTextField()`, to be sure the widget type is correct. In addition, the function is more careful about dereferencing the multi-level pointer in the call data structure. Each pointer is tested before each dereference to be sure the pointer is non-`NULL`. Here is the modified function:

```
/******************************************************
 * CompleteFileCallback.c: Complete a file name.
 ******************************************************/
#include <Xm/Xm.h>
#include <Xm/TextF.h>

/*
 * Replace the contents of the text field with the complete
 * name of a file that matches the current text.
 */

extern char *GetCompleteFileName ( char * );

void CompleteFileCallback ( Widget    w,
                            XtPointer clientData,
                            XtPointer callData )
{
    XmTextVerifyCallbackStruct *cbs =
                 ( XmTextVerifyCallbackStruct * ) callData;
    char completionChar = ( char ) clientData;

   /*
    * This function only works for modify verify callbacks
    * registered with XmTextField widgets!
    */

    if ( !( cbs &&
            cbs->reason == XmCR_MODIFYING_TEXT_VALUE &&
            XmIsTextField ( w ) ) )
        return;

    if ( cbs && cbs->text && cbs->text->ptr &&
         cbs->text->ptr[0] == completionChar )
    {
       char *str = XmTextFieldGetString ( w );
       XmTextFieldSetString ( w, GetCompleteFileName ( str ) );
    }
}
```

This modified function still doesn't work correctly for the situations discussed in Chapter 1, but at least it will no longer cause a fatal error. This implementation will simply cause programs that try to use it inappropriately to not work as intended. This is not a perfect solution, but at least it is an improvement. If the programmer doesn't discover that the function doesn't work as expected, users will suffer some minor inconvenience, but the program will still be usable.

Another approach is to try to make the function more general so it can handle a wider range of cases. The following implementation continues to perform the sanity checks introduced above, but expands the function to work with the XmText widget and to work as an `XmNactivateCallback`.

```
/*****************************************************
 * CompleteFileCallback.c: Complete a file name.
 *****************************************************/
#include <Xm/Xm.h>
#include <Xm/TextF.h>
#include <Xm/Text.h>

/*
 * Replace the contents of the text field with the complete
 * name of a file that matches the current text.
 */

extern char *GetCompleteFileName ( char * );

void CompleteFileCallback ( Widget    w,
                            XtPointer clientData,
                            XtPointer callData )
{
    XmTextVerifyCallbackStruct *cbs =
                  ( XmTextVerifyCallbackStruct * ) callData;
    char completionChar = ( char ) clientData;

   /*
    * Function only works with XmText and XmTextField widgets!
    */

    if ( !XmIsTextField ( w ) && !XmIsText ( w ) )
       return;

   /*
    * If the callback is a modifyverify callback, check
    * that the entered character is the completion character.
    * If the callback is an activate callback, just expand.
    */
```

```
    if ( cbs && cbs->reason == XmCR_MODIFYING_TEXT_VALUE &&
         cbs->text && cbs->text->ptr &&
         cbs->text->ptr[0] == completionChar )
    {
       char *str = XmTextGetString ( w );
       XmTextSetString ( w, GetCompleteFileName ( str ) );
    }
    else if ( cbs && cbs->reason == XmCR_ACTIVATE )
    {
       char *str = XmTextGetString ( w );
       XmTextSetString ( w, GetCompleteFileName ( str ) );
    }
}
```

This version of `CompleteFileCallback()` simply gives up if the specified widget is not a text field or text widget. However, this implementation takes advantage of the fact that Motif allows the XmText functions to be used with an XmTextField widget (but not vice-versa). By assuming an XmText widget, `CompleteFileCallback()` can work with either an XmText or XmTextField widget. Also, this version can be registered as an `XmNactivateCallback`. This implementation basically does what Programmer B expected in the original scenario described in Chapter 1.

There are several problems with this second approach, however. The biggest problem is that the function has grown considerably more complex. If the function was really intended to be used primarily with an XmTextField widget's `XmNmodifyVerifyCallback`, then the additional complexity of this implementation adds overhead and size to all programs, even when the new functionality is not needed. Also, the function handles more cases, but we cannot be sure we have thought of every case in which this function might be useful. So the original problem remains. Finally, because the function is now more complex and tries to handle more cases, the odds that there is a bug in this function itself has been greatly increased. Because the function is useful in more situations, there may be more ways to break it than there were in the original. This version looks safe, but so did the original implementation.

Passive and Aggressive Defensive Programming

Although the variations of `CompleteFileCallback()` described in the previous section do a better job of defending against misuse than the original, they both have one major flaw. They both fail silently when misused, which puts the burden on the caller to test carefully to be sure the function does what it is expected to do. Although testing should certainly be done, it would be more effective if the `CompleteFileCallback()` function could help programmers who use it (or abuse it) discover any errors as soon as possible.

What the previous implementations do might be called *passive defensive programming*. These functions protect themselves and their callers against fatal errors, but do it silently and unobtrusively. It is usually better if errors occur noisily and obviously, at least while a program is under development. One way to make errors more obvious is to practice a more aggressive style of defensive programming. For example, the following version of `CompleteFileCallback()` issues a warning message when any of the arguments are incorrect. For simplicity, this example reverts to the limitation of working with the `XmNmodifyVerifyCallback`, although both XmText and XmTextField widgets are supported.

```
/**************************************************
 * CompleteFileCallback.c: Complete a file name.
 **************************************************/
#include <Xm/Xm.h>
#include <Xm/TextF.h>
#include <Xm/Text.h>

/*
 * Replace the contents of a text field with the complete
 * name of a file that matches the current text.
 */

extern char *GetCompleteFileName ( char * );

void CompleteFileCallback ( Widget    w,
                            XtPointer clientData,
                            XtPointer callData )
{
    XmTextVerifyCallbackStruct *cbs =
                 ( XmTextVerifyCallbackStruct * ) callData;
    char completionChar = ( char ) clientData;
   /*
    * This function only works for modify verify callbacks
    * registered with XmText and XmTextField widgets!
    */
    if ( !cbs || cbs->reason != XmCR_MODIFYING_TEXT_VALUE )
    {
        fprintf ( stderr, "%s %s",
                  "CompleteFileName must be called",
                  "as a ModifyVerifyCallback" );
        return;
    }
```

```
    if ( !XmIsText ( w ) && !XmIsTextField ( w ) )
    {
        fprintf ( stderr, "%s %s",
                  "CompleteFileName is only designed to",
                   "work with XmText and XmTextField widgets" );
        return;
    }

    if ( completionChar == NULL )
    {
        fprintf ( stderr,
                  "CompleteFileCallback requires a \
                   non-null completion character" );
        return;
    }

    if ( cbs && cbs->text && cbs->text->ptr &&
          cbs->text->ptr[0] == completionChar )
    {
       char *str = XmTextGetString ( w );
       XmTextSetString ( w, GetCompleteFileName ( str ) );
    }
}
```

An alternate approach is to use `XtWarning()` to report the error, or to use `XtError()`. `XtWarning()` simply prints a message, but it has an advantage over `printf()`, because custom error handler functions can be installed to catch the warnings (See Chapter 4). `XtError()` prints a message and exits, which is a sure way to get the attention of any programmer who misuses this function.

This approach has a few shortcomings. For example, while a programmer may see the messages while testing a program, it will not be immediately obvious where the messages are coming from. A programmer may have to spend a great deal of time tracing the source of the message. An even more aggressive approach is to call the function `abort()` after printing the message. This function deliberately causes a program to core dump, which allows a programmer to use a debugger to find the exact sequence of function calls that lead to the error.

A version of this function that aborts when an error occurs could be written as follows:

```
/**************************************************
 * CompleteFileCallback.c: Complete a file name.
 **************************************************/
#include <Xm/Xm.h>
#include <Xm/TextF.h>
#include <Xm/Text.h>

/*
 * Replace the contents of a text field with the complete
 * name of a file that matches the current text.
 */

extern char *GetCompleteFileName ( char * );

void CompleteFileCallback ( Widget     w,
                            XtPointer clientData,
                            XtPointer callData )
{
    XmTextVerifyCallbackStruct *cbs =
                 ( XmTextVerifyCallbackStruct * ) callData;
    char completionChar = ( char ) clientData;
   /*
    * This function only works for modify verify callbacks
    * registered with XmText and XmTextField widgets!
    */
    if ( cbs &&
         cbs->reason != XmCR_MODIFYING_TEXT_VALUE     ||
         ( !XmIsText ( w) && !XmIsTextField ( w ) ) ||
         completionChar == NULL )
    {
        fprintf ( stderr,
                  "Incorrect use of CompleteFileCallback" );
        abort();
    }

    if ( cbs && cbs->text && cbs->text->ptr &&
         cbs->text->ptr[0] == completionChar )
    {
       char *str = XmTextGetString ( w );
       XmTextSetString ( w, GetCompleteFileName ( str ) );
    }
}
```

This implementation combines all tests into a single error message, because a programmer can now use a debugger to quickly identify the source of the error. However, this version of `CompleteFileCallback()` still has some shortcomings. In particular, programs that use this function will pay the price of the additional tests (in performance and code size) long after any errors have been found. Also, the additional code for each test has the potential to introduce bugs of its own, and adds maintenance overhead. While the cost of the tests in this example may be low, the impact of many tests can add up. The following section describes a way to overcome many of these objections.

2.2 Conditional Compilation and Assertions

The previous section shows ways to write a function so that it provides some assistance at identifying problems caused by incorrect or unintended use. One problem with this approach is that the tests add to the complexity of the function, and degrade performance even when the function is being used correctly. This section shows how an application can support debugging, but allow the support to be removed easily once the application has been tested.

Conditional Compilation

One simple way to avoid degrading performance with code needed only during development is to use preprocessor conditional statements that can be activated or deactivated as needed, by recompiling. For example, the following implementation of `CompleteFileCallback()` encloses all the tests inside a conditional `ifndef` statement that can be removed by compiling with the symbol `NDEBUG`[1] defined.

```
/*****************************************************
 * CompleteFileCallback.c: Complete a file name.
 *****************************************************/
#include <Xm/Xm.h>
#include <Xm/TextF.h>
#include <Xm/Text.h>
#include <stdlib.h>

/*
 * Replace the contents of the text field with the complete
 * name of a file that matches the current text.
 */
```

1 The double-negative approach of combining `NDEBUG` with an `ifndef` preprocessor directive is used for consistency with the `assert()` macro. This macro is discussed on page 37.

```
13  extern char *GetCompleteFileName ( char * );
14
15  void CompleteFileCallback ( Widget    w,
16                              XtPointer clientData,
17                              XtPointer callData )
18  {
19      XmTextVerifyCallbackStruct *cbs =
20                      ( XmTextVerifyCallbackStruct * ) callData;
21      char completionChar = ( char ) clientData;
22
23  #ifndef NDEBUG
24     /*
25      * This function only works for modify verify callbacks
26      * registered with XmText and XmTextField widgets!
27      */
28
29      if ( cbs &&
30           cbs->reason != XmCR_MODIFYING_TEXT_VALUE ||
31           ( !XmIsText ( w) && ! XmIsTextField ( w ) ) ||
32           completionChar == NULL )
33      {
34          fprintf ( stderr,
35                    "Incorrect use of CompleteFileCallback" );
36          abort();
37      }
38  #endif
39      if (
40  #ifndef NDEBUG
41           cbs && cbs->text &&
42  #endif
43           cbs->text->ptr &&
44           cbs->text->ptr[0] == completionChar )
45      {
46         char *str = XmTextGetString ( w );
47         XmTextSetString ( w, GetCompleteFileName ( str ) );
48      }
49  }
```

Notice that even the tests on line 41 are enclosed between conditional compilation statements. If the function is used correctly, the call data structure will always be valid, so the additional overhead of these tests can be eliminated. If this function is compiled normally, the debugging tests will be left in. If the function is compiled as:

```
cc -c -DNDEBUG complete.c
```

the debugging code will be removed.

One common way to use this technique is to create two versions of all libraries, one for debugging and the other for production use. The debugging version would typically contain many debugging tests, and might also be compiled with the compiler's `-g` flag to better support debugging:

```
cc -c -g complete.c
```

A production version can be created by removing all debugging support and also compiling the code with compiler optimization turned on:

```
cc -c -O -DNDEBUG complete.c
```

One problem with this approach is that the code remains very cluttered, and the conditional compiler statements may even introduce errors. It is critical that such statements not change the behavior of the function. Unfortunately, it is easy to change the block structure of a function when the `ifdef` statements are present. For example, consider the following function, which retrieves the character data from a label widget's `XmNlabelString` resource:

```
char *GetTextOfLabel ( Widget w )
{
    char     *text = NULL;
    XmString xmstr;

    XtVaGetValues ( w, XmNlabelString, &xmstr, NULL );

    if ( xmstr && XmStringGetLtoR ( xmstr,
                                    XmFONTLIST_DEFAULT_TAG,
                                    &text ) )
#ifndef NDEBUG
        printf ( "Retrieved text = %s\n", text );
#endif
        return ( text );
}
```

This function's logic changes depending on the setting of the `NDEBUG` compilation flag. When `NDEBUG` is not defined, `printf()` reports the value of the retrieved text if `XmStringGetLtoR()` is successful. Because `text` is initialized to `NULL`, the function works correctly in debug mode. If the retrieval is unsuccessful, the value of `text`, which has been initialized to `NULL`, is returned. However, if `NDEBUG` is defined, the value of `text` is returned only if the string is valid. If `NDEBUG` is defined and the expression in the `if` statement is `FALSE`, the function's return value is undefined.

This function is almost the same as the original, except for the four `assert()` statements, which are well-isolated. The `assert()` macros provide a clear, concise, and easily maintained declaration of the assumptions made by this function. Each assertion reports an individual error, which can be easily understood and traced when an error occurs.

For example, attempting to call the `CompleteFileCallback()` as the result of an `XmNactivateCallback` would produce a core file and a message like this:

```
assertion failed,line 25,cbs->reason==XmCR_MODIFYING_TEXT_VALUE
abort(core dump)
```

The `assert()` macro has significantly less impact on the logic of a function, and is less error-prone because the code is less cluttered. Because the `assert()` macro is compact and easy to use, programmers are more likely to add a full set of tests. For example, the function `GetTextOfLabel()` could be written as follows:

```
char *GetTextOfLabel ( Widget w )
{
    char     *text = NULL;
    XmString xmstr;
    Boolean  result;

    assert ( XmIsLabel ( w ) );

    XtVaGetValues ( w, XmNlabelString, &xmstr, NULL );

    assert ( xmstr );

    result = XmStringGetLtoR ( xmstr,
                               XmFONTLIST_DEFAULT_TAG,
                               &text ) );

    assert ( result && text );
    return ( text );
}
```

The use of the `assert()` macro in this function makes the function cleaner, simpler, and easier to understand. With the assertions, the `if` statement that tests to see if `XmStringGetLtoR()` has succeeded is no longer necessary, and can be removed. Any failure would indicate a memory problem or other serious error, and would be caught by the assertion.

Assertions and conditional debugging statements do not prevent an application from calling a function with the wrong arguments. However, this approach causes failures that make the cause obvious, instead of producing problems that might be overlooked until later. When a function fails because of an assertion, it should be clear that the caller has used the function incorrectly.

Useful Xt and Motif Test Functions

Xt and Motif provide several functions and macros that can be used very effectively with the `assert()` macro. Motif defines functions and macros for each widget class that can be used to determine if a widget belongs to that class. For example, `XmIsLabel()` evaluates to `TRUE` if its argument is an XmLabel widget or any subclass (XmPushButton, XmToggleButton, etc.). `XmIsRowColumn()` evaluates to true if its argument is an XmRowColumn widget, or a subclass. Each type of widget and gadget has an equivalent macro. These macros can be used like any expression, of course, but are particularly useful as arguments to `assert()`.

The macros that identify Motif and Xt abstract classes can also be useful. For example, imagine a function that expects to operate on any primitive widget, but that does not work correctly for manager widgets. Such a function could include an assertion:

```
assert ( XmIsPrimitive ( w ) );
```

`XmIsManager()` evaluates to `TRUE` when its argument is a manager widget. `XmIsGadget()` determines whether its argument is a gadget rather than a widget.

Xt also implements functions and macros for the classes it defines. `XtIsWidget()` can be used to determine if a given widget is a subclass of the Core widget class. `XtIsComposite()` checks for widgets that are subclasses of Composite, and so on. In addition, Xt supports other functions, like `XtIsRealized()` and `XtIsManaged()`, that can be useful inside an assertion.

One particularly useful function defined by Xt is `XtIsObject()`. The other functions and macros (`XtIsWidget()`, `XmIsPrimitive()`, and so on) simply test the class of the given argument, on the assumption that the argument is a type of widget. However, `XtIsObject()` performs a series of tests to determine if an arbitrary pointer is really a widget or gadget. Every widget contains a member that points to itself, and various other members that are expected to have non-`NULL` values. `XtIsObject()` checks these members to see if the values are reasonable. If a pointer is not a widget, or if the widget has been destroyed, `XtIsObject()` will return `FALSE`. `XtIsObject()` returns `TRUE` if tests determine that the pointer is a valid widget.

Notice that the other functions described here do not call `XtIsObject()` as part of their tests. So, calling `XmIsManager()` with an arbitrary object, or even an old pointer to a widget that has been destroyed may produce an error. A more robust approach would be to check pointers with `XtIsObject()` before testing them with a specific Motif type-testing function. For example:

```
assert ( XtIsObject ( w ) && XmIsManager ( w ) );
```

`XtIsObject()` is an ideal function to place inside a macro like `assert()`. This function is not completely fool-proof and some inputs can cause the program to crash. (Try `XtIsObject(25)`, for example.) Therefore, `XtIsObject()` may not be appropriate for use as a permanent fixture inside a program. However, inside a conditional macro like `assert()`, where the test is executed only during debugging, this function provides meaningful tests most of the time. If the function itself fails, an error condition has certainly been found, and the assertion would have failed anyway.

2.3 The Advantages of Type Checking

Using ANSI C or C++, both of which provide better type checking than older pre-ANSI C compilers, can also help avoid many errors that would otherwise go undetected. For example, consider the following function, written in pre-ANSI C:

Bug!

```
void GoToEnd ( textWidget )
    Widget textWidget;
{
     Position last = XmTextGetLastPosition ( textWidget );
    XmTextShowPosition ( textWidget, last );
}
```

This function attempts to move or scroll a text widget so that it displays the last character in the widget's text buffer. This code works fine as long as the text widget does not contain very much text. However, `Position` is not the correct return type for `XmTextGetLastPosition()`, which returns a value of type `XmTextPosition`. The sizes of the types `Position` and `XmTextPosition` may vary on different platforms, but on most machines, `Position` is likely to be a short, while `XmTextPosition` is most likely to be a long. In this example, the value returned by `XmTextGetLastPosition()` is assigned to a variable of type `Position`. On any system on which the size of `Position` is less than the size of `XmTextPosition`, the value of `last` may overflow if the text buffer grows large enough. When this happens, the buffer will start scrolling to the wrong location. Such errors might easily go undetected for a long time. The type checking offered by ANSI C or C++ would detect this problem at compile time.

Type Checking and Callbacks

One area that seems to cause confusion among Motif programmers involves the type signature of callbacks and event handlers. Callbacks are usually registered by calling `XtAddCallback()`, whose type declaration is:

```
void XtAddCallback ( Widget,
                     String,
                     XtCallbackProc,
                     XtPointer );
```

Programmers who switch from a traditional C compiler to ANSI C or C++ may be puzzled by warnings (in ANSI C) or errors (with C++) involving the callback functions passed to `XtAddCallback()`. The error varies from compiler to compiler, but usually says something about an "incorrect type of argument number 3, XtCallbackProc expected".

Looking at the header file Intrinsic.h, we can see that `XtCallbackProc` is a typedef, defined as:

```
typedef void (*XtCallbackProc)( Widget, XtPointer, XtPointer );
```

This declaration is often misunderstood, and in an attempt to get rid of warnings, some programmers mistakenly declare their callbacks as[2]:

Wrong!

```
XtCallbackProc MyCallback ( Widget, XtPointer, XtPointer );
```

[2] This error is so common that, until recently, this mistaken declaration was common inside Motif itself.

This declaration is wrong, of course. This statement declares a function, `MyCallback()`, which takes three arguments, and returns a *pointer to a function* that takes three arguments. Programmers who try this approach find that the compiler still complains about the type.

Another common approach to using callbacks is to declare the arguments as the type that will be used in the function. For example, if `MyCallback()` is to be registered as an `XmNactivateCallback` for an XmPushButton widget, and expects a widget as client data, some programmers might declare the function as:

```
void MyCallback ( Widget   w,
                  Widget   clientdata,
                  XmPushButtonCallbackStruct *callData )
```

This declaration takes advantage of C's ability to implicitly cast the parameters to the expected type. However, attempting to register this function as a callback, when using ANSI C or C++ also produces a warning or error about a type mismatch.

Another source of confusion is that in older versions of Xt, callbacks were declared as:

Obsolete Style

```
void MyCallback ( Widget, caddr_t, caddr_t )
```

Of course, old code that uses this style still exists. Attempting to register a function with this type signature will also cause an error or warning with an ANSI C or C++ compiler.

C programmers have historically been somewhat careless about types, because of C's lack of type checking. Some programmers even exploit the ability to pass arbitrary pointers to use functions and data in unexpected ways. For example, you may have encountered examples that register functions like `XtManageChild()` or `XtDestroyWidget()` as callbacks, taking advantage of the assumption that these functions ignore all but the first argument, which will be a widget. Of course, this type of "creativity" can be the source of many hard-to-find errors, and should be avoided.

It is important to handle callback functions correctly to allow the compiler to help you avoid bugs. The basic problem with all the above mistakes is that programmers generally cast to get rid of the error or warning. It is common to see code that looks like this:

Wrong!

```
XtAddCallback ( w, XmNactivateCallback,
                ( XtCallbackProc ) MyCallback, NULL );
```

If you see code like this, you know that the programmer has been unable to get rid of the warnings and has simply decided to cast to silence the compiler. The cast should be a clear danger signal. Once a cast has been introduced, more serious errors may go unnoticed.

The best way to declare callbacks is the way that allows your compiler to help you the most, which generally means declaring types as correctly as possible, and using the fewest casts. Some programmers prefer to cast the callback when it is registered because it allows them to declare the expected types used as arguments to the callback. However, this approach involves three casts, the explicit cast used in `XtAddCallback()`, and two implicit casts used in the function itself. Furthermore, there is no way to be sure that all casts are correct.

The safest way to declare a callback is as follows:

1. Declare the callback exactly as expected by `XtAddCallback()`. For example:

   ```
   void MyCallback ( Widget    w,
                     XtPointer clientData,
                     XtPointer callData );
   ```

   If you are using C++, and `MyCallback()` is a member function of a class, it must be a static member function, declared as:

   ```
   class MyClass {
       // Other declarations

       static void MyCallback ( Widget    w,
                                XtPointer clientData,
                                XtPointer callData );
   };
   ```

2. Register the callback without casting the function. The client data may be cast, if needed. For example:

   ```
   XtAddCallback ( w, XmNactivateCallback,
                   MyCallback, ( XtPointer ) aWidget );
   ```

   In C++, a member function callback would be added as follows:

```
XtAddCallback ( w, XmNactivateCallback,
                &MyClass::MyCallback,
                ( XtPointer ) aWidget );
```

3. In the callback, cast any arguments needed by the function to their expected types. If there is any possibility of an error (and there always is), use assertions to test the type of each argument. For example:

```
void MyCallback ( Widget    w,
                  XtPointer clientData,
                  XtPointer callData )
{
    XmPushButtonCallbackStruct *cbs =
              ( XmPushButtonCallbackStruct * ) callData;
    Widget aWidget = ( Widget ) clientData;

    assert ( cbs && cbs->reason == XmCR_ACTIVATE );
    assert ( XtIsObject ( aWidget ) );

    /* Other callback operations */
}
```

This approach reduces the chances for errors to a minimum because it reduces the number of casts, and checks the validity of those items that must still be cast explicitly.

Although this discussion focuses on callbacks, the same concepts apply to event handlers, timeout callbacks, input callbacks, work procedures, error and warning handlers, and action procedures. Xt and Motif make heavy use of function pointers and indirection. Any code that manipulates function pointers should be treated with caution. Never cast a function pointer to get rid of a compiler warning. Declaring the function properly will help avoid costly bugs in the future.

2.4 Dangling Pointers and Widget Destruction

All C programs that use dynamically allocated memory are susceptible to dangling pointers. A dangling pointer is a pointer to memory that is no longer valid, or that is no longer being used for the same purpose it was formerly.

For example, consider the following program, which contains an obvious bug:

```
 1 /*********************************************************
 2  * dangling.c: A buggy program with a dangling pointer
 3  *********************************************************/
 4 #include <Xm/Xm.h>
 5 #include <Xm/DrawingA.h>
 6
 7 void main ( int argc, char **argv )
 8 {
 9     Widget       shell, canvas;
10     XtAppContext app;
11
12     shell = XtAppInitialize ( &app, "Dangling", NULL, 0,
13                               &argc, argv, NULL, NULL, 0 );
14
15     canvas = XtCreateWidget ( "canvas", xmDrawingAreaWidgetClass,
16                               shell, NULL, 0 );
17
18     XtDestroyWidget ( canvas );
19
20     XtManageChild ( canvas );      Bug!
21
22     XtRealizeWidget ( shell );
23     XtAppMainLoop ( app );
24 }
```

Here, the `canvas` widget is destroyed on line 18, and the memory associated with that widget is reclaimed. However, `canvas` continues to point to the address that once contained the widget. Additional references to that memory location, such as that on line 20, can cause a program to fail because there is no way to be sure what lies at that memory location.

Such bugs may be hard to catch because it is possible for the data stored in that memory location to remain unchanged for some period of time, even after the data has been freed. For example, in the above program, it is likely that no additional memory has been allocated between the time the widget is destroyed and the attempt to manage it. On some systems, this program may execute without error. However, different memory usage patterns, which may emerge as a program changes and grows, can cause this bug to appear.

Dangling pointers are particularly likely in programs that destroy widgets. Normally, dangling pointers occur when a program has two or more references to the same memory location. The most obvious way to reduce the chances of such problems is to disallow multiple references to an address. It is also a good idea to localize references so they can easily cleaned up when the associated memory is destroyed.

Multiple references are often introduced into a program by passing a widget as client data to a callback. For example, [Young94] describes a technique that uses a work procedure to display and remove a busy dialog with a single function call, made only at the beginning of a busy period. The function that displays a busy cursor is written as follows:

```
void DisplayBusyCursor ( Widget w )
{
    static cursor = NULL;

    if ( !cursor )
      cursor = XCreateFontCursor ( XtDisplay ( w ), XC_watch );

    XDefineCursor ( XtDisplay ( w ), XtWindow ( w ), cursor );

    XFlush ( XtDisplay ( w ) );

    XtAppAddWorkProc ( XtWidgetToApplicationContext ( w ),
                       RemoveBusyCursor, ( XtPointer ) w );
}
```

Xt invokes the work procedure added by this function when the program returns to the event loop. The work procedure simply removes the busy cursor by calling `XUndefineCursor()`.

```
Boolean RemoveBusyCursor ( XtPointer clientData )
{
    Widget w = ( Widget ) clientData;

    XUndefineCursor ( XtDisplay ( w ), XtWindow ( w ) );

    return ( TRUE );
}
```

Notice, however, that `RemoveBusyCursor()` relies on the widget passed as client data. One potential danger when using this function is that the widget passed as client data might be destroyed as part of the lengthy operation for which the busy cursor is being displayed. If this were to occur, the client data would be a dangling pointer to memory that no longer represents a valid widget.

This function could benefit from some tests to be sure the widget passed as client data is valid at the time the function is called. For example, `Remove-BusyCursor()` could be written as:

```
Boolean RemoveBusyCursor ( XtPointer clientData )
{
    Widget w = ( Widget ) clientData;

    assert ( w && XtIsObject ( w ) );
    assert ( XtDisplay ( w ) );
    assert ( XtWindow ( w ) );

    XUndefineCursor ( XtDisplay ( w ), XtWindow ( w ) );

    return ( TRUE );
}
```

Dangling pointers are possible even when a program contains only a single reference to a widget, because a widget is destroyed when its parent is destroyed. In some cases, destroying a widget in one part of a program can leave a dangling reference in a seemingly unrelated part of the program. The problem is that, even if a program minimizes the number of references to any individual widget, Xt and Motif have additional pointers to each widget.

Consider the following function, which implements a simple digital clock that can be added to any other program. This function is adapted from an example in [Young 94]. The function `CreateClock()` just creates an XmLabel widget and calls a function, `UpdateTime()`, that initiates a sequence of Xt timeout callbacks to implement a clock.

```
/*********************************************************
 * CreateClock:  A convenience function to create a clock
 *               that can be placed in any widget hierarchy.
 *********************************************************/
#include <Xm/Xm.h>
#include <Xm/Label.h>
#include <time.h>
#include <stdio.h>

static void UpdateTime ( XtPointer     clientData,
                         XtIntervalId *id );

Widget CreateClock ( Widget parent )
{
    Widget face;

    face = XtCreateManagedWidget ( "face", xmLabelWidgetClass,
                                   parent, NULL, 0 );
    UpdateTime ( ( XtPointer ) face, NULL );
}
```

```
static void UpdateTime ( XtPointer clientData, XtIntervalId *id )
{
    Widget w =  ( Widget ) clientData;
    long   tloc, rounded_tloc, next_minute;
    char   buffer[100];

   /*
    * Get the system time.
    */

    time ( &tloc );

   /*
    * Convert the time to a string and display it,
    * after rounding it down to the last minute.
    */

    rounded_tloc = tloc / 60 * 60;

    sprintf ( buffer, "%s", ctime ( &rounded_tloc ) );

    XtVaSetValues ( w,
                    XtVaTypedArg, XmNlabelString, XmRString,
                    buffer, strlen ( buffer ) + 1, NULL );

   /*
    * Adjust the time to reflect the time until
    * the next round minute.
    */

    next_minute =  ( 60 - tloc % 60 ) * 1000;

   /*
    * Xt removes timeouts when they occur,
    * so re-register the function.
    */

    XtAppAddTimeOut ( XtWidgetToApplicationContext ( w ),
                      next_minute, UpdateTime,
                      ( XtPointer )  w );
}
```

This function appears to be implemented correctly. If used in a simple program that just displays a clock, no problems are likely to be found. For example, the following program exhibits no apparent bugs.

```
/*****************************************************
 * xclock: Use CreateClock() to implement a digital
 *         clock program.
 *****************************************************/
#include <Xm/Xm.h>

extern Widget CreateClock ( Widget parent );

void main ( int argc, char **argv )
{
    Widget       shell, clock;
    XtAppContext app;

    shell = XtAppInitialize ( &app, "XClock", NULL, 0,
                              &argc, argv, NULL, NULL, 0 );

    clock = CreateClock ( shell );

    XtRealizeWidget ( shell );
    XtAppMainLoop ( app );
}
```

However, consider what might happen if `CreateClock()` is used in a more complex application in which the program destroys an ancestor of the widget used for the clock. For example, the following simple program pops up a dialog that displays the clock. When the user dismisses the dialog, the dialog widget is destroyed.

```
/*****************************************************
 * xclock2: Use CreateClock() in a program that
 *          displays a clock in a dialog.
 *****************************************************/
#include <Xm/Xm.h>
#include <Xm/PushB.h>
#include <Xm/MessageB.h>

extern Widget CreateClock ( Widget parent );
void ShowClock ( Widget, XtPointer, XtPointer );
void DestroyDialog ( Widget, XtPointer, XtPointer );

void main ( int argc, char ** argv )
{
    Widget       shell, button;
    XtAppContext app;

    shell = XtAppInitialize ( &app, "XClock", NULL, 0,
                              &argc, argv, NULL, NULL, 0 );
```

```
    /*
     * Create a button that, when clicked, launches a dialog.
     */

     button =  XtCreateManagedWidget ( "show_clock",
                                       xmPushButtonWidgetClass,
                                       shell, NULL, 0 );

     XtAddCallback ( button, XmNactivateCallback,
                     ShowClock, NULL );

     XtRealizeWidget ( shell );
     XtAppMainLoop ( app );
}

void ShowClock ( Widget    w,
                 XtPointer callData,
                 XtPointer clientData )
{
     Widget dialog, child;

    /*
     * Create a dialog and remove current work area child.
     */

     dialog = XmCreateInformationDialog ( w, "clock", NULL, 0 );
     child = XmMessageBoxGetChild ( dialog,
                                    XmDIALOG_MESSAGE_LABEL );
     XtUnmanageChild ( child );

    /*
     * Add the clock to the dialog.
     */

     CreateClock ( dialog );

    /*
     * Destroy the dialog when the user dismisses it.
     */

     XtAddCallback ( dialog, XmNokCallback,
                     DestroyDialog, NULL );

    /*
     * Display the dialog.
     */

     XtManageChild ( dialog );
}
```

```
69 void DestroyDialog ( Widget     w,
70                      XtPointer callData,
71                      XtPointer clientData )
72 {
73     XtDestroyWidget ( w );
74 }
```

This program posts a dialog when the user clicks on the button in the main window. The dialog displays the current time, using the `CreateClock()` function to install a digital clock in the dialog. Everything is fine, until the user dismisses the dialog. At this point, the dialog widget is destroyed, which automatically destroys the dialog's children, including the XmLabel widget created by the `CreateClock()` function. However, Xt still calls the timeout callback set up by the `UpdateTime()` function at regular intervals. As a result, this function tries to display some text in the XmLabel widget, which has been destroyed.

Eventually, this program will almost certainly crash. The program may die the first time the `UpdateTime()` function is called after the XmLabel widget has been destroyed, or the program may proceed for some time before an error occurs. The problem might manifest itself as a core dump when the program tries to access memory that has been previously freed, or the program may encounter an X error when trying to display text in a window that has been destroyed.

In any case, the program will eventually fail and the real source of the problem may be difficult to determine from the symptoms. It is unlikely that anything will point directly to the call to `XtDestroyWidget()` on line 73, which is the most immediate cause of the problem.

Such problems are particularly troublesome when using convenience functions that might be placed in a library for general use. A programmer might write a function like `CreateClock()` without ever considering what might happen if the XmLabel widget's parent were to be destroyed. If the function is intended only for use in a simple program like the `xclock` example, there might be no need to think about widget destruction. However, if this function is made widely available, someone else may decide to use it without being aware of the restrictions and assumptions made in the implementation.

One way to make `CreateClock()` more robust is to install an `XmNdestroyCallback` that detects the destruction of the XmLabel widget. An `XmNdestroyCallback` could be used in several ways. The simplest approach is to remove the timeout callback if the XmLabel widget is destroyed. The following version of the `CreateClock()` module demonstrates this strategy. There are several subtle changes to this version. The `face` widget is declared as a static variable that is accessible to several callbacks. `CreateClock()` installs an `XmNdestroyCallback` function immediately after creating the widget, and `UpdateTime()` checks that the face widget is not `NULL` before proceeding. Changes from the previous version are shown in bold.

```
/*********************************************************
 * CreateClock:  A convenience function to create a clock
 *               that can be placed in any widget hierarchy.
 *               This version guards against unplanned
 *               widget destruction.
 *********************************************************/
#include <Xm/Xm.h>
#include <Xm/Label.h>
#include <time.h>
#include <stdio.h>

static void UpdateTime ( XtPointer    clientData,
                         XtIntervalId *id );
static void DestroyCallback ( Widget    w,
                              XtPointer callData,
                              XtPointer clientData );
static Widget  face; /* Note: static variable prevents
                        multiple clocks */

Widget CreateClock ( Widget parent )
{
   /* Widget face; Now a static global */

    face = XtCreateManagedWidget ( "face", xmLabelWidgetClass,
                                   parent, NULL, 0 );
   /*
    * Add a callback to detect when this widget is destroyed.
    */

    XtAddCallback ( face, XmNdestroyCallback,
                    DestroyCallback, NULL );

    UpdateTime ( NULL, NULL ); /* face is now global */
}
```

The callback function `DestroyCallback()` is called any time the XmLabel widget created by this module is destroyed. It simply sets the `face` widget, which is now a static variable available to all functions in this file, to `NULL`.

```
static void DestroyCallback ( Widget    w,
                              XtPointer callData,
                              XtPointer clientData )
{
    face = NULL; /* Set the face widget to NULL, to be
                    detected when the clock is updated */
}
```

The function `UpdateTime()` is similar to the version described earlier, but this implementation displays the time in the `face` widget, which is globally available in this file. Before updating the time, the function checks to see if `face` is `NULL`. If so, `UpdateTime()` stops the clock by not installing the next timeout.

```
static void UpdateTime ( XtPointer clientData, XtIntervalId *id )
{
 /* Widget w =  ( Widget ) clientData; face is now a global */
    long   tloc, rounded_tloc, next_minute;
    char   buffer[100];

   /*
    * If the face widget has been destroyed, just return,
    * ending cycle of timeouts.
    */

    if ( !face )
        return;

   /*
    * Get the system time.
    */

    time ( &tloc );

   /*
    * Convert the time to a string and display it,
    * after rounding it down to the last minute.
    */

    rounded_tloc = tloc / 60 * 60;

    sprintf ( buffer, "%s", ctime ( &rounded_tloc )  );

    XtVaSetValues ( face,
                    XtVaTypedArg, XmNlabelString, XmRString,
                    buffer, strlen ( buffer ) + 1, NULL );

```

```
    /*
     * Adjust the time to reflect the time until
     * the next round minute.
     */

     next_minute =  ( 60 - tloc % 60 ) * 1000;

    /*
     * Xt removes timeouts when they occur,
     * so re-register the function.
     */

     XtAppAddTimeOut ( XtWidgetToApplicationContext ( face ),
                       next_minute, UpdateTime, NULL );
}
```

This example demonstrates one way to use an `XmNdestroyCallback` to make a module more robust, but there are other approaches that could be used. For example, if destroying the XmLabel widget should be considered an error, the destroy callback could print an error message and then call `abort()` to force a core dump. Alternately, an assertion could be used, in the destroy callback, or in the `UpdateTime()` function. In this way, the `CreateClock()` module could assist programs that use the module by making problems obvious and more easily detected.

There is a limitation in the approach demonstrated above. Because `face` is declared as a global variable, `CreateClock()` can only be called to create one clock at a time. If this module is used to create two clocks, the `face` widget will indicate the second XmLabel widget, breaking the first clock. A more robust implementation should either avoid this problem and support multiple clocks, or anticipate the problem and guard against bugs that could result from this limitation. For example, `face` could be initialized to `NULL`, and `CreateClock()` could test that it is not already set, as follows:

```
/*************************************************************
 * CreateClock:  A convenience function to create a clock
 *               that can be placed in any widget hierarchy.
 *               This version guards against unplanned
 *               widget destruction and prevents callers
 *               from creating multiple clocks
 *************************************************************/
#include <Xm/Xm.h>
#include <Xm/Label.h>
#include <time.h>
#include <assert.h>
```

```
static void UpdateTime ( XtPointer     clientData,
                         XtIntervalId  id );
static void DestroyCallback ( Widget    w,
                              XtPointer callData,
                              XtPointer clientData );

static Widget  face = NULL;

Widget CreateClock ( Widget parent )
{
    assert ( !face );

    face = XtCreateManagedWidget ( "face", xmLabelWidgetClass,
                                   parent, NULL, 0 );

   /*
    * Add a callback to detect when this widget is destroyed.
    */

    XtAddCallback ( face, XmNdestroyCallback,
                    DestroyCallback, NULL );

    UpdateTime ( NULL, NULL ); /* face is now global */
}
```

Yet another way to deal with this issue is to return to the original model, without the global `face` widget, and arrange for the `XmNdestroyCallback` to remove the next timeout event. This would require the program to make both the `face` widget and the current timeout identifier available to `DestroyCallback()`.

2.5 Architectural Design Issues

Many bugs in Motif programs are a direct result of not following the programming model supported by X and Motif. All X programs are meant to be event driven. Properly designed X applications are designed to receive an event, process the event quickly, and return to the event queue to wait for the arrival of the next event. Applications should have a single central event loop, and respond to individual events. Applications that attempt to circumvent this model often exhibit very hard to find bugs.

Similarly, Xt and Motif applications are expected to use callbacks and the translation manager to be notified of user input. Programmers that attempt to use other models can easily get into trouble. One common problem involves using multiple event loops instead of relying on the main event loop. It is often necessary to make limited use of secondary event loops, and some examples of how to use events loops effectively are presented in later chapters. However, secondary event loops can have surprising effects, and must be used carefully.

For example, consider the following program, which is a poorly implemented version of the `xlogobug` program introduced in Chapter 1. This version attempts to solve some of the drawing programs by making several changes that, on the surface seem harmless, even if they are not effective. The first step is to move the creation of the graphics context into an event handler that is invoked when the window is mapped. This step reduces the time the application spends before the window is placed on the screen. Because the X server guarantees that a `MapNotify` event will be sent before the first `Expose` event is generated, we can be sure the GC used to draw the lines will be created before it is needed.

The second step is to call `XmUpdateDisplay()` to try to force the window to be drawn quickly. This (incorrectly) modified program can be written as follows:

```
/******************************************************
 * xlogobug.c: Mis-architected program
 ******************************************************/
#include <Xm/Xm.h>
#include <Xm/DrawingA.h>
GC  gc;

void ExposeCallback ( Widget   w,
                      XtPointer clientData,
                      XtPointer callData )
{
    int width, height;

   /*
    * Determine the size of the canvas widget to allow
    * the lines to be drawn.
    */

    XtVaGetValues ( w,
                    XmNwidth,  &width,
                    XmNheight, &height,
                    NULL );
```

```

    /*
     * Draw an X into the canvas widget's window, using the
     * widget's size to draw a line diagonally between
     * each corner.
     */

    XDrawLine ( XtDisplay ( w ), XtWindow ( w ), gc,
                0, 0, width, height);

    XDrawLine ( XtDisplay ( w ), XtWindow ( w ), gc,
                width, 0, 0, height);
}

void WindowMapped ( Widget w, XtPointer clientData,
                    XEvent *event, Boolean *flag )
{
    Widget    canvas = ( Widget ) clientData;
    XGCValues values;

    if ( event->type == MapNotify )
    {
        /*
         * Get the colors to use in a graphics context.
         */

        XtVaGetValues ( canvas,
                        XmNforeground, &values.foreground,
                        NULL );

        gc = XtGetGC ( canvas, GCForeground, &values );
    }
}

void main ( int argc, char **argv )
{
    Widget       shell, canvas;
    XtAppContext app;

    /*
     * Initialize Xt and create a shell widget.
     */

    shell = XtAppInitialize ( &app, "Xlogobug", NULL, 0,
                              &argc, argv, NULL, NULL, 0 );
    /*
     * Create a drawing area widget in which to display
     * a pair of lines that form an X.
     */
```

```
    canvas = XtCreateManagedWidget ( "canvas",
                                     xmDrawingAreaWidgetClass,
                                     shell, NULL, 0 );
   /*
    * Add a callback to be invoked when the contents of
    * the canvas widget should be drawn.
    */

    XtAddCallback ( canvas, XmNexposeCallback,
                    ExposeCallback, NULL );
   /*
    * Add an event handler to create the GC when the window
    * is first mapped.
    */

Problem
    XtAddEventHandler ( canvas, StructureNotifyMask, 0,
                        WindowMapped, ( XtPointer ) canvas );

   /*
    * Realize all widgets so the drawing area widget's
    * window will exist.
    */

    XtRealizeWidget ( shell );

   /*
    * Call XmUpdateDisplay() to force the window to be drawn
    */

Problem
    XmUpdateDisplay ( shell );

   /*
    * Start handling events.
    */

    XtAppMainLoop ( app );
}
```

This program now has an interesting bug that may or may not appear on a given system, depending on the speed of the X server, the program, and the window manager. Under certain conditions, it is possible for the calls to `XDrawLine()` in the `ExposeCallback()` function to be called with an invalid GC. This problem seems to indicate that the function `WindowMapped()` was not called, which might make you suspect a bug in the X server. The program should not receive an `Expose` event before a `MapNotify` event.

However, the real problem is a mis-architected program. The primary source of the bug is the call to `XmUpdateDisplay()`, although the `WindowMapped()` event handler plays a role as well. `XmUpdateDisplay()` enters an event loop that retrieves and dispatches all pending `Expose` events. This function looks ahead in the event queue and removes all `Expose` events, but leaves other non-`Expose` events on the queue. Therefore, if the `canvas` widget's window has been mapped and some `Expose` events have been generated before `XmUpdateDisplay()` returns, it is possible for the `ExposeCallback()` function to be called while the `MapNotify` event is still in the event queue. The X server reports the events correctly, in sequence, but the application's architecture changes the order in which events are processed.

This program demonstrates a problem introduced by "trying too hard" when using Motif. Most tasks involving the user interface can be written in a fairly straight-forward manner. If you find that you need to go to great lengths to accomplish what should be a simple task, the chances are that you are taking the wrong approach. Programs that "fight the system" presented by X and Motif are often more complex and buggier than those that use X and Motif's intended model. In many cases, time spent learning more about the functionality of X and Motif reveals a straight-forward way to perform almost any operation.

Choosing the Easiest Path

One source of confusion for Motif programmers is that there is often more than one way to perform any given task. The features of X, Xt, and Motif libraries are not mutually exclusive, and there is some redundancy. For example, you can create a graphics context using the Xlib function `XCreateGC()`, or the Xt function `XtGetGC()`. You can create an atom by calling the Xlib function `XInternAtom()`, or the Motif function `XmInternAtom()`.

It is difficult to make general statements about which facility to use, because in many cases there are subtle differences between the mechanisms supported by each layer. For example, `XtGetGC()` caches graphics contexts, while `XCreateGC()` does not. Which function should be used depends on your needs. `XmInternAtom()` was also created for the same reason, to provide caching for atoms. Now, however, Xlib also caches atoms, so the Motif function is truly redundant, and adds an additional, unnecessary expense.

Lacking specific information about which alternative to use, it is probably best to choose the "path of least resistance", and use the approach that is the most straightforward. As mentioned in the previous section, if a simple operation seems to require a lot of unnecessary steps, you may be taking the wrong approach.

Some programmers have been known to resist using various Motif convenience facilities in an attempt to maintain more control by working with as many low-level facilities as possible. While there is nothing inherently wrong with this approach, it offers far more opportunities for something to go wrong. Often, Motif provides convenience routines for commonly performed operations, or operations that are easy to implement incorrectly. If you simply allow Motif to do the work for you in these cases, you have a better chance of avoiding bugs.

For example, consider the following program, which was inspired by a real situation. The function `PopupWarningDialog()` posts a Motif warning dialog when it is called. This example tries to avoid using the Motif convenience functions and tries to use the Xt dialog model to construct and post a Motif dialog.

```
/*******************************************************
 * buggydialog.c: Attempt to post a dialog
 *******************************************************/
#include <Xm/Xm.h>
#include <Xm/DialogS.h>
#include <Xm/MessageB.h>

void PopupWarningCallback ( Widget    parent,
                            XtPointer clientData,
                            XtPointer callData )
{
    Arg      args[2];
    int      n;
    Widget   warn,
             dialog;
    XmString xmstr;

   /*
    * Create a shell for the dialog, associated with parent.
    */

    n = 0;
Error
    XtSetArg ( args[n], XmNtransientFor, parent ); n++;
    dialog = XtmCreateWidget ( "dialog",
                               xmDialogShellWidgetClass,
                               parent, args, n );

```

```
    /*
     * Create a compound string and display it in a MessageBox.
     */

     xmstr = XmStringCreateLocalized ( "Watch out" );

     n = 0;
     XtSetArg ( args[n], XmNmessageString, xmstr ); n++;
     messagebox = XtCreateWidget ( "messagebox",
                                   xmMessageBoxWidgetClass,
                                   dialog, args, n );
     XmStringFree ( xmstr );

    /*
     * Popup the dialog, and manage the message box.
     */

```

Wrong order

```
     XtPopup ( dialog, XtGrabExclusive );
     XtManageChild ( messagebox );
}
```

This code may not appear to contain any obvious bugs, although it seems like a lot of work to create and post a dialog. The function creates a shell and an XmMessageBox widget individually, establishes the widget passed to the dialog as the "transientFor" window, and uses the Xt function `XtPopup()` to post the dialog.

We can test this function with a simple driver program that pops up the dialog when a button is pressed. This driver can be written as follows:

```
/************************************************************
 * dialogposter.c: driver program to post a warning dialog
 ***********************************************************/
#include <Xm/Xm.h>
#include <Xm/PushB.h>
extern void PopupWarningCallback ( Widget, XtPointer,XtPointer );

void main ( int argc, char **argv )
{
    Widget       shell, button;
    XtAppContext app;

    shell = XtAppInitialize ( &app, "Dialogposter", NULL, 0,
                              &argc, argv, NULL, NULL, 0 );

    button = XtCreateManagedWidget ( "popup",
                                     xmPushButtonWidgetClass,
                                     shell, NULL, 0 );
```

```
    XtAddCallback ( button, XmNactivateCallback,
                    PopupWarningCallback, NULL );

    XtRealizeWidget ( shell );

    XtAppMainLoop ( app );
}
```

When this dialog is posted, the program crashes, leaving behind a core file. Examining the core file shows that an error has occurred deep in Motif, in an internal function named `_XmGetFocusData()`. Because we have no idea what this function is, and debugging Motif itself is outside the domain of the application programmer, it is difficult to know how to proceed. This could be a bug in Motif, or the program could be doing something wrong.

One way to proceed in such cases, is to simply "try things," and eliminate various steps until the problem goes away or changes to something we can understand. This isn't a very scientific approach, and later chapters will suggest better ways to deal with such problems. But for now, let's try removing the `XmNtransientFor` resource from the dialog, on the vague hunch that perhaps the error is related to focus in some way. (Because of the crash in `_XmGetFocusData()`).

With this resource removed, the program no longer core dumps, but the dialog exhibits some very strange behavior. It appears for an instant in the upper left corner of the screen but is quickly centered over the program's window. However, the dialog window is so small that the dialog itself cannot be seen. Resizing the dialog window shows the complete dialog.

Later chapters present tools and techniques that could be used to debug these problems. However, debugging this program is really a waste of time. Neither of these problems would not occur in the first place if we had simply created the dialog using the straight-forward mechanisms provided by Motif.[3]

A far easier, less error prone way to write the `PopupWarning-Callback()` function is shown below. This version uses the simplest approach, and just calls the Motif function `XmCreateWarningDialog()` to create the dialog. Using Motif conventions, this dialog is displayed by simply calling `XtManageChild()`. This version of the callback does not get involved with creating a shell, setting `XmNtransientFor` resources, popping up

[3] If you are curious: The geometry problem occurs because the dialog is not managed until after the shell is popped up. The original core dump seems to occur when the value of the `XmN-transientFor` resource is a non-shell widget.

widgets with exclusive grabs, and so on. The code is simpler, cleaner, easier to understand, and most importantly, it works the first time.

```
/**********************************************************
 * notbuggydialog.c: Straight-forward way to create
 *                    and post a simple dialog.
 **********************************************************/
#include <Xm/Xm.h>
#include <Xm/MessageB.h>

void PopupWarningCallback ( Widget    parent,
                            XtPointer clientData,
                            XtPointer callData )
{
    messagebox = XmCreateWarningDialog ( parent, "messagebox",
                                         NULL, 0 );

    XtVaSetValues ( messagebox,
                    XtVaTypedArg, XmNmessageString, XmRString,
                    "Watch Out", strlen ( "Watch Out") + 1,
                    NULL );

    XtManageChild ( messagebox );
}
```

2.6 Avoiding Layout Problems

Although much of the discussion in this chapter focuses on ways to avoid errors that would cause a program to crash in some way, there are other types of errors that can occur in a program that has a graphical user interface. For example, a common problem faced by Motif programmers involves the physical location of the various widgets in the interface. Often, getting an interface to look right on the screen can be a significant challenge. Chapter 6 discusses some ways to debug such problems when they occur. However, as with other errors, it is often easier to get the layout right in the first place than to debug it later.

Using a User Interface Builder

One way to minimize layout problems is to use a user interface builder to create the widget hierarchy and layout. A user interface builder is an interactive tool that allows developers to experiment with widget layouts easily. Builders are particularly useful when a layout is complex or not well understood. Using a builder can help you discover and understand potential layout difficulties quickly. Limitations of various manager widgets, resize behavior, spacing issues, and so on become apparent quickly, instead of after many lines of code have been written.

A builder can also be helpful when designing or prototyping the user interface layout, because a builder can allow you to see and interact with many different interfaces quickly. A prototype interface can be shown to potential users so that the final design can be chosen at an early stage. It is far easier to implement a widget layout once than to have to make major changes later.

Once a layout has been completed, most user interface builders can generate code. Depending on the builder, and the needs of your application, this code may become the basis of your program. In some cases, the structure, style, or quality of the code generated by the builder may not fit well with the architecture planned for your program. However, even if the code generated by a builder cannot be used directly, a builder allows a developer to experiment until a satisfactory layout has been achieved. Most Motif programs are usually easier to write once the layout is well understood. In many cases, at least some portion of the code can be used, which reduces the chances of making errors when implementing the widget hierarchy or setting resources.

Building a Complex UI From Small Modules

Most real applications create interfaces that contain many widgets. Programmers often have trouble evolving from a small simple interface to a large, complex interface. Extremely simple programs, like the programs described in most books, for example, often use a single manager widget as the basis of an interface. Real interfaces can seldom be based on a single manager widget, and attempts to do so often introduce bugs.

The XmForm widget is the most complex, and most widely used Motif manager widget because it offers the most flexibility in its layout. It is often possible to create even very complex layouts using a single XmForm widget to manage a collection of primitive widgets. However, setting up the constraint resources to specify a complex layout can be extremely error-prone. Often, a layout is almost completed, and seems to be working correctly, when adding one more attachment suddenly breaks the entire layout. Once the layout stops working, it is often difficult to identify the cause or a solution. It is also common to have trouble with the dynamic behavior of the children of a form widget, even when the desired initial layout is achieved.

It is often more effective, and less error-prone, to compose interfaces in small, easy-to-understand units. By building complex interfaces from smaller building blocks, the behavior of each individual unit can be tested before combining the pieces, thus eliminating bugs before they occur. Usually, each unit is managed by a single manager widget. Each Motif manager widget is designed to handle a specific type of layout, and most complex interfaces combine multiple manager widgets to achieve the overall layout of an application.

Let's consider a simple example. Figure 2.1 shows a mock-up drawing of a planned user interface for a simple drawing editor.

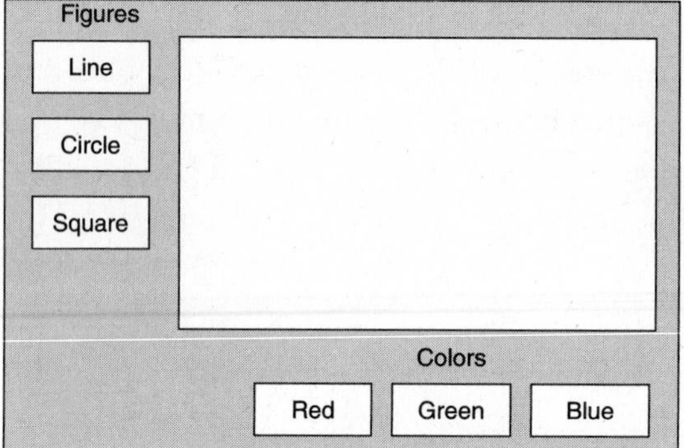

Figure 2.1 A typical user interface layout.

There are many ways this layout could be implemented, each with its own advantages and disadvantages. Before choosing the widgets required to implement this layout, some additional decisions must be made. In this program, we will assume that the buttons along the bottom and left side should have a fixed size, but the large area used as a drawing canvas should stretch as the overall window changes size. The easiest way to implement this behavior is to use an XmForm widget as the main manager widget.

The layout shown in Figure 2.1 is not visually complex, and it seems reasonable to try to implement it with a single XmForm widget, using various attachments to place all buttons, labels, and the canvas area. Figure 2.2 shows one of the many possible sets of attachments that could be used to create this layout.

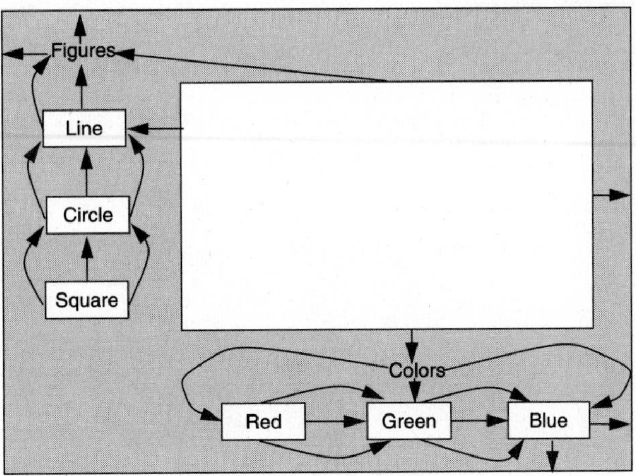

Figure 2.2 Possible form attachments for Figure 2.1.

The attachments in Figure 2.2 are surprisingly complex. The attachments are designed to be sure that the buttons within each related set are aligned. The buttons along the left side are meant to be positioned under the "Figures" title, and the "Colors" label is also centered over the bottom row of buttons. The column of buttons in the upper left do not resize, and stay in the upper left corner. The row of buttons along the bottom always stay in the lower right corner, and do not change size. The area in the center of the window stretches to fill the remainder of the window. The XmForm widget is very flexible and there are other attachments that could implement this layout and dynamic behavior, but these are typical.

When using this approach, the widget hierarchy is flat, with all non-manager widgets created as children of a single manager widget, as shown in Figure 2.3.

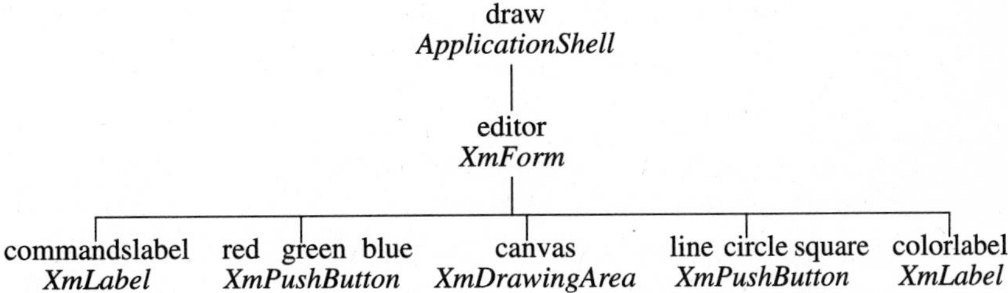

Figure 2.3 Flat widget hierarchy for the layout in Figure 2.1.

Implementing the widget hierarchy and attachments described in Figure 2.2 and Figure 2.3 produces the window shown in Figure 2.4.

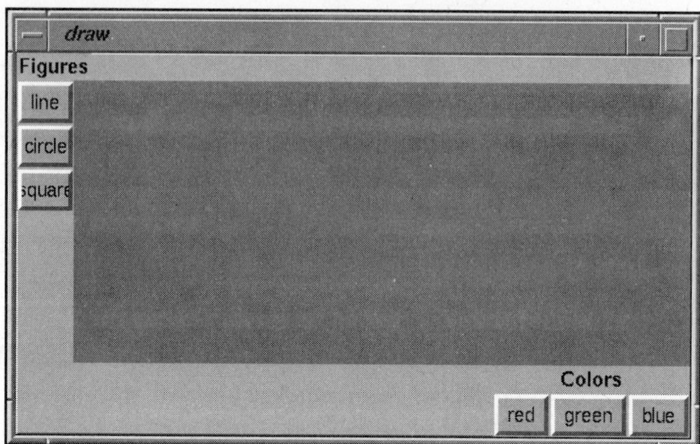

Figure 2.4 Appearance of attachments in Figure 2.2.

Notice that this layout is not very aesthetically pleasing. The buttons are cramped, and spacing is very poor. The text in the button labeled "square" is clipped on both the beginning and end and the "Figures" label protrudes past the buttons and over the canvas, which looks odd.

These problems can all be fixed, of course. Offsets can be used to provide more spacing, and some attachments can be changed. However, these changes are likely to be error-prone because of the high degree of interaction between the various widgets in the layout, and certain hidden assumptions in the implementation. For example, the "square" label is clipped is because of an implicit assumption that the size of each button under the Figures label should be tied to the size of the "line" button. This restriction was not an explicit goal of the original layout, it just fell out of the particular approach to attachments used to implement the layout. (In other words, it's a bug!)

Modifying this layout to meet the needs of future evolution of the program is likely to be difficult as well. It is hard to see what unplanned assumptions may be hidden in this complex form layout, but it is not hard to imagine that they exist. Even if we fix the problems in the current interface, it is difficult to know what problems may turn up as changes are made in the future. The size of labels can be particularly troublesome if the application is expected to be localized for other languages. An internationalizable application cannot make assumptions about the size, or relative size of labels, as this example does.

Fortunately, there is another way to approach widget layout in Motif that is less error-prone, easier to understand and implement, and easier to maintain. For all but the simplest widget layouts, it is best to use a hierarchical approach that breaks functional parts of the user interface into self-contained subsystems. This approach is analogous to the hierarchical composition and decomposition approaches that are a core part of nearly every software engineering design and construction technique.

Usually, each logically related part of the program can be implemented as a self-contained module. In the portion of a program that deals with the user interface, a module often encapsulates a portion of the user interface with the associated functionality. For example, Figure 2.5 shows a portion of the `draw` program's interface that could be built as a stand-alone module. This collection of widgets could be placed in a manager widget, which in turn is placed in the overall drawing program. If done correctly, the buttons and labels in this subsystem can be completely hidden from the rest of the program.

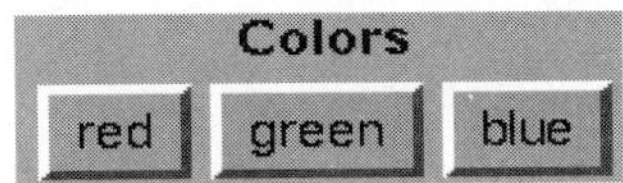

Figure 2.5 The color panel subsystem.

If the buttons under the "Figures" label are also placed in a separate widget hierarchy, the layout of the main window can be greatly simplified. For example, compare the attachments diagrammed in Figure 2.6 with the original version in Figure 2.2. The simplified version is less likely to be a source of bugs now, and in the future.

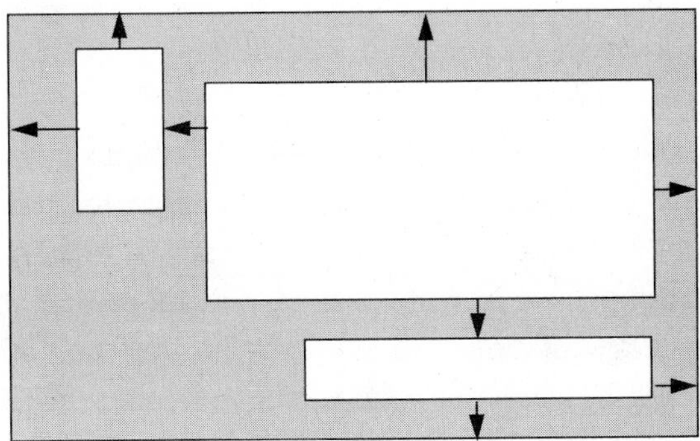

Figure 2.6 Form attachments for modular, hierarchical layout.

Let's look at a partial implementation of this program, in which the various parts of the interface are treated as subsystems managed within their own widget hierarchy. To begin with, the main program is made much simpler. The program simply initializes Xt, calls a function to create the contents of the program's window, and enters the event loop.

```
/*****************************************************
 * draw.c: Sample widget layout for a draw program.
 *****************************************************/
#include <Xm/Xm.h>
#include <Xm/PushB.h>
#include <Xm/Label.h>
#include <Xm/DrawingA.h>
#include <Xm/Form.h>
#include <Xm/RowColumn.h>
Widget CreateEditor ( const char *, Widget shell );
Widget CreateFigures ( const char *, Widget shell );
Widget CreateColors ( const char *, Widget shell );
Widget CreateCanvas ( const char *, Widget shell );
void main ( int argc, char **argv )
{
    Widget       shell;
    XtAppContext app;
    shell = XtAppInitialize ( &app, "Draw", NULL, 0,
                              &argc, argv, NULL, NULL, 0 );
    CreateEditor ( "editor", shell );
    XtRealizeWidget ( shell );
    XtAppMainLoop ( app );
}
```

The function `CreateEditor()` creates an XmForm widget that handles the large-scale layout of the drawing editor's interface. It calls three other functions to create and lay out each of the subsystems in the interface, including the drawing canvas. Notice that `CreateEditor()` has no knowledge of any widgets in the interface, other than the single widget returned by each subsystem creation functions. Each subsystem is a "black box", the contents of which is unknown. `CreateEditor()` specifies form attachments diagrammed in Figure 2.6 to handle the layout of each subsystem, but the layout of the components within each subsystem is handled independently.

```
Widget CreateEditor ( const char *name, Widget shell )
{
    Widget form, figures, colors, canvas;

    form = XtCreateManagedWidget ( name, xmFormWidgetClass,
                                   shell, NULL, 0 );

    figures = CreateFigures ( "figures", form );
    colors = CreateColors ( "colors", form );
    canvas = CreateCanvas ( "canvas", form );

    XtVaSetValues ( colors,
                    XmNtopAttachment,    XmATTACH_NONE,
                    XmNbottomAttachment, XmATTACH_FORM,
                    XmNleftAttachment,   XmATTACH_NONE,
                    XmNrightAttachment,  XmATTACH_FORM,
                    NULL );

    XtVaSetValues ( canvas,
                    XmNtopAttachment,    XmATTACH_FORM,
                    XmNrightAttachment,  XmATTACH_FORM,
                    XmNbottomAttachment, XmATTACH_WIDGET,
                    XmNbottomWidget,     colors,
                    XmNleftAttachment,   XmATTACH_WIDGET,
                    XmNleftWidget,       figures,
                    NULL );

    XtVaSetValues ( colors,
                    XmNtopAttachment,    XmATTACH_NONE,
                    XmNbottomAttachment, XmATTACH_FORM,
                    XmNleftAttachment,   XmATTACH_NONE,
                    XmNrightAttachment,  XmATTACH_FORM,
                    NULL );

  return ( form );
}
```

The function `CreateColors()` implements the subsystem that contains a labeled set of buttons used to select a color for the drawing canvas. This subsystem consists of an XmForm widget that manages the label and an XmRowColumn widget. The XmRowColumn widget provides an easier, more robust way to manage the buttons than the form attachments used earlier. Figure 2.7 shows the widget hierarchy created by this module.

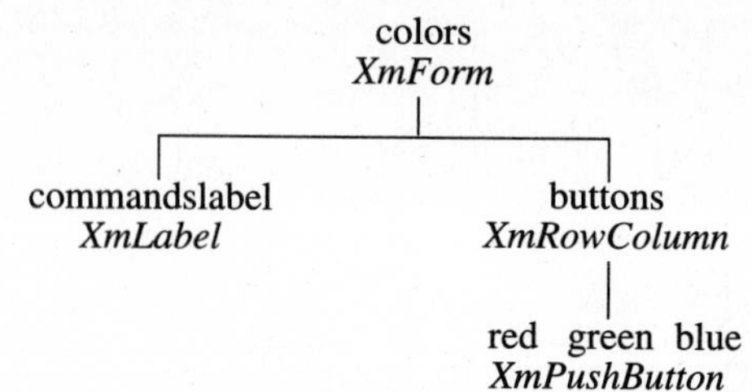

Figure 2.7 Widget hierarchy of colors subsystem.

The function `CreateColors()` takes a name and a parent widget and creates the widget hierarchy shown in Figure 2.7.

```
Widget CreateColors ( const char *name, Widget parent )
{
    Widget form, colorlabel, rowColumn, red, green, blue;

    form = XtCreateManagedWidget ( name, xmFormWidgetClass,
                                   parent, NULL, 0 );

    colorlabel = XtVaCreateManagedWidget ( "colorlabel",
                        xmLabelWidgetClass, form,
                        XmNtopAttachment,    XmATTACH_FORM,
                        XmNbottomAttachment, XmATTACH_NONE,
                        XmNleftAttachment,   XmATTACH_FORM,
                        XmNrightAttachment,  XmATTACH_FORM,
                        NULL );

    rowColumn = XtVaCreateManagedWidget ( "buttons",
                      xmRowColumnWidgetClass, form,
                      XmNorientation,      XmHORIZONTAL,
                      XmNtopAttachment,    XmATTACH_WIDGET,
                      XmNtopWidget,        colorlabel,
                      XmNbottomAttachment, XmATTACH_FORM,
                      XmNleftAttachment,   XmATTACH_FORM,
                      XmNrightAttachment,  XmATTACH_FORM,
                      NULL );

    red = XtCreateManagedWidget ( "red",
                                  xmPushButtonWidgetClass,
                                  rowColumn, NULL, 0 );

    green = XtCreateManagedWidget ( "green",
                                    xmPushButtonWidgetClass,
                                    rowColumn, NULL, 0 );

```

```
    blue = XtCreateManagedWidget ( "blue",
                                   xmPushButtonWidgetClass,
                                   rowColumn, NULL, 0 );

    return ( form );
}
```

Although the canvas area of the drawing editor may be a single widget, it is useful to treat it as an independent subsystem as well. It is possible that this widget could be replaced with a more complex hierarchy. In any case, the canvas could be used as a part of a subsystem that includes additional functionality.

```
Widget CreateCanvas ( const char *name, Widget parent )
{
    Widget canvas;

    canvas = XtCreateManagedWidget ( name,
                                     xmDrawingAreaWidgetClass,
                                     parent, NULL, 0);

    return ( canvas );
}
```

The final portion of the interface is created by `CreateFigures()`, which creates an XmRowColumn widget that manages the "Figures" label and all the buttons below it. The XmRowColumn widget automatically sizes itself to hold the largest child, so the clipping problem in the original layout should not occur.

```
Widget CreateFigures ( const char *name, Widget parent )
{
    Widget rowColumn, commandslabel, line, circle, square;

    rowColumn = XtCreateManagedWidget ( name,
                                        xmRowColumnWidgetClass,
                                        parent, NULL, 0);

    commandslabel = XtCreateManagedWidget ( "commandslabel",
                                            xmLabelWidgetClass,
                                            rowColumn, NULL,0 );

    line = XtCreateManagedWidget ( "line",
                                   xmPushButtonWidgetClass,
                                   rowColumn, NULL, 0 );

```

```
    circle = XtCreateManagedWidget ( "circle",
                                     xmPushButtonWidgetClass,
                                     rowColumn, NULL, 0 );

    square = XtCreateManagedWidget ( "square",
                                     xmPushButtonWidgetClass,
                                     rowColumn, NULL, 0 );

    return ( rowColumn );
}
```

Figure 2.8 shows the layout created by this program.

Figure 2.8 Result of a more hierarchical layout approach.

Although not particularly exciting, this new layout has none of the obvious flaws observed in Figure 2.4. Furthermore, making adjustments to this layout will be much easier. The layout of each subsystem can be tested separately, so changes in spacing between the major parts of the interface can be separated from modifications within individual subsystems.

By isolating and encapsulating functionally related elements of the interface within separate subsystems, it becomes much easier to make minor, or even major, changes to parts of the program. For example, the Color subsystem could be redesigned to be more visually interesting without affecting the rest of the program. Figure 2.9 shows a modified panel that consists of an XmFrame widget that contains the XmRowColumn widget in this subsystem. The `colorlabel` widget has been designated as the title of the frame.

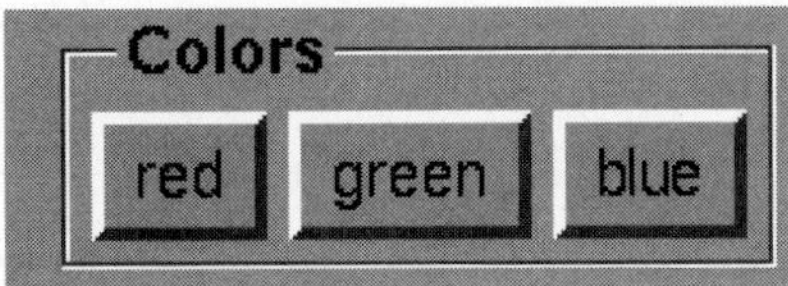

Figure 2.9 Changing the color panel appearance.

The following implementation of `CreateColors()` shows the changes needed to create the appearance in Figure 2.9.

```
Widget CreateColors ( const char *name, Widget parent )
{
    Widget frame, colorlabel, rowColumn, red, green, blue;

    frame = XtCreateManagedWidget ( name,
                                    xmFrameWidgetClass,
                                    parent, NULL, 0 );

    colorlabel =
          XtVaCreateManagedWidget ( "colorlabel",
                                xmLabelWidgetClass, frame,
                                XmNchildType, XmFRAME_TITLE_CHILD,
                                NULL );

    rowColumn = XtVaCreateManagedWidget ( "buttons",
                                     xmRowColumnWidgetClass,
                                     frame,
                                     XmNorientation, XmHORIZONTAL,
                                     NULL );

    red = XtCreateManagedWidget ( "red",
                                  xmPushButtonWidgetClass,
                                  rowColumn, NULL, 0 );

    green = XtCreateManagedWidget ( "green",
                                    xmPushButtonWidgetClass,
                                    rowColumn, NULL, 0 );


    blue = XtCreateManagedWidget ( "blue",
                                   xmPushButtonWidgetClass,
                                   rowColumn, NULL, 0 );

    return ( frame );
}
```

Other subsystems could be changed just as easily, without disturbing the overall layout of the program. For example, Figure 2.10 shows the results of re-implementing all three subsystems to put a frame around each major component. The function `CreateEditor()` would not need to be changed at all, and the attachments described in Figure 2.6 continue to work as before.

Figure 2.10 Drawing program layout with modified subsystems.

Unlike the original implementation, this new implementation is quite flexible, and can adapt to significant changes in the size or shape of the various subsystems. For example, Figure 2.11 shows the result of replacing the text labels in the program with iconic representations.

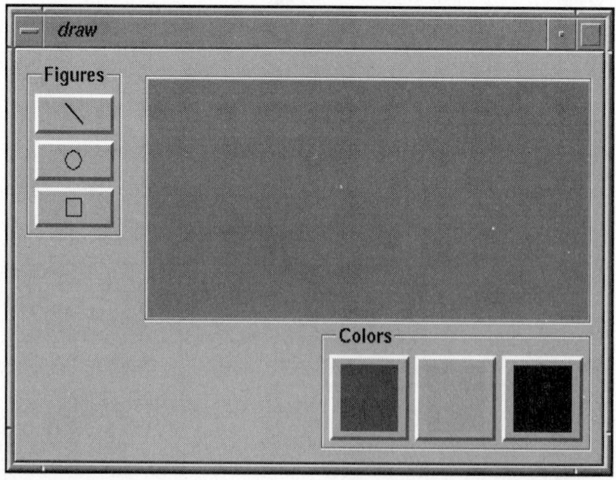

Figure 2.11 Changes to subsystem sizes does not break layout.

Modularity and Program Architecture

One of the challenges when developing a Motif program involves the connections between various elements of the program. For example, the program in the previous section ignores the operations performed by the various buttons in the drawing editor. When the user selects a color by clicking on one of the buttons at the bottom of the program's window, that information somehow needs to affect figures drawn in the canvas area.

Too often, the need to connect various parts of a program is addressed by making widgets accessible throughout a program, either as global variables, or by passing widgets to other functions. For example, in the original implementation, one might be tempted to install a `SetColorCallback()` function with each color button, passing the `canvas` widget as client data. The `SetColorCallback()` could just change the `canvas` widget's `XmNforeground` resource, which could then be used by drawing routines.

This approach has several shortcomings. First, it introduces multiple pointers to the `canvas` widget, which can lead to problems if widgets are destroyed. (For example, perhaps someday the program might support multiple canvases, which are dynamically created and destroyed.) Depending on non-obvious connections leads to code that is difficult to maintain, and subtle and hard-to-find bugs. In general, client data should be used cautiously, and passing widgets as client data is particularly error-prone.

Another problem is that the single-function architecture of the original design in unlikely to be supportable as the program develops. The modular approach described in the previous section is not just for the user interface layout; organizing programs as a collection of well-defined modules is simply good software engineering practice. However, it is harder to access widgets when the program is broken into separate encapsulated subsystems. Programmers who are used to passing arbitrary widgets as client data, or accessing globally-defined widgets inside callbacks may struggle with the walls created by a more modular approach.

The best approach is to consider the creation of the widget layout and hierarchy as an integrated part of the program's structural design. Each subsystem should be implemented as a self-contained module that exports a public interface. Each module implements whatever functionality it requires, along with its own self-contained widget hierarchy.

For example, the draw program could be composed of at least three separate modules: a Canvas module, a FigureControl module, and a ColorControl module. Each module should have at least one implementation file, and at least a public header file that exports an interface for interacting with the module. For example, the Canvas module might support a `SetColor()` function that accepts an RGB value to be used for drawing new figures. The public header file for this module would look something like:

```
/*************************************************************
 * Canvas.h: Public functions for Canvas module.
 *************************************************************/
extern Widget CreateCanvas ( const char *name, Widget parent );
extern void SetColor ( int red, int green, int blue );
```

With this interface, the ColorControl module can create the buttons used to set colors, register callbacks, and so on without any assumptions about the implementation of the Canvas module, except for the existence of the `SetColor()` function. If we replace the XmDrawingArea widget used in this implementation with a completely different type of widget (perhaps a custom widget that understands Postscript, OpenGL, PEX, or another rendering mechanism), the program should still work correctly, assuming the Canvas module is re-implemented correctly.

For example, a ColorControl module might be written like this:

```
/*************************************************************
 * ColorControl.c: ColorControl module for draw program.
 *************************************************************/
#include <Xm/Xm.h>
#include <Xm/Frame.h>
#include <Xm/RowColumn.h>
#include <Xm/Label.h>
#include <Xm/PushB.h>
#include "Canvas.h" /* Canvas module interface */

static void SelectColorCallback ( Widget,
                                  XtPointer,
                                  XtPointer );

Widget CreateColors ( char *name, Widget parent )
{
    Widget frame, colorlabel, rowColumn, red, green, blue;

   /*
    * Create a labeled frame for all widgets.
    */

    frame = XtCreateManagedWidget ( name, xmFrameWidgetClass,
                                    parent, NULL, 0 );
```

```

    colorlabel = XtVaCreateManagedWidget ( "colorlabel",
                             xmLabelWidgetClass, frame,
                             XmNchildType, XmFRAME_TITLE_CHILD,
                             NULL );
   /*
    * Place the three color buttons in a row column widget.
    */

    rowColumn = XtVaCreateManagedWidget ( "rowColumn",
                                   xmRowColumnWidgetClass,
                                   frame,
                                   XmNorientation, XmHORIZONTAL,
                                   NULL );

    red = XtCreateManagedWidget ( "red",
                                   xmPushButtonWidgetClass,
                                   rowColumn, NULL, 0 );

    XtAddCallback ( red, XmNactivateCallback,
                    SelectColorCallback, "red" );

    green = XtCreateManagedWidget ( "green",
                                    xmPushButtonWidgetClass,
                                    rowColumn, NULL, 0 );

    XtAddCallback ( red, XmNactivateCallback,
                    SelectColorCallback, "green" );

    blue = XtCreateManagedWidget ( "blue",
                                   xmPushButtonWidgetClass,
                                   rowColumn, NULL, 0 );

    XtAddCallback ( red, XmNactivateCallback,
                    SelectColorCallback, "blue" );

    return ( frame );
}
```

The function `SelectColorCallback()` is registered with each button in the color panel. This function retrieves the name of a color from the client data passed to the callback. Once the color has been allocated, and the RGB components are known, the callback calls the external `SetColor()` function to set the current drawing color. The ColorControl module does not have to know about the Canvas module, and the Canvas module does not need to understand how the ColorControl module is implemented.

```
static void SelectColorCallback ( Widget    w,
                                  XtPointer clientData,
                                  XtPointer callData )
{
    char      *colorName = ( char * ) clientData;
    Display   *dpy       = XtDisplay ( w );
    int        scr       = DefaultScreen ( dpy );
    Colormap   cmap      = DefaultColormap ( dpy, scr );
    XColor     color,
               ignore;

   /*
    * Allocate the named color and retrieve
    * the color components.
    */

    XAllocNamedColor ( dpy, cmap, colorName,
                       &color, &ignore );

   /*
    * Call Canvas module's interface to set drawing color.
    */

    SetColor ( color.red,
               color.green,
               color.blue );
}
```

When thinking about program design from this perspective, the use of hierarchy in the widget layout is a natural fallout of the program design. As a side effect, layout problems can be minimized, or at least more easily isolated when they do occur.

Subsystems and Widget Hierarchies in C++

For those who are familiar with C++, it is probably clear that the modular approach described in this section can be implemented using C++ classes. A C++ class can be used to implement each subsystem, hiding all widgets and other details in the private or protected portions of each class. Each class can export a public interface that can be used by other classes by defining public member functions. For example, a Canvas class might be defined as follows:

```
//////////////////////////
// Canvas.h
//////////////////////////
#include <Xm/Xm.h>

class Canvas {

    public:

        Canvas ( const char *name, Widget parent );
        ~Canvas();

        void setColor ( int r, int g, int b );

     private:

        Widget _frame;
        Widget _canvas;

    // other internal data, widgets, functions
};
```

The class constructor could create the widgets supported within the module, and perform other initialization as needed:

```
/////////////////////////
// Canvas.C:
/////////////////////////
#include "Canvas.h"
#include <Xm/Frame.h>
#include <Xm/DrawingA.h>

Canvas::Canvas ( const char *name, Widget parent )
{
    _frame = XtCreateManagedWidget ( name, xmFrameWidgetClass,
                                     parent, NULL, 0 );

    _canvas = XtCreateManagedWidget ( "canvas",
                                      xmDrawingAreaWidgetClass,
                                      frame, NULL, 0 );

    // Add callbacks, etc.
}
```

The rest of the class implementation would provide the additional private and public features of the module.

2.7 Conclusion

Debugging occupies a large percentage of a typical programmer's work day. Although the existence of some number of bugs is inevitable, debugging is at best a tedious process of finding and fixing errors that should not have been made to begin with. Good software engineering techniques, along with careful design and coding, can help prevent many, although not all, bugs from being introduced.

Because debugging is so time consuming, it is worthwhile to anticipate the inevitable existence of bugs and plan to make it easy to find them when they do occur. Modern software techniques result in systems that consist of independent modules with well-defined interfaces. If each of these modules is written to help report and identify mistakes, erroneous assumptions, and general misuses, many bugs can be found quickly and easily. By anticipating the types of bugs that might occur, many bugs will be found during development, when they are relatively cheap and easy to fix.

One factor that contributes to many bugs in Motif applications is lack of time spent learning before beginning to code. Graphical user interfaces are relatively new, but users increasingly expect applications to provide them. Many programmers, who may be experienced in other areas, are just starting to learn Motif or other user interface toolkits. The complexity of X and Motif presents a significant learning curve. New Motif programmers need to have some patience and allow time to learn before expecting to develop production-quality user interface code. The time spent learning will be more than regained in time not spent debugging.

3

Debugging Tools

In spite of best efforts, bugs occur in even the most carefully written programs. Even if the techniques described in Chapter 2 are used, mistakes, false assumptions, and logic errors will still be made. Furthermore, the X, Xt and Motif libraries are of little help in debugging. They do not check arguments types, provide assertions, nor generally report any but the most obvious errors. Because the X and Motif libraries are so large, and because the Motif and X functions can be combined in nearly endless ways, most Motif programmers will introduce bugs in spite of anything they do to prevent them.

When bugs are encountered, programmers need tools to gather enough information to identify the source of the bugs. The more information a programmer has available, the better his or her chances at finding the problem quickly. This chapter discusses some tools that can provide information that can be useful when debugging X and Motif applications. Some of these tools are general purpose, like debuggers, while others are special purpose tools that are uniquely suited for X and Motif debugging.

3.1 Debuggers

The primary, and most frequently used tool for debugging is, of course, a debugger. All systems support at least some type of debugger that allows programmers to run a program and examine the state of the program at various points. On UNIX platforms, the dbx debugger is widely available, in one form or another. The dbx debugger provides a character-oriented interface that dates from the pre-GUI days of UNIX. Figure 3.1 shows a typical dbx session.

Stepping

Print call stack

```
% dbx xclock
Process  5444 (xclock) started
[2] Process  5444 (xclock) stopped at [main:23 ,0x400c50]
  23   shell = XtAppInitialize  (  &app, "XClock",   NULL, 0,
(dbx) Step
Process  5444 (xclock) stopped at [main:26 ,0x400c90]
  26   face = XtCreateManagedWidget ( "face",
(dbx) Step
Process  5444 (xclock) stopped at [main:33 ,0x400cbc]
  33   UpdateTime (   ( XtPointer )  face, NULL );
(dbx) Step
Process  5444 (xclock) stopped at [UpdateTime:42 ,0x400d4c]
  42   Widget w =   ( Widget )  clientData;
(dbx) Step
Process  5444 (xclock) stopped at [UpdateTime:50 ,0x400d58]
  50   time ( &tloc );
(dbx) where
>  0 UpdateTime(clientData = 0x1001a770, id = (nil)) ["xclock.c":5
0x400d58]
   1 main(argc = 1, argv = 0x7fffaf14) ["xclock.c":33, 0x400ccc]
```

Figure 3.1 The dbx debugger.

Many platforms also support more modern and powerful debuggers, which often have graphical interfaces and are sometimes easier to use. These debuggers often offer significant advantages over simpler debuggers like dbx. The purpose of any debugger is to provide a programmer with information about the current state of a program and to help the programmer understand how the program arrived at this state. Modern debuggers can take advantage of graphical interface technology to provide more information, presented more effectively, to help the programmer find problems quickly.

For example, Figure 3.2 shows a debugger that exploits the X environment to provide the developer with as much information as possible. This debugger (Silicon Graphics' CaseVision® WorkShop) allows programmers to see the state of many parts of a program at once. As shown, this debugger displays a source view of the program being debugged, the current callstack, a graph of some data structures, and a spreadsheet that continuously evaluates expressions in the current frame of reference. One window even provides a three-dimensional plot of the values in one of the program's data structures. A collection of views displays a variety of information about the program. All views are kept up-to-date as values change, allowing the programmer to understand the state of the program at any point, and to see relationships between data that would be difficult to obtain in a more primitive debugger.

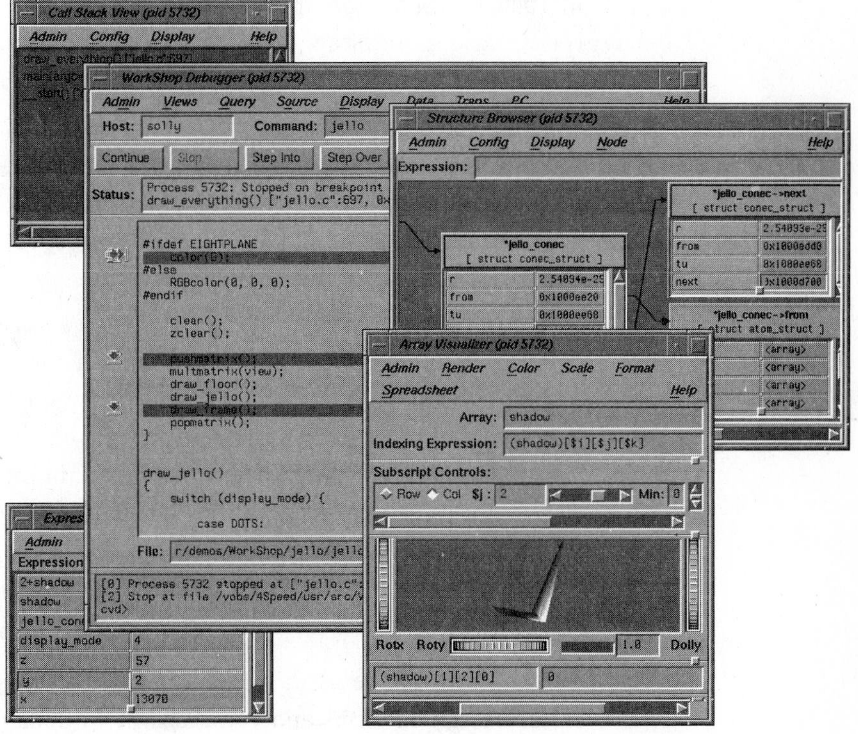

Figure 3.2 A contemporary commercial debugger.

While lacking the power of more contemporary debuggers, a simple debugger like `dbx` can be used effectively to find many bugs that occur in X applications. The `dbx` debugger also has the advantage of being widely available on most platforms. The examples in this book use `dbx`, along with other simple tools, although the basic techniques should be applicable to any debugger you have available.

It is worthwhile to take the time to learn how to make the most effective use of any debugger you have. However, in most situations, knowing how to perform a few key operations should be sufficient. The examples in this book assume you know how to perform a few simple operations, including:

- Setting breakpoints: A breakpoint can be set at any point of the program, which causes the debugger to stop the program before that point is executed. Typically, debuggers allow breakpoints to be set upon entering or leaving a function, or at a specific line number. Some debuggers allow conditional breakpoints to be set, so the program only stops if some condition (usually based on the value of a variable) is true. Some debuggers can also monitor a variable and stop the program if the value of the variable changes.

- Displaying a call stack: A callstack shows the functions currently being executed in order to reach a particular point. Usually, the values of arguments can be displayed as well. Most debuggers allow the programmer to move up and down the callstack to inspect the state of the program at various points in the current call frame.

- Examining core files: Under some circumstances, a program that encounters an error will produce a core file. When a core file is available, examining the program under a debugger normally shows the callstack at the point of the error. Often, the ability to see the callstack is sufficient to understand the source of the problem with no additional effort.

- Stepping: When a program is stopped, most debuggers allow execution to continue one line at a time. Programmers can execute individual lines of code, stepping into each function call that occurs, or they may skip over function calls.

- Evaluate expressions: A key part of debugging involves examining the values of various expressions and variables. Most debuggers allow the values of structures and arrays to be examined, as well as the values of simple data types.

In this book, all examples of debugging techniques can be performed using only simple operations, like those listed above, using the `dbx` debugger. Programmers with access to more sophisticated debuggers should be able to perform the same operations, possibly more easily, and will most likely have access to additional features as well.

Debuggers and Grabs

One difficulty programmers often encounter when using a debugger[1] with X applications involves server *grabs*. At various times, Motif applications grab the pointer or the server, which means that all input is directed to that application until the grab is released. If a programmer uses a debugger to set a breakpoint between the point at which the grab is initiated and the point at which the grab is released, the programmer can be locked out of interacting with either program.

When this situation occurs, the debugger cannot receive input because all input is being grabbed by the program being debugged. However, because the debugger has stopped the program, the program cannot release the grab. The programmer cannot interact with either the debugger or the application being debugged, and the server is effectively frozen. The only solution at this point is to log on from another machine or terminal and kill the process that established the grab.

It is often difficult to know exactly when an application might initiate a grab, and it is surprisingly easy to get caught in this trap. Code related to popup menus is particularly susceptible to this problem. For example, consider the following simple program, adapted from [Young94], which posts a popup menu when the user holds down mouse button three in an XmBulletinBoard widget:

```
/******************************************************
 * popupmenu.c: Demonstrate how to create a popup.
 ******************************************************/
#include <Xm/Xm.h>
#include <Xm/RowColumn.h>
#include <Xm/PushB.h>
#include <Xm/BulletinB.h>

static void PostMenu ( Widget     w,
                       XtPointer clientData,
                       XEvent    *event,
                       Boolean   *flag );

```

[1] Some commercial debuggers provide special support for X-based applications to avoid the problem described in this section.

```
void CreatePopupMenu ( Widget parent );

void main ( int argc, char ** argv )
{
    Widget       shell, bboard;
    XtAppContext app;

   /*
    * Initialize Xt and create a widget.
    */

    shell = XtAppInitialize (  &app, "Popupmenu", NULL, 0,
                               &argc, argv, NULL, NULL, 0 );

    bboard = XtCreateManagedWidget ( "bboard",
                                     xmBulletinBoardWidgetClass,
                                     shell, NULL, 0 );
   /*
    * Create a popup menu, as a child of the bulletin board.
    */

    CreatePopupMenu ( bboard );

    XtRealizeWidget ( shell );
    XtAppMainLoop ( app );
}

void CreatePopupMenu ( Widget parent )
{
    Widget menu, button1, button2;

   /*
    * Create a popup menu. Add an event handler
    * to the given widget to pop up the menu when
    * a mouse button is pressed.
    */

    menu = XmCreatePopupMenu ( parent, "menu", NULL, 0 );

    XtAddEventHandler ( parent, ButtonPressMask, FALSE,
                        PostMenu, menu );

   /*
    * Add buttons to the pane.
    */

    button1 = XtCreateManagedWidget ( "Item1",
                                      xmPushButtonWidgetClass,
                                      menu, NULL, 0 );
```

```
    button2 = XtCreateManagedWidget ( "Item2",
                                      xmPushButtonWidgetClass,
                                      menu, NULL, 0 );
}

static void PostMenu ( Widget     w,
                       XtPointer  clientData,
                       XEvent    *event,
                       Boolean   *flag )
{
    Widget  menu = ( Widget )  clientData;

    if ( event->xbutton.button == Button3 )
    {
        /*
         * Position the menu over the pointer and post.
         */

        XmMenuPosition ( menu,
                         ( XButtonPressedEvent * ) event );
        XtManageChild ( menu );
    }
}
```

Server grabbed

In this program, the grab problem occurs if, for any reason, you need to debug the function `PostMenu()` and attempt to set a breakpoint in that function. This function is called in response to a `ButtonPress` event. A grab is in effect by the time the function is called. Because the grabbing application is stopped by the debugger, the entire system is effectively locked.

To avoid such situations, it is necessary to use two displays or a second terminal. By running the debugger on one display and the program being debugged on the other, the server will not be frozen when the application being debugged grabs the server.

3.2 X Protocol Monitors

Besides general tools like debuggers, there are tools written specifically for X that can be useful when debugging X and Motif applications. One type of tool that is unique to X is the protocol monitor. The MIT X distribution includes a program named `xscope` that prints a trace of all events and requests sent between an application and the server. This program allows programmers to see exactly what events the server generates and what requests an application makes. `Xscope` connects to the X server, like any application, but then allows other applications to connect to it, instead of connecting directly to the X server. `Xscope` simply forwards events and requests to and from the X server, as shown in Figure 3.3.

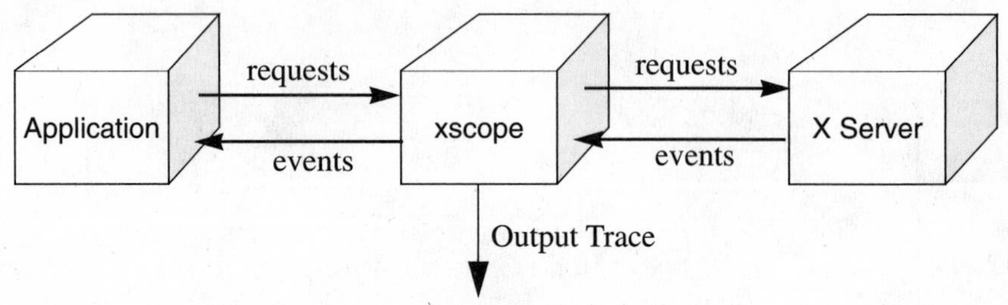

Figure 3.3 Architecture of `xscope`.

`Xscope` prints a trace of all events and requests that pass through it, which provides detailed information about the events and requests that pass between any client and the X server. Figure 3.4 shows a sample of the output produced by `xscope`.

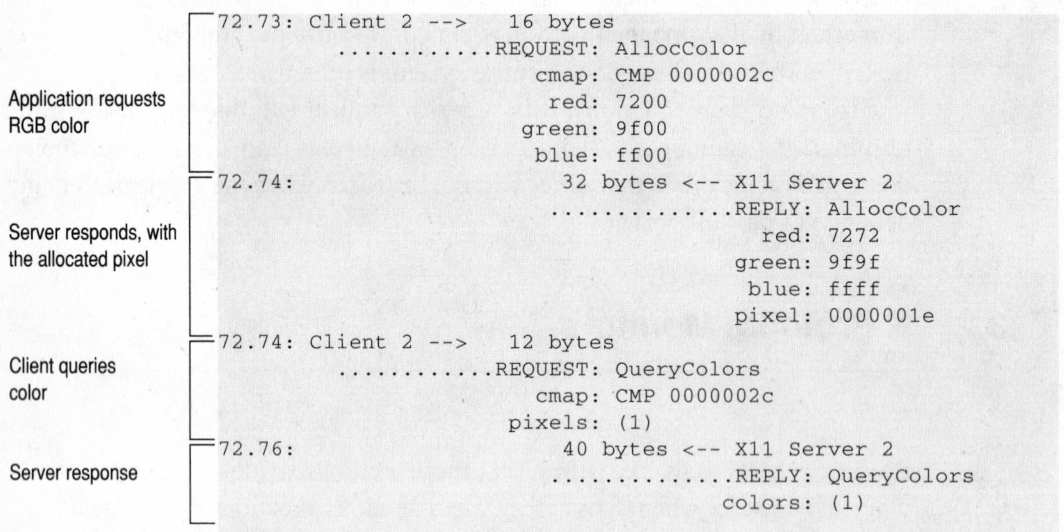

Figure 3.4 Example `xscope` output.

Although `xscope` is useful, the amount of output from this program can be overwhelming. Starting with X11R5, the "contrib" section of the MIT X distribution contains a utility named xmon, which provides a similar, but more flexible capability. Xmon is really two separate programs, `xmonui` and `xmond`. These programs are run as a pair; `xmonui` allows the programmer to control the level of detail reported by `xmond`.

Figure 3.5 shows the `xmonui` interface. The controls in this window allow the user to select categories of events and requests to be traced, specify the level of detail reported for each event, and also gather statistics about events, request, and errors. It is possible to trace individual types of events or requests or to simply print a summary of how many events and requests of each type have occurred. Besides being useful for debugging, `xmond` and `xmonui` are useful for performance tuning, and are discussed further in later chapters.

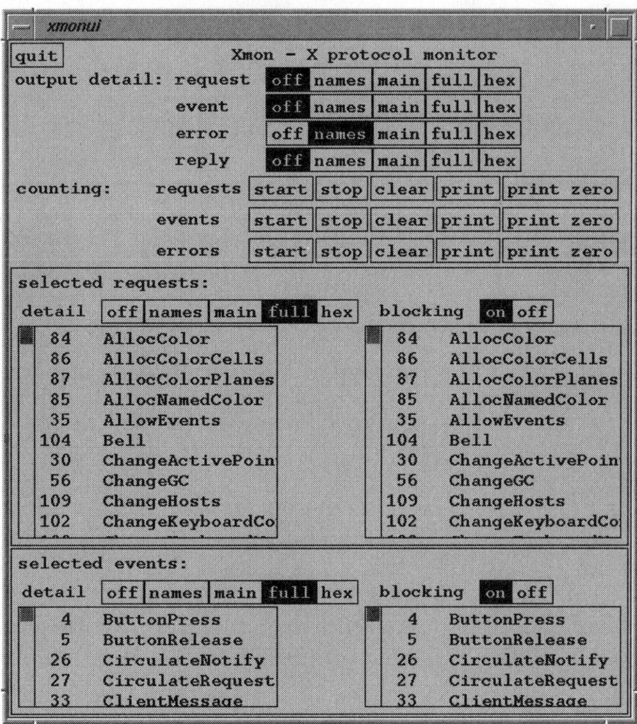

Figure 3.5 The `xmonui` interface.

Like `xscope`, `xmond` is inserted between an application and the X server, as shown in Figure 3.6. Instead of sending requests to the X server, the application sends requests to `xmond`, which forwards them to the X server. `Xmond` can print each request as it passes between the application and the server. Events are handled similarly. The X server sends events to `xmond`, which forwards them to the applications connected to xmon. The `xmonui` program simply sends commands to `xmond` to control how it reports the events and requests that are routed through it.

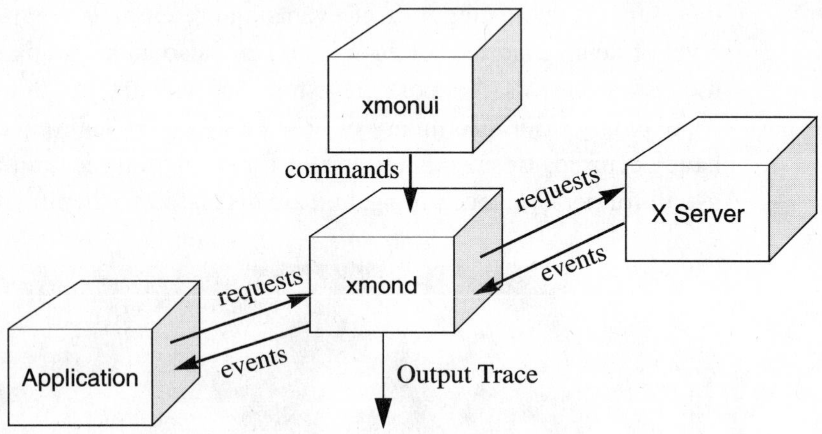

Figure 3.6 Architecture of the xmon facility.

To use this protocol monitor, `xmond` and `xmonui` must be started before the program to be debugged. These programs can be run as follows:

```
% xmonui | xmond -port 1
```

The `port` argument allows the caller to specify what X display an application can use to connect to `xmond`. Next, the program to be debugged can be run using the display number specified as the port instead of the default display number zero. For example, the `xclock` program described in Chapter 2 could be run on a machine named "gizmo" as follows:

```
% xmonui | xmond -port 1 &
% xclock -display gizmo:1.0
```

The set of controls labeled "output detail" at the top of the `xmonui` window allow the user to request a trace of the events and requests that flow between an application and the X server. Events and request tracing can be completely turned off, the names of individual requests or events can be printed as they occur, or complete information about each event and request can be printed. For example, Figure 3.7 shows a sequence of requests that occur upon start-up of a simple program. Only the names of requests and replies are reported:

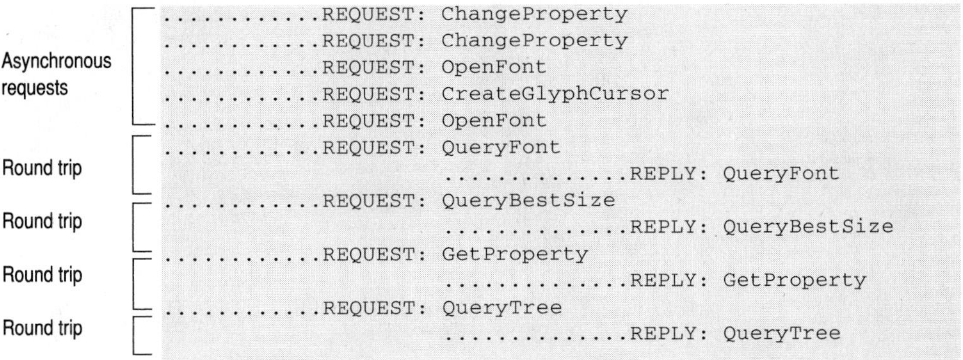

Figure 3.7 Output excerpt from `xmond`.

The output in Figure 3.7 shows a sequence of requests being sent to the X server, including requests for properties to be changed, fonts to be opened, and so on. The first five requests in this sequence are asynchronous, and do not require a reply. However, the `QueryFont` request requires a round trip to the server, which triggers a reply. `GetProperty` and `QueryTree` requests also require replies.

Xmon also allows the user to see more detail about each request, reply, and event. Selecting the "main" option for requests and replies on `xmonui`'s upper panel produces output similar to that shown in Figure 3.8.

The top of Figure 3.8 shows a client requesting the server to allocate a color. The information in the request shows the ID of the colormap and the RGB values to be installed in the allocated color cell. The reply shows the RGB values actually used, along with the pixel allocated for this request. The second request shown in Figure 3.8 asks the X server to create a graphics context. The information printed by `xmond` shows the GC's ID, the drawable associated with this GC, and the mask and values to be set in the GC. Notice that creating a GC does not require a reply. Xlib assigns the identifier based on a strategy that guarantees unique numbers, so that the server does not have to reply to this request. Requests to create windows are handled similarly.

Client request to allocate RGB color

Server response with allocated pixel

Client request to create a graphics context

```
............REQUEST: AllocColor
              cmap: CMP 00000033
               red: ff00
             green: ff00
              blue: 0000
                           ..............REPLY: AllocColor
                                             red: ffff
                                           green: ffff
                                            blue: 0000
                                           pixel: 00000003
............REQUEST: CreateGC
     graphic-context-id: GXC 05400010
               drawable: DWB 00000035
             value-mask: background | font | graphics-exposure
             value-list:
                   background: 00000070
                         font: FNT 0540000f
             graphics-exposures: False
```

Figure 3.8 More detailed information trace from `xmond`.

For some uses, it is sufficient to know how many events and requests have occurred. The `xmonui` panel labeled "counting" allows users to print a summary of the events, requests, or errors that have occurred since the last time the category was "cleared". Pressing the "print" button produces a table, as shown in Figure 3.9.

```
requests received:
code   count   name
 70      2     PolyFillRectangle
events received:
code   count   name:
  7     13     EnterNotify
  8     14     LeaveNotify
  9      1     FocusIn
 10      1     FocusOut
no errors received
```

Figure 3.9 Event and request summary from `xmond`.

Here, `xmond` reports that an application has made 2 `PolyFillRect-angle` requests. The server has generated 13 `EnterNotify` events, 14 `LeaveNotify` events, one `FocusIn` and one `FocusOut` event. No error events were received during the interval of this report.

The bottom section of the xmonui interface allows users to select specific events and requests for tracing. The user can control which events and requests are reported, and with what level of detail the operation should be reported. The bottom panel also allows the user to select specific request and events that should be blocked, or not transmitted between the real server and clients.

One interesting way to use xmon is to run a program under a debugger, with the display set so that the program is connected to xmond. Then, you can use the debugger to step through the program while watching xmond's output to provide a clear picture of what code produces which requests.

3.3 Tools for Inspecting the User Interface

It is often useful to be able to examine the appearance and externally visible characteristics of a program's user interface in greater detail, particularly when dealing with visual problems and layout bugs. This section describes some tools that can help programmers inspect the visual aspects of a running program's interface, and gather other X-specific information.

editres

Editres is a unique tool that can be extremely useful when debugging user interfaces. This program, which is distributed with X11R5, provides an easy way to examine the widget hierarchy created by a running application. Editres can also be used to highlight any widget in a running application.

Editres relies on an inter-client protocol based on selections and client messages. If editres doesn't work with your version of Motif, editres support can be added easily. To add editres support, an application must add an event handler for the shell returned by XtAppInitialize(), as follows:

```
XtAddEventHandler ( shell, ( EventMask ) 0, TRUE,
                    _XEditResCheckMessages, NULL );
```

The function _XEditResCheckMessages() is defined in libXmu.a, which is part of the MIT X distribution. Applications that use the editres protocol must link with this library in addition to the other Motif and X libraries.

Figure 3.10 shows the editres program as it displays the widget hierarchy of a simple program.

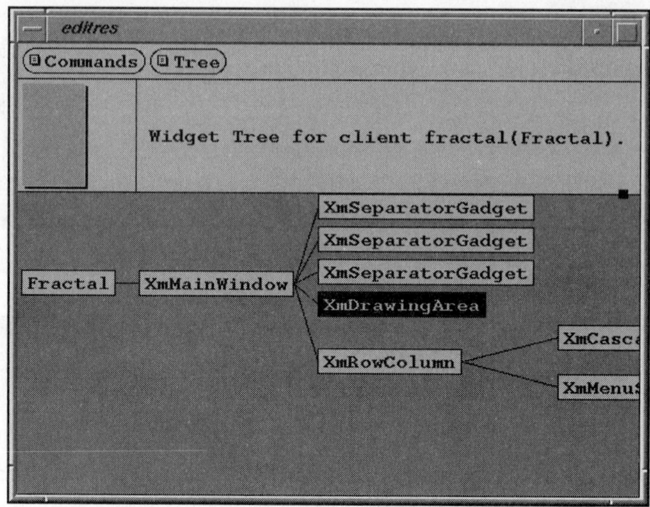

Figure 3.10 The editres program.

The following "hello world" program adds editres support:

```
/**********************************************
 * hello.c: Display "Hello World" in a window
 **********************************************/
#include <Xm/Xm.h>
#include <Xm/Label.h>

extern XtEventHandler _XEditResCheckMessages;

void main ( int argc, char **argv )
{
    Widget       shell, msg;
    XtAppContext app;
    XmString     xmstr;

    shell = XtAppInitialize ( &app, "Hello", NULL, 0,
                              &argc, argv, NULL, NULL, 0 );

   /*
    * Install event handler for editres protocol.
    */

```

Hook for editres

```
    XtAddEventHandler ( shell, ( EventMask ) 0, TRUE,
                               _XEditResCheckMessages, NULL);

    xmstr = XmStringCreateLocalized ( "Hello World" );

    msg = XtVaCreateManagedWidget ( "hello",
                                    xmLabelWidgetClass, shell,
                                    XmNlabelString,     xmstr,
                                    NULL );


    XmStringFree ( xmstr );
    XtRealizeWidget ( shell );
    XtAppMainLoop ( app );
}
```

This program must be linked with libXmu.a, as follows:

```
cc -o hello hello.c -lXm -lXmu -lXt -lX11
```

xmag

Another program that can be useful when working with visual problems and layout bugs is `xmag`. `Xmag`, shown in Figure 3.11, is a simple interactive program that displays a small portion of the screen at a magnified scale. `Xmag` makes it easy to examine the color values of individual pixels, and can be useful when investigating layout, rendering, and other visual problems.

Figure 3.11 An `xmag` close-up of a window manager border.

The XtGeo Library

Another tool that can be useful when investigating geometry and layout problems is the XtGeo library. This library, developed at the Open Software Foundation, modifies the internal Xt geometry management functions to print information about how a widget's geometry is managed as a program runs. The XtGeo library is freely available as contributed software. To use libXtGeo, the program to be inspected must be relinked with the XtGeo library specified before the Xt library. For example, the `xclock` program discussed in Chapter 2 could be compiled as follows (some systems may require additional libraries).

```
cc -o xclock xclock.c -lXm -lXtGeo -lXt -lX11
```

To see detailed information about how the widgets in a program are sized and positioned, it is necessary to run the program with the resource `geoTattler` set to "`on`". For example, the `xclock` program could be run as follows:

```
xclock -xrm "*geoTattler: on"
```

Running this command produces the output shown in Figure 3.12.

Start geometry management process	`xclock -xrm "*geoTattler: on"`
	`Call "xclock"[1,1]'s realize proc`
	`Child "face"[30,18] is marked managed`

Face requests its desired size	`XtSetValues sees some geometry changes for "face".`
	`    "face" is making a geometry request to its parent "xcl`
	`        Asking for a change in width: from 30 to 158.`

Xt allows size	`        Parent "xclock" is not realized yet.`
	`        Copy values from request to widget.`
	`    and return XtGeometryYes.`
	`    XtSetValues calls "face"'s resize proc.`

Parent told about new child	`Call "xclock"[0,0]'s changemanaged`
	`"face" is being configured by its parent "xclock"`
	`    No change in configuration`

Create windows	`Call "xclock"[158,18]'s realize proc` `Call "face"[158,18]'s realize proc`
Redraw face	`XtSetValues calls ClearArea on "face".`

Figure 3.12 Trace of `xclock`'s geometry management, produced by XtGeo.

The output in Figure 3.12 traces the steps performed internally by the Xt geometry management facilities to determine the final size and position of each widget. In the `xclock` program, the management starts when the shell widget is realized. Xt checks all children for any widgets marked as managed. Each widget determines its desired size, and communicates with its parent if necessary, to request that size. If widgets are not yet realized, Xt simply grants the request without consulting the parent. Finally, after all geometries have been established, windows are created for each widget.

The geometry management process shown in Figure 3.12 is extremely simple. For more complex widget hierarchies, XtGeo can produce enormous amounts of output, which can be much more difficult to understand. With some practice, however, XtGeo can provide invaluable information about the geometry management of any application. In some cases you can limit the amount of output by limiting the trace to specific widgets. The `geoTattler` resource can be activated for individual widgets or widget hierarchies using the resource manager's pattern matching abilities. For example, `xclock` could be run as follows, to show only the geometry management that involves the face widget:

```
xclock -xrm "*face*geoTattler: on"
```

appres

Problems with widget layout or other visual characteristics of an application are often related to resources. Applications pick up resources from several places, from the application's app-defaults file to the user's .Xdefaults file. It is often useful to know what resources an application loads into its resource database. The MIT X distribution includes a simple program that can report the resources loaded by any application from all locations. This program, named `appres`, allows a user to specify a class and instance name to see what resources would be picked up by a program with that name and class.

For example, the resources that would affect the `xclock` program could be determined by running `appres` as follows:

```
appres XClock xclock
```

xprop

X and Motif applications use properties to communicate with the window manager. In some cases, it is useful to know exactly what properties are set, and to examine the values of those properties. The `xprop` program allows a user to select a window by clicking on the window using the mouse. The program then reports all properties associated with that window. Figure 3.13 shows the output of `xprop` when used to examine the `xclock` program described in Chapter 2.

The information in Figure 3.13 shows that `xclock`'s window is currently in a normal state (not iconified) and that the program responds to several Motif protocol messages. It also shows that `xclock`'s class name is "XClock", that the machine on which the program is running is named "gizmo", and that `xclock` does not accept input focus. Depending on the problem you are trying to solve, some or all this information may be useful.

For example, I recently encountered a problem in which an application appeared to not respond to resources set in its app-defaults file. Running `appres` showed that the resource should exist. However, checking the window manager properties with `xprop` showed that the class name of the application had been misspelled, which explained why the expected app-defaults file was not being loaded.

```
WM_STATE(WM_STATE):
                window state: Normal
                icon window: 0x1000579
_MOTIF_WM_MESSAGES(ATOM) = _MOTIF_WM_OFFSET
WM_PROTOCOLS(ATOM): protocols _MOTIF_WM_MESSAGES, WM_DELETE_WINDOW
WM_CLASS(STRING) = "xclock", "XClock"
WM_HINTS(WM_HINTS):
                Client accepts input or input focus: False
                Initial state is Normal State.
WM_NORMAL_HINTS(WM_SIZE_HINTS):
                program specified location: 0, 0
                program specified size: 158 by 18
                window gravity: NorthWest
WM_CLIENT_MACHINE(STRING) = "gizmo"
WM_COMMAND(STRING) = { "xclock" }
WM_ICON_NAME(STRING) = "xclock"
WM_NAME(STRING) = "xclock"
```

Figure 3.13 Example `xprop` output.

xwininfo

Another program that can be used to gather information about the state of a program and its windows is `xwininfo`. This program allows the user to query the server for various information about a specific window. By default, the window is selected interactively by clicking on the window whose characteristics are to be reported.

Figure 3.14 shows a typical session with `xwininfo`. After a window has been selected, `xwininfo` reports the window's geometry, depth, visual type, and other information.

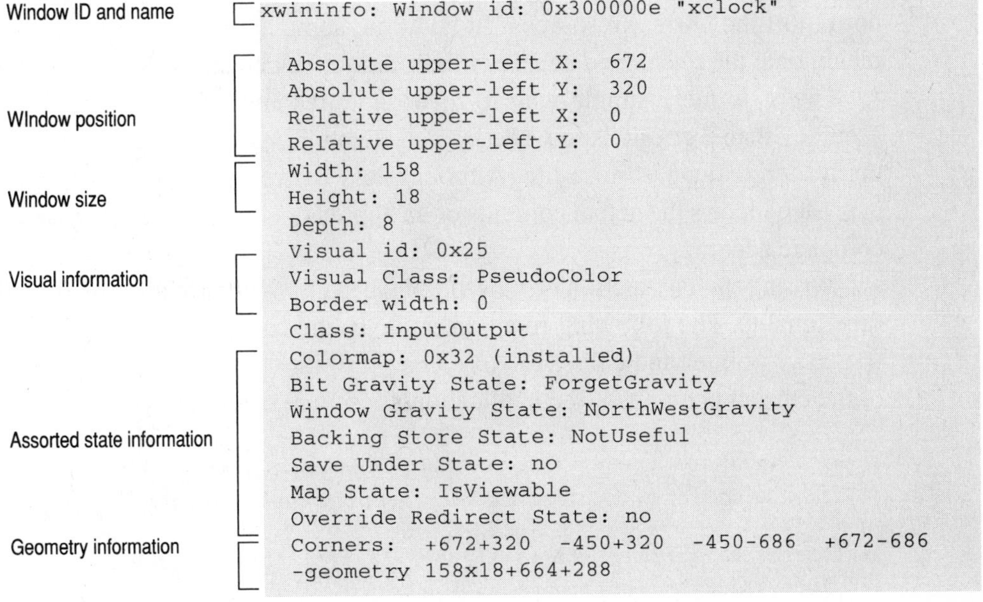

Window ID and name
WIndow position
Window size
Visual information
Assorted state information
Geometry information
xwininfo: Window id: 0x300000e "xclock"
Absolute upper-left X: 672
Absolute upper-left Y: 320
Relative upper-left X: 0
Relative upper-left Y: 0
Width: 158
Height: 18
Depth: 8
Visual id: 0x25
Visual Class: PseudoColor
Border width: 0
Class: InputOutput
Colormap: 0x32 (installed)
Bit Gravity State: ForgetGravity
Window Gravity State: NorthWestGravity
Backing Store State: NotUseful
Save Under State: no
Map State: IsViewable
Override Redirect State: no
Corners: +672+320 -450+320 -450-686 +672-686
-geometry 158x18+664+288

Figure 3.14 Information reported by `xwininfo`.

3.4 Home Grown Tools

Although most of the tools described in this chapter are stand-alone programs, many programmers develop collections of useful functions and utilities that are useful for solving specific problems during debugging. Sometimes these tools are system-dependent and exploit features of a particular system. Others may simply be too fragile, special purpose, or undocumented to be generally useful, and are therefore not distributed to wider audiences. This section explores a few simple ideas for such special purpose functions and facilities.

A Resource Dumper

The `appres` program reports the resources that an application should load when it is run. However, there is always a possibility that the output of `appres` will not exactly match the contents of an application's resource database. For example, as mentioned earlier, if a program's class name is spelled differently in the program than when `appres` is used, `appres` will not report the correct resources. In addition, some applications may directly manipulate the resource database, which cannot be detected by `appres`.

One extremely simple way to investigate resource problems with more accuracy than `appres` is to write a small function that dumps the contents of the resource database to a file. Although less convenient than `appres`, this approach reports the actual contents of an application's resource database with complete accuracy.

Writing such a function is quite simple, because Xlib provides the required functionality. The following function retrieves the resource database from the `Display` pointer and calls `XrmPutFileDatabase()` to write a text version of the current contents of the application's resource database.

```
/*******************************************************
 *  DumpResources.c: Save resource database contents
 *                   to a file.
 *******************************************************/
#include <X11/Intrinsic.h>
#include <stdio.h>

void DumpResources ( Display *dpy )
{
    char *name, *className, buf[100];
    XrmDatabase db = XtDatabase ( dpy );

   /*
    * Generate file name from application name.
    */

    XtGetApplicationNameAndClass ( dpy, &name, &className );
    sprintf ( buf, "/usr/tmp/database.%s", name );

```

```
    /*
     * Save database to file.
     */

    XrmPutFileDatabase ( db, buf );
}
```

Function Wrappers

Chapter 2 shows how the `assert()` macro allows programmers to write code that makes errors easier to find. Assertions are an effective way to catch function calls that provide incorrect parameters. It would be extremely useful if all libraries were available in debugging versions that use the `assert()` macro. Unfortunately, none of the X and Motif libraries use assertions, and the X and Motif functions rarely check the values passed to them.

There are several ways to add additional type checking to functions in libraries. First, the sources to Xlib and Xt are readily available, so you could go through these libraries and add assertions and other tests to create your own debugging versions. However, this task is tedious and may require a greater understanding of the X and Xt internals than you have, or wish to have. Furthermore, Motif source code is not usually available.

Warning! System-dependent technique

There is an interesting approach that can be used on systems that support UNIX SVR4-style dynamic shared libraries. On these systems, it is possible to write a wrapper around an existing function that has the same name as the existing function. The wrapper can perform any tests required, and then use the shared library technology to load and call the real function. Although wrapping each function in Xt and Motif would be a formidable task, this technique could be used to add tests to crucial functions that appear to be involved in a specific problem under investigation.

For example, suppose that a program crashes shortly after creating some widgets, and you suspect that some bad data is being passed to `XtCreateWidget()` at some point. Possible bad parameters might include a parent that has already been destroyed, a `NULL` widget name, or an `ArgList` that contains bad entries, or whose size is given incorrectly. Unfortunately, Xt does not check for any of these things, and using a debugger to check every value passed to every call to `XtCreateWidget()` would be extremely tedious.

Instead, the following function wrapper could be written and linked with your program before the Xt library. This function is highly system-dependent, but works on at least Silicon Graphics' IRIX 5.0 or later and Sun's Solaris operating system. HP's HPUX 9.0 or later has similar capabilities, but provides a slightly different API. Other systems may or may not have the required dynamic loading capabilities to support this technique.

A function wrapper that can be substituted for `XtCreateWidget()`, while performing additional checks, can be written as follows:

```
/*****************************************
 * CreateWidgetWrapper.c:
 *****************************************/
#ifndef NDEBUG
#include <dlfcn.h>
#include <assert.h>
#include <X11/Intrinsic.h>
#include <ctype.h>

/*
 * Typedef needed to cast return value of dlsym(). Type
 * declaration is taken from Intrinsic.h.
 */

typedef Widget ( *createfunc ) ( _Xconst _XtString,
                                 WidgetClass, Widget,
                                 ArgList, Cardinal );
/*
 * If linking is handled correctly, this function
 * will be called instead of the real XtCreateWidget.
 */

Widget XtCreateWidget ( _Xconst _XtString name,
                        WidgetClass      widgetclass,
                        Widget           parent,
                        ArgList          args,
                        Cardinal         numArgs )
{
    Widget     w;
    void      *handle;
    createfunc fptr;
    int        i;

   /*
    * Xt seems to accept NULL names, but it is a bad idea
    * because resources cannot be retrieved properly.
    */
```

Check name

```
    assert ( name && *name );

   /*
    * Make sure the parent is legitimate.
    */
```

```
Valid     44       assert ( XtIsObject( parent ) && XtIsComposite ( parent ) );
widget?   45
          46       for ( i = 0; i < numArgs; i++ )
          47       {
          48           /*
          49            * Check each argument for a NULL name. There's no
          50            * way to check for good values, because all values
          51            * could be valid. This test tries to  confirm that
          52            * numArgs is less than or equal to the number of
          53            * non-NULL resources in the arglist.
          54            */
          55
          56           assert ( args && args[i].name &&
          57                    isascii ( args[i].name[0] ) );
          58       }
          59
          60      /*
          61       * Load Xt. Location may vary from system to system.
          62       */
          63
          64       handle = dlopen ( "/usr/lib/libXt.so", RTLD_LAZY );
Is Xt     65       assert ( handle );
loaded?   66
          67      /*
          68       * Get a pointer to XtCreateWidget, in the newly
          69       * loaded library.
          70       */
          71
          72       fptr = ( createfunc ) dlsym ( handle, "XtCreateWidget" );
Function  73       assert ( fptr );
found?    74
          75      /*
          76       * Call the real Xt function.
          77       */
          78
          79       w =  (*fptr)( name, widgetclass, parent, args, numArgs );
          80
          81      /*
          82       * Check the return value.
          83       */
          84
Widget    85       assert ( w && XtIsObject ( w ) );
created?  86       return ( w );
          87  }
          88  #endif
```

This function is declared exactly like `XtCreateWidget()`, with the same name, arguments, and return type. In addition, line 15 declares a type that represents a function whose type signature matches `XtCreateWidget()`. This declaration is needed for a cast that is required later. The body of the function performs several tests, making heavy use of the `assert()` macro. The function tests that a valid string has been provided as a name, and that the given parent is a valid composite widget. The tests that begin on line 46 attempt to check whether the length of the argument array matches the specified length. This test could fail to catch some error conditions, but it serves as a sanity check.

Finally, if all tests succeed, the wrapper function calls `dlopen()` on line 64 to load the real Xt library. The function `dlopen()` returns a handle that can be used to identify this library. An assertion confirms that Xt was loaded successfully. Next, on line 72, the wrapper uses the function `dlsym()` to obtain a pointer to the implementation of `XtCreateWidget()` defined by the Xt library. Once a pointer to `XtCreateWidget()` has been successfully retrieved, the real function is invoked on line 79. The wrapper then checks the value returned by the real `XtCreateWidget()`, using an assertion, before returning the widget.

Once written, this function can be linked with a program to test the added assertions. It is important that when resolving calls to `XtCreateWidget()`, the linker uses the wrapper function rather than the one found in Xt. Normally, the correct function will be used if you simply link the file containing the function as part of your program, before the Xt library, although this behavior is system-dependent. Notice that the entire file shown above is contained inside an conditional compilation statement. If `NDEBUG` is defined, the file will be effectively empty and the program will automatically pick up the real `XtCreateWidget()` instead of the wrapper.

Wrapping every Xt and Motif function as demonstrated here would be extremely time-consuming and probably not worth the effort. However, for specific hard-to-debug situations, selective use of this technique may be valuable.

A Simple Widget "Lint" Facility

One general tool that is often useful to C programmers is "lint". Lint is a program that can be run over C source code to look for certain classes of errors or questionable style that the C compiler may not catch. Such situations include not testing return values, passing incorrect data types to functions, not returning values from functions, and so on.

It might be useful to apply the same basic approach to Motif programs. There are certain classes of errors that should be easy to detect, but that are idiomatic to Motif or X, and therefore not something that a compiler would detect. A series of tests based on domain knowledge of Motif should be able to detect some common problems more easily than waiting for an error to appear in a program.

This section describes a simple framework for implementing such a facility. This mechanism, which we will call "WL" (**W**idget**L**int), allows applications to call a single function, `WLRunTests()`, from anywhere within a program. This function, which takes a widget and an identifying string as arguments, traverses the widget hierarchy, invoking a collection of tests on each widget. As described here, WL does not implement any specific tests initially, but instead supports the process of walking through the widget hierarchy, and invoking test functions on each widget. Various test functions can be added easily. Each test is independent, and new test functions can be written for specific conditions without affecting the other tests. Some tests might check for serious error conditions, while others might implement rules of thumb that should usually not be broken.

The WL library requires programs to be modified before they can run these tests, but this requirement should not cause a significant problem. The mechanism is intended primarily for use during development, to help catch errors at the earliest possible stage. The package is written so that when `NDEBUG` is defined, the code completely disappears, allowing applications to leave the tests in production versions. Even when `NDEBUG` is not defined, the tests are only executed when a resource, `*WLint`, is set to "on".

Programs that use this facility should include the file wlint.h, which simply provides the definition of the `WLRunTests()` function.

```
/***********************************************************
 * wlint.h: External interface for "Widget Lint" tester.
 ***********************************************************/

/* Allow this module to be removed by defining NDEBUG. */

#ifndef NDEBUG
extern void _WLRunTests ( Widget, const char * );
#define WLRunTests(w, str) _WLRunTests ( w, str )
#else
#define WLRunTests(w,str)
#endif
```

The WL framework, and any test functions to be added to it, needs several definitions, which are contained in a private header file, wlintP.h. This header file declares the type of each test function, a data structure used internally in the framework, and a function that can be used to add new tests. The private header file also defines an enumerated type, whose values are used when installing a new test. Test functions added to the WL framework can specify that they should be called for all widgets, only primitive widgets, only manager widgets, only shell widgets, or only gadgets. It is also possible to specify that a test function should only be invoked one time, instead of once for every widget in the application's widget hierarchy.

```
/*******************************************************
 * wlintP.h: Declarations for use inside WL library
 *           and related test functions.
 *******************************************************/
#include <X11/Intrinsic.h>

typedef enum { SHELL,      /* Test only shells */
               MANAGER,    /* Test only managers */
               PRIMITIVE,  /* Test primitives and gadgets */
               GADGET,     /* Test only gadgets */
               ALL,        /* Test all widget types */
               JUSTONCE    /* Don't traverse widget tree */
             } TestType;

typedef enum { INIT, RUNTEST, POSTOP } ActionType;

typedef void ( *WLTestProc )( Widget, ActionType );

typedef struct {
    char        *name;  /* Name of the test */
    TestType    type;   /* Widget types to be tested */
    WLTestProc  func;   /* Test function to be executed */
} TestData;

/*
 * Convenience function for adding tests to
 * internal TestData array.
 */

extern void WLAddTest ( char        *name,
                        TestType    type,
                        WLTestProc  func );
```

The file wlint.c contains the core of the WL framework, including the implementation of the `_WLRunTests()` function. This function calls an external function that installs all current tests, and then loops through a list of tests. For each test, an optional message reports the beginning of the test. Then, the test function is called once with the second argument specified as `INIT`. This allows each test function to perform any initialization it might require. Next, `RunTest()` is called for each widget in the hierarchy. `RunTest()` arranges for each test to be performed on any or all types of widgets, as needed. Each individual test is responsible for all output associated with the test. Finally, the test function is invoked a final time, with a value of `POSTOP`, to allow the function to perform any required clean-up, report any accumulated data, or anything else the test requires.

```
/**************************************
 * wlint.c: Driver for WL framework.
 **************************************/
#include "wlintP.h"
#include <X11/IntrinsicP.h>
#include <Xm/Xm.h>
#include <Xm/MenuShell.h>
#include <Xm/Display.h>
#include <stdio.h>

extern void WLRegisterTests ( void );
static void RunTest ( Widget w,
                      TestType type,
                      WLTestProc func );
static void InitializeTests ( void );

static TestData *testList = NULL;
static int       numTests = 0;

void _WLRunTests ( Widget w, const char *str )
{
    int      i;
    char     *opt = NULL;
    Boolean  verbose = FALSE;
    char     *name, *appClass;

   /*
    * Only allow this test to be run for shell widgets.
    * Disallow the XmDisplay shell used for drag and drop
    * and menu shells as starting points.
    */

```

```
    if ( !XtIsShell ( w ) ||
         XmIsDisplay ( w ) ||
         XmIsMenuShell ( w) )
       return;

   /*
    * Get the name of the application to allow resources
    * to be retrieved.
    */

    XtGetApplicationNameAndClass ( XtDisplay ( w ),
                                   &name, &appClass );
   /*
    * Find out if the tests should be run, and if verbose
    * mode should be turned on.
    */

    opt = XGetDefault ( XtDisplay ( w ), name, "WLint" );

    if ( opt == NULL ||
         strcasecmp ( opt, "on" ) != 0 )
      return;

    opt = XGetDefault ( XtDisplay ( w ), name, "WLverbose" );

    if ( opt != NULL &&
         strcasecmp ( opt, "true" ) == 0 )
       verbose = TRUE;

    if ( verbose )
    {
       /*
        * Set up the tests. Print any message provided.
        */

        fprintf ( stderr, "\n\n" );
        fprintf ( stderr, "****************************\n" );
        if ( str )
            fprintf ( stderr, "Starting test %s\n", str );
        fprintf ( stderr, "****************************\n" );
    }

   /*
    * Initialize data structures, and install functions
    * to be executed.
    */

    InitializeTests();
    WLRegisterTests();
```

```

    /*
     * Report each test as it begins, and fire off the test.
     */

     for ( i = 0; i < numTests; i++ )
     {
         ( *testList[i].func ) ( NULL, INIT );

         if ( verbose )
         {
              fprintf ( stderr, "\n\n" );
              fprintf ( stderr, "**********************\n" );
              if ( testList[i].name )
                  fprintf ( stderr, "TEST: %s\n",
                            testList[i].name );
              fprintf ( stderr, "***********************\n" );
         }

         RunTest ( w, testList[i].type, testList[i].func );

        /*
         * Run each test function one last time.
         */

         ( *testList[i].func ) ( NULL, POSTOP );
     }
}
```

The function RunTest() does the real work of this package, by invoking a test for any widget that matches the criteria for which the test was registered. RunTest() calls itself recursively to traverse the entire widget hierarchy, unless the type of a test is JUSTONCE.

```
static void RunTest ( Widget      w,
                      TestType    type,
                      WLTestProc func)
{
    unsigned int i;

    if ( !w )  /* End the recursive test */
        return;

    /*
     * Compare the type for which each test has been
     * with the type of the current widget, and execute
     * the test function, as appropriate.
     */
```

```
    switch ( type )
    {
      case SHELL:
        if ( XtIsShell ( w ) )
            ( *func )( w, RUNTEST );
        break;
      case MANAGER:
        if ( XmIsManager ( w ) )
            ( *func )( w, RUNTEST );
        break;
      case PRIMITIVE:
        if ( XmIsPrimitive ( w ) || XmIsGadget ( w ) )
            ( *func )( w, RUNTEST );
        break;
      case GADGET:
        if ( XmIsGadget ( w ) )
            ( *func )( w, RUNTEST );
        break;
      case ALL:
        ( *func )( w, RUNTEST );
        break;
      case JUSTONCE:
        ( *func )( w, RUNTEST );
        return;
    }

   /*
    * If this widget can have children, call RunTest()
    * recursively for each child.
    */
    if ( XtIsComposite ( w ) )
    {
        CompositeWidget cw = ( CompositeWidget ) w;
        for ( i = 0; i < cw->composite.num_children; i++ )
            RunTest ( cw->composite.children[i], type, func );
    }

   /*
    * Any widget (but not gadgets) can have popup
    * children. Run the test for these as well.
    */

    if ( XtIsWidget ( w ) )
        for ( i = 0; i < w->core.num_popups; i++ )
        {
            Widget child = w->core.popup_list[i];
            RunTest ( child, type, func );
        }
}
```

The function `InitializeTests()` simply initializes the array of test data to `NULL` and sets the number of tests to `NULL`.

```
173 static void InitializeTests (void )
174 {
175     numTests = 0;
176 
177     if ( testList )
178         XtFree ( ( char * ) testList );
179 
180     testList = NULL;
181 }
```

The remaining function is `WLAddTest()`, which just provides a convenient way to register a test function with the WL framework. This function expects a name, the type of test being added, and a test function to be executed.

```
182 void WLAddTest ( char *name, TestType type, WLTestProc func )
183 {
184     numTests++;
185 
186     testList = ( TestData* )
187                    XtRealloc ( ( char * ) testList,
188                                   sizeof ( TestData ) * numTests );
189 
190     if ( name )
191         testList[numTests-1].name = XtNewString ( name );
192     else
193         testList[numTests-1].name = NULL;
194 
195     testList[numTests-1].type = type;
196     testList[numTests-1].func = func;
197 }
```

The second file used in the WL framework defines the function `WLRegisterTests()`. `_WLRunTests()` calls this function on line 81, on page 110, to register all test functions. At this point, `WLRegisterTests()` is an empty stub. As tests are added, each test must be registered by calling `WLAddTest()` from within this function. We will see examples of how this function is used shortly.

```
/*****************************************************
 * register.c: Register all test functions with WL
 *****************************************************/
#include "wlintP.h"

/* Declare new external test functions here */
void WLRegisterTests ( void )
{
    /* Add new tests here by calling WLAddTest() */
}
```

Writing Test Functions

Before the WL framework described in the previous section can be useful, tests must be added. WL is designed to allow simple, easy-to-write tests to be added individually. A good test should look for a single, well-defined situation, and report any potential errors. Each test must be written carefully, to avoid introducing errors into the program, or affecting other tests. However, the task performed by each test is limited only by your imagination.

There are only a few rules to be followed by any test function. First, the function should be declared as a void function with no return value. Each test should take a two arguments. The first is a widget to be tested, while the second indicates why the particular function is being called. Each function is called once before any widgets are processed, with the second argument given as `INIT`, to allow for any initialization. Each test function is then called for each widget in the hierarchy that matches the way the function was registered. The value of the second argument is given as `RUNTEST` when a widget has been provided as a test subject.

Finally, the function is called one last time with the second argument given as `POSTOP`, to allow any post-processing to be performed after all tests. Some tests might report some cumulative data at this point, or do some cleanup. Any information to be reported should be written to `stderr`.

The following example demonstrates the form of a typical test function:

```
/*******************************************************
 * sample.c: Demonstrate the form of a WL test function
 *******************************************************/
#include <X11/IntrinsicP.h>
#include <stdio.h>
#include "wlintP.h"

void SampleTest ( Widget w, ActionType action )
{
```

```
    if ( action == INIT )
    {
       /* Optional: Perform any initialization here */

        return;
    }

    if ( action == POSTOP )
    {
       /* Optional: report any summary data */

        return;
    }

    /* Perform any tests here, reporting errors to stderr. */
}
```

As an example, let's look at a simple function that tests whether or not a given widget reference has been destroyed or corrupted. By installing this function in the WL framework, it is possible to test the validity of every widget in the widget hierarchy. The `ValidWidgetTest()` function simply returns when the `action` argument is `INIT` or `POSTOP`. Otherwise, it calls `XtIsObject()` to test whether the widget reference is valid. If the test fails, an error message is reported.

Normally, a test function would simply return after reporting an error, but in this case, the error is so severe that `ValidWidgetTest()` just aborts. The resulting core file allows the programmer to use a debugger to investigate further. Once an invalid widget reference exists in the widget tree, it is likely that additional tests will fail anyway. This function does try to provide some clue by saving the last widget examined so its name can be reported when an error occurs. It is difficult to know for sure what relationship this widget would have to the trashed widget, but having an identifiable landmark before the point of error can be useful.

If a widget passes the `XtIsObject()` test, `ValidWidgetTest()` also tests to see if a widget is in the process of being destroyed. Notice that this test requires that the private file IntrinsicP.h be included, to allow access to the internal members of a widget. The fact that a widget is being destroyed may or may not be an error. The presence of this test allows the WL framework to report this situation at any time. It is up to the programmer to decide if the report indicates a problem or not.

The first test function, `ValidWidgetTest()` can be written as follows:

```
/*******************************************************
 * ValidWidgetTest.c: Test integrity of each widget.
 ******************************************************/
#include <X11/IntrinsicP.h>
#include <stdio.h>
#include <stdlib.h>
#include "wlintP.h"

static Widget lastWidget = NULL;

void ValidWidgetTest ( Widget w, ActionType action )
{
    if ( action == INIT ||
        action == POSTOP )
    {
        lastWidget = NULL;
        return;
    }

    if ( !XtIsObject ( w ) ) /* Is widget trashed? */
    {
        fprintf ( stderr, "Non object in widget hierarchy\n" );
        if ( lastWidget )
            fprintf ( stderr, "last valid widget = %s\n",
                      XtName ( lastWidget ) );
        abort();
    }
    else if ( w->core.being_destroyed )
        fprintf ( stderr, "%s is being destroyed\n",
                            XtName ( w ) );
    lastWidget = w;
}
```

Adding this function to the WL framework requires modifying the file register.c. Each new test function should be declared at the top of resource.c, before calling `WLAddTest()` inside the body of `WLRegisterTests()`. For example, the `ValidWidgetTest()` function can be added as follows:

```
/***************************************************
 * register.c: Register all test functions with WL
 **************************************************/
#include "wlintP.h"
extern void ValidWidgetTest ( Widget, ActionType );

void WLRegisterTests ( void )
{
   /* Add new tests here by calling WLAddTest() */

```

```
11      WLAddTest ( "Testing for invalid and destroyed widgets ",
12                  ALL, ValidWidgetTest );
13  }
```

The call to `WLAddTest()` on line 11 provides a string that explains the purpose of the test. The second argument indicates that the test should be performed on all widgets and gadgets, and the third specifies the function to be called.

With this single function added, the WL framework can now be used to examine a program. It is easiest to create a library to contain the core WL functions, as well as all test functions. Then, the WL library can be linked with applications that use it. A library can be built from the current set of files as follows:

```
cc -c wlint.c register.c  ValidWidgetTest.c
ar ruv libWL.a wlint.o register.o ValidWidgetTest.o
```

The function `WLRunTests()` can now be called at any point in a program. A common place for such tests might be right before entering the event loop, but it might be useful to run the tests from multiple places in a program. A simple use of the WL framework would look like this:

```
/***********************************************
 * label.c: Display a label widget in a window.
 ***********************************************/
#include <Xm/Xm.h>
#include <Xm/Label.h>
#include "wlint.h"

void main ( int argc, char **argv )
{
    Widget       shell, msg;
    XtAppContext app;

    shell = XtAppInitialize ( &app, "Label", NULL, 0,
                              &argc, argv, NULL, NULL, 0 );

    msg = XtCreateManagedWidget ( "msg",
                                  xmLabelWidgetClass, shell,
                                  NULL, 0 );
    XtRealizeWidget ( shell );
    WLRunTests ( shell, "Before Main Loop" );

    XtAppMainLoop ( app );
}
```

Run tests

Running this program produces the output shown in Figure 3.15. The WL framework reports the beginning of the test sequence, printing the string given to `WLRunTests()`, and reports each test as it executes. No problems were found in this example, as we would expect.

```
% label -xrm "*WLint: on" -xrm "*WLverbose: true"
*****************************
Starting test Before Main Loop
*****************************

*****************************
TEST: Testing for invalid and destroyed widgets
*****************************
```

Figure 3.15 WL output with `ValidWidgetTest()` function installed.

We can test the newly added function by introducing a deliberate error in the program. For example, the following program explicitly trashes the pointer to the XmLabel widget.

```
/***********************************************
 * label.c: Display a label in a window
 ***********************************************/
#include <Xm/Xm.h>
#include <Xm/Label.h>
#include <stdio.h>
#include "wlint.h"

void main ( int argc, char **argv )
{
    Widget       shell, msg;
    XtAppContext app;

    shell = XtAppInitialize ( &app, "Label", NULL, 0,
                              &argc, argv, NULL, NULL, 0 );

    msg = XtCreateManagedWidget ( "msg", xmLabelWidgetClass,
                                  shell, NULL, 0 );
   /*
    * Deliberately overwrite the widget so we can test
    * the WL function.
    */

     sprintf ( ( char * ) msg, "A silly code overwrite" );

    WLRunTests ( shell, "Before Main Loop" );
```

Code Overwrite

```
    XtRealizeWidget ( shell );
    XtAppMainLoop ( app );
}
```

If the `ValidWidgetTest()` function works as intended, the WL framework should find and report the trashed widget in this program. Figure 3.16 shows the output of WL when this program is run. The output reports the beginning of a new test sequence, followed by the beginning of the test for invalid widgets. As expected, a trashed widget is discovered in the hierarchy. The error is reported and the test aborts to allow a debugger to be used to examine the problem. A trashed widget is too serious an error to continue, even if there were more tests registered with the framework.

```
* label -xrm "*WLint: on" -xrm "*WLverbose: true"
*****************************
Starting test Before Main Loop
*****************************


*****************************
TEST: Testing for in-valid and destroyed widgets
*****************************
Non object in widget hierarchy
last valid widget = label
Abort(coredump)
```

Figure 3.16 WL output with a trashed widget in the hierarchy.

Adding WL Automatically

If your system supports dynamic shared libraries, you can borrow the same technique used to create function wrappers, on page 103, to automatically add the WL framework to any program without modifying the code. The easiest way to accomplish this is to redefine `XtRealizeWidget()` and add the new definition to the WL library. This version of `XtRealizeWidget()` uses `dlopen()` and `dlsym()` to find and invoke the real `XtRealizeWidget()` and then calls `WLRunTests()`.

Warning! System-dependent technique

The `XtRealizeWidget()` replacement can be implemented as follows, on systems that support these functions:

```
/**********************************************************
 * realize.c: XtRealizeWidget wrapper to automatically
 *            run WL tests. WARNING: Assumes SVR4 shared
 *            library support.
 **********************************************************/
#ifndef NDEBUG
#include <dlfcn.h>
#include <assert.h>
#include <Xm/Display.h>
#include "wlint.h"

/*
 * Declare a function type so we can cast.
 */

typedef void ( *realize )( Widget );

void XtRealizeWidget ( Widget   shell )
{
    void   *handle;
    realize fptr;

   /*
    * Load the real Xt.
    */

    handle = dlopen ( "/usr/lib/libXt.so", RTLD_LAZY );
    assert ( handle );

   /*
    * Find the address of XtRealizeWidget in the Xt library.
    */

    fptr = ( realize ) dlsym ( handle, "XtRealizeWidget" );
    assert ( fptr );

   /*
    * Call the real XtRealizeWidget function.
    */

    ( *fptr )( shell );

   /*
    * Invoke the WL test functions.
    */

    WLRunTests ( shell, "After Realization" );
}
#endif
```

Once this function has been added to the WL library, it is only necessary to specify the WL library before Xt on a program's list of libraries to run the tests automatically when the program calls `XtRealizeWidget()`. Because it may be useful to run the tests at other times as well, one might also call `WLRunTests()` directly from different parts of a program.

An Unmanaged Children Test

The tests to be added to the WL framework can be quite simple, and can report more than just serious errors. For example, this section describes a function that reports any widgets that are unmanaged. It is possible for widgets to be unmanaged intentionally at various points in a program. However, a common error is to forget to manage a widget, particularly when the Motif convenience functions are used. The `UnmanagedTest()` function reports such situations, which allows the programmer to consider whether the report indicates an error, or a proper condition.

This function uses the final `POSTOP` call to provide a final status report, based on an accumulated count. Notice that the `UnmanagedTest()` function does not require internal access to the private parts of a widget, so only Intrinsic.h is included.

```
/*************************************************
 * UnmanagedTest.c: Report all unmanaged widgets.
 *************************************************/
#include <X11/Intrinsic.h>
#include <stdio.h>
#include "wlintP.h"
static int count;

void UnmanagedTest ( Widget w, ActionType action )
{
    if ( action == INIT )
    {
        count = 0;
        return;
    }
    if ( action == POSTOP ) /* Last time */
    {
        if ( count )
            fprintf ( stderr,
                      "Number of unmanaged widgets = %d\n",
                      count );
        return;
    }
```

```

    /*
     * Shells are never managed, so only look at non-shells.
     */

    if ( !XtIsManaged ( w ) && !XtIsShell ( w ) )
    {
        fprintf ( stderr, "%s is unmanaged\n", XtName ( w ) );
        count++;
    }
}
```

This function can be added to the WL framework, by modifying register.c, the same as before.

```
/*****************************************************
 * register.c: Register all test functions with WL
 *****************************************************/
#include "wlintP.h"
extern void ValidWidgetTest ( Widget, ActionType );
extern void UnmanagedTest ( Widget, ActionType );

void WLRegisterTests ( void )
{
   /* Add new tests here by calling WLAddTest(). */

    WLAddTest ( "Testing for Invalid and destroyed widgets ",
                ALL, ValidWidgetTest );

    WLAddTest ( "Unmanaged Widget Test ",
                 ALL, UnmanagedTest );
}
```

Name and Class Name Tests

Test functions do not necessarily need to limit themselves to examining individual widgets. Given one widget, a function can investigate the widget's parent, children, or any other widget up or down the widget hierarchy. In some cases, tests might not even involve widgets at all. For example, I recently encountered a program that had a NULL class name. The NULL class name caused no problem until we tried to set some resources by what we supposed was the class name of the application. The following test would help catch this error:

```
/**************************************************************
 * nullclassname.c: Check for NULL application class name.
 **************************************************************/
#include <X11/Intrinsic.h>
#include <ctype.h>
#include <stdio.h>
#include "wlintP.h"

void NULLClassNameTest ( Widget shell, ActionType action )
{
    char *name, *appClass;

    if ( action == INIT ||
         action == POSTOP )
        return;

    if ( !XtIsShell ( shell ) )
        return;

   /*
    * Retrieve the name and class name from the shell
    * and see if it is non-NULL.
    */

    XtGetApplicationNameAndClass ( XtDisplay ( shell ),
                                   &name, &appClass );

    if ( !appClass )
    {
        fprintf ( stderr,
                 "Application has a NULL class name\n" );
    }
}
```

One of the bugs mentioned earlier involved an application whose class name had been misspelled. The following test catches situations in which a class name has either been misspelled, or does not match. Note that a mismatch is not necessarily an error, but it is worth checking in case the mismatch is unintentional.

```
/*************************************************************
 * classnametest.c: See if class name matches application
 *************************************************************/
#include <X11/Intrinsic.h>
#include <ctype.h>
#include <stdio.h>
#include "wlintP.h"
```

```
void ClassNameTest ( Widget shell, ActionType action )
{
    char *name, *appClass;

    if ( action == INIT ||
         action == POSTOP )
        return;

    if ( !XtIsShell ( shell ) )
       return;

   /*
    * Retrieve the name and class name of the application
    */

    XtGetApplicationNameAndClass ( XtDisplay ( shell ),
                                   &name, &appClass );
   /*
    * Compare the names and class names. By convention, these
    * should nominally be the same, except for case, unless
    * a user changes the name of the executable.
    */

    if ( name && appClass )
    {
        if ( strcasecmp ( name, appClass ) != 0 )
        {
            fprintf ( stderr,
                     "Application name/class name mismatch:");
            fprintf ( stderr,
                      "name = %s class = %s\n",
                      name, appClass );
        }
    }
}
```

The WL framework can also be used to enforce certain guidelines that you or your organization would like to follow. For example, some groups have coding standards that include the format of widget names, which could be easily tested. If internationalization is a concern, it is possible to write a test to determine if the `XmNlabelString` resource of an XmLabel widget (or subclass) has been set programmatically, or read from a resource file. The test function could simply try to retrieve the value of the widget's label from the resource database and see if the retrieved value matches the widget's current label. Chapter 6 demonstrates this technique in a slightly different situation.

The following function is one practical example of a test that enforces a stylistic guideline. This function tests that the class name follows the X conventions of having the class name be the same as the name, but with the first letter changed to uppercase, unless the name of the program starts with x. If the first letter starts with x, the `CapitalizationTest()` function tests that the class name consists of a capital X, followed by a capitalized second letter.

```
/**************************************************************
 * classconventions.c: Test conformance to X conventions
 **************************************************************/
#include <X11/Intrinsic.h>
#include <ctype.h>
#include <stdio.h>
#include "wlintP.h"

void CapitalizationTest ( Widget shell, ActionType action )
{
    char *name, *appClass;

    if ( action == INIT ||
         action == POSTOP )
        return;

    if ( !XtIsShell ( shell ) )
        return;

   /*
    * Retrieve the name and class name of the application.
    */

    XtGetApplicationNameAndClass ( XtDisplay ( shell ),
                                   &name, &appClass );
   /*
    * If the name is long enough, check that the class name
    * follows X conventions. The first letter of class name
    * should be capitalized, unless the name begins with X, in
    * which case, the first two letters should be capitalized.
    */

    if ( name && appClass && strlen ( name ) > 2 )
    {
        if ( name [0]     == 'x' &&
             appClass[0] != 'X' &&
             name[1]      != tolower ( appClass[1] ) )
        {
            fprintf ( stderr,
                  "Unconventional Application class name\n" );
```

```
            fprintf ( stderr, "Classname should be " );
            if ( strlen ( name ) > 2 )
                fprintf ( stderr, "X%c%s",
                                  toupper ( name[1] ),
                                  &name[2] ) );
            else
                fprintf ( stderr, "X%c",
                          toupper ( name[1] ) );
        }
        else if ( name [0] != tolower ( appClass[0] ) )
        {
            fprintf ( stderr,
                  "Unconventional Application class name\n" );
            fprintf ( stderr, "Classname should be " );
            fprintf ( stderr, "%c%s",
                      toupper ( name[0] ),
                      &name[1] );
        }
    }
}
```

All these tests need be executed once, each time the test suite is executed, so they can be added to the WL framework by calling `WLAddTest()` with the value `JUSTONCE` as the second argument. These tests will be run once each time `WLRunTests()` is called, but will not be called for each widget in the hierarchy.

```
/*******************************************************
 * register.c: Register all test functions with WL
 *******************************************************/
#include "wlintP.h"
extern void ValidWidgetTest ( Widget, ActionType );
extern void UnmanagedTest ( Widget, ActionType );
extern void ClassNameTest ( Widget, ActionType );
extern void CapitalizationTest ( Widget, ActionType );

void WLRegisterTests ( void )
{
   /* Add new tests here by calling WLAddTest() */
    WLAddTest ( "Testing for Invalid and destroyed widgets ",
                ALL, ValidWidgetTest }
    WLAddTest ( "Unmanaged Widget Test ", ALL, UnmanagedTest );
    WLAddTest ( "Name/class name mismatch",
                JUSTONCE, ClassNameTest );
    WLAddTest ( "Checking classname conventions",
                JUSTONCE, CapitalizationTest );
}
```

The tests demonstrated here are just a few examples of the types of homegrown tests that can be written. Tests can be simple or complex, and can attempt to catch common errors, enforce guidelines, or provide reminders. You might write tests for errors you know you commonly make. Although the tests shown here may seem trivial, the cost of running the tests is relatively low, and, like lint, if they catch an error even once in a while, they can save time that would be spent debugging.

Once the basic framework has been incorporated in your development environment, adding tests incrementally should be fairly painless. It may be worthwhile to try to add tests to catch any bugs you encounter through other techniques. If you have made a particular mistake at one place in a program, it is possible that you or someone else have made the same error elsewhere. The tests can also function as part of a regression test sequence; running the tests after changes have been made ensures that old bugs have not returned.

The WL framework also lends itself to finding certain performance problems caused by misuse of Motif. Later chapters continue to add tests to aid in debugging as well as pointing out potential performance problems.

3.5 Conclusion

Tools are an essential part of any debugging activity. To isolate and fix a bug, a programmer needs all available information about a program's state to isolate and fix the bug. Traditional tools like debuggers are almost always the first choice in any debugging situation, but programmers should not ignore other tools at their disposal. Debuggers only provide information about one aspect of a program. Particularly with X and Motif applications, a great deal of information can be gathered with other tools like `xscope`, `xprop`, `xmond`, and so on. This information is simply not accessible from within a debugger.

Although more information is usually better than not enough information, sometimes the task of debugging a large Motif program can be overwhelming because there are simply too many issues to consider. For example, trying to locate a trashed pointer in a Motif application by examining every data structure in a debugger would be unrealistic. In such cases, invasive tools that use the speed of the computer to check the program's state from inside the program itself can be useful. The WL framework, whose basic mechanisms are described in this chapter, is an example of an invasive tool specifically aimed at detecting problems that relate to widgets.

Another type of invasive tool that was not discussed in this chapter is a debugging `malloc()` library. Errors related to abuse of pointers or dynamically allocated memory are a frequent problem in Motif applications, and these can often be detected with modified implementations of `malloc()`. Chapter 5 addresses this topic in detail.

Later chapters use the tools described in this chapter to gather information that can be used to debug typical problems. Some of the tools will also be useful when examining the performance characteristics of Motif programs in Chapters 7 though 12.

Although this chapter describes simple tools that are widely available, many programmers also have access to commercial quality tools. The fact that this book cannot cover all the commercial tools available on various platforms should not be viewed as an indication that these tools are not useful. On the contrary, you generally get what you pay for, and a good set of quality programming tools can pay for themselves very quickly. Debugging is a difficult task at best. Using the best tools you can find can make the job easier.

4

Characterizing Bugs

When a bug occurs in an X or Motif program, one of the first challenges is to identify the true source of the problem. Bugs may be difficult to isolate in any type of program, but many programmers seem to have particular difficulty correctly interpreting the symptoms associated with certain Motif and X bugs. Most bugs that occur in Motif programs are the result of an error in the application itself, but these bugs often manifest themselves as errors in the various libraries. The connection between the point of failure and the real cause is often somewhat obscure.

There are several characteristics of X and Motif that make bugs difficult to understand and diagnose:

- **Complexity**. Programmers who write graphical interfaces using Motif face the daunting task of working with three libraries that together provide over 700 functions that must be mixed, matched and combined to create a complete application. Many of these functions have inconsistent behavior, have surprising side-effects, or can only be used in specialized cases. For example, many publicly available functions in Xt are really intended only for use inside widgets, or inside Xt. Calling these functions from an application can compromise the internal consistency of the widgets in the program, but there is no way to know, other than reading the documentation, which functions should be used and which should not.

- **Customization**. The 50 or so widget classes supported by Motif can be extensively customized, not only by programmers, but by end-users, who also have access to the approximately 500 resources recognized by a typical Motif application. This makes testing difficult because it is hard to guarantee a reliable, consistent environment, or to anticipate what effect an end-user's customizations might have.
- **Library layering**. All Motif applications use at least three libraries, X, Xt, and Motif. Each has its own purpose, but there is some duplication. Also, applications and libraries do not strictly adhere to the layering. For example, applications may sometimes call Xlib directly, Xlib calls may come from Xt, or they may come from Motif. This architecture sometimes makes it very difficult to understand what has gone wrong when a symptom seems to point to a lower-level library.
- **Control flow and indirection**. Most applications use callbacks, event handlers, and other types of indirection that can greatly complicate the task of debugging. These features are used by applications and are also used internally by Xt and Motif. In certain cases, it is possible for actions by an application to affect the behavior of internal callbacks and event handlers, unintentionally.
- **X's asynchronous, multi-process model**. Some errors are difficult to repeat because of hard-to-duplicate interactions with window managers, the X server, and other clients running on the same machine. All rendering and window manipulation is performed by the X server, which is not normally accessible to a programmer debugging an application. The fact that X applications normally run asynchronously with respect to the server and other applications can also make it difficult to isolate some bugs.
- **Data abstraction**. Many of the data structures used in a Motif program are opaque and cannot be accessed from within an application. The internal structure of server resources, like windows, pixmaps, and so on, are completely unavailable to an application because they are maintained in a separate process. While data abstraction is normally a desirable characteristic, anything that hides information makes debugging more difficult.

These characteristics all contribute to the difficulties many programmers face when they encounter a problem in a Motif program. This chapter examines some symptoms that can occur in typical Motif programs and suggests ways to isolate various types of problems to find the true cause. This chapter also continues to explore how the debugging tools discussed in Chapter 3 can be used effectively to solve problems.

Many of the source code examples in this chapter may seem a little silly. Most of these examples are contrived to demonstrate a specific type of problem, such as accessing a widget that has already been destroyed, and to show the symptoms that occur as a result. These situations are usually demonstrated in as straight-forward a manner as possible — calling `XtDestroyWidget()` twice in a row for example! Unfortunately, bugs in real programs will not be so easy to spot.

Nevertheless, once you have traced through many thousands of lines of the complex logic in your own program searching for a bug, the ultimate source of the problem will reduce to something quite basic: a trashed pointer, a widget destroyed twice, a widget that was not realized, and so on. By becoming familiar with the symptoms of each of these problems, you may at least have some idea what you are searching for when bugs occur.

4.1 Debugging with Layered Libraries

One challenge many programmers face when they encounter a bug is understanding the multiple layers of libraries used in any Motif program. Programmers often tend to think about the Motif library as the main toolkit they are using, but of course, Motif builds on Xt, which builds on Xlib, which relies on the X server. In addition, applications may call some Xt and Xlib functions, although other Xt and Xlib functions are almost never used directly. Furthermore, there is some redundancy between the libraries, and some duplication or near duplication of functionality.

Bugs that cause an application to core dump are ordinarily the easiest fix, because a debugger can be used to find exactly where the program failed. However, when debugging Motif programs, the layering and architecture of X and Motif libraries can result in very deep call stacks that can be very misleading.

When examining a core dump in a Motif application, one of the first things to consider is that the real bug is most likely in the application, in spite of what the call stack shows. For example, just because a program dies with a core dump inside a call to `XtCreateWidget()` does not necessarily mean that there is a bug in Xt. A core dump in `XtCreateWidget()` could be caused by a bug in the widget being created, or by an error in the arguments passed to the function. In fact, the error may not be related in any way to the code currently being executed. Because Xt and Motif make heavy use of dynamically allocated memory, any misuse of `malloc()` or `free()` can produce errors in functions like `XtCreateWidget()`, even if the real problem lies in a completely different part of the program.

It is useful to become familiar with some basic call stacks that are commonly encountered in Xt and Motif-based programs. For example, Figure 4.1 shows a callstack produced by running the `xclock` program under a debugger and then interrupting the program. This callstack does not indicate a bug, of course; it just shows the function the program was executing when the program was interrupted. Starting from the bottom of the callstack, the program was executing the function `XtAppMainLoop()`, which was called from `main()`. `XtAppMainLoop()` loops endlessly handling events, and had called the Xt function `XtAppNextEvent()` when this interrupt occurred. `XtAppNextEvent()` had called `_XtWaitForSomething()`, an internal Xt function that waits for an event to occur. `_XtWaitForSomething()` had called `select()`, a UNIX system call that blocks while waiting for input from a file, in this case, the socket connection to the X server.

```
% dbx xclock
Process 22584 (xclock) started
[2] Process 22584 (xclock) stopped at [main:27 ,0x402620]
  27  shell = XtAppInitialize  (  &app, "XClock",   NULL, 0,
(dbx) run
Interrupt
(dbx) where
>  0 _select(0x4, 0x7fffad2c, 0x7fffacac, 0x7fffac2c, 0x7fffadc8) [
   1 _XtwaitForSomething(0x0, 0x0, 0x0, 0x1, 0x0) ["NextEvent.c":22
   2 XtAppNextEvent(0x0, 0x7fffae40, 0x1000a160, 0x4026a0, 0x1) ["N
   3 XtAppMainLoop(0x0, 0x7fffae40, 0x0, 0x0, 0x0) ["Event.c":1200,
   4 main(argc = 1, argv = 0x7fffaf14) ["xclock.c":42, 0x4026cc]
```

Waiting for an event

Event loop

Figure 4.1 Callstack of an interrupted program.

Once a program completes its initialization, creates the widgets used in the user interface, and so on, it spends most of its time in an event loop. Therefore, nearly any problem will involve a callstack that contains `XtAppMainLoop()`. If the program is waiting for, or processing a new event, `XtAppNextEvent()` is likely to be on the callstack, as it is in Figure 4.1.

When a program is not waiting for an event, it is usually dispatching the last event received. In most Motif programs, almost anything that happens, other than retrieving an event, happens as a result of dispatching an event. Figure 4.2 shows an example of a callstack resulting from an error in a callback function.

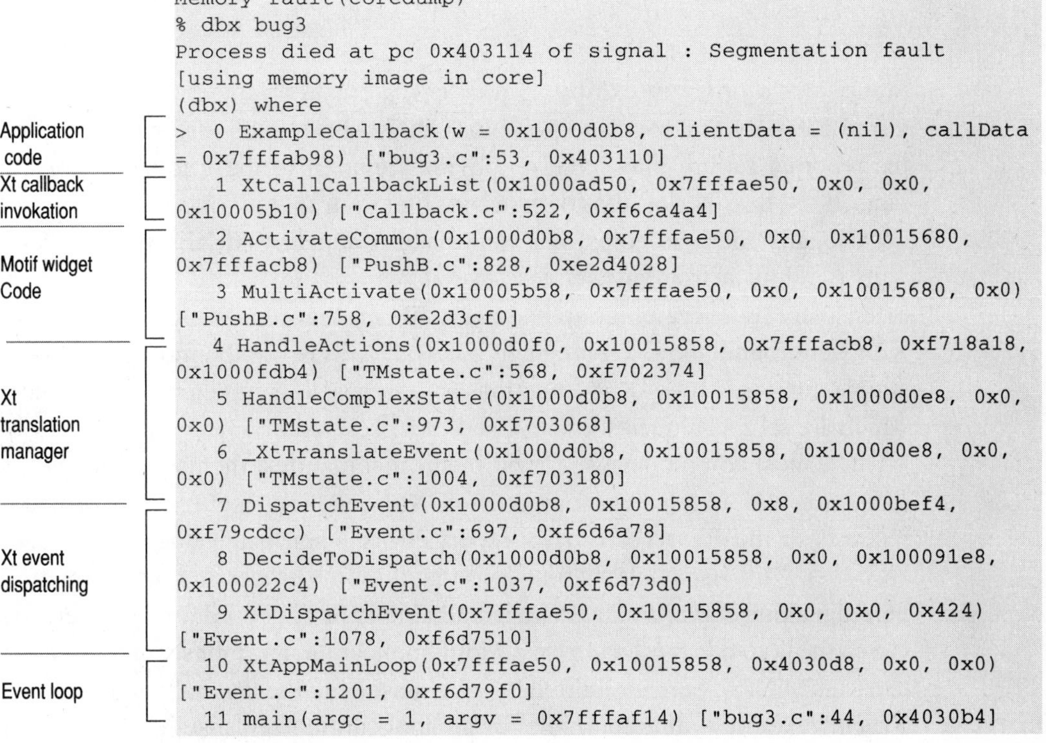


```
Memory fault(coredump)
% dbx bug3
Process died at pc 0x403114 of signal : Segmentation fault
[using memory image in core]
(dbx) where
>  0 ExampleCallback(w = 0x1000d0b8, clientData = (nil), callData
= 0x7fffab98) ["bug3.c":53, 0x403110]
   1 XtCallCallbackList(0x1000ad50, 0x7fffae50, 0x0, 0x0,
0x10005b10) ["Callback.c":522, 0xf6ca4a4]
   2 ActivateCommon(0x1000d0b8, 0x7fffae50, 0x0, 0x10015680,
0x7fffacb8) ["PushB.c":828, 0xe2d4028]
   3 MultiActivate(0x10005b58, 0x7fffae50, 0x0, 0x10015680, 0x0)
["PushB.c":758, 0xe2d3cf0]
   4 HandleActions(0x1000d0f0, 0x10015858, 0x7fffacb8, 0xf718a18,
0x1000fdb4) ["TMstate.c":568, 0xf702374]
   5 HandleComplexState(0x1000d0b8, 0x10015858, 0x1000d0e8, 0x0,
0x0) ["TMstate.c":973, 0xf703068]
   6 _XtTranslateEvent(0x1000d0b8, 0x10015858, 0x1000d0e8, 0x0,
0x0) ["TMstate.c":1004, 0xf703180]
   7 DispatchEvent(0x1000d0b8, 0x10015858, 0x8, 0x1000bef4,
0xf79cdcc) ["Event.c":697, 0xf6d6a78]
   8 DecideToDispatch(0x1000d0b8, 0x10015858, 0x0, 0x100091e8,
0x100022c4) ["Event.c":1037, 0xf6d73d0]
   9 XtDispatchEvent(0x7fffae50, 0x10015858, 0x0, 0x0, 0x424)
["Event.c":1078, 0xf6d7510]
  10 XtAppMainLoop(0x7fffae50, 0x10015858, 0x4030d8, 0x0, 0x0)
["Event.c":1201, 0xf6d79f0]
  11 main(argc = 1, argv = 0x7fffaf14) ["bug3.c":44, 0x4030b4]
```

Figure 4.2 A callstack caused by a core dump in a callback function.

This callstack shows the dispatching side of the event loop. `XtApp-MainLoop()` calls `XtDispatchEvent()`, which calls the internal Xt function, `DecideToDispatch()`, which determines how the event should be routed within the application. In Figure 4.2, the event is passed to the Xt translation manager. The translation manager maps the event to an action procedure registered by the Motif XmPushButton widget, which eventually calls an Xt function, `XtCallCallbackList()` to invoke the application's callback function.

It is interesting to notice how the flow of control moves back and forth between the application, Xt, and Motif. Xlib is also involved, although it does not show up on the callstack in Figure 4.2. All four are interlocked, working together rather than flowing strictly top to bottom or bottom to top.

4.2 Symptoms That Involve Xlib

Sometimes a program exhibits a problem, a crash, an unexpected exit, or a visual anomaly that seems to point to Xlib. In such situations, the location of the reported failure may have no obvious relation to the true source of the bug. It is rare for a programmer to find a true bug in Xlib, although occasionally the symptoms of a bug make it appear that Xlib has a defect. Xlib is rarely a true suspect for several reasons. First, this library is used extensively by every program and every library that runs on X. Most bugs in Xlib were found and fixed long ago. Second, Xlib is, for the most part, a very simple library. Many Xlib functions simply pack parameters into packets which are sent as requests to the X server.

The most common cause for problems that manifest themselves in Xlib is a function call with incorrect arguments. Xlib functions that result in protocol requests to the X server usually report errors when bad values are passed. However, Xlib also contains functions that do some processing of information before making server requests, so not all abuses of Xlib produce server errors. Given the layered architecture of a Motif application, it might seem reasonable to assume that any error reported by Xlib must be in the layer above it, namely Xt. However, it is quite possible for an application to misuse Motif or Xt so that Xlib is also misused.

This section examines some common errors that involve Xlib in some way, and demonstrates how to identify the true cause.

Debugging in an Asynchronous Environment

Bugs that involve X requests or events can be very tricky to isolate because X normally runs in asynchronous mode. When the server receives an invalid request, it simply reports an error, which the application detects the next time it reads the event queue. The results can be deceiving and it may be difficult to map a specific error to the code that actually made the request.

For example, consider the following program, which contains an obvious flaw. This program creates a widget and then tries to draw a line in the widget's window before the widget has been realized.

```
/*******************************************************************
 * drawline.c: Demonstrate a bug involving Xlib and widgets
 *******************************************************************/
#include <Xm/Xm.h>
#include <Xm/DrawingA.h>

void main ( int argc, char **argv )
{
    Widget       shell, canvas;
    XtAppContext app;
    GC           gc;

    shell = XtAppInitialize ( &app, "Drawline", NULL, 0,
                              &argc, argv, NULL, NULL, 0 );

    canvas = XtCreateManagedWidget ( "canvas",
                                     xmDrawingAreaWidgetClass,
                                     shell, NULL, 0 );

    gc = XtGetGC ( canvas, NULL, 0 );

   /*
    * BUG. Try to draw to an unrealized widget.
    */

    XDrawLine( XtDisplay ( canvas ), XtWindow ( canvas ),
               gc, 0, 0, 20, 20 );

    XtRealizeWidget ( shell );
    XtAppMainLoop ( app );
}
```

Bug!

Figure 4.3 shows the error message produced by running this program. The message reports that a `BadDrawable` error has occurred as the result of an `X_PolySegment` request. The error message also includes assorted other information, including the resource `ID` involved in the request.

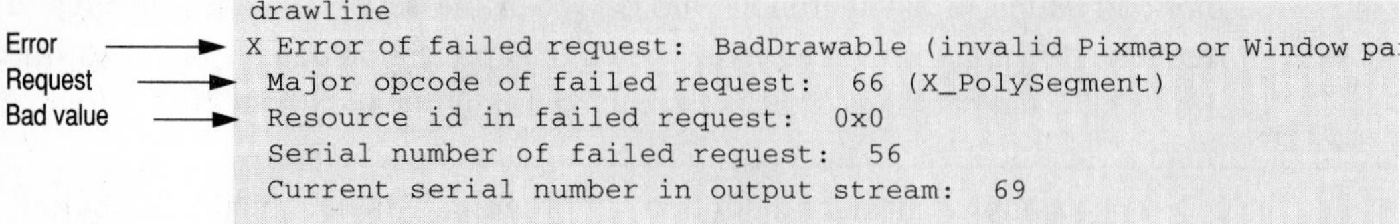

Error
Request
Bad value
drawline
X Error of failed request: BadDrawable (invalid Pixmap or Window pa
 Major opcode of failed request: 66 (X_PolySegment)
 Resource id in failed request: 0x0
 Serial number of failed request: 56
 Current serial number in output stream: 69

Figure 4.3 An X protocol error caused by drawing into an unrealized widget.

Newcomers to X often find such errors less than helpful because there is no indication of the source of the error. The program exits cleanly without leaving a core file, so there is little to go on when trying to investigate further.

In this simple program, the error cannot be too difficult to find; there are only a few executable statements. However, in a larger program, the inability to associate the error with a specific line of code presents a more difficult problem. Also notice that the error complains about an `X_PolySegment` request. Xlib function calls do not always map directly to corresponding request names. In this example, Xlib makes an `X_PolySegment` request because the application called `XDrawLine()`. [Scheifler92] can be helpful when trying to understanding protocol requests.

The easiest way to examine such errors before the program exits is to run the program under the control of a debugger. By default, X errors are reported by an Xlib function, `_XError()`. Therefore, it is possible to examine the steps that lead up to the error by running the program from within a debugger, after setting a breakpoint on entry to `_XError()`. Alternately, you may be able to set a breakpoint in `exit()`, which is called by `_XError()`.

Figure 4.4 shows a debugging session in which an X error is trapped before the error message shown in Figure 4.3 is printed. This is an improvement, because the program no longer exits, and we have a chance to use the debugger to gather more information. However, notice that the stack trace in Figure 4.4 shows nothing to indicate the true source of the problem. It merely shows that the error occurred while processing an event.

If you have not seen this type of error before, it is easy to be mislead. You might even suspect that there is a bug in `_XEventsQueued()` because of the call stacks shown in Figure 4.4. To those used to more synchronous systems, it may seem that the bug could not be caused by anything in the application itself, because only Xt and Xlib functions are on the call stack. However, because X is an asynchronous system, the call to `_XError()` is not made at the point of the error. Instead, `_XError()` is called when the application receives an error event from the server. This error reports a problem in some previous server request, which may have happened at any point in the program.

Default error handler: frames 0

Xlib event handling: frames 1–2

Xt Event loop: frames 3–5

```
% dbx drawline
Process  6224 (drawline) started
[2] Process  6224 (drawline) stopped at [main:13 ,0x400b98]
  13  shell = XtAppInitialize ( &app, "Drawline", NULL, 0,
(dbx) stop in _XError
Process  6224: [3] stop in _XError
(dbx) run
Process  6225 (drawline) started
[3] Process  6225 (drawline) stopped at [_XError:1708 ,0xf7967b8]
         Source (of XlibInt.c) not available for Process  6225
(dbx) where
>  0 _XError(0x10006458, 0x7fffa368, 0x120, 0x0, 0xfb5a220)
["XlibInt.c":1708, 0xf7967b8]
   1 _XEventsQueued(0x10006458, 0x7fffa368, 0x120, 0x0, 0xfb5a220)
["XlibInt.c":369, 0xf7941f4]
   2 XEventsQueued(0x10006458, 0x7fffa368, 0x120, 0x0, 0x0)
["XPending.c":29, 0xf77f148]
   3 _XtwaitForSomething(0x0, 0x0, 0x0, 0x1, 0x0) ["NextEvent.c":3:
0xf6e2768]
   4 XtAppNextEvent(0x0, 0x7fffae40, 0x1, 0x7fffaf14, 0x1)
["NextEvent.c":739, 0xf6e381c]
  5 XtAppMainLoop(0x0, 0x7fffae40, 0x10017af0, 0x0, 0x0) ["Event.c":
0xf6d79d8]
   6 main(argc = 1, argv = 0x7fffaf14) ["drawline.c":30, 0x400ca4]
```

Figure 4.4 Using a debugger to trace the source of an X error.

The real problem can be found easily by running the program in synchronous mode. In synchronous mode, all Xlib functions wait for the X server to process each request before returning. Any errors that occur are reported immediately. All Xt applications can be executed synchronously by running the program with a `-synchronous` flag. For example, Figure 4.5 shows the results of rerunning the `drawline` program with a `synchronous` flag (or just `synch`). The stack trace above `_XError()` clearly shows that the error occurred during a call to `XDrawLine()`. Examining the arguments to `XDrawLine()`, as reported by the debugger, shows that the second argument is `0x0`, which is an invalid window ID. This call is clearly responsible for the original error, which reported a window ID of `0x0`.

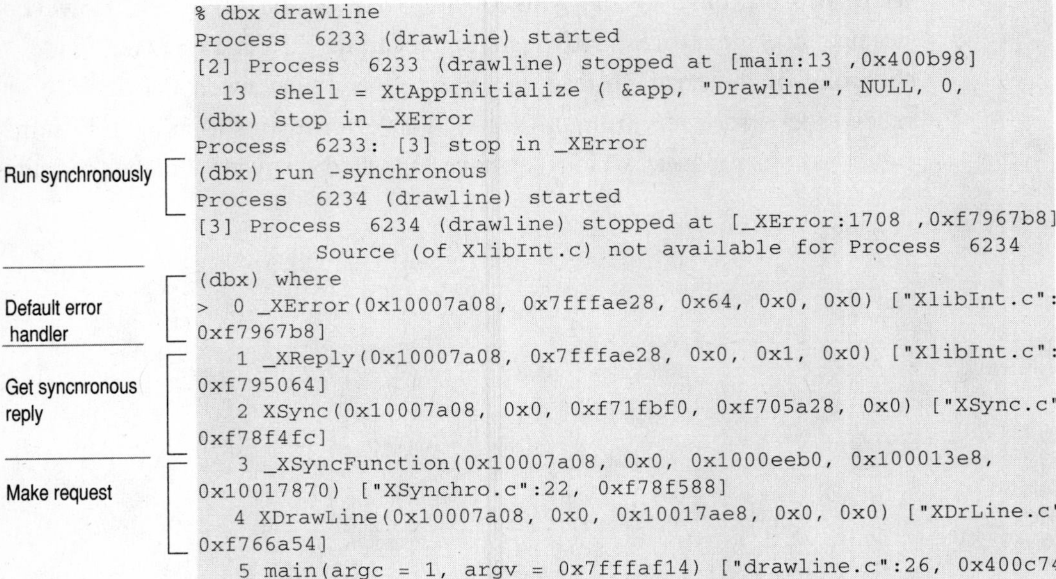


```
% dbx drawline
Process  6233 (drawline) started
[2] Process  6233 (drawline) stopped at [main:13 ,0x400b98]
  13  shell = XtAppInitialize ( &app, "Drawline", NULL, 0,
(dbx) stop in _XError
Process  6233: [3] stop in _XError
(dbx) run -synchronous
Process  6234 (drawline) started
[3] Process  6234 (drawline) stopped at [_XError:1708 ,0xf7967b8]
         Source (of XlibInt.c) not available for Process  6234
(dbx) where
>  0 _XError(0x10007a08, 0x7fffae28, 0x64, 0x0, 0x0) ["XlibInt.c":
0xf7967b8]
   1 _XReply(0x10007a08, 0x7fffae28, 0x0, 0x1, 0x0) ["XlibInt.c":
0xf795064]
   2 XSync(0x10007a08, 0x0, 0xf71fbf0, 0xf705a28, 0x0) ["XSync.c"
0xf78f4fc]
   3 _XSyncFunction(0x10007a08, 0x0, 0x1000eeb0, 0x100013e8,
0x10017870) ["XSynchro.c":22, 0xf78f588]
   4 XDrawLine(0x10007a08, 0x0, 0x10017ae8, 0x0, 0x0) ["XDrLine.c'
0xf766a54]
   5 main(argc = 1, argv = 0x7fffaf14) ["drawline.c":26, 0x400c74
```

Figure 4.5 Tracing the source of an X error in a synchronous application.

Error Handlers as Debugging Aids

Both Xlib and Xt allow applications to install error handlers, which can be used to support debugging. Error handlers are functions that can be registered with X or Xt, to be called when an error occurs. The message printed in Figure 4.3 is produced by Xlib's default error handler, but custom error handlers can change this behavior,

Xlib supports two types of error handlers, for two types of errors. The first is called when a protocol error occurs. These errors generally occur when a server request contains invalid parameters. The error shown in Figure 4.3 is an example of this type of error. Applications can install a new error handler for such errors by calling the Xlib function `XSetErrorHandler()`. `XSetIOErrorHandler()` can be called to install a new handler function for IO errors, which are errors that occur when the application cannot communicate with the X server.

When using Motif, the Xt library also supports custom error and warning handlers that report errors encountered within Xt or Motif. A function can be installed to handle Xt warnings by calling `XtAppSetWarningHandler()`, Error handlers can be installed by calling `XtAppSetErrorHandler()`.

The ability to install custom error and warning handlers offers several possibilities for debugging. Some applications may wish to install error handlers that print additional information. Because error handlers can be installed at any time, an application might install a special error handler before entering a critical region of code, which could report the state of the program at the point of error. Another possibility is to install error handler functions that abort, producing a core dump when an error or warning occurs.

This technique can be useful when delivering an application to someone in a different environment. If the error handlers are installed conditionally, any customer who encounters an error can be told to activate the error handlers to produce a core dump, which can then be debugged. For example, the following module includes a function that allows an application to install error handlers based on the value of a resource.

```
/***********************************
 * SetupErrorHandlers.c
 ***********************************/
#include <X11/Intrinsic.h>
#include <stdio.h>
#include <string.h>

/*
 * The following error handlers abort when called
 * to produce a core dump that can be used for debugging
 */

static void MyXtErrorHandler ( String msg )
{
   fprintf ( stderr, msg );
   abort();
}

static int MyXIOErrorHandler ( Display *dpy )
{
   fprintf ( stderr, "X IO Error\n" );
   abort();
}

static int MyXErrorHandler ( Display *dpy, XErrorEvent *ev )
{
   fprintf ( stderr, "X error\n" );
   abort();
}


```

```
/*
 * Install the above error handlers if the "abortOnErrors"
 * resource is true.
 */

void SetupErrorHandlers ( Widget w, char *name )
{
    Display *display = XtDisplay ( w );
    XtAppContext appContext =
                          XtWidgetToApplicationContext ( w );

    char *opt = XGetDefault ( display, name,
                              "abortOnErrors" );

    if ( opt && !strcasecmp ( opt, "true" ) )
    {
       XtAppSetWarningHandler ( appContext, MyXtErrorHandler );
       XtAppSetErrorHandler ( appContext, MyXtErrorHandler );
       XSetErrorHandler ( MyXErrorHandler );
       XSetIOErrorHandler ( MyXIOErrorHandler );
    }
}
```

4.3 Symptoms That Involve Xt

Errors that involve the Xt library in some way are far more common than Xlib or X server errors. Most Motif applications make heavy use of Xt functions, and nearly all Motif operations involve Xt one way or another. Unlike Xlib, Xt does a great deal of work itself. Although heavily used, it is both more complex and less heavily used than Xlib. Therefore it is possible to encounter a true bug in Xt. However, it is still much more likely that bugs that appear to point to Xt are actually caused by the application's misuse of Xt.

Xt implements an object oriented architecture that supports creating and manipulating widgets. Like most object-oriented architectures, Xt relies heavily on pointers and dynamically allocated memory. Therefore, all applications based on Xt are highly susceptible to errors related to memory use. Applications can easily cause Xt to fail simply by misusing memory, even in a completely unrelated part of the program. This topic is sufficiently important that a separate chapter is devoted to the problems of memory use and abuse.

If a program fails while calling an Xt function that allocates memory, like `XtCreateWidget()` or `XtGetGC()`, there is a good chance that the program has corrupted memory, which can cause `malloc()` to fail. On the other hand, core dumps in functions that operate on widgets, like `XtManageChild()` or `XtSetValues()`, often indicate that the widget given as an argument is invalid. The problem could be due to memory corruption, bad arguments, or it could be caused by passing one of these functions a dangling reference to a widget that has been destroyed.

For example, consider the following, obviously flawed program:

```
1   /******************************************************
2    * buggy.c: Show the impact of passing bad data
3    *          to an Xt function
4    ******************************************************/
5   #include <Xm/Xm.h>
6   #include <Xm/PushB.h>
7
8   void main ( int argc, char **argv )
9   {
10     Widget       shell, button;
11     XtAppContext app;
12
13     shell = XtAppInitialize ( &app, "Buggy", NULL, 0,
14                               &argc, argv, NULL, NULL, 0 );
15
16     XtFree ( shell );   /* BUG */
17
18     button = XtCreateManagedWidget ( "button",
19                                      xmPushButtonWidgetClass,
20                                      shell,
21                                      NULL, 0 );
22     XtRealizeWidget ( shell );
23     XtAppMainLoop ( app );
24  }
```

Error! (line 16)

Use of corrupt widget (lines 19–21)

This program frees the memory associated with the shell widget before passing it to `XtCreateWidget()`. Notice that, in this contrived experiment, the shell widget is not cleanly destroyed by calling `XtDestroyWidget()`. `XtFree()` simply deallocates the memory used by the widget, without cleaning up. This is certainly an unlikely scenario, exactly as written, but the effect is very much like what happens when the memory used by a widget is corrupted, which can and does happen all the time in C programs.

The exact way this error will manifest itself is hard to predict, but the resulting error will certainly not point to line 16, where the shell widget's memory is freed. Instead, running this program is likely to cause a core dump whose callstack resembles that in Figure 4.6. Here, the callstack indicates a failure on line 358 of an internal Xt function, `_XtCreateWidget()`. In a less obviously flawed program, one might be tempted to think the bug was in Xt itself.

```
% buggy
Memory fault(coredump)
% dbx buggy
Process died at pc 0xf6d23b8 of signal : Segmentation fault
[using memory image in core]
(dbx) where
>  0 _XtCreateWidget(0x10000008, 0xe3d684c, 0xe3d684c, 0x0, 0xC
["Create.c":358, 0xf6d23b4]
   1 XtCreateWidget(0x1, 0x1000a7a8, 0xe3d684c, 0xf6c9244, 0x0)
["Create.c":403, 0xf6d2500]
   2 XtCreateManagedWidget(0x7fffaeec, 0x10000000, 0xe3d684c, 0x
0x0) ["Create.c":428, 0xf6d2538]
   3 main(argc = 1, argv = 0x7fffaf14) ["buggy.c":18, 0x400b78]
```

Figure 4.6 A core dump while creating a widget.

Examples like this are one reason the `ValidWidgetTest()` function, discussed in Chapter 3 as part of the WL test framework, can be valuable. Once a widget's memory has been corrupted, the program can fail at any time. Of course, one can also try to understand such problems using a debugger. Not all errors involve a widget whose memory has been completely trashed. Often, there are more subtle problems that involve widgets.

Investigating a widget that appears to be suspect can be tricky because `Widget` is an opaque type. Because the true definition of `Widget` is not available, debuggers can't normally be used to examine a widget's structure in application code. One way around this problem is to include IntrinsicP.h in the application to provide the true definition of the `Widget` structure. It is generally inappropriate to include private headers, but they may be needed for debugging.

For example, let's return to the `xlogobug` program described in Chapter 1. Although several bugs have been fixed, this program still has unresolved problems. When the program is run, a window like that in Figure 4.7 appears. What should appear as an X that spans the window from corner to corner shows up as some small lines in the upper left corner.

Figure 4.7 The `xlogobug` program.

We might start to debug this problem by adding a print statement to the `ExposeCallback()` function, which draws the lines in the window. The following function is the same as the implementation in Chapter 1, except for the print statement, which reports the values of `width` and `height`.

```
void ExposeCallback ( Widget    w,
                      XtPointer clientData,
                      XtPointer callData )
{
    int width, height;

   /*
    * Determine the size of the canvas widget to allow
    * the lines to be drawn.
    */

    XtVaGetValues ( w,
                    XmNwidth,  &width,
                    XmNheight, &height,
                    NULL );

    printf ( "width = %d height = %d, width, height );

   /*
    * Draw an X into the canvas widget's window, using the
    * widget's size to draw a line diagonally between
    * each corner.
    */

```

```
33      XDrawLine ( XtDisplay ( w ), XtWindow ( w ), gc,
34                  0, 0, width, height);
35
36      XDrawLine ( XtDisplay ( w ), XtWindow ( w ), gc,
37                  width, 0, 0, height);
38  }
```

Now, when the `xlogobug` program is executed, the print statement on line 25 confirms that something is wrong with the values passed to `XDrawLine()`. The reported values for the width and height of the XmDrawingArea widget are clearly incorrect, as shown in Figure 4.8.

```
% xlogobug
width = 65536 height = 95108
% xlogobug -geometry =200x200
width = 13107200 height = 1316772
```

Figure 4.8 Running the `xlogobug` program.

In an initial attempt to investigate, we might use a debugger like `dbx` to try to examine the values stored in the widget itself. Figure 4.9 shows a typical session with `dbx`, in which an attempt is made to debug this problem.

```
% dbx xlogobug
Process  1240 (xlogobug) started
[2] Process  1240 (xlogobug) stopped at [main:48 ,0x402774]
  48  shell = XtAppInitialize ( &app, "Xlogohbug", NULL, 0,
```

Set breakpoint

```
(dbx) stop in ExposeCallback
Process  1240: [3] stop in ExposeCallback
(dbx) run -geometry =200x200
```

```
[3] Process  1241 (xlogobug) stopped at [ExposeCallback:20
,0x40263c]
  15  XtVaGetValues ( w,
```

Try to inspect widget

```
(dbx) print w
0x1000c670
(dbx) print *w
@1000c670
```

```
(dbx) Step
Process 1241 (xlogobug) stopped at [ExposeCallback:31 ,0x40266c]
  2312  XDrawLine ( XtDisplay ( w ), XtWindow ( w ), gc,
```

print geometries

```
(dbx) print width
13107232
(dbx) print height
13107202
```

Figure 4.9 Trying to inspect the contents of a widget.

After the XmDrawingArea widget has been created, the value of the `canvas` variable is printed. The value `0x1000c670` is a pointer, which seems appropriate for a widget. To see the contents of the widget, it is necessary to dereference this pointer. However, evaluating "`*canvas`" shows only `@0x1000c670`, which indicates "the value stored at `0x1000c670`", which is less than helpful. The debugger cannot provide more information because the definition of type `Widget` is unknown.

Going on to inspect the values of `width` and `height` confirms that the values are much larger than expected. However, there is no way to find out what values the widget maintains internally.

To inspect the data contained in a widget, it is necessary to include <X11/IntrinsicP.h> and recompile the program. Figure 4.10 shows the result of running the modified program under a debugger.

```
% dbx xlogobug
Process  1224 (xlogobug) started
[2] Process  1224 (xlogobug) stopped at [main:48 ,0x4026c8]
  48  shell = XtAppInitialize ( &app, "Xlogohbug", NULL, 0,
(dbx) stop in ExposeCallback
Process  1224: [3] stop in ExposeCallback
(dbx) run -geometry =200x200
Process  1224 (xlogobug) terminated
Process  1225 (xlogobug) started
[3] Process 1225 (xlogobug) stopped at [ExposeCallback:31 ,0x4025e4]
  31  XtVaGetValues ( w,
(dbx) print w
0x1000c670
(dbx) print *w
struct _WidgetRec {
    core = struct _CorePart {
        self = 0x1000c670
        widget_class = 0xe3d2738
        parent = 0x1001f4c0
        xrm_name = 1012
        being_destroyed = '\000'
        destroy_callbacks = 0x10004238
        constraints = (nil)
        x = 0
        y = 0
        width = 200
        height = 200
        border_width = 0
```

Widget's geometry

Figure 4.10 Inspecting a widget in a program built with private headers.

Again, printing the value of `canvas` shows an address. However, inspecting `*canvas` now provides far more useful results, and all members of the widget's instance record are reported. From the instance record, we can see that the widget's size is 200 by 200, as expected. So, we know that the widget is not part of the problem, and the original problem must have another cause.

Although it is not obvious from this figure, there is still a degree of abstraction present in the `canvas` widget's instance record. The `canvas` variable is declared to be type `Widget`, and including IntrinsicP.h provides the definition of the `Widget` data type. However, the `canvas` widget is really of type `XmDrawingAreaWidget`, which has additional members beyond those included in the Core `Widget` structure. However, these members cannot be viewed in the debugger. To see the complete contents of the `canvas` widget, the program would have to include <Xm/DrawingAP.h> and declare `canvas` as type `XmDrawingAreaWidget`.

At this point, the problem exhibited by the `xlogobug` program remains unsolved. We will return to it shortly, after discussing some errors that can occur when setting resources.

ArgList Errors

A large part of any Motif program involves manipulating resources. Unfortunately, resources are the source of many errors. It is particularly easy to introduce errors into a program when using the Xt resource mechanism to set resources programmatically.

Resources are typically passed in fixed size `Arg` arrays to `XtSetValues()`, `XtGetValues()`, and all widget creation functions. One common mistake is to attempt to store more resources than the array has been declared to hold. Such errors may be difficult to find because they may simply cause a memory corruption that turns up much later. Errors can also occur if the length of the `Arg` list does not match the length given to the Xt function used to set or retrieve resources.

One problem with such errors is that they may not even show up during development, or may cause different errors on different machines. A program that contains these bugs may work fine for a long time, and then suddenly manifest a bug when built on a different system, built with a different compiler, linked with different libraries, or even when a resource setting changes.

For example, the following program worked fine for a long time before it suddenly started crashing following a compiler upgrade.

```
             1  /***********************************************
             2   * initbug.c: Demonstrate a common type of bug
             3   ***********************************************/
             4  #include <Xm/Xm.h>
             5  #include <Xm/Label.h>
             6
             7  void main ( int argc, char **argv )
             8  {
Not          9      Arg          args[10];
initialized 10      int          n;
            11      Widget       shell;
            12      XtAppContext app;
            13
Bug!        14      shell = XtAppInitialize ( &app, "Initbug", NULL, 0,
            15                                &argc, argv, NULL, args, n );
            16
            17      n = 0;
            18      XtSetArg ( args[n], XmNwidth, 100 ); n++;
            19      XtCreateManagedWidget ( "test", xmLabelWidgetClass,
            20                              shell,
            21                              args, n );
            22
            23      XtRealizeWidget ( shell );
            24
            25      XtAppMainLoop ( app );
            26  }
```

The problem is the two initialized variables passed to `XtAppInitialize()` on lines 9 and 10. The values stored in the variables `arg` and `n` when `XtAppInitialize()` is called are completely undefined. If `n` is non-zero, Xt will try to use whatever garbage is in the uninitialized `Arg` array to initialize the shell widget, with possibly disastrous results. Of course, if `n` just happens to be zero, no error will occur. The `XtCreateWidget()` wrapper described in Chapter 2 tries to detect this error, among others.

Array overruns, in which more values are stored in an array than the array was declared to hold, can also cause memory problems. A likely place to find array overruns is the `XtSetArg()` macro, because this macro is used to store resource values into a fixed length array. `Arg` arrays are often accidently overrun when modifying an existing program by adding “just one more” argument to a list, without checking to be sure the array is large enough. The following program contains an obvious array overrun.

```
/****************************************************
 * tooshort.c: Show an ArgList overrun
 ****************************************************/
#include <Xm/Xm.h>
#include <Xm/PushB.h>

void main ( int argc, char **argv )
{
    Widget       shell, button;
    XtAppContext app;
    Arg          args[2];
    int          n;

    shell = XtAppInitialize ( &app, "Tooshort", NULL, 0,
                              &argc, argv, NULL, NULL, 0 );

    n = 0;
    XtSetArg ( args[n], XmNwidth, 100 ); n++;
    XtSetArg ( args[n], XmNheight, 25 ); n++;
    XtSetArg ( args[n], XmNrecomputeSize, FALSE ); n++;   /* 3rd entry */
    button = XtCreateManagedWidget ( "button",
                                     xmPushButtonWidgetClass,
                                     shell,
                                     args, n );

    XtRealizeWidget ( shell );

    XtAppMainLoop ( app );
}
```

This type of bug can be insidious because this program will most likely run without reporting any errors. Therefore, such problems often go unnoticed until new features, new libraries, a new compiler, or some other change alters the memory usage patterns of the program and the array overrun causes a failure. When this bug does cause an error, the symptoms will probably not indicate the true point of the error. The problem is particularly likely to occur if the array overrun is in a function in a large program or in a library, where any given address is more likely to be used eventually.

Although simple mistakes like the array overrun in the above program do occur, `Arg` arrays are often used in ways that make such errors harder to detect. For example, the following function initializes an `Arg` list differently depending on the value of certain parameters. The complexity of the logic makes it hard to see whether the `Arg` list could overflow in any given situation.

```
/*********************************************************
 * toocomplex.c: Show an ArgList overrun due to
 *               confusing misuse of arg arrays inside
 *               tangled conditional statements
 *********************************************************/
#include <Xm/Xm.h>
#include <Xm/PushB.h>

Widget CreateLabel ( Widget parent,
                     char  *name,  char *label,
                     int    width, int   height,
                     Pixmap pix )
{
   Widget   label;
   XmString xmstr;
   Arg      args[3];
   int      n;

   n = 0;
   if ( label && !pix )
   {
        xmstr = XmStringCreateLocalized ( label );
        XtSetArg ( args[n], XmNlabelString, xmstr ); n++;
   }
   else if ( pix )
   {
      int w, h;

      XGetGeometry ( XtDisplay ( parent ), pix, &w, &h );
      XtSetArg ( args[n], XmNlabelPixmap, pix ); n++;
      XtSetArg ( args[n], XmNwidth, w ); n++;
      XtSetArg ( args[n], XmNheight, h ); n++;
   }
   if ( ( width || height ) && !pix )
   {
      if ( height )
      {
          XtSetArg ( args[n], XmNheight, height ); n++;
      }
      else
      {
          XtSetArg ( args[n], XmNheight, 10 ); n++;
      }
      XtSetArg ( args[n], XmNwidth, width ); n++;
   }
   else
   {
       XtSetArg ( args[n], XmNrecomputeSize, FALSE ); n++;
   }
```

```
50      label = XtCreateManagedWidget ( "button",
51                                      xmPushButtonWidgetClass,
52                                      parent,
53                                      args, n );
54  }
```

Is there a condition in which the number of entries in the `Arg` array could exceed the declared size of the array? It's difficult to know for sure, and such a function could contain errors that would go unnoticed for a long time. Such combinations of conditional statements and `Arg` arrays are best avoided, although they are common in many Motif programs.

One way to catch errors in examples like this is to use an assertion. Adding the statement:

```
assert ( n <= XtNumber  (  args ) );
```

before the call to `XtCreateManagedWidget()` on line 50 would detect an array-overrun in this function. This only works when the `Arg` array is statically declared.

Another common error when using `Arg` arrays with `if` statements is to forget the trailing counter that is typically used in sets of calls to `XtSetArg()`. For example, consider the following code segment:

```
n=0;
if ( w < 100 )
   XtSetArg ( args[n], XmNwidth, 100 ); n++;
if ( h > 200 )
   XtSetArg ( args[n], XmNheight, h ); n++;
button = XtCreateManagedWidget ( "button",
                                  xmPushButtonWidgetClass,
                                  shell, args, n );
```

The problem here is that `n` is incremented whether the `XtSetArg()` statements are executed or not. If both conditions in this code segment are `TRUE`, then `n` will be set to 2, and there will be two arguments in the array. However, if either of the statements is `FALSE`, `n` will still be set to 2, but there will be fewer than two arguments in the `Arg` array.

Using Vararg Resource Functions

These problems can be avoided by using vararg functions, like `XtVaSetValues()`, to specify resources. Some programmers prefer not to use these functions because they carry a slight performance cost, although the cost is extremely small. However, they are usually more convenient, and somewhat less error-prone. Still, when using vararg functions, there is the risk of forgetting the required terminating `NULL`, with equally disastrous results. In addition, vararg functions cannot be used with conditional statements, like those demonstrated by the `CreateLabel()` function described earlier.

Consider the following program, which neglects the terminating `NULL` when calling `XtVaSetValues()`. The program creates an XmRowColumn widget that contains a button and a label. Each time the user presses a button, a callback function is supposed to change the string in the label.

```
/******************************************************
 * vararg.c: Demonstrate the error resulting from a
 *           non-terminated vararg function.
 ******************************************************/
#include <Xm/Xm.h>
#include <Xm/Label.h>
#include <Xm/PushB.h>
#include <Xm/RowColumn.h>
#include <stdio.h>

void Callback ( Widget    w,
                XtPointer clientData,
                XtPointer callData)
{
    Widget   label = ( Widget ) clientData;
    XmString xmstr;
    static   int count = 0;
    char     buf[100];

    sprintf ( buf, "Called %d times", count++ );
    xmstr = XmStringCreateLocalized ( buf );
Bug XtVaSetValues ( label, XmNlabelString, xmstr );
    XmStringFree ( xmstr );
}

void main ( int argc, char **argv )
{
    Widget       shell, label, button, rc;
    XtAppContext app;

    shell = XtAppInitialize ( &app, "Varargbug", NULL, 0,
                              &argc, argv, NULL, NULL, 0 );

    rc = XtCreateManagedWidget ( "rc", xmRowColumnWidgetClass,
                                 shell, NULL, 0 );

```

```
    label = XtCreateManagedWidget ( "label",
                                    xmLabelWidgetClass,
                                    rc, NULL, 0 );
    button = XtCreateManagedWidget ( "button",
                                     xmPushButtonWidgetClass,
                                     rc, NULL, 0 );
    XtAddCallback ( button, XmNactivateCallback,
                    Callback, label );
    XtRealizeWidget ( shell );
    XtAppMainLoop ( app );
}
```

Figure 4.11 shows the callstack of a segmentation violation that might occur when this program runs.

Processing the varargs

SetValues

Application callback

Invoking the callback

```
% vararg
Memory fault(coredump)
% dbx vararg
Process died at pc 0xfb0d8e4 of signal : Segmentation fault
(dbx) where
>  0 strcmp(0x43616c6c, 0xf717a98, 0x7fffaa64, 0x10016dbe, 0x1)
[0xfb0d8e0]
   1 _XtCountVaList(0x43616c6c, 0xf717a98, 0x7fffaa64,
0x10016dbe, 0xf705be8) ["Varargs.c":77, 0xf706b5c]
   2 XtVaSetValues(0x1001cb50, 0xe3f3f05, 0x10016db8,
0x10016dbe, 0xfbd18d0) ["VarCreate.c":222, 0xf705c24]
   3 Callback(w = 0x1001e5a0, clientData = 0x1001cb50, callData
= 0x7fffab90) ["vararg.c":25, 0x400d10]
   4 XtCallCallbackList(0x10006458, 0x3, 0x7fffaaa8, 0x1001e5a0,
0x7fffab90) ["Callback.c":522, 0xf6ca4a4]
   5 ActivateCommon(0x1001e5a0, 0x7fffae48, 0x0, 0x1001d8f8,
0x7fffacb0) ["PushB.c":828, 0xe16c4ac]
   6 Activate(0x0, 0xf702ea8, 0x10005620, 0xffffffff, 0x0)
["PushB.c":727, 0xe178d90]
   7 HandleActions(0x1001e5d8, 0x0, 0x1001fcfc, 0xf718a18,
0x1001fcfc) ["TMstate.c":568, 0xf702374]
   8 HandleComplexState(0x1001e5a0, 0x1001d8f0, 0x1001e5a0, 0x0,
0x0) ["TMstate.c":973, 0xf703068]
   9 _XtTranslateEvent(0x1001e5a0, 0x1001d8f0, 0x1001e5a0, 0x0,
0x0) ["TMstate.c":1004, 0xf703180]
  10 DispatchEvent(0x1001e5a0, 0x1001d8f0, 0x8, 0x1000756c,
0xf77ca04) ["Event.c":697, 0xf6d6a78]
  11 DecideToDispatch(0x1001e5a0, 0x1001d8f0, 0x0, 0x10005620,
0xf6d79a4) ["Event.c":1037, 0xf6d73d0]
  12 XtDispatchEvent(0x7fffae48, 0x1001d8f0, 0xfbe0008, 0x2b,
0xf6d79a4) ["Event.c":1078, 0xf6d7510]
  13 XtAppMainLoop(0x7fffae48, 0x1001d8f0, 0x0, 0x10006cf4, 0x0)
["Event.c":1201, 0xf6d79f0]
  14 main(argc = 1, argv = 0x7fffaf14) ["vararg.c":54, 0x400e78]
```

Figure 4.11 Callstack from non-terminated vararg function.

As usual, the program dies in a library function rather than at the point at which the error really occurs. At least in this example, following the callstack back to the last point in the application source does lead to the line of code responsible for the error.

Setting and Retrieving Values

Besides the errors that can occur by initializing `Arg` arrays incorrectly, there are other problems that are related to resources. One potential problem is that the `XtGetValues()`/`XtSetValues()` functions are very sensitive to the size of the data passed as resource values. For example, consider the `xlogobug` program, first seen in Chapter 1, which has a problem we have still not identified. The last version, discussed earlier in this chapter prints obviously erroneous values for the width and height of a widget, as retrieved by `XtGetValues()`.

The debugging session shown in Figure 4.10 has already determined that the values stored inside the widget are correct, so it seems that there must be a problem in retrieving the values. Using a debugger to look at the `xlogobug` program more closely provides the answer. Figure 4.12 shows a debugging session in which the value of the `width` variable is examined in the debugger.

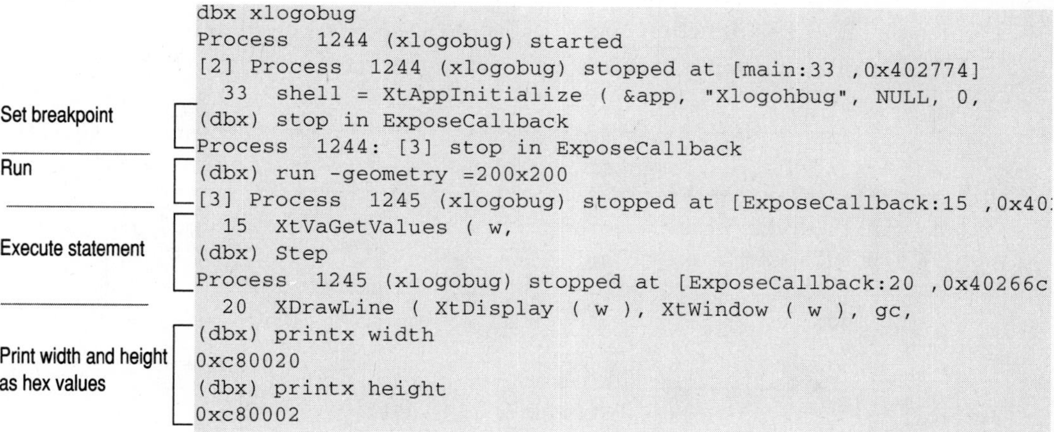


```
dbx xlogobug
Process  1244 (xlogobug) started
[2] Process  1244 (xlogobug) stopped at [main:33 ,0x402774]
  33  shell = XtAppInitialize ( &app, "Xlogohbug", NULL, 0,
(dbx) stop in ExposeCallback
Process  1244: [3] stop in ExposeCallback
(dbx) run -geometry =200x200
[3] Process  1245 (xlogobug) stopped at [ExposeCallback:15 ,0x40:
  15  XtVaGetValues ( w,
(dbx) step
Process  1245 (xlogobug) stopped at [ExposeCallback:20 ,0x40266c
  20  XDrawLine ( XtDisplay ( w ), XtWindow ( w ), gc,
(dbx) printx width
0xc80020
(dbx) printx height
0xc80002
```

Figure 4.12 Examining values returned from `XtVaGetValues()`.

Printing the value of `width` as a decimal shows the same value reported by `printf()`. However, displaying `width` as a hexadecimal value shows the value to be 0xc80020. This is interesting because the hexadecimal value 0xc8 is equal to 200 in decimal, which is the expected size of the widget. However, the value has been shifted by the difference between the size of an `int` and the size of a `Dimension`, which makes the value be 0xc80000, or 13107200. Notice that the value reported by `dbx` also has some uninitialized data in the lower bits, which causes further confusion. Referring back to the original code on page 143, we can see that `width` is declared as an `int`. But the `XmNwidth` resource expects a variable of type `Dimension`. `XtGetValues()` uses `bcopy()` to copy the bits directly from the widget to the provided address. The address is simply off by two bytes.

Changing the declaration of `width` from an `int` to a `Dimension` fixes the problem. Notice that the size of various data types is system-dependent. If the size of an `int` is equal to the size of a `Dimension` on a particular system, this bug would not appear on that system. This bug would also not appear on a little endian machine. This is a good example of a bug that may appear when porting to a new system. It is common to see bug reports that say "my program runs fine on Vendor X's machine, but crashes when I recompile on Vendor Y's system. What is wrong with Vendor Y's Motif?" The answer, of course, is there may be nothing wrong with Vendor Y's system; the bug is in the program, but just didn't show up on Vendor X's system.

Now that we understand the problem, the `xlogobug` program can finally be written so the X appears correctly. The following version of the `ExposeCallback()` function correctly declares the types of `width` and `height` as `Dimension`, and retrieves the correct size of the widget.

```
/***********************************************************
 * xlogobug.c: A buggy program,correctly retrieving size
 ***********************************************************/
#include <Xm/Xm.h>
#include <Xm/DrawingA.h>

GC  gc;

void ExposeCallback ( Widget    w,
                      XtPointer clientData,
                      XtPointer callData )
{
    Dimension width, height;

    /*
     * Determine the size of the canvas widget to allow
     * the lines to be drawn.
     */
```

```

    XtVaGetValues ( w,
                    XmNwidth,  &width,
                    XmNheight, &height,
                    NULL );

   /*
    * Draw an X into the canvas widget's window, using the
    * widget's size to draw a line diagonally between
    * each corner.
    */

    XDrawLine ( XtDisplay ( w ), XtWindow ( w ), gc,
                0, 0, width, height );

    XDrawLine ( XtDisplay ( w ), XtWindow ( w ), gc,
                width, 0, 0, height );
}
```

Figure 4.13 shows the `xlogobug` program as it was intended to appear on the screen, now that this bug has been found and fixed.

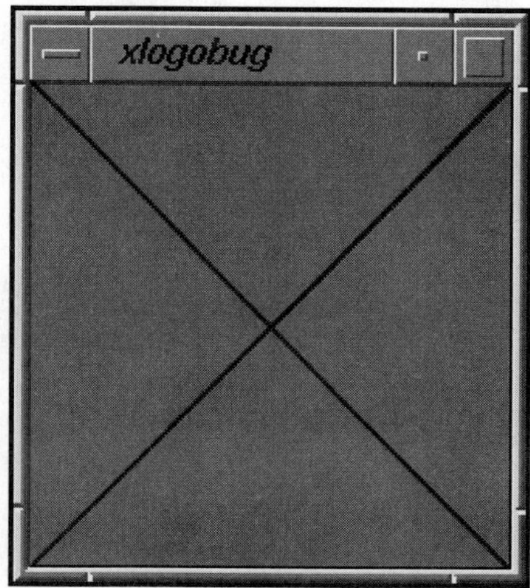

Figure 4.13 Correctly working `xlogobug` program.

Figure 4.14 shows the corrected program being executed under the control of a debugger. This time, printing the values of `width` and `height` reports the correct value.

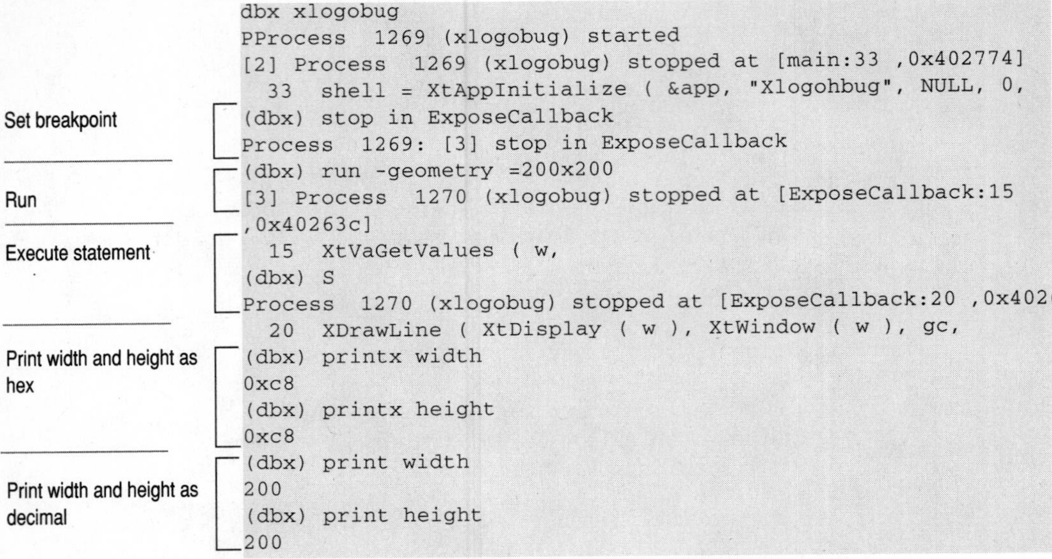


```
dbx xlogobug
PProcess  1269 (xlogobug) started
[2] Process  1269 (xlogobug) stopped at [main:33 ,0x402774]
  33  shell = XtAppInitialize ( &app, "Xlogohbug", NULL, 0,
(dbx) stop in ExposeCallback
Process  1269: [3] stop in ExposeCallback
(dbx) run -geometry =200x200
[3] Process  1270 (xlogobug) stopped at [ExposeCallback:15
,0x40263c]
  15  XtVaGetValues ( w,
(dbx) s
Process  1270 (xlogobug) stopped at [ExposeCallback:20 ,0x402
  20  XDrawLine ( XtDisplay ( w ), XtWindow ( w ), gc,
(dbx) printx width
0xc8
(dbx) printx height
0xc8
(dbx) print width
200
(dbx) print height
200
```

Figure 4.14 Examining values returned from `XtVaGetValues()`.

Drawing and Redisplay Problems

Although the initial problems with the `xlogobug` program have finally been solved, there are still some remaining errors. For example, if the window shown in Figure 4.13 is resized, the resulting program has some unexpected behavior, as shown in Figure 4.15.

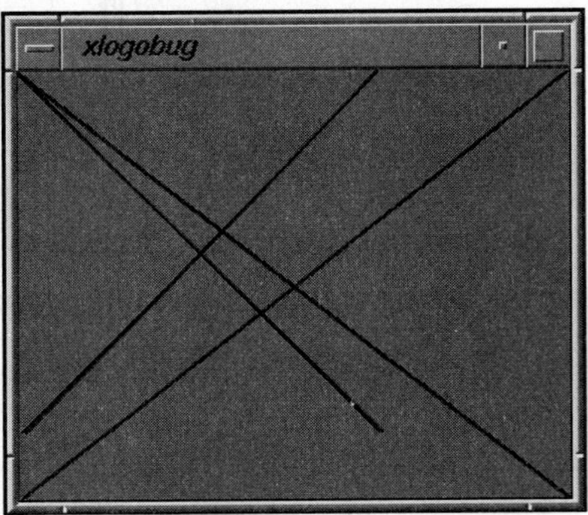

Figure 4.15 Drawing problem in `xlogobug` program.

It is fairly easy to guess what the problem is in this example, because there are only a few possibilities. The lines in the window match the new dimensions as well as the previous size. It could be a rendering problem, in which the lines are being drawn twice, or the original lines might not have been erased. We can use a protocol monitor to investigate. Figure 4.16 shows the events and requests made by this program, beginning with the point at which the window is resized.

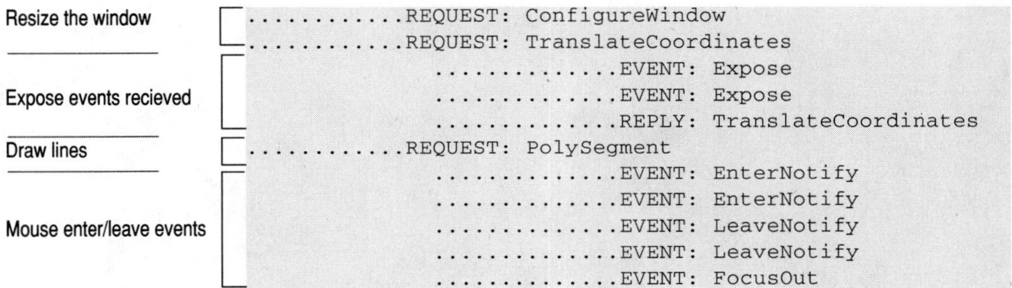
Resize the window
Expose events recieved
Draw lines
Mouse enter/leave events
............REQUEST: ConfigureWindow
............REQUEST: TranslateCoordinates
.............EVENT: Expose
.............EVENT: Expose
.............REPLY: TranslateCoordinates
............REQUEST: PolySegment
.............EVENT: EnterNotify
.............EVENT: EnterNotify
.............EVENT: LeaveNotify
.............EVENT: LeaveNotify
.............EVENT: FocusOut

Figure 4.16 Trace of drawing requests in `xlogobug` program.

From this information, we can see that the server generated two `Expose` events after the window was resized. Strangely, the program makes only one drawing request in response to the `Expose` events. This is a bit unexpected, because we know the program draws at least two lines. However, Xlib sometimes collapses multiple drawing operations into a single server request. So in this example, the calls to `XDrawLine()` are probably being collapsed into a single `PolySegment` request. Because Figure 4.16 shows only the names of requests, we cannot determine how many lines are being drawn.

However, it is easy to use xmon to gather more detailed information. Figure 4.17 shows the details of the `PolySegment` request made when the `xlogobug` program is resized.

```
............REQUEST: PolySegment
        sequence number: 75
         request length: 000b
               drawable: DWB 0440000b
                     gc: GXC 0440000c
               segments: (4)
                        x1: 0
                        y1: 0
                        x2: 235
                        y2: 222
                        ---
                        x1: 235
                        y1: 0
                        x2: 0
                        y2: 222
                        ---
                        x1: 0
                        y1: 0
                        x2: 235
                        y2: 222
                        ---
                        x1: 235
                        y1: 0
                        x2: 0
                        y2: 222
```

Figure 4.17 Detailed trace of drawing requests.

From the trace in Figure 4.17, we can see that the single `X_PolySegment` request is drawing four lines with a single request. However, the second pair of lines are duplicates. Apparently, `xlogobug` is drawing once for each `Expose` event it receives. Although the multiple redraws might be a problem for some programs, this does not account for the four lines we can see in the window.

The two `Expose` events are probably generated because the `xlogobug` window has been resized in two dimensions at once, so the server has to report `Expose` events for two regions. We can confirm this by resizing `xlogobug` in only one dimension and examining the requests, as shown in Figure 4.18.

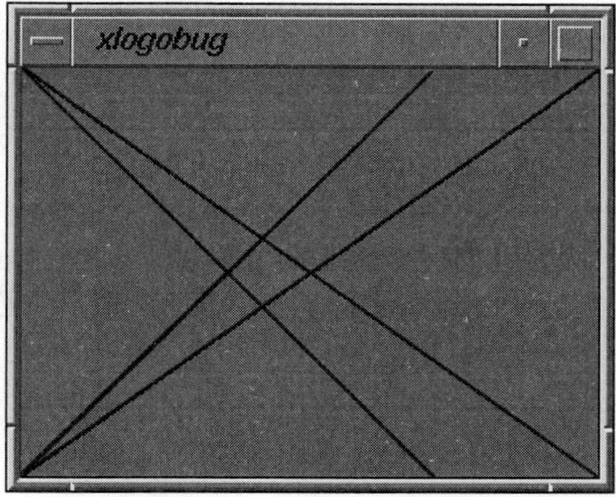

Figure 4.18 Resizing `xlogobug` in only one dimension.

Just increasing the width of the `xlogobug` window produces only one `Expose` event, and the program makes the requests shown in Figure 4.19.

```
............REQUEST: PolySegment
    sequence number: 76
     request length: 0007
           drawable: DWB 0440000b
                 gc: GXC 0440000c
           segments: (2)
                         x1: 0
                         y1: 0
                         x2: 281
                         y2: 200
                         ---
                         x1: 281
                         y1: 0
                         x2: 0
                         y2: 200
```

Figure 4.19 Requests made for window in Figure 4.18.

From the `xmond` output, it is clear that `xlogobug` draws only the lines that span the window's diagonals. The remaining two lines must be left from when the window was smaller. In other words, the window is not being erased. When a window is resized, the X server generates `Expose` events for any newly exposed areas, but it does not necessarily clear the existing area of the window. Furthermore, if a window's size is reduced, the application receives a

ConfigureNotify event, but may not receive an Expose event, because no new areas are exposed by such a change. For this program to render the window contents correctly, it is necessary to add a callback to clear the window when the window is resized. This can be done easily, by writing a Resize-Callback() function, like this:

```
void ResizeCallback ( Widget    w,
                      XtPointer clientData,
                      XtPointer callData )
{
    if ( XtIsRealized ( w ) )
        XClearArea ( XtDisplay ( w ), XtWindow ( w ),
                     0, 0, 0, 0, TRUE );
}
```

The last argument to XClearArea() requests the server to generate an Expose event for the entire window when it is erased. The callback can be registered with the XmDrawingArea widget by adding the following line to the xlogobug program:

```
    XtAddCallback ( canvas, XmNresizeCallback,
                    ResizeCallback, NULL );
```

It is important to be careful when triggering exposures with XClearArea() to avoid multiple redraws. Some widgets compress Expose events, but some do not. When using a widget that does not compress Expose events, (including the XmDrawingArea widget), it is usually best to check the Expose event structure and redraw only when the count member is set to zero.

Referencing Destroyed Widgets

One bug that seems to occur regularly in Motif programs involves references to widgets after they have been destroyed. Usually, such bugs are the result of a logic error, or a dangling pointer. Although one might think that such problems could be identified quickly, such errors can sometimes be quite elusive. In part, the complexity of the Xt widget destruction process makes errors hard to find.

For example, it is possible, in some situations, for a widget to be destroyed multiple times without causing any obvious problem. Xt uses a two-phase destroy process that can exhibit subtly different behavior depending on the current state of the program, which further complicates debugging. For example, consider the following program, which contains an obvious bug, in which the same widget is destroyed twice in a row:

Bug!

```
 1  /*****************************************************
 2   * doubledestroy.c: Show results of destroying a
 3   *                  widget twice.
 4   *****************************************************/
 5 #include <Xm/Xm.h>
 6 #include <Xm/PushB.h>
 7 #include <stdio.h>
 8
 9 void main ( int argc, char **argv )
10 {
11     Widget       shell, button;
12     XtAppContext app;
13
14     shell = XtAppInitialize ( &app, "Doubledestroy", NULL, 0,
15                               &argc, argv, NULL, NULL, 0 );
16
17     button = XtCreateManagedWidget ( "button",
18                                      xmPushButtonWidgetClass,
19                                      shell, NULL, 0 );
20    /*
21     * Destroy the button once
22     */
23
24     XtDestroyWidget ( button );
25
26    /*
27     * Bug! Destroy the button widget again!
28     */
29
30     XtDestroyWidget ( button );
31
32     XtRealizeWidget ( shell );
33     XtAppMainLoop ( app );
34 }
```

This program normally runs without reporting any errors. Because the program destroys the button before entering the event loop, it displays only an empty shell, but the program does not core dump, nor produce any error messages. This is because `XtDestroyWidget()` checks a flag maintained by the widget to determine if it is already in the process of being destroyed. If so, `XtDestroyWidget()` simply returns. So, in this example, the second call to `XtDestroyWidget()`, on line 30, simply returns.

Of course, in this example, the widget is not in the process of being destroyed when the second call to `XtDestroyWidget()` is made. The widget is completely destroyed in the first call on line 24, and the memory associated with the widget is freed. However, because no additional memory is allocated or freed between the two calls to `XtDestroyWidget()`, there is little chance that the memory used by the widget has been disturbed. In most cases, the second call can access the internal widget data without causing an error. This behavior is completely dependent on the `malloc()` implementation being used. The program could suddenly begin to exhibit problems if a different version of `malloc()` is used, something changes about the memory usage pattern of the program, or the destroyed widget is referenced in some other way.

For example, consider the following slight variation of the above program. This version also destroys the same widget twice, but in this version, the second call to `XtDestroyWidget()` is not made until after `XtRealizeWidget()`.

```
1   /******************************************************
2    * doubledestroy2.c: Show results of destroying a
3    *                   widget twice.
4    ******************************************************/
5   #include <Xm/Xm.h>
6   #include <Xm/PushB.h>
7   #include <stdio.h>
8
9   void main ( int argc, char **argv )
10  {
11      Widget       shell, button;
12      XtAppContext app;
13
14      shell = XtAppInitialize ( &app, "Doubledestroy", NULL, 0,
15                                &argc, argv, NULL, NULL, 0 );
16
17      button = XtCreateManagedWidget ( "button",
18                                       xmPushButtonWidgetClass,
19                                       shell, NULL, 0 );
20     /*
21      * Destroy the button once
22      */
23
24      XtDestroyWidget ( button );
25
26      XtRealizeWidget ( shell );
27
```

Bug!

```
    /*
     * Bug! Destroy the button widget again!
     */

    XtDestroyWidget ( button );

    XtAppMainLoop ( app );
}
```

In this program, because `XtRealizeWidget()` allocates additional memory, the memory formerly used by the button widget is more likely to have been altered, and the second call to `XtDestroyWidget()` may cause a core dump.

The exact behavior of this example program is highly system dependent. For example, Figure 4.20 shows the callstack reported by `dbx` when this program is executed on a Silicon Graphic's Indy workstation, running IRIX 5.2. Here, the destroy process proceeds into several lower level functions before some memory access to the destroyed widget fails.

```
% dbx doubledestroy
Process died at pc 0xf6d2d8c of signal : Segmentation fault
[using memory image in core]
(dbx) where
>  0 XtPhase2Destroy(0x1001b400, 0x1001b400, 0x7fffae3c, 0x10006178
0x10005620) ["Destroy.c":127, 0xf6d2d88]
   1 _XtDoPhase2Destroy(0x1001b400, 0x1001b400, 0x7fffae3c, 0x100061
0xf716191) ["Destroy.c":237, 0xf6d31a4]
   2 XtDestroyWidget(0x1001b400, 0x1001b400, 0x7fffae3c, 0x10006178
0x7fffaef8) ["Destroy.c":288, 0xf6d3394]
   3 main(argc = 1, argv = 0x7fffaf14) ["doubledestroy.c":32, 0x4014
```

Figure 4.20 Callstack of core dump from destroying a widget twice.

However, on a Sun Sparc 10, running Solaris 2.0, `dbx` reports a different callstack, as shown in Figure 4.21. On this system, the program crashes immediately inside the call to `XtDestroyWidget()`. In either case, however, the basic principle is the same, the only difference is the pattern of memory use.

```
% dbx doubledestroy
program terminated by SEGV (segmentation violation)
(dbx) where
XtWidgetToApplicationContext(0x152980, 0x440000f, 0x14d900, 0, 0x1,
0x141fac) at 0xac640
XtDestroyWidget(0x152980, 0x440000f, 0x145cec, 0x13fe10, 0, 0) at
0xab7b8
main(0x1, 0x145c78, 0xeffffe5c, 0x138c00, 0, 0x152980) at 0x25bcc
```

Figure 4.21 Callstack of core dump from destroying a widget twice.

The examples above explicitly destroy a widget twice, which few programs would do, exactly as shown. However, similar situations can occur in real programs, in ways that may be harder to detect. For example, destroying a manager widget before destroying one of its children produces a similar problem.

Problems that occur as a result of destroying widgets dynamically after a program is running can also be difficult to find. Once a program is running, most changes occur directly or indirectly because of user input. User input is communicated to the application via events, of course. Xt's two phase destroy sequence interacts with an application's event loop in various ways that can make problems caused by improperly destroying widgets much harder to understand.

When a widget is destroyed, the first phase of the destruction includes the following steps:

- If the widget is marked as being destroyed, `XtDestroyWidget()` returns immediately. (This is why the first `doubledestroy` program, described above, did not display any problems.)
- Otherwise, `XtDestroyWidget()` recursively descends the widget tree and marks all normal and pop-up children as being destroyed.
- Next, `XtDestroyWidget()` adds the widget to a list of widgets to be destroyed when it is safe to do so. It is possible to have multiple event handlers and callbacks that must be called to handle the current event, so the widget cannot be destroyed immediately.

In some cases, phase two of the widget destruction occurs immediately following phase one, in other cases, it may not occur until later. If the application is currently inside `XtDispatchEvent()`, and there are additional event handlers or action routines that should be executed because of the current event, phase two is delayed until all these functions have been called. In this situation, phase two begins just before `XtDispatchEvent()` returns. Otherwise, phase two begins immediately.

Phase two of the destroy sequence performs the following steps:

- Any destroy callbacks registered with the destroyed widget or its children are invoked. Callbacks registered with children are called before those registered with their parents.
- If the destroyed widget's parent is not being destroyed, the widget is unmanaged, and removed from the parent's internal list of children.
- The internal `destroy()` method supported by all widgets is called to clean up any memory allocated by the widget.
- The widget's window is destroyed. The X server recursively destroys the windows of all children.
- The windows of all pop-up children are destroyed,
- The memory associated with the widget is freed.

Figure 4.20 on page 163 shows a callstack that shows the second phase destruction when it takes place immediately.

Xt's two phase destroy sequence can be confused by using nested event loops in conjunction with destroying widgets, so secondary event loops should be used with caution. Many programmers like to use nested event loops to simulate a blocking effect for modal dialogs. Calling `XmUpdateDisplay()` also produces a nested event loop.

Detecting Erroneous Calls to XtDestroyWidget()

It can often be difficult to catch situations that lead to destroying widgets that have been corrupted, or previously destroyed. By the time the error is detected it is often not clear which widget was involved in the error. One way to make it easier to find such errors is to use the wrapper technique described in Chapter 3 to create a less forgiving version of `XtDestroyWidget()`. For those who have UNIX SVR4 dynamic shared libraries, such a wrapper can be implemented as shown below.

```
/******************************************************
 * Destroy.c: Debugging wrapper for XtDestroyWidget()
 ******************************************************/
#ifndef NDEBUG
#include <dlfcn.h>
#include <assert.h>
#include <X11/IntrinsicP.h>

typedef void ( *destroyfunc )( Widget );

void XtDestroyWidget ( Widget w )
{
    void        *handle = NULL;
    destroyfunc fptr = NULL;

   /*
    * Signal an error if the pointer passed in is not
    * a valid, un-destroyed widget.
    */

    assert ( w );
    assert ( XtIsObject ( w ) );
    assert ( !w->core.being_destroyed );

   /*
    * Load the real Xt library
    */

    handle = dlopen ( "/usr/lib/libXt.so", RTLD_LAZY );
    assert ( handle );

   /*
    * Get a pointer to the real XtDestroyWidget() function
    */

    fptr = ( destroyfunc ) dlsym(handle, "XtDestroyWidget" );
    assert ( fptr );

   /*
    * Invoke Xt's XtDestroyWidget() to destroy the widget
    */

    (*fptr)( w );
}
#endif
```

This function uses an `assert()` statement to check that the given widget is non-`NULL`, that it passes the tests performed by `XtIsObject()` and that it is not in the process of being destroyed. These tests are not fool-proof, but they catch most cases, including those demonstrated in this section. Once all tests have succeeded, the wrapper locates the real `XtDestroyWidget()` and calls it to do the real work.

If your system does not support dynamic shared libraries, there are several alternatives to this approach. You could get the source to Xt and modify it directly, adding similar `assert()` statements to those above. Another approach is to use `assert()` macros directly in your code to check the state of a widget each time you call `XtDestroyWidget()`. For example a callback used to destroy a widget could be written as follows:

```
void DestroyWidgetCallback ( Widget w,
                             XtPointer callData,
                             XtPointer clientData )
{
    Widget button = ( Widget ) clientData;
    assert ( XtIsObject ( button ) );

    XtDestroyWidget ( button );
}
```

Of course, as discussed in Chapter 2, it is always a good idea to test the arguments passed to a callback. However, testing a widget before calling `XtDestroyWidget()` is less thorough than using the wrapper function described earlier. Adding assertions can only catch problems in your own code, and, Xt, Motif, and other libraries may also call `XtDestroyWidget()`. The wrapper approach tests all calls to `XtDestroyWidget()`, without modifying any code.

4.4 Errors That Involve Motif

Because so much of a program's interaction with Motif uses the facilities provided by Xt, many errors encountered in a Motif program involve Xt. However, there are a few features of Motif that do not use Xt, and some errors that tend to show up as Motif-specific problems. This section discusses problems that relate to Motif convenience functions, gadgets, and widget appearance. Chapter 6 explores some the problems associated with geometry management, which also tend to be Motif-specific.

Motif Convenience Functions

Motif provides many types of convenience functions for creating and manipulating widgets. Although easy-to-use, these functions are often the source of errors. For example, a common error is to create a widget using a Motif convenience function and forget to manage it. If you are used to using `XtCreateManagedWidget()`, it can be very easy to forget that you must explicitly manage a widget created by calling `XmCreateScrolledText()`. The resulting bug is normally easy to spot, and easy to find. The widget simply does not appear on the screen as expected. The easiest way to investigate this problem is to use `editres` to inspect the widget hierarchy and locate a widget on the screen. If you attempt to select a widget that is not on the screen, `editres` will warn you that the widget's window is not mapped. Most of the time, this means the widget has not been managed.

Testing for Unmanaged Widgets

The WL framework, described in Chapter 3, provides an easy way to generate warnings about unmanaged widgets. While not a difficult problem, some time can be saved with a simple test and warning. The following test function reports the total number of unmanaged widgets, if any were found. Notice that having unmanaged widgets does not necessarily indicate an error, if the widgets are unmanaged intentionally.

```
/*******************************************
 * UnmanagedCheck.c
 *******************************************/
#include <X11/Intrinsic.h>
#include <stdio.h>
#include "wlintP.h"

static int count;

void UnmanagedCheck ( Widget w, ActionType action )
{
    if( action == INIT )
    {
        count = 0;
        return;
    }

    if( action == POSTOP )
    {
        if ( count )
```

```
            fprintf ( stderr,
                      "Number of unmanaged widgets = %d\n",
                      count );
        else
            fprintf ( stderr, "No unmanaged widgets found\n" );
         return;
    }

    if ( !XtIsManaged( w ) && !XtIsShell ( w ) )
    {
        fprintf ( stderr, "%s is unmanaged\n", XtName ( w ) );
        count++;
    }
}
```

This function can be registered as part of the WL framework test suites by adding the following line to the WL library:

```
WLAddTest ( "Looking for unmanaged widgets",
            ALL, UnmanagedCheck );
```

Gadgets

The most common problems with using gadgets occur when a program does not obey the restrictions associated with gadgets. For example, in Motif 1.2 gadgets cannot support different colors, so attempts to change a gadget's color will fail. Gadgets also do not have windows, so any operation that assumes that a widget has a window will fail. For example, `XtWindow()` returns `NULL` if passed a gadget, so attempting to use Xlib functions to draw in a gadget will generate an X server error.

There are other, less obvious situations in which the lack of a window can cause problems as well. For example, the Xt functions `XtMapWidget()` and `XtUnmapWidget()` are sometimes considered to be an alternative to setting `XmNmappedWhenManaged` to `TRUE` or `FALSE`. Gadgets do support this resource, but `XtMapWidget()` is just a macro that expands to:

```
XMapWindow ( XtDisplay ( w ), XtWindow ( w ) );
```

Because gadgets do not have a window to map, this function will obviously fail.

Even more troublesome is the fact that the gadget structure is slightly different from that of widgets. Therefore, certain other Xt functions do not work correctly with gadgets. For example, calling `XtMapWidget()` on a gadget does not fail with an X server error, as you might expect. Instead, the program is more likely to core dump in the call to `XtDisplay()` before the call to `XMapWindow()` is even made. `XtDisplay()` cannot be used with gadgets. Instead, Display pointers must be retrieved from gadgets with `XtDisplayOfObject()` or `XtDisplay(XtParent(gadget))`. This restriction often causes problems in callbacks, where it may not be clear whether the invoking widget is truly a widget or is a gadget instead.

Update Problems

Motif programs sometimes exhibit visual problems of one kind or another. Two types of visual problems are common. One involves geometry management and layout, and the other involves widgets, text, or graphics that fail to draw properly. Chapter 6 discusses geometry management in detail, while this section presents some examples that demonstrate the second type of problem.

When programming with Motif, it is important to remember that an application must always return to the event loop as often and as rapidly as possible. It is easy to forget that, although programs do not need to render the labels and shadows provided by Motif, these visuals are being drawn by Motif, and therefore indirectly by the program. The program must respond to events continuously to allow Motif to maintain the visual appearance of its widgets.

For example, consider the following simple program, which displays a dialog while performing a simulated lengthy task. When the user clicks on a button, the program posts the dialog, which informs the user that the program is busy, and then performs the task. When the task has been completed, the program removes the dialog from the screen, and returns to the event loop.

```
/**********************************************************
 * busy.c: Display a dialog while the program is busy
 **********************************************************/
#include <Xm/Xm.h>
#include <Xm/MessageB.h>
#include <Xm/PushB.h>
#include <stdlib.h>

void BusyCallback ( Widget    w,
                    XtPointer clientData,
                    XtPointer callData );

void main ( int argc, char **argv )
```

```
{
    Widget       shell, button;
    XtAppContext app;

    shell = XtAppInitialize ( &app, "Busy", NULL, 0,
                              &argc, argv, NULL, NULL, 0 );

   /*
    * Create a button and add a callback to start the task
    */

    button = XtCreateManagedWidget ( "Start",
                                     xmPushButtonWidgetClass,
                                     shell, NULL, 0 );

    XtAddCallback ( button, XmNactivateCallback,
                    BusyCallback, NULL );

    XtRealizeWidget ( shell );
    XtAppMainLoop ( app );
}
```

The `BusyCallback()` function creates the dialog and simulates a lengthy task by calling `sleep()` for ten seconds.

```
#define BUSYMSG "Busy, Please wait"

void BusyCallback ( Widget    w,
                    XtPointer clientData,
                    XtPointer callData )
{
    static Widget dialog = NULL;

    if ( !dialog )
    {
       /*
        * Create the dialog if it doesn't already exist.
        */

        dialog = XmCreateWorkingDialog ( w, "dialog",
                                         NULL, 0 );

        XtVaSetValues ( dialog,
                        XtVaTypedArg, XmNmessageString,
                        XmRString,
                        BUSYMSG, strlen ( BUSYMSG )+1,
                        NULL );
    }
```

```

    /*
     * Display the dialog
     */

     XtManageChild ( dialog );

    /*
     * Simulate a lengthy task.
     */

     sleep ( 10 );

    /*
     * When the task is complete, remove the dialog
     */

     XtUnmanageChild ( dialog );
}
```

The behavior of this example can be puzzling the first time it is encountered. Most of the time, the dialog never appears! The reason is obvious if we consider the X client-server architecture. The X server does not necessarily process all requests immediately. Because the `busy` program makes no further requests until after it unmanages the dialog, and Xlib buffers requests, the X server does not receive the request to display the dialog until after the busy period is completely over. At that point, the program immediately requests that the dialog be removed. With the delays caused by the window manager interaction, it is unlikely that the dialog will be seen by the user at all. At most, it may flash on the screen for a brief moment.

One way to understand what happens in this situation is to look at the events and requests that flow between the application and the X server, using `xscope` or xmon. Figure 4.22 shows a slightly abbreviated trace of events and requests that occur between the time the `busy` program receives a `ButtonPress` event and the time the dialog is dismissed. Some unrelated events and requests have been removed from this list for clarity. The first sequence of requests and events is related to the Motif XmPushButton widget being pressed. The button must redraw its text and background color to change its appearance to the armed state and back to its normal state. The application receives a `LeaveNotify` event when the pointer leaves the area occupied by the button. Then, no requests are made while the application is busy.

Once the application returns from its busy state and returns to the event loop, pending requests are sent to the X server. The first request maps the dialog, but a subsequent request unmaps the same window. Once all requests have been sent to the X server, the application reads the pending events, which include a `MapNotify` event indicating that the dialog window has been mapped. But of course, it is too late, and the application has already requested that the dialog be removed from the screen, probably before the user can even see it.

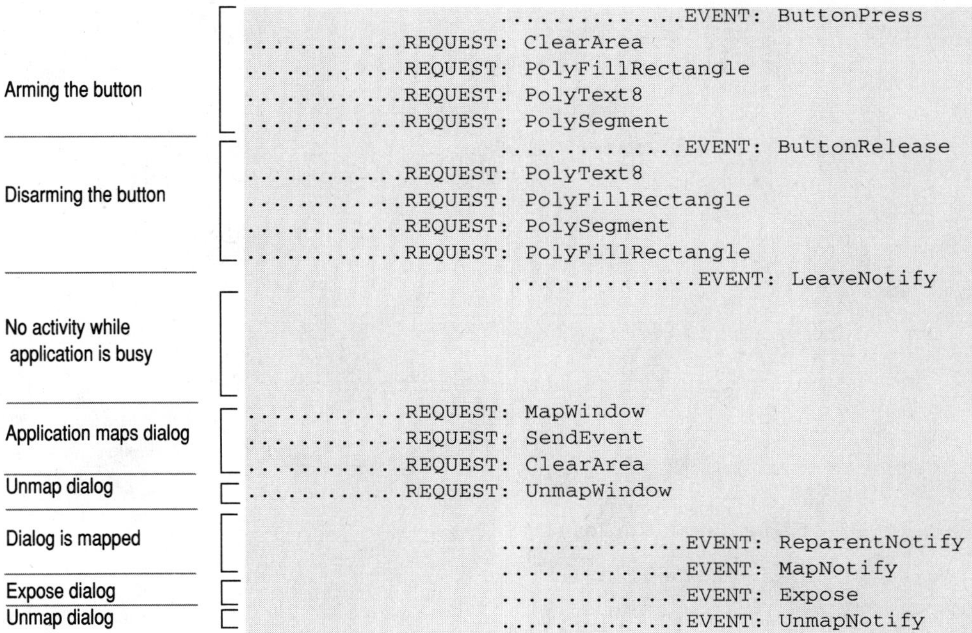

Arming the button
Disarming the button
No activity while application is busy
Application maps dialog
Unmap dialog
Dialog is mapped
Expose dialog
Unmap dialog
..............EVENT: ButtonPress
............REQUEST: ClearArea
............REQUEST: PolyFillRectangle
............REQUEST: PolyText8
............REQUEST: PolySegment
..............EVENT: ButtonRelease
............REQUEST: PolyText8
............REQUEST: PolyFillRectangle
............REQUEST: PolySegment
............REQUEST: PolyFillRectangle
..............EVENT: LeaveNotify
............REQUEST: MapWindow
............REQUEST: SendEvent
............REQUEST: ClearArea
............REQUEST: UnmapWindow
..............EVENT: ReparentNotify
..............EVENT: MapNotify
..............EVENT: Expose
..............EVENT: UnmapNotify

Figure 4.22 Abbreviated `xmond` event trace of busy dialog error.

Obviously, it is important to be sure that certain requests are processed as quickly as possible, particularly if the application cannot return to the event loop immediately. The Xlib function `XFlush()` forces all requests to be sent to the X server immediately, so one possible solution to the problem demonstrated above might be to call `XFlush()` after displaying the dialog. A new version of `BusyCallback()` could be written as follows:

```
#define BUSYMSG "Busy, Please wait"

void BusyCallback ( Widget    w,
                    XtPointer clientData,
                    XtPointer callData )
{
    static Widget dialog = NULL;

    if ( !dialog )
    {
        /*
         * Create the dialog if it doesn't already exist.
         */

        dialog = XmCreateWorkingDialog ( w, "dialog",
                                         NULL, 0 );

        XtVaSetValues ( dialog,
                        XtVaTypedArg, XmNmessageString,
                        XmRString,
                        BUSYMSG, strlen ( BUSYMSG ) + 1,
                        NULL );
    }

   /*
    * Display the dialog, flushing the request queue
    */

    XtManageChild ( dialog );

    XFlush ( XtDisplay ( dialog ) );

   /*
    * Simulate a lengthy task.
    */

    sleep ( 10 );

   /*
    * When the task is complete, remove the dialog
    */

    XtUnmanageChild ( dialog );
}
```

Unfortunately, this attempt to fix the initial problem reveals a slightly different problem. With the addition of the call to `XFlush()`, the dialog appears immediately, but it appears as only a blank window that contains no text, no shadows, and no buttons. The dialog stays on the screen, blank, for as long as the program is busy, and then disappears. Using xmon again to look at the events and requests can help explain why this occurs.

Figure 4.23 shows an abbreviated trace of the events and requests from this example. Again, the program makes requests to change the button to its armed appearance, and back to its normal state. However, this time the request to map the dialog is processed immediately. The server generates an `Expose` event to tell the application to redraw the contents of the dialog. Unfortunately, the application does not return to the event loop, and therefore never processes the event. The application does not make any requests to draw the contents of the dialog, because it never handles the `Expose` event. The next request, to unmap the dialog, comes after the application is no longer busy. The application removes the dialog from the screen before it even has a chance to draw the dialog's contents

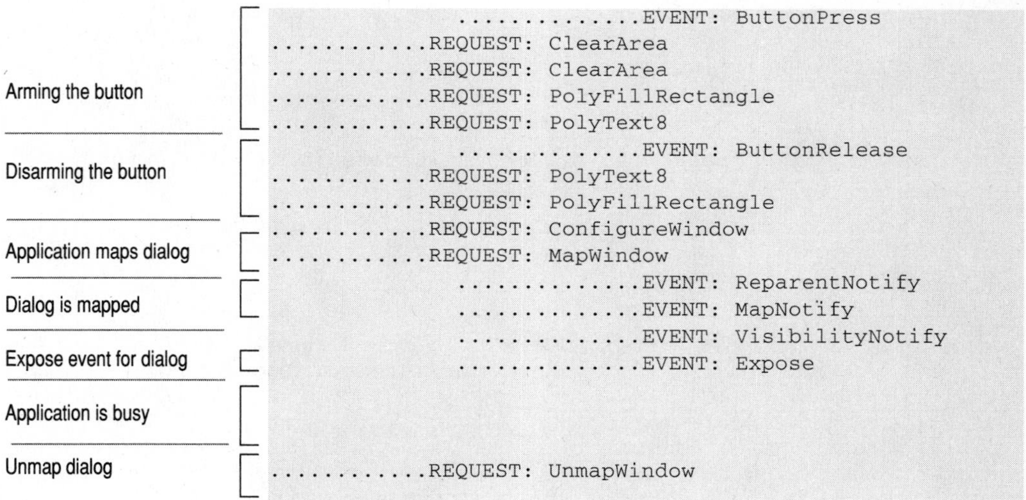
Arming the button
..............EVENT: ButtonPress
............REQUEST: ClearArea
............REQUEST: ClearArea
............REQUEST: PolyFillRectangle
............REQUEST: PolyText8
Disarming the button
..............EVENT: ButtonRelease
............REQUEST: PolyText8
............REQUEST: PolyFillRectangle
Application maps dialog
............REQUEST: ConfigureWindow
............REQUEST: MapWindow
Dialog is mapped
..............EVENT: ReparentNotify
..............EVENT: MapNotify
..............EVENT: VisibilityNotify
Expose event for dialog
..............EVENT: Expose
Application is busy
Unmap dialog
............REQUEST: UnmapWindow

Figure 4.23 Abbreviated `xmond` event trace of busy dialog error.

To ensure that the dialog's contents are displayed properly, the application must wait for the dialog to be mapped and then handle all pending events before entering the busy state. In some cases, calling the function `XmUpdate-Display()` after managing the dialog is sufficient. This function reads and processes all pending `Expose` events and then returns. If the window manager can display the dialog quickly enough, the dialog may be posted before `XmUpdateDisplay()` has finished processing pending `Expose` events.

To be safe, however, it is necessary to be sure the dialog is actually mapped before proceeding. One way to ensure the dialog is mapped is to enter a short custom event loop that processes all events until a `MapNotify` event is received. Once the `MapNotify` event is received, it is safe to exit the event loop, and call `XmUpdateDisplay()` to process all pending `Expose` events. A version of `BusyCallback()` that implements this behavior can be written as follows:

```
#define BUSYMSG "Busy, Please wait"

void BusyCallback ( Widget    w,
                    XtPointer clientData,
                    XtPointer callData )
{
    static Widget dialog = NULL;
    Boolean       mapped;
    XtAppContext  app = XtWidgetToApplicationContext ( w );

    if ( !dialog )
    {
       /*
        * Create the dialog if it doesn't already exist.
        */

        dialog = XmCreateWorkingDialog ( w, "dialog",
                                         NULL, 0 );

        XtVaSetValues ( dialog,
                        XtVaTypedArg, XmNmessageString,
                        XmRString,
                        BUSYMSG, strlen ( BUSYMSG )+1,
                        NULL );
    }

   /*
    * Display the dialog
    */

    XtManageChild ( dialog );

   /*
    * Initialize mapped to FALSE before entering an event
    * loop. The loop exits when mapped is set to TRUE
    * after a MapNotify event is recieved.
```

```
     *
     * Note: A more general solution would be to register an
     * event handler to be called when the dialog is mapped.
     * The loop below could conceivably exit before the
     * dialog appears, if some other window were mapped first,
     * or if a MapNotify event were still in the event
     * queue from mapping a previous window. These problems are
     * unlikely in this simple example, but could occur in
     * real programs.
     */

    mapped = FALSE;

    while ( XtIsManaged ( dialog ) && !mapped )
    {
        XEvent event;

        XtAppNextEvent ( app, &event );
        XtDispatchEvent ( &event );
        if ( event.type == MapNotify )
            mapped = TRUE;
    }

    XmUpdateDisplay ( dialog );

   /*
    * Simulate a lengthy task.
    */

    sleep ( 10 );

   /*
    * When the task is complete, remove the dialog
    */

    XtUnmanageChild ( dialog );
}
```

Notice that the contents of the dialog are only drawn when the dialog initially appears. If the program remains busy for a long time, and the user covers and uncovers the dialog in any way, the dialog will again be empty. Applications that need to be away for the event loop for extended periods of time must take special precautions to keep windows up-to-date.

Similar problems can also occur in other situations. For example, consider the following program, which creates an XmMainWindow widget containing a message window. The program performs some lengthy task, but this time the program uses the message window to keep the user informed of the progress of the task. As the task proceeds, an XmLabel widget in the message window is updated, reporting “10% Done”, “20% Done”, and so on.

```
/***********************************************
 * busy2.c: simulate a busy application that
 *          reports status in a message area
 ***********************************************/
#include <stdio.h>
#include <Xm/Xm.h>
#include <Xm/MainW.h>
#include <Xm/Label.h>
#include <Xm/DrawingA.h>

void main ( int argc, char **argv )
{
    Widget        shell, canvas, msg, mainw;
    XtAppContext  app;
    int           i;

    shell = XtAppInitialize ( &app, "Busy", NULL, 0,
                              &argc, argv,
                              NULL, NULL, 0 );

   /*
    * Create a main window to hold a message and work area
    */

    mainw = XtCreateManagedWidget ( "mainWindow",
                                    xmMainWindowWidgetClass,
                                    shell, NULL, 0 );

   /*
    * Create a label widget to be used as the message area
    */

    msg = XtCreateManagedWidget ( "message",
                                  xmLabelWidgetClass,
                                  mainw, NULL, 0 );

    canvas = XmCreateDrawingArea ( mainw, "canvas", NULL, 0 );

    XtManageChild ( canvas );

   /*
    * Install the main window widget's children
    */

```

```
    XtVaSetValues ( mainw,
                    XmNworkWindow, canvas,
                    XmNmessageWindow, msg,
                    NULL );
   /*
    * Realize the widgets and call XmUpdateDisplay() to force
    * the window to appear and do its initial drawing.
    */

    XtRealizeWidget ( shell );

    XmUpdateDisplay ( shell );

   /*
    * With the window visible, do the initial tasks,
    * periodically reporting progress in the message window.
    */

    for ( i = 0; i < 10; i++ )
    {
        char      buf[100];
        XmString xmstr;

        sleep( 2 );

        sprintf ( buf, "%d%% Done", ( i + 1 )* 10 );

        xmstr = XmStringCreateLocalized ( buf );
        XtVaSetValues ( msg, XmNlabelString, xmstr, NULL );

        XmStringFree ( xmstr );
    }

    XtAppMainLoop ( app );
}
```

In this program, the message window also remains blank throughout the busy period, suddenly displaying "100% Done" when the task has been completed. Here, we know that the window has been displayed, and the program is producing a steady stream of requests. However, the requests do not seem to be taking effect. Figure 4.24 shows the problem in this case. Again, the requests are being buffered and not being sent to the server until after the application is no longer busy. Once the application returns to the event loop, all ten `ClearArea` requests are made, which generate ten `Expose` events. Then the label widget is redrawn in response to the `Expose` events.

Window appears	..............EVENT: MapNotify ....EVENT: VisibilityNotify ....EVENT: VisibilityNotify ....EVENT: Expose ....EVENT: Expose
Application is busy	
ClerArea reqquests generated by XtSetValues() are sent to the server	............REQUEST: ClearArea ....REQUEST: ClearArea ....REQUEST: ClearArea ....REQUEST: ClearArea ....REQUEST: ClearArea ....REQUEST: ClearArea ....REQUEST: ClearArea ....REQUEST: ClearArea ....REQUEST: ClearArea ....REQUEST: ClearArea
Server generates Expose events in response to ClearArea requests	..............EVENT: Expose ....EVENT: Expose ....EVENT: Expose ....EVENT: Expose ....EVENT: Expose ....EVENT: Expose ....EVENT: Expose ....EVENT: Expose ....EVENT: Expose ....EVENT: Expose
program draws label	............REQUEST: PolyText8

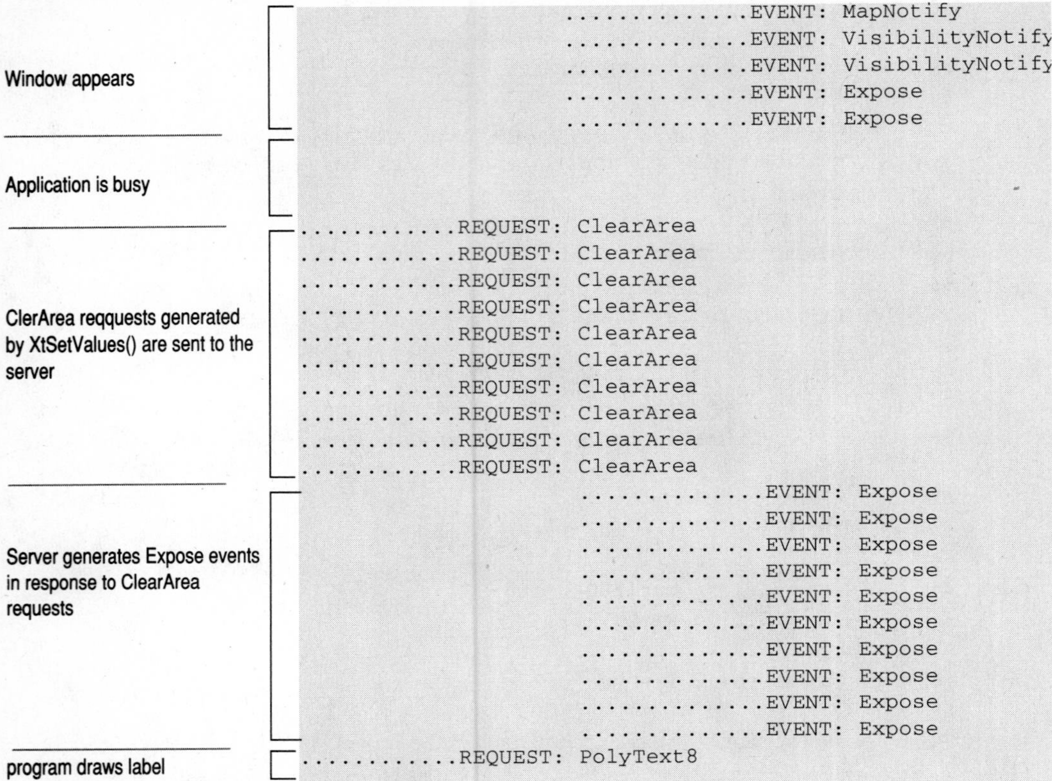

Figure 4.24 Abbreviated `xmond` event trace of `busy2` program.

We could alter this behavior by adding a call to `XFlush()` after each call to `XtVaSetValues()`, as follows:

```
for ( i = 0; i < 10; i++ )
{
    char buf[100];
    XmString xmstr;

    sleep ( 2 );

    sprintf ( buf, "%d%% Done", ( i +1 )* 10 );
    xmstr = XmStringCreateLocalized ( buf );
    XtVaSetValues ( msg, XmNlabelString, xmstr, NULL );
    XmStringFree ( xmstr );
    XFlush ( XtDisplay ( msg ) );
}
```

However, this change has no effect on the visual behavior of the program. Looking at the events and requests, as shown in Figure 4.25, we can see that `ClearArea` request are being sent to the server as the program tries to update the label, and the server immediately generates an `Expose` event for each request. However, because the program is not handling events, it cannot receive and process these events. Once the program returns to the event loop, it processes the `Expose` events and issues a `PolyText8` request to update the label.

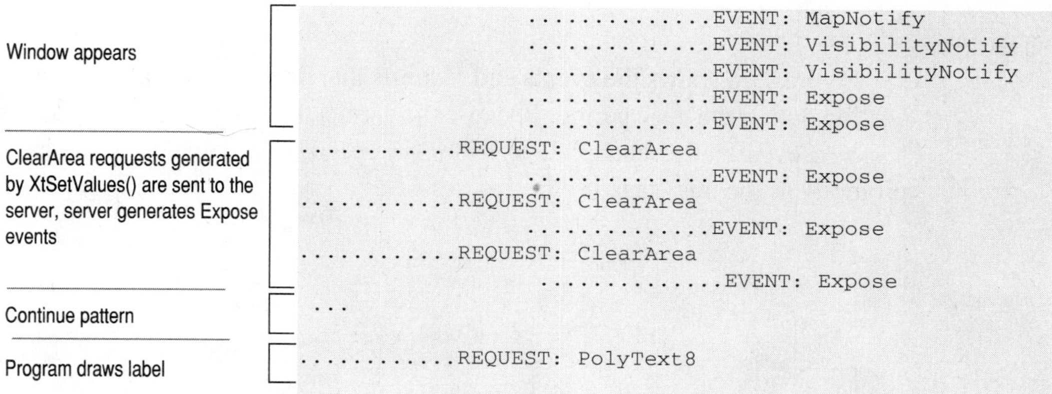

Figure 4.25 Result of adding `XFlush()` to `busy2` program.

As we can see from the event and request traces above, the XmLabel widget's internal `SetValues()` function relies on the application to handle events to draw labels each time the text displayed by a widget is changed. When an application calls `XtVaSetValues()` to change a label, the label widget stores the new label, and informs Xt that it needs to be redrawn. Xt makes an `XClearArea()` request, which causes the X server to generate an `Expose` event. When the `Expose` event is received and dispatched, the XmLabel widget redraws itself using the new label. Because this program does not process the `Expose` events until the program enters the main event loop in line 78, the widget does not draw the label during the busy period.

The solution to this problem is simple. Calling `XmUpdateDisplay()` after calling `XtVaSetValues()` processes all pending `Expose` events and updates the label text as the task progresses. The code segment in the above example should be written as:

```
for ( i = 0; i < 10; i++ )
{
    char buf[100];
    XmString xmstr;

    sleep ( 2 );

    sprintf ( buf, "%d%% Done", ( i +1 )* 10 );
    xmstr = XmStringCreateLocalized ( buf );
    XtVaSetValues ( msg, XmNlabelString, xmstr, NULL );
    XmStringFree ( xmstr );
    XmUpdateDisplay ( msg );
}
```

Figure 4.26 shows the events and requests that flow between this modified version during the busy period. Because the application receives and processes `Expose` events after each call to `XtVaSetValues()`, the label is updated promptly as the busy task progresses.

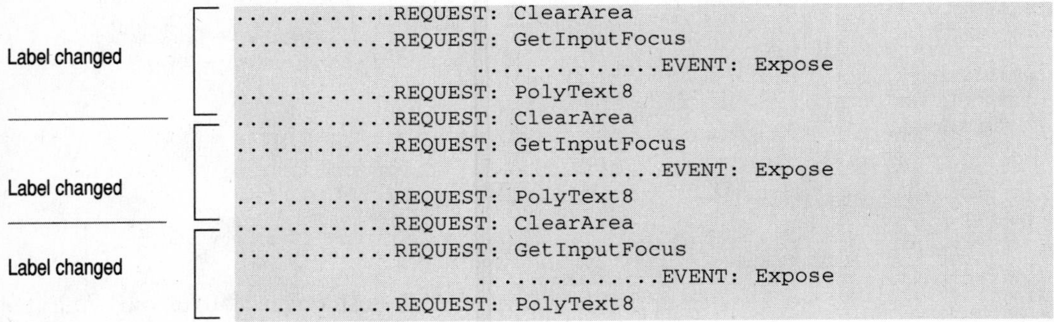

Figure 4.26 Using `XmUpdateDisplay()` to `busy2` program.

4.5 Errors That Involve Resources

Most Motif programs make extensive use of resources. Some of these may be set programmatically while others may be set in resource files. Earlier sections have discussed some of the problems that can occur when setting resources programmatically. However, problems that relate to resources set in resource files can be particularly baffling because there is little one can do to debug the problem.

Probably the most common problem encountered when using resources involves a resource that does not appear to take effect. Most often, when a resource does not take effect, it is because the resource has been overridden by another resource specification. For example, suppose we want to set the color of the clock face in the `xclock` program described in Chapter 2. This could be done as follows:

```
*face*foreground: blue
```

Assuming you have a color display, enough colors are available in the colormap, and you have no other resources set anywhere, this resource specification should result in a blue `xclock` the next time the program is run.

However, this specification could fail to take effect for any number of reasons. For example, if you have a similar specification (say, `*face*foreground: red`) later in your .Xdefaults file, or in any file loaded later than the one in which you have placed this specification, the later specification will win. On the other hand, a specification that is more specific in any resource file loaded by the `xclock` program will override this resource. For example, the following resources all take precedence over the desired setting.

```
XClock*Foreground: green
*face.foreground:  orange
xclock*foreground: red
```

If you cannot understand why a resource isn't taking effect, don't forget to look at the app-defaults, files specified by the `XUSERFILESEARCHPATH`, a file named "XClock" in your home directory, the `RESOURCE_MANAGER` property on the root window, the file .Xdefaults-<host>, and so on. Of course, don't ignore the possibility that the resource is hard coded within the program.

Resource files can also have other hard-to-spot errors, and neither X nor Xt provide much help for spotting errors. For example, trailing blanks to the right of the value are not stripped off. A color specification of "red " (with a trailing space) will fail because this is not the same as "red". Misspelled resource names are another trivial, but hard-to-find problem. Any string can potentially be a resource name, and the resource database is not cross-checked against known resources.

Several vendors have additional features in their Motif environment that may affect the resource precedence rules. Both Hewlett-Packard and Silicon Graphics support facilities known as "schemes", which allow applications to apply a complete palette of colors to their application easily. These facilities are generally very useful, and add a professional look to all Motif applications automatically, without requiring the programmer to spend time choosing colors and fonts. However, they tend to override certain resource specifications that would normally work in other Motif environments.

On HP machines, the scheme mechanism is turned on by default; in the Silicon Graphics environment, schemes are off by default. Programmers who wish to use schemes on Silicon Graphics can explicitly activate the scheme mechanism. If you encounter trouble with resources taking effect when using an environment that supports this or similar features, consider the possibility that the preset resources are overriding your resources.

Another common problem related to resources involves missing files or improper installation. If your application relies on resources set in an application defaults file, it is a good idea to guard against the possibility that a user might remove or not properly install this file. One easy way to protect yourself against this problem is to include a resource specification whose value is a known string. For example, you might add a line like the following to an app-defaults file:

```
!! Don't remove this line
*versionString:  xclock, Release 1.1.3
```

Then, an application can retrieve the value of the `versionString` resource and test it against the expected value, as demonstrated by the following code segment:

```
opt = XGetDefaults ( dpy, "xclock", "versionString");
if ( !opt || strcmp ( opt, "xclock, Release 1.1.3" ) )
    XtError ( "Application is not properly installed" );
```

Errors that are caused by the presence or absence of resource or other initialization files often show up as bugs that only affect one user on a particular system. If someone reports a problem that you cannot reproduce, it may be useful to ask them to reproduce it using a different login account. It is also useful to test software under different accounts (log in as “guest”, for example), to eliminate dependencies on your environment.

4.6 Conclusion

One way to become proficient at debugging Motif applications is to learn to recognize the symptoms of bugs that commonly occur. Although many of the problems described in this chapter may appear on the surface to indicate bugs in the underlying libraries, these symptoms are usually caused by an application that misuses the libraries. Once you have learned to recognize a pattern or symptom, it becomes easier to know what tool or tools to use to gather more information, and what sort of problems to look for.

The examples in this chapter tend to contain rather obvious bugs, which can usually be found by simple code inspection. Unfortunately, real applications will be much more complex and code inspection is far less effective. However, the basic errors, and symptoms of those errors are often the same, regardless of the size and complexity of the program. You probably won't encounter a program that calls `XtDestroyWidget()` twice in subsequent lines of code. However, it is easy for a large program to destroy a widget that has already been destroyed in less obvious ways, due to the more complex logic and organization of the program.

Chapter 5 discusses ways to address another common type of problem encountered in Motif applications, errors that involve dynamic memory allocation and de-allocation. Memory allocation is related to some of the issues discussed in this chapter, particularly widget destruction.

5

Debugging Memory Problems

Many of the bugs discussed in previous chapters are caused by programs that deal with dynamically allocated memory incorrectly. Because Motif relies heavily on pointers to dynamically allocated memory, errors associated with the use or abuse of `malloc()` and its related functions are particularly common in Motif applications. This chapter examines some of these errors, and suggests ways to debug `malloc()` problems.

5.1 Types of Malloc Errors

Most malloc-related errors involve modifying an area of memory that should not have been modified. Such problems can arise because of errors in arithmetic involving pointers or array bounds, but can also occur because of logic errors in how `malloc()` is used. Some of the more common errors, their symptoms and causes are discussed in the following sections

Array Overruns

Stuffing four items into an array meant to hold three changes the value of the memory location just beyond the bounds of array. If an array is statically declared, the overwritten memory location is probably associated with a nearby variable declaration, although this is compiler dependent. However, if the array was dynamically allocated, overwriting the array modifies the location that follows the array in the `malloc()` arena. This location could represent anything at all, a widget, a compound string, or any other dynamically allocated data structure. It could also overwrite internal information maintained by `malloc()` that can cause `malloc()` to fail at a later time.

For example, consider the following simple program:

```
/**************************************************
 * mem.c: A simple demonstration of the effects
 *        of array overruns.
 **************************************************/
#include <malloc.h>
#include <stdio.h>

main()
{
    /* Allocate enough space for "hello" and "world" */

     char *a = ( char * ) malloc ( 6 );
     char *b = ( char * ) malloc ( 6 );

    /* Print addresses of allocated memory */

     printf ("0x%x 0x%x\n", a, b );

    /* Copy "hello world" into two strings. */

     strcpy ( a, "hello" );
     strcpy ( b, "world" );

    /* Print the strings */

     printf("%s %s\n", a, b);

    /* Copy a long string into the first address. */

     strcpy ( a, "So long, fare well, goodbye cruel" );

    /* Print the results. */

```

```
    printf("%s %s\n", a, b);

   /* Free allocated memory */

    free(a);
    free(b);
}
```

This program allocates enough memory for the words "hello" and "world", and copies these words into these strings. The program also prints the address of each allocated piece of memory. After confirming the contents of both strings, the program copies a new phrase into the first piece of memory, and then prints both strings. Figure 5.1 shows the output produced by running the program. Notice that the program does not crash, or report any error, but the final phrase is incorrect.

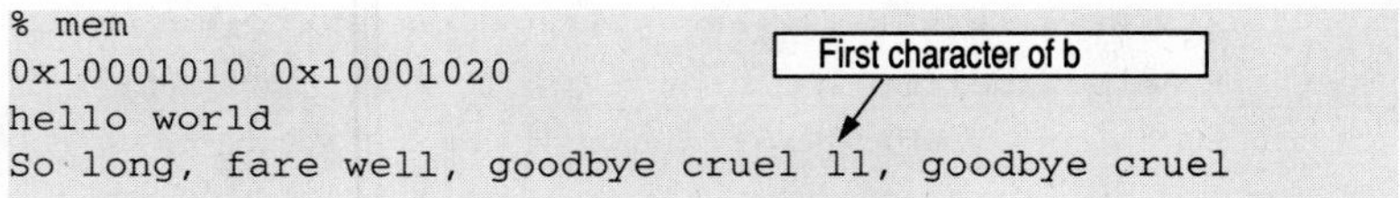

% mem
0x10001010 0x10001020
hello world
So long, fare well, goodbye cruel ll, goodbye cruel
First character of b

Figure 5.1 Output of mem program.

Notice the addresses allocated by `malloc()`. Because this is a small program, with only these two calls to `malloc()`, the addresses are contiguous. However, the program requests 6 bytes, and the addresses are 16 bytes apart. This is clearly an implementation-dependent behavior on the part of the `malloc()` used in this example. Perhaps this `malloc()` implementation allocates memory on some type of boundary. Of course, all `malloc()` implementations must maintain information about the allocated memory, which is sometimes placed between the memory being allocated.

Figure 5.1 shows the type of problem that can be caused by writing data past the bounds of allocated memory. When the program write a long string into variable `a`, it simply starts at address `0x10001010`, and proceeds from there. Once the long string has been stored at `a`'s address, printing `b` shows that the former contents of `b` have been overwritten.

As serious as this problem appears, this simple program hides the danger that can be encountered in a real program. In a complex program, there is no guarantee that two sequential calls to `malloc()` will return sequential addresses. The memory location that lies just beyond a's 6 bytes might be a widget, a compound string, the Xlib event queue, or any other dynamically allocated data structure. Furthermore, although this example makes it look as if there is some room for error (extra bytes seem to be allocated), one cannot depend on this behavior.

Dangling Pointers

A dangling pointer is a pointer to memory that has already been freed. The danger of a dangling pointer is that `malloc()` may reallocate the memory this pointer represents. Any attempt to modify the contents of the memory through the dangling pointer may corrupt the memory in unexpected ways. Like array overruns, the effect is hard to detect because the memory being modified could be used anywhere in a program. Depending on how the memory is currently being used, modifying memory through a dangling pointer could have no affect at all, or cause a core dump. Bizarre effects are also possible in some situations. For example, one could image that if the memory being modified just happened to be the foreground member inside a widget that a widget could be drawn using the wrong color.

The following example demonstrates how errors can be introduced by a dangling pointer. A string is allocated, and then freed. Then a second string, the same size as the first, is allocated. In this simple program, most malloc implementations are likely to reuse the address of the first string when allocating space for the second string. Because the first pointer still points to the address it formerly used, modifying the dangling pointer modifies the second string.

```
/***********************************************************
 * mem2.c: A simple demonstration of a dangling pointer
 ***********************************************************/
#include <malloc.h>
#include <stdio.h>

main()
{
   /*
    * Allocate room for "hello"
    */

    char *a = ( char * ) malloc ( 6 );
    char *b;

   /*
    * Store "hello" in a.
    */
```

```

     strcpy ( a, "hello" );

    /*
     * Print address allocated for a and value stored in a.
     */

     printf ( "0x%x\n", a );
     printf ( "a = %s", a );

    /*
     * Free the memory. Note: a still points to address.
     */

     free ( a );

    /*
     * Allocate space for b and store "world" in b.
     */

     b = ( char * ) malloc ( 6 );
     strcpy ( b, "world" );

    /*
     * Print address allocated for b and value stored in b.
     */

     printf ( "0x%x\n", b );

     printf ( "b = %s\n", b );

    /*
     * Modify a, which has been freed, but still points to
     * its former memory.
     */

     strcpy ( a, "goodbye" );

     printf ( "b = %s\n",  b );
}
```

Figure 5.2 shows the output from running this program. We can see that the variable `b` is given the same address formerly used by `a`. Modifying `a`, which is a dangling pointer, modifies the memory pointed to by `b`.

```
% mem2
0x10003048
a = hello
0x10003048
b = world
b = goodbye
```

Figure 5.2 Output of `mem2` program.

Operating on Uninitialized Data.

Frequently, the value of an uninitialized variable is zero, as discussed in Chapter 4. In some cases, dynamically allocated memory also contains zeros when returned by `malloc()`. However, the value of any uninitialized piece of memory is completely undetermined. Programs that depend on a value being automatically initialized to zero can fail when the program's memory patterns change, unless the value is explicitly set.

For example, the following simple program is likely to run without errors:

```
/****************************************************************
 * mem3.c: A simple demonstration of uniitialized memory
 ****************************************************************/
#include <malloc.h>
#include <stdio.h>

typedef struct {
  char *name;
  char *addr;
} Info;

main()
{
    Info *a = ( Info * ) malloc ( sizeof ( Info ) );

   /*
    * Bug! Assumes initialized memory.
    */

    if ( a && a->name )
        a->name[3] = 'x';
}
```

Bug!

The values stored in the members of `a` are completely undefined. Because this is the first call to `malloc()` in this program, it is possible that the values will be zero, although this is far from certain. In a larger program, the values stored in allocated memory are purely arbitrary, a function of the `malloc()` algorithm and the program's pattern of memory use. Sooner or later, a code segment like this will fail.

Double Free

Freeing memory twice is another common problem. Usually this occurs because of a logic error, or because of a dangling pointer. Freeing the same memory twice tends to corrupt the `malloc()` arena and confuse the `malloc()` algorithms. In some cases, the memory may have been re-allocated in one or possibly multiple chunks. The error typically shows up much later, during a `malloc()` operation. Because Motif makes heavy use of `malloc()`, such problems may show up while creating a widget, creating a compound string, or even destroying a widget.

Freeing Static or Automatic Variables

Freeing an address that was not allocated by `malloc()` can also corrupt the `malloc()` arena and confuses the `malloc()` algorithm in much the same way as freeing memory twice.

Leaks

Memory leaks degrade performance by increasing a program's size and making future `malloc()` operations slower. Leaks can be very dangerous in Motif programs because most interactive programs are designed to be run for a long period of time. Even a small leak can cause problems for a program that runs for hours, days, or even weeks.

5.2 Avoiding Malloc Bugs

`Malloc()` problems can be very difficult to find once they are introduced so it is best to try to avoid them as much as possible. Many of the techniques suggested in Chapter 2 are meant to avoid memory-related errors associated with Motif. The following list summarizes some of the techniques that can be used specifically to reduce memory errors.

- Don't destroy widgets unnecessarily. Many of the memory-related bugs Motif programmers encounter are caused by destroying widgets. Not destroying widgets reduces the chances of introducing a bug and may improve performance in some cases. Motif is known to have occasional problems when destroying many widgets, as well.
- Use the `XmNdestroyCallback` callback list for widgets that could be dynamically destroyed, or descendants of widgets that could be destroyed. As discussed earlier, it is not necessary to explicitly destroy a widget to have a problem with widget destruction, particularly if you write code that can be used by others.
- Use the `assert()` macro liberally to check return values, function arguments, types, and so on. Because the `assert()` macro can be removed from production code, you can afford to check everything without degrading performance.
- Check widgets with `XtIsObject()` inside an `assert()` statement. This technique can catch references to many corrupted or destroyed widgets.
- Be careful about modifying pointers returned by Motif functions. Some must not be modified, while others must be freed to avoid leaks. In general, most Motif convenience functions allocate memory and return copies of resources. For example, `XmListGetSelectedItems()` calls `malloc()` to allocate space for a list of all selected items and returns a list of compound strings, which are also copies of the items maintained by the list widget. Therefore, an application that calls this function should free each item on the list, and then the list itself, when the list is no longer needed. However, if a program retrieves a list of selected items by calling `XtGetValues()`, the caller receives a direct pointer to the list maintained by the list widget. If this list is freed, or altered in any way, the program may fail at some later time.

  In general, values retrieved using `XtGetValues()` are direct pointers to internal memory and should not be freed. One exception is compound strings. Widgets generally make a copy of all compound strings to be returned by `XtGetValues()`. Similarly, most values passed to a widget using `XtSetValues()` are not copied, and must continue to exist as long as the widget needs the data. Motif widgets copy compound strings, however. Of course, integer values are not a problem, but pixmaps, bitmaps, certain lists of items, and so on require careful attention.

- Minimize multiple pointers to the same object. In Xt, there are always multiple pointers to widgets. Each manager widget has a pointer to each child, each child has a pointer to its parent, and so on. However, a program can at least reduce the chances of dangling pointers by not creating unnecessary pointers to widgets. Dangling pointers are often created by passing widgets as client data in callbacks, work procedures, and so on. Using a modular design that does not expose the widgets in a module helps minimize references as well.
- Initialize all variables and initialize the contents of dynamically allocated memory.
- Set all pointers to `NULL` after calling freeing the memory they represent.
- Using C++ can help programmers deal with memory management issues because C++ provides more tools for handling memory allocation and deallocation and also encourages encapsulation, which helps avoid dangling pointers.

5.3 Tools for Debugging Malloc Problems

Because memory problems are so common in C programs, many programmers have written tools to help debug these problems. The most common tool is a modified `malloc()` library that supports debugging in some way. It seems that every organization has a modified `malloc()` library of some kind, and you may be able to find several different libraries from which to choose.

A typical debugging `malloc()` library maintains additional information about each chunk of allocated memory, which can be used to periodically examine the program's dynamic memory (known as the *malloc arena*) to look for problems. Some debugging `malloc()` implementations check all allocated memory every time `malloc()` or `free()` are called. While thorough, this approach can be very slow when used with Motif programs that use large amounts of memory.

One important (and unfortunate) characteristic of most debugging `malloc()` libraries is that they find errors that have already occurred. While better than not finding errors at all, detecting errors after they have occurred can be confusing. The effect is not unlike the asynchronous error events associated with an Xlib error. The callstack indicates where the error was detected, which may have little or nothing to do with where the error actually occurred.

Because memory behavior is so complex and unpredictable, few debugging `malloc()` libraries catch every error. In fact, it is often useful to test with as many versions of `malloc()` as you can find, whether they are designed for debugging or not. Because different `malloc()` libraries may use different allocation strategies, memory layout, and so on, errors may show up with one library, but not another. A debugging `malloc()` library is one case where a single tool is seldom enough. The more `malloc()` libraries you have available, the more likely one of them will find a bug that the others miss.

Commercial Malloc Tools

Recently, a number of commercial products that can help debug memory problems have become available. Although this book does not focus on commercial tools, it is worth mentioning a few of the types of tools that are available. One of the best known commercial tools for finding memory problems is Purify®, from Pure Software. This product takes a unique approach that differentiates it from the more typical debugging `malloc()` libraries. Unlike most debugging `malloc()` libraries, Purify is able to detect certain types of problems at the point of the error, instead of uncovering the problem on a later call to `malloc()`. This ability can make debugging much easier.

Purify gained some acclaim among the X community because it was able to identify a serious error in the Xt phase 2 destroy code that had gone unnoticed for several major releases of Xt. (This bug existed in X11R4, but has been fixed in newer versions. Most vendors who still ship X11R4 have applied a patch to fix this bug in the older version, as well.)

Insight, from ParaSoft is another commercial tool that can help find errors related to `malloc()` and other abuses of pointers. Insight works, in part, by preprocessing your source code, adding various tests that can catch errors. Insight also “knows” about Xlib, Xt, and Motif functions, and checks various arguments, in a way that is somewhat reminiscent of the function wrappers described in Chapter 4.

Although most malloc tools simply print warnings which must be investigated with a debugger, other commercial tools help programmers inspect a program’s memory interactively. For example, Figure 5.3 shows a commercial product (Silicon Graphics' CaseVision®) that allows programmers to visualize various characteristics of a program's memory use.

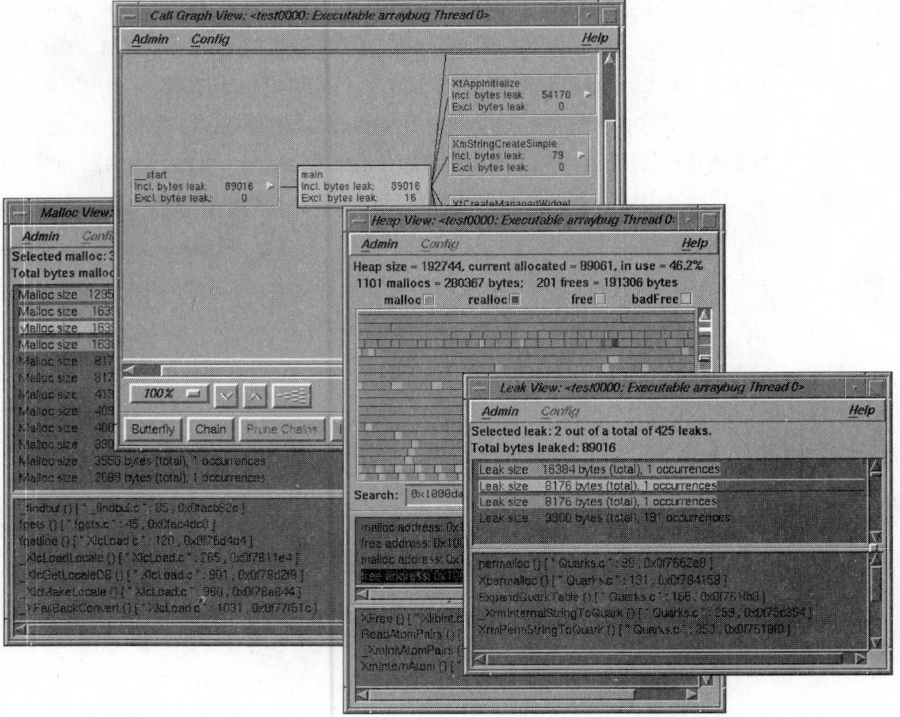

Figure 5.3 An interactive tool for debugging memory problems.

The window in the lower left displays a list containing each piece of memory allocated by `malloc()` and can display the callstack of the point in the program that allocated the memory. The window in the lower right provides a similar capability, listing all leaks. The upper window displays a dynamic call graph of the program, annotated with the bytes allocated by each function. The remaining window presents a visual map of the program's dynamic memory space. A programmer can see the `malloc()`, `free()` and `realloc()` history of any given address, along with all call stacks associated with each event. This tool also allows programmers to view the memory allocated or freed in any segment of a program, only within a particular function, or between any two arbitrary lines of code.

A Typical Debugging Malloc Library

This chapter explores ways to debug memory problems, using a typical public domain `malloc()` library that is widely available. This library, libdbmalloc, uses a fairly traditional approach, but is quite powerful. This library has been used extensively and has helped many programmers find bugs. The author of this library also produces an even more powerful version of this library as a commercial product known as SENTINEL®. The dbmalloc library has many features that can help find memory corruption, uninitialized pointers, dangling pointers, and memory leaks. The library differs from the normal malloc library in the following ways:

1. Each chunk of memory allocated by `malloc()` contains a "magic number." When a pointer is freed, `free()` checks this magic number to verify that the pointer represents a valid `malloc()` segment.

2. Each chunk of memory allocated by `malloc()` is filled with a non-zero pattern. This makes it easy to find code that operates on uninitialized variables on the incorrect assumption that the contents of memory allocated by `malloc()` is set to `NULL`. Any code that depends on uninitialized memory being set to zero will fail.

3. The size of an allocated chunk of memory is at least 1 byte larger than requested. The extra bytes are filled with a non-zero pattern which allows `free()` to check for array boundary overruns and similar errors.

4. When a pointer is freed, the memory is filled with a non-zero pattern to catch any attempts to use previously freed data.

5. The functions `strcmp()`, `strcpy()` and other similar functions are modified to perform tests based on the information maintained by the `malloc()` library.

6. Each time `malloc()` or `free()` are called, the library checks the integrity of all previously allocated memory.

The dbmalloc library prints a warning when any error is detected. Because of the information maintained by the library, it can provide some hints about where the error may have occurred, but cannot always be correct.

This debugging library supports several options that affect the library's behavior. These can be set several different ways, but it is usually easiest to set environment variables. The environment variables recognized by dbmalloc include:

- `MALLOC_WARN`: If this environment variable is non-zero, the dbmalloc library aborts, producing a core file when any warning condition is encountered.
- `MALLOC_FATAL`: If this environment variable is non-zero, the dbmalloc library aborts, producing a core file when any error condition is encountered.
- `MALLOC_CKCHAIN`: If this environment variable is non-zero, the dbmalloc library checks the entire chain of `malloc()` information each time `malloc()` or `free()` are called.

An Example

Let's examine a program with an obvious bug to see how this library can help. The following program destroys a widget and then tries to manage it. This program will usually run with no error, as long as memory used by the `canvas` widget remains intact after the widget is destroyed. In a simple program like this, with some `malloc()` implementations, this is likely to be true. However, as the program grows or libraries are changed, this error can cause a noticeable bug to just "appear".

```
/**************************************************
 * dangling.c: A buggy program
 **************************************************/
#include <Xm/Xm.h>
#include <Xm/DrawingA.h>

void main ( int argc, char **argv )
{
    Widget       shell, canvas;
    XtAppContext app;

    shell = XtAppInitialize ( &app, "Dangling", NULL, 0,
                              &argc, argv, NULL, NULL, 0 );

    canvas = XtCreateWidget ( "canvas",
                              xmDrawingAreaWidgetClass,
                              shell, NULL, 0 );

    XtDestroyWidget ( canvas );

    XtManageChild ( canvas ); /* BUG!! */
```

```
22
23      XtRealizeWidget ( shell );
24      XtAppMainLoop ( app );
25  }
```

Linking with a debugging malloc library can help find this error. To use the debugging version of `malloc()`, the program must explicitly specify the dbmalloc library when linking the program. The `-u` option supported by most linkers can be useful because it forces any other versions of `malloc()` to be ignored:

```
cc -o dangling dangling.c -lXm -lXt -lX11 -u malloc -ldbmalloc
```

When linked with the debugging `malloc()` library, running this program produces a core dump. Examining the program with a debugger shows that the program died when calling `XtManageChild()` on line 21. Figure 5.4 shows the debugging session.

```
% dangling
Bus error(coredump)
% dbx dangling
Process died at pc 0xf6d7170 of signal : Bus error
[using memory image in core]
(dbx) t
>   0 XtManageChildren(0x7fffaee0, 0x1, 0x0, 0x1, 0x7fffaf4c)
["Manage.c":138, 0xf6d716c]
    1 XtManageChild(0x1002f388, 0x1, 0x0, 0x1, 0x0)
["Manage.c":231, 0xf6ec148]
    2 main(argc = 1, argv = 0x7fffaf44) ["dangling.c":22,
0x402590]
```

Figure 5.4 Examining core dump when linked with libdbmalloc.

Why does this program core dump when linked with libdbmalloc and not with the normal malloc library? To see why, we must include IntrinsicP.h in the program and recompile, so we can examine the contents of the `canvas` widget. Figure 5.5 shows a debugging session that moves up the callstack to the point where the program calls `XtManageChild()`. Printing the `canvas` widget shows some interesting data. Nearly all the fields are set to a repeating pattern of hex 0x02. This is the pattern libdbmalloc uses to fill memory that has been freed. Because `canvas` now points to memory that does not look like a widget, the function `XtManageChild()` dies trying to dereference various fields within the widget.

```
% dangling
Bus error(coredump)
1% dbx dangling
Process died at pc 0xf6d7170 of signal : Bus error
[using memory image in core]
(dbx) t
>  0 XtManageChildren(0x7fffaee0, 0x1, 0x0, 0x1, 0x7fffaf4c)
["Manage.c":138, 0xf6d716c]
   1 XtManageChild(0x1002f388, 0x1, 0x0, 0x1, 0x0)
["Manage.c":231, 0xf6ec148]
   2 main(argc = 1, argv = 0x7fffaf44) ["dangling.c":22,
0x402590]
(dbx) up
XtManageChild:   Source (of Manage.c) not available for
Process     0
(dbx) up
main:  22  XtManageChild ( canvas );
(dbx) (dbx) p canvas
0x1002f388
(dbx) p *canvas
struct _WidgetRec {
    core = struct _CorePart {
        self = 0x2020202
        widget_class = 0x2020202
        parent = 0x2020202
        xrm_name = 33686018
        being_destroyed = '^B'
        destroy_callbacks = 0x2020202
        constraints = 0x2020202
```

Figure 5.5 Examining `canvas` widget after core dump.

Example 2

The dbmalloc library can also help catch attempts to free memory that was not allocated by calling `malloc()`. For example, the `busy2` program described on page 178 in Chapter 4 contains a loop like this:

```
for ( i = 0; i < 10; i++ )
{
    char      buf[100];
    XmString xmstr;

    sleep( 2 );

    sprintf ( buf, "%d%% Done", ( i +1 )* 10 );
    xmstr = XmStringCreateLocalized ( buf );
```

```
        XtVaSetValues ( msg, XmNlabelString, xmstr, NULL );
        XmStringFree ( xmstr );
        XmUpdateDisplay ( shell );
    }
```

When I first wrote this example, however, what I actually wrote was the following:

```
for ( i = 0; i < 10; i++ )
    {
        char     buf[100];
        XmString xmstr;

        sleep( 2 );

        sprintf ( buf, "%d%% Done", ( i +1 )* 10 );
        xmstr = XmStringCreateLocalized ( buf );
        XtVaSetValues ( msg, XmNlabelString, xmstr, NULL );
        XmStringFree ( buf ); /* BUG */
        XmUpdateDisplay ( shell );
    }
```

This program crashes, producing a core file. Figure 5.6 shows the callstack reported by `dbx` for the crash. The error seems to point to a problem in `XmUpdateDisplay()`. However, looking at the call to `XmUpdate-Display()` shows nothing obvious wrong.

```
(dbx) >  0 realfree(0x803fbab8, 0x7fffaed4, 0x400be4,
0x400be5, 0x7fffafa4) ["malloc.c":476, 0xfb3cf60]
   1 __malloc(0x803fbab8, 0x7fffaed4, 0x400be4, 0x400be5,
0x10007a08) ["malloc.c":245, 0xfb3c894]
   2 _malloc(0x64, 0x7fffaed4, 0x400be4, 0x400be5,
0x10007a08) ["malloc.c":134, 0xfb3c568]
   3 _XEnq(0xfb5a220, 0x7fffad80, 0x400be4, 0x400be5, 0x0)
["XlibInt.c":1094, 0xf795388]
   4 _XReply(0xfb5a220, 0xf6c90c0, 0x0, 0x1, 0x8)
["XlibInt.c":998, 0xf795090]
   5 XSync(0x7fffafa4, 0x0, 0xfb5a220, 0xfb3d79c, 0x0)
["XSync.c":33, 0xf78f4fc]
   6 XmUpdateDisplay(0x1001d608, 0xe3f3ee5, 0x1001eb78, 0x0,
0x1001d608) ["Manager.c":2861, 0xe39db84]
   7 main(argc = 1, argv = 0x7fffaf04) ["updatebug.c":45,
0x400e94]
```

Figure 5.6 Callstack of `updatebug` core dump.

The true source of this bug was caught by linking with the dbmalloc library and running the program with the `MALLOC_WARN` environment variable set, as shown in Figure 5.7.

```
% setenv MALLOC_WARN 1
% updatebug
MALLOC Warning from free():
Pointer is not within malloc area
Abort(coredump)
```

Figure 5.7 Running with `malloc()` warnings activated.

Looking at the core dump with a debugger, we can see the source of the error, as shown in Figure 5.8. Although the dbmalloc library cannot indicate why the call to `XmStringFree()` fails, we can at least inspect the right line of code to see that the program is attempting to free a statically declared array.

```
% dbx updatebug
Process died at pc 0xfb03e0c of signal : Abort
[using memory image in core]
(dbx) where
>  0 _kill(0x5a0c, 0x6, 0x7fffa858, 0x0, 0x0) [0xfb03e08]
   1 raise(0x6, 0x6, 0x7fffa858, 0x0, 0x0) ["raise.c":22,
0xfb0449c]
   2 abort(0x6, 0x6, 0x7fffa858, 0x0, 0x0) ["abort.c":37,
0xfac31b0]
   3 malloc_abort() ["abort.c":41, 0x410198]
   4 malloc_err_handler(level = 1) ["malloc.c":1246,
0x40a080]
   5 malloc_warning(funcname = 0x100002a8, file = (nil),
line = 0, mptr = (nil)) ["malloc.c":967, 0x40892c]
   6 DBFfree(func = 0x100002a8, type = 256, counter = 598,
file = (nil), line = 0, cptr = 0x7fffae6c) ["free.c":116,
0x406ae4]
   7 debug_free(file = (nil), line = 0, cptr = 0x7fffae6c)
["free.c":63, 0x406988]
   8 free(cptr = 0x7fffae6c) ["free.c":50, 0x4068fc]
   9 XtFree(0xf71fbf0, 0x0, 0x1010101, 0x0, 0x1)
["Alloc.c":130, 0xf6c9240]
  10 XmStringFree(0x1001e588, 0x0, 0x10039258, 0x0,
0x1001e588) ["XmString.c":5302, 0xe370bd8]
  11 main(argc = 1, argv = 0x7fffaf04) ["updatebug.c":44,
0x40283c]
```

Figure 5.8 Callstack of memory error detected by libdbmalloc.

Example 3

Consider a simple program that corrupts memory by copying a string into a buffer that is too small. This common occurrence can easily go unnoticed for a long time. The error is likely to show up only in a large program, and will probably cause a crash in a completely unrelated part of the program. The following program dynamically allocates a string to contain a short message and the name of the program. However, the string is too short to hold the entire message.

```
      1  /******************************************************
      2   * overwrite.c: eomstrate an array overrun.
      3   ******************************************************/
      4  #include <Xm/Xm.h>
      5  #include <Xm/PushB.h>
      6  #include <stdio.h>
      7
      8   void main ( int argc, char **argv )
      9   {
     10       Widget        shell, button;
     11       XtAppContext app;
     12       char         *buf;
     13
     14       shell = XtAppInitialize ( &app, "Overwrite", NULL, 0,
     15                                  &argc, argv, NULL, NULL, 0 );
     16
Bug! 17       buf = XtMalloc ( strlen ( argv[0] ) );
     18       sprintf ( buf, "This program's name is %s", argv[0] );
     19
     20       button = XtVaCreateManagedWidget ( "button",
     21                                 xmPushButtonWidgetClass, shell,
     22                                 XtVaTypedArg, XmNlabelString,
     23                                 XmRString, buf, strlen ( buf ),
     24                                 NULL );
     25       XtRealizeWidget ( shell );
     26       XtAppMainLoop ( app );
     27  }
```

Running this program is unlikely to produce any error, and the memory corruption caused by line 18 could go undetected for a long time. However, if the program is linked with the dbmalloc library, running the program produces the message shown in Figure 5.9. One of dbmalloc's tests has detected a problem in the program's address space while performing a `memcopy()`, probably while creating the widget. Although debugging `malloc()` libraries like dbmalloc can only detect errors after they occur, dbmalloc maintains enough information that it tries to guess where the corrupted memory was originally allocated.

```
MALLOC Warning from memcpy():
Pointer within malloc region, but outside of malloc data bounds
This error is *probably* associated with the following
allocation:

        A call to malloc for 9 bytes in an unknown file.
        This was the 686th call to malloc.
```

Figure 5.9 Malloc warning message.

Although libdbmalloc has identified an error, the provided information does not identify the exact location of the error. We do know which call to `malloc()` may have allocated the piece of memory that was later corrupted in some way. Most debuggers allow you to specify that the program should be stopped after a certain point is reach a given number of times. So, if we did not know what call to `malloc()` was associated with the problem, we could find the call in question by setting a breakpoint in `malloc()` for the 686th time it is called.

The dbmalloc library can provide better information if the program includes the header file dbmalloc.h, which is distributed with the `malloc()` package. After including dbmalloc.h and rebuilding the program, the program produces the information shown in Figure 5.10.

```
MALLOC Warning from memcpy():
Pointer within malloc region, but outside of malloc data bounds
This error is *probably* associated with the following
allocation:

     A call to XtMalloc for 9 bytes in overwrite.c on line 17.
      This was the 333rd call to XtMalloc.
```

Figure 5.10 Warning message with malloc header included.

This information is much more useful because it accurately reports the exact line and file in which the memory in question was allocated. The dbmalloc library knows about Xt, and, with the header included, actually reports the call to `XtMalloc()` correctly. Notice that dbmalloc still does not report the point at which the error occurred, however. In a small program, the error might be found by inspecting all uses of the variable associated with the call to `malloc()` reported by dbmalloc. For larger programs, or more subtle errors, this may be tedious and non-productive.

If your debugger has the ability to "watch" an address or variable for modification, there is a more reliable way to find the true source of error, starting with the information reported by dbmalloc. For example, `dbx` supports a trace command that can provide a notification when the value of a variable changes.

Figure 5.11 shows a `dbx` session that demonstrates how this feature can be used. First, we can set a breakpoint on line 17, as indicated by `dbmalloc()`. Then, step over this statement to allocate the array and assign a pointer to `buf`. Now that `buf` has been allocated, we can use `dbx`'s trace command to watch for modifications to the address just beyond the end of `buf`. We could watch any value, of course, but it seems likely that we are dealing with a code overwrite, so the location just beyond the allocated memory seems like a good place to start. Continuing the program, we can see that dbmalloc again reports the error, and then `dbx` reports that `buf[9]` has been modified, and changed to the character `'r'`. The modification occurs on line 18, which we could have found by inspection in this simple program. Errors in large, complex programs will seldom be so obvious, but the techniques remain the same, regardless of the size of a program.

One problem with `dbx`'s trace command is that it can be extremely slow. For large complex programs like most Motif applications, this feature may be too slow to be useful. This is particularly true if the problem occurs in a part of the program that requires user interaction. If the problem is time-dependent, the slow performance of the tracing process may render it useless. In such cases, the ability to detect the exact point of failure, offered by some commercial tools, becomes much more valuable. Some debuggers can also watch for changes to an address without performance degradation.

```
% dbx overwrite
(dbx) stop at 17
Process      0: [2] stop at "overwrite": 17
(dbx) run
Process  9856 (overwrite) started
Process  9856 (overwrite) stopped at [main:17 ,0x4027b0]
  17  buf = XtMalloc ( strlen ( argv[0] ) );
(dbx) Step
  18  sprintf ( buf, "This program's name is %s", argv[0] );
(dbx) trace buf[9]
Process  9856: [3] trace buf + 9 * 1 in main
(dbx) continue
MALLOC Warning from memcpy():
Pointer within malloc region, but outside of malloc data bounds
This error is *probably* associated with the following
allocation:

     A call to XtMalloc for 9 bytes in overwrite.c on line 17.
      This was the 337th call to XtMalloc.

[3] buf + 9 * 1 changed before [main: line 18]:
                new value = 'r';
```

Figure 5.11 Tracing a memory location.

5.4 Conclusion

Memory related errors are among the most common types of problems encountered in a Motif program. Memory problems are particularly troublesome because they may not show up immediately. Often, problems exist without showing any symptoms. Like a dormant virus, they lie just below the surface waiting for the worst possible moment to appear.

Fortunately, there are many tools that can be used to help find memory problems. If you are fortunate enough to have some of the commercial-quality tools that are available, you may have a better chance to find memory bugs. However, there are also many public domain malloc libraries that can be used to find errors. Because there are so many ways for a program to misuse memory, few malloc libraries or tools can catch everything. Therefore, it is often worthwhile to test with several different `malloc()` implementations. Besides the fact that each debugging malloc library has different strengths and weaknesses, the difference in algorithms used by each `malloc()` implementation can help turn up any errors that exist.

6

Layout Problems and Other Visual Bugs

One of the most frustrating types of bugs encountered when writing a Motif program involves an interface whose visual appearance is wrong. Such problems are often difficult to solve because programmers cannot inspect a program's layout using familiar tools like a debugger. Many factors contribute to an interface's appearance and dynamic behavior, and not all are easily accessible. For example, a program's resource database includes resources loaded from several different locations. Because of complex precedence rules, multiple resources files, and so on, it is difficult to be sure exactly what resource specifications affect the appearance of any given widget. It is also difficult to investigate the state of individual widgets because the `Widget` data type is opaque and cannot be readily inspected using a debugger. Programmers may also have trouble understanding the algorithmic process that leads to the final position and size of each individual widget.

However, there are many other techniques that can be useful for addressing layout and visual problems. Chapter 3 introduces some tools that can help gather information about a program's interface when something goes wrong. These include `editres`, `appres`, `xwininfo`, `xprop` and the XtGeo library. The WL test framework described in Chapter 3 is a more invasive testing tool that supports tests that could detect errors in some layouts.

This chapter explores ways to apply some of these tools to identify and fix layout bugs. Section 6.1 presents a simple case study involving a very small program that has a layout problem. Section 6.2 explores a second example that illustrates the process of isolating and fixing a commonly encountered error. Section 6.3 explores some ideas for adding new test functions to the WL framework originally described in Chapter 3. These new functions help detect common errors that affect widget layout, including those discussed in the earlier sections.

6.1 An Example: Debugging a Layout Problem

Let's look at a very simple example and examine the types of layout problems that could occur. This example starts with a simple design and an implementation of a widget layout that has some problems. We will trace each step of a typical process that could be used to debug the problems. Experienced developers may detect the source of the problems quickly, and might skip many of the steps shown in this example, when debugging a real program. However, the exercise in this section takes the problem one step at a time, to demonstrate many of the tools and techniques at our disposal.

Figure 6.1 shows a layout for a small panel that contains an XmScale widget and a label.

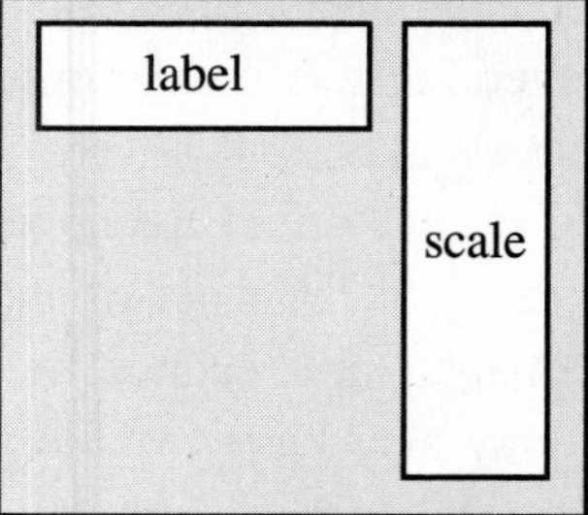

Figure 6.1 A simple layout for a labeled scale.

The XmScale widget supports a title, but the XmScale widget's built-in title appears on the right side of the scale widget. There are times when it is worthwhile to allow the capabilities and limitations of Motif to influence a program's visual design. However, there may also be situations in which there is an important reason to deviate from the default Motif appearance or behavior. For this example, we will assume that it is really important to have the title be on the left side of the XmScale widget, as shown in Figure 6.1.

The layout in Figure 6.1 could be created by placing a label and a scale widget in a manager widget, such as a form. Figure 6.2 shows a set of form attachments designed to implement this layout. The layout and attachments shown here may seem too simple to cause many problems. However, some of the most frustrating layout problems often involve seemingly simple layouts. For purposes of discussion, imagine that this layout is just a small piece of a much larger widget tree,

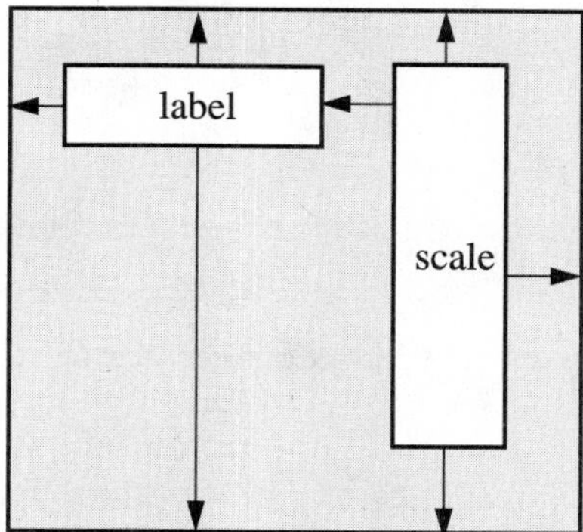

Figure 6.2 Form attachments for layout in Figure 6.1.

A small program intended to implement this layout could be written as follows:

```
/**********************************************
 * scale.c: Create a labeled scale in a form
 **********************************************/
#include <Xm/Xm.h>
#include <Xm/Form.h>
#include <Xm/Label.h>
#include <Xm/Scale.h>

void main ( int argc, char ** argv )
{
    Widget        shell, form, label, scale;
    XtAppContext app;
    int           i;
```

```

    shell = XtAppInitialize ( &app, "Scale", NULL, 0,
                              &argc, argv, NULL, NULL, 0 );

    form = XtCreateManagedWidget ( "form", xmFormWidgetClass,
                                   shell, NULL, 0 );

   /*
    * The label goes to the left.
    */

    label = XtVaCreateManagedWidget ( "label", xmLabelWidgetClass,
                           form,
                           XmNtopAttachment,    XmATTACH_FORM,
                           XmNbottomAttachment, XmATTACH_FORM,
                           XmNleftAttachment,   XmATTACH_FORM,
                           XmNrightAttachment,  XmATTACH_FORM,
                           NULL );

   /*
    * The scale is attached to the right side of the label.
    */

    scale = XtVaCreateManagedWidget ( "scale", xmScaleWidgetClass,
                          form,
                          XmNtopAttachment,    XmATTACH_FORM,
                          XmNbottomAttachment, XmATTACH_FORM,
                          XmNleftAttachment,   XmATTACH_WIDGET,
                          XmNleftWidget,       label,
                          XmNrightAttachment,  XmATTACH_FORM,
                          NULL );

    XtRealizeWidget ( shell );
    XtAppMainLoop ( app );
}
```

Compiling and running this program produces the window shown in Figure 6.3.

Figure 6.3 First run of the `scale` program.

Clearly, something is wrong, because the window in Figure 6.3 looks nothing like the intended layout. In fact, the XmScale widget isn't even visible. The window fills the entire screen, with the label centered in the window.

Besides the incorrect appearance, there is a warning message printed to the shell window from which the program was run. The message, shown in Figure 6.4, reports an internal error in the XmForm widget, and a suggestion to check for "contradictory constraints" in the form constraint resources.

```
% scale
Warning:
  Name: form
  Class: XmForm
  Bailed out of edge synchronization after 10,000 iterations.
 Check for contradictory constraints on the children of this form.
```

Figure 6.4 The error message reported by XmForm.

When any problem is encountered in a such a simple example, the first step should be to review the code. In fact, any time a bug is found, it is a good idea to review at least the most-recently written code. Starting with the layout design, the constraints designed in Figure 6.2 do not appear to be contradictory. However, looking at the source code more carefully, we can see that the constraints on the XmScale widget do not match the specification in Figure 6.2. The right side of the `label` widget is attached to the right side of the form, but the `scale` widget's left side is attached to the right side of `label`. The right side of the `scale` widget is also attached to the right side of its parent, which effectively attaches both sides of `scale` to the same point. This simple coding error explains why the XmScale widget is not visible.

This problem can be fixed by changing the value of the label widget's `XmNrightAttachment` resource, on line 30, to `XmATTACH_NONE`, as was originally intended. Although `XmATTACH_NONE` is the default value, this attachment should be specified explicitly. If an attachment is left unspecified, it is possible for a program to pick up another value inadvertently from the user's resource files.

The revised program below shows the change in bold. We can now be more confident that the implementation matches the design specification.

```
/*************************************************
 * scale.c: Create a labeled scale in a form
 *************************************************/
#include <Xm/Xm.h>
#include <Xm/Form.h>
#include <Xm/Label.h>
#include <Xm/Scale.h>

void main ( int argc, char ** argv )
{
    Widget       shell, form, label, scale;
    XtAppContext app;
    int          i;

    shell = XtAppInitialize ( &app, "Scale",  NULL, 0,
                              &argc, argv, NULL, NULL, 0 );

    form = XtCreateManagedWidget ( "form", xmFormWidgetClass,
                                   shell, NULL, 0 );

   /*
    * The label goes to the left.
    */

    label =
        XtVaCreateManagedWidget ( "label", xmLabelWidgetClass,
                     form,
                     XmNtopAttachment,    XmATTACH_FORM,
                     XmNbottomAttachment, XmATTACH_FORM,
                     XmNleftAttachment,   XmATTACH_FORM,
                     XmNrightAttachment,  XmATTACH_NONE,
                     NULL );

   /*
    * The scale is attached to the right side of the label.
    */

    scale = XtVaCreateManagedWidget ( "scale", xmScaleWidgetClass,
                  form,
                  XmNtopAttachment,    XmATTACH_FORM,
                  XmNbottomAttachment, XmATTACH_FORM,
                  XmNleftAttachment,   XmATTACH_WIDGET,
                  XmNleftWidget,       label,
                  XmNrightAttachment,  XmATTACH_FORM,
                  NULL );

    XtRealizeWidget ( shell );
    XtAppMainLoop ( app );
}
```

Corrected Constraint

After making this change, running the modified program produces the layout shown in Figure 6.5.

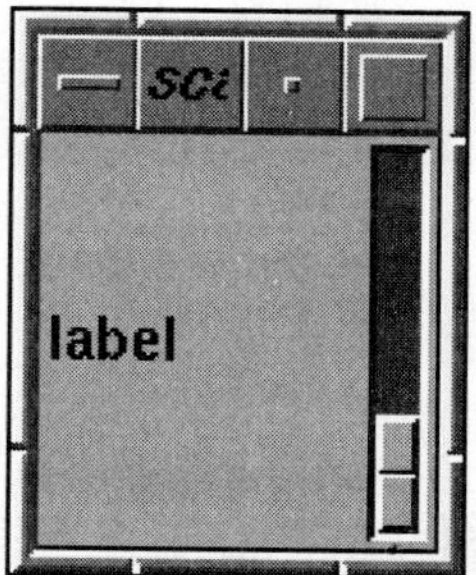

Figure 6.5 The `scale` program after fixing the left attachment error.

Although the window in Figure 6.5 is much closer to the intended layout, the appearance is still not entirely correct. The program may be implementing the attachments in Figure 6.2 correctly, but the program's layout does not match that in Figure 6.1. The label should be positioned at the top of the XmForm widget, but instead, it is centered in the form. There could be several possible reasons for this error, but before exploring further, it would be useful to know exactly where the label is and how big it is. Because labels have no visible edges, the label widget could be occupying the entire form, or perhaps it is just centered in the form.

One way to see where the label is really positioned is to use `editres` to display the widget tree and locate the bounds of some specific widgets. Depending on your version of Motif, you may need to modify the program to support `editres`, as described in Chapter 3. The following version of the `scale` program adds `editres` support.

```
/*************************************************
 * scale.c: Create a labeled scale in a form
 ************************************************/
#include <Xm/Xm.h>
#include <Xm/Form.h>
#include <Xm/Label.h>
#include <Xm/Scale.h>

extern XtEventHandler _XEditResCheckMessages;

void main ( int argc, char ** argv )
{
```

Editres Hook

```
    Widget        shell, form, label, scale;
    XtAppContext app;
    int           i;

    shell = XtAppInitialize ( &app, "Scale",  NULL, 0,
                              &argc, argv, NULL, NULL, 0 );

    XtAddEventHandler ( shell, ( EventMask ) 0, TRUE,
                        _XEditResCheckMessages, NULL );

    form = XtCreateManagedWidget ( "form", xmFormWidgetClass,
                                   shell, NULL, 0 );

   /*
    * The label goes to the left.
    */

    label = XtVaCreateManagedWidget ( "label", xmLabelWidgetClass,
                              form,
                              XmNtopAttachment,    XmATTACH_FORM,
                              XmNbottomAttachment, XmATTACH_FORM,
                              XmNleftAttachment,   XmATTACH_FORM,
                              XmNrightAttachment,  XmATTACH_NONE,
                              NULL );

   /*
    * The scale is attached to the right side of the label.
    */

    scale = XtVaCreateManagedWidget ( "scale", xmScaleWidgetClass,
                            form,
                            XmNtopAttachment,    XmATTACH_FORM,
                            XmNbottomAttachment, XmATTACH_FORM,
                            XmNleftAttachment,   XmATTACH_WIDGET,
                            XmNleftWidget,       label,
                            XmNrightAttachment,  XmATTACH_FORM,
                            NULL );

    XtRealizeWidget ( shell );
    XtAppMainLoop ( app );
}
```

Figure 6.6 shows an `editres` window that displays the widget hierarchy of the `scale` program. The user can click on the box named "label" in the `editres` window and then choose the "Flash Selected Widgets" item from the Tree menu pane. This command causes the area occupied by the selected widget or widgets to be highlighted in the program under inspection.

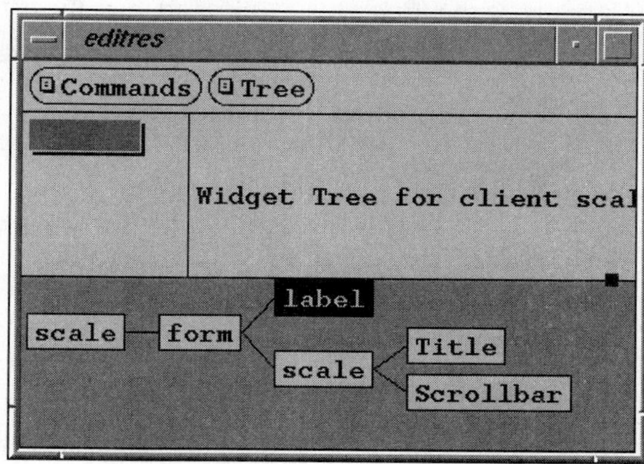

Figure 6.6 Using `editres` to examine the label widget in the scale program.

Figure 6.7 shows the `scale` program when `editres` flashes the label widget. The grey box on the left side of the window shows the area occupied by the label widget. It is easy to see that the widget spans the form widget from top to bottom.

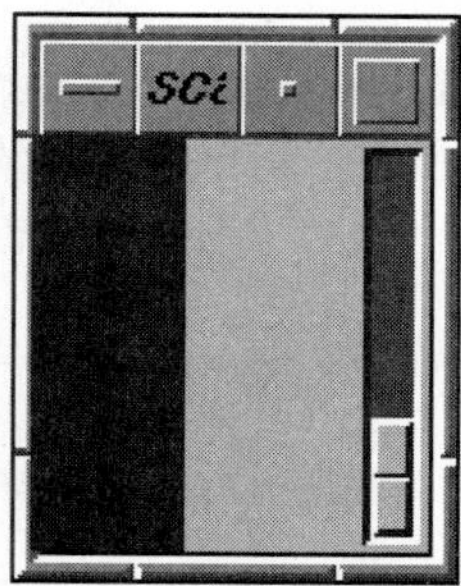

Figure 6.7 The `scale` program, with the label widget flashing.

So why is the label so tall? One possibility is that the label widget's `XmNheight` resource has been set in such a way that the label is taller than intended. For example, an unintended resource could have been picked up from the user's .Xdefaults file. As a quick test, the program could be run again, explicitly setting the label's height to a small value. The label's height can be set by using the `-xrm` command line argument to set the resource as follows:

```
scale -xrm "*label.height: 20"
```

However, executing this command has no effect, and the program still appears as shown in Figure 6.5. So, the next puzzle is "why does the label ignore an explicit height setting?"

There are several possible reasons why a widget would not respond to a geometry setting. For example, the resource manager precedence rules make it possible for some other resource specification to override the one given on the command line. Because resources can come from so many places in a Motif program, it is hard to be sure just what resources are being applied to a program. An easy way to check the contents of an application's resource database is to use `appres`, described in Chapter 3. Figure 6.8 shows the results of running appres, with the arguments used for the scale program. The program is picking up some colors from somewhere, probably the .Xdefaults file, and also reports the `XmNheight` resource set on the command line.

```
appres Scale scale -xrm "*label.height: 20"
*label.height:  20
*foreground:    black
*background:    grey50
```

Figure 6.8 Appres output.

Although it seems unlikely in this simple case, `appres` could be wrong. To be more thorough, we can modify the program to call `DumpResources()`, described in Chapter 3, just before the program enters event loop:

```
/**********************************************
 * scale.c: Create a labeled scale in a form
 **********************************************/
#include <Xm/Xm.h>
#include <Xm/Form.h>
#include <Xm/Label.h>
#include <Xm/Scale.h>

extern void DumpResources ( Display *dpy );
extern XtEventHandler _XEditResCheckMessages;

void main ( int argc, char ** argv )
{
    Widget       shell, form, label, scale;
    XtAppContext app;
    int          i;


```

```
    shell = XtAppInitialize ( &app, "Scale",  NULL, 0,
                              &argc, argv, NULL, NULL, 0 );

    XtAddEventHandler ( shell, ( EventMask ) 0, TRUE,
                        _XEditResCheckMessages, NULL );

    form = XtCreateManagedWidget ( "form", xmFormWidgetClass,
                                   shell, NULL, 0 );

   /*
    * The label goes to the left.
    */

   label = XtVaCreateManagedWidget ( "label", xmLabelWidgetClass,
                                    form,
                                    XmNtopAttachment,    XmATTACH_FORM,
                                    XmNbottomAttachment, XmATTACH_FORM,
                                    XmNleftAttachment,   XmATTACH_FORM,
                                    XmNrightAttachment,  XmATTACH_NONE,
                                    NULL );

   /*
    * The scale is attached to the right side of the label.
    */

    scale = XtVaCreateManagedWidget ( "scale", xmScaleWidgetClass,
                                    form,
                                    XmNtopAttachment,    XmATTACH_FORM,
                                    XmNbottomAttachment, XmATTACH_FORM,
                                    XmNleftAttachment,   XmATTACH_WIDGET,
                                    XmNleftWidget,       label,
                                    XmNrightAttachment,  XmATTACH_FORM,
                                    NULL );

    DumpResources ( XtDisplay ( shell ) );

    XtRealizeWidget ( shell );

    XtAppMainLoop ( app );
}
```

DumpResources() prints the entire contents of the resource database to a file, where it can be inspected. The contents of the scale program's resource database are shown in Figure 6.9. As would be true in most cases, there is no difference in the resources reported by appres, and what is in the program's database.

```
*label.height:   20
*foreground:     black
*background:     grey50
```

Figure 6.9 The `scale` program's resource database.

It seems clear that the command-line option is being added to the resource database, and there does not appear to be any other resource that could be overriding the setting, so there must be some other explanation for the layout problem.

Another tool that is useful for investigating geometry bugs is the XtGeo library, described in Chapter 3. To use libXtGeo, the `scale` program must be relinked with the XtGeo library specified ahead of the Xt library, as follows

```
cc -o scale scale.c -lXm -lXtGeo -lXt -lX11
```

To see detailed information about how each widget's size and position is determined, the `scale` program can be run with the resource `geoTattler` set to "`on`", as follows:

```
scale -xrm "*label.height: 20" -xrm "*geoTattler: on"
```

This command produces the output shown in Figure 6.10.

The XtGeo library produces a large amount of information, and it is often more convenient to redirect the output to a file for easier browsing. For this small program, however, the output is manageable. The trace begins by reporting that all widgets are being realized and being marked as managed. Next, the `scale` widget makes a request to its parent to grow to 19 pixels wide and 104 pixels tall. The `form` widget is not yet realized, so Xt automatically grants the request and returns `XtGeometryYes`. The `scale` widget then resizes its internal scrollbar component. In the next section, the `form` widget requests a change in size. The `form` widget's parent, a shell, is also not realized yet, so Xt grants the request. Both the XmScale and XmForm widget are now 104 pixels tall.

Next, the `label` widget is configured by its parent, the XmForm widget. The trace reports that `label` is changed from 20 pixels tall to 104 pixels. This information is significant, because it appears that setting the `label` widget's height resource to 20 did take effect. The `label` is initially 20 pixels tall, as requested by the resource specified on the command line. However, we can see from Figure 6.10 that the `form` widget is explicitly forcing `label` to be the same height as the XmScale widget.

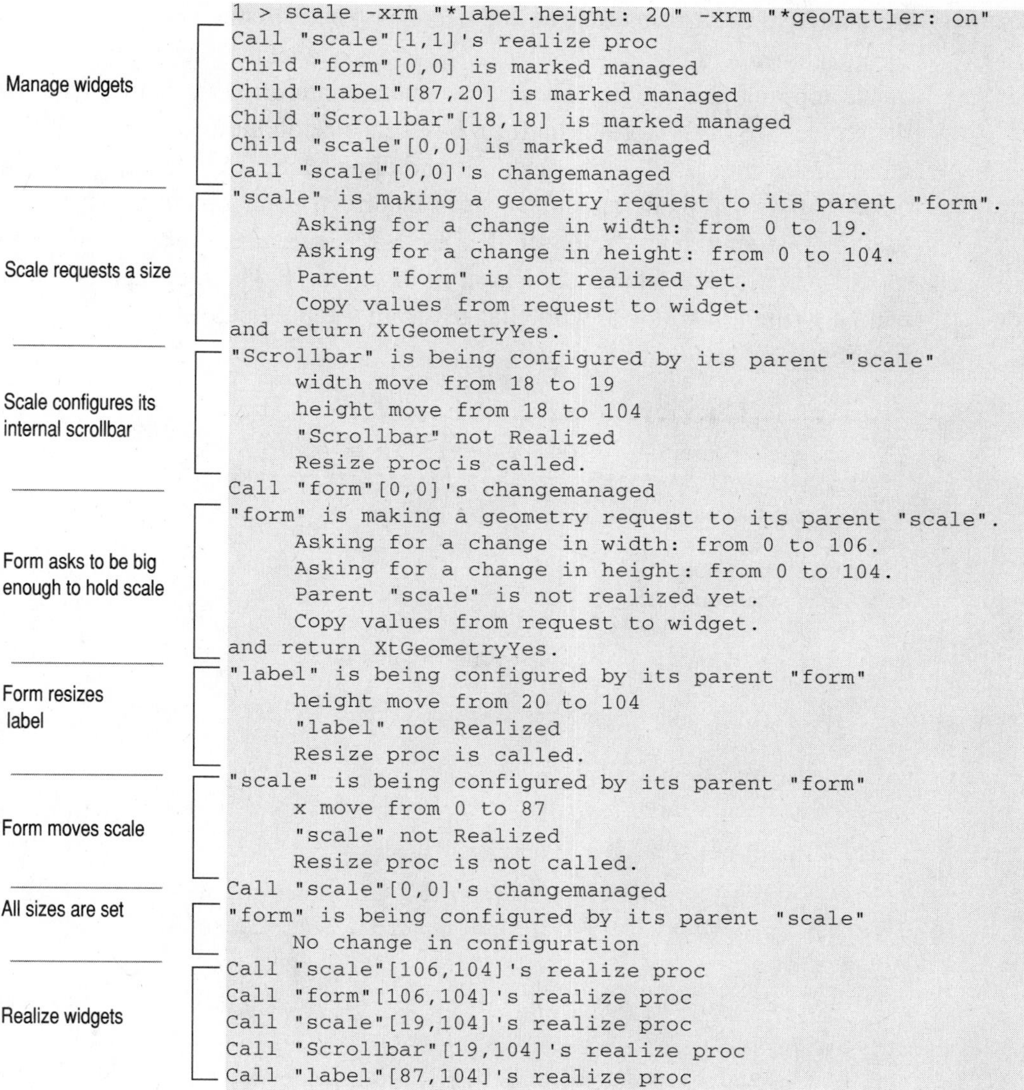


```
1 > scale -xrm "*label.height: 20" -xrm "*geoTattler: on"
Call "scale"[1,1]'s realize proc
Child "form"[0,0] is marked managed
Child "label"[87,20] is marked managed
Child "Scrollbar"[18,18] is marked managed
Child "scale"[0,0] is marked managed
Call "scale"[0,0]'s changemanaged
"scale" is making a geometry request to its parent "form".
     Asking for a change in width: from 0 to 19.
     Asking for a change in height: from 0 to 104.
     Parent "form" is not realized yet.
     Copy values from request to widget.
and return XtGeometryYes.
"Scrollbar" is being configured by its parent "scale"
     width move from 18 to 19
     height move from 18 to 104
     "Scrollbar" not Realized
     Resize proc is called.
Call "form"[0,0]'s changemanaged
"form" is making a geometry request to its parent "scale".
     Asking for a change in width: from 0 to 106.
     Asking for a change in height: from 0 to 104.
     Parent "scale" is not realized yet.
     Copy values from request to widget.
and return XtGeometryYes.
"label" is being configured by its parent "form"
     height move from 20 to 104
     "label" not Realized
     Resize proc is called.
"scale" is being configured by its parent "form"
     x move from 0 to 87
     "scale" not Realized
     Resize proc is not called.
Call "scale"[0,0]'s changemanaged
"form" is being configured by its parent "scale"
     No change in configuration
Call "scale"[106,104]'s realize proc
Call "form"[106,104]'s realize proc
Call "scale"[19,104]'s realize proc
Call "Scrollbar"[19,104]'s realize proc
Call "label"[87,104]'s realize proc
```

Figure 6.10 Geometry management trace produced by XtGeo.

The geometry behavior of this example illustrates an important point to remember when designing and debugging layouts. A widget can request to be a specific size, but each widget's parent has the final say. The size and position of each widget in a Motif widget hierarchy is determined by the way each manager widget's layout algorithm interacts with other widgets.

Now that we know that the form widget is controlling the label's height, the source of the error is easy to find. Referring back to the original design of the attachments in Figure 6.2, we can see that the label is attached to the form at the top and the bottom. These attachments naturally stretch the label to match the size of the form. The form bases its size on the height of its tallest child, and computes all other positions and dimensions from the attachments. Now that we know the attachments are incorrect, the problem can be fixed easily. Changing line 29 to set the `XmNbottomAttachment` resource to `XmATTACH_NONE` produces the layout in Figure 6.11. The modified program can be written as follows, with changes from the previous version shown in bold:

```
1  /*************************************************
2   * scale.c: Create a labeled scale in a form
3   *************************************************/
4  #include <Xm/Xm.h>
5  #include <Xm/Form.h>
6  #include <Xm/Label.h>
7  #include <Xm/Scale.h>
8
9  extern XtEventHandler _XEditResCheckMessages;
10
11 void main ( int argc, char ** argv )
12 {
13     Widget       shell, form, label, scale;
14     XtAppContext app;
15     int          i;
16
17     shell = XtAppInitialize ( &app, "Scale",  NULL, 0,
18                               &argc, argv, NULL, NULL, 0 );
19
20     XtAddEventHandler ( shell, ( EventMask ) 0, TRUE,
21                        _XEditResCheckMessages, NULL );
22
23     form = XtCreateManagedWidget ( "form", xmFormWidgetClass,
24                                   shell, NULL, 0 );
25    /*
26     * The label goes to the left.
27     */
28
29     label = XtVaCreateManagedWidget ( "label", xmLabelWidgetClass,
30                         form,
31                         XmNtopAttachment,    XmATTACH_FORM,
```

```
                         XmNbottomAttachment, XmATTACH_NONE,
                         XmNleftAttachment,   XmATTACH_FORM,
                         XmNrightAttachment,  XmATTACH_NONE,
                         NULL );
    /*
     * The scale is attached to the right side of the label.
     */

    scale = XtVaCreateManagedWidget ( "scale", xmScaleWidgetClass,
                         form,
                         XmNtopAttachment,    XmATTACH_FORM,
                         XmNbottomAttachment, XmATTACH_FORM,
                         XmNleftAttachment,   XmATTACH_WIDGET,
                         XmNleftWidget,       label,
                         XmNrightAttachment,  XmATTACH_FORM,
                         NULL );

    XtRealizeWidget ( shell );
    XtAppMainLoop ( app );
}
```

With these corrections, the `scale` program looks much better and the layout matches the layout sketched in Figure 6.1.

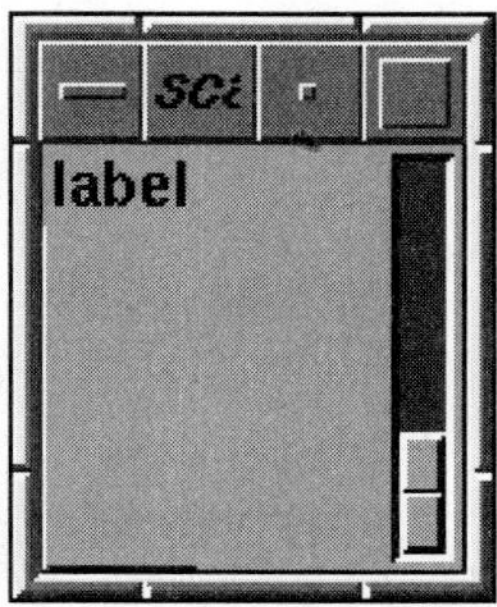

Figure 6.11 The `scale` program after fixing the label's attachments.

However, although the basic layout now seems correct, there is still a small problem with the window in Figure 6.11. Notice that there seems to be an odd-looking black line along the left half of the bottom of the window. Although this problem is not as serious as the initial layout bugs, the unintended line mars the appearance of the program and needs to be fixed, if the program is to look its best.

The `xmag` program can be used to take a closer look at the problem. Running `xmag` and selecting the region at the lower left corner of the `scale` program's window produces the window in Figure 6.12. This figure shows the window manager frame and an inner border between the window manager frame. The magnified view confirms the existence of a partial, nearly black line along the lower left side of the window. The line seems to extend from the far left side of the form to about the `label` widget's right side, although it is hard to be sure exactly where the `label` widget's right side is.

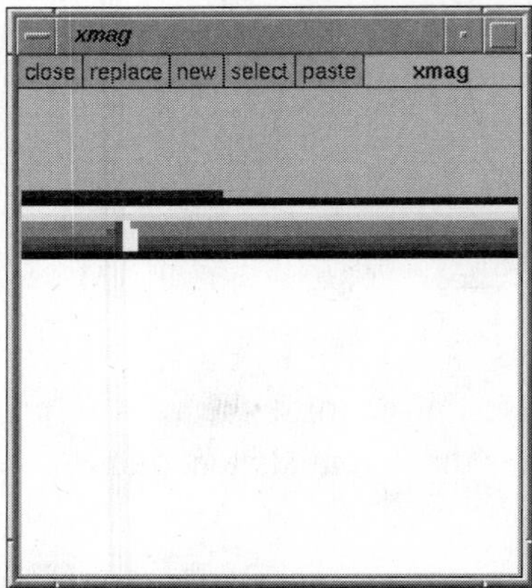

Figure 6.12 Using `xmag` to examine the problem.

Using `editres` to locate the bounds of the `label` widget confirms that the line has approximately the same width as the `label` widget. Figure 6.13 shows the `scale` program with the `label`, in its new position, flashing under the control of `editres`.

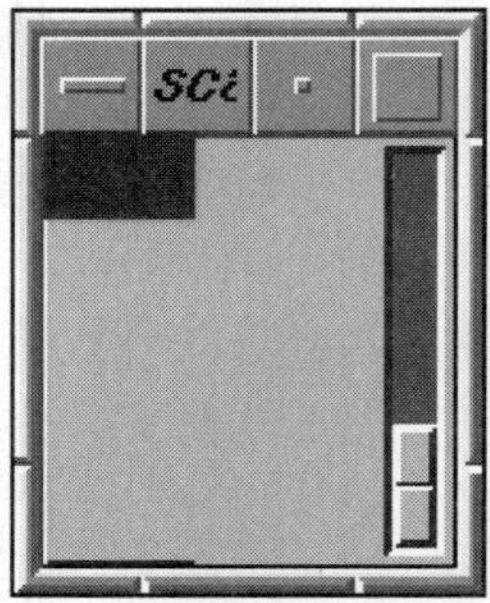

Figure 6.13 Highlighting the label with `editres`.

Although it is interesting that the line has the same width as the `label` widget, it is not clear that this widget has anything to do with the line. The bottom of the `label` widget is far from where the line appears. However, because this widget's right side coincides with the point at which the line ends, it is also true that the XmScale widget begins where the line ends. `Editres` can be used to confirm that the XmScale widget extends to the point at which the line ends. Figure 6.14 shows the results of flashing the XmScale widget using `editres`.

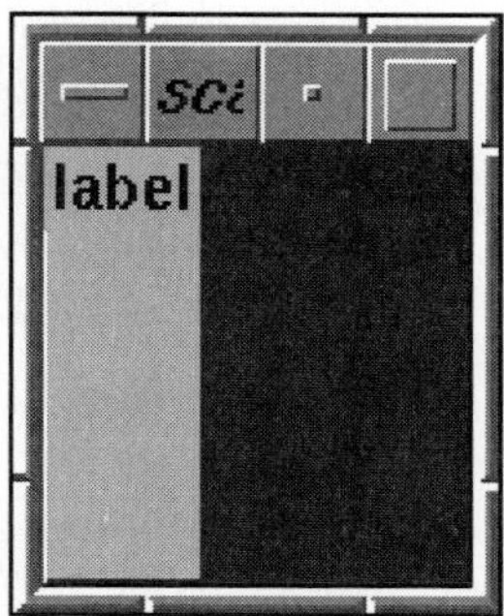

Figure 6.14 Extent of the XmScale widget, highlighted by `editres`.

Based on this evidence, it appears that the `form` widget may have a shadow that is being overdrawn by the XmScale widget because the `scale` widget is attached directly to the bottom side of its parent. The line appears on the left side because the `label` widget is unattached on the bottom and does not overdraw its parent's shadow. So the real problem is not the visible line, but the absence of the bottom shadow in the remaining half of the `form` widget.

Now that we understand this problem, a closer look reveals a second shadow-related problem. The label covers its parent's shadow along the form's left edge. Actually, the `scale` and `label` widgets are covering the `form` widget's shadows everywhere they make contact with the edges of the `form` widget. The problem is only apparent because the `form` widget's lower left corner is unoccupied.

There are several ways to fix the visual anomalies in this program. The form widget's shadow thickness could be set to zero, the form's top and bottom shadow colors could be set to match the widget's background color, or an offset could be specified for the various attachments.

The last approach is probably the easiest to test. Running the `scale` program with the following arguments provides a two pixel offset between all attachments, and produces the window in Figure 6.15:

```
scale -xrm "*Offset: 2"
```

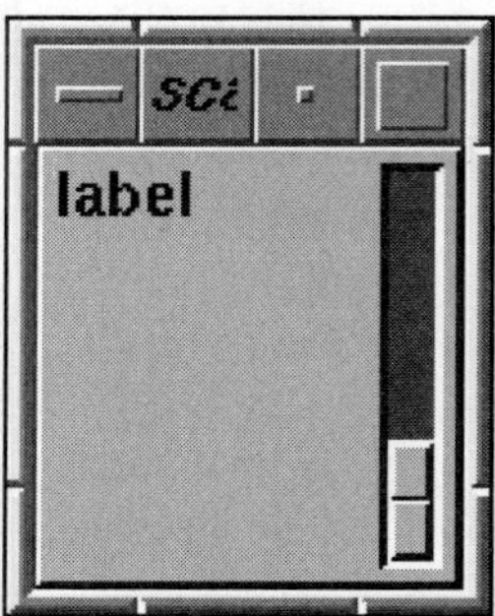

Figure 6.15 The final scale layout.

With these changes, the labeled scale finally has the appearance originally planned. Although extremely simple, this example demonstrates some techniques that can be used to solve any layout problem. Unlike this example, which involves only three widgets, many real-world interface problems may involve dozens, or even hundreds of widgets. More widgets tend to involve more complex interactions between widgets, and therefore produce more problems. Still, the same techniques demonstrated in this simple example can be applied to more complex problems, as well.

6.2 An Example: Extending an Existing Interface

It is particularly easy to create bugs when modifying an existing program. When modifying or extending an existing interface, particularly one you did not write yourself, the original interface may not be not well understood. It is quite easy to introduce bugs when you do not take the time to step through the original program line by line to understand the logic, widgets, or layout used. This scenario serves as the inspiration for a second case study on identifying and fixing layout bugs.

The original program comes from [Young94]. The `chooseone` program is a simple program that takes a list of arguments from its command line and displays them in a scrolled list. The user is expected to select one item from the list, and the program echoes that item to `stdout`. This program is meant to be used in shell scripts, to prompt a user to choose from a list of items. The program returns the selected item for further use in the shell script. Figure 6.16 shows the layout of the original program.

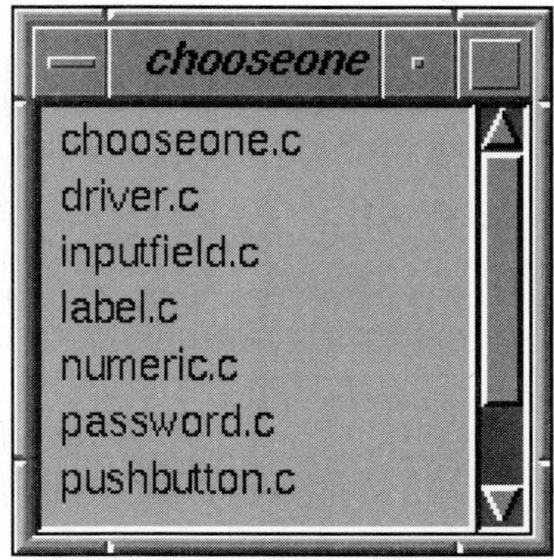

Figure 6.16 The original `chooseone` program.

The body of the original program, which creates the window shown in Figure 6.16, is written as follows:

```
/**********************************************************
 * chooseone.c: Allow the user to select from a list
 *              of command-line arguments
 **********************************************************/
#include <Xm/Xm.h>
#include <Xm/List.h>
#include <stdio.h>
#include <stdlib.h>

static void BrowseCallback ( Widget    widget,
                             XtPointer clientData,
                             XtPointer callData );

const char usageString[] =
             "Usage: chooseone <non-zero list of choices>";

```

```
void main ( int argc, char **argv )
{
    Widget       shell, list;
    int          i;
    XmString    *xmstr;
    XtAppContext app;

    shell = XtAppInitialize ( &app, "Chooseone",  NULL, 0,
                              &argc, argv, NULL, NULL, 0 );

    if ( argc <= 1 )
    {
        fprintf ( stderr, usageString );
        exit ( -1 );
    }

   /*
    * Convert all command-line arguments to an array of
    * type XmString, ignoring argv[0].
    */

    xmstr = ( XmString * ) XtMalloc ( sizeof ( XmString ) *
                                        ( argc - 1 ) );
    for ( i = 1; i < argc; i++ )
        xmstr [i - 1] = XmStringCreateLtoR ( argv[i],
                                        XmFONTLIST_DEFAULT_TAG );
   /*
    * Create the list widget and register a browse callback.
    */

    list = XmCreateScrolledList ( shell, "list", NULL, 0 );
    XtManageChild ( list );

    XtVaSetValues ( list,
                    XmNitems,             xmstr,
                    XmNitemCount,         argc - 1,
                    XmNvisibleItemCount, 20,
                    NULL );

    XtAddCallback ( list, XmNbrowseSelectionCallback,
                    BrowseCallback, NULL );

    XtRealizeWidget ( shell );
    XtAppMainLoop ( app );
}
```

```
static void BrowseCallback ( Widget    w,
                             XtPointer clientData,
                             XtPointer callData)
{
   XmListCallbackStruct *cbs =
                         ( XmListCallbackStruct * ) callData;
   Boolean  result;
   char     *text;

  /*
   * Retrieve the character data from the compound string
   */

   if ( ( result = XmStringGetLtoR ( cbs->item,
                                     XmFONTLIST_DEFAULT_TAG,
                                     &text ) ) == TRUE )
   {
       /*
        * If some text was retrieved, print it. Normally, this
        * data should be freed, but the program is going to
        * exit, anyway.
        */

        printf ( "%s\n", text );
   }

   exit ( 0 );
}
```

Although this program works as-is, it is missing some features that would make it more useful. For example, the program always forces the user to choose one item from the list. In some situations, it would be useful to allow the user to cancel the operation instead of choosing an item. There are other features that could be added as well, but let's add just this one simple feature to the program.

The original example simply creates a list widget as a child of the shell, adds each item found on the command line to the list, and installs a callback with the list widget. Adding a new button requires a more complex widget hierarchy. We must manage the list in another manager widget, like an XmForm widget, and also add a cancel button. Figure 6.17 shows a set of form attachments that can be used to achieve a reasonable layout for the modified interface.

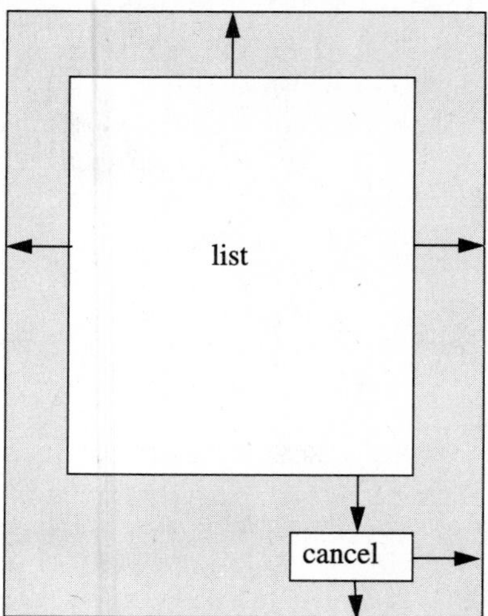

Figure 6.17 Form attachments for modified `chooseone` layout.

The modified program is shown below. The changes and additions required to add the cancel button are shown in bold. The changes simply create a form widget and change the list widget to be a child of the form widget. A cancel button is also added as a child of the form widget, and the attachments shown in Figure 6.17 are set up.

```
/*****************************************************
 * chooseone.c: Allow the user to select from a list
 *             of command-line arguments.
 *              Modified to add a cancel button.
 *****************************************************/
#include <Xm/Xm.h>
#include <Xm/List.h>
#include <Xm/Form.h>
#include <Xm/PushB.h>
#include <stdio.h>
#include <stdlib.h>

static void BrowseCallback ( Widget    widget,
                             XtPointer clientData,
                             XtPointer callData );

static void CancelCallback ( Widget widget,
                             XtPointer clientData,
                             XtPointer callData );
```

```
const char usageString[] =
              "Usage: chooseone <non-zero list of choices>";

void main ( int argc, char **argv )
{
    Widget       shell, list, form, cancel;
    int          i;
    XmString    *xmstr;
    XtAppContext app;

    shell = XtAppInitialize ( &app, "Chooseone",  NULL, 0,
                              &argc, argv, NULL, NULL, 0 );
    if ( argc <= 1 )
    {
        fprintf ( stderr, usageString );
        exit ( -1 );
    }

   /*
    * Create a form widget to manage the list and button.
    */

    form = XtCreateManagedWidget ( "form",
                                   xmFormWidgetClass,
                                   shell, NULL, 0 );
   /*
    * Convert all command-line arguments to an array of
    * type XmString, ignoring argv[0].
    */

    xmstr = ( XmString * ) XtMalloc ( sizeof ( XmString ) *
                                      ( argc - 1 ) );
    for ( i = 1; i < argc; i++ )
        xmstr [i - 1] = XmStringCreateLtoR ( argv[i],
                                       XmFONTLIST_DEFAULT_TAG );
   /*
    * Create the list widget and register a browse callback.
    */

    list = XmCreateScrolledList ( form, "list", NULL, 0 );
    XtManageChild ( list );

   /*
    * Add a cancel button and a cancel callback.
    */

    cancel = XtCreateManagedWidget ( "cancel",
                                     xmPushButtonWidgetClass,
                                     form, NULL, 0 );
```

```
    XtAddCallback ( cancel, XmNactivateCallback,
                    CancelCallback, NULL );

   /*
    * This setvalues call was already here. Just add the form
    * attachments to make the list span the top half of the
    * program's window.
    */

    XtVaSetValues ( list,
                    XmNitems,              xmstr,
                    XmNitemCount,          argc - 1,
                    XmNvisibleItemCount,   20,
                    XmNtopAttachment,      XmATTACH_FORM,
                    XmNbottomWidget,       cancel,
                    XmNbottomAttachment,   XmATTACH_WIDGET,
                    XmNleftAttachment,     XmATTACH_FORM,
                    XmNrightAttachment,    XmATTACH_FORM,
                    NULL );
   /*
    * Attach the button to the lower right corner of th window
    */

    XtVaSetValues ( cancel,
                    XmNtopAttachment,      XmATTACH_NONE,
                    XmNbottomAttachment,   XmATTACH_FORM,
                    XmNleftAttachment,     XmATTACH_NONE,
                    XmNrightAttachment,    XmATTACH_FORM,
                    NULL );

    XtAddCallback ( list, XmNbrowseSelectionCallback,
                    BrowseCallback, NULL );

    XtRealizeWidget ( shell );
    XtAppMainLoop ( app );
}
```

The `CancelCallback()` function is a new callback, to be called if the user cancels the operation. It should print the value “None”, and exit.

```
static void CancelCallback ( Widget    w,
                             XtPointer clientData,
                             XtPointer callData)
{
    printf ( "None" );
    exit( 0 );
}
```

The `BrowseCallback()` function is unchanged from the original. This function simply retrieves the text from the selected item, prints it to standard out, and exits.

With these modifications, we can now test the new version of the program. Running the program with a single argument:

```
chooseone test
```

displays the window shown in Figure 6.18. This window, of course, does not look quite as expected. The scrollbars may be missing because there aren't enough items to scroll. But the button was supposed to be at the bottom, and the list was supposed to span the window.

Figure 6.18 First test of the modified `chooseone` program.

To further complicate things, additional tests produce somewhat different results. For example, running the command:

```
chooseone /usr/include/X11/*
```

produces the window shown in Figure 6.19. Here, the scrollbar has appeared, and the list correctly spans the entire window. However, the `cancel` button has disappeared.

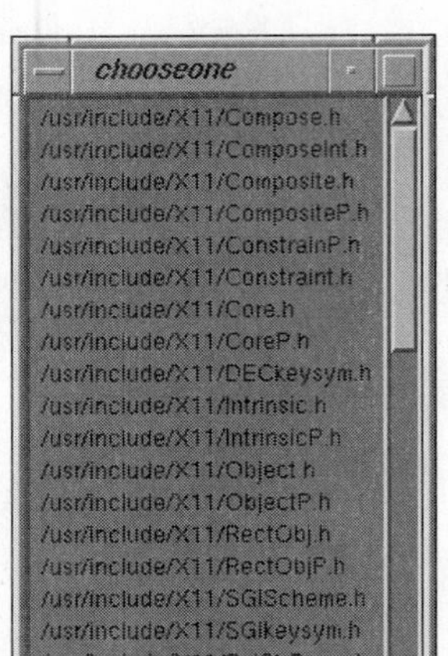

Figure 6.19 Second test of the modified `chooseone` program.

We can start to investigate this behavior by using `editres` to display the program's widget hierarchy, as shown in Figure 6.20. The `cancel` button is clearly present in the hierarchy.

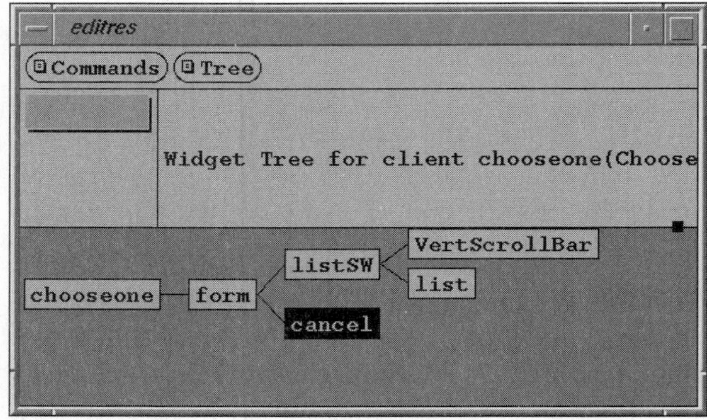

Figure 6.20 Using `editres` to inspect the `chooseone` widget hierarchy.

We can select the `cancel` button in `editres`, and use `editres` to highlight the location of the missing `cancel` button. Figure 6.21 shows the area highlighted by `editres`. The `cancel` button is apparently where it should be, but it is covered by the `list` widget.

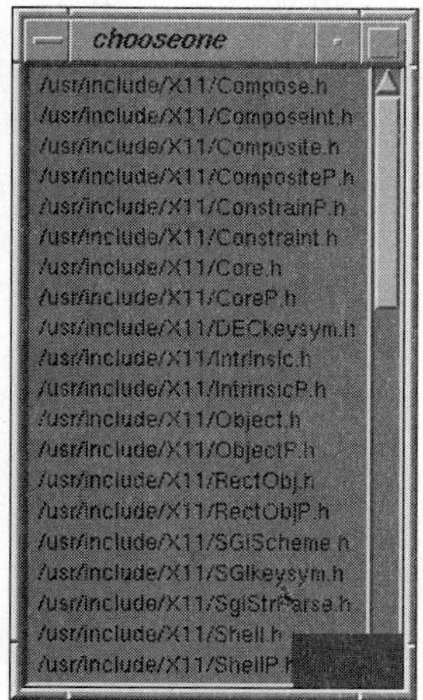

Figure 6.21 The `cancel` button location revealed by `editres`.

It might be useful to see how this program behaves when the window is resized. Figure 6.22 shows the window after it has been resized.

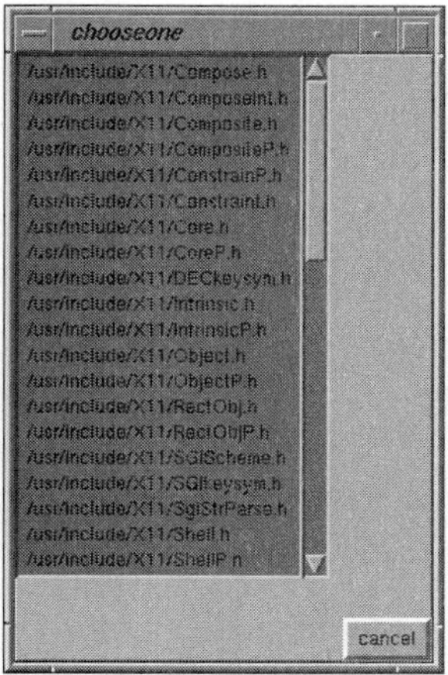

Figure 6.22 A resized `chooseone` window.

Interestingly, stretching the window so that it is larger reveals the cancel button, attached to the bottom right corner as it should be. However, the list widget does not change size with the rest of the window. Clearly something is wrong with the program's geometry management.

The tool that can provide the most detail information about a program's geometry management is the XtGeo library. Let's run the modified `chooseone` again, after linking with this library. The program can be run as follows to trace the geometry management process:

```
chooseone /usr/include/X11/*.h -xrm "*geoTattler: on"
```

We will examine the XtGeo output in two stages. Figure 6.23 shows the first part of the XtGeo output.

Manage all widgets

```
Call "chooseone"[1,1]'s realize proc
Child "form"[0,0] is marked managed
Child "listSW"[100,100] is marked managed
Child "list"[24,27] is marked managed
Child "cancel"[60,30] is marked managed
Child "VertScrollBar"[18,18] is marked managed
```

Establish the desired size of the list

```
XtSetValues sees some geometry changes for "list".
     "list" is making a geometry request to its parent "listSW
          Asking for a change in width: from 24 to 191.
          Asking for a change in height: from 27 to 347.
          Parent "listSW" is not realized yet.
          Copy values from request to widget.
     and return XtGeometryYes.
     XtSetValues calls "list"'s resize proc.
```

listSW computes its desired size and requests that size from its parent

```
Call "listSW"[100,100]'s changemanaged
"listSW" is making a geometry request to its parent "form".
     Asking for a change in width: from 100 to 209.
     Asking for a change in height: from 100 to 347.
     Parent "form" is not realized yet.
     Copy values from request to widget.
and return XtGeometryYes.
```

listSW sets the final size of the list widget

```
"listSW" is asking its preferred geometry to "list".
     with the following constraints:
      width = 209
      height = 347
      using core x = 0.
      using core y = 0.
      using core width = 191.
      using core height = 347.
      using core border_width = 0.
"list" returns XtGeometryYes to "listSW".
"list" is being configured by its parent "listSW"
     No change in configuration
```

listSW sets the final size of the vertical scrollbar

```
"VertScrollBar" is being configured by its parent "listSW"
     x move from 0 to 191
     height move from 18 to 347
     "VertScrollBar" not Realized
     Resize proc is called.
```

Figure 6.23 First portion of `chooseone`'s geometry trace.

Once all widgets are marked as managed, the `list` widget determines its desired size. A width of 191 and height of 347 probably corresponds to the size of the list in Figure 6.19, and the widget is probably trying to be wide enough to display the path names in the list.

Next, a widget named `listSW` asks its parent, `form`, if it can grow to 209x347. This is interesting because the `chooseone` program does not create a widget named `listSW`. Looking again at the list widget's geometry request, we can see that `listSW` is apparently the `list` widget's parent, and is responsible for its geometry. Continuing, we can see that `listSW` eventually determines the size of both the list and the vertical scrollbar associated with the list.

Figure 6.24 continues the output produced by the XtGeo library.

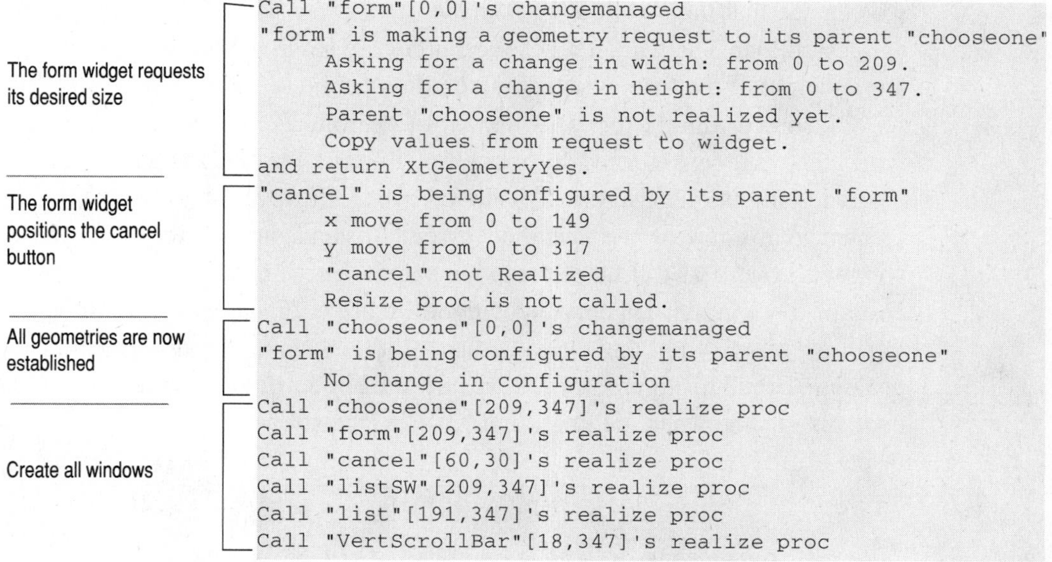


```
Call "form"[0,0]'s changemanaged
"form" is making a geometry request to its parent "chooseone"
     Asking for a change in width: from 0 to 209.
     Asking for a change in height: from 0 to 347.
     Parent "chooseone" is not realized yet.
     Copy values from request to widget.
and return XtGeometryYes.
"cancel" is being configured by its parent "form"
     x move from 0 to 149
     y move from 0 to 317
     "cancel" not Realized
     Resize proc is not called.
Call "chooseone"[0,0]'s changemanaged
"form" is being configured by its parent "chooseone"
     No change in configuration
Call "chooseone"[209,347]'s realize proc
Call "form"[209,347]'s realize proc
Call "cancel"[60,30]'s realize proc
Call "listSW"[209,347]'s realize proc
Call "list"[191,347]'s realize proc
Call "VertScrollBar"[18,347]'s realize proc
```

Figure 6.24 Second part of `chooseone`'s geometry management trace.

Here, the `form` widget requests a size large enough to hold its children. Notice that the requested size is the same as the size of the `listSW` widget. Also notice that the `cancel` button has not been involved in any geometry negotiations so far. However, the next step is to position the `cancel` button. The `form` widget moves the `cancel` button to 149,317, which is 60 pixels from the right edge and 30 pixels from the bottom of the form.

The next stage notifies the program's shell widget that it has managed children, and indicates that no geometry management changes are needed. Finally, all windows are created. The numbers reported in this stage indicate the final size of each widget. Notice that `form` is the same size as `listSW`, which is as wide as `list` plus the width of the scrollbar. Also notice that the `cancel` widget is 60 pixels wide and 30 pixels tall.

From this trace of the geometry management, it is clear that the `form` widget does not do what we expect. It has deliberately placed the `cancel` button at the bottom right corner of the form, as expected. However, it really has done nothing with the list, except to grow large enough to contain it. Furthermore, we noticed that an unexpected widget, `listSW`, was involved in the geometry management, and in fact seems to be inserted between the list and the form widget. We should have noticed this widget when we examined the hierarchy using `editres`, of course. Indeed, referring back to Figure 6.20, we can see that the scrolled list is made up of three widgets, `list`, `listSW`, and a scrollbar. The widget whose resources are set in the program is actually a grandchild of the form widget, not the direct child.

Of course, this is the way the Motif "scrolled" convenience functions work. The widget returned by these functions is the widget that would be created without the "scrolled" characteristic. However, the widget is not created as a child of the specified parent. Instead, an XmScrolledWindow widget is created as a child of the given parent, and the new widget becomes a child of the XmScrolledWindow widget. Figure 6.25 shows `editres` again, this time displaying the class names of the widgets in the `chooseone` program. From this figure, we can see how the XmScrolledWindow widget has been inserted between the `form` and `list` widgets.

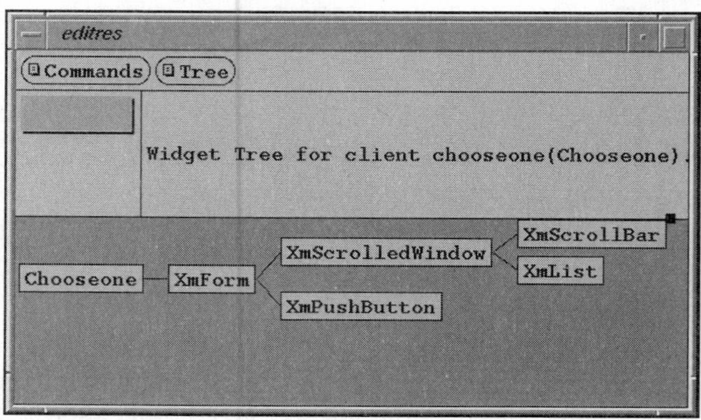

Figure 6.25 The class names of the `chooseone` widgets.

Based on this information, it is fairly easy to conclude that the constraint resources specified in the call to `XtVaSetValues()` on line 78 of the modified program have not taken effect. They cannot, because the resources are being passed to the `list` widget, which is not even a child of the `form` widget. Instead, the attachments must be made to the `list` widget's parent, which is a direct child of the `form` widget. The following code segment creates the correct attachments:

```
73      /*
74       * Specify the list widget resources.
75       */
76
77       XtVaSetValues ( list,
78                       XmNitems,             xmstr,
79                       XmNitemCount,         argc - 1,
80                       XmNvisibleItemCount, 20,
81                       NULL );
82
83      /*
84       * Add the form attachments to make the list
85       * span the top half of the program's window. Note
86       * that the attachments must be made to the list's parent.
87       */
88
89       XtVaSetValues ( XtParent ( list ),
90                       XmNtopAttachment,     XmATTACH_FORM,
91                       XmNbottomWidget,      cancel,
92                       XmNbottomAttachment, XmATTACH_WIDGET,
93                       XmNleftAttachment,    XmATTACH_FORM,
94                       XmNrightAttachment,   XmATTACH_FORM,
95                       NULL );
96
97      /*
98       * Attach the button to the lower right corner of th window
99       */
100
101      XtVaSetValues ( cancel,
102                      XmNtopAttachment,     XmATTACH_NONE,
103                      XmNbottomAttachment, XmATTACH_FORM,
104                      XmNleftAttachment,    XmATTACH_NONE,
105                      XmNrightAttachment,   XmATTACH_FORM,
106                      NULL );
107
```

Making these changes allows the `form` widget to perform the expected geometry management. Figure 6.26 shows the corrected `chooseone` window layout, with the added `cancel` button.

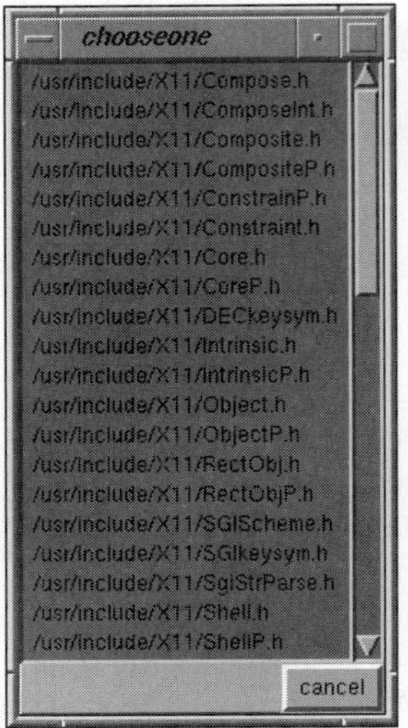

Figure 6.26 The debugged `chooseone` window layout.

6.3 Debugging Layouts with the WL Framework

The "widget lint" framework described in Chapter 3 can also be useful when solving layout problems. For example, some of the problems encountered in the examples in this chapter could be caught by tests that can be added to the framework. Difficulties you encounter once are likely to be encountered again, and we may save some time and effort by writing tests to detect such problems as they occur. This section examines some simple additions to the WL framework designed to detect and report potential layout problems.

Checking for Overdrawn Shadows

One of the easiest tests to add is one that addresses the shadow problem found in the `scale` example in Section 6.1. The following function calls `XtParent()` to access the parent of the widget being tested. The function then retrieves the dimensions of the child and parent, and the thickness of the parent's shadow. If the shadow thickness is greater than zero, the function tests to see if the child's position or size causes it to overlap the parent's shadow. If so, a warning is issued.

```
/**********************************************
 * ShadowClobberTest.c: Detect shadow overlays
 **********************************************/
#include <Xm/Xm.h>
#include <stdio.h>
#include "wlintP.h"

void ShadowClobberTest ( Widget w, ActionType action )
{
    Widget    parent;
    Position  x, y;
    Dimension width, height, pwidth, pheight;
    Dimension shadow;

    if( action == INIT ||
        action == POSTOP )
        return;

   /*
    * Make sure this widget has a managed Motif manager
    * widget as a parent. Shells can have a Motif manager
    * as a parent, but they are not interesting because
    * a shell can only be a popup child, which would not
    * cover any shadows.
    */

    if ( ( parent = XtParent ( w ) ) == NULL )
        return;

    if ( !XmIsManager ( parent ) || XtIsShell ( w ) )
        return;

    if ( !XtIsManaged ( w ) || !XtIsManaged ( parent ) )
        return;

   /*
    * Get the dimensions of parent and child.
    */

    XtVaGetValues ( w,
                    XmNx, &x,  XmNy, &y,
                    XmNwidth,  &width,
                    XmNheight, &height,
                    NULL );
```

```
    XtVaGetValues ( parent,
                    XmNwidth,             &pwidth,
                    XmNheight,            &pheight,
                    XmNshadowThickness, &shadow,
                    NULL );

   /*
    * If the parent has a shadow, see if the child
    * covers any part of it.
    */

    if ( shadow == 0 )
        return;

    if ( x < shadow || y < shadow      ||
         x + width  > pwidth - shadow ||
         y + height > pheight - shadow )
    {
        fprintf ( stderr, "%s covers shadow of parent %s\n",
                          XtName ( w ), XtName ( parent ) );
    }
}
```

This function can be registered as part of the WL framework test suites by adding the following line to the WL library:

```
WLAddTest ( "Checking for shadow overlap",
            ALL, ShadowClobberTest );
```

Installing this function in the WL library and running it over the `scale` program without setting the `Offset` resource produces the output shown in Figure 6.27.

```
scale -xrm "*WLint: on"
Title is unmanaged
Number of unmanaged widgets = 1
label covers shadow of parent form
scale covers shadow of parent form
Scrollbar covers shadow of parent scale
```

Figure 6.27 Output of WL shadow test.

The test for unmanaged widgets reports that the Title widget, which is used internally by the XmScale widget, is unmanaged, although this is expected. The WL output then reports that both the `label` and `scale` widgets are covering the edges of `form` widget, which causes the visual problem we detected in Figure 6.11. The test also reports that the XmScale widget's internal scrollbar widget covers the `scale` widget's shadow. While interesting, this does not appear to be causing any visible problem in this program.

Checking Form Attachments

One area that many programmers have trouble with, as demonstrated by the examples in this chapter, involves form attachments. The XmForm widget is one of the most powerful manager widgets in Motif, but offers many ways to introduce errors. The XmForm widget does report some error conditions, but often in somewhat less than useful ways. For example, the initial error message reported in the `scale` example simply warned of an inconsistency and suggested checking resources. This message does supply the name of the form widget involved, but does not identify the specific error, nor the name of the child involved.

It is not hard to do better than the XmForm widget's built-in checking. One way is to add some tests to the WL framework that use some simple rules of thumb to detect possible errors. For example, the following guidelines provide a starting place for detecting form errors that involve attachments:

1. When using positional attachments (`XmATTACH_POSITION`), the top and bottom position attachments should not specify the same position. The same is true of the left and right attachments. Of course, the top position could be the same as the bottom if different offsets were specified for each attachment. However, this would be an unusual and hard-to-maintain use of positions and offsets, and should probably be handled differently.

2. The position specified in a positional attachment should not be greater than the value of the `XmNfractionBase` resource of the parent XmForm widget.

3. A bottom positional attachment should not be less than the top attachment. A similar rule applies to left and right attachments.

4. In general, when using `XmATTACH_WIDGET`, a widget should not be attached to a widget whose corresponding side is attached to anything else. For example, the left side of the XmScale widget in the scale example was originally attached to the right side of the label, which was

in turn attached to the form. This error is what caused the inconsistent constraint error in the scale example. This rule does not apply to XmATTACH_OPPOSITE_WIDGET.

5. The widget corresponding to any widget attachment must be non-NULL. When using widget attachments, the order in which widgets are created is very important, and easy to get wrong. The XmForm widget does not report such errors, it simply dies with a core dump. This rule includes XmATTACH_OPPOSITE_WIDGET attachments, of course.

These guidelines are not complete, and represent just a few assumptions about how an XmForm widget should be used. For example, the "rubber positioning" mode of the form is not addressed, nor are attachments of type XmATTACH_OPPOSITE_FORM. There are also potential problems with the form widget that cannot easily be detected. For example, the default form attachment is XmATTACH_NONE. Allowing default values to be assigned automatically can be dangerous, because an unintended value could be picked up from a resource file. However, the XmForm widget converts all top and left XmATTACH_NONE attachments to type XmATTACH_FORM with an offset equal to the widget's position. Once the form widget makes this change, there is no reliable way for a test function to detect an original default attachment of type XmATTACH_NONE.

The following function tries to detect violations of the rules of thumb outlined above. Like many of the WL tests, these tests are not conclusive proof that a program has or does not have errors. The function points out possible sources of errors that should be investigated. This function uses auxiliary functions to shorten and simplify some of the tests, which must be performed on each of four sides of each widget.

```
/*******************************************************
 * formattachments.c: Tests for form attachments
 *******************************************************/
#include <Xm/Xm.h>
#include <Xm/Form.h>
#include <stdio.h>
#include "wlintP.h"

static void TestPosition ( Widget        w,
                           int           fractionBase,
                           unsigned char attachment,
                           char         *sideName,
                           int           position )
```

```
{
    /*
     * Make sure any positional attachment is within
     * a reasonable range.
     */

     if ( attachment  == XmATTACH_POSITION &&
          position > fractionBase )
         fprintf ( stderr,
                   "%s's %s position is too large\n",
                   XtName ( w ), sideName );
}

static void TestOppositeAttachment( Widget        w,
                                    unsigned char attachment,
                                    char         *sideName,
                                    Widget        widget )
{
    /*
     * If attached to a widget, make sure the widget
     * has been specified.
     */

     if ( attachment == XmATTACH_OPPOSITE_WIDGET )
     {
         if ( widget == NULL )
             fprintf ( stderr,
                       "%s attached to NULL %s widget\n",
                       XtName ( w ), sideName );
     }
}

static void TestAttachment ( Widget        w,
                             unsigned char attachment,
                             char         *sideName,
                             Widget        widget,
                             char         *otherside )
{
    /*
     * If attached to a widget, make sure the widget
     * has been specified properly, and that the attachment
     * point is not also attached.
     */
     if ( attachment == XmATTACH_WIDGET )
     {
         if ( widget == NULL )
             fprintf ( stderr,
                       "%s attached to a NULL %s widget\n",
                       XtName ( w ), sideName );
```

```
        else
        {
            unsigned char attach;

            XtVaGetValues ( widget,
                            otherside, &attach,
                            NULL );

            if ( attach != XmATTACH_NONE )
            {
                fprintf ( stderr,
                         "%s is attached on the %s to %s ",
                         XtName ( w ), sideName,
                         XtName ( widget ) );
               fprintf ( stderr,
               "whose %s resource is not set to attach_none\n",
                        otherside );
            }
        }
    }
}

/*
 * The WL test function.
 */

void FormAttachmentsTest ( Widget w, ActionType action )
{
    unsigned char top, bottom, left, right;
    int           topPosition,  bottomPosition,
                  leftPosition, rightPosition;
    int           fractionBase;
    Widget        topWidget,  bottomWidget,
                  leftWidget, rightWidget;

    if ( action == INIT ||
         action == POSTOP )
        return;

   /*
    * Be sure this widget has a parent. No shells.
    */

    if ( !XtParent ( w ) || XtIsShell ( w ) )
        return;

   /*
    * See if the parent is a form widget.
    */
```

```
    if ( !XmIsForm ( XtParent ( w ) ) )
        return;

   /*
    * Get all attachment values from the widget and parent.
    */

    XtVaGetValues ( XtParent ( w ),
                    XmNfractionBase, &fractionBase,
                    NULL );

    XtVaGetValues ( w,
                    XmNleftAttachment,   &left,
                    XmNrightAttachment,  &right,
                    XmNtopAttachment,    &top,
                    XmNbottomAttachment, &bottom,
                    XmNtopPosition,      &topPosition,
                    XmNbottomPosition,   &bottomPosition,
                    XmNleftPosition,     &leftPosition,
                    XmNrightPosition,    &rightPosition,
                    XmNtopWidget,        &topWidget,
                    XmNbottomWidget,     &bottomWidget,
                    XmNleftWidget,       &leftWidget,
                    XmNrightWidget,      &rightWidget,
                    NULL );

   /*
    * Check position attachments
    */

    TestPosition ( w, fractionBase, left,
                   "left", leftPosition );
    TestPosition ( w, fractionBase, right,
                  "right", rightPosition );
    TestPosition ( w, fractionBase, top,
                   "top", topPosition );
    TestPosition ( w, fractionBase, bottom,
                   "bottom", bottomPosition );
   /*
    * Check that left/top positions are less than
    * right/bottom positions.
    */

    if ( left  == XmATTACH_POSITION &&
         right == XmATTACH_POSITION &&
         leftPosition >= rightPosition )
        fprintf ( stderr,
                  "invalid left/right positions: %s\n",
                  XtName ( w ) );
```

```

    if ( top    == XmATTACH_POSITION &&
         bottom == XmATTACH_POSITION &&
         bottomPosition <= topPosition )
       fprintf ( stderr,
                 "Invalid top/bottom positions: %s\n",
                 XtName (  w ) );
   /*
    * Test each widget attachment
    */

    TestAttachment ( w, top, "top",
                     topWidget, XmNbottomAttachment );
    TestAttachment ( w, bottom, "bottom",
                     bottomWidget, XmNtopAttachment );
    TestAttachment ( w, left, "left",
                     leftWidget,  XmNrightAttachment );
    TestAttachment ( w, right,"right",
                     rightWidget, XmNleftAttachment );
   /*
    * Test each opposite widget attachment
    */

    TestOppositeAttachment ( w, top,
                             "top",    topWidget );
    TestOppositeAttachment ( w, bottom,
                             "bottom", bottomWidget );
    TestOppositeAttachment ( w, left,
                             "left",   leftWidget );
    TestOppositeAttachment ( w, right,
                             "right",  rightWidget );
}
```

This function can be registered as part of the WL testing framework by adding the following line to the WL library:

```
WLAddTest ( "Checking Form attachments",
            ALL, FormAttachmentsTest );
```

We can test the `FormAttachment()` function by trying it on the original `scale` program, described on page 209. Figure 6.28 shows the output produced when `WLRunTests()` is called just after `XtRealizeWidget()`.

XmForm widget error message

Attachment problem

```
scale -xrm "*WLint: on"
Warning:
    Name: form
    Class: XmForm
    Bailed out of edge synchronization after 10,000 iterations.
   Check for contradictory constraints on the children of this fc

Title is unmanaged
Number of unmanaged widgets = 1
scale is attached on the left to label whose rightAttachment
resource is not set to attach_none
label covers shadow of parent form
scale covers shadow of parent form
Scrollbar covers shadow of parent scale
```

Figure 6.28 Output of WL with the `FormAttachment()` test.

With this test function, the original problem with the `scale` program is quickly and precisely identified.

Form Attachments and Scrolled Windows

The problem demonstrated by the `chooseone` example in Section 6.2 is a fairly common error. Once you have encountered it, it is usually easy to catch, but it takes time nevertheless. This situation is not too hard to detect, so it is useful to be able to warn the programmer quickly about the problem when it occurs. The following WL test function looks for situations in which an XmForm manages an XmScrolledWindow widget, and in which the XmScrolledWindow widget does not appear to have any form attachments specified.

We cannot detect this situation with one hundred percent accuracy, but when a child of a form has no attachments whatsoever, the form widget assigns left and top attachments of `XmATTACH_FORM`, and right and bottom attachments of `XmATTACH_NONE`. In such cases, the widget will most likely have offset values of zero. We can detect this situation by simply looking at the widget hierarchy and widget attachments, and issue a warning if the attachments match this profile.

```
/*************************************************************
 * ScrolledTest.c: Catch attempts to set form attachments
 *                 on a child of a scrolled window created
 *                 by a Motif convenience function.
 *************************************************************/
#include <Xm/Xm.h>
#include <Xm/Form.h>
#include <Xm/ScrolledW.h>
#include <stdio.h>
#include "wlintP.h"

void ScrolledTest ( Widget w, ActionType action )
{
    unsigned char top, bottom, left, right;
    int           topOffset, bottomOffset,
                  leftOffset, rightOffset;
    int x;

    if( action == INIT ||
        action == POSTOP )
        return;

   /*
    * The widget must have some parent to be of interest.
    */

    if ( !XtParent ( w ) )
        return;

   /*
    * See if the situation we are looking for exists. The
    * widget must be a scrolled window widget whose parent
    * is a form widget.
    */

    if ( !( XmIsForm ( XtParent ( w ) ) &&
            XmIsScrolledWindow ( w ) ) )
        return;

   /*
    * Get the form attachments for the scrolled window widget.
    */

    XtVaGetValues ( w,
                    XmNleftAttachment,   &left,
                    XmNrightAttachment,  &right,
                    XmNtopAttachment,    &top,
                    XmNbottomAttachment, &bottom,
                    XmNtopOffset,        &topOffset,
```

```
                    XmNbottomOffset,      &bottomOffset,
                    XmNleftOffset,        &leftOffset,
                    XmNrightOffset,       &rightOffset,
                    NULL );

    /*
     * Look for the default resource values that indicate
     * that no form attachments were set for the scrolled
     * window widget, possibly indicating an error.
     */

    if ( topOffset    == 0 &&
         bottomOffset == 0 &&
         leftOffset   == 0 &&
         rightOffset  == 0 &&
         left         == XmATTACH_FORM &&
         top          == XmATTACH_FORM &&
         bottom       == XmATTACH_NONE &&
         right        == XmATTACH_NONE )
    {
        fprintf ( stderr, "Attachments *may* have been placed\
                  on form grandchild\n");
        fprintf ( stderr, "Form = %s scrolled window = %s\n",
                  XtName ( XtParent ( w ) ), XtName ( w ) );
    }
}
```

Resource Sanity Checks

The previous section mentions that there is a potential danger when leaving an attachment resource set to its default value. Very simply, a program picks up resources from many places. Unless critical resources like form attachments are specified programmatically, there is always a possibility that a user might set a resource in his or her .Xdefaults that can affect your program in ways you did not anticipate. Alternately, there is a possibility that you are relying on a setting in your own resource files during testing without realizing it. If so, a program may work fine on your machine, but fail unexpectedly when installed in a clean environment. Although colors, fonts, and labels should almost never be specified programmatically, resources that control the layout usually should be hard-coded in a program. It is unlikely that any end-user would have a legitimate need to customize a program's layout, or that such customizability could be supported adequately.

There is no conclusive way to tell if positional information like attachment resources have been set programmatically or picked up from a resource file.

There is a heuristic way to determine if a resource has been loaded from a file, however. The idea is to query the resource database for the resource the widget would find, and then to compare that value to the value stored in the widget. It is possible that the widget's resource has been set programmatically, and simply happens to match a value in the resource database, but this test can at least catch some cases.

The `GeometryResourceTest()` function, shown below, looks for situations in which `XmNx`,[1] `XmNy`, `XmNwidth`, `XmNheight`, or various form attachments appear to have been set in a resource file. A warning is issued for any resource value that matches the value retrieved from a file.

This test function requires a way to retrieve a resource relative to a widget, using the same resource database query the widget itself would use. This task can be performed by a simple function, `GetResourceFromDatabase()`. This function depends on `XtGetSubResources()`, an Xt function that retrieves a resource from the application's resource database by combining the requested resource name and class and given widget. The caller must also provide a string that indicates the desired type (`XmRString`, `XmRInt`, and so on), and the size of the desired resource type. Given this information, `GetResourceFromDatabase()` can perform any necessary type conversion between the String format of the database and the desired type.

```
/***************************************************************
 * GetResourceFromDatabase.c: Retrieve a resource relative
 *                            to a widget.
 ***************************************************************/
#include <Xm/Xm.h>
#include <assert.h>
#include <Vk/XtHacks.h>


XtPointer GetResourceFromDatabase ( Widget w,
                                    const  char *name,
                                    const  char *className,
                                    const  char *desiredType,
                                    int    size )
{
```

[1] The `XmNx`, `XmNy`, `XmNwidth` and `XmNheight` resources should almost never be set explicitly in a Motif application. In most cases, the correct way to define a layout involves choosing appropriate manager widgets and hierarchies. Setting explicit positions and hard-coded sizes programmatically or in resource files is generally a bad idea, and should be avoided if at all possible. Sizes and positions could be wrong if labels or fonts change due to customization or localization.

```
    static XtPointer returnValue = NULL;
    XtResource requestResources;

    assert ( size <= sizeof ( XtPointer ) );
    assert ( w );

   /*
    * Fill out the resource structure.
    */

    requestResources.resource_name   = ( char* ) name;
    requestResources.resource_class  = ( char* ) className;
    requestResources.resource_type   = ( char*) desiredType;
    requestResources.resource_size   = size;
    requestResources.default_type    = XmRImmediate;
    requestResources.resource_offset = 0;
    requestResources.default_addr    = ( XtPointer ) NULL;

   /*
    * Retrieve the value relative to the given widget.
    */

    XtGetSubresources(  w,
                        ( XtPointer ) &returnValue,
                        NULL, NULL, &requestResources,
                        1, NULL, 0 );
   /*
    * Different sizes require different treatment.
    */

    if ( !strcmp ( desiredType, XmRString ) )
        return ( returnValue );
    else if ( size == sizeof ( long ) )
        return ( ( XtPointer ) *( long* ) &returnValue );
    else if ( size == sizeof( short ) )
        return ( ( XtPointer ) *( short* ) &returnValue );
    else if (size == sizeof ( char ) )
        return (( XtPointer ) *( char* ) &returnValue );
    else if ( size == sizeof ( XtArgVal ) )
        return ( *( XtPointer* ) &returnValue );

    return ( returnValue );
}
```

The function `GeometryResourceTest()` uses `GetResourceFromDatabase()` to determine if a widget's geometry resource has been specified in a file. The test is not foolproof, but does provide a checklist of resources that should be examined. The function retrieves the resources from the widget under test, and also retrieves each resource from the resource database. If the two values are the same, a warning is issued. Various convenience functions are used to reduce repetition in the tests.

```
/*************************************************************
 * GeometryResourceTest.c: Test for geometry resources
 *                         in resource files.
 *************************************************************/
#include <Xm/Xm.h>
#include <Xm/Form.h>
#include <stdio.h>
#include "wlintP.h"

extern XtPointer GetResourceFromDatabase ( Widget w,
                                           const  char *,
                                           const  char *,
                                           const  char *,
                                           int );

static void PositionTest ( Widget w,
                           int    value,
                           char  *resname )
{
     Position pos;

    /*
     * See if the retrieved position resource matches the
     * widget's current value. Ignore values of zero.
     */

     pos =  ( Position ) GetResourceFromDatabase ( w,
                                                  resname,
                                                  XmCPosition,
                                                  XmRPosition,
                                                  sizeof( Position ) );

     if ( value == pos && pos != 0 )
         fprintf ( stderr,
                   "%s's XmN%s resource *may* come from file\n",
                   XtName ( w ), resname );
}

static void SizeTest ( Widget    w,
                       Dimension value,
                       char     *resname )
{
     Dimension size;

```

```
    /*
     * See if the retrieved dimension resource matches the
     * widget's current value.
     */

     size = ( Dimension ) GetResourceFromDatabase ( w,
                                   resname, XmCDimension,
                                   XmRDimension,
                                   sizeof ( Dimension ) );

     if ( value == size )
         fprintf ( stderr,
                "%s's XmN%s resource *may* come from file\n",
                XtName ( w ), resname );
}


static void AttachmentTest ( Widget        w,
                             unsigned char value,
                             char         *attachment )
{
     unsigned char dbvalue;

    /*
     * Check the form attachment resource
     */

     dbvalue = ( unsigned char ) GetResourceFromDatabase ( w,
                                   attachment,  XmCAttachment,
                                   XmRInt,
                                   sizeof ( unsigned char ) );

     if ( dbvalue == value )
         fprintf ( stderr,
                   "%s's XmN%s resource *may* come from file\n",
                   XtName ( w ), attachment );
}


static void  PositionAttachmentTest ( Widget w,
                                      int    value,
                                      char  *attachment)
{

    /*
     * See if the retrieved position attachment matches the
     * widget's current value.
     */

```

```
     int position = ( int ) GetResourceFromDatabase ( w,
                                                     attachment,
                                                     XmCAttachment,
                                                     XmRInt,
                                                     sizeof ( int ) );
    if ( position == value )
       fprintf ( stderr,
                 "%s's XmN%s resource *may* come from file\n",
                 XtName ( w ), attachment );
}

/*
 * WL test function
 */

void GeometryResourceTest ( Widget w, ActionType action )
{
    unsigned char top, bottom, left, right, dbattachment;
    int           topPosition, bottomPosition,
                  leftPosition, rightPosition, dbposition;
    Widget        topWidget, bottomWidget,
                  leftWidget, rightWidget, dbwidget;
    Position      x, y, dbpos;
    Dimension     width, height, dbsize;

    if( action == INIT ||
        action == POSTOP )
        return;

    if ( !XtParent ( w ) )
        return;

   /*
    * Retrieve all positional resources.
    */

    XtVaGetValues ( w,
                    XmNx,                  &x,
                    XmNy,                  &y,
                    XmNwidth,              &width,
                    XmNheight,             &height,
                    XmNleftAttachment,     &left,
                    XmNrightAttachment,    &right,
                    XmNtopAttachment,      &top,
                    XmNbottomAttachment,   &bottom,
                    XmNtopPosition,        &topPosition,
                    XmNbottomPosition,     &bottomPosition,
                    XmNleftPosition,       &leftPosition,
                    XmNrightPosition,      &rightPosition,
```

```
                        XmNtopWidget,         &topWidget,
                        XmNbottomWidget,      &bottomWidget,
                        XmNleftWidget,        &leftWidget,
                        XmNrightWidget,       &rightWidget,
                        NULL );

   /*
    * Test each widget's x,y,width and height resources.
    */

    PositionTest ( w, x, XmNx );
    PositionTest ( w, y, XmNy );
    SizeTest ( w, width, XmNwidth );
    SizeTest ( w, height, XmNheight );

   /*
    * If the parent is a form widget,
    * test attachment resources
    */

    if ( XmIsForm ( XtParent ( w ) ) )
    {
        AttachmentTest ( w, left,  XmNleftAttachment );
        AttachmentTest ( w, right, XmNrightAttachment );
        AttachmentTest ( w, top,   XmNtopAttachment );
        AttachmentTest ( w, bottom,XmNbottomAttachment );

        if ( left == XmATTACH_POSITION )
            PositionAttachmentTest ( w, leftPosition,
                                        XmNleftPosition );
        if ( right == XmATTACH_POSITION )
            PositionAttachmentTest ( w, rightPosition,
                                        XmNrightPosition );
        if ( top == XmATTACH_POSITION )
            PositionAttachmentTest ( w, topPosition,
                                        XmNtopPosition );
        if ( bottom == XmATTACH_POSITION )
            PositionAttachmentTest ( w, bottomPosition,
                                        XmNbottomPosition );
    }
}
```

The following program can be used to test this WL function. The program specifies some form attachments in the application, but others are specified in a resource file. The program is intended to align three label widgets across the top of an XmForm widget, as shown in Figure 6.29.

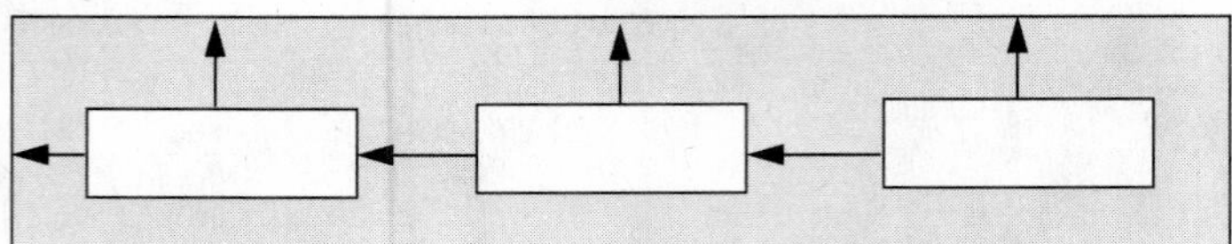

Figure 6.29 Layout of the `labels` example.

The test program can be written as follows:

```
/*************************************************
 * labels.c: Three labels in a form
 *************************************************/
#include <Xm/Xm.h>
#include <Xm/Form.h>
#include <Xm/Label.h>

void main ( int argc, char ** argv )
{
    Widget       shell, form, label1, label2, label3;
    XtAppContext app;
    int          i;

    shell = XtAppInitialize ( &app, "Labels", NULL, 0,
                              &argc, argv, NULL, NULL, 0 );

   /*
    * Create a form to hold the other two widgets
    */

    form = XtCreateManagedWidget ( "form",
                                   xmFormWidgetClass,
                                   shell, NULL, 0 );

    label1 = XtVaCreateManagedWidget ( "label1",
                              xmLabelWidgetClass, form,
                              XmNleftAttachment,  XmATTACH_FORM,
                              XmNrightAttachment, XmATTACH_NONE,
                              NULL );

    label2 = XtVaCreateManagedWidget ( "label2",
                             xmLabelWidgetClass, form,
                             XmNleftWidget,      label1,
                             XmNleftAttachment, XmATTACH_WIDGET,
                             XmNrightAttachment,XmATTACH_NONE,
                             NULL );
```

```

    label3 = XtVaCreateManagedWidget ( "label3",
                           xmLabelWidgetClass, form,
                           XmNleftWidget,      label2,
                           XmNleftAttachment,  XmATTACH_WIDGET,
                           XmNrightAttachment, XmATTACH_NONE,
                           NULL );

    XtRealizeWidget ( shell );

    XtAppMainLoop ( app );
}
```

The application's app-defaults file contains the following resources, which apply to the label widgets in this program.

```
*XmLabel*topAttachment:    attach_form
*XmLabel*bottomAttachment: attach_none
```

Assume that the user's .Xdefaults file also contains a few resources, which include the following:

```
*label1*topAttachment: attach_position
*topPosition: 25
*XmLabel*bottomAttachment: attach_form
```

These might be resources meant for some other program, but which just happen to be set globally.

Figure 6.30 shows the results of running the test program.

```
% labels -xrm "*WLint: on"
label1's XmNrightAttachment resource *may* come from file
label1's XmNtopAttachment resource *may* come from file
label1's XmNbottomAttachment resource *may* come from file
label1's XmNtopPosition resource *may* come from file
label2's XmNrightAttachment resource *may* come from file
label2's XmNtopAttachment resource *may* come from file
label2's XmNbottomAttachment resource *may* come from file
label3's XmNrightAttachment resource *may* come from file
label3's XmNtopAttachment resource *may* come from file
label3's XmNbottomAttachment resource *may* come from file
```

Figure 6.30 Output of position tests.

This test shows that the program depends on some geometry resources being set in a resource file. Furthermore, in this example, the user's .Xdefaults file interferes with the intended layout of the program by overriding some of the resources in the app-defaults file.

Notice that not all the warnings in Figure 6.30 indicate errors, although most do. For example, the `XmNrightAttachment` resource of each label just happens to be set to `XmATTACH_NONE`, which Motif represents using the value zero. Unfortunately zero is also the value returned by `XtGetSubResources()` if no resource is found. Therefore, there is no way to be sure whether this value was truly set in a resource file, or if the widget's default value just coincides with no value being set in the resource database. We could enhance the WL function to provide some indication of the probability that a value is really set in a resource database, or just ignore all values of zero as likely false alarms.

6.4 Conclusion

This chapter concludes the discussion on debugging techniques by presenting some ideas on how to debug layout problems. Layout problems can be difficult to solve because there are few tools for mapping what we see on the screen to the algorithms that produce the layout. Even with tools like XtGeo, the layout algorithms may be so complex that it is difficult to trace the process in any useful way. However, by applying all the tools available, it is usually possible to isolate and fix visual bugs.

7

Performance Considerations for Motif Applications

Once a program works correctly, with no errors, the next area of concern for many programmers is performance. This chapter lays some ground work for discussions about how to achieve maximum performance when writing programs using Motif. Later chapters present examples and discuss specific tools and techniques for measuring and improving performance.

It is extremely important for interactive applications to perform efficiently, because users perform tasks by directly manipulating these programs while they are running. If a program does not respond to user input immediately, and consistently, the interaction will be clumsy and awkward.

The desired performance characteristics of interactive applications and the demands these applications place on a system are substantially different from those of non-interactive applications. Programs that run in batch mode, (compilers for example), typically start, execute in a relatively sequential manner, and then exit when their tasks are completed. Although there is always a desire for such programs to run as fast as possible, users generally start these programs and do another task while the program runs. For such programs, the total time required to execute the program is the primary concern.

Interactive applications differ in several significant ways. First, interactive applications may run almost indefinitely, so measuring the total time required to execute a program has little meaning. However, users expect to have a more or less continuous interaction with these applications, so the responsiveness of the system is critical. For example, consider Motif's 3D button illusion. If an XmPushButton widget cannot respond to a mouse button press and change its appearance almost instantaneously, the illusion that the user is pressing a real button will be broken. Similarly, menus, dialogs and secondary windows must appear quickly to give a user the impression that the system is responding to his or her commands. One of the most important performance characteristics of an interactive application is a predictable correspondence between user actions and the program's responses.

In fact, the most useful performance goal for an interactive application has little to do with raw measurements or execution times. For an interactive application, it is more effective to optimize the time required for a user to complete a particular task than to focus on traditional measurements such as CPU time, I/O, and so on. In this respect, improving the performance of a Motif application often involves user interface and "usability" issues at least as much as it concerns efficient use of machine resources.

With this in mind, it is important not to lose sight of the real goal as we consider various characteristics of Motif performance in the following chapters. It is easy to get bogged down in numbers and measurements and forget the user. For example, programmers who are concerned with X/Motif performance often place a heavy emphasis on reducing the number of events and requests sent to the X server, and indeed later chapters discuss this aspect of application performance in detail. However, reducing the time it takes a user to perform a specific task is more important than reducing server requests. In some cases, providing users with a more efficient, enjoyable and productive environment may even increase the number of server requests, CPU utilization, and so on.

Of course, all other things being equal, a program that runs more efficiently is better than one that does not. Consistent, snappy performance is an important characteristics of a program that is pleasant to use. A program that has inconsistent or sluggish response characteristics is almost always irritating to users. A program that uses fewer machine resources also allows other applications in the user's environment to perform better.

7.1 General Performance Tuning and Analysis

In some ways, Motif programs are no different than other applications when it comes to performance. Just as a Motif program can exhibit bugs that have nothing to do with Motif, a Motif program can also have poor performance characteristics that have nothing to do with the user interface.

To many programmers, performance tuning primarily means reducing the number of instructions that must be executed by an application. Books that discuss code tuning techniques usually contain examples of minimizing computations that occur inside loops, eliminating loops, eliminating common expressions in calculations, using inexpensive operations like addition instead of multiplication, and so on. One can also improve the performance of a program by replacing a poor algorithm, like a linear search, with a faster approach, like a hash table.

Most interactive programs contain some modules that have traditional algorithmic characteristics. For these portions of a program, it may be appropriate to apply these techniques to produce more efficient code. Basic UNIX performance measurement tools, like `prof`, can sometimes help with this task.

Because a user views an interactive program through its user interface, the user (and perhaps the programmer) will often blame the user interface for any performance problems that appear. Of course, the user interface is just one part of a typical application. Programmers should always be sure that any performance difficulties they may encounter are not being caused by the application-specific parts of a program before trying to tune the user interface.

For example, it is not at all unusual to encounter a Motif application that contains buttons that do not respond to user input for long periods of time. A normal Motif application can easily respond to input within these buttons, and provide instantaneous response. If a Motif XmPushButton widget does not respond, it is probably because the application is not handling events at that time. Usually, this is because the application is busy doing something else, and unable to process events. To allow the user interface to respond, any other tasks performed by the program must also be handled efficiently, to allow the application to return to the event loop as quickly as possible.

Although all programs, including Motif programs, can suffer from fundamental performance problems such as those mentioned in this section, Motif applications have some unique characteristics. This book focuses on those aspects of performance that are unique to Motif, on the assumption that you are already familiar with fundamental performance issues. There are several books that discuss basic techniques for creating efficient programs. If you need information on general performance issues, the following sources may be useful places to start:

Books that discuss basic performance tuning

Bently, Jon, *Writing Efficient Programs*, Prentice Hall, 1982.

Dowd, Kevin, *High Performance Computing*, O'Reilly & Associates, 1993.

McConnell, Steve, *Code Complete*, Microsoft Press, 1993.

Smith, Connie U., *Performance Engineering of Software Systems*, Addison-Wesley 1990.

7.2 The X Environment and Performance

Before examining an application's performance characteristics, it is important to understand how various aspects of the user's UNIX and X environment can affect an application's performance. Obviously, CPU speed has a significant effect on performance, but there are other factors as well. Although many factors that affect performance may be beyond the control of the application programmer, it is important to take the time to understand some of the issues. Because certain characteristics of a user's environment can affect performance, a user might not see the performance you believe your application can achieve.

The following are just a few of the factors that can affect the performance of a Motif application, but that are generally beyond a programmer's control:

- **Basic system performance**. Obviously, CPU speed, virtual memory characteristics, disk access speed, graphics display speed, the amount of memory available, and other system characteristics affect the performance of all applications. These are, for the most part, beyond the control of the application programmer. If you know your application requires certain minimum features or hardware performance characteristics, it is best to set the user's expectations in advance.
- **System load**. It is always possible to run more applications on a multitasking system than the system can handle. A program that starts up

instantly when a system is relatively unused may take a very long time to start upon a heavily loaded system. If a program exhibits poor performance, be sure you understand the state of the entire system at the time of the problem.

- **Server speed**. Different implementations of the X server may have different performance characteristics. However, it is usually difficult to say categorically that one server is "faster" than another. One server may be much faster at creating windows but much slower at drawing lines. Another may be faster at copying small pixmaps, but slower at manipulating large pixmaps. There are benchmark programs that can be used to measure the characteristics of an X sever, but this is the domain of those few programmers who support X servers. This information is rarely useful to an application programmer. Unless your user base is limited to a specific X server implementation and a specific hardware configuration, it is almost impossible to take advantage of such information.
- **Transport mechanism**. Many systems support more than one way to connect to the X server. For example, on a machine named "gizmo," setting the `DISPLAY` environment variable to `gizmo:0` causes applications to connect to the server using a network connection. Setting `DISPLAY` to `unix:0`, `:0`, or `localhost:0` causes the application to connect to the local display via UNIX-domain sockets, which is a more direct mechanism. Some systems may support shared memory connections, which may be faster yet.

  If an application is connected to a remote display, other system characteristics are involved. The performance is obviously dependent on the speed of the network connection as well as the characteristics of the two machines involved. Sometimes, the fact that the X server is executing on a different machine than the client can actually improve performance, in spite of a potentially slower network connection because multiple CPUs can be used.
- **User customizations**. Users can use various resource files to customize applications. Large resource files may have some effect on application performance due to the number of resources that must be loaded, and contents of the files can also contribute. For example, if a user configures a program to use many fonts, the program will request the server load those fonts, which may have an impact on the application's performance. Some fonts may also require longer to load than others.

Tuning your system and X environment for greatest efficiency is a topic worthy of a separate discussion. However, because users, not programmers control the environment in which a program runs, we will ignore most of these issues in this book. The following sources may be useful to those who would like more information on how the user's environment can affect performance:

Information about tuning your X environment

Niall Mansfield, *The Joy of X*, Addison Wesley, 1993.

Art Mulder, *How To Maximize the Performance of X*, monthly posting to comp.windows.x newsgroup.

7.3 Code Tuning vs. Architecture

For most contemporary, interactive programs, traditional code tuning techniques designed to reduce the number of instructions a program executes are not directly relevant, except in the broadest sense. Traditional tuning techniques are best when applied to programs that are computationally intensive. Tuning a typical Motif application tends be an exercise in maximizing the throughput and responsiveness of a system architecture. As discussed in Chapter 1, a Motif program is really only one small part of a multi-process system. When attempting to improve the performance of such an application, one cannot ignore the other components of the system by applying code-tuning techniques to just one process.

It is common, when examining a Motif application using tools meant for traditional performance tuning (See Chapter 8) to conclude that the program is not doing anything. Often, the program itself is not consuming CPU cycles, yet certain operations may be unacceptably slow. The missing time may be accounted for by looking at the X server, the window manager, the inter-process communication mechanism, and even the operating system. No X program can perform any operation that involves interacting with the user by itself. Instead, each program works in tandem with the X server by sending requests and processing events. Therefore, any attempt to understand and improve performance must consider the entire architecture of the system. In addition to the CPU time spent in the process, it is important to consider the speed of the connection to the X server, the server's ability to handle certain requests, the number of context switches between the program and the server, and so on.

Because there is such a close connection between any X program and the X server, it is important to follow the architectural model that X was designed to support. For example, it is important to not circumvent the event-driven model provided by X. Applications written for different systems and then ported to X may have originally used different models. These applications sometimes perform poorly when they are ported without adapting the architecture to that expected by X.

Xt was designed to work well with X, and it also has a specific architectural model that applications should follow as closely as possible. Performance problems and many types of bugs can easily occur in applications that attempt to force a different model on an Xt or Motif application. Just as X applications are expected to be event driven, all Xt applications should use a main event loop, and register callbacks, action procedures, event handlers, and so on to handle input. Xt provides mechanisms for receiving input from other sources, implementing background tasks, and performing repeated operations. If a program implements these features as expected by Xt, Xt can help the program work most efficiently. Problems often arise from attempting to go around these mechanisms in some way.

Let's consider a very simple example of how a misuse of the X and Xt model can degrade performance. Suppose we need to post a dialog in a program that is about to start a lengthy task. The dialog is to be used to inform the user that the program will be unable to respond for a while. We have already looked at such a program in Chapter 4. We know that simply calling `XtManageChild()` to display the dialog before entering the busy state does not work well. The dialog is unlikely to appear until the program returns to the event loop. We also know that the program needs to wait for the dialog to appear by entering a secondary event loop and watching for a `MapNotify` event.

Inefficient example

The following function shows one possible way to implement such a loop:

```
void WaitForDialog ( Widget w )
{
    XtAppContext app = XtWidgetToApplicationContext ( w );
    XEvent       event;
    Boolean      mapped = FALSE;

```

```
            /*
             * Poor use of X and Xt model.
             */
Wrong!      while (  !mapped  )
            {
Wrong!          if ( XtAppPending ( app ) )
                {
                    XtAppNextEvent ( app, &event );
                    XtDispatchEvent ( &event );
                    if ( event.type == MapNotify )
                        mapped = TRUE;
                }
            }
        }
```

Bad approach!

This function is intended (incorrectly) to accomplish several things. First, the loop is meant to run as quickly as possible. The test to terminate the `while` loop is very cheap. Furthermore, the program does not waste time blocking in `XtAppNextEvent()` unless there is actually an event to read. The overall goal is to find out as quickly as possible when the dialog appears on the screen.

Unfortunately, the above code segment is based on erroneous assumptions, and can be very inefficient because it does not allow the application and the X server to work together as a system. The function does work, in the sense that it returns after the dialog is displayed. However, this loop consumes a large percentage of the machine's CPU cycles between events. `XtAppPending()` returns very quickly, and is called repeatedly and rapidly until an event arrives in the queue.

Because the program consumes so many CPU resources, the X server may not be able to get its share to perform the task the program is waiting for. The program won't exit the loop until the dialog appears, but the X server and window manager must fight for a chance to display the dialog because the loop is loading down the machine. To get the dialog up as quickly as possible, we must change the program to give up control and allow the X server to have its share of machine resources.

Better approach

To work with the system instead of against it, this function should request the X server to provide a service, and then relinquish the CPU by calling `XtAppNextEvent()`. `XtAppNextEvent()` blocks until an event is available on the event queue, which allows other processes, including the X server, to use the CPU. The server performs the work, and then notifies the client that it has completed the task. An implementation of the `WaitForDialog()` function that makes more efficient use of the X architecture can be written as follows:

```
void WaitForDialog ( Widget w  )
{
    XtAppContext app = XtWidgetToApplicationContext ( w );
    XEvent        event;
    Boolean       mapped = FALSE;

   /*
    * Better use of X and Xt model.
    */

    while ( !mapped )
    {
       /*
        * Block while waiting for server
        */

        XtAppNextEvent ( app, &event );
        XtDispatchEvent ( &event );
        if ( event.type == MapNotify )
            mapped = TRUE;
    }
}
```

Block while X server works

7.4 Performance Characteristics of Motif Applications

There are usually two primary areas of concern when considering the performance of Motif-based applications. The first is *start-up time*, which is the amount of time required for a newly executed program to be ready to interact with the user. It is often appropriate to treat the time required to display secondary windows as start-up time, because many of the issues are similar, from a user's perspective, at least.

The second area is *run-time* performance, which involves measuring and improving the responsiveness of an application or an entire system once a program is running. The most important criteria in either case is user perception, which can be difficult to characterize because perception may change from user to user, and from task to task. Users may have some preconceived notion of how long a given task should take, and may be more willing to wait for some operations to be performed than others.

For applications that have difficulty achieving adequate performance, programmers can use user perception to their advantage. If a user can see that a program is responding, the user will generally be more patient. Simple techniques such as animated busy cursors, periodic messages that report the program's status, and so on, can help reduce the impact of an otherwise slow operation.

Basic principles of good user interface design can also help improve runtime performance, or at least the user's perception of performance. For example, the *Motif Style Guide* suggests that menu items that post dialogs or display other windows should have ellipsis after the item's label. This tells the user that a new window will be displayed if this item is chosen, which serves as a hint that a relatively major operation is involved, compared to other menu commands. By setting user expectations before a command is issued, the user's perception of performance can be improved.

Providing accelerators for frequently used operations can also improve the user's ability to use an application quickly. Users may feel that a program's performance is inadequate if the program requires long sequences of repetitive user actions to accomplish a task. Providing expert modes and other short-cuts can improve a program's performance by making fewer demands on the interface while simultaneously improving the user's ability to use the program effectively.

Most simple, well-written applications should have little problem providing adequate performance when handling basic Motif interactions like pushing buttons and displaying dialogs. The most difficult part of writing a good interactive application usually involves the challenges of performing useful tasks while staying responsive. Real applications have real work to do, which can sometimes interfere with an application's ability to respond to user input at all times. Such applications must be designed carefully to maximize performance and responsiveness.

7.5 Psychological Aspects of Performance Tuning

Whether you are trying to design a new application to have good performance or trying to tune an existing application, it will eventually be necessary to measure the performance of an application to understand how well you have succeeded. Chapter 8 describes some simple tools and techniques that can be used to measure performance, and the rest of this book provides many examples. However, before attempting to measure the performance of any application, there are less intangible aspects of the performance analysis process that should be considered. This section discusses how certain human psychological characteristics can affect the performance tuning process.

Setting Goals

One of the first steps that should be taken before beginning to tune an application is to establish a set of performance goals. Goals are sometimes difficult to set because it is difficult to predict what performance characteristics will be acceptable, particularly for an application that has not yet been written. (See "How Fast is Fast?" on page 271.)

However, it is important to establish performance goals to define a fixed target. Without concrete goals, it is easy to fall into traps in which you arbitrarily decide that something is "fast enough" with no data to verify the claim. Alternately, you may waste time trying to squeeze the last ounce of performance out of a program when the performance is already within acceptable limits. When setting goals, it is important to be specific. The goals should include the hardware configuration, software environment, techniques used to make measurements, and specific tasks being performed. Without a fixed frame of reference, it is difficult to make comparisons. Without valid comparisons, it is impossible to know if any given change had a positive effect, negative effect, or no effect at all.

Setting concrete goals also helps eliminate some undesirable consequences of user perception. Typically, as programmers work on an application, they lose perspective on the features, performance, and other characteristics of the program. Over time, frequent users become "trained," either to avoid operations that don't work as expected, or to ignore certain deficiencies. While you probably won't mind if your users learn to overlook certain deficiencies, developing such blind spots yourself can prevent you from noticing and fixing performance problems (or bugs) while the program is under development.

Expectations and beliefs can influence everything from the initial software design to the way a user perceives the finished application's performance. If you have simply heard that "all X/Motif programs are big and slow," you may make assumptions that will affect your judgement not only during implementation and design, but when measuring performance. Solid goals, accompanied by well-designed, repeatable tests can provide hard evidence that is more useful than such subjective opinions, so you can achieve the best possible performance.

Of course, it is important to set goals that are realistic and achievable in the environment in which your program will be running. This requires an understanding of what is possible and what is not, as well as what you can control and what you cannot. For example, if a Motif-based "hello world" program requires a quarter of a second to start-up on your system, it is unlikely that you can achieve a 1/10th second start-up time for a Motif-based word processor, which is much more complex.

It is also unlikely that you can guarantee consistent start-up times on a multi-tasking multi-user system. There are too many variables, ranging from background daemons to demands on the system from other users, to ensure a consistent minimum start-up time. Expecting the same consistent performance in a UNIX environment that might be achievable on a single-tasking personal computer of similar power is unrealistic, and only leads to frustration. In a multi-tasking environment, the performance of any single application is deliberately compromised in favor of the benefits offered by multi-tasking.

Measuring What You Want to See and Other Dangers

There are several intrinsic problems with measuring the performance of any application. The first is the well known fact that by the act of observing, the observer changes the behavior of the entity being observed. Even adding a print statement to a program changes the execution pattern of the program slightly. Adding system calls to measure elapsed time adds overhead and has some affect on performance. All commercially-available tools for measuring performance alter the performance characteristics of the program being measured. It is impossible to gather data without affecting the program, or at least the environment in which the program is run. At best, the effect can be minimized or at least recognized.

Chapter 8 describes several techniques for measuring elapsed time in a Motif program. To introduce some consistency and to be sure all measurements include the time required for the server to process requests, these techniques sometimes involve flushing the event queue, receiving and processing events, and so on. These techniques have the potential to alter the behavior of a program dramatically. (See the discussion in Chapter 4, starting on page 170, for example.) This intrusion does not usually affect the measurement process, but it is important to be aware of potential consequences.

Another challenge when trying to understand and improve performance involves the mind-set of the person performing measurements and experiments. Users are not the only ones who are influenced by perception. Programmers must beware of various psychological factors that can lead to mistaken assumptions, and erroneous measurements. For example, measurements can be affected by optimism on the part of a programmer. Suppose a programmer believes he or she has identified the source of a performance problem, and has rewritten a portion of the code to fix the problem. At this point, the programmer *wants* to believe the problem has been found. The programmer may unintentionally influence the measurement process to prove what he or she wants to believe.

Any preconceived notion can be dangerous. Without meaning to, programmers can easily design experiments to "prove" what they expect to see. In addition, most programs are affected by so many variables that it is easy to misinterpret the results of any measurement. It is important to keep an open mind during experiments and measurements, and to look for unexpected factors that might contribute to the behavior being observed.

It is also important not to leap to conclusions not directly supportable by the tests. For example, one experiment in Chapter 10 shows that a particular combination of widgets and gadgets produces a larger program than using widgets alone. From this, one might leap to the conclusion that "gadgets are bigger and slower than widgets", but this is not supported by the measurements. The test only shows size measurements for a specific program with a specific combination of widgets and gadgets. Other combinations might produce different results, and speed is not even considered in that experiment.

7.6 How Fast is Fast?

The previous section discusses the importance of setting goals. The obvious questions prompted by this discussion include "What is a reasonable goal?" and "How fast is fast enough?" There are, unfortunately, no universal answers to these questions. You may have certain goals that are driven by needs of the application you are building, but beyond that, the answer depends on many factors.

It is well known that human perception has interesting weaknesses that can be exploited. For example, motion pictures depend on the fact that the human eye cannot distinguish individual images, when displayed sequentially at a rate of about 1/30th of a second. It has been shown that the human eye can only distinguish between limited shades of grey. And everyone requires a discrete amount of time to respond to any event. These human limitations provide a window within which programs can perform tasks without forcing the user to wait.

For example, various studies [Foley82] established long ago that users perceive actions that occur in a short amount of time (typically 0.1 to 0.2 seconds) as instantaneous.[1] The exact time varies with the task and user expectations. For example, users may accept a a slightly longer time, perhaps 0.3 second or less, for large-scale user interface actions. This applies to major events, like displaying or moving windows, popping up dialogs, and so on. It obviously does not apply to continuous events like tracking the mouse cursor or typing. For purposes of discussion, this book assumes that an application should be able to start-up and respond to significant user commands in less than 0.3 second.

However, all applications are different, and the real test of performance is user satisfaction. For example, start-up time is often considered a critical aspect of application performance. For many applications, this is true. Users expect to start a desktop utility like a calculator quickly, use it, and dismiss it. On the other hand, in a multi-tasking environment, many applications are left running most of the time. For example, a mail program might be started when a user logs in and left running as long as the user remains logged in. Because the program is always running, the initial start-up is less important than its interactive response time and its impact on the system while it is running. The program could require seconds or even minutes to start up without annoying the user under normal circumstances.

Another way to set performance goals is to consider other similar applications in the user's environment. While establishing ideal, aggressive benchmarks without regard to the limitations of other programs may be a noble goal, it is often sufficient to be no slower than similar programs. While faster is always be better in theory, settling for "fast enough" allows time to work on other characteristics of a program.

Another way to decide what is "fast enough" is to consider the task a user will perform with your program. If your program allows a user to perform a task that simply cannot be performed any other way, performance is probably

[1] We can get a better idea of what these times mean by considering the time required to enter text. If an extremely fast typist could enter text at 120 words per minute (600 characters per minute), a program would need to be able to process the input and display each character in 0.1 second to keep from falling behind.

not even an issue (until someone else writes a competing program that runs faster!) If your program allows a user to perform a function that was previously done some other way (another program, manually, etc.), then the true test is whether your program allows that task to be completed quickly enough to justify the cost of your program. Of course, few conscientious programmers want to produce programs that are only marginally adequate.

Because the purpose of this book is to provide information that can be used to make Motif programs run as fast as possible, the following chapters cannot fall back on the "fast enough" argument. For the examples in this book, we will set an explicit goal that all applications should be able to provide a response in 0.3 second, at all times. We must keep in mind, of course, that this figure is highly dependent on the machine and environment in which the measurements are made. On some machines, this goal is simply not achievable. On some very high-performance (and expensive) machines, achieving such a goal might be trivial. Section 7.8 describes the system used for the measurements in this book.

Performance of any application can vary widely from experiment to experiment even on the same machine, due to variations that are inherent in the multi-tasking environment. In fact, the start-up goal should be stated more clearly: It should be *possible* for an application to respond in 0.3 second or less under ideal circumstances. This time cannot be established as a worst case goal, and in fact it would be difficult to specify any worst case goal. It is always possible for a multi-tasking machine to be so loaded down by other processes that any goal we might set would not be achievable.

7.7 Alternate Views of Performance Tuning

Before discussing specific ways to improve the performance of Motif applications, it is worthwhile to consider some alternate views of performance measurement and tuning. System and application performance is often a "hot" issue, and discussions can sometimes turn into intense debates. There is a great deal of what might be called "conventional wisdom" about application and system performance that sometimes makes it difficult to distinguish fact from fiction. As with most folklore, there is sometimes at least a grain of truth behind various beliefs, although it is easy to mis-apply or over generalize any given statement. When tuning, it is important to not be blinded by beliefs, rumors, or even someone else's experience. Measure what your program is doing, and then question your own measurements. Even measurements and statistics can lie, unless evaluated carefully.

The following sections discuss some commonly held ideas about performance.

Improving Performance with Faster Hardware

A common developer's response to complaints about a program that performs poorly is to tell the user to "upgrade to a faster machine". While such statements are often ridiculed as a software developer's excuse for writing inefficient code, there may be some justification for this recommendation. Hardware prices continue to drop at a phenomenal rate, seemingly just as fast as CPU speeds increase. Increased productivity might very well compensate for the cost of a faster system, and a new machine may be substantially cheaper than the cost of the manpower needed to improve the performance of the software. Of course, even if buying new hardware would be the ideal answer, in many cases, your users will simply not have the budget.

A software developer's responsibility should be to make a program run as efficiently as possible, within reasonable limits, and to inform the user of the minimum hardware and system requirements to run the software adequately. Clearly, it is to your benefit to be able to run on the least expensive hardware possible.

Features or Performance?

It is not unusual to hear programmers decry the continual growth in size and decline of a program's performance[2] due to "creeping featurism." Typically, a program is relatively small and lightweight when it begins its lifecycle. If the program is successful, users begin to request new features and other improvements. Eventually, the developer adds so many features that the once simple, efficient program becomes large, slow, and loaded with obscure features.

One explanation for this phenomena can be found by properly defining the meaning of "performance" as it applies to software. The goal of a good program is to maximize the *user's* performance. In many cases, the engineering time spent shaving a few seconds off the start-up of an application, or improving the time required to display a dialog or redraw an image, might

2 In other programmers' programs, of course!

be better spent adding a new feature that would save a user hours instead of seconds.

It is also important to realize that complaints that a program is "slow" and has "too many features", may actually mean that the program is "awkward" and "difficult to use," which are different issues. In some situations, designing a more usable interface may be more effective that improving performance, assuming the performance is within tolerable limits.

When (and If) to Tune

There are several distinct schools of thought on when performance tuning should be scheduled during software development. The first holds that tuning should never be done until there is a problem. This idea is based in part on the "80/20" rule, which, applied to performance, states that a typical application spends 80% of its time executing 20% of the code. Only after a program is finished and measurements are taken, is it possible to identify problem areas. These few small problems can them be fixed quickly and easily. This idea is also based on the adage "If it isn't broken, don't fix it". There is no reason to spend time squeezing the last ounce of performance from a routine that does not cause any perceptible performance problem.

Another school of thought says that performance must be included as a core part of the entire development effort, starting with the design stage. Often, performance problems are caused by a poorly designed architecture, mistaken assumptions or other fundamental aspects of the design. In such cases, it is not usually possible to tune the problem later because doing so would require a complete redesign and re-implementation. Such problems sometimes show up as a system that is generally slow, but with no clear bottleneck. In other cases, the bottleneck is clear, but the problem is so fundamental to the design that it cannot be changed.

Another group says that you should never tune at all because tuning tends to produce unmaintainable code, and may not even achieve the intended goal. Tuning is often done by cutting corners or making certain assumptions to reduce the amount of work that must be performed. Such changes are always risky, and can easily introduce bugs. We have already discussed the argument that users may benefit more from new features than from better performance. If tuning does not add significant value, and simultaneously introduces bugs, or makes maintenance even more time-consuming, it may not be worthwhile.

Tuning the Underlying Systems

Another frequently heard opinion is that applications do not need to be tuned because underlying software is the real cause of any problems. If we consider Motif, Xt, Xlib, the X server, UNIX, the compiler, and so on, it is easy to believe that any or all of these are responsible for any performance problems observed in an application. It also makes sense to tune the lowest layers of software, because better performance at this level means better performance for all applications. Of course, most suppliers of these systems do strive to provide the best possible performance.

However, one cannot place the entire burden of improving performance on the underlying software. From a practical perspective, one cannot escape the need to focus on application-level performance. Even if the lower layers of software were greatly improved, it would always be possible to write a program that uses these layers inefficiently. The following chapters provide many examples that demonstrate this fact. Even more to the point, the only part of the system you, as an application programmer control directly is your application. You can hope that the engineers who supply your platform provide better and better performance with each release, but you can actually do something about the way your application uses or misuses the libraries it depends on.

Striking a Balance

So, which of the often conflicting opinions described in the previous sections are correct? The "right" answer, clearly, is that all are true to some extent, and none are true all the time. Programers must make trade-offs between features and performance, between time spent designing for performance versus waiting to see if a problem even exists, and so on.

In many cases, the answer depends on the type of program and the type of user. For many programs, there is a minimum performance threshold that must be met. Above that threshold, the program is uncomfortable to use. If a program cannot meet that requirement, performance considerations outweigh all other issues. Once a program meets minimum requirements, performance ceases to be an important issue compared to features, cost, quality, time to market, and so on.

On the other hand, users also have a set of minimum expectations with regard to features, below which you cannot slip. The expected set of features is continually changing as new products emerge. Unless you have the minimum features a user needs, no amount of speed, or even quality and cost, will help. For example, today it is almost unthinkable to produce a program without a graphical interface. People sometimes complain about the slowness of programs with graphical interfaces. Yet, if application performance is truly the most important characteristic of a program, replacing the graphical interface with a character-based interface certainly provides a solution. No one takes such drastic steps because sheer *application* speed is simply not the only, nor the most important, consideration.

The issue of when to tune depends to some extent on the type of program involved. The performance of a Motif program depends heavily on the application's architecture. Therefore, it may be beneficial to consider performance, at least to a certain extent, as early as possible. Applications, or parts of applications, that tend to be more computationally intensive are often better candidates for the 80/20 approach to tuning, assuming that the basic architecture is reasonably efficient to begin with.

Having described some of the alternate views and potential pitfalls of tuning, the remainder of this book assumes you have decided to spend some time improving the performance of your Motif applications. The ideas, techniques, and information described in the following chapters should be helpful whether you decide to plan for performance from the beginning, or tune later. It may even help you decide when it is simply appropriate to tell the user to buy more hardware. The goal is to show how to obtain information about a program's performance and to make the interface as efficient as possible. What you do with the information is a decision only you can make.

7.8 Reference Systems and Tests

Any discussion of performance is necessarily dependent on the system and environment used to run the software being examined. Although X allows applications to be written in a portable manner, it in no way guarantees consistent performance between different platforms. It is important to understand the environment in which an application is expected to run and to plan accordingly to achieve adequate performance in that environment.

It is also important to understand that any statement regarding absolute or relative performance of any application may only be valid with respect to a particular machine or software environment. Performance is subject to variations from system to system, and even from test to test on the same system.

In spite of these challenges, there is much to be learned from looking at performance characteristics, and to do that, specific tests must be made on specific systems. Accordingly, the following chapters use performance measurements to compare the effects of various implementation techniques. All measurements reported in this book are based on experiments run in one of two environments. These are referred to in chapters 8-12 as System A and System B. The characteristics of these systems are:

System A: A Silicon Graphics IRIS Indy workstation, with a MIPS R4000 processor, 64 Megabytes of RAM, and an 8 bit color display, running Silicon Graphic's 5.2 release of the IRIX operating system. All tests were performed locally, with the applications running on the same machine as the X server.

System B: An outdated NCD monochrome X terminal, connected to the system above. Therefore, tests made using System B differ from those made using System A only in the X server and display hardware used.

All examples in this book are based on Motif 1.2.3 and X11R5. All examples are written in ANSI C and, except for the debugging examples, compiled using full optimization, unless otherwise noted. In addition, all examples were linked with shared library implementations of the X, Xt and Motif libraries.

During each test, every effort was made to maintain a stable and repeatable environment. Load on the system was kept to a minimum, but realistic, level. Typically, several other applications were running during tests, including a mail program, various terminal emulators, an editor, and so on. Care was taken to avoid running large compilations, or other time-consuming tasks that could interfere with the measurements. All experiments were performed while running Motif's `mwm` window manager. Unless otherwise noted, there was no .Xdefaults file, no `RESOURCE_MANAGER` property on the root window, and no application resource file for any test cases.

All programs were executed many times and attempts were made to understand and eliminate significant variations between tests. The times reported for various examples in later chapters are averages of multiple tests. For each reported measurement, the experiment was performed twelve times. The single highest and single lowest measurements were rejected, and the remaining ten times were averaged. This process eliminates most of the effects of paging, to produce the most consistent results (See Section 9.6 and Section 10.4 for discussions of the impact of paging on an application's performance.)

Because performance is so dependent on the underlying hardware and software environment, the various programs discussed in this book were also tested on several other platforms. This book does not report the times measured on any of these platforms, because the purpose of this book is not to compare the performance characteristics of different vendors' machines. The reason for measuring performance on these other machines was to be sure the information reported in this book was not skewed by using only one vendor's environment.

For example, one could imagine that a particular implementation of the X server could be sufficiently different that a technique that improves performance on one platform could make the performance worse on another. In general, the measurements on these other platforms were unremarkable, and no such cases were discovered. As one might expect, performance was better on faster machines, and worse on slower machines. There were no unexplained anomalies between these platforms, and the relative behavior of the programs described in the following chapters seems to vary little from machine to machine.

The other machines on which tests were performed were:

- A Hewlett-Packard 735 workstation with 64 Megabytes of RAM, a color display and running HPUX 9.0. All tests were performed locally, with the applications running on the same machine as the X server.
- A Hewlett-Packard 715 workstation with 32 Megabytes of RAM, a color display and running HPUX 9.0. All tests were performed locally, with the applications running on the same machine as the X server.
- A Silicon Graphics IRIS Indigo workstation, with a MIPS R3K processor, 56 Megabytes of RAM, a color display, and running Silicon Graphic's 5.2 release of the IRIX operating system. All tests were performed locally, with the applications running on the same machine as the X server.
- A Sun Sparc 10 workstation with 32 Megabytes of RAM, a color display, and running the Solaris operating system. All tests were performed locally, with the applications running on the same machine as the X server.

7.9 Getting More Information

This book focuses on performance issues that relate directly to Motif applications, which includes many topics related to general X performance. However, space does not allow all aspects of X performance to be addressed in this book. Useful information about performance measuring and tuning is often difficult to find, but there are a few sources. Those interested in learning more about performance issues related to X may find the following articles useful:

Other sources of information about X performance

Ralph Droms and A. Wayne Dyksen, "Performance Measurements of the X Window System Protocol", *Software Practice and Experience*, Vol. 20, No. S2, October, 1990.

Joel McCormack, "Writing Fast X Servers for Dumb Color Frame Buffers", *Software Practice and Experience*, Vol. 20, No. S2, October, 1990.

Chris Peterson and Sharon Chang, "Improving X Application Performance", *The X Resource*, Issue 3, Summer 1992.

Ken Lee, "Software Engineering for X Application Performance", *The X Journal*, Vol. 3, No. 5, May/June 1994.

7.10 Conclusion

This chapter introduces some basic issues related to performance tuning Motif programs. Although Motif is not known for its speed, it is possible to write fast, responsive Motif applications. Most simple, well-written applications should have little trouble providing adequate performance when handling basic operations like posting menus and dialogs. The most difficult challenge of writing responsive Motif applications involves handling those times when an application must perform significant application-specific tasks. However, there are many choices that can be made, with respect to how an application uses Motif, that can affect performance.

The following chapters introduce some tools and techniques that can be used to measure and understand the performance of Motif applications. We will explore typical problems, examine options, and develop and measure various approaches that can be used to improve performance. Through the various examples, some common themes emerge that can be applied during the design and implementation phase of various Motif programs.

While considering the various measurements of CPU cycles, server requests, and elapsed time described in the following chapters, it is important to keep one thought in mind: the most important consideration when developing any application is the user. Graphical interfaces are supposed to make a task easier, faster, or more enjoyable. Ultimately, the real measure of performance is how much an application improves the user's ability to perform tasks efficiently.

8

Tools for Performance Tuning

To talk about performance in anything other than vague terms, and to make meaningful improvements in an application's performance, it is necessary to be able to make measurements. Many systems support sophisticated commercial-quality tools that can be used to gather data to be used in performance tuning. However, simple tools that are readily available on all platforms can be used quite effectively. The examples in this book show how basic, widely-available tools can be used to measure and understand the performance of Motif applications. The following sections briefly introduce the tools used throughout the remainder of this book.

8.1 Measuring Elapsed Time

One of the easiest and simplest ways to characterize performance is to measure the time required for a particular task to be completed. Measuring "wall clock time" is sometimes regarded as a poor substitute for more sophisticated measurements. However, when making coarse grained measurements of interactive systems, *elapsed time* is often more meaningful than more sophisticated measurements for one reason: For interactive systems, the key measure of performance is user perception, which is heavily dependent on elapsed time.

If making a change to a program reduces the number of CPU cycles consumed or the number of requests to the X server, but increases the elapsed time as seen by the user, the change has not improved program's performance from the user's perspective. Users really don't care about CPU utilization, server requests, or any other metric. Elapsed time is the best characterization of what a user experiences when using a program.

Measuring elapsed time is also particularly useful in a client-server system, which all Motif applications are. If a program makes excessive use of the X server, elapsed time required to complete an operation could be high while the CPU time consumed by the application could be quite low. A program can easily manipulate the X server so that the X server consumes CPU time rather than the program itself. Tools that can properly measure system performance in a client-server environment are rare, and measuring elapsed time is one of the best techniques available for client-server systems.

To interpret elapsed time measurements successfully, it is important to make multiple tests. Often, on virtual memory systems with demand paging, the first time a program is run, the elapsed time will be greater than if the measurement is made a second time. This is generally because new pages are being loaded into memory during the first run. On subsequent tests, these pages may already be loaded. Depending on how a program is expected to be used, the first measurement may be most important, or it may be more useful to time several consecutive tests. Elapsed time measurements must be treated as rough indications of performance. Small variations between tests are not relevant, and system behavior sometimes produces wide variations from test to test.

In general, it is best to test on a system that is in a known state to minimize unexpected interactions. For example, the system on which tests are being made should not have multiple users, because of the possibility for drastic changes in the load on the system from test to test. Of course, a program should normally be tested in the environment in which it will run. If a program is normally used while other large processes are executing, or while the system is under an extreme load, then measurements should be made under those conditions.

Using a Stopwatch

It is easy to get started measuring elapsed time using only a clock, or a stopwatch. For many operations, such basic tools are adequate, at least for an initial rough attempt to gather data. Of course, one must beware of human response time and resulting inaccuracies. Although sometimes useful, stopwatches leave room for human error, and to time short operations or to get more reliable measurements, better tools are needed.

Using the System Clock

One simple, but reliable, tool that is available to almost everyone is the system clock. For example, on UNIX platforms, the function `gettimeofday()` returns the time, in seconds and microseconds, since January 1, 1970. The exact granularity of the time is system dependent, but should not be worse than 10 milliseconds. This function can be used to measure the elapsed time between various points in a program.

Another useful way to measure time from within an application is to use the `times()` function. This function returns the elapsed time in units of clock ticks since the system started. The number of clock ticks per second is a system-dependent parameter, `CLK_TCK`, which is defined in the header file limits.h. This function expects a single argument, which is a pointer to a structure of type `struct tms`. This structure is defined as:

```
struct tms {
    clock_t tms_utime;
    clock_t tms_stime;
    clock_t tms_cutime;
    clock_t tms_cstime
};
```

When `times()` returns, these members contain the time, in clock ticks, spent executing the process. The `tms_utime` member indicates the amount of time spent in the "user" portion of the program, while `tms_stime` reports the time spent executing system calls on behalf of this process. The "user" time indicates the amount of time the system spent in user mode executing this process. Together, these two numbers indicate the CPU time of the process, which is the total time spent by the CPU executing this process. The last members, `tms_cutime` and `tms_cstime`, provide the same information about any child processes of the calling program.

The information obtained from the `times()` function can be useful in many ways. For example, it is interesting to compare the total CPU time reported by this function with the elapsed time obtained by the same call. Normally, the elapsed time will be greater than the CPU time. If these times are substantially different, the system must have been doing something else besides executing this program during the measured time period. In most cases, the system was probably doing one of three things: executing another process, handling I/O, or paging in or out portions of the program. In multitasking systems, each program shares the CPU with other programs, so not all the time is spent executing any individual program.

All these possibilities are likely, when looking at the performance of Motif applications. Motif programs are large, and paging is often an issue. All Motif applications interact with the X server and perhaps the window manager, so other processes are almost guaranteed to need the CPU while a Motif program is running. Finally, all Motif applications perform I/O, to send requests to and receive events from the X server.

Convenience Functions for Reporting Time

It is convenient to write some utility functions that use the information obtained from `times()` to compute and report elapsed time from within a program. For example, the following function allows applications to mark a specific point in a program, by printing a message along with the time used by the program since the last time the function was called. The elapsed time, user time, and system time are reported in seconds and milliseconds. The function takes two arguments, a string to be printed along with the time, and a Boolean value. If the second argument is `FALSE`, the function simply prints the given message and records the current time. If the second argument is `TRUE`, the function reports the time elapsed since the last time the function was called.

This function, `ReportTime()`, is fairly lightweight, and should have a negligible effect of a program's performance as long as it is not called too frequently.

```
/*******************************************************
 * TimerTools.c: Simple functions to measure time.
 *******************************************************/
#include <stdio.h>
#include <sys/times.h>
#include <limits.h>
#include <unistd.h>
#include <X11/Intrinsic.h>
```

```
void ReportTime ( String msg, Boolean report )
{
    static int firstTime = TRUE;
    static struct tms  last;
    static struct tms  now;
    static clock_t     current, prev;

   /*
    * Always print the message, if it exists.
    */

    if ( msg )
        printf ( "%s:\n", msg );

   /*
    * Report the time since the last call.
    */

    if ( !firstTime && report )
    {
        int user, sys, elapsed;

       /*
        * Get the current time.
        */

        current = times ( &now );

       /*
        * Convert to milliseconds since the last call.
        */

        user = 1000 *
                 ( now.tms_utime - last.tms_utime ) / CLK_TCK;
        sys  = 1000 *
                 ( now.tms_stime - last.tms_stime ) / CLK_TCK;
        elapsed = 1000 * ( current - prev ) / CLK_TCK;

       /*
        * Print the information in seconds and milliseconds.
        */

        printf ( "    Elapsed Time = %d.%03d\n",
                 elapsed / 1000, elapsed % 1000 );
        printf ( "    User Time    = %d.%03d\n",
                 user / 1000, user % 1000 );
        printf ( "    System Time  = %d.%03d\n",
                 sys / 1000, sys % 1000 );
    }
```

```

        firstTime = FALSE;
      /*
       * Get the current time to be used in the next calculation.
       */

       prev = times ( &last );
   }
```

It can be difficult to obtain meaningful elapsed time measurements for X-based programs because X runs asynchronously with respect to the client application. The X architecture makes it hard to know, at any stage of a program, exactly what events and requests have been processed. For example, let's look at how we might measure the time required to create and display a dialog. A code segment that uses `ReportTime()` could be written like this:

```
ReportTime ( "Creating Dialog", FALSE );

dialog = XmCreateErrorDialog ( "error", parent, NULL, 0 );
XtManageChild ( dialog );

ReportTime ( "Dialog Posted", TRUE );
```

Because of the way X requests and events are processed, it is likely that the reported time will be very misleading, depending on what you expect to measure. When the second call to `ReportTime()` is made, the data structure associated with the dialog widget will have been allocated and initialized, but the X server may or may not have processed the request to create the dialog window. In addition, the dialog is certainly not fully displayed at the time of the second call to `ReportTime()` because the dialog must be drawn in response to an `Expose` event, and the application has not yet returned to an event loop.

So, as written, this code segment reports the time required to create and manage a widget, and to place some unknown number of requests into the X request queue. The reported time does not include the time required to create the necessary windows, display and refresh the dialog, and so on. It is generally more relevant, when trying to tune an interactive application, to measure the time required to make a dialog visible to a user.

To get a more useful indication of the time required for such operations, a program can call `XSync()` to request the X server to handle all pending requests and place all events in the application's event queue. Finally, an event loop that processes all events in the event queue before moving on allows the application to process all events necessary to complete the task being measured.

The following function can be used to perform these steps.

```
66  void HandleEvents ( Widget w )
67  {
68      XtAppContext app;
69      XEvent       event;
70      XtInputMask  mask;
71
72      app = XtWidgetToApplicationContext ( w );
73
74      XSync ( XtDisplay ( w ), 0 );
75
76      while ( mask = XtAppPending ( app ) )
77      {
78          XtAppNextEvent ( app, &event );
79          XtDispatchEvent ( &event );
80
81      }
82  }
```

This function is rather expensive because of the call to `XSync()` as well as the events that may be processed. However, it provides more reproducible and realistic behavior than if we just ignore the interaction with the X server. You would not want to leave calls to this function in a final product, but as a measuring tool, it can be very useful.

Another difficulty that must be solved when trying to measure the user's view of elapsed time is the potential for a race condition between the application, the window manager, and the server. If we were to call `HandleEvents()` after managing a dialog, for example, the call to `XSync()` on line 74 would force the X server to handle the various requests involved in posting the dialog. However, because the window manager is also involved in placing a window on the screen, there is no way to guarantee that the dialog will have appeared by the time `XtAppNextEvent()` is called on line 78. In fact it is highly unlikely that the dialog will appear consistently within this time. If there are no events caused by the dialog being displayed, the event loop in `HandleEvents()` will simply terminate, even before the dialog has been displayed.

To guarantee that the program measures the time required to display a dialog on the screen, it is necessary to wait until the server has sent a

MapNotify event to indicate that the dialog's window has actually been mapped. This task can be handled with the following simple function.

```
void WaitForWindow ( Widget w )
{
    XtAppContext app;
    XEvent       event;
    XtInputMask  mask;

    app = XtWidgetToApplicationContext ( w );

    XSync ( XtDisplay ( w ), 0 );

    while ( TRUE )
    {
        XtAppNextEvent ( app, &event );
        XtDispatchEvent ( &event );

        if ( event.xany.type == MapNotify &&
             event.xany.window == XtWindow ( w ) )
          return;
    }
}
```

This function calls XSync() to force all requests to be sent to the server and then enters an event loop that is terminated only when a MapNotify event is received. Obviously, this function should be used with care, and called only when a MapNotify event will positively be received.

With these functions, the total time required to display a dialog can be measured as follows:

```
ReportTime ( "Creating Dialog", FALSE );

dialog = XmCreateErrorDialog ( "error", parent, NULL, 0 );
XtManageChild ( dialog );

WaitForWindow ( XtParent (dialog ) );
HandleEvents ( dialog );

ReportTime ( "Dialog Posted", TRUE );
```

Figure 8.1 shows the output that would be produced by this code segment, if it were executed as part of a program.

```
% dialog
Creating Dialog:
Dialog Posted:
   Elapsed Time = 0.14
   User Time    = 0.050
   System Time  = 0.020
```

Figure 8.1 Measuring the time required to post a dialog.

The following header file can be included by applications that use the functions described above.

```
/**********************************************************
 * TimerTools.h: Simple functions to measure time.
 **********************************************************/
extern void ReportTime ( char * message, Boolean report );
extern void HandleEvents ( Widget w );
extern void WaitForWindow ( Widget shell );
```

The functions described here should allow consistent and meaningful measurements to be made. However, adding these functions to a program definitely alters the behavior of the program, so they must be used with care, to avoid skewing the measurements. For example, flushing the request and events queues by calling `XSync()` is an expensive operation, so if these functions are called too often, they may impact the performance of the program being measured. It is also possible for secondary event loops to alter a program's behavior and even introduce unexpected bugs (See Chapter 4).

At best, the extra event loop causes an application to process events in a different way than it normally would. For example, imagine investigating the problem discussed in Chapter 4, in which a dialog does not appear immediately because the application never returns to an event loop. The techniques described here will not measure the time required to pop up the dialog correctly, because calling `WaitForWindow()` and `HandleEvents()` will suddenly make the dialog appear more quickly.

External Timing Functions

One of the problems with using the functions described in the previous section is that a program must be modified to use them. Most systems support a `time` command which can be used to execute a program and report the time used by that program, without modifying the program. For example, Figure

8.2 shows the results of using the `time` command to measure the time required to execute `ls`.

```
% time ls TimerTools.h
TimerTools.h

real   0m0.11s
user   0m0.01s
sys    0m0.04s
```

Figure 8.2 Using the `time` command.

The first line is, of course, the output of `ls`. After `ls` terminates, `time` reports that `ls` took zero minutes and 0.11 second to execute, measured in real, "wall clock" time. The `ls` command used zero minutes and 0.01 second of user time, and used 0.04 second of system time.

Unfortunately, the `time` command is most useful for measuring the time required to execute a program that starts up, executes and terminates. The function is seldom directly useful for measuring the times of interactive programs, because these programs do not exit upon completion of a task.

However, we can easily borrow the basic idea of the `time()` command to create a program that can measure the start-up time of an interactive X application. The following program executes a program given as an argument, and reports the time from the point the second program is launched until a window appears on the screen. The program determines when a window appears on the screen by watching for `SubStructureNotify` events on the root window.

```
/*********************************************************
 * maptime.c: Report the time required to start an X
 *             application and map the first window.
 *********************************************************/
#include <sys/types.h>
#include <sys/time.h>
#include <X11/Xlib.h>
#include <unistd.h>
#include <stdio.h>

void main ( int argc, char **argv )
{
    Display *dpy;
    XEvent   event;
    struct   timeval start, finish;
    int      msec;
```

```

    /*
     * Open the default display.
     */

     dpy = XOpenDisplay ( NULL );

    /*
     * Request SubstructureNotify events for the root window.
     * This will include MapNotify events for all children.
     */

     XSelectInput ( dpy, DefaultRootWindow ( dpy ),
                    SubstructureNotifyMask );
    /*
     * Get the starting time.
     */

     gettimeofday ( &start, NULL );

    /*
     * Launch the process by forking and calling execvp().
     */

     if ( fork() == 0 )
     {
        /*
         * In child process.
         */

         close ( ConnectionNumber ( dpy ) );
         execvp ( argv[1], argv + 1 );
         exit ( -1 );
     }

    /*
     * In parent process, watch for a MapNotify event from a
     * child of the root window. Note that we could get the
     * wrong child, as there is no way to be sure the window
     * is created by the process just launched. But normally,
     * in a controlled test, the next window to be mapped would
     * the window we are waiting for.
     */

     for ( ; ; )
     {
         XNextEvent ( dpy, &event );

         if ( event.type == MapNotify )
```

```
        {
            /*
             * Get the current time, and compute the difference
             * between the time measured before the process
             * was started.
             */

            gettimeofday ( &finish, NULL );
            msec = finish.tv_sec * 1000 +
                                    finish.tv_usec / 1000;
            msec -= start.tv_sec * 1000 +
                                    start.tv_usec / 1000;

            /*
             * Report time and exit.
             */

            printf ( "Startup time: %d milliseconds\n", msec );
            exit ( 0 );
        }
    }
}
```

This simple program, which we will name `maptime`, provides an easy way to measure the initial start-up time of any program, without modifying the source. Notice that this program defines start-up time as the time required for an initial window to be mapped. When measuring start-up time with `WaitForWindow()`, followed by `HandleEvents()` and `ReportTime()` as described earlier, start-up time is defined a bit differently. When these functions are used to measure start-up time, the measurement includes the time to process most, if not all, initial events received by the program. The basic difference is that `maptime` program does not include the time required to draw the contents of a window, while the function-based approach does. In most cases, the difference is relatively unimportant, as long as the same measurement technique is used consistently.

Figure 8.3 shows how `maptime` can be used to measure the start-up time of the `xclock` program.

```
% maptime xclock
  Startup time: 290 milliseconds
```

Figure 8.3 Using the `maptime` program.

8.2 Measuring Application Size

The size of a Motif application plays an important role in its performance. Large applications can place demands on a system that can result in slower performance for the application itself and also impact the performance of other applications running on the system. The effect of application size on performance is a complex issue that will be discussed in later chapters. Unfortunately, there are few widely available tools that provide the information we need to evaluate this aspect of Motif performance properly.

However, the simple UNIX command `ps` provides one way to gather some basic information about the size of a process. With some ingenuity, this simple utility can provide a surprising amount of information about a program. Although the format and usage of this command may vary from system to system, most versions of `ps` can report the size of a process, as well as how long it has been running. For example, Figure 8.4 shows part of the output of the `ps` command when executed on System A.

```
% ps -elf
 F S UID  PID PPID C PRI NI  P  SZ:RSS WCHAN    STIME    TTY TIME COMD
30 S root 435 1    0  0  20  * 733:249 8038a708 11:36:30 ?  0:00 xdm
```

Figure 8.4 Typical `ps` output.

Many of the fields in this output can be ignored, but others provide valuable data. The field labeled SZ:RSS indicates the total size and the *resident size* of each process. An application's resident size indicates the amount of physical memory used by the program, which is generally far less than the total size of the program, in a virtual memory system. Here, the process named `xdm` has a total size of 733 pages, and 249 pages are currently resident in memory. On System A, a page is 4096 bytes, so `xdm` is using a total of 3,002,360 bytes, of which 1,019,904 bytes are resident in memory.

Some other useful information can also be gathered using `ps`. For example, the field labeled STIME indicates the time at which the process was started, and the TIME field reports the total CPU time the process has consumed so far.

The fields, formats, command line flags, and other characteristics of `ps` vary from system to system. Check the man page for `ps` on your system to learn what information your implementation provides. For example, on a Sun system, `ps` reports only the resident size of a process, under the heading SZ. It is also important to be very careful about interpreting the information produced by `ps`. Page sizes vary on different systems, and in some cases the numbers reported may be misleading. This is especially true if shared libraries are involved. It is not enough to obtain a number, you must be sure you understand exactly what the number means, and what factors might be contributing to the reported information.

8.3 Xscope and Xmon

Chapter 3 introduces `xscope`, `xmonui`, and `xmond` as aids for debugging. These programs can also be useful when tuning applications. The most obvious use of these programs is to investigate the number of server requests an application makes, when attempting to reduce the traffic between the application and the X server. However, more subtle, but potentially useful information can also be gleaned from the output of these tools.

In addition to the number of events and requests, looking at the nature of an application's interaction with the X server can provide insights into the performance characteristics of a program. For example, a large number of sequential configuration requests may indicate problems with geometry management. Similarly, it may be easier to detect multiple redraws by looking at the requests being sent to the X server than by visually observing the program's interface. Most modern X servers are fast enough that redrawing a window several times may not be noticeable. However, the cumulative effect of such errors can reduce the responsiveness of the application. Programs that repaint windows multiple times may have other logical errors or efficiency problems that cause the program to consume unnecessary CPU cycles in addition to generating more server traffic.

Xmon can also be used to detect unnecessary allocation of server resources. In a complex program, it is easy to inadvertently create pixmaps that are not used, graphics contexts that are unneeded, or even colors that are never used. The output of `xmond` cannot automatically identify unnecessary requests, but combined with a working knowledge of the program being tuned, the protocol trace can help bring potential problems to light. It is usually easiest to start with a summary of the requests and events that have occurred, and look for anything that seems unusual. From there, individual requests or events can be monitored in more detail, if necessary.

Another thing to watch for is synchronous requests that require replies. Good performance on an X system depends on being able to stream requests and events asynchronously between the X server and each application. If an application makes requests in such a way that asynchronous requests are interspersed with requests that require round trips, performance will suffer. The reference book *X Window System*, by Bob Scheifler and Jim Gettys, can help in understanding which requests require round trips.

8.4 Traditional Performance Tools

Most UNIX-based systems include some standard tools for obtaining performance profiles of an application. These tools come in two basic flavors, *statistical program counter sampling* and *basic block counting*. Each type is described below. As we will see, these tools are normally of limited use for measuring the performance of a Motif application.

The first type of tool works by periodically sampling the program counter and providing a statistical sample of where your program spent its time. This facility is available on most systems as an integrated part of the compiler. The information can be obtained by executing the commands `prof` or `gprof`. To use `prof`, you must compile your program using a special flag, usually `-p`, run the program, and then run `prof`. The `prof` command prints a summary of the time spent, using a data file produced when the program being tested exits. The `gprof` command works similarly, but provides somewhat different information. See the man pages for these tools for specific details on your system.

Figure 8.5 shows an example of how `prof` can be used to profile the `xclock` program described in Chapter 2. First, the program is compiled with the `-p` flag, and executed. The program must be exited cleanly, so that `exit()` is called. Then, running `prof` with the program to be profiled as an argument produces a summary of the time spent in various statistically sampled functions.

```
--------------------------------------------------------------------------
Profile listing generated Sat Mar 26 12:43:34 1994
   with:         prof xclock
--------------------------------------------------------------------------

samples   time    CPU    FPU    Clock   N-cpu  S-interval Countsize
    13  0.13s  R4000  R4010 100.0MHz   1      10.0ms      2(bytes)

Each sample covers 4 bytes for every 10.0ms ( 7.69% of 0.1300sec)

--------------------------------------------------------------------------
  -p[rocedures] using pc-sampling.
  Sorted in descending order by the number of samples in each proce
  Unexecuted procedures are excluded.
--------------------------------------------------------------------------

samples   time(%)       cum time(%)      procedure (file)

      2  0.02s( 15.4) 0.02s( 15.4)         _select (libc.so.1:select
      1  0.01s(  7.7) 0.03s( 23.1) _XWaitForReadable (libX11.so.1:X
      1  0.01s(  7.7) 0.05s( 38.5)            _read (libc.so.1:read.s
      1  0.01s(  7.7) 0.06s( 46.2) XrmQGetResource (libX11.so.1:Xrm
      1  0.01s(  7.7) 0.07s( 53.8)           XSync (libX11.so.1:XSyr
      1  0.01s(  7.7) 0.08s( 61.5)          XtFree (libXt.so:Alloc.c
      1  0.01s(  7.7) 0.09s( 69.2) ParseTranslationTable (libXt.so:
      1  0.01s(  7.7)   0.1s( 76.9)         Resolve (libXt.so:Intrins
      1  0.01s(  7.7) 0.11s( 84.6)           _free (libc.so.1:malloc
      1  0.01s(  7.7) 0.12s( 92.3) ExpandQuarkTable (libX11.so.1:Qu
      1  0.01s(  7.7) 0.13s(100.0) _XrmInternalStringToQuark (libX1

     13  0.13s(100.0) 0.13s(100.0)              TOTAL
```

Figure 8.5 Using `prof` to measure the performance of `xclock`.

Notice that the information in Figure 8.5 is not particularly useful, nor probably what you would hope to see when profiling this program. One might expect to see functions called directly by the program, like `XtCreateWidget()`, `XtRealizeWidget()`, or even `XtSetValues()`. The problem with prof is that it takes samples at regular intervals, which on this machine are 10 milliseconds apart. Ten milliseconds is a very long time in CPU terms, and the samples can easily miss entire functions on a reasonably fast machine. `Prof` is most useful for programs that iterate over sequences of operations for a very long time. If `xclock` was run for a very long time, we might get some relevant data, although the data would probably show that most of the time was being spent in `select()`. For most Motif applications, the information provided by `prof` is virtually useless.

The second type of tool found on many UNIX systems performs basic block counting during a program's execution. The technique used by these tools is to compute the number of instructions (or machine cycles) used by each line of code in the program. These tools rely on additional statements inserted into the executable in some way to determine which blocks of code are actually executed. With this information, these tools can report exactly which lines of code were executed and how many machine instructions were executed for each line of code. Different hardware vendors have different tools that fit into this category. For example, Sun systems have a tool named `tcov` which uses the compiler to add the code needed to trace the execution of the program. On MIPS-based systems, like the Silicon Graphics machines used for the tests in this book, the `pixie` program instruments an executable after it has been compiled.

Unlike `prof`, basic block counting tools like `tcov` and `pixie` are not based on statistical sampling, so they do not miss functions. These tools can tell you exactly what functions and what lines of code were executed each time the program is run. However, these tools only report the instructions executed by the application. Time spent elsewhere is not considered or reported. CPU usage is not normally the most significant issue in Motif applications, although it can be useful to see what code is executed.

For those fortunate enough to have them, there are also many commercial tools that can be used to provide even more performance information about a program. There are tools that can provide insight into more esoteric behavior such as the number of page faults, number of context switches, the size of a program over time, the working set (the number of pages of executable code that must be in memory at any given time), memory use, and so on.

For example, Figure 8.6 shows one example of an integrated set of commercial tools that can be used to measure many characteristics of program performance. The window in the middle displays a list of functions along with the time used by each function. A strip-chart shows various characteristics of the program and the system, and a timeline allows a programmer to examine any segment of time during the program's execution. The window to the right displays a dynamic call graph of the functions executed by the program, annotated with information about the performance of each function call. The window to the right displays additional data in stripchart form.

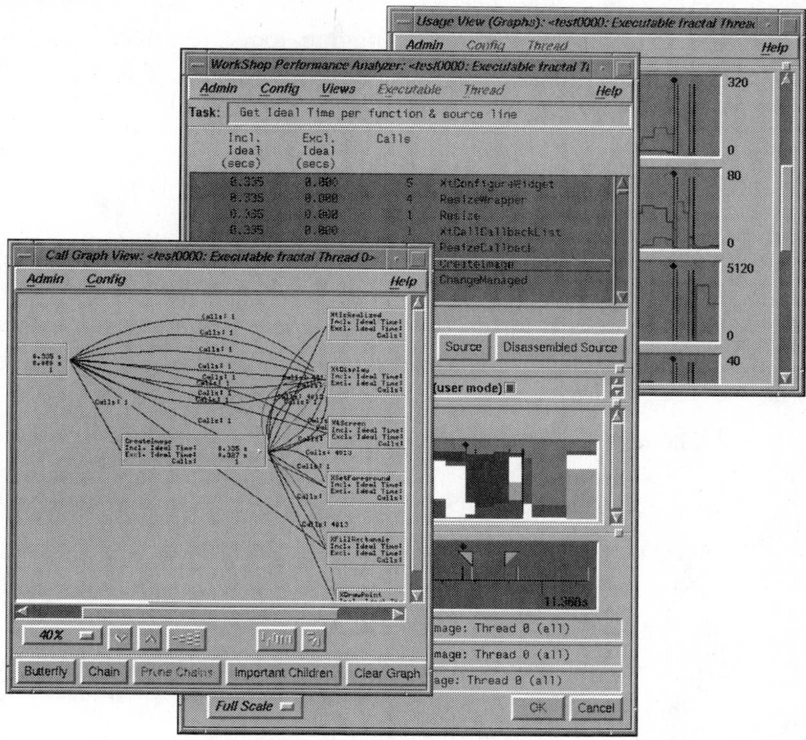

Figure 8.6 A commercial performance analyzer.

Because such tools are generally associated with specific systems, a detailed discussion of these tools and their associated techniques is beyond the scope of this book. All measurements in this book rely as much as possible on simple tools that are universally available, such as the system time, `xmon`, `ps`, `editres`, and so on. If you have access to commercial-quality performance tools, however, they can be very useful when trying to understand performance issues.

8.5 Other Tools

A great deal of information about a program's performance can be gathered using only the simple tools described above. However, when investigating performance, one needs all the tools available to gather information. For example, nearly all the debugging tools described in Chapter 2 can help gather information that relates to performance. This section briefly describes some other tools that can be used to help in any performance effort.

Debuggers as Performance Tools

Although not normally thought of as a performance tool, even a debugger can be used effectively to look for performance problems. For example, stepping through critical pieces of code may reveal surprising information about what is really happening in a program. While tedious, a line by line code review of a program's dynamic behavior can be surprisingly effective for finding inefficiencies in isolated pieces of code.

A debugger can also be used in conjunction with other programs to identify problem areas. For example, one of the difficulties with using `xmond` involves associating sequences of asynchronous requests with the code that produces them. Running a program under a debugger while watching the output of `xmond` can help solve this problem.

One approach is to start a program under a debugger, making sure that the program sends requests to the xmon display. Set breakpoints at periodic intervals and run the program in synchronous mode. Now, each time the program runs between breakpoints, the output of `xmond` can be correlated with the section of code just executed. If any anomalies are observed, breakpoints can be set at finer and finer grained intervals to narrow the search. If necessary, the program can be stepped through line at a time to see the requests generated by each line of code.

A debugger provides a great deal of control over a program's execution, which can be exploited in some interesting ways. For example, Chapter 10 demonstrates how a debugger can be used with `ps` to measure the amount of physical memory needed to complete a simple operation.

Memory Use

Memory use is an area of great concern when writing Motif programs. Although `ps` can be used to show the current size of the program, it is also useful to have more detailed information about memory use within a program. Fortunately, there are many tools available for analyzing memory use. The most powerful of these tools are commercial quality (and commercially priced) products. If you are fortunate to have such tools available to you, they can be a great help. However, as discussed in Chapter 5, there are public domain `malloc()` libraries that can be used effectively as well. A good library can help detect leaks (memory that is allocated and never freed), abuses of memory, such as freeing memory that was not allocated by `malloc()`, and some can also provide statistics that can be used to identify excessive or inefficient use of `malloc()`. All of this information can be useful when trying to improve a program's performance.

XtGeo and editres

The XtGeo library and the `editres` program were introduced in Chapter 3 as tools that can help debug layout problems. In many cases, a Motif program's performance is affected greatly by the widget hierarchy, widgets used, or the geometry management process. Therefore, these tools have a place in any suite of performance tools. These tools don't measure time or memory use, but they do provide information that can help a programmer understand the behavior of an application.

The Widget Lint Library

The first part of this book developed a simple set of functions that can be used to look for common misuses of Motif. In some situations, this same technique can be used to uncover problems that could result in decreased performance. Like `editres` and XtGeo, the WL framework cannot provide numerical information about time spent in different parts of the program. However, if it is possible to identify specific ways that Motif can be used inefficiently, one could conceivably write test functions to detect such situations.

To write such tests, it is necessary to identify static characteristics of the program's widget hierarchy that represent potential performance problems. Later chapters provide a few examples of situations in which this can be done.

Another interesting idea, not explored in this book, is to modify XtGeo to detect dynamic situations that could cause performance problems. For example, it might be helpful to report widgets that are frequently resized, situations that seem to involve excessive or unusual geometry requests, and so on.

8.6 Conclusion

Information that can help a programmer understand and improve performance is difficult to obtain for any type of program. The task is even harder for Motif applications because of the asynchronous multi-process environment in which they operate. In addition, the tools available for performance analysis are limited, compared to the large number of tools available for debugging. Nevertheless, in most cases, a few simple tools can be used quite effectively. The following chapters demonstrate how the tools described in this chapter can be used to evaluate the performance of some typical Motif applications.

9

Improving Start-up Time

One of an interactive program's most noticeable performance characteristics is the time required to start the program. *Start-up time* is the length of time that elapses before a new process is ready to interact with the user. A lengthy start-up time can interrupt the flow of the user's work. In addition, many issues associated with start-up performance also affect an application's runtime performance. This chapter explores start-up time, while Chapter 10 examines ways to investigate and improve runtime performance.

For the discussions in this book, we will set an explicit goal that all applications should be able to start up and be ready to respond to user input in three tenths of a second or less on System A. If best efforts to achieve this goal fail, an initial start-up time of one second or less will be considered an acceptable compromise, as long as the user receives some feedback quickly. Of course an application's performance will always vary in a multi-tasking environment like UNIX. The goal must be to make it *possible* for an application to meet the goal on a reasonably normal system. We cannot guarantee that a program will always meet the goal.

9.1 Measuring Minimum Start-up Times

Before attempting to improve the start-up time of a specific program, it is useful to understand some basic performance characteristics of all Xt programs. For example, it is useful to know the minimum time required to connect to the X server and initialize Xt on the targeted system. No matter how much we tune application-specific code, there is little an application programmer can do to make an Xt program start up faster than the following simple program:

```
/**********************************************
 * timetest.c: Test Xt initialization time
 **********************************************/
 #include <Xm/Xm.h>
 #include "TimerTools.h"

  void main ( int argc, char **argv )
  {
     Widget       shell;
     XtAppContext app;

     ReportTime ( "Starting", FALSE );

     shell = XtAppInitialize ( &app, "Timetest", NULL, 0,
                               &argc, argv, NULL, NULL, 0 );

     HandleEvents ( shell );
     ReportTime ( "Finished", TRUE );
}
```

Start Timing (beside line 12–13); Stop Timing (beside lines 17–18)

This program uses the tools described in Chapter 8 to measure the amount of time required to execute `XtAppInitialize()`. The measurements do not include any system time required to start the process.

On System A, with no app-defaults file, no .Xdefaults file, and no `RESOURCE_MANAGER` property on the root window, the `timetest` program executes in 0.11 second, as shown in Figure 9.1.

```
% timetest
Starting:
Finished:
   Elapsed Time = 0.11
   User Time    = 0.040
   System Time  = 0.040
```

Figure 9.1 Start-up time for `timetest` program.

It is also worthwhile to consider the system overhead required to launch the process. For example, running the `timetest` program using the UNIX utility `time` produces the information shown in Figure 9.2.

```
                % time timetest
                Starting:
                Finished:
Internally     ┌   Elapsed Time = 0.11
measured       │   User Time    = 0.040
time           └   System Time  = 0.040
               ┌real   0m0.16s
Reported by    │user   0m0.06s
"time"         └sys    0m0.06s
```

Figure 9.2 Start-up time for `timetest`, plus information from `time`.

Here, the `time` command, which outputs its measurements after the program exits, reports that the `timetest` program executed in 0.16 second (real, elapsed time), used 0.06 second of user time, and 0.06 second of system time. Notice the discrepancy between the time measured from within the program (0.11 second) and the elapsed time reported by the `time` command (0.16 second). The `time` command includes the overhead of starting the process, paging in the code required to execute the process, and so on, which cannot be measured from within the program. There are few widely available tools that can provide additional information about the missing time, and because it is a system issue, there is little an application programmer can do to reduce the time required to launch a process. Although the difference is quite small in this particular example, it is important to keep the potential impact of system overhead in mind as additional performance tests are made.

It is useful to try to understand exactly where the time is being spent in this example program. `XtAppInitialize()` is a convenience function that calls several other Xt function to perform the basic initialization of a program. It is also possible to perform these steps individually. The following program, `timetest2`, is functionally equivalent to the `timetest` example shown above. This program, however, times each phase of the initialization.

```
        /**********************************************
         * timetest2.c : Test Xt initialization time.
         **********************************************/
        #include <Xm/Xm.h>
        #include "TimerTools.h"

        void main ( int argc, char **argv )
        {
            Widget       shell;
            XtAppContext app;
            Display     *dpy;

Start       ReportTime ( "Starting", FALSE );
Timing
            XtToolkitInitialize();

Report      ReportTime ( "Xt inited", TRUE );

            app = XtCreateApplicationContext();

Report      ReportTime ( "App context created", TRUE );

            dpy = XtOpenDisplay ( app, NULL, NULL, "Timetest",
                                  NULL, 0, &argc, argv );

Report      ReportTime ( "Display opened", TRUE );

            shell = XtAppCreateShell ( NULL, "shell",
                                       applicationShellWidgetClass,
                                       dpy, NULL, 0 );

Report      ReportTime ( "Shell created", TRUE );
            HandleEvents ( shell );
Final       ReportTime ( "Finished", TRUE );
Time    }
```

Running this program on System A produces the measurements shown in Figure 9.3.

```
% timetest2
Starting:
Xt inited:
    Elapsed Time = 0.010
    User Time    = 0.000
    System Time  = 0.010
App context created:
    Elapsed Time = 0.000
    User Time    = 0.000
    System Time  = 0.000
Display opened:
    Elapsed Time = 0.045
    User Time    = 0.020
    System Time  = 0.020
Shell created:
    Elapsed Time = 0.070
    User Time    = 0.030
    System Time  = 0.020
Finished:
    Elapsed Time = 0.000
    User Time    = 0.000
    System Time  = 0.000
```


Figure 9.3 Start-up time measurements for `timetest2`.

From the measurements in Figure 9.3, we can see that the slowest single part of the initialization sequence is the call to `XtAppCreateShell()`. Creating the shell widget takes well over half the total time. All Motif applications perform some global initialization when the first shell is created. This initialization includes some setup for drag and drop, some global data structures, and so on. Most of these steps are performed by the Motif VendorShell class, of which the ApplicationShell widget class is a subclass. Opening a connection to the X server is the next most expensive operation.

Start-up Server Requests

One thing that affects the performance of Motif applications is the number and type of requests the application sends to the X server. The measurements reported in Figure 9.1show that CPU utilization accounts for only part of the total time required to execute the `timetest` example. It is possible that some of the remaining time is spent communicating with the X server. Figure 9.4 shows a summary of the requests made by the `timetest` program, as reported by `xmond`. The requests that require a server round trip are shown in italics.

Request	# of Requests	Request	# of Requests
CreateWindow	1	*QueryFont*	2
QueryTree	1	CreateGC	1
InternAtom	5	CreateGlyphCursor	1
ChangeProperty	6	*QueryBestSize*	1
GetProperty	7	*QueryExtension*	2
ListProperties	2	*GetKeyboardMapping*	1
GetInputFocus	4	*GetModifierMapping*	1
OpenFont	3		

Figure 9.4 Requests issued when `XtAppInitialize()` is called.

Figure 9.4 shows that there are several requests that require round trips, which can be relatively expensive. Unfortunately, there is little an application can do to eliminate these requests, because these are generated by Xt and Motif. In any case, it is likely that these round trip requests account for some of the application's start-up time. A few of these requests might be worth investigating (why are two fonts being queried, for example?), but fixing such problems would probably involve changes to Motif, Xt, or Xlib, which is beyond the domain of this book, as well as most development projects.

The four calls to `GetInputFocus`, shown in Figure 9.4 are worth discussing. One certainly might wonder why this program needs to request input focus four times when no window is on the screen. Actually, `GetInputFocus` is one of the cheapest round trip requests, and it therefore used to force all events and requests to be processed when `XSync()` is called. So at least one of these requests can be traced to the `HandleEvents()` function. The others must be coming from Motif, Xt or Xlib.

Slower Systems

It is also useful to look at the minimum start-up time of these programs on other systems, particularly those that are significantly different from the primary test machine. For example, System B involves an X terminal, and could have very different start-up behavior for all X applications. Figure 9.5 shows the results of displaying the `timetest` example on this system.

```
% timetest
Starting:
Finished:
   Elapsed Time = 0.510
   User Time    = 0.040
   System Time  = 0.050
```

Figure 9.5 The `timetest` start-up on an X terminal.

The start-up time shown in Figure 9.5 is nearly five times slower than that measured on System A, and clearly shows that no Motif application can be expected to achieve the same start-up performance possible on System A. It is interesting to notice that neither the user time nor the system time, as reported by the `times()` function, are significantly worse than on System A. However, an additional four tenths of a second are being spent somewhere.

Running the `timetest2` program on System B produces some more detailed information, shown in Figure 9.6.

```
% timetest
Starting:
Xt inited:
   Elapsed Time = 0.000
   User Time    = 0.000
   System Time  = 0.000
App context created:
   Elapsed Time = 0.000
   User Time    = 0.000
   System Time  = 0.000
Display opened:
   Elapsed Time = 0.120
   User Time    = 0.020
   System Time  = 0.030
Shell created:
   Elapsed Time = 0.480
   User Time    = 0.030
   System Time  = 0.020
Finished:
   Elapsed Time = 0.000
   User Time    = 0.000
   System Time  = 0.000
```


Figure 9.6 The `timetest2` program's start-up on System B.

Again, the time required to create the shell dominates the measurements. As before, it seems likely that the program is waiting for the X terminal's server to load fonts, perform round trips, and so on. Apparently this server, or the connection to the server, is slower than the server on System A.

Hello World

Although interesting as a way to establish a base line from which to pursue other measurements, the `timetest` program discussed above is of no practical use, so it is difficult to know how this example's start-up time relates to real programs. To gather more information, we need to examine some more realistic examples.

As a first step, the following program, hello.c, is one of the simplest possible programs that does anything useful. The program simply displays a label that says "Hello World". With minor changes, this program could be changed to display any arbitrary message.

The `hello` program includes calls to `ReportTime()`, `WaitForWindow()`, and `HandleEvents()` to measure the time required to display the program's window.

```
/*****************************************************
 * hello.c: Display"hello world" on the screen.
 *****************************************************/
#include <Xm/Xm.h>
#include <Xm/Label.h>
#include "TimerTools.h"

void main ( int argc, char **argv )
{
    Widget          shell, label;
    XtAppContext app;
    XmString        xmstr;
```

Start timing

```
    ReportTime ( "Starting", FALSE );

    shell = XtAppInitialize ( &app, "Hello", NULL, 0,
                              &argc, argv, NULL, NULL, 0 );

    xmstr = XmStringCreateLtoR ( "Hello World",
                                 XmFONTLIST_DEFAULT_TAG );

   /*
    * Create a Motif XmLabel widget to display the string.
    */
```

```
    label = XtVaCreateManagedWidget ( "label",
                                      xmLabelWidgetClass, shell,
                                      XmNlabelString, xmstr,
                                      NULL );

    XmStringFree ( xmstr );  /* Free the compound string. */

    XtRealizeWidget ( shell );

    WaitForWindow ( shell );
    HandleEvents ( shell );
    ReportTime ( "Up", TRUE );
    XtAppMainLoop ( app );
}
```

Report elapsed time

This program does substantially more work than the `timetest` example. In this example, a Motif label widget is created, a compound string is created and displayed, two widgets are realized (windows are created) and some simple geometry management is performed. In addition, fonts must be loaded, colors allocated, and many widget resources initialized.

In spite of the additional work, the program is only slightly slower than the `timetest` program. Running the program on System A with no resource files reports a total start-up time of 0.20 second, as shown in Figure 9.7.

```
% hello
Starting:
Up:
   Elapsed Time = 0.20
   User Time    = 0.060
   System Time  = 0.050
```

Figure 9.7 Start-up time of “hello world”.

Running the same example on System B reports a total time of 0.76 second, as shown in Figure 9.8. This slower start-up time is consistent with the performance of the `timetest` program, measured earlier.

```
% hello
Starting:
Up:
   Elapsed Time = 0.760
   User Time    = 0.200
   System Time  = 0.080
```

Figure 9.8 Start-up time of “hello world” on an X terminal.

The Effect of Resource Files

The measurements in the previous sections were made without allowing the programs to load any resource files. It is interesting to see what effect adding resource files has on a simple program like the hello world example described above. If an app-defaults file or Xdefaults file is provided, any resources in these files will be loaded and stored in the program's resource database, even if the program will never need the resources.

As a first test, let's add a 300-line application defaults file, which is fairly realistic for a small Motif program, and a 100-line .Xdefaults file. The resources in these files are all designed to be picked up by the program, and are not qualified by program name. There is some duplication of resources, because the hello program does not really use hundreds of resources. Figure 9.9 shows the time required to start the `hello` example on System A with these files present.

```
% hello
Starting:
Up:
    Elapsed Time = 0.24
    User Time    = 0.060
    System Time  = 0.050
```

Figure 9.9 Hello world with 300-line app-defaults file.

As seen in Figure 9.9, loading 400 lines of resources from two files increases the start-up time of the `hello` program to 0.24 second on System A. A difference of four hundredths of a second is barely significant, and may easily be due to variations in the system or errors in measurement, rather than the impact of loading the resources. Notice that the CPU time has not increased.

Let's see what happens if we load even more resources. Figure 9.10 shows the results of running the `hello` program with a 100-line .Xdefaults file and a 1000-line app-defaults file:

```
% hello
Starting:
Up:
    Elapsed Time = 0.26
    User Time    = 0.080
    System Time  = 0.050
```

Figure 9.10 Hello world with a 1000-line app-defaults file.

Adding a 1000-line app-defaults file increases the program's start-up time to 0.26 second. This additional time is still nothing to be concerned about, but it seems that loading a large number of resources does have a small, but measurable impact on the program's start-up time.

To test that assumption further, let's load an unrealistic 10,000 lines of resources. Figure 9.11 shows the results of running `hello` with a 10,000-line app-defaults file, plus a 100-line .Xdefaults file.

```
% hello
Starting:
Up:
   Elapsed Time = 0.39
   User Time    = 0.190
   System Time  = 0.070
```

Figure 9.11 Hello world with a 10,000-line app-defaults file.

It is also interesting to consider how loading resources files into the program's resource database affects the program's size. Using `ps` to observe the initial size of this program shows that the total size of `hello` with no resource files is 1072 pages, of which 410 are resident. Adding a 1000-line app-defaults file produces no measurable change. The program still requires 1072 pages, with 410 resident pages. However, loading 10,000 lines of resources causes the program to grow to 1102 pages total size and 459 resident pages.

Clearly resource files have some impact on the overall start-up time, as well as the size of an application. However, for realistic numbers of resources, the effect is negligible. Even in an extreme case, loading 10,000 lines of resources only increases the `hello` program's start-up time from 0.20 to 0.39 second. Of course, no program should have a 10,000 line app-defaults file, and more reasonably-sized files seem to have only a small impact on performance. Obviously programmers should not add unnecessary entries to their app-defaults files, but neither should they be afraid to use reasonably sized resource files when they are needed.

Of course, the exact content of resource files and the nature of the program can have an impact that is not shown by these experiments. If a program uses many fonts or colors, for example, the impact of these resources could be much greater than shown here. However, any increase in start-up time would be due to the steps required to process the resources, rather than to load them into the resource database. For example, if a resource file specifies many fonts, the application will have to request the server to load these fonts, which can affect performance. Some fonts may be more expensive to load than others as well.

For example, suppose we set a single resource that affects the `hello` program:

```
*fontList: -*-helvetica-bold-o-*-*-*-160-75-75-*-*-iso8859-1
```

This font does not exist on System A, but the X11R5 scalable font mechanism can create one to match the given specification. Setting this single resource in the .Xdefaults file increases the start-up time of the `hello` program to 0.78 second, as shown in Figure 9.12.

```
% hello
Starting:
Up:
   Elapsed Time = 0.780
   CPU Time     = 0.080
   System Time  = 0.060
```

Figure 9.12 Hello world start-up time with a scalable font.

Notice that the additional start-up time is not really reflected in the CPU time or system time, but the elapsed time has increased by over half a second. The application is waiting for the X server to scale the font during the missing time.

9.2 Basic Strategies for Improving Start-up Time

From the measurements reported in the previous section, we can see that, at least on System A, an extremely simple Motif application can be started up in as little as 0.20 second, which is more than acceptable. This start-up time should appear to be instantaneous to a user.

Unfortunately, few real Motif applications start up in 0.20 second. You need only launch your favorite Motif-based word processor, mail program, or other program to see dramatically longer start-up times on most systems. The time required to display the simple `hello` program should be considered to be the minimum time that can realistically be achieved on a given system and treated as a goal to be strived for when developing larger programs.

Motif applications that have slow start-up times may have one or more of the following problems:

- The application's user interface may be overly complex. Some programs create many widgets, generate a great deal of X server traffic, and allocate large amounts of memory.

  Naturally, any useful program will be more complex than the `timetest` and `hello` programs discussed so far. However, interfaces should use the least number of widgets possible to provide the desired functionality. More complex interfaces naturally use more system resources and take longer to start-up. Each widget created by a program generates server requests to load fonts, allocate colors, create windows, and so on. Each widget requires memory to be allocated dynamically, which makes the program larger. To the extent possible, applications should reduce the number of widgets created at start-up time.

- The application may be performing other tasks besides displaying the user interface during start-up.

  Much of the time, the reason an application starts up slowly has nothing to do with Motif or X. Real applications usually have other tasks to perform upon start-up, in addition to creating the user interface. One way to improve the user's perception of start-up time is to make the interface appear as quickly as possible, delaying other tasks until after the interface has appeared. For example, an application that has to open a database should be sure to get the application's window on the screen before opening the database. The application can display a busy cursor or a message while waiting. As long as an application provides some indication of progress periodically, users will probably be satisfied.

  Although Motif has gained somewhat of a reputation for being slow, much of this reputation is undeserved or misplaced. Motif could certainly be much faster, but its reputation for sluggishness can often be traced to applications that make poor use of Motif. In many cases, these applications are actually slow at performing non-user interface operations without providing suitable feedback to the user.

- The program may not be using Motif in an optimal way.

  When writing a simple program like hello.c, it is hard to do anything seriously wrong, with respect to performance. As a program becomes more complex it is much easier to misuse Motif in ways that introduce performance problems. Many examples in the remainder of this book show the improvements that can be achieved by simple changes to the way in which an application treats widgets.

- The system may be underpowered, running other programs, or have insufficient memory to run the program efficiently.

  The start-up time of a program is heavily influenced by the environment in which it runs. Most of the measurements reported in this book assume a lightly loaded machine, with adequate memory and power. Start-up time can be affected by a program's size. Section 9.6 discusses these topics in more detail.

Applications that have these characteristics can be improved in many ways, which are discussed at length throughout this and the following chapters. There are ways to reduce the number of widgets used, ways to use widgets more efficiently, and ways to structure a program to prevent lengthy operations from interfering with the user's perception of start-up time. There are some specific ways to take advantage of Motif to get maximum performance. Even the case of the underpowered or overworked system can be addressed to some extent by decreasing the demands a program makes on the system.

Many of the techniques that can provide better performance require detailed discussion and explanation. However, there are a few rules of thumb that all programmers should consider as a starting point when working on start-up performance. These rules include:

1. Make the most efficient use of Motif widgets.

   Some Motif widgets must be handled with great care to achieve the best results. For example, adding items one at a time to an XmList widget will take far longer than adding all items at once.

   Some widgets are also cheaper to use than others. For example, it is far cheaper to display read-only text in an XmLabel widget or gadget than to use an XmText widget set to read-only mode. A label widget can be created and initialized much more quickly than a text widget. The label widget's runtime performance is likely to be better as well. (See Section 10.6.) The improvement is unlikely to be noticeable if only a single widget is involved. With many widgets, the cumulative effect may be quite noticeable.

Each widget class must be initialized the first time a widget that belongs to that class is created. For some classes, this initialization time can be significant. For example, the XmText and XmTextField widgets create cursors when the first widget of the class is created. Therefore, applications should probably not create a previously unused type of widget if another type, already in use, will do. For example, it might be cheaper for a program that already contains one XmText widget to create a second XmText widget than to create an XmTextField. Of course, if a program really needs the functionality of a different widget class, the performance cost is seldom worth the loss of functionality.

There may be other performance issues with specific releases of Motif, or versions of Motif on specific platforms, as well. For example, the drag and drop support in initial versions of Motif 1.2 caused geometry management to be more expensive when drag and drop is used (the default) than when it is not.

Gadgets can also be used in some situations to greatly improve start-up performance. In other cases, gadgets may actually reduce performance. The effect of gadgets on performance is investigated in detail later.

2. Be sure the application is dealing with geometry management in the most efficient manner.

   Each time a widget is managed, the widget's parent is notified, *if* the parent is realized. Depending on the parent's geometry management policy, the parent may recompute the layout of all children each time it is notified that its set of managed children has changed. Changes in a layout may require changes in the parent's size, which may prompt configuration requests even further up the widget hierarchy. If the widgets involved in these configuration changes are realized, the process may generate a large amount of X server traffic as well.

   As a rule of thumb, all children added after a widget is realized should be managed at once, by calling `XtManageChildren()`. Widgets should be managed beginning with the bottom of the hierarchy, and all management, as well as all geometry manipulations, should be completed before the widgets are realized. If widgets are not yet realized when children are managed, there should be no loss of performance from managing children individually.

3. Use the shallowest widget hierarchy possible.

Xt's geometry management is a complex process than involves computing each widget's desired size and propagating geometry requests up and down the widget hierarchy. The deeper the widget hierarchy, the more computations and geometry requests may be involved. Depending on when the geometry management occurs, this process may also generate a large amount of traffic between the application and the X server. Best performance will usually be achieved by using the smallest number of manager widgets possible to create any given layout.

4. Minimize the user's perception of start-up by delaying non-essential operations until after the user interface is running.

   If start-up speed is the goal, it is important to architect an application with user perception in mind. Programmers should plan for start-up performance by thinking from the user's perspective rather than from the program's view. For example, when an application first appears, the user typically sees a window and a menu bar. The window may have something displayed in it, or it may not. Even if a window will eventually have some contents, a user's perception of start-up time can sometimes be improved by simply displaying an empty window as quickly as possible. A busy cursor can be displayed, if necessary, until the rest of the application is ready.

   Even more interesting is what the user cannot see. For example, when a window first appears, the user can see the title of each pane in the menu bar. However, he or she cannot see the items in the menu panes. Applications that need to minimize start-up time can create menu items after the interface is visible. In CPU terms, it takes a very long time for a user to focus on a new window, identify the desired menu pane and move the mouse to select the menu. A program can easily create the menu items during this time, to create the illusion of faster start-up time. Instead of creating such items while the user is waiting for the program, they can be created while the program would be waiting for the user.

5. Use the fastest `malloc()` implementation available.

   Like any object-oriented system, Motif is highly dependent on dynamically allocated memory. All Motif widgets are structures that are created by calling `malloc()`, and many other features of Motif and X allocate memory, as well. Even placing events on an application's event queue may require space to be allocated by calling `malloc()`. Therefore the performance of `malloc()` itself can have an important effect on the performance of a Motif application.

Most systems support several variations of `malloc()`, and one of these may provide better performance than the others. However, patterns of memory use vary widely from application to application, so it is difficult to identify any single `malloc()` implementation as "best" for all applications. It is also important to consider the long term behavior of any `malloc()` library. The fact that a particular implementation of `malloc()` improves start-up time does not necessarily mean that it will have the best overall behavior over the lifetime of a program.

These points are explored further in the following sections, along with examples, measurements, and suggestions for ways to implement these guidelines.

9.3 Managing Widgets and Gadgets

The previous section mentions that it is more efficient to manage widgets before their parents are realized, or to manage them in groups after their parents are realized. The following example program serves as a test case to explore the performance characteristics associated with various approaches to creating and managing widgets. The program simply creates a collection of push buttons as children of an XmRowColumn widget. The XmRowColumn widget is a child of a form, just to add some typical geometry management into the test.

The `widgettest` program accepts several command line arguments, to allow different tests to be performed easily without modifying or recompiling the program. The command line arguments recognized by `widgettest` are:

- `numWidgets`: This flag allows the user to specify the number of widgets to be created.
- `manageAll`: This flag changes the program to manage all children at once using `XtManageChildren()`. Without this flag, the program manages all children individually when they are created, using `XtCreateManagedWidget()`.

- afterRealize: This flag changes the program's behavior so that the push buttons are created and managed after their parent is realized and visible on the screen.
- useGadgets: When this flag is present, the program creates XmPushButton gadgets. If the program is run without this flag, XmPushButton widgets are created.
- unmanagedParent: When this option is specified, the row column widget is managed after its children are managed. Without this flag, the row column widget is managed before the children are created.

In summary, the widgettest program can create any number of widgets or gadgets, managed individually or as a group. The program can realize the shell before or after the buttons are created, and manage the XmRowColumn parent before or after its children. The widgettest program uses the ReportTime(), WaitForWindow() and HandleEvents() functions described earlier to report the time required to create and display all widgets. The first call to ReportTime() occurs right after the XmRowColumn widget is created, because everything leading up to this point is the same in all cases. Here is the program:

```
/**********************************************************
 * widgettest.c: Experiment with creating many widgets.
 **********************************************************/
#include <Xm/Xm.h>
#include <Xm/RowColumn.h>
#include <Xm/Form.h>
#include <Xm/PushB.h>
#include <Xm/PushBG.h>
#include "TimerTools.h"

int          numWidgets      = 100;
Boolean      manageAll       = FALSE;
Boolean      useGadgets      = FALSE;
Boolean      afterRealize    = FALSE;
Boolean      unmanagedParent   = TRUE;

/*
 * Set up command-line arguments.
 */

static XtResource resources[] = {
{ "numWidgets", "NumWidgets", XmRInt, sizeof(int),
        ( Cardinal )  &numWidgets,  XmRImmediate,
        ( XtPointer )  100 },
```

```
{ "manageAll", "ManageAll", XmRBoolean, sizeof  ( Boolean ),
        ( Cardinal ) &manageAll,  XmRString, "FALSE" },
{ "afterRealize", "AfterRealize", XmRBoolean, sizeof  ( Boolean ),
        ( Cardinal ) &afterRealize,  XmRString, "FALSE"},
{ "useGadgets", "UseGadgets", XmRBoolean, sizeof  ( Boolean ),
        ( Cardinal ) &useGadgets,  XmRString, "FALSE" },
{ "unmanagedParent", "UnmanagedParent", XmRBoolean,
        sizeof  ( Boolean ), ( Cardinal ) &unmanagedParent,
        XmRString, "TRUE" },
};

XrmOptionDescRec options[] = {
  {"-numWidgets",   "*numWidgets",   XrmoptionSepArg, NULL },
  {"-useGadgets",   "*useGadgets",   XrmoptionNoArg, "TRUE"},
  {"-manageAll",    "*manageAll",    XrmoptionNoArg, "TRUE"},
  {"-afterRealize", "*afterRealize", XrmoptionNoArg, "TRUE"},
  {"-unmanagedParent", "*unmanagedParent",
                                     XrmoptionNoArg, "FALSE"},
};

void main ( int argc, char **argv )
{
    Widget       shell, rowcol, form;
    XtAppContext app;
    int          i;
    WidgetList   widgets;
    WidgetClass  widgetType = xmPushButtonWidgetClass;

    shell = XtAppInitialize ( &app, "Widgettest",
                              options, XtNumber ( options ),
                              &argc, argv, NULL, NULL, 0 );
   /*
    * Load options.
    */

    XtGetApplicationResources ( shell, 0, resources,
                                XtNumber ( resources ),
                                NULL, 0  );

   /*
    * Allocate a list in which to keep all children.
    */

    widgets = ( WidgetList ) XtMalloc ( sizeof( Widget ) *
                                        numWidgets );

   /*
    * If gadgets are to be used, change the class pointer.
    */
```

Start timing

```

    if ( useGadgets )
        widgetType = xmPushButtonGadgetClass;

   /*
    * Create the manager widgets.
    */

    form = XtVaCreateManagedWidget ( "form",
                                     xmFormWidgetClass,
                                     shell, NULL );

    rowcol = XtVaCreateWidget ( "rowcol",
                                xmRowColumnWidgetClass, form,
                                XmNnumColumns, 20,
                                NULL );

   /*
    * Start timing from the point after the parents have
    * been created.
    */

    ReportTime ( "Row Column Created", FALSE );

   /*
    * Manage the parent now, if this option is not selected.
    */

    if ( !unmanagedParent )
        XtManageChild ( rowcol );

   /*
    * If we are measuring the effect of managing children of
    * a realized widget, realize the shell now.
    */

    if ( afterRealize )
    {
        XtRealizeWidget ( shell );
    }

   /*
    * Create the children of the XmRowColumn widget. If
    * children are to be managed in groups, store each child
    * in an array  and then call XtManageChildren().
    * Otherwise, just call XtCreateManagedWidget().
    */


```

```
    if ( manageAll )
    {
        for ( i = 0; i < numWidgets; i++ )
            widgets[i] = XtCreateWidget ( "button", widgetType,
                                          rowcol, NULL, 0 );
        XtManageChildren ( widgets, numWidgets );
    }
    else
       for ( i = 0; i < numWidgets; i++ )
           XtCreateManagedWidget ( "button", widgetType,
                                   rowcol, NULL, 0 );
   /*
    * Now that all children are managed, handle the parent,
    * depending on the options specified. Manage and/or
    * realize, if necessary.
    */

    if ( unmanagedParent )
        XtManageChild ( rowcol );

    if ( !afterRealize )
        XtRealizeWidget ( shell );
   /*
    * Now wait for the shell to appear on the screen.
    * Handle all pending events, to ensure
    * repeatable behavior for measurements.
    */

    WaitForWindow( shell );
    HandleEvents ( shell );
    ReportTime ( "UP", TRUE );

}
```

End timing

Running this program with one hundred widgets and gadgets and various command line arguments produces the table shown in Figure 9.13.

When managed	Operation	Widgets	Gadgets
Before realize	Individually managed	0.448	0.354
Before realize	Managed as a group	0.439	0.321
After realize	Individually managed	0.695	0.521
After realize	Managed as a group	0.461	0.307
After realize	Manage as a group, parent unmanaged	0.425	0.309

Figure 9.13 Times reported by `widgettest` for 100 children.

Figure 9.14 shows the information reported in Figure 9.13, plotted as a bar graph. The cross-hatched bars represent gadgets, while the solid grey bars represent widgets.

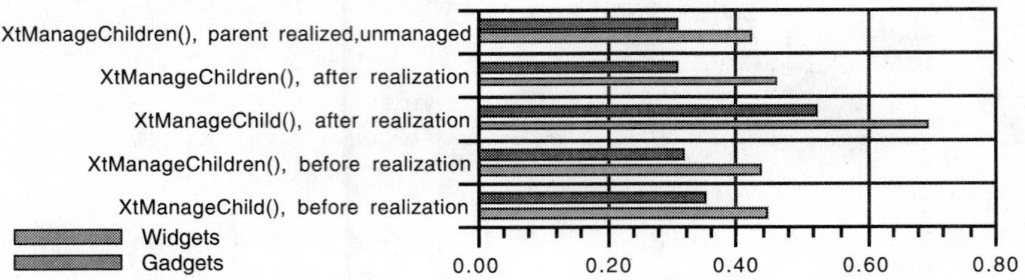

Figure 9.14 Graph of data in Figure 9.13 (100 children).

Although the differences between the various approaches are very small in this example, there are several clear trends. It appears that managing individual children before their parent is realized is faster than managing individual widgets afterward. It also appears that managing as a group is more efficient than managing individually when the children's parent is already realized. Gadgets also seem to be slightly faster than widgets in each case.

However, notice that managing as a group is virtually the same as individual management when all children are managed before their parent is realized. This measurement is consistent with the architecture of Xt. When the child of an unrealized widget is managed, Xt does not notify the parent until the parent is realized. Applications that can manage widgets before realization do not need to take special precautions. However, applications that need to create and manage widgets after the parent is realized need to exercise more care, as these numbers show.

The comparison of widgets and gadgets is also interesting. Gadgets were originally designed to be "cheap" widgets. However, over the years, widgets have become cheaper, mostly because X servers have become better at creating windows. In recent years, many programmers have concluded that gadgets are actually more expensive that widgets. Certainly, the difference in start-up time is not dramatically better for gadgets than widgets in this test case, although the gadgets do clearly and consistently produce slightly faster start-up times in this example. The relationships shown in this experiment held true on each of the test machines described in Chapter 7.

There are other aspects of gadget performance that need to be explored in relation to runtime behavior, but this experiment seems to indicate that using gadgets might improve start-up performance in some situations. Remember, of course, that this particular exercise demonstrates a rather contrived situation. Few real programs would create 100 push buttons in a single row column widget, although such situations do occur.

It is interesting to see how the `widgettest` program behaves when different numbers of children are created. For example, Figure 9.15 and Figure 9.16 shows the results of a more realistic test that creates 25 widgets, while Figure 9.17 and Figure 9.18 show the measurements for 500 widgets.

When managed	Operation	Widgets	Gadgets
Before realize	Individually managed	0.175	0.127
Before realize	Managed as a group	0.174	0.128
After realize	Individually managed	0.188	0.142
After realize	Managed as a group	0.165	0.122
After realize	Manage as a group, parent unmanaged	0.159	0.120

Figure 9.15 Times reported by `widgettest` program for 25 children.

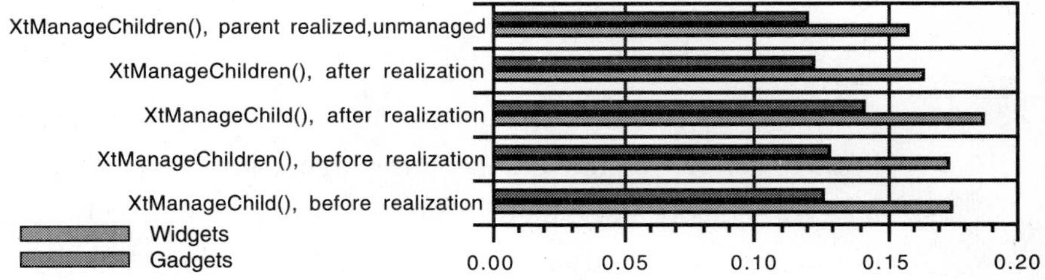

Figure 9.16 Graph of data in Figure 9.15 (25 children).

In each experiment, the same basic relationships exhibited by the first series of tests continue to hold true. Gadgets seem to be marginally faster than widgets, and managing individual widgets before realization is definitely faster than managing afterward. Once the parent has been realized, managing children in groups is faster than managing them individually. For the case involving only 25 widgets, notice that the difference between managing before and after realization is very small. However, the effect is quite pronounced with larger numbers of widgets.

When managed	Operation	Widgets	Gadgets
Before realize	Individually managed	1.95	1.329
Before realize	Managed as a group	1.902	1.329
After realize	Individually managed	7.223	5.815
After realize	Managed as a group	2.319	1.317
After realize	Manage as a group, parent unmanaged	1.938	1.328

Figure 9.17 Times reported by `widgettest` program for 25 children.

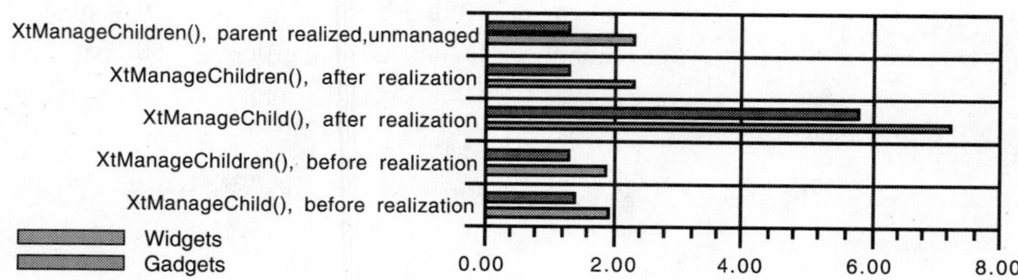

Figure 9.18 Graph of data in Figure 9.17 (500 children)

These measurements indicate that performance of this program is not linearly related to the number of widgets involved. The time required to manage widgets individually after their parent is realized is particularly non-linear. With 25 children, as seen in Figure 9.15, managing children individually takes 1.14 times the amount of time to manage them in a group. When using 100 widgets, as seen in Figure 9.13, managing children individually takes 1.5 times as long as managing them in a group. When 500 widgets are involved, the ratio becomes even greater. Managing 500 children individually takes 3.11 times as long as managing all children at once.

Also notice that the gap between using gadgets and widgets becomes more significant when the buttons are managed as a group after the parent is realized. With 25 widgets, the difference between using gadgets and widgets is 0.043 second, which is not significant. With 100 widgets, the difference is 0.154

second. In the extreme case of creating 500 buttons, the difference between using gadgets and widgets rises to 1 second.

Given the restrictions associated with gadgets, one might choose to not use gadgets for a potential gain of only hundredths of a second, but if an application requires hundreds of buttons or labels, it appears that gadgets might be worth considering.

Another important point to consider when examining these figures is the difference between the fastest possible way to display a set of buttons and the worst possible way. First, within any given set of figures, using gadgets, managed all at once before the parent is realized is significantly faster than the worst case, in which widgets are managed individually after the parent is realized. With only 25 widgets, the difference between the best and worst case, is 0.073 second, which is not large. However, when creating 500 widgets, the difference is 5.89 second, which is far more significant. Although the differences between the various other approaches are less dramatic, it should be clear that there is one way to set up an interface that produces noticeably poorer performance.

Menus

Although the example program described in the previous section may seem too contrived to apply directly to a real application, the situation simulated by the `widgettest` program is not uncommon. For example, applications routinely create hundreds of buttons as children of row column widgets in menus. A typical menu bar with six menu panes, each of which contain 10 items, including one submenu in each pane, creates 120 buttons. The only difference is that in such a menu, each set of 10 buttons is managed in a separate row column widget.

Let's examine the performance of the following program, which creates six menu panes that contain ten items each in a menu bar. The example creates sixty XmPushButton widgets and six XmCascadeButton widgets. The program also creates seven XmRowColumn widgets, including the menubar. One XmMenuShell widget is also created as part of the menu structure. The first part of the program creates some simple convenience routines that create menu panes, and a menu bar.

```
/*********************************************************
 * menu.c: measure time required to create menu panes.
 *********************************************************/
#include <Xm/Xm.h>
#include <Xm/MainW.h>
#include <Xm/CascadeB.h>
#include <Xm/RowColumn.h>
#include <Xm/PushB.h>
#include "TimerTools.h"

void CreatePane ( Widget parent )
{
    Widget cascade, submenu;
    int    i;

   /*
    * Create a menu pane with 10 items. Assume
    * parent is a menu bar or menu pane.
    */

    submenu = XmCreatePulldownMenu ( parent, "Submenu",
                                     NULL, 0 );

    cascade = XtVaCreateManagedWidget ( "Submenu",
                                   xmCascadeButtonWidgetClass,
                                   parent,
                                   XmNsubMenuId, submenu,
                                   NULL );
    for ( i = 0; i < 10; i++ )
        XtCreateManagedWidget ( "Item",
                               xmPushButtonWidgetClass,
                               submenu, NULL, 0 );
}

Widget CreateMenu ( Widget parent )
{
    Widget menu;
    int    i;

    /* Create a menu bar with six panes. */

    menu = XmCreateMenuBar ( parent, "menu", NULL, 0 );

    for ( i = 0; i < 6; i++ )
        CreatePane ( menu );

    XtManageChild ( menu );
    return ( menu );
}
```

The body of the program simply creates an XmMainWindow widget and calls `CreateMenu()` to add a menu bar with six menu panes to the window. The program calls `ReportTime()` before calling `XtAppInitialize()`, and again after the window appears on the screen.

```
void main ( int argc, char ** argv )
{
    Widget       shell, mainWindow, menu;
    XtAppContext app;

```

Start timing

```
    ReportTime ( "Starting", TRUE );

    shell = XtAppInitialize (  &app, "Menu", NULL, 0,
                               &argc, argv, NULL, NULL, 0 );

    mainWindow = XtCreateManagedWidget ( "mainWindow",
                                         xmMainWindowWidgetClass,
                                         shell, NULL, 0 );
   /*
    * Create a menubar and install it into the main window.
    */

    menu =  CreateMenu ( mainWindow );
    XtVaSetValues ( mainWindow,
                    XmNmenuBar, menu,
                    NULL );

    XtRealizeWidget ( shell );
```

Process events

```
    WaitForWindow ( shell );
    HandleEvents ( shell );

```

Stop timing

```
    ReportTime ( "Up", TRUE );

    XtAppMainLoop ( app );
}
```

Figure 9.19 shows the start-up times reported by running this program on System A.

```
% menu
Starting:
Up:
   Elapsed Time  = 0.69
   User Time     = 0.340
   System Time   = 0.070
```

Figure 9.19 Start-up times of the `menu` program, with six menu panes.

As shown in Figure 9.19, this program requires 0.69 second to create the menu and display the window. Although this is still a very short period of time, this simple program's start-up time does not meet the 0.3 second goal we established. This program is more realistic than earlier examples, in terms of the number of widgets used. The program never manages more than ten widgets as children of an XmRowColumn widget, which is far more conservative than the hundreds of widgets measured in the earlier tests. Even so, start-up time has increased significantly compared to the `hello` program described earlier in this chapter. We should be concerned that this program's start-up time is slower than we would like, because this program is still extremely simple. Real programs need to do even more, both creating more widgets, and performing application-specific tasks.

Figure 9.20 shows the start-up times reported by running this program on System B, the X terminal. As expected, the reported start-up time is substantially longer on this system. Notice the difference between the elapsed time and the CPU time, in particular.

```
% menu
Starting:
Up:
   Elapsed Time = 3.530
   User Time    = 0.320
   System Time  = 0.070
```

Figure 9.20 Menu start-up times on an X terminal.

We can attempt to improve the `menu` program's start-up time by applying what we learned in the previous section. An important thing to know is that `XmCreatePulldownMenu()` creates a menu pane and immediately realizes the widget. Therefore, the menu panes in this program represent the worst-case scenario described in the last section. Each entry in each menu pane is a widget, and is managed individually as a child of a realized parent.

Therefore, as a first step toward improving the `menu` program's start-up time, we can change the program to manage menu entries in groups. For example, `CreatePane()` could be written as follows:

```
void CreatePane ( Widget parent )
{
    Widget cascade, submenu;
    Widget buttons[10];
    int    i;
```

```
    submenu = XmCreatePulldownMenu ( parent, "Submenu",
                                     NULL, 0 );

    cascade = XtVaCreateManagedWidget ( "Submenu",
                                    xmCascadeButtonWidgetClass,
                                    parent,
                                    XmNsubMenuId, submenu,
                                    NULL  );
    for ( i = 0; i < 10; i++ )
      buttons[i] = XtCreateWidget ( "Item",
                                    xmPushButtonWidgetClass,
                                    submenu, NULL, 0 );

    XtManageChildren ( buttons, 10 );
}
```

Running this modified version of `menu` produces the times shown in Figure 9.21.

```
% menu
Starting:
Up:
   Elapsed Time  = 0.63
   User Time     = 0.310
   System Time   = 0.070
```

Improvement of 0.06 sec.

Figure 9.21 Start-up times for `menu`, managing children in groups.

Managing the menu items in groups does not produce a large improvement, but it is a start. As we learned earlier, changing the program to use gadgets may also help. Gadgets are particularly effective in menus, because the limitations associated with gadgets are seldom a problem in this situation. Modifying `CreatePane()` again to use gadgets reduces the total start-up time to 0.52 second, as shown in Figure 9.22, for a total savings of 0.17 second over the original version:

```
% menu
Starting:
Up:
   Elapsed Time  = 0.52
   User Time     = 0.250
   System Time   = 0.060
```

Total improvement = 0.17

Figure 9.22 Start-up times for menu, managing gadgets in groups.

The start-up time on System B, the X terminal, remains slower than System A, as expected. However, the improvement over the previous X terminal times is more noticeable. Figure 9.23 shows that changing this program to use gadgets and managing in groups shaves 0.82 second from the start-up time on System B.

Total improvement = 0.82

```
% menu
Starting:
Up:
   Elapsed Time = 2.710
   User Time    = 0.280
   System Time  = 0.070
```

Figure 9.23 Menu start-up, using gadgets on an X terminal.

Even with these changes, this program is slower than the `hello` example described earlier in this chapter. The most likely explanation for the difference in performance is the much larger number of widgets created in this example. It is also possible that the XmMainWindow widget used in this example takes a significant amount of time to create. The XmMainWindow widget is a fairly complex widget, and different widgets do require different amounts of time to create and initialize. In any case, every widget is needed, and there is nothing to remove and no remaining straight-forward improvements to be made. Fortunately, there are some techniques that can be used to improve the user's perception of start-up time in situations like this. These techniques, which use work procedures to delay certain operations, are explored in Section 9.7.

9.4 Creating Economical User Interfaces

The tests in the previous section demonstrate that the time required to create and manage large numbers of children can be significant. Part of a program's start-up time is spent creating and managing widgets, part is spent loading resources and so on. Some applications truly require a large number of widgets to implement their user interface. In other cases, the number of widgets can be significantly reduced with some attention to the design of the interface.

There are many benefits to thinking economically when designing a user interface. Often, the first interface that comes to mind is not the best interface in terms of both efficiency and usability. This section explores a simple program and shows how a user interface design can affect an application's performance.

Example: A File Permissions Panel

Let's design an interface for a simple program that might be provided as part of a desktop environment and that allows a user to change the access permissions of a file. On UNIX systems, there are three types of users who can be granted access to a file: the owner, the members of a group, and all others. Each type of user may have different access privileges. Each may have permission to read a file, to modify a file, or to execute a file (assuming the file is executable). The interface should display the current state of each characteristic of the file, for each type of person, and should allow each aspect to be changed.

An initial design of an interface to address these needs might look like the window shown in Figure 9.24.

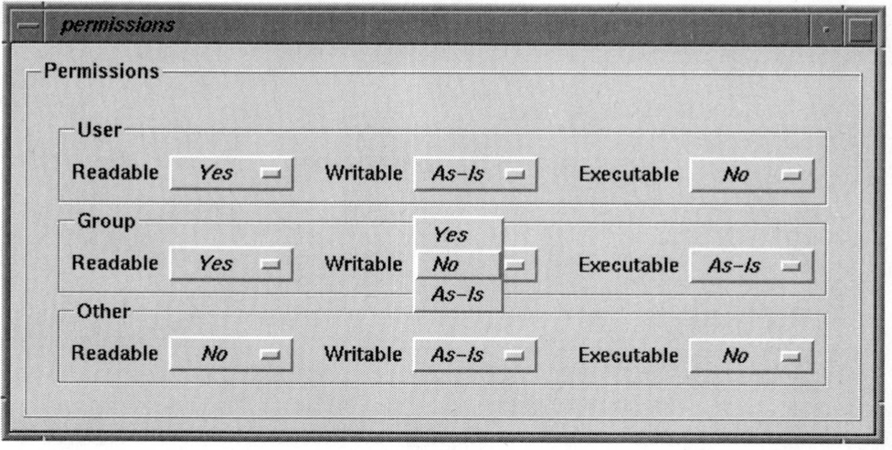

Figure 9.24 First interface for changing file permissions.

The interface in Figure 9.24 is meant to be very "user friendly," and aesthetically pleasing Everything is nicely labeled and laid out in related groups. XmFrame widgets can be used to offset and label related areas. For each type of user, each type of permission can be controlled by an option menu. The option menu allows the current value of each field to be displayed, and allows the user to change the item if desired. Each option menu allows a choice of "Yes", "No", or "As-Is" for each type of permission. The "As-Is" option allows the user to leave any given permission unchanged without specifying exactly what it is.

Ignoring the underlying functionality, a program that implements this interface can be written fairly easily. The following short program creates the layout shown in Figure 9.24. The first function creates the option menu used for each individual item in the panel.

```
/***********************************************************
 * permissions.c: Layout for permissions panel design.
 ***********************************************************/
#include <Xm/Xm.h>
#include <Xm/Label.h>
#include <Xm/Frame.h>
#include <Xm/Form.h>
#include <Xm/RowColumn.h>
#include <Xm/PushB.h>
#include "TimerTools.h"

Widget CreateOption ( Widget parent, char *name )
{
    Arg    args[2];
    Widget pane, option, yes, no, asis;

   /*
    * Create a single Yes/No/As-Is option menu.
    */

    pane = XmCreatePulldownMenu ( parent, "pane", NULL, 0 );

    XtSetArg ( args[0], XmNsubMenuId, pane );
    option = XmCreateOptionMenu ( parent, name, args, 1 );

    XtManageChild ( option );

    yes = XtCreateManagedWidget ( "Yes",
                                  xmPushButtonWidgetClass,
                                  pane, NULL, 0);

    no = XtCreateManagedWidget ( "No",
                                 xmPushButtonWidgetClass,
                                 pane, NULL, 0);

```

```
    asis = XtCreateManagedWidget ( "As-Is",
                                   xmPushButtonWidgetClass,
                                   pane, NULL, 0);
    return( option );
}
```

The function `CreateRWE()` creates a framed set of option menus to handle the values of the "readable', "writable", and "executable" attributes of each type of user.

```
Widget CreateRWE ( Widget parent, char *name )
{
    Widget frame, label, rowcolumn;

   /*
    * Create a labeled frame containing a row of option menus
    */

    frame = XtVaCreateManagedWidget ( "frame",
                             xmFrameWidgetClass, parent,
                             XmNshadowType, XmSHADOW_ETCHED_IN,
                             NULL );

    label = XtVaCreateManagedWidget ( name,
                              xmLabelWidgetClass, frame,
                              XmNchildType, XmFRAME_TITLE_CHILD,
                              NULL );

    rowcolumn = XtVaCreateManagedWidget ( "rowColumn",
                           xmRowColumnWidgetClass,frame,
                           XmNorientation,   XmHORIZONTAL,
                           XmNpacking,       XmPACK_COLUMN,
                           XmNchildType, XmFRAME_WORKAREA_CHILD,
                           NULL );

    CreateOption ( rowcolumn, "Readable" );
    CreateOption ( rowcolumn, "Writable" );
    CreateOption ( rowcolumn, "Executable" );

    return ( frame );
}
```

The function `CreatePermissionsPanel()` creates a labeled frame, which holds an XmRowColumn widget. The XmRowColumn widget manages three rows, one for each of users, groups, and others. Each row is created by calling `CreateRWE()`.

```
Widget CreatePermissionPanel ( Widget parent)
{
    Widget form1, frame1, form, rowColumn1,
           label, user, group, other;

    form1 = XtCreateManagedWidget ( "form", xmFormWidgetClass,
                                    parent, NULL, 0 );

    frame1 = XtVaCreateManagedWidget ( "frame1",
                    xmFrameWidgetClass,  form1,
                    XmNshadowType,       XmSHADOW_ETCHED_OUT,
                    XmNtopAttachment,    XmATTACH_FORM,
                    XmNbottomAttachment, XmATTACH_FORM,
                    XmNleftAttachment,   XmATTACH_FORM,
                    XmNrightAttachment,  XmATTACH_FORM,
                    XmNtopOffset,        10,
                    XmNbottomOffset,     10,
                    XmNleftOffset,       10,
                    XmNrightOffset,      10,
                    NULL );

    label = XtVaCreateManagedWidget ( "Permissions",
                            xmLabelWidgetClass, frame1,
                            XmNchildType, XmFRAME_TITLE_CHILD,
                            NULL );

    form = XtVaCreateManagedWidget ( "form",
                         xmFormWidgetClass, frame1,
                         XmNchildType, XmFRAME_WORKAREA_CHILD,
                         NULL );

    rowColumn1 = XtVaCreateManagedWidget ( "rowColumn1",
                          xmRowColumnWidgetClass, form,
                          XmNtopAttachment,    XmATTACH_FORM,
                          XmNbottomAttachment, XmATTACH_FORM,
                          XmNleftAttachment,   XmATTACH_FORM,
                          XmNrightAttachment,  XmATTACH_FORM,
                          XmNtopOffset,        20,
                          XmNbottomOffset,     20,
                          XmNleftOffset,       20,
                          XmNrightOffset,      20,
                          NULL );

    user =  CreateRWE ( rowColumn1, "User" );
    group = CreateRWE ( rowColumn1, "Group" );
    other = CreateRWE ( rowColumn1, "Other" );

    return ( form1 );
}
```

The following simple program serves as a driver to launch the panel. The permissions panel might be used as a stand-alone program, but it is more likely to be created as a dialog that is posted from within another program. The calls to `ReportTime()` report the initial start-up, and measure the time required to create and display the panel.

```
void main ( int argc, char **argv )
{
    Widget          shell;
    XtAppContext    app;

    ReportTime ( "Starting", FALSE );

    shell = XtAppInitialize ( &app, "Permissions", NULL, 0,
                              &argc, argv, NULL, NULL, 0 );

    ReportTime ( "Creating panel", TRUE );

    CreatePermissionPanel ( shell );

    XtRealizeWidget ( shell );

    WaitForWindow ( shell );
    HandleEvents ( shell );

    ReportTime ( "Panel up", TRUE );

    XtAppMainLoop ( app );
}
```

Figure 9.25 shows the times reported by running the `permissions` program on System A. The panel itself can be created and displayed in 0.52 second. The Xt initialization and program start-up adds an additional 0.13 second.

```
% permissions
Starting:
Creating Panel:
   Elapsed Time = 0.13
   User Time    = 0.040
   System Time  = 0.040
Panel up:
   Elapsed Time = 0.52
   User Time    = 0.280
   System Time  = 0.030
```

Figure 9.25 Start-up times for the `permissions` program.

Notice that a total of 0.31 second (0.28 + 0.03) of CPU time is required to create and display the panel. This program is doing more work than previous programs we have examined. Presumably, part of the time is spent creating widgets, performing geometry management, and so on.

Start-up time on the X terminal is substantially slower, as shown in Figure 9.26.[1]

```
% permissions
Starting:
Creating panel:
   Elapsed Time = 0.500
   User Time    = 0.040
   System Time  = 0.040
Panel up:
   Elapsed Time = 2.310
   User Time    = 0.260
   System Time  = 0.040
```

Figure 9.26 Permissions start-up on an X terminal.

Examining the `permissions` program's use of the X server with `xmond` and `xmonui` reveals some interesting data about this panel. The program makes 380 requests to display the permissions panel and the server generates 158 events. Reducing these events and requests is unlikely, by itself, to improve performance measurably, but the events and requests do provide clues to the underlying complexity of the interface. Changing the interface or the implementation to reduce the number of requests may improve performance in other ways.

Of the requests made by this program, those shown in Figure 9.27 are the most relevant and interesting.

[1] Looking at this example with some performance tools that can provide information about instruction counts and other data also provides some interesting insight into the `permissions` program's performance. Although experiments in this book do not rely on tools that are not widely available, the following information is worth considering. The `preference` program makes 87 calls to various widgets' internal `change_managed` methods, which is interesting because the geometry management process can sometimes be expensive. The call to `CreatePermissionsPanel()` executes 7,451,575 CPU instructions. While executing `CreatePermissionsPanel()`, the program calls `malloc()` 3207 times to allocate 125,306 bytes memory, of which 82,909 are not freed.

Request	# of Requests
CreateWindow	70
ChangeWindowAttributes	19
MapWindow	37
MapSubwindows	20
ConfigureWindow	45
CreateGC	8
PolySegment	108
PolyFillRectangle	9
PolyText8	13

Figure 9.27 Some requests made by `permissions` program.

The X server also generates 158 events when this program is executed, as shown in Figure 9.28.

Event Type	# of Events
Expose	69
MapNotify	42
ReparentNotify	1
ConfigureNotify	46

Figure 9.28 Events received by `permissions` program.

The `ConfigureNotify` events are perhaps the most interesting, because these could potentially trigger changes in geometry layouts that could be quite expensive. Alternately, the `ConfigureNotify` events could be the result of the panel's geometry management rather than a cause. Referring to Figure 9.27, we can see that the application makes 45 `ConfigureWindow` requests, so the latter assumption is more likely.

The number of `Expose` events is also interesting. Taking a naive view, one might suppose that when a window is displayed, the application is notified and simply redraws the entire window. The 69 `Expose` events sent to this relatively simple panel indicate that the real behavior is much more complex.

Counting Widgets

It is interesting to consider the number of widgets created by this example, because each widget adds to the work a program must perform. Figure 9.28 shows that the application receives 42 `MapNotify` events, which probably means that at least 42 windows are mapped when the program starts up. Figure 9.27 shows that the application creates 70 windows, and the other performance measurements show that various `change_managed` methods are called 87 times. Although the permissions panel does not appear to be very complex, this interface seems to use a surprising number of widgets (and corresponding windows).

It would be useful to have an easy way to count the widgets in a program. One way to determine the number of widgets in a program is to use `editres` to display the widgets, and to manually count them. However, for large programs, this can quickly become tedious and error-prone. `Editres` also has the ability to dump the widget hierarchy to a file, so you could save the widget hierarchy and use `wc` to count the widgets. The `xwininfo` program can also print a hierarchy of windows, which could be used with `wc` to determine the number of windows in the program, but gadgets would not be included.

The WL framework introduced in Chapter 3 provides another easy way to determine how many widgets a program creates. It is straight-forward to add a function to the WL framework that just counts all widgets in a hierarchy. The following function counts each widget, and also keeps track of how many shells, managers, primitive widgets, and gadgets a program creates.

```
/******************************************************
 * CountWidgets.c: Count the widgets in a program.
 ******************************************************/
#include <Xm/Xm.h>
#include <stdio.h>
#include "wlintP.h"

static int numManagers;
static int numPrimitive;
static int numGadgets;
static int numShells;
static int total;

void CountWidgets ( Widget w, ActionType action )
{
    Cardinal   numChildren;
    WidgetList children;

```

```
    if ( action == INIT )
    {
        numManagers = numPrimitive = 0;
        numGadgets  = total = numShells = 0;
        return;
    }

    if ( action == POSTOP )
    {
        printf ( "Total number of widgets = %d\n", total );
        printf ( "Total number of manager widgets = %d\n",
                 numManagers );
        printf ( "Total number of shells = %d\n",
                 numShells );
        printf ( "Total number of primitive widgets = %d\n",
                 numPrimitive );
        printf ( "Total number of gadgets = %d\n",
                 numGadgets );
        return;
    }

    if ( XmIsGadget ( w ) )
        numGadgets++;
    else if ( XmIsManager ( w ) )
        numManagers++;
    else if ( XmIsPrimitive ( w ) )
        numPrimitive++;
    else if ( XtIsShell ( w ) )
        numShells++;

    total++;
}
```

Besides the number of widgets created by a program, it is also interesting to know the depth of a program's widget hierarchy. The depth of the widget hierarchy provides some indication of the amount of geometry management the program must do. It is trivial to write a WL test function to determine the depth of the widget hierarchy. A function designed to perform this task, `ReportDepth()`, can be written as follows:

```
/*****************************************************
 * ReportDepth.c: Report the depth of deepest part
 *                of the widget hierarchy.
 *****************************************************/
#include <Xm/Xm.h>
#include <stdio.h>
#include "wlintP.h"
```

```

static int depth;

void ReportDepth ( Widget w, ActionType action )
{
    int count;

    if ( action == INIT )
    {
        depth = 0;
        return;
    }

    if ( action == POSTOP )
    {
        fprintf ( stderr,"Greatest widget tree depth = %d\n",
                  depth );
        return;
    }

    count = 1;

    while ( w = XtParent ( w ) )
        count++;

    if ( count > depth )
        depth = count;
}
```

Adding these functions to the WL framework and using the framework to examine the `permissions` program produces the information shown in Figure 9.29.

```
% permissions -xrm "*WLint: on" -xrm "*WLverbose: true"
*****************************
TEST: Count Widgets Test
*****************************
Total number of widgets = 87
Total number of manager widgets = 28
Total number of shells = 10
Total number of primitive widgets = 31
Total number of gadgets = 18
*****************************
TEST: Depth Test
*****************************
depth = 10
```

Figure 9.29 Widget count and depth information for `permissions` program.

From the data reported by the new WL functions, we can confirm that the `permissions` program creates 87 widgets, with a maximum hierarchy depth of 10. It is also interesting to see that the program creates 18 gadgets. Because these gadgets were not created explicitly in the program, we must assume they were created by Motif, probably as part of the option menus. (This assumption could be confirmed using `editres`, of course.)

A First Attempt at Tuning

Although the start-up time of the `permissions` program is not unreasonable, it could be improved. The program requires nearly two thirds of a second to start-up, which is well over our goal of three tenths of a second. The data gathered regarding events, requests, and widgets (and gadgets) in the interface also seems surprising. The task this panel is meant to perform is very simple, and the data seems to indicate that more work is being done than should be necessary.

As a first step, we can try to apply some of the techniques learned in earlier experiments, and change the program to manage widgets in groups and to use gadgets in the menus. The only place that managing in groups matters is in the creation of the individual option menus, because the other widgets' parents are not realized when they are managed.

Rewriting the function `CreateOption()` is sufficient to make these changes. The new version can be written as follows:

```
Widget CreateOption ( Widget parent, char *name )
{
    Arg    args[2];
    Widget pane, option;
    Widget widgets[3];

    pane = XmCreatePulldownMenu ( parent, "pane", NULL, 0 );

    XtSetArg ( args[0], XmNsubMenuId, pane );
    option = XmCreateOptionMenu ( parent, name, args, 1 );
    XtManageChild(option);

    widgets[0] = XtCreateManagedWidget ( "Yes",
                                          xmPushButtonGadgetClass,
                                          pane, NULL, 0);

    widgets[1] = XtCreateManagedWidget ( "No",
                                          xmPushButtonGadgetClass,
                                          pane, NULL, 0 );
```

```
    widgets[2] = XtCreateManagedWidget ( "As-Is",
                                         xmPushButtonGadgetClass,
                                         pane, NULL, 0 );

    XtManageChildren ( widgets, 3 );

    return ( option );
}
```

Figure 9.30 shows the times reported by running this version of the program. Changing the menus to use gadgets, and managing the buttons in each option menu in groups reduces the panel display time to 0.49 second, for an improvement of only 0.03 second. The complete program still requires 0.62 second to start-up.

```
% permissions
Starting:
Creating Panel:
   Elapsed Time  = 0.13
   User Time     = 0.040
   System Time   = 0.040
Panel up:
   Elapsed Time  = 0.49
   User Time     = 0.280
   System Time   = 0.030
```

Improvement = 0.03

Figure 9.30 Start-up times for gadget-based permissions panel.

The "improvement" shown in Figure 9.30 is too small to be worthwhile, and the program is still not as fast as we would like. We could gather the same data collected for the original version and see if there is something else that could be done to improve the start-up time. However, it seems likely that we can only shave milliseconds off the start-up time with this approach. A better way to improve the performance of this panel is to go back and reconsider the original design.

A More Economical Design

In spite of best efforts, the permission panel whose interface is shown in Figure 9.24 does not perform as well as we might like. It seems as if we should be able to display a simple panel to change permissions on a file very quickly. Users will be unlikely to use this interface if it takes substantially longer to launch than the command line equivalent (the UNIX command `chown`). The various statistics gathered to evaluate this program's performance are more surprising. For example, surely this simple task can be handled with fewer than 87 widgets and gadgets. In addition, after some use, the interface itself seems clumsy. Considering only the visual aspect of the interface, the interface itself seems rather busy. Perhaps a more compact design could solve all problems at once.

The interface shown in Figure 9.31 represents a second design for a panel that performs the same task. Here, the nested frames have been removed and the labels for each type of person have simply been placed along the left side of the widow. Instead of nine individual option menus that present the user with three choices each, a toggle button represents each individual attribute. The toggles make it easy to see if an item is set or not. The "as-is" concept is completely gone, because all a user has to do to leave any given setting "as-is" is to leave it alone. The entire panel is still surrounded by a single XmFrame widget which, while not necessary, lends a nice visual touch and provides a way to label the panel as a whole. A fully functional implementation might use this label to identify the file whose permissions are represented, so this label has a purpose. Appearance is also important, and we should not have to throw out all visual features to get performance, any more than we should clutter the interface with too many unnecessary features.

Figure 9.31 A second permissions panel interface.

This panel can be implemented using two functions. The function `CreatePermissionsPanel()` must be re-written, and `CreateRWE()` must be reimplemented as well. The function `CreateOption()` is no longer needed. The remaining two functions can be re-written as follows:

```
/***************************************************************
 * permissions2.c: Layout for second design.
 **************************************************************/
#include <Xm/Xm.h>
#include <Xm/LabelG.h>
#include <Xm/Frame.h>
#include <Xm/Form.h>
#include <Xm/RowColumn.h>
#include <Xm/ToggleBG.h>
#include "TimerTools.h"

Widget CreateRWE ( Widget parent, char *name )
{
    Widget label, readable, writable, executable;

    Widget rc = XtVaCreateManagedWidget ( "rc",
                                 xmRowColumnWidgetClass,
                                 parent,
                                 XmNorientation, XmHORIZONTAL,
                                 XmNpacking, XmPACK_COLUMN,
                                 NULL );

    label = XtCreateManagedWidget ( name,
                                   xmLabelGadgetClass, rc,
                                   NULL, 0);

    readable = XtCreateManagedWidget ( "Readable",
                                   xmToggleButtonGadgetClass,
                                   rc, NULL, 0 );

    writable = XtCreateManagedWidget ( "Writable",
                                   xmToggleButtonGadgetClass,
                                   rc, NULL, 0);

    executable = XtCreateManagedWidget ( "Executable",
                                   xmToggleButtonGadgetClass,
                                   rc, NULL, 0);
    return ( rc );
}


Widget CreatePermissionPanel ( Widget parent )
{
    Widget  form1, frame1, form, rowColumn1, label;

    form1 = XtCreateManagedWidget ( "permissions",
                                   xmFormWidgetClass,
                                   parent, NULL, 0);

```

```
    frame1 = XtVaCreateManagedWidget ( "frame1",
                        xmFrameWidgetClass,  form1,
                        XmNshadowType,       XmSHADOW_ETCHED_OUT,
                        XmNtopAttachment,    XmATTACH_FORM,
                        XmNbottomAttachment, XmATTACH_FORM,
                        XmNleftAttachment,   XmATTACH_FORM,
                        XmNrightAttachment,  XmATTACH_FORM,
                        XmNtopOffset,        10,
                        XmNbottomOffset,     10,
                        XmNleftOffset,       10,
                        XmNrightOffset,      10,
                        NULL );

    label = XtVaCreateManagedWidget ( "Permissions",
                        xmLabelWidgetClass, frame1,
                        XmNchildType, XmFRAME_TITLE_CHILD,
                        NULL );

    rowColumn1 = XtVaCreateManagedWidget ( "rowColumn1",
                        xmRowColumnWidgetClass,
                        frame1,
                        XmNorientation,    XmVERTICAL,
                        NULL );

    CreateRWE ( rowColumn1, "User" );
    CreateRWE ( rowColumn1, "Group" );
    CreateRWE ( rowColumn1, "Other" );

    return( form1 );
}
```

Figure 9.32 shows the start-up times for the new implementation of the permissions panel. The panel itself can be created and displayed in 0.17 second, which is less than half the time of the original version, and well under the 0.3 second goal. Adding 0.12 second for initialization brings the total start-up time of this program to 0.29 second.[2]

---

[2] Using the same performance tools applied to the earlier version of the permission panel confirms that the new implementation makes only 20 calls to various widgets' `change_managed` methods, as we might expect. Calling the rewritten version of `CreatePermissionsPanel()` executes 2,242,928 CPU instructions (approximately one third of the original). During the execution of `CreatePermissionsPanel()` the program makes 1184 calls to `malloc()` to allocate 68,498 bytes (less than half the memory allocated by the original). Of this, 46,368 bytes remain in use after the panel is displayed.

Total improvement = 0.35 secs

```
% permissions2
Starting:
Creating Panel:
    Elapsed Time = 0.12
    User Time    = 0.040
    System Time  = 0.040
Panel up:
    Elapsed Time = 0.17
    User Time    = 0.080
    System Time  = 0.020
```

Figure 9.32 Start-up time of second permissions panel on System A.

The performance on the X terminal system has also improved dramatically. As shown in Figure 9.33, the panel can now be displayed in 1.14 second, a reduction of 1.16 second.

Total improvement = 1.16 secs

```
% permissions2
Starting:
Creating panel:
    Elapsed Time = 0.510
    User Time    = 0.040
    System Time  = 0.040
Panel up:
    Elapsed Time = 1.140
    User Time    = 0.080
    System Time  = 0.020
```

Figure 9.33 Start-up time of second permissions panel on X terminal.

It is interesting to compare the various performance metrics that can be gathered for this panel with the original design. The new design is much simpler, and this should show up in all aspects of the panel's performance. While the original panel requires 87 widgets, the new design uses only 20. It is reasonable to expect that reducing the number of widgets from 87 to 20 might have some impact on the start-up time of this panel.

Figure 9.34 shows the output of the WL framework, using the tests added earlier in this section. The data in Figure 9.34 confirms that the total number of widgets has been reduced to 20. The number of managers and shell have been dramatically reduced. The depth of the widget hierarchy has also been reduced.

```
*****************************
TEST: Count Widgets Test
*****************************
Total number of widgets = 20
Total number of manager widgets = 6
Total number of shells = 1
Total number of primitive widgets = 0
Total number of gadgets = 13
******************************
TEST: Depth Test
*****************************
depth = 6
```

Figure 9.34 Widget count and depth information for `permissions` program.

Looking this program's behavior with `xmond` and `xmonui` shows that displaying the second panel involves 132 requests and 25 events compared to 380 and 158, respectively, for the original version. A comparison of the specific requests made and events generated by each implementation is also interesting. Figure 9.35 shows only the requests that are different between the implementations. Notice that in all but one case, the simpler version makes fewer requests than the original.

Requests	Simpler version	Original Design
CreateWindow	8	70
ChangeWindowAttributes	1	19
MapWindow	1	37
MapSubwindows	7	20
PolySegment	24	108
PolyText8	13	13
ConfigureWindow	0	45
CreateGC	10	8
SetClipRectangles	0	9
FreeGC	0	2

Figure 9.35 Comparison of requests for `permission` implementations.

Figure 9.36 compares the events generated for each implementation of the permissions panel. Only events that are different are shown. Clearly, the simpler version places fewer demands on the X server.

Event	Simpler Version	Original Design
Expose	21	69
MapNotify	2	42
ConfigureNotify	1	46

Figure 9.36 Comparison of events for `permissions` programs.

Performance and Usability

The discussion in the previous section focuses on performance, as measured in terms of clock times and server traffic. However, there are important differences between the two implementations that have been ignored. The second version if not really a more efficient version of the original. We have changed the functionality of the panel. It is often necessary to let performance characteristics or other pragmatic concerns influence a design, although it is important to balance usability, visual design, and implementation issues. The way a user interacts with an interface can be at least as important as the start-up time, or any other performance characteristic.

For example, we might conclude that second permissions panel design is simpler, cleaner, and easier to understand. For setting permissions on single files, the second interface should be far easier to use, which makes the user more efficient at performing his or her task. However, this example considered only the interface without considering the task the panel would actually perform. Neither version of the program actually operates on a file, and it is not clear from this example how the panel fits into a user's environment.

If, for example, the panel is intended to allow a user to change the permissions on multiple files at once, the "as-is" concept in the original version might be important. Because the second implementation does not support this model, a user who wants to change only one class of permission on a group of files would have to post a dialog for each individual file. In this case, the fact that the dialog comes up a bit faster would be dwarfed by the fact that the user would have to post multiple dialogs. In fact, depending on how the panel is meant to be used, one might use the information that the original implementation is 0.35 seconds slower to conclude that the advantages of the first user model outweigh the loss of performance.

So, without understanding how a particular set of widgets will be used, it is difficult to make design trade-offs between features and performance. However, measuring and understanding the performance characteristics of different approaches provides the basic information needed to make such decisions.

9.5 Geometry Management

One of the tasks every Motif application performs during the start-up phase is geometry management. We have already seen how different approaches to managing children can affect a program's performance. However, even when handled as efficiently as possible, a program performs a great deal of work when the initial widget hierarchy is created and managed. Each manager widget must determine the desired size of each of its children, and compute its own desired size. Then, if necessary, the manager must ask to be resized, and finally arrange all children, once the manager's parent has determined its size. This process is performed for each level in the widget hierarchy, and may be expensive, in some cases.

For example, consider the two versions of the `permissions` program described in the previous section. The original program, which had 87 widgets in a hierarchy 10 levels deep consumed 0.28 second of CPU time. On a 100 MIP machine, 28 milliseconds of CPU time represents a large number of instructions! It is likely that many of those cycles were consumed doing geometry management. The simpler `permissions` implementation, which creates only 20 widgets in a hierarchy only 6 levels deep consumes only 0.08 second of CPU time.

One tool that can be used to inspect the geometry management process is the XtGeo library, introduced in Chapter 3. Although normally used as a debugging tool, this library can be used to obtain some insight about the complexity of the geometry management process. Unfortunately, the output of this tool tends to be overwhelming when used to examine a complete program, so we may need to rely on statistics and filtering to obtain useful performance information from XtGeo.

The UNIX utility `grep` provides one simple way to extract useful information from XtGeo. For example, each time a widget requests a change in geometry, XtGeo produces a message similar to this:

```
"other" is making a geometry request to its parent "rowColumn1".
     Asking for a change in width: from 16 to 603.
     Asking for a change in height: from 16 to 33.
     Parent "rowColumn1" is not realized yet.
     Copy values from request to widget.
and return XtGeometryYes.
```

To find out how many geometry requests are made, we can use `grep` and the UNIX `wc` utility to filter the output of XtGeo and produce a count. For example, to compare the geometry requests made by each version of `permissions`, we could set the resource `*geoTattler` to "`on`", and execute the following commands:

```
permissions  | grep "geometry request" | wc -l
        64

permissions2  | grep "geometry request" | wc -l
        6
```

So the widgets in the original version made 64 geometry requests, compared to only 6 requests in the simpler version.

Another crude metric that could provide some insight is the sheer amount of data produced by XtGeo for each version. We could estimate the complexity of each program's total geometry management process as follows:

```
permissions   | wc -l
        3477

permissions2  | wc -l
         642
```

Unnecessary Manager Widgets

Because geometry management takes time and generates server requests, it makes sense to minimize it wherever possible. We have already found that reducing the number of widgets improves a program's performance. Of course, we cannot always just eliminate widgets. Some applications are complex and simply require many controls, labels, and so on. One error that programmers commonly make, however, involves using layers of manager widgets that serve no useful purpose. It is not uncommon, for example, to see programs that contain manager widgets that each contain only a single child.

Nested hierarchies and redundant managers often occur because of abstractions used within a program. For example, Chapter 2 discusses the advantages of creating widget hierarchies that form small self-contained modules. While this technique is good for maintainability and debugging, such techniques can also create inefficient widget hierarchies. In many cases, the programmer may not even be aware that the program has redundant managers or extremely deep widget hierarchies.

One way to reduce the amount of geometry management a program must perform is to identify and eliminate unnecessary manager widgets. The WL framework provides one way to help detect such problems. The following function, which can be installed in the framework, looks for manager widgets that contain a single child that is also a manager widget. It might be useful to search for managers with only one child of any type, as well. However, there are many legitimate uses for managers with only one child, so such a test would raise many false alarms, unless written to account for all expectations to the rule. There is seldom (although occasionally) a good reason for a manager that contains only another manager widget.

The following function warns about any widget hierarchy that appears to contain redundant managers.

```
/*******************************************************
 * RedundantManagerTest.c: test for unneeded managers
 *******************************************************/
#include <Xm/Xm.h>
#include <Xm/Frame.h>
#include <stdio.h>
#include "wlintP.h"

void RedundantManagerTest ( Widget w, ActionType action )
{
    if ( action == INIT || action == POSTOP )
        return;

    if ( XmIsManager ( w ) && !XmIsFrame ( w ) )
    {
        Cardinal   numChildren;
        WidgetList children;
        XtVaGetValues ( w,
                        XmNnumChildren, &numChildren,
                        XmNchildren,    &children,
                        NULL );
```

```

        if ( numChildren == 1 && XmIsManager ( children[0] ) )
            printf( "%s manages only %s, which is a manager\n",
                    XtName ( w ), XtName ( children[0] ) );
    }
}
```

9.6 Program Size and Start-up Performance

A very important factor in the start-up speed of any application involves the size of the process being executed. Motif programs are generally quite large, which can have serious consequences throughout the execution of the program. The effect of application size at runtime can be difficult to understand (See Chapter 10). However, the impact of size on start-up behavior is relatively simple. Before a program can be executed, the code to be run must be loaded from disk into memory. The longer it takes to load the instructions and data needed to execute the program, the slower the program's start-up time is going to be.

Several factors contribute to the time required to load an executable image into memory. The speed of the CPU plays a role, as does the speed of the disk and memory. The operating system's ability to manipulate pages also plays a role, particularly if the system has a limited amount of physical memory. Depending on how much physical memory is available, the operating system may have to unload some pages of physical memory before the pages needed by the new executable can be loaded.

The other factor is obviously the size of the program itself. The smaller a program is, the fewer pages the system has to load. It is important to understand that "size", as used here has little or nothing to do with the disk space occupied by the program, as reported by `ls`. A program's runtime size is the amount of space the program needs in physical memory to execute its instructions and access and manipulate data. This space may consist of instructions (text) from the program or libraries, or data needed by the program (dynamically allocated memory, like widgets, for example.)

Because Motif applications tend to be large, the time needed to load the initial pages of a program into memory can play a significant role in the start-up speed. Programmers have little control over most of the factors that contribute to this time. The one area in which programmers can exert some control is the size of the program. Even there, Motif, Xlib, and Xt tend to dominate the size of many programs, particularly simple ones.

This scenario is complicated by the behavior of the virtual memory system as well as shared libraries, on those systems that support them. Because the system requires time to load pages into memory, most virtual memory systems attempt to cache recently used pages. Therefore, it is possible to observe dramatically different performance depending on whether a program has been executed recently, leaving portions of its text loaded in memory. When using shared libraries, applications share portions of the text of various libraries, like Motif. If some pages of Motif are already loaded because an other application is using them, or has recently used them, a new Motif application may need fewer new pages.

Performance also depends on the amount of memory a system has. For example, if a system does not have enough physical memory to contain the pages needed by an application as well as those needed by the window manager and the X server, performance may be greatly impaired. In an extreme scenario, a system might have to unload pages needed by an application before loading the portions of the X server required to respond to a request, and then unload the X server pages to reload the application's pages. All systems require a minimum amount of memory to run X and Motif applications successfully. In some cases, you might improve a machine's performance more by adding memory than by upgrading to a faster CPU.

Let's design a simple experiment to measure the impact of these system characteristics. The behavior of different systems will vary dramatically, so this example shows just one possible behavior.

For this test, we will run the `hello` program described in Section 9.1. Recall that we measured the start-up time of the hello program as 0.20 second, based on an average of multiple runs. Those tests were performed in a "normal" environment that included several other Motif applications, and measurements were taken only after the program had been executed several times.

Let's try running this program in a somewhat different environment. First, we will exit all Motif-based applications, including the `mwm` window manager. The following experiments were performed without any window manager, executing all programs from an attached terminal to avoid unintended interaction with the system. Executing `hello`, the program reports start-up in 0.16 second. (As one might expect, the program appears to be slightly faster without the window manager interaction.)

Now, we need to find a way to force the system to "page out" all cached pages for the `hello` program, Motif, and so on. An easy way to force all cached pages out of memory is to run a program that allocates as much memory as possible and then touches each page of the allocated memory, to force it to be loaded into physical memory. If enough pages must be brought in for this program, other program's pages will be forced out. The following small program can handle this task:

```
/***************************************************
 * memhog.c: Try to force pages out of memory.
 ***************************************************/
#include <malloc.h>
#define PAGESIZE 4096

void main ( int argc, char **argv )
{
    int   size = atoi ( argv[1] ) * 1024 * 1024;
    char *pages = ( char * ) malloc ( size );
    int   i, j;

   /*
    * Touch all pages.
    */

    for ( i = 0; i < size ; i += PAGESIZE )
        pages [ i ] = i;
}
```

This program, which we will call `memhog`, allocates a large array, whose size can be specified as a command line argument, given in megabytes. The program assigns a value to one entry on each page of the allocated memory to force each page into memory.

After running `memhog` several times to be sure all pages have been forced from physical memory, we can run `hello` again. First, to be sure we are seeing only the effect of paging in the `hello` program, we should run a program that uses only Xlib before starting `hello` again. This step ensures that at least some portions of the X server are loaded, to avoid distorting the measurements with time required to page in the server. Also, because some pages may need to be loaded before the program can even call `ReportTime()`, we will use the `maptime` program described in Chapter 8 to measure the start-up time of the `hello` program. These steps produce the times reported in Figure 9.37.

```
% memhog 64
% xhw
% maptime hello
Starting:
Startup time = 2126 milliseconds
Up:
   Elapsed Time = 1.670
   User Time    = 0.60
   System Time  = 0.60
```

Figure 9.37 Hello program start-up, with all memory cleared.

Notice that the time required to start this program has increased by an order of magnitude. Notice that the difference between the internally reported time and the time reported by `maptime` is much greater than when the system does not have to bring in so many pages just to begin to execute the program.

Now, we can run the program again. This time, the measurements show the results of the system's caching behavior. Some pages used by the program, as well as parts of Motif and Xt required by this program, are already loaded in memory. With this second run, the program's start-up has returned to its previous, much faster time, as shown in Figure 9.38.

```
% maptime hello
Starting:
Startup time = 187 milliseconds
Up:
   Elapsed Time = 0.17
   User Time    = 0.060
   System Time  = 0.050
```

Figure 9.38 Hello program start-up, run a second time.

Now, let's try something a little different. Once again, we can run `memhog` several times to page out all memory. Remember that no Motif programs are running at this point, although the X server is running. After clearing physical memory, this time we will run several other Motif programs, including a desktop manager and a mail program. Finally, running `hello` twice in a row produces the start-up times shown in Figure 9.39.

```
% memhog 64
% fm &
% zmail -gui &
% maptime hello
Starting:
Startup time = 248 milliseconds
Up:
   Elapsed Time = 0.21
   User Time    = 0.060
   System Time  = 0.060
% hello
Starting:
Up:
   Elapsed Time = 0.17
   User Time    = 0.060
   System Time  = 0.050
```

Figure 9.39 Hello program start-up with Motif environment running.

In this sequence of tests, `hello`'s initial start-up time is much faster than in the first series of tests. This may be because parts of Motif and Xt needed by the `hello` program have already been loaded by the other Motif applications running in the second test. Another possibility is that additional parts of the of the X server were brought in by these other programs. In any case, it is easy to see that the environment in which a program is executed has a great deal to do with its performance.

Most measurements in this book factor out the impact of the operating system by running each program multiple times, and eliminating the slowest reported time from any sequence of tests. The behavior demonstrated in this experiment is too system dependent and too unreliable to serve as a basis for most performance decisions. However, it is important to understand the issues raised in this section. We have been working to shave off a few *milliseconds*, eliminate a few server requests, and so on. Meanwhile, the state of the operating system, along with the other programs in a user's environment can easily add or subtract entire *seconds* from a program's start-up time, effectively overshadowing any other steps we might take. It is also important to realize that these tests were performed on a machine with more than enough memory to handle these programs. A system with extremely limited memory would magnify the effect demonstrated here.

9.7 Sleight of Hand Techniques

You may find that once all obvious improvements have been made, your program still takes too long to start up. Some applications are inherently complex and heavy-weight. Some absolutely require the use of many widgets. Some applications may even have difficulty managing widgets in groups, or managing widgets before realization. Or your program may be expected to run on hardware that is not powerful enough to provide good performance. For such hard-to-solve situations, programmers can resort to techniques that take advantage of the fact that the user's perception of start-up time is more important than the actual start-up time.

Many people have compared creating user interfaces to creating movies, in which various production techniques are applied to lead the viewer along, while cleverly hiding distractions and unnecessary details. However, another reasonable analogy is to compare a programmer to a magician. Magicians seem to make things appear and disappear instantly. We all know it isn't possible, but the effect is undeniable. Magicians know how to control and manipulate an audience's perception so that they see what the magician wants them to see.

The following sections explore several ways to alter a user's perception of start-up time, for those cases where it is not possible to improve the actual performance. There are undoubtedly other techniques that fit this category as well.

Delaying Non-essential Tasks

Often, a minor rearrangement of the steps a program performs as it starts up can have a significant effect on the user's perception of an application's start-up time. Most applications not only create widgets, but must read files, process data, and so on, as part of an application's initialization. However, it is usually possible to delay non-essential steps until after the program's interface is visible. By displaying the application's interface as quickly as possible, the user's perception of start-up time can be improved.

If only a small amount of additional work remains after the interface is displayed, the work may be completed by the time the user responds and begins to try to use the application. The application can take advantage of the time the user takes to react to complete any initialization that needs to be done.

Even simple applications can benefit from the technique of delaying non-essential tasks. For example, the following program reads a file, given as a command line argument, and displays it in a text editor, after adding line numbers to the beginning of each line.

```
/**********************************************************
 * fileviewer.c: Display a file with line numbers
 **********************************************************/
#include <stdio.h>
#include <Xm/Xm.h>
#include <Xm/Text.h>
#include <Xm/MainW.h>
#include "TimerTools.h"

void main ( int argc, char ** argv )
{
    XtAppContext app;
    Widget       text, shell , mainwindow;
    int          i;
    FILE        *fp;

    ReportTime ( "Starting", FALSE );

    shell = XtAppInitialize ( &app, "Fileviewer", NULL, 0,
                              &argc, argv, NULL, NULL, 0 );

    mainwindow = XtVaCreateManagedWidget ( "mainwindow",
                                           xmMainWindowWidgetClass,
                                           shell, NULL, 0 );

    text = XmCreateScrolledText ( mainwindow, "text", NULL, 0 );
    XtManageChild ( text );

    XtVaSetValues ( text,
                    XmNcolumns, 80,
                    XmNrows,    24,
                    XmNeditMode, XmMULTI_LINE_EDIT,
                    NULL );

    XtVaSetValues ( mainwindow,
                    XmNworkWindow, XtParent ( text ),
                    NULL );

    if ( argc > 1 && ( fp = fopen ( argv[1], "r" ) ) != NULL )
    {
       char buf[500];
       char buf2[600];
       int count = 0;
```

```

        while ( fgets ( buf, 500, fp ) )
        {
            sprintf ( buf2, "%d %s", count++, buf );
            XmTextInsert ( text, XmTextGetLastPosition ( text ),
                                 buf2);
         }
        fclose ( fp );
    }

    XtRealizeWidget ( shell );
    WaitForWindow ( shell );
    XmUpdateDisplay ( shell );
    ReportTime ( "Up",  TRUE );

    ReportTime ( "Ready" ,  TRUE );
    XtAppMainLoop ( app );
}
```

Using this program to display a file produces the start-up times shown in Figure 9.40.

```
% fileviewer fileviewer.c
Starting:
Up:
   Elapsed Time = 0.500
   User Time    = 0.320
   System Time  = 0.090
Ready:
   Elapsed Time = 0.000
   User Time    = 0.000
   System Time  = 0.000
```

Figure 9.40 Start-up time of original `fileviewer` program.

Rearranging the code slightly can help improve the user's perception of start-up time by getting the window on the screen more quickly. The changes, shown below, involve moving the call to `XtRealizeWidget()` to the point before the file is read and processed. To be sure the window is drawn properly, it is necessary to call a function like `XmUpdateDisplay()` to handle pending events.

In some cases, additional precautions must be taken to avoid the problems caused by changes to widgets after realization. In this example, moving the call to `XtRealizeWidget()` to before the file is read allows the user to see the scrollbars being adjusted as each line is added to the XmText widget. The scrollbar motion is visually distracting, and also causes an unacceptable degradation of the performance. An easy way to fix this problem is to delay managing the XmText widget until after the file is loaded. For large files, a busy cursor could be displayed as well.

```
/*******************************************************
 * fileviewer2.c: Display a file with line numbers
 *******************************************************/
#include <stdio.h>
#include <Xm/Xm.h>
#include <Xm/Text.h>
#include <Xm/MainW.h>
#include "TimerTools.h"

void main ( int argc, char ** argv )
{
    XtAppContext app;
    Widget       text, shell, mainwindow;
    int          i;
    FILE        *fp;

    ReportTime ( "Starting", FALSE );

    shell = XtAppInitialize ( &app, "Fileviewer", NULL, 0,
                              &argc, argv, NULL, NULL, 0 );

    mainwindow = XtVaCreateManagedWidget ( "mainwindow",
                                   xmMainWindowWidgetClass,
                                   shell, NULL, 0 );
    XtRealizeWidget ( shell );
    WaitForWindow ( shell );
    XmUpdateDisplay ( shell );
    ReportTime ( "Up",  TRUE );

    text = XmCreateScrolledText ( mainwindow, "text", NULL, 0 );

    XtVaSetValues ( text,
                    XmNcolumns, 80,
                    XmNrows,    24,
                    XmNeditMode, XmMULTI_LINE_EDIT,
                    NULL );

    XtVaSetValues ( mainwindow,
                    XmNworkWindow, XtParent ( text ),
                    NULL );

```

```
    if ( argc > 1 && ( fp = fopen ( argv[1], "r" ) ) != NULL )
    {
       char buf[500];
       char buf2[600];
       int count = 0;

       while ( fgets ( buf, 500, fp ) )
       {
           sprintf ( buf2, "%d %s", count++, buf );
           XmTextInsert ( text, XmTextGetLastPosition ( text ),
                          buf2);
        }
       fclose ( fp );
    }

    XtManageChild ( text );
    ReportTime ( "Ready" ,  TRUE );
    XtAppMainLoop ( app );
}
```

Making these changes produces the start-up times shown in Figure 9.41.

```
fileviewer2 fileviewer.c
Starting:
Up:
   Elapsed Time = 0.330
   User Time    = 0.120
   System Time  = 0.080
Ready:
   Elapsed Time = 0.410
   User Time    = 0.260
   System Time  = 0.010
```

Figure 9.41 Start-up time of modified `fileviewer` program.

Notice that the total time required to start-up this program has increased slightly. However, because the window appears more quickly, the user's perception will be improved. The longer the task to be performed at start-up, the more effective this technique should be.

Start-up Screens

One simple way to improve the user's perception of start-up time is to use a *start-up screen*. Start-up screens are a standard feature of most personal computer software, but are almost unknown in UNIX and Motif-based software. The idea is to display a simple window upon start-up before the real application interface is ready. Measurements reported at the beginning of this chapter show that it is possible to display a simple window in less than a quarter of a second. Even if an application cannot be ready for a substantial amount of time, the start-up screen can be displayed to provide instantaneous response to the user. A start-up screen can reassure the user that the program is responding by displaying some kind of information while the rest of the application is starting.

Start-up screens can be used in many different ways, and can become an exercise in creativity. At a minimum, they might contain status information to allow the user to understand what the program is doing. On personal computers, start-up screens are often treated like the credits of a movie. They may contain copyright information, information about the programmers who created the product, ordering or support information, or even instructions to novices. Many applications try to make start-up screens entertaining as well. A simple animation, displayed as part of a start-up screen, can provide a pleasant distraction, while the application performs the real work in the background.

To use a start-up screen, it is necessary to architect the application so that the window that serves as a start-up screen can be displayed as quickly as possible, before the real window is created. In Motif, the easiest way to structure a program to use a start-up screen is to create an initial shell widget that is never displayed, and to create all other windows as popup children of this shell. The following program demonstrates this approach. The program includes calls to `ReportTime()` to measure how long the start-up screen takes to appear.

```
/*******************************************************
 * startupscr.c: Demonstrate a startup screen.
 *******************************************************/
#include <Xm/Xm.h>
#include <Xm/MainW.h>
#include <Xm/MessageB.h>
#include "TimerTools.h"

static Boolean startupScreenVisible = FALSE;

void DialogMapped ( Widget w,
                    XtPointer clientData,
                    XtPointer callData)
{
    startupScreenVisible = TRUE;
```

```
}
void main ( int argc, char **argv )
{
    Widget       hiddenShell, shell, dialog;
    XtAppContext app;
    Display      *dpy;

```

Start timing

```
    ReportTime ( "Starting", TRUE );

   /*
    * Initialize Xt and create a hidden shell that is never
    * seen. Set XmNmappedWhenManaged to FALSE to allow this
    * shell to serve as the parent of a dialog.
    */
    hiddenShell = XtVaAppInitialize ( &app, "Startupscr",
                                      NULL, 0, &argc, argv, NULL,
                                      XmNmappedWhenManaged, FALSE,
                                      NULL );
    dpy = XtDisplay ( hiddenShell );

   /*
    * Position the shell in the middle of the screen so
    * dialogs will be centered on the screen.
    */
    XtVaSetValues ( hiddenShell,
                    XmNx, DisplayWidth (dpy, 0 )  / 2,
                    XmNy, DisplayHeight ( dpy, 0 ) / 2,
                    NULL );
   /*
    * Realize the shell. Because XmNmappedWhenManaged is
    * FALSE, the shell does not appear.
    */
    XtRealizeWidget ( hiddenShell );

   /*
    * Create a dialog that serves as a simple startup screen.
    */
```

Create start-up screen

```
   dialog = XmCreateInformationDialog ( hiddenShell,
                                        "startupscreen",
                                        NULL, 0 );
   /*
    * Add a callback to be called when the widget is mapped.
    */
    XtAddCallback ( dialog, XmNmapCallback,
                    DialogMapped, ( XtPointer ) NULL );

   /*
    * Manage the dialog to make it appear.
    */
```

```
    XtManageChild ( dialog );

   /*
    * Without extra steps, the dialog will not actually
    * appear, or be redrawn until the application reaches
    * the event loop. To make the dialog appear as soon
    * as possible, call XSync  and then enter an event loop.
    * The event loop can be exited when the dialog is mapped,
    * as determined by the value of startupScreenVisible,
    * which is set in the DialogMapped callback.
    */

    XSync ( XtDisplay ( hiddenShell ), 0 );
    while ( !startupScreenVisible )
    {
        XEvent event;
        XtAppNextEvent ( app, &event );
        XtDispatchEvent ( &event );
    }
```

Start-up screen appears

```
    XmUpdateDisplay ( hiddenShell );
    ReportTime ( "Startup Screen Visible", TRUE );

   /*
    * Simulate a lengthy task by sleeping for a while.
    */
    sleep ( 15 );

    /*
     * Create the rest of the program's user interface.
     */

    shell = XtCreatePopupShell ( "shell1",
                                 topLevelShellWidgetClass,
                                 hiddenShell, NULL, 0 );

    XtCreateManagedWidget ( "Widget", xmMainWindowWidgetClass,
                            shell, NULL, 0 );

   /* Other UI and application setup. */

    XtPopup ( shell, XtGrabNone );

   /* Dismiss the start-up dialog. */
```

Remove start-up screen

```
    XtUnmanageChild ( dialog );

    XtAppMainLoop ( app );
}
```

Running this program produces the output shown in Figure 9.42. For this program, the start-up screen (a simple dialog) appears almost instantaneously, in 0.28 second. Once the start-up screen is displayed, the program can perform other tasks needed to display the complete interface. In this example, the start-up screen is very simple, and just displays a static message. The text displayed in the dialog can be set in a resource file. Of course, applications might also choose to create more complex start-up screens, instead of using a standard Motif dialog. The same basic approach applies in any case.

```
% startupscr
Starting:
Startup screen visible:
   Elapsed Time = 0.28
   User Time    = 0.090
   System Time  = 0.060
```

Figure 9.42 Time required for the start-up screen to appear.

A dialog is just one type of feedback that can help reduce user-perceived start-up time, and other approaches are possible. For example, even a busy cursor provides some reassurance to the user that a program is responding. If the feedback is continuous, the effect is even better. For example, a busy cursor can be animated as a program proceeds. A start-up screen can be used to display periodic updates, or to display simple animations.

In some applications, it may be possible to integrate some type of animation with the program's real task. For example, consider a program that displays sequences of large images, such as a presentation, or slide-making program. Switching between images might be quite time consuming, particularly if it involves reading a large image from the disk. However, if the program provides various transition effects (fading between images, dissolving the current image, and so on), the user may consider these transition effects to be simply part of the process. Meanwhile, under the cover of the interesting, but non-essential effect, the program can perform the real task of reading and initializing the next image.

Another way to improve a user's perception of start-up time is to take advantage of any audio capabilities a system might have. Some applications play music or make other sounds when launched. Sound is easily misused and can become annoying when overused. However, when used carefully, sound can be used to reassure the user that an application is responding and can be used to fill gaps between visual responses to make the response time seem shorter than it really is.

In the best case, start-up screens, cursors, audio, visual effects and other transitions can be combined to present the user with continuous feedback designed to divert the user's attention from the time required to perform a lengthy operation.

Using Work Procedures

The first example in this section shows that the user's perceived start-up time can sometimes be improved by delaying certain operations until after a window has been displayed on the screen. Another way to accomplish the same effect is to use work procedures. Work procedures can be registered at any time, but will not be invoked until the application has entered the event loop, retrieved and processed any pending events, and is waiting for the next event. Although usually described as a mechanism for implementing background tasks, applications can use work procedures as a way to delay an operation until after an application is running.

For example, consider the `menu` program described earlier in this chapter. In spite of using the most efficient techniques available to us, this example was unable to create and manage a large number of widgets in a menu within the desired start-up time. However, it is not really necessary to create the panes in a menu bar during start-up because the user cannot see the contents of the menu panes when the interface first appears. Once the interface is up, the application can use the time required for the user to move to the menu bar to create the contents of the menu bar.

The following functions demonstrate this technique. This code segment shows how the function `CreatePane()`, first described on page 328, can be modified to install a work procedure to create each pane. The program begins by declaring a structure that can be used to store two widgets. This structure is used as client data to a work procedure.

```
/**************************************************
 * menu.c: Show how work procedures can be used
 *         to delay menu creation.
 *************************************************/
#include <Xm/Xm.h>
#include <Xm/MainW.h>
#include <Xm/CascadeBG.h>
#include <Xm/RowColumn.h>
#include <Xm/PushBG.h>
```

```
#include "TimerTools.h"

typedef struct {
  Widget menubar;
  Widget cascade;
} WidgetPair;

Boolean CreatePaneWorkProc ( XtPointer clientData );
```

`CreatePane()` is still called from the `CreateMenu()` function during start-up. However, this function now simply sets up the work procedure and returns quickly, instead of creating the entire pane. One problem that must be dealt with involves the order of the panes in the menu. Work procedures are called in the inverse of the order in which they were installed. Therefore, if we defer the entire process of adding a pane to a menu until the work procedure is called, the menu items will be in the wrong order. The easiest way around this problem is to create the XmCascadeButton gadget used by each pane directly in `CreatePane()`. Then, the `WidgetPair` structure can be used to indicate which cascade widget each specific pane should be attached to.

```
void CreatePane ( Widget parent )
{
   /*
    * Allocate a structure to be used for info needed by
    * work procedure.
    */
    WidgetPair *wp = ( WidgetPair* )
                            XtMalloc ( sizeof( WidgetPair ) );
   /*
    * Create a cascade button for this pane. Store menubar
    * and cascade in the structure.
    */

    wp->menubar = parent;
    wp->cascade = XtCreateManagedWidget ( "Submenu",
                                 xmCascadeButtonGadgetClass,
                                 parent, NULL, 0  );
   /*
    * Register a work procedure to create the rest of the pane
    * when the application has a chance.
    */

    XtAppAddWorkProc ( XtWidgetToApplicationContext ( parent ),
                       CreatePaneWorkProc,
                       ( XtPointer ) wp );
}
```

The function `CreatePaneWorkProc()` creates a menu pane. Like the earlier example, this function simply creates a typical pane. A real program would be more complex because it would create specific menu items in multiple work procedures. Here, the same work procedure is used to create all panes. The function casts the `clientData` to a structure of type `WidgetPair` and uses the widgets in that structure as the basis of each menu pane.

```
Boolean CreatePaneWorkProc ( XtPointer clientData )
{
    WidgetPair *wp = ( WidgetPair* ) clientData;
    Widget      submenu, buttons[10];
    int         i;

   /*
    * Create a pulldown menu pane
    */

    submenu = XmCreatePulldownMenu ( wp->menubar, "Submenu",
                                     NULL, 0 );
   /*
    * Attach the menu pane to the cascade specified in the
    * client data structure.
    */

    XtVaSetValues ( wp->cascade, XmNsubMenuId, submenu, NULL );

   /*
    * Add items to the menu pane.
    */

    for ( i = 0; i < 10; i++ )
        buttons[i] = XtCreateWidget ( "Item",
                                      xmPushButtonGadgetClass,
                                      submenu, NULL, 0 );

    XtManageChildren ( buttons, 10 );

   /*
    * Free the client data structure, because this is
    * only place we know that we are done with this memory.
    */

    XtFree ( ( char * ) wp );
    ReportTime ( "Pane Created", TRUE );

    return ( TRUE );
}
```

Stop timing

Figure 9.43 shows the start-up time of the `menu` program after integrating these changes into the rest of the program.

Time to display main window and menu bar

0.24 second required to complete menu panes.

```
% menu
Starting:
Up:
    Elapsed Time = 0.36
    User Time    = 0.10
    System Time  = 0.060
Pane Created:
    Elapsed Time = 0.040
    User Time    = 0.030
    System Time  = 0.000
Pane Created:
    Elapsed Time = 0.040
    User Time    = 0.030
    System Time  = 0.000
Pane Created:
    Elapsed Time = 0.040
    User Time    = 0.030
    System Time  = 0.000
Pane Created:
    Elapsed Time = 0.040
    User Time    = 0.030
    System Time  = 0.000
Pane Created:
    Elapsed Time = 0.040
    User Time    = 0.030
    System Time  = 0.000
Pane Created:
    Elapsed Time = 0.040
    User Time    = 0.030
    System Time  = 0.000
```

Figure 9.43 Start-up time with delayed menu creation.

With this change, the program's window appears on the screen in 0.36 second. Each menu pane is created in approximately 0.04 second, and the entire menubar is constructed and ready for interaction in 0.24 second, which is fast enough to prevent the user from using the menus before they are ready.

Notice that the total start-up time, if menu creation is included, has not really changed significantly. However, the user's perception of start-up time should be improved.

9.8 Conclusion

This chapter discusses various ways to improve the start-up time of an application. In many cases, these techniques help in fairly small ways. Used together, however, the effect can often be a substantial improvement in user-perceived start-up time, particularly for large programs. We can summarize the main points made in this chapter as follows:

- Whenever possible, try to get the application's window on the screen as quickly as possible. If the application itself cannot be displayed, consider start-up screens or other similar techniques. It is better to provide some response than nothing at all.
- Delay creating parts of the user interface that are not visible until the parts of the interface a user will see are ready. Use work procedures, if necessary, to delay some actions.
- At least as far as start-up time is concerned, gadgets appear to provide better performance than widgets, especially if many widgets or gadgets are being used. For small numbers of widgets, any gain may be small.
- Don't create widgets you don't need, and don't create widgets until you need them. Each widget created during start-up increases the start-up time of the application.
- Use the smallest number of widgets possible to achieve the interface you want. Simpler, shallower widget hierarchies produce faster start-up times than more complex widget hierarchies.
- Manage widgets or gadgets before their parents are realized.
- If it is not possible to create and manage widgets before realization, be sure to manage all children in groups using `XtManageChildren()`.
- Be sure not to overlook performance problems in parts of the program besides the user interface.

Although these points were discussed in the context of start-up time, many of these suggestions apply to the runtime performance of a program as well. Chapter 10 assumes these points are understood, and examines additional issues that affect an application's runtime performance. Chapters 11 and 12 also include further examples and discussions of start-up performance in the context of more complete case studies.

10

Improving Runtime Performance

The previous chapter discusses ways to improve the start-up time of Motif applications. While start-up time is important, runtime performance is often even more critical. Many Motif applications are designed to be left running an extended period of time. In such cases, the difference of a few seconds here and there in starting an application is unlikely to become an issue. However, the need for a responsive interface remains an ongoing concern for as long as the application is running.

Besides being responsive at all times, any X application should also avoid causing problems for other applications running in a user's environment. All applications in a multi-tasking environment must compete for resources. Resources that are shared among applications include the X server, the mouse and keyboard, the color map or maps, system memory, and of course, the CPU. Most programmers know, for example, that well-behaved applications must not grab the X server or the pointer for extended periods of time, and must not use so many colors that none are left for other applications. However, applications should also try not to degrade the performance of the rest of the system by placing heavy demands on the server.

This chapter discusses issues related to runtime performance, and demonstrates ways that applications can maximize their responsiveness while reducing their impact on the performance of the overall system. Many runtime issues are similar to those discussed in previous chapter, and the same tools used to measure and improve start-up can be applied to runtime issues.

Goals of Runtime Performance

The goals of start-up performance are fairly easy to quantify. Ideally, programs should be ready for interaction within a certain, measurable period of time. Failing that, programs should be able to provide ongoing feedback to the user within a reasonably short time. Runtime performance is often more difficult to characterize with specific numbers. Most of the time, the user simply wants a program to feel "snappy" and responsive, which often means truly instantaneous response.

Unlike start-up, runtime performance often involves multiple operations, which have to be performed in an acceptable amount of time. User interface design plays an important role in the user's perception of runtime performance, because a poor user interface design can make a program seem slow even if individual operations are executed quickly. If a user has to post a dialog or menu occasionally, any lag in response time may be forgiven. But if the user has to post dialogs repeatedly to perform a simple task, any performance problem will become intolerable.

In addition, the time a user finds acceptable may vary from task to task. A user may accept delays while a program sorts items in a list, opens files, or posts dialogs. However, if a Motif button does not respond to a mouse button press immediately, the system will be seen as unresponsive. Similarly, a program must allow a user to drag a scrollbar thumb or post a menu with no noticeable delay.

Some runtime operations can be characterized and treated as start-up operations for purposes of performance. For example, the general rules of start-up performance can be applied to opening secondary windows or dialogs. As long as feedback is provided within a reasonable amount of time, such operations do not usually need to be instantaneous. In general, of course, the more quickly the application can respond to any user action, the more responsive the application will feel.

10.1 Basic Techniques

There are several strategies that can be employed to ensure that a Motif application is always as responsive as possible. The basic rule of thumb can be stated as follows:

> *Never let an application be so busy that is cannot handle Expose events, configuration events, and basic interaction events (ButtonPress, KeyPress, MotionNotify) immediately.*

Because most real applications must do something besides wait in an event loop for user input, some ingenuity may be required to achieve this goal. One way to handle this requirement is to organize applications into two distinct components, a user interface component and an underlying "engine" that actually performs the work. The role of the interface in such an architecture is to send commands to the engine, and to display data provided by the engine to the user. The interface portion also handles events and makes server requests, without waiting for the engine. In some cases, the engine and user interface may be implemented as separate processes, although some applications can achieve a similar effect by using work procedures or time-out events. When multiple processes are used, communication between the user interface and the engine can be handled by pipes or sockets. The user interface portion can use `XtAppAddInput()` to handle information received from the engine in the same way it handles events from the X server.

Besides the application's architecture, runtime performance can also be affected by choices made when designing the user interface. For example, consider a program that needs to display status messages at fairly frequent intervals. All of the following approaches are possible, and have been used in one or more applications:

1. Create a dialog to display each message and destroy the dialog when the user dismisses it.

2. Post a previously built dialog and unmanage it when the user dismisses it.

3. Manage a label widget in a predetermined position and unmanage it to remove the message.

4. Map a label widget in a predetermined position unmap the label to remove the message.

5. Change the string in a label widget that is always displayed. Display an empty string when the message is no longer needed.

The above steps show how the same basic task can be accomplished in many ways. Options 4 and 5 are the most efficient way to handle this task because they involve the least geometry management and the fewest number of server requests. Not only are they more efficient in terms of machine utilization, they are also the most efficient from the perspective of user interaction. The only negative aspect of these two approaches is that the label widget always occupies some screen space, even when it is not being used.

This is just one example of the types of choices a programmer can make when implementing a program or designing an interface. There are usually many ways to implement a given feature, and some choices are more efficient than others.

10.2 Dynamic Configuration Changes

Many simple programs create their entire user interface during start-up and make few, if any, changes while the program is running. However, more complex applications may need to create, destroy, or reconfigure widgets after the program's initial interface has been displayed. Such applications must be designed carefully to avoid performance problems.

Chapter 9 demonstrated that creating and managing widgets after a program is running, and all parents are realized, can be dramatically more expensive than creating and managing widgets before realization. Applications that make dynamic changes to widget layout face the same challenges. Often, such operations are not necessary. The previous section described several alternatives to managing and unmanaging widgets, for example. However, there may be times when making a widget appear and disappear is the right thing to do. In these cases, it is important to understand the various trade-offs between creating and destroying, managing and unmanaging, mapping and unmapping, and other such operations.

Creating widgets to perform specific tasks and destroying them when the task is completed is very time-consuming. If the idea is to display a new user interface component quickly, then managing or mapping a previously created widget will always be faster than creating new widgets while the user is waiting. Destroying a widget is also expensive because it requires time to free all resources, recompute layouts, and so on. Widgets can be removed from the screen by unmapping or unmanaging them rather than destroying them, so they are ready to be displayed again, when needed.

On the other hand, each widget requires memory, so widgets that are no longer needed should not be kept around if memory usage is an issue. If a widget is unlikely to be used again, destroying it can release memory for other uses. An example of a widget that could definitely be destroyed would be a start-up screen, as described in Section 9.7. Once an application is running, any widgets used to implement a start-up screen should no longer be needed. Dialogs that report rare or unusual errors are also good candidates for dynamic creation and destruction. There is no reason to create a dialog in advance for an error that is unlikely to occur, nor is there any reason to keep such a dialog if it is unlikely to be used again. (Of course, we know from earlier chapters that destroying widgets can be a source of bugs, so it is important to be careful.)

Mapping and unmapping widgets can be a much faster way to change an interface. However, there are several restrictions about when this technique can be used. For example, a widget can only be mapped (by calling `XtMapWidget()`) after it is realized. `XtMapWidget()` calls `XMapWindow()` with the widget's window as an argument, and does not test that the window exists. The same is true of `XtUnmapWidget()`. Therefore, a gadget cannot be mapped or unmapped with these functions. Another approach is to set the resource `XmNmappedWhenManaged` to `TRUE` to display a widget or gadget, and `FALSE` to remove it from the screen.

It is also important to understand the layout implications of creating and destroying widgets dynamically as opposed to managing and unmanaging or mapping and unmapping. When a widget is destroyed, it is removed from its parent's managed set, and the parent rearranges the remaining children. If a new widget is created and managed, the parent also recomputes its layout to position the new child. When a widget is unmanaged or managed, the parent also rearranges all remaining children. However, unmapping a widget leaves a widget managed, and the parent continues to maintain a layout that includes space for the child. The space will simply be empty. Therefore, deciding whether to map/unmap, manage/unmanage, or create/destroy involves more than performance. The right choice also depends on what effect you are trying to achieve.

For example, consider the following simple program, which manages seven XmPushButton widgets as children of an XmRowColumn widget. One child, `target`, can be manipulated by clicking on the remaining buttons. One button unmanages the target button, another unmaps it, and so on.

```
/***********************************************
 * manage.c : Show the effect of unmanaging
 *            vs. unmapping vs. destroying.
 ***********************************************/
#include <Xm/Xm.h>
#include <Xm/PushB.h>
#include <Xm/RowColumn.h>

static void UnmanageCallback ( Widget, XtPointer,
                                       XtPointer );
static void ManageCallback ( Widget, XtPointer,
                                     XtPointer );
static void UnmapCallback ( Widget, XtPointer,
                                    XtPointer );
static void MapCallback ( Widget, XtPointer,
                                  XtPointer );
static void DestroyCallback ( Widget, XtPointer,
                                      XtPointer );
static void CreateCallback ( Widget, XtPointer,
                                     XtPointer );

Widget target = NULL;

void main ( int argc, char **argv )
{
    Widget       shell, rc, create, destroy;
    Widget       map, manage, unmanage, unmap;
    XtAppContext app;

    shell = XtAppInitialize ( &app, "Manage", NULL, 0,
                              &argc, argv, NULL, NULL, 0 );

   /*
    * Create a RowColumn widget.
    */

    rc = XtCreateManagedWidget ( "rc",
                                 xmRowColumnWidgetClass,
                                 shell, NULL, 0 );


   /*
    * Add children to the Row widget.
    */
```

```
    map = XtCreateManagedWidget ( "map",
                                  xmPushButtonWidgetClass,
                                  rc, NULL, 0 );
    unmap = XtCreateManagedWidget ( "unmap",
                                    xmPushButtonWidgetClass,
                                    rc, NULL, 0 );
    target = XtCreateManagedWidget ( "target",
                                     xmPushButtonWidgetClass,
                                     rc, NULL, 0 );
    manage = XtCreateManagedWidget ( "manage",
                                     xmPushButtonWidgetClass,
                                     rc, NULL, 0 );
    unmanage = XtCreateManagedWidget ( "unmanage",
                                       xmPushButtonWidgetClass,
                                       rc, NULL, 0 );
    create = XtCreateManagedWidget ( "create",
                                     xmPushButtonWidgetClass,
                                     rc, NULL, 0 );
    destroy = XtCreateManagedWidget ( "destroy",
                                      xmPushButtonWidgetClass,
                                      rc, NULL, 0 );

    XtAddCallback ( map, XmNactivateCallback,
                    MapCallback, NULL );
    XtAddCallback ( unmap, XmNactivateCallback,
                    UnmapCallback, NULL );
    XtAddCallback ( manage, XmNactivateCallback,
                    ManageCallback, NULL );
    XtAddCallback ( unmanage, XmNactivateCallback,
                    UnmanageCallback, NULL );
    XtAddCallback ( create, XmNactivateCallback,
                    CreateCallback, ( XtPointer ) rc );
    XtAddCallback ( destroy, XmNactivateCallback,
                    DestroyCallback, NULL );

    XtRealizeWidget ( shell );
    XtAppMainLoop ( app );
}

void CreateCallback ( Widget    w,
                      XtPointer clientData,
                      XtPointer callData )
{
    Widget parent = ( Widget ) clientData;

    target = XtCreateManagedWidget ( "target",
                                     xmPushButtonWidgetClass,
                                     parent, NULL, 0 );
}
```

```
void DestroyCallback ( Widget    w,
                       XtPointer clientData,
                       XtPointer callData )
{
    XtDestroyWidget ( target );

    target = NULL;
}

void ManageCallback ( Widget    w,
                      XtPointer clientData,
                      XtPointer callData )
{
    if ( target )
        XtManageChild ( target );
}

void UnmanageCallback ( Widget    w,
                        XtPointer clientData,
                        XtPointer callData)
{
    if ( target )
        XtUnmanageChild ( target );
}

void MapCallback ( Widget    w,
                   XtPointer clientData,
                   XtPointer callData )
{
    if ( target )
        XtMapWidget ( target );
}

void UnmapCallback ( Widget    w,
                     XtPointer clientData,
                     XtPointer callData )
{
    if ( target )
        XtUnmapWidget ( target );
}
```

Figure 10.1 shows the layout of this program when it first appears. The XmRowColumn widget has placed each button in the order in which it was created. The `target` button is near the middle.

Figure 10.1 Initial layout with all children managed.

Figure 10.2 shows this program's widget layout after the `unmanage` button has been selected. The `target` button has been removed from the screen, and the remaining widgets have been repositioned to fill the gap left by the target widget.

Figure 10.2 Unmanaging the `target` widget.

Selecting the `manage` button at this point restores the `target` button in its original location, repositioning the other widgets to make room for the target widget.

Figure 10.3 shows the layout after the `unmap` button has been selected. Once again, the `target` widget has been removed from the screen. However, there has been no change to the XmRowColumn widget's layout. The remaining widgets are positioned exactly where they were, and the space formerly occupied by the `target` widget is left empty.

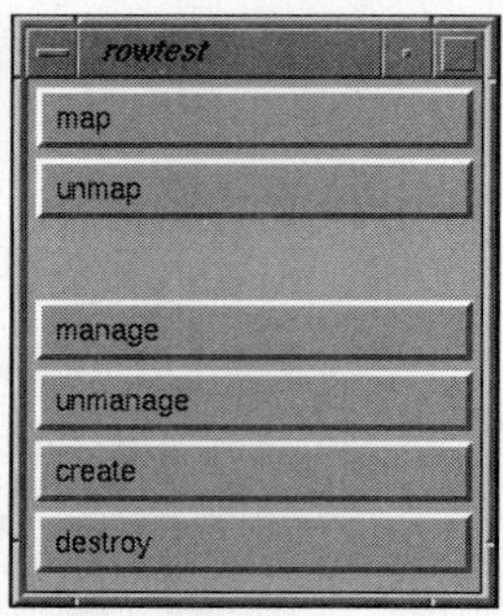

Figure 10.3 Unmapping the `target` widget.

Figure 10.4 shows the layouts produced by selecting the `destroy` button followed by the `create` button. When the `create` button is selected, the XmRowColumn widget positions the new `target` button after all other children. Therefore, the new widget does not have the same position as the original `target` widget. This behavior is dependent on the management policy of the parent.

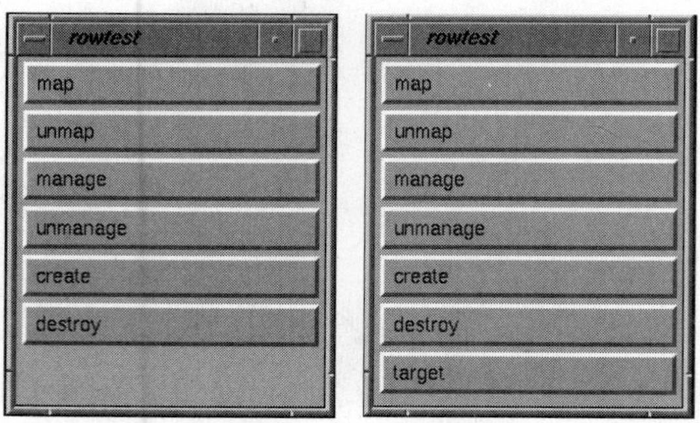

Figure 10.4 Destroying and recreating the `target` widget.

As this example demonstrates, there are multiple ways to remove and show a widget on the screen. Mapping and unmapping the widget is the fastest alternative provided by this program. However, when choosing an approach, you must consider the layout effect you wish to achieve in addition to performance issues.

10.3 Gadgets and Runtime Performance

Many programmers have pointed out that, although gadgets can be used to improve start-up performance, they can sometimes degrade the runtime performance of a system. The extent to which this is true depends on how gadgets are used and the characteristics of the system on which the program runs. The basic problem is that gadgets cannot receive any events from the X server, because they don't have windows. A gadget's parent must track input focus, mouse motion, and button events and direct the appropriate events to the correct child. This definitely adds overhead and additional computation requirements to any parent that manages gadgets.

In addition, manager widgets that have gadget children must request `MotionNotify` events so they can track pointer focus and simulate Enter/Leave events. On low performance X servers, or systems that run over low-bandwidth lines, the additional server traffic can be a potential problem.

For example, consider the `permissions` program described in Chapter 9. The second implementation of the program uses gadgets, but it is easy to create yet another version that uses widgets. Figure 10.5 shows a comparison of the events generated by moving the mouse cursor into the window and clicking on each toggle button in both versions of this program.

Events	Widgets	Gadgets
ButtonPress	9	9
ButtonRelease	9	9
MotionNotify	0	291
EnterNotify	37	19
LeaveNotify	39	19
FocusIn	5	5
FocusOut	6	1

Figure 10.5 Events generated by mouse motion in `permissions` programs.

Clearly, the gadget version results in a large number of `MotionNotify` events while the version that uses widgets generates none. The widget version generates more `EnterNotify` and `LeaveNotify` events, but not nearly enough to balance the 291 additional `MotionNotify` events in the gadget version. The X server generates 105 events for the widget version of this program, compared to 353 for the gadget version.

Figure 10.6 shows the requests made by each version of the program for the same operation. Here, the differences are small, with gadgets having a slight edge. The widget version makes a total of 158 requests, while the gadget version makes 131.

Requests	Widgets	Gadgets
ClearArea	0	40
PolySegment	56	36
PolyFillRectangle	84	46
PolyText8	18	9

Figure 10.6 Requests made in `permissions` programs.

So, at least in this example, gadgets do add to the traffic between a client and the X server. This program produces several hundred more events when gadgets are used. Based strictly on measured data, this impairs runtime performance while only marginally improving start-up performance. Subjectively, the runtime response of these two programs seems acceptable, in both cases. On System B, the X terminal, the effect of the additional `MotionNotify` events is noticeable, although only slightly. On System A, there is no perceptible difference in the interactive feel of the two programs.

If we compare the initial start-up time of these two versions, we can see that using widgets instead of gadgets seems to add very slightly to the start-up time. Figure 10.7 shows the time required to start each implementation, measured on System A. The widget version consistently takes 0.02 seconds longer to start than the gadget version. This is, of course, too small a difference to be significant.

Widgets

```
% permissions2
Starting:
Creating panel:
   Elapsed Time = 0.120
   User Time    = 0.040
   System Time  = 0.040
Panel up:
   Elapsed Time = 0.200
   User Time    = 0.080
   System Time  = 0.020
```

Gadgets

```
% permissions3
Starting:
Creating panel:
   Elapsed Time = 0.120
   User Time    = 0.040
   System Time  = 0.040
Panel up:
   Elapsed Time = 0.220
   User Time    = 0.090
```

Figure 10.7 Start-up times of `permissions` program, widgets vs. gadgets.

10.4 Memory Use

The way an application uses memory can have a significant effect on performance. The correlation between a program's use of memory and performance is complex and involves both the memory allocated by the application, and the memory required for instructions and data the system needs to execute the program. Performance can be affected by the speed at which memory can be dynamically allocated, how much memory the program allocates, and whether the application frees dynamically allocated memory when it is no longer needed. An application's performance can also be affected by the size of the program, and by the program's patterns of memory access. The following sections explore each of these topics.

Malloc() Performance

All Motif and Xt-based applications make extensive use of dynamically allocated memory. The object-oriented architecture supported by Xt is based on the ability to dynamically allocate "objects", which are ultimately created by calling `malloc()`. Chapter 5 describes how bugs can be caused by misusing `malloc()`. However, the way a program uses `malloc()` can also have a significant impact on the application's performance. Because Motif makes such heavy use of `malloc()`, one obvious way to improve performance is to use a faster implementation of `malloc()`. This is particularly true when trying to improve start-up time, as discussed in Chapter 9. Many systems support several different `malloc()` implementations available, and it is worthwhile to experiment with each version.

Unfortunately, when considering ongoing runtime performance, it is more difficult to define the characteristics of a "fast" `malloc()`. If only start-up performance is considered, the fastest `malloc()` implementation would be one that allocates new memory as quickly as possible. However, because process size is often a problem for Motif applications, it may be better for some applications to use a `malloc()` library that makes efficient use of space. It may be difficult to find an implementation of `malloc()` with both characteristics.

Some implementations of `malloc()` allow programmers to set options that affect the algorithms used by `malloc()`. If the memory use patterns of a particular application are sufficiently well understood, these options can be used to tune the `malloc()` algorithm to the needs of the program.

Unfortunately, most Motif programs use dynamically allocated memory so heavily that it is hard to identify any specific pattern. Furthermore, Motif programmers who wish to make better use of `malloc()` usually find that most of their program's dynamically allocated memory is allocated by Motif, Xt, or Xlib. Application programmers are only in indirect control.

Leaks

One frequently encountered problem in Motif applications involves memory leaks. A *leak* is memory that has been allocated but not freed, even though it is no longer needed. In non-interactive programs, memory leaks are often of lesser importance. Batch-style programs start-up, allocate memory, execute, and then exit, at which point all memory is returned to the system. In contrast, interactive applications tend to execute for a long time. Programs may be run for hours, days, or even weeks. Over time, even the simplest memory leak can cause a program's size to grow to the point that the program runs more slowly, or may degrade the performance of the system as a whole by keeping memory that other applications need.

Because memory may be allocated on behalf of a program by Motif functions, it is important to know what functions allocate memory. Of course, because Motif is based on a dynamic object model, one can almost assume that every Motif operation allocates some memory. However, many of these functions also free the memory when it is no longer needed. Problems arise when the programmer is expected to free memory explicitly.

For example, consider the following implementation of `UpdateTime()` used in the `xclock` program discussed in Chapter 2. Unlike the original version, which uses `XtVaSetValues()` to create and free a compound string automatically, this version creates a compound string directly. The string is created by calling `XmStringCreateLocalized()` within the call to `XtVaSetValues()`, shown on line 45, below. This function creates a new string each time it is called, but never frees the string, causing the program to grow steadily in size. To see the effect more rapidly, this program updates the clock every 100 milliseconds, instead of every minute as in the previous version. Changes from the previous implementation are shown in bold.

```
      22  static void UpdateTime ( XtPointer clientData, XtIntervalId id )
      23  {
      24      Widget w =  ( Widget ) clientData;
      25      long   tloc, rounded_tloc, next_minute;
      26      char   buffer[100];
      27
      28     /*
      29      * Get the system time.
      30      */
      31
      32      time ( &tloc );
      33
      34     /*
      35      * Convert the time to a string and display it,
      36      * after rounding it down to the last minute.
      37      */
      38
      39      rounded_tloc = tloc / 60 * 60;
      40
      41      sprintf ( buffer, "%s", ctime ( &rounded_tloc ) );
      42
      43      XtVaSetValues ( w,
      44                      XmNlabelString,
Leak! 45                      XmStringCreateLocalized ( buffer ),
      46                      NULL );
      47
      48     /*
      49      * Adjust the time to reflect the time until
      50      * the next round minute.
      51      */
```

```
    next_minute =  ( 60 - tloc % 60 ) * 100;

   /*
    * Xt removes timeouts when they occur,
    * so re-register the function.
    */

    XtAppAddTimeOut ( XtWidgetToApplicationContext ( w ),
                      next_minute, UpdateTime,
                      ( XtPointer )  w );
}
```

This leak is very small, so it may not seem that it should represent a serious problem. However, a small desktop utility like a clock usually runs continuously while the user is logged in. Many users do not log out daily, and such a program might run indefinitely. To see the impact of this leak, we can use `ps` to measure the program's size periodically. Upon start-up, `ps` reports that the program requires a total size of 1074 pages, or 4,399,104 bytes and has a resident size (the amount of memory actually kept in physical memory) of 486 pages, or 1,990,656 bytes. After approximately fours hours of operation, `ps` reports that `xclock` has grown to 1174 total pages and 606 resident pages. That is a growth of 409,600 bytes in total size, or approximately 100K per hour.

Clearly, even this tiny leak can cause a major problem over time. Left running indefinitely, this program would exceed the capacity of the system and crash with a `malloc()` error, or be killed by the system. Long before that, the additional memory use would tend to degrade the performance of this program, and possibly others. For large programs that use more widgets, more compound strings and so on, leaks can quickly become a significant problem.

There are many commercial products that can help detect memory leaks, as well as some public domain `malloc()` libraries that can help isolate leaks. Of course, it is often difficult to be certain exactly what constitutes a leak. Most of these products can provide a list of memory locations that have been allocated and not freed, but much of the memory in a Motif application is needed as long as the application is running.

In theory, you could identify leaks by freeing every thing used in a program before exiting. This would include destroying all widgets, closing the X server connection, and so on. In practice, this does not work well. A complete cleanup takes unnecessary time, and many internal tables, lists and other data structures in X, Xt, and Motif are simply not freed because there is no reason for them to be.

Many leaks can be detected or avoided with careful planning and by remembering which Motif and Xt functions allocate memory that must be freed. As a rule of thumb, `XtGetValues()` does not allocate memory when used to retrieve integers and other similar values. However, it does allocate memory when used to retrieve compound strings or character strings from a text widget. In either of these cases, Motif makes a copy of its internal string and returns the copy to the caller.

`XtSetValues()` is similar to `XtGetValues()` in that most resources are used directly, and not copied by the widgets. However, all compound strings are copied by the Motif widgets. Therefore, once a compound string has been passed to `XtSetValues()` or `XtCreateWidget()`, the string can be freed.

Many Motif convenience functions also allocate memory that the caller is expected to free. For example, `XmListGetSelectedItems()` allocates a list of compound strings that must be freed by the caller. Other functions do not allocate memory, and the return values must not be freed. For example, `XmFontListGetFontEntry()` returns a pointer to an entry in a font list, not a copy.

Memory allocated by Xt or Motif can often be freed by calling `XtFree()`. `XtFree()` is just a convenience function that calls `free()` after checking for a `NULL` address. (Similarly, `XtMalloc()` is just a convenience function that calls `malloc()` and then calls `XtError()` if the request fails.)

Some types of memory should be freed using special-purpose functions. For example, compound strings must be freed using `XmStringFree()`. A compound string is a complex data structure that has members that are dynamically allocated. Destroying a compound string by calling `XtFree()` does not cause an error, but it does cause a leak, because the outer compound string data structure is freed, but internal members are not. Widgets, of course, must be destroyed by calling `XtDestroyWidget()`, and graphics contexts created with `XtGetGC()` or `XtAllocateGC()` must be freed by calling `XtReleaseGC()`.

When in doubt, check the Motif man pages for any particular function or widget resource to see if values should or should not be freed.

Virtual Memory, Working Sets, and Locality of Reference

One of the most difficult performance issues when developing Motif-based applications involves dynamic memory behavior. In a multi-tasking, virtual memory environment like those in which most Motif applications are used, both the amount of memory used, and the patterns in which memory is allocated and accessed during the execution of the program can greatly affect the application's performance. Furthermore, the runtime characteristics of an application's memory use can affect, and be affected by, other applications running on the system.

The primary reason runtime memory issues are so complex is due to the existence of *virtual memory.* Virtual memory systems allow the total amount of memory required by all applications currently running on a system to exceed the amount of physical memory supported by the hardware. In some cases, the difference between the maximum amount of virtual memory and the physical memory available can be substantial. Virtual memory systems are based on the assumption that any given program does not require all of its instructions and data to be available at once, and that the amount of physical memory required by all running programs at any given time will not exceed the physical memory available on the system.

Most systems load memory in units of a *page*. When a program needs instructions or data that are not currently loaded into physical memory, a *page fault* occurs, and the system must quickly load the page that contains the required portion of the program. Some systems may also load other pages that surround the page that is needed. Naturally, the application must wait until the new page or pages are loaded before it can proceed. Section 9.6 describes how the need to load instructions and data from disk can affect start-up time. The same behavior can be observed any time new pages are needed during a program's execution.

Several other characteristics of virtual memory are important when considering the performance of Motif applications. First, it is important to realize that in a multi-tasking environment, many programs may compete to have memory loaded at any given time. If the amount of memory required by all programs exceeds the physical memory available, the system must discard some of the pages currently loaded. Unloading pages takes time, particularly if they must be reloaded when they are needed again.

The granularity with which memory can be loaded is also important. On the systems used for the tests described in this book, a page is 4096 bytes. Therefore, even if a program requires only a single byte of memory at any given location, the virtual memory system will always load a minimum of 4096 bytes, thereby tying up 4096 bytes of physical memory that might be needed by some other application.

Motif applications can exhibit interesting behavior on virtual memory systems for several reasons. The first has to do with *locality of reference*.

Locality of reference simply refers to the likelihood that the next memory reference a program makes will be on the same page as the last reference. To a certain extent, virtual memory is based on the assumption that when a program begins executing instructions on a particular page, it is likely to continue executing instructions on that page for some period of time. For certain types of applications, this assumption is often true. Such programs are said to have good locality of reference.

In a multi-layered, object-oriented architecture like that implemented by Xt and Motif, the flow of control is unlikely to result in individual pages of memory being used for extended periods of time. Motif programs typically have very poor locality of reference. Even a simple operation often involves many parts of Motif, Xt, and Xlib, and may require many pages to be resident.

For example, we can design an experiment to help us estimate how many pages are involved when performing a simple operation like setting a resource. Let's begin by modifying the hello.c program discussed in Chapter 9, adding a call to `XtVaSetValues()` to change the color of a widget after it has been displayed. Because changing a widget's color involves redisplaying the widget, we will also add a call to `XmUpdateDisplay()`. We can bracket these changes with calls to `ReportTime()`, so we can see just how long this operation takes to be completed. The additions to this program are shown in bold, below.

```
/*************************************************
 * hello.c: Display"hello world" on the screen.
 *************************************************/
#include <Xm/Xm.h>
#include <Xm/Label.h>
#include "TimerTools.h"

void main ( int argc, char **argv )
{
    Widget       shell, label;
    XtAppContext app;
    XmString     xmstr;

    ReportTime ( "Starting", FALSE );

    shell = XtAppInitialize ( &app, "Hello", NULL, 0,
                              &argc, argv, NULL, NULL, 0 );

    /* Create a string in the form expected by Motif. */

    xmstr = XmStringCreateLtoR ( "Hello World",
```

```
       22                                       XmFONTLIST_DEFAULT_TAG );
       23
       24      /*
       25       * Create a Motif XmLabel widget to display the string.
       26       */
       27
       28       label = XtVaCreateManagedWidget ( "label",
       29                                          xmLabelWidgetClass, shell,
       30                                          XmNlabelString, xmstr,
       31                                          NULL );
       32
       33       XmStringFree ( xmstr );  /* Free the compound string. */
       34
       35       XtRealizeWidget ( shell );
       36
       37       WaitForWindow ( shell );
       38       HandleEvents ( shell );
       39       ReportTime ( "Up", TRUE );
       40
Start  41       ReportTime ( "Change Color", FALSE );
timing 42
       43       XtVaSetValues ( label, XmNforeground, 15, NULL );
       44
       45       XmUpdateDisplay ( shell );
Report 46       ReportTime ( "Change Color", TRUE );
       47       XtAppMainLoop ( app );
       48  }
```

Now, we can run this program under the control of a debugger, setting breakpoints at lines 41 and 48, before and after the call to `XtVaSetValues()`, and including the calls to `ReportTime()`. First, we can simply run the program, as shown in Figure 10.8, to be sure the program is written correctly. Notice that the label widget's foreground color is changed so quickly that the elapsed time is reported as zero.

Set breakpoints

Time to execute lines 1-40

Time to execute lines 41-46

```
 % dbx hello
Process  6732 (hello) started
[2] Process  6732 (hello) stopped at [main:16 ,0x400e64]
  16  ReportTime("Starting", FALSE);

(dbx) stop at 49
Process  6732: [3] stop at "hello.c":41

(dbx) stop at 57
Process  6732: [4] stop at "hello.c":48

(dbx) run
Starting:
Running:
   Elapsed Time = 0.160
   User Time    = 0.060
   System Time  = 0.060

Process  6674 (hello) stopped at [main:41 ,0x400f30]

(dbx) continue
Change color:
Done:
   Elapsed Time = 0.000
   User Time    = 0.000
   System Time  = 0.000
[4] Process  6735 (hello) stopped at [main:48 ,0x40101c]
  57  XtAppMainLoop ( app );
```

Figure 10.8 Set up to measure pages needed to execute `XtSetValues()`.

Next, we can re-run the program. This session is shown in Figure 10.9.

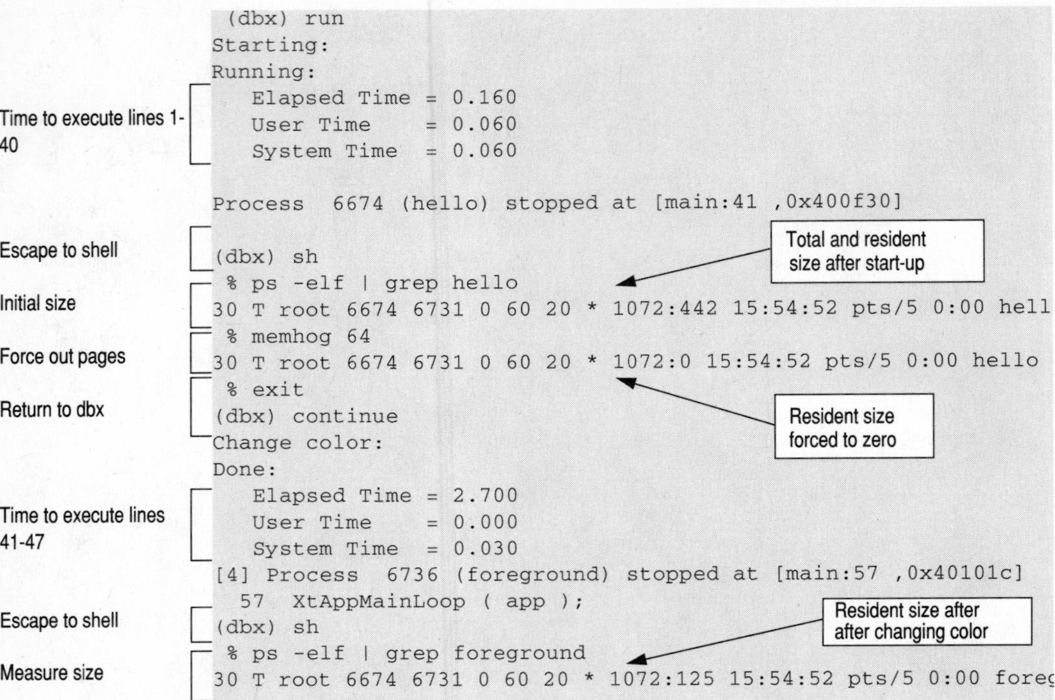
(dbx) run
Starting:
Running:
Time to execute lines 1-40
Elapsed Time = 0.160
User Time = 0.060
System Time = 0.060
Process 6674 (hello) stopped at [main:41 ,0x400f30]
Escape to shell
(dbx) sh
Total and resident size after start-up
% ps -elf | grep hello
Initial size
30 T root 6674 6731 0 60 20 * 1072:442 15:54:52 pts/5 0:00 hell
% memhog 64
Force out pages
30 T root 6674 6731 0 60 20 * 1072:0 15:54:52 pts/5 0:00 hello
% exit
Return to dbx
(dbx) continue
Resident size forced to zero
Change color:
Done:
Time to execute lines 41-47
Elapsed Time = 2.700
User Time = 0.000
System Time = 0.030
[4] Process 6736 (foreground) stopped at [main:57 ,0x40101c]
57 XtAppMainLoop (app);
Escape to shell
(dbx) sh
Resident size after after changing color
% ps -elf | grep foreground
Measure size
30 T root 6674 6731 0 60 20 * 1072:125 15:54:52 pts/5 0:00 foreg

Figure 10.9 Measuring pages needed to execute `XtSetValues()`.

This time, when `dbx` stops at the first break point, we will escape to a shell by typing "`sh`". In the shell, we can use `ps` to get the number of pages currently in memory for the `hello` program. It appears that `hello` has a total size of 1072 pages, or 4,390,912 bytes of which 442 pages, or 1,810,432 bytes are resident in memory. Not all of these pages are necessarily needed at this time, many may have been needed at some point, and have not been unloaded. The system simply hasn't needed the space yet. Now that the program is stopped, we can run the `memhog` program described in Chapter 9 to force all pages out of memory. This program may need to be run several times, until finally `ps` reports that `hello`'s resident size has shrunk to zero.

Once `hello`'s resident pages have been forced out of the system, we can exit the shell, and return to the debugger. In the debugger, we can continue to the next breakpoint. At this point, the program will have changed the color of the label widget and redrawn the widget. Notice, first that the time to perform this operation has taken 2.7 seconds, compared to nearly zero during the initial test. The additional time is clearly the time required to bring load the necessary pages into memory.[1]

At this point, we can once again escape to a shell and check the size of the `hello` program. According to `ps`, the program has a resident size of 125 pages, or 512,000 bytes. This is the number of pages that must be in memory to accomplish the operation of changing the color of the widget. (Ignoring the impact of the calls to `ReportTime()`, and other intrusions necessary to make this measurement.)

There is some other interesting data that could be gathered from this experiment. For example, how many pages does the X server use to process any requests that arise out of this call to `XtVaSetValues()`? Does the window manager get involved in any way? Because the X server and window manager are also forced out of memory by the `memhog` program, all we have to do to answer these questions is check the resident size of these programs after the second breakpoint.

Rerunning the original experiment with this extra measurement shows that the window manager is not involved at all; it does not change size after the call to `XtVaSetValues()`. However, `ps` reports that the X server's total size is 2604 pages, of which 6 pages remained in memory after the `memhog` program was run. (It is often hard to force *everything* out.) After stopping at the second breakpoint, `ps` reports that the X server's resident size has increased to 116 pages, while its total size remains the same. So, we can estimate that approximately 110 pages, or 450,506 bytes, are loaded to allow the X server to process the requests associated with this color change.

These measurements are quite crude, and more detailed information could shed more light on the patterns of memory use involved in this procedure. Clearly, however, the runtime performance of a Motif program can be severely impacted by the amount of memory available in a system. If a system has enough physical memory to keep many of the pages commonly needed by a program available, the performance will be faster than if these pages have to be loaded each time an operation is performed. Pages might have to be

---

[1] Of course, the 2.7 seconds required to change the widget's color cannot be attributed entirely to the cost of loading the pages need by `hello`. Parts of the X server have to be paged in as well. We can eliminate the X server's contribution to the measured time, and achieve a more realistic indication of the time potentially involved in this operation, by running an Xlib program after all pages have been forced out, but before returning to the debugger. This loads at least some parts of the server and the window manager. Performing the test in this way, the time required to page in the code needed to change the color of the widget is 1.21 seconds.

removed from physical memory if the system does not have enough physical memory to meet the needs of all processes running on the system.

The term *working set* is often used to characterize memory usage in a virtual memory environment. An application's working set is the amount of physical memory that the application needs to perform any given operation. In the example above, we could say the working set required to change the color of the label in the `hello` program is 125 pages.

As long as the total of all applications' working sets is less than the available physical memory, each individual application should perform as well if it were running alone, at least as far as memory behavior is concerned. (Ignoring the effect of multiple applications competing for CPU cycles and X server facilities). However, if the sum of all application's minimum working sets exceeds the physical memory on the system, the virtual memory system begins to have a strong impact on the performance of the system.

Programmers have relatively little direct control over the size of their application's working sets. However, being aware of the issues, and results of tests like that described above, can help programmers in some critical cases. For example, it seems likely that keeping calls to Motif, X or Xt functions somewhat localized when possible might be helpful.

Some systems support tools that can help reduce the size of an application's working set. These tools usually rearrange the code in an executable in an attempt to pack the instructions in a more meaningful way. For example, in the worst case, it is possible that the `hello` program needs to execute only 125 functions (or less) to change the color of its label, but each function lies on a separate page. Each of these functions might be quite small and occupy far less than a page. By packing the instructions for these functions together, it might be possible to greatly reduce the number of pages used for this operation. The tools to accomplish this task are highly vendor specific and do not tend to be widely available.

Another interesting area to pursue with respect to an application's size and working set involves the use of gadgets. Some programmers have speculated that the additional code required to handle gadgets may have a negative impact on the memory behavior, and therefore the performance, of applications that use them. It would be impractical to remove all the code to support gadgets from Motif to test this theory. However, we can devise a test to measure one effect of using gadgets. The test can be performed as follows:

1. Run the `permissions3` example, which uses only widgets.
2. Cover the program's interface with another window.
3. Run the `memhog` program to force out all pages used by the program. Use `ps` to be sure the program's resident set size has gone to zero.
4. Uncover the `permissions3` program's interface by lowering or moving the window that covers it.
5. Use `ps` to measure the current resident set size. This number should be the number of pages required to execute the code that redraws the program's interface.
6. Now, move the mouse cursor into the window and click on each of the nine buttons.
7. Again use `ps` to measure the current resident set size.
8. Repeat the test with the version of the `permissions` program that uses gadgets.
9. Repeat the test with a modified version of `permissions` that uses 6 gadgets and 4 widgets.

Figure 10.10 shows the results of this experiment.

Program	Working Set (pages) after Redisplay	Working Set (pages) after selecting buttons
Widgets only	90	179
Gadgets only	91	196
Widgets and Gadgets	98	215

Figure 10.10 Comparison of working sets for gadgets and widgets.

The data only measures the exact scenario described in the test, and different operations or different widgets could produce quite different working sets. These numbers indicate that, for this program, using gadgets alone requires a slightly larger working set than using widgets alone. However, mixing XmToggleButton gadgets and XmToggleButton gadgets is more expensive than using either alone. Presumably this is because different code is needed to deal with each case. For example, both the XmToggleButton widget's redisplay code and the XmToggleButtonGadget's redisplay code are needed. So, the difference in size demonstrated in this example probably has less to do with gadgets, per se, than the introduction of an additional widget class.

From Figure 10.10, we could conclude that using gadgets could increase a program's size and therefore be a source of some performance degradation, at least on systems that have limited memory. It is hard to avoid using gadgets completely because Motif itself uses gadgets in dialogs, and some other places, and an application has no way to force Motif to use widgets. Perhaps a compromise would be to say that in any given panel, it seems unwise to mix widgets and gadgets if you are concerned about working set size. In any case, using gadgets when only a few widgets are needed certainly does not appear to offer any benefits.

However, this experiment measures a very specific scenario, and we should not leap to any general conclusions based on this limited data. For example, this experiment does not consider any possible growth in the X server's working set when widgets are used. There is also nothing in this test to indicate that the size of the working set has any actual impact on performance, although we know that performance could be affected if memory is in such short supply that pages must be loaded to complete these tasks.

Shared Libraries

Another consideration when investigating the role that memory plays in the performance of Motif applications is shared libraries. Many, although not all, systems support shared libraries, which allow the text, and perhaps some data, of a library to be shared between multiple applications that link with the library.

To understand how this effects the memory usage, consider the gadget-based `permissions` program whose total size is 4.3 Megabytes, of which perhaps 1 Megabyte is kept in memory during normal operation. For a small program like this, which is entirely user interface, most of this space can be attributed to Motif, Xt or Xlib. In particular, the resident size of this program, once it is running, should consist almost entirely of Motif, Xt and Xlib. Without shared libraries, running a second permissions program would require an additional 4 Megabytes total, and an additional 1 Megabyte resident. Clearly, this memory use can add up quickly. However, if even half of this space is text or read-only data that can be shared between other Motif programs, then each instance of the permissions program would only use an additional 500K of memory. Furthermore, if the 500K that is shared among applications is always loaded, the runtime performance of all programs may be improved.

Shared libraries greatly complicate the task of understanding any given application's use of memory. Although reducing the memory needs of any given application by reducing the size of the application's working set is generally a desirable goal, it is harder to measure the impact of a specific change to any one program. For example, if the nature of the programs running on a system is such that large parts of any given library are always present in physical memory, then reducing the part of any one application's working set that comes from that library is unlikely to have any impact on performance, because those pages will need to be loaded anyway.

10.5 Runtime Performance and the X Server

An important aspect of runtime performance involves the way an application uses the X server, the window manager, and any other application it may communicate with. We have already seen that reducing requests and events can improve an application's start-up performance. It may be less obvious that reducing requests and events can improve the performance of other applications, but because the X server must handle all processes, optimizing an application's interaction with the X server can benefit all applications in the user's environment.

X depends on being able to handle requests asynchronously to provide best performance, so performance can be degraded by applications that make frequent calls to `XFlush()` or `XSync()`. Figure 10.11 shows the effect of running a program in synchronous mode. In this example, the `permissions` program takes about 50% longer to create its panel when run synchronously. Frequent calls to `XFlush()` or `XSync()` can have a similar effect.

Asynchronous

```
% permissions2
Starting:
Creating Panel:
   Elapsed Time = 0.12
   User Time    = 0.040
   System Time  = 0.040
Panel up:
   Elapsed Time = 0.17
   User Time    = 0.080
   System Time  = 0.020
```

Synchronous

```
% permissions2 -sync
Starting:
Creating Panel:
   Elapsed Time = 0.19
   User Time    = 0.060
   System Time  = 0.050
Panel up:
   Elapsed Time = 0.27
   User Time    = 0.090
   System Time  = 0.040
```

Figure 10.11 Asynchronous vs. synchronous performance.

Xlib attempts to minimize the traffic sent to the X server by buffering many requests. For example, multiple calls to `XDrawLine()` that use the same window and same graphics context may be grouped into a single request to draw multiple segments. Calling `XFlush()` or `XSync()` destroys the effect of the buffering by forcing each request to be handled immediately. However, the buffering can also be disturbed in other less obvious ways. For example, if multiple lines are to be drawn in two windows, it would be faster to draw all lines in one window first and then draw the lines in the second window. Alternating between windows would prevent the server from buffering the requests.

It is also easy for applications to abuse the server by misusing server resources, which include windows, graphics contexts, fonts, and pixmaps. For example, we have already seen the effect memory leaks can have on an application. An application can also "leak" memory by not freeing server resources when they are no longer needed. Because resources like windows, graphics contexts, and pixmaps, are not stored in an application's address space, the leak will not be evident in the size of the application. Instead, the X server will grow. Because the X server runs for a long time, and services many applications, even a small leak can have a serious effect. Chapter 12 provides an example of this type of leak.

10.6 Using Motif Widgets Efficiently

Some Motif widgets must be used very carefully to achieve the best performance. Earlier examples have shown how managing widgets in groups can be faster than managing them individually. The general principle, that performing multiple operations in a batch mode is better than repeated individual calls, applies to other situations as well.

For example, the Motif XmList widget provides several ways to add items to a list. A list of compound strings can be added using `XtSetValues()`, items can be added one at a time by calling `XmListAddItem()`, or multiple items can be added at once by calling `XmListAddItems()`. For very small lists, the user is unlikely to notice any difference in the performance of any of these approaches. However, many applications need to display rather large lists. For large lists, the difference between these different approaches can be dramatic.

Consider the following program, which creates a list containing the number of items specified as a command-line argument.

```
/**********************************************
 * listtest.c: Examine the performance of
 *             various ways to display a list.
 **********************************************/
#include <Xm/Xm.h>
#include <Xm/List.h>
#include <stdlib.h>
#include "TimerTools.h"

Widget CreateList ( Widget parent, int nitems );

void main ( int argc, char **argv )
{
    Widget       shell, list;
    XtAppContext app;

    shell = XtAppInitialize ( &app, "List", NULL, 0,
                              &argc, argv, NULL, NULL, 0 );

    list = CreateList ( shell, atoi ( argv[1] ) );
    XtRealizeWidget ( shell );

    XtAppMainLoop ( app );
}
```

The function `CreateList()` creates an XmList widget by calling `XmCreateScrolledList()` and adds the specified number of entries to the list. Let's consider three ways to implement this function. The first uses the convenience function `XmListAddItem()` to add items to the list.

```
Widget CreateList ( Widget parent, int nItems )
{
    int i;
    Widget list;
    XmString xmstr;

    list = XmCreateScrolledList ( parent, "list", NULL, 0 );
    XtManageChild ( list );
```

Start timing

```
    ReportTime ("Starting to add items", FALSE );

    for ( i = 1; i < nItems; i++ )
    {
        xmstr = XmStringCreateLocalized ( "A String" );
        XmListAddItem ( list, xmstr, 0 );
        XmStringFree ( xmstr );
    }
```

End timing

```
    ReportTime ( "Done", TRUE );

    return ( list );
}
```

The second implementation uses `XmListAddItems()` to add an array of compound strings to the list.

```
Widget CreateList (Widget parent, int nItems )
{
    int      i;
    Widget   list;
    XmString *xmstr;

    list = XmCreateScrolledList ( parent, "list", NULL, 0 );
    XtManageChild ( list );

    xmstr = ( XmString * ) XtMalloc ( sizeof ( XmString ) *
                                            nItems );
```

Start timing

```
    ReportTime ("Starting to add items", FALSE );

    for ( i = 0; i < nItems; i++ )
        xmstr[i] = XmStringCreateLocalized ( "A String" );
```

```

    XmListAddItems ( list, xmstr, nItems, 0 );

    for ( i = 0; i < nItems; i++ )
        XmStringFree ( xmstr[i] );
    XtFree ( ( char * ) xmstr );

```

End timing

```
    ReportTime ( "Done", TRUE );

    return ( list );
}
```

The final version of `CreateList()` calls `XtVaSetValues()` to install a list of new items in the XmList widget.

```
Widget CreateList ( Widget parent, int nItems )
{
    int i;
    Widget list;
    XmString *xmstr;

    list = XmCreateScrolledList ( parent, "list", NULL, 0 );
    XtManageChild ( list );

    xmstr = ( XmString * ) XtMalloc ( sizeof ( XmString ) *
                                              nItems );

```

Start timing

```
    ReportTime ("Starting to add items", FALSE );

    for ( i = 0; i < nItems; i++ )
        xmstr[i] = XmStringCreateLocalized ( " A String" );

    XtVaSetValues ( list,
                    XmNitems,     xmstr,
                    XmNitemCount, nItems,
                    NULL );

    for ( i = 0; i < nItems; i++ )
        XmStringFree ( xmstr [ i ] );
    XtFree ( ( char * ) xmstr );
```

End timing

```
    ReportTime ( "Done", TRUE );

    return ( list );
}
```

Figure 10.12 shows the time required to run each version of this program to display various numbers of items. It is clear from these measurements that when adding large numbers of items to a list, it is much faster to use `XtSetValues()`. For very small lists, the difference is less important.

# of Items	XmListAddItem()	XmListAddItems()	XtSetValues()
10	0.01	0.01	0.01
100	0.08	0.02	0.01
1000	1.66	0.21	0.09
10000	76.12	2.29	1.13

Figure 10.12 Comparisons of different ways to add items to a list.

Why do the functions `XmListAddItem()` and `XmListAddItems()` exist if `XtSetValues()` is so much faster? `XtSetValues()` can only be used to install all items in a list. `XmListAddItem()` and `XmListAddItems()` can be used to insert items at any point in an existing list. When adding a single item to an existing list, `XmListAddItem()` is the preferred mechanism. `XmListAddItems()` should be used to insert reasonable numbers of items into an existing list.

However, for creating the initial contents of a list widget, or completely replacing the current contents, `XtSetValues()` is the fastest possible approach. `XtSetValues()` may also be worth considering if a single item is to be added to a large list. In this case, the list widget would recreate the entire list just to add the new item, so it might be just as fast for the application to create and install a completely new list.

Displaying Text

The XmList widget is frequently a source of performance problems, but there are other widgets that can cause problems if not used carefully. For example, consider a program that needs to display many fields of text that must be updated rapidly with various values. Such a panel might be used as a digital readout used to display some real-time data. There are several ways to implement such a panel. For example, the text could be displayed in label widgets, label gadgets, XmText widgets, or XmTextField widgets.

Let's explore the performance of each of these options by devising a stress test to determine which approach is the most efficient. The following simple program just displays a set of 10 widgets in an XmRowColumn widget. The program installs a work procedure to update the text in each widget as rapidly as possible. Each time the work procedure is called, it simply updates each label with a new value. The value alternates between a short string and a long string to include the effect of variable-sized data. The following sections show the results for label widgets and gadgets and the XmText and XmTextField widgets.

Label Widgets

The first version of the program, which uses XmLabel widgets, is shown below. The program measures the time from before `XtAppInitialize()` is called until each label widget has been updated 100 times.

```
/*****************************************************
 * widgetlabels.c: Rapidly update a grid of labels.
 *****************************************************/
#include <Xm/Xm.h>
#include <Xm/Label.h>
#include <Xm/RowColumn.h>
#include <Xm/TextF.h>
#include "TimerTools.h"

Widget labels[10];

Boolean UpdateLabels ( XtPointer clientData );

void main ( int argc, char **argv )
{
    Widget       rc, shell;
    XtAppContext app;
    int          i;

```

Start timing

```
    ReportTime ( "Starting", FALSE );

    shell = XtAppInitialize ( &app, "Widgetlabels", NULL, 0,
                              &argc, argv, NULL, NULL, 0 );

    rc = XtVaCreateManagedWidget ( "rc",
                                   xmRowColumnWidgetClass,
                                   shell,
                                   XmNnumColumns, 2,
                                   XmNpacking, XmPACK_TIGHT,
                                   NULL );

    for ( i = 0; i < 10; i++ )
       labels[i] = XtCreateManagedWidget ( "label",
                                           xmLabelWidgetClass,
                                           rc, NULL, 0 );
```

```
36      XtRealizeWidget ( shell );
37
38     /*
39      * Install a work procedure to update each label
40      * as quickly as possible.
41      */
42
43      XtAppAddWorkProc ( app, UpdateLabels, NULL );
44
45      XtAppMainLoop ( app );
46  }
```

UpdateLabels() is a work procedure that will be called as often as possible. This function converts a text string to a compound string and installs it as the new label for each XmLabel widget. The size of the label is changed each time this function is called to simulate the effect of displaying real, arbitrarily sized data. The test on line 80 terminates the work procedure after updating each label 100 times.

```
47  Boolean UpdateLabels ( XtPointer clientData )
48  {
49      static int count = 0;
50      XmString   xmstr;
51      int        i;
52      char       buf[20];
53
54     /*
55      * Create a varying label to display.
56      */
57
58      sprintf ( buf, "%d", count %2 ? 10 : 1000000000 );
59
60     /*
61      * Display the label in each widget.
62      */
63
64      for ( i = 0; i < 10; i++ )
65      {
66          xmstr = XmStringCreateLocalized ( buf );
67
68          XtVaSetValues ( labels[i],
69                          XmNlabelString, xmstr,
70                          NULL );
71
72          XmStringFree ( xmstr );
73      }
74
```

```
    /*
     * Terminate the test if the labels have been
     * updated 100 times.
     */

    if ( count++ > 100 )
    {
        ReportTime ( "Done", TRUE );
        return ( TRUE );
    }

    return ( FALSE );
}
```

Stop timing

This program uses `ReportTime()` to measure the amount of time required to update the labels 100 times. We might suspect that one cost of this program is creating the compound string each time the work procedure is called, and it is tempting to optimize this aspect of the program. However, the function should create a compound string for each label each time because we are trying to simulate what would happen if each text field was updated with assorted values.

Figure 10.13 shows the results of running this program.

```
% widgetlabels
Starting:
Done:
   Elapsed Time = 1.480
   User Time    = 1.030
   System Time  = 0.100
```

Figure 10.13 Time required to update 10 labels 100 times.

According to these figures, each call to the work procedure takes approximately 0.0014 seconds, which seems reasonable, although the overall effect is not as smooth or fast as one might like. One interesting aspect of this program's behavior can be observed by watching it run. The labels are not seen updating smoothly. Instead the text seems to jump a bit, leaping between values on occasion. It might be worthwhile to investigate this program's behavior more completely, to see if it can be improved.

Figure 10.14 shows a partial listing of some of the more frequent requests generated by this program, as reported by `xmond`. `XtSetValues()` generates a `ClearArea` request to redisplay the widget each time a label is changed, so the 1010 `ClearArea` requests should not be surprising. A few of the other requests are surprising, though. For example, the 260 changes to a graphics context are difficult to explain. Also, the are 61 `ConfigureWindow` requests, which seems odd since there are only ten labels and they do not change size. These geometry requests are time-consuming because of the server traffic.

Request Name	# of Requests
ConfigureWindow	61
ChangeProperty	15
CreateGC	8
ChangeGC	260
SetClipRectangles	260
ClearArea	1010
PolyText8	450

Figure 10.14 Some of the requests made by `widgetlabels` program.

We could try to understand why these `ConfigureWindow` requests are being made by linking with the XtGeo library and examining the geometry management process. After relinking, we could set the `geoTattler` resource to "`on`", and run the `widgetlabels` program as follows:

```
widgetlabels | grep "geometry request" | wc -l
     2021
```

It appears that this program is making a rather large number of geometry requests, which must occur when the size of the displayed string changes. The performance of this example might be improved if this geometry management could be eliminated.

Fortunately, many of the Motif widgets support resources that control their behavior with respect to geometry management. For example, all shell widgets support an `XmNallowShellResize` resource. By default, this resource is set to `FALSE`, which means that the shell does not attempt to grow or shrink in response to requests from a child. The XmRowColumn widget also supports two resources, `XmNresizeHeight` and `XmNresizeWidth`. If these are `TRUE`, the default, the XmRowColumn widget attempts to honor resize requests from its children. Finally, the XmLabel widget supports an `XmNrecomputeSize` resource that determines if the widget should request a new size when the size of its label changes. This resource is also `TRUE` by default.

In the previous test, all resources were set to their default values, which might account for the geometry behavior observed while running the program. To see if it is possible to improve the performance by preventing the widgets from attempting to recompute their sizes, we can run the program again, with appropriate resources set to `FALSE`. Figure 10.15 shows the results.

```
% widgetlabels -xrm "*resizeWidth: false" \
-xrm "*recomputeSize: false"
Starting:
Done:
   Elapsed Time = 1.090
   User Time    = 0.710
   System Time  = 0.090
```

Figure 10.15 Update 10 labels 100 times, resizing disabled.

With these resources set, the overall effect is somewhat smoother and the program runs slightly faster. The number of requests is also reduced by this change. Figure 10.16 compares the requests made by this program with and without allowing the widgets to recompute their geometries.

Request	**# of Requests**	
	Resizable	**Non-Resizable**
ConfigureWindow	61	11
ChangeProperty	15	15
ChangeGC	260	160
SetClipRectangles	260	160
ClearArea	1010	1010
PolyText8	450	320

Figure 10.16 Requests made by `widgetlabels`.

It might also be useful to examine the geometry management by linking with the XtGeo library and running the program again, with the resize resources set to `FALSE`. The results show that the number of geometry requests has been reduced to a single request:

```
widget labels -xrm "*resizeWidth: false" \
-xrm "*recomputeSize: false" | grep "geometry request" | wc -l
       1
```

The next step is to create a version of this program that uses gadgets and run the same tests. Figure 10.17 shows the times reported by this version, allowing the program to perform the same geometry management as in the original test. Although the gadgets seem to be slightly faster, the difference is inconsequential.

```
% gadgetlabels
Starting:
Done:
   Elapsed Time = 1.430
   User Time    = 1.040
   System Time  = 0.080
```

Figure 10.17 Updating 10 label gadgets 100 times.

Figure 10.18 shows the times measured for the gadget version with the geometry management of the various widgets and gadgets disabled. This program is almost identical, in terms of time, to the widget version. It appears that gadgets are no faster to update than widgets.

```
% gadgetlabels -xrm "*resizeWidth: false" \
-xrm "*recomputeSize: false"
Starting:
Done:
   Elapsed Time = 1.110
   User Time    = 0.760
   System Time  = 0.080
```

Figure 10.18 Update 10 label gadgets 100 times, resizing disabled.

The requests made by the gadget version are not substantially different from those made by the widget version. Figure 10.19 shows the results when the `XmNresizeWidth` and `XmNrecomputeSize` resources are set to `TRUE` and `FALSE`. From these measurements, it does not appear that gadgets offer any significant advantage in this situation.

Request	# of Requests	
	Resizable	Non-Resizable
ConfigureWindow	1	1
ChangeProperty	15	15
ChangeGC	290	170
SetClipRectangles	290	170
ClearArea	1039	990
PolyText8	470	330

Figure 10.19 Some of the requests made by `gadgetlabels` program.

Text Widgets

Having gathered the data for label widgets and gadgets, the task of measuring text widgets remains. The XmText and XmTextField widgets have the advantage that they do not, in Motif 1.2, use compound strings, so it seems that there might be considerably less expense involved in updating these widgets. On the other hand, these widgets are meant to support editing, and may carry considerably more baggage than needed for this simple task.

The following program is similar to the `widgetlabels` program in the previous section. This version has been modified to use XmText widgets instead of XmLabel widgets.

```
/*************************************************************
 * textlabels.c: Rapidly update a grid of XmText widgets.
 *************************************************************/
#include <Xm/Xm.h>
#include <Xm/Label.h>
#include <Xm/RowColumn.h>
#include <Xm/Text.h>
#include "TimerTools.h"

Widget labels[10];

Boolean UpdateLabels ( XtPointer clientData );


void main ( int argc, char **argv )
{
    Widget       rc, shell;
    XtAppContext app;
    int          i;
```

Start timing

```
    ReportTime ( "Starting", FALSE );


    shell = XtAppInitialize ( &app, "Labels",
                              NULL, 0,
                              &argc, argv, NULL, NULL, 0 );

    rc = XtVaCreateManagedWidget ( "rc",
                                   xmRowColumnWidgetClass,
                                   shell,
                                   XmNnumColumns, 2,
                                   XmNpacking, XmPACK_TIGHT,
                                   NULL);

    for ( i = 0; i < 10; i++ )
      labels[i] = XtCreateManagedWidget ( "label",
                                          xmTextWidgetClass,
                                          rc, NULL, 0 );
    XtRealizeWidget ( shell );
    XtAppAddWorkProc ( app, UpdateLabels, NULL );
    XtAppMainLoop ( app );
}

Boolean UpdateLabels ( XtPointer clientData )
{
    static int count = 0;
    XmString   xmstr;
    int        i;
    char       buf[20];

    sprintf ( buf, "%d", count %2 ? 10 : 10000000 );

    for ( i = 0; i < 10; i++ )
        XtVaSetValues ( labels[i], XmNvalue, buf, NULL );

    if ( count++ > 100 )
    {
```

Stop timing

```
        ReportTime ( "Done", TRUE );
        return ( TRUE );
    }

    return ( FALSE );
}
```

Although we have already been alerted to the issue of allowing resizable windows, let's run this test case exactly as is, to see if the same effect can be observed with XmText widgets. Figure 10.20 shows the results of running this program. Surprisingly, the XmText widgets require substantially more time to complete this operation than either the label widgets or the label gadgets.

```
% textlabels
Starting:
Done:
   Elapsed Time = 3.980
   User Time    = 1.530
   System Time  = 0.280
```

Figure 10.20 Updating 10 XmText widgets 100 times.

Like the XmLabel widget, the XmText widget also supports a resource that prevents it from attempting to resize when the text inside the widget changes. For the XmText widget, this resource is a boolean, `XmNresizeWidth`. It's default value is `FALSE`, although the XmRowColumn widget's resource is still set to `TRUE`. Geometry management should not be a significant issue in this example, as long as the XmText widget's `XmNresizeWidth` resource remains set to `FALSE`.

Next, we can try the XmTextField widget. The XmTextField widget is intended to be a lightweight version of the XmText widget. It offers nearly the same interface, but can support only a single row of text. Because of the simpler demands on this widget, it is meant to be less expensive, and was designed for the type of situation represented by this example. The example can be changed to use XmTextField widgets by simply including TextF.h instead of Text.h and instantiating XmTextField widgets instead of XmText widgets.

Figure 10.21 shows the results of running this program.

```
% textfieldlabels
Starting:
Done:
   Elapsed Time = 8.780
   User Time    = 2.080
   System Time  = 0.810
```

Figure 10.21 Updating 10 XmTextField widgets 100 times.

Surprisingly, the performance of the version using XmTextField widgets is considerably worse than the XmText version in this experiment. Of course, in both cases, the XmTextField widget produces significantly worse performance than the XmText widget. To try to understand why, we can look at the events and requests involved in each version of the program.

Figure 10.22 shows some of the more interesting requests generated by each program. This table shows the requests generated for both the XmText and XmTextField versions.

It is obvious from the information reported by `xmond` that a large number of requests are being made. Far more requests are made by either of the text widgets than by the XmLabel and XmLabelGadget implementations. Furthermore, many of these requests require round trips to the server. Although fewer in number than some of the requests, `GetWindowAttributes`, `GetGeometry`, and `QueryColors` can be quite expensive because of the synchronous round trips they require. `GetSelectionOwner` also requires a round trip, and the XmTextField widget generates over 1000 of these! This request alone may account for the poorer performance of the XmTextField widget. Some other requests are made in staggering numbers, including over 12,000 `SetClipRectangles` requests for the XmTextField widget and between 4,000 and 7,000 `ChangeGC` requests for the different variations.

Request Names	**# of Requests**	
	XmText	**XmTextField**
GetWindowAttributes	208	208
GetGeometry	208	208
ChangeProperty	26	28
SetSelectionOwner	0	1010
GetSelectionOwner	0	1010
ChangeGC	4209	7147
SetClipRectangles	7172	12296
ClearArea	1150	10
CopyArea	4191	5090
PolySegment	81	21
PolyFillRectangle	3673	3623
PolyText8	1060	1020
AllocColor	108	108
QueryColors	105	105

Figure 10.22 Some requests made by XmText and XmTextField widgets.

Figure 10.23 summarizes the times and the total number of requests and events involved in each of the four cases measured here. It seems likely that the large numbers of requests generated by the XmText and XmTextField versions accounts for their markedly slower times. The XmTextField widget seems to be slower than the XmText widget, even though it generates fewer requests. Although there could be many reasons for the difference in performance, we must remember that the type of request (i.e round-trip versus asynchronous) can have a significant effect.

	Label Widget	**Label Gadget**	**Text**	**Text Field**
Time Resizable	1.48	1.43	3.98	8.78
Time Not Resizable	1.09	1.11	N/A	N/A
Total Events Resizable	1049	1048	N/A	N/A
Total Events Not Resizable	1029	999	37	17
Total Requests Resizable	2121	2158	N/A	N/A
Total Requests Not Resizable	1739	1429	45397	32392

Figure 10.23 Summary of times, events and requests.

This experiment clearly shows the importance of choosing and configuring widgets carefully, particularly for time-critical tasks. Of course, the exact information measured in this section might easily change from one version of Motif to the next. For example, some aspects of the XmText and XmTextField widgets' behavior seem like possible bugs. For example, it is difficult to think of a valid reason for thousands of `ChangeCG` requests, or even the 105 `QueryColors` requests in this experiment. The `SetSelectionOwner` and `GetSelectionOwner` requests also seem suspicious, because the XmTextField widget makes them, while the XmText widget does not. Such problems could easily be fixed in future versions of Motif, or even some vendor's current versions.

If you do encounter runtime performance problems with Motif, it is worthwhile to spend some time trying different approaches. Although, as an application developer, you may not be able to alter a Motif widget to improve its performance, you can make choices about what widgets you use, and how they are configured.

10.7 Conclusion

Runtime performance is a complex issue that involves the architecture of an application, what widgets are selected and how they are used, the server traffic generated, and much more. The single most critical issue is the program's ability to handle events. Most well-written applications should have little trouble providing responsive menus, dialogs, and so on, if the application is able to process events in a timely manner. Designing a program for an event-driven environment is a basic part of learning how to program with X and Motif. Suggestions and examples of how to write programs properly for an event-driven architecture can be found in most of the Motif and X tutorials mentioned in this book. The case studies in the following two chapters also discuss additional techniques for improving both start-up and runtime performance.

Assuming a program is architected correctly, a program's runtime performance often is determined by various system characteristics, such as the load on the system, the amount of memory the system has, and so on. While programmers do not have much direct control over such aspects of the user's environment, they can try to reduce the burden their own programs place on the system. Selecting the most efficient Motif widgets, eliminating unnecessary widgets, and making efficient use of the widgets that are used can make a significant difference.

As always, usability issues and user interface design can also play an important role. If the user can perform a task in one step instead of two or three, the user benefits directly, and at the same time, the number of server requests, widgets used, and so on, may also be reduced. It is also important to separate the task being performed from its visual indication. In many cases, the user can be presented with continuous visual feedback and interaction, while the real task is performed in the background.

11

Case Study #1: A Fractal Generator

Previous chapters explore various ways to improve Motif performance by looking at small examples or isolated aspects of typical Motif programs. The final two chapters of this book examine two complete programs in an attempt to apply everything we have discussed so far to more realistic cases. This chapter examines a program originally presented in [Young94], a simple fractal generator, which presents some unique challenges with respect to performance. Chapter 12 presents a simple file and directory browser application that might be found on a contemporary desktop.

The `fractal` program discussed in this chapter is interesting because it has performance characteristics that are often encountered in certain types of real applications. The example contains a modest user interface that consists of a rendering area and a few menu items. The program also has a moderately complex dialog that can be used to set user preferences. The most significant, and most challenging aspect of the fractal example is that the program performs a time-consuming task in addition to presenting a panel of widgets to the user. The program offers few of the straight-forward opportunities for performance improvement described in previous chapters. There are no large collections of widgets to be managed as a group, or converted to gadgets. There are no deep hierarchies of widgets that might introduce performance penalties. In fact, there are not very many widgets in this program. The challenge presented by the fractal generator is to create a program is truly interactive and responsive to the user, while still performing a task that is inherently time consuming.

This chapter begins by examining the initial version of the fractal program, which is a slightly modified version of the program described in [Young94]. The next step is to measure the performance of the initial version of the program. Then, based on the measurements, we will explore ways to improve the program's responsiveness, if necessary.

11.1 The Basic Fractal Program

The program examined in this chapter is a simple fractal generator. The program displays a Mandelbrot image in a window, shown on the left in Figure 11.1.

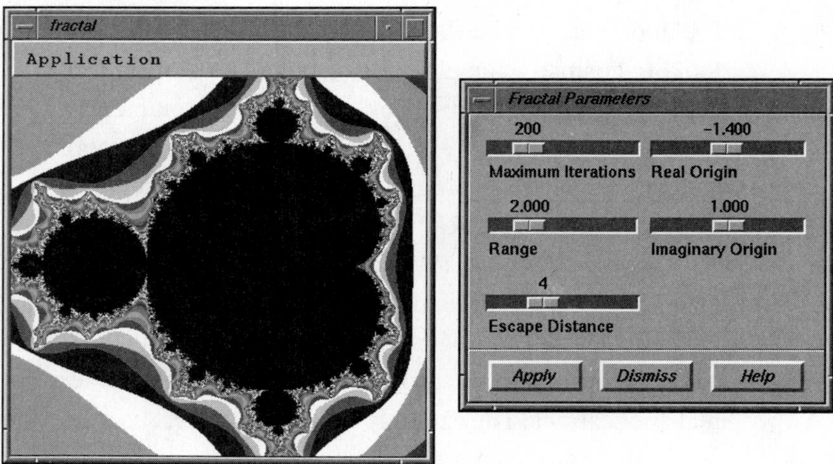

Figure 11.1 The `fractal` program.

The user can manipulate various parameters that affect the appearance of the fractal image using sliders on a preference panel, which appears on the right in Figure 11.1. This panel is optional and can be displayed by choosing a

"Preferences..." item on the Application menu pane in the main window. The preference panel allows the user to zoom or pan the image, control the number of iterations involved in the fractal, and so on. Any changes made to the controls on the preference panel take effect when the user clicks on the panel's "Apply" button.

The `fractal` program is designed to allow interactive exploration, and, in addition to the preference dialog, supports a more direct way to zoom into a specific part of the image. The user can sweep out an area of the fractal in the main rendering area, using the mouse to draw a rubberbanded rectangle. The selected area is then expanded to fill the entire window. Figure 11.2 illustrates this process. The window on the left shows a full fractal image, with a selected area. The image on the right shows the program after the selected area has been drawn in full scale.

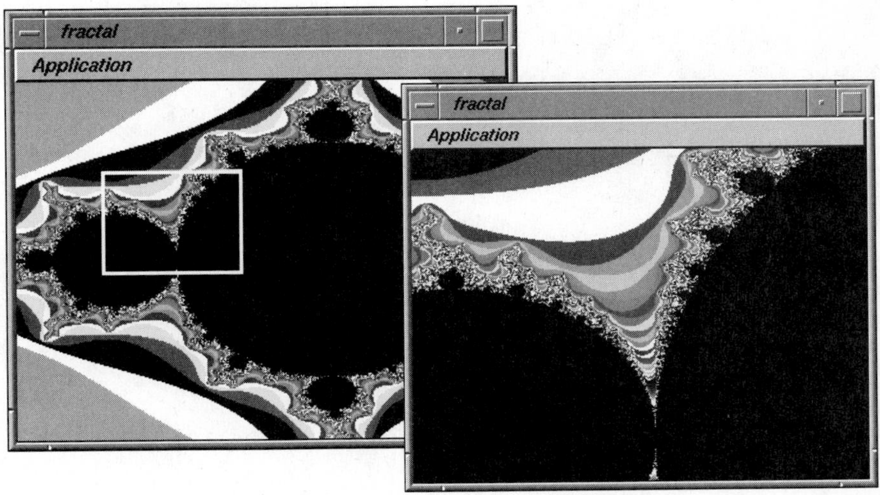

Figure 11.2 Interactively selecting an area for a closer view.

[Young94] discusses the fractal algorithm used in this example, as well as the implementation of the program in some detail. There are also many books that discuss the mathematics of fractal images for those who are interested in the concepts that underlie this program. For this discussion, these details are unimportant. We can approach this program as if we are tuning a program written by someone else. We need to examine it, understand its performance, and focus on any areas that need to be improved.

Implementation Overview

We can begin by looking at the complete program in its initial state. The version of the program described in this section differs slightly from the one described in [Young94]. Some features have been removed for simplicity, and calls to the timing functions used throughout this book have been added.

The fractal program consists of four files, one file that implements the main window and the fractal drawing functions, a file that implements a preference panel, a header file that contains definitions that must be shared between the other two modules, and a resource file.

The header file contains definitions of data structures used throughout the program:

```
/*************************************************************
 * fractal.h: Type declarations for the fractal program.
 *************************************************************/
#include <Xm/Xm.h>

typedef struct {
     double  real, imag;
} ComplexNumber;

/*
 * Assorted information needed to generate and draw the image.
 */

typedef struct {
    Widget          canvas;
    Pixmap          pixmap;
    GC              gc;
    GC              xorGC;
    Dimension       width, height;
    int             depth, ncolors;
    double          range, maxDistance;
    ComplexNumber   origin;
} ImageData;
```

The file fractal.c contains functions that create the main fractal window and its menu bar. This file also contains the fractal rendering functions and various callbacks and event handlers used by the program.

```
/*************************************************************
 * fractal.c: Main window and rendering code for fractal.
 *************************************************************/
#include <Xm/Xm.h>
#include <Xm/DrawingA.h>
#include <Xm/MainW.h>
#include <Xm/RowColumn.h>
#include <Xm/CascadeB.h>
#include <Xm/PushB.h>
#include <stdlib.h>
#include "fractal.h"
#include "TimerTools.h"

extern ShowPreferences ( Widget parent, ImageData *data );

static void InitData ( Widget w, ImageData *data );
static void ResizeCallback ( Widget    w,
                             XtPointer clientData,
                             XtPointer callData );
static void RedisplayCallback ( Widget    w,
                                XtPointer clientData,
                                XtPointer callData );
static void ShowPreferencesCallback ( Widget    w,
                                      XtPointer clientData,
                                      XtPointer callData );
static void QuitCallback ( Widget    w,
                           XtPointer clientData,
                           XtPointer callData );

/*
 * Function called from preference module
 */

void CreateImage ( ImageData *data );

/*
 * Functions that support rubberband selection of a region.
 */

static void StartRubberBand ( Widget    w,
                              XtPointer clientData,
                              XEvent   *event,
                              Boolean  *flag );

static void TrackRubberBand ( Widget    w,
                              XtPointer clientData,
                              XEvent   *event,
                              Boolean  *flag );

```

```
static void EndRubberBand ( Widget    w,
                            XtPointer clientData,
                            XEvent   *event,
                            Boolean   *flag );

static int startX, startY, lastX, lastY;
```

The function `CreateMenu()` creates a menu bar that contains one menu pane. The menu pane contains items that allow the user to quit and to post a preference dialog.

```
Widget CreateMenu ( Widget parent, ImageData *data )
{
    Widget menu, pref, quit;
    Widget cascade, submenu;
    int    i;

    menu = XmCreateMenuBar ( parent, "menu", NULL, 0 );
    XtManageChild ( menu );

    submenu = XmCreatePulldownMenu ( menu,
                                     "Application",
                                     NULL, 0 );

    cascade = XtVaCreateManagedWidget ( "Application",
                                    xmCascadeButtonWidgetClass,
                                    menu,
                                    XmNsubMenuId, submenu,
                                    NULL  );

    pref = XtCreateManagedWidget ( "Preferences",
                                   xmPushButtonWidgetClass,
                                   submenu, NULL, 0 );

    quit = XtCreateManagedWidget ( "Quit",
                                   xmPushButtonWidgetClass,
                                   submenu, NULL, 0 );

    XtAddCallback ( pref, XmNactivateCallback,
                    ShowPreferencesCallback,
                    ( XtPointer ) data);

    XtAddCallback ( quit, XmNactivateCallback,
                    QuitCallback, NULL );

    return ( menu );
}
```

The main part of the `fractal` program creates an XmMainWindow widget and a Motif XmDrawingArea widget in which the fractal is drawn. The program also registers various callbacks and event handlers with the drawing area widget, and initializes some data structures. To measure the start-up time of this program, `ReportTime()` is called as the first statement in `main()`, and called again after the shell has been mapped and the initial events have been processed.

Start timing

```
void main ( int argc, char **argv )
{
    Widget       shell, canvas, mainWindow, menu;
    XtAppContext app;
    ImageData    data;

    ReportTime ( "Starting", TRUE );

    shell = XtAppInitialize ( &app, "Fractal", NULL, 0,
                              &argc, argv, NULL, NULL, 0 );

    mainWindow = XtCreateManagedWidget ( "mainWindow",
                                         xmMainWindowWidgetClass,
                                         shell, NULL, 0 );
   /*
    * Create the widget in which to display the fractal.
    */

    canvas = XtCreateManagedWidget ( "canvas",
                                     xmDrawingAreaWidgetClass,
                                     mainWindow, NULL, 0 );

   /*
    * Create the GCs needed by the fractal program.
    */

    InitData ( canvas, &data );

   /*
    * Create the menu bar and set up the window layout.
    */

    menu = CreateMenu ( mainWindow, &data );

    XtVaSetValues ( mainWindow,
                    XmNmenuBar,    menu,
                    XmNworkWindow, canvas,
                    NULL );

```

```
    /*
     * Add callbacks to handle resize and exposures.
     */

     XtAddCallback ( canvas, XmNexposeCallback,
                         RedisplayCallback, ( XtPointer ) &data );
     XtAddCallback ( canvas, XmNresizeCallback,
                         ResizeCallback, ( XtPointer )  &data );
   /*
    * Add event handlers to track the mouse and allow
    * the user to select a region with rubberband rectangle.
    */

    XtAddEventHandler ( canvas, ButtonPressMask, FALSE,
                            StartRubberBand, &data );
    XtAddEventHandler ( canvas, ButtonMotionMask, FALSE,
                            TrackRubberBand, &data );
    XtAddEventHandler ( canvas, ButtonReleaseMask, FALSE,
                            EndRubberBand, &data );

    XtRealizeWidget ( shell );
    WaitForWindow ( shell );
    HandleEvents ( shell );
    ReportTime ( "Up", TRUE );

    XtAppMainLoop ( app );
}
```

Stop timing

The following callbacks are installed in the `fractal` program's menu items. The first posts the preference dialog, while the second simply exits.

```
static void ShowPreferencesCallback ( Widget    w,
                                      XtPointer clientData,
                                      XtPointer callData )
{
     ImageData *data = ( ImageData * ) clientData;

    /* Call external function to display pereference panel. */

     ShowPreferences ( XtParent ( w ), data );
}

static void QuitCallback ( Widget    w,
                           XtPointer clientData,
                           XtPointer callData )
{
    exit ( 0 );
}
```

`InitData()` initializes a data structure used to control the fractal image, and creates the graphics contexts used in the program.

```
static void InitData ( Widget w, ImageData *data )
{
    XGCValues values;

    /*
     * Get the size of the drawing area.
     */

     XtVaGetValues ( w,
                    XmNwidth,       &data->width,
                    XmNheight,      &data->height,
                    XmNbackground, &values.foreground,
                    NULL );

     data->canvas      = w;
     data->depth       = 200;
     data->origin.real = -1.4;
     data->origin.imag = 1.0;
     data->range       = 2.0;
     data->maxDistance = 4.0;
     data->pixmap      = NULL;

    /*
     * Find out how many colors we have to work with, and
     * create a default, writable, graphics context.
     */

     data->ncolors = XDisplayCells ( XtDisplay ( w ),
                        XDefaultScreen ( XtDisplay ( w ) ) );

     data->gc = XCreateGC ( XtDisplay ( w ),
                        DefaultRootWindow ( XtDisplay ( w ) ),
                        NULL, NULL );

   /*
    * Create a second GC set to XOR mode to use in the
    * rubberbanding functions that select a region.
    */

    values.function = GXxor;

    data->xorGC = XtGetGC ( w,
                          GCForeground | GCFunction,
                          &values );
}
```

The following event handlers are installed to handle mouse motion in the XmDrawingArea widget. Together, these functions provide the ability to sweep out an area to be displayed in full resolution.

```
static void StartRubberBand ( Widget    w,
                              XtPointer clientData,
                              XEvent    *event,
                              Boolean   *flag )
{
    lastX = startX = event->xbutton.x;
    lastY = startY = event->xbutton.y;
}

static void TrackRubberBand ( Widget    w,
                              XtPointer clientData,
                              XEvent    *event,
                              Boolean   *flag )
{
    int        height;
    ImageData *data = ( ImageData* ) clientData;

   /*
    * If a non-zero sized rectangle has been previously drawn,
    * erase it by drawing again in XOR mode.
    */

    if ( lastX - startX > 0 || lastY - startY > 0 )
        XDrawRectangle ( XtDisplay ( w ), XtWindow ( w ),
                         data->xorGC,
                         startX, startY,
                         lastX - startX, lastY - startY );

   /*
    * Update the last point. Force an aspect ratio that
    * matches the shape of the window.
    */

    lastX  =  event->xmotion.x;
    height = data->height *
                   ( lastX - startX ) / data->width;
    lastY  =  startY + height;

    if ( lastX < startX )
        lastX = startX;

    if ( lastY < startY )
        lastY = startY;

```

```
    /*
     * Draw a rectangle in XOR mode so it can be easily erased.
     */

     XDrawRectangle ( XtDisplay ( w ), XtWindow ( w ), data->xorGC,
                      startX, startY,
                      lastX - startX, lastY - startY );
}

static void EndRubberBand ( Widget     w,
                            XtPointer clientData,
                            XEvent    *event,
                            Boolean   *flag )
{
    int        height;
    ImageData *data = ( ImageData* ) clientData;

    /*
     * If a non-zero sized rectangle has been previously
     * drawn, erase it by drawing again in XOR mode.
     */

     if ( lastX - startX > 0 || lastY - startY > 0 )
         XDrawRectangle ( XtDisplay ( w ), XtWindow ( w ),
                          data->xorGC, startX, startY,
                          lastX - startX, lastY - startY );
    /*
     * Update the last point. Force an aspect ratio that
     * matches the shape of the window.
     */

     lastX  = event->xmotion.x;
     height = data->height * ( lastX - startX ) / data->width;
     lastY  = startY + height;

    /*
     * Unless a non-zero sized region was selected, return.
     */

     if ( lastX <= startX || lastY <= startY )
         return;

    /*
     * Convert the pixel-based corrdinates to the real
     * coordinates used to compute the fractal image.
     */

     data->origin.real += data->range *
                          ( double ) startX / ( double ) data->width;
```

```
    data->origin.imag -= data->range *
                       ( double )  startY / ( double ) data->height;

    data->range = data->range *
                 ( double ) ( lastX - startX ) / ( double ) data->width;

   /*
    * Create a new image, based on the selected range and
    * origin. Keep the preference panel in sync.
    */

    CreateImage ( data );
    UpdatePreferences ( data );
}
```

The function `CreateImage()` generates the fractal image. This function uses three nested `for` loops to evaluate the fractal expression and to determine the color of each pixel in the window. Once the color of a particular pixel has been determined, `CreateImage()` calls `XDrawPoint()` to draw a single pixel of the fractal image. `CreateImage()` draws each point twice: once in the XmDrawingArea widget and once in a pixmap. The pixmap is used to restore the image when the window is exposed. Rather than forcing the program to recompute the image for each `Expose` event, the appropriate portion of the pixmap is copied to the window. The image only needs to be recomputed if some aspect of the image changes.

```
void CreateImage ( ImageData *data )
{
    Widget w = data->canvas;
    int    x, y, iteration;

   /*
    * If the canvas is realized, erase it.
    */

    if ( XtIsRealized ( w ) )
        XClearArea ( XtDisplay ( w ), XtWindow ( w ),
                     0, 0, 0, 0, TRUE );

   /*
    * Erase the pixmap by filling it with black.
    */

    XSetForeground ( XtDisplay ( w ), data->gc,
                     BlackPixelOfScreen ( XtScreen ( w ) ) );

```

```
    XFillRectangle ( XtDisplay ( w ), data->pixmap,
                     data->gc, 0, 0,
                     data->width,  data->height );

   /*
    * For each pixel on the window....
    */

    for ( y = 0; y < data->height; y++ )
    {
        ComplexNumber z, k;

        for ( x = 0; x < data->width; x++ )
        {

            /*
             * Initialize K to a normalized, floating
             * coordinate in the x, y plane.
             * Initialize Z to ( 0.0, 0.0 ).
             */

             z.real =  z.imag = 0.0;

             k.real =  data->origin.real +
                 ( double ) x / ( double ) data->width *
                       data->range;

             k.imag =  data->origin.imag -
                 ( double ) y / ( double ) data->height *
                       data->range;

            /*
             * Calculate z =  z * z + k over and over.
             */

             for ( iteration = 0;
                    iteration < data->depth;
                    iteration++ )
             {
                 double   real;
                 int      distance;

                 real   = z.real;
                 z.real = z.real * z.real -
                                  z.imag * z.imag + k.real;
                 z.imag = 2 * real * z.imag + k.imag;

                 distance = ( int ) ( z.real * z.real +
                                      z.imag * z.imag );
```

```
                /*
                 * If the z point has moved off the plane,
                 * set the current foreground color to
                 * the distance (cast to an int and modulo
                 * the number of colors available), and
                 * draw a point in the window and the pixmap.
                 */

                if ( distance  >= data->maxDistance )
                {
                    Pixel color;

                    color = ( Pixel )iteration % data->ncolors;

                    XSetForeground ( XtDisplay ( w ),
                                     data->gc, color );

                    XDrawPoint ( XtDisplay ( w ),
                                 data->pixmap,
                                 data->gc, x, y );

                    if ( XtIsRealized ( w ) )
                        XDrawPoint ( XtDisplay ( w ),
                                     XtWindow ( w ),
                                     data->gc,x,y );
                    break;
                }
            }
        }
    }
}
```

The callback function `RedisplayCallback()` copies a region of the pixmap to the `canvas` widget's window when an `Expose` event is received.

```
static void RedisplayCallback ( Widget    w,
                                XtPointer clientData,
                                XtPointer callData )
{
    ImageData *data = ( ImageData * ) clientData;
    XmDrawingAreaCallbackStruct *cb =
                        ( XmDrawingAreaCallbackStruct * ) callData;
    XExposeEvent *event = ( XExposeEvent * ) cb->event;

   /*
    * Extract the exposed area from the event and copy
    * from the saved pixmap to the window.
    */
```

```
    XCopyArea ( XtDisplay ( w ), data->pixmap,
                XtWindow ( w ), data->gc,
                event->x, event->y,
                event->width, event->height,
                event->x, event->y );
}
```

ResizeCallback() frees the current pixmap and creates a new pixmap each time the fractal program's drawing area is resized. Once a new pixmap is ready, this function calls CreateImage() to generate a new fractal image.

```
static void ResizeCallback ( Widget    w,
                             XtPointer clientData,
                             XtPointer callData )
{
    ImageData *data = ( ImageData * ) clientData;

   /*
    *  Get the new window size.
    */

    XtVaGetValues ( w,
                    XmNwidth,  &data->width,
                    XmNheight, &data->height,
                    NULL );
   /*
    * Clear the window, forcing an Expose event to be generated
    */

    if ( XtIsRealized ( w ) )
        XClearArea ( XtDisplay ( w ), XtWindow ( w ),
                     0, 0, 0, 0, TRUE );

   /*
    *  Free the old pixmap and create a new pixmap
    *  the same size as the window.
    */

    if ( data->pixmap )
        XFreePixmap ( XtDisplay ( w ), data->pixmap );

    data->pixmap = XCreatePixmap ( XtDisplay ( w ),
                         DefaultRootWindow ( XtDisplay ( w ) ),
                         data->width, data->height,
                         DefaultDepthOfScreen ( XtScreen ( w ) ) );

    XSetForeground ( XtDisplay ( w ), data->gc,
                     BlackPixelOfScreen ( XtScreen ( w ) ) );
```

```
    XFillRectangle ( XtDisplay ( w ), data->pixmap,
                     data->gc, 0, 0,
                     data->width,  data->height );

   /*
    * Generate a new image.
    */

    CreateImage ( data );
}
```

The second part of the `fractal` program is the preference panel. The preference panel is implemented in a separate file, preference.c, as an independent module. The module consists of a function that creates and displays the preference dialog and also includes several callbacks.

```
/************************************************************
 * preference.c: Implement a preference dialog to allow
 *               customization of the fractal image.
 ************************************************************/
#include <Xm/Xm.h>
#include <Xm/Scale.h>
#include <Xm/ToggleB.h>
#include <Xm/MessageB.h>
#include <Xm/RowColumn.h>
#include <math.h>
#include "fractal.h"

typedef struct  {
  char    *name;
  float    multiplier;
  Widget   w;
  int      value;
} SliderData;

static void OkCallback ( Widget    w,
                         XtPointer clientData,
                         XtPointer callData );
static void CancelCallback ( Widget    w,
                             XtPointer clientData,
                             XtPointer callData );
extern void CreateImage ( ImageData *data );
extern void SetupColorMap ( Widget     shell,
                            ImageData *data,
                            Boolean    ramp );
void  UpdatePreferences ( ImageData *data );
typedef enum { DEPTH, RANGE, DIST, REAL,
               IMAG, NCOLORS } PreferenceTypes;
```

```

static SliderData sliders [] = {
  { "depth"      },
  { "range"      },
  { "distance"   },
  { "realOrigin" },
  { "imagOrigin" }
};

static Widget dialog = NULL;
```

The function `ShowPreferences()` creates and displays a custom preference dialog. Because this function creates and displays a window, we will insert calls to `ReportTime()` at the beginning and end to measure the time required to display the window.

Start timing

```
void ShowPreferences ( Widget parent, ImageData *data )
{
    Widget rowColumn;
    int    i;

    ReportTime ( "Posting Preference Dialog", FALSE );

    /*
     * If this is the first time this function has been
     * called, create the preference dialog.
     */

    if ( !dialog )
    {
        Arg args[1];

       /*
        * Use a message box dialog widget, and remove the
        * symbol and label areas. This dialog is designed
        * to allow the user to apply data or to dismiss the
        * dialog, so XmNautoUnmanage is also set to FALSE.
        */

        XtSetArg ( args[0], XmNautoUnmanage, FALSE );
        dialog = XmCreateMessageDialog ( parent, "preferences",
                                         args, 1 );
        XtUnmanageChild (  XmMessageBoxGetChild ( dialog,
                                           XmDIALOG_SYMBOL_LABEL ) );
        XtUnmanageChild ( XmMessageBoxGetChild ( dialog,
                                          XmDIALOG_MESSAGE_LABEL ) );

       /* Create the work area */
```

```

    rowColumn =
            XtVaCreateManagedWidget ( "rowColumn",
                                     xmRowColumnWidgetClass,
                                     dialog,
                                     XmNorientation,XmVERTICAL,
                                     XmNpacking, XmPACK_COLUMN,
                                     XmNnumColumns,  2,
                                     NULL );

  /* Create sliders to control variable values */

   for ( i = 0; i < XtNumber ( sliders ); i++ )
   {
       short decimalPoints;

       sliders[i].w =
              XtCreateManagedWidget ( sliders[i].name,
                                      xmScaleWidgetClass,
                                      rowColumn,
                                      NULL, 0 );

      /*
       * Because the range of each slider can be
       * specified in a resource file, the program
       * must determine the number of decimal points
       * to be used when evaluating a slider position.
       * Get the value, and convert to a power of ten.
       */

       XtVaGetValues ( sliders[i].w,
                       XmNdecimalPoints, &decimalPoints,
                       NULL );
       sliders[i].multiplier = powf ( 10.0,
                                      ( double ) decimalPoints );

    }

   /*
    * Add callbacks to apply new values and to dismiss
    * the dialog without applying changes.
    */

    XtAddCallback ( dialog, XmNokCallback,
                    OkCallback, ( XtPointer ) data );
    XtAddCallback ( dialog, XmNcancelCallback,
                    CancelCallback, ( XtPointer ) data );
}

```

```
    /*
     * Post the dialog, first setting all sliders to the
     * current values of the corresponding data.
     */

     UpdatePreferences ( data );
     XtManageChild ( dialog );

     WaitForWindow ( XtParent ( dialog ) );
     HandleEvents ( dialog );
     ReportTime ( "Preference Panel Up", TRUE );
}
```

Stop timing

`UpdatePreferences()` sets the initial value of each slider in the preference panel.

```
void UpdatePreferences ( ImageData *data )
{
    int i;

   /*
    * Don't try to update if the dialog doesn't exist yet.
    */

    if ( !dialog )
        return;

   /*
    * Multiply each value by the multiplier for each scale
    * to get the correct integer value for each scale.
    */

    sliders[DEPTH].value   = data->depth *
                                    sliders[DEPTH].multiplier;
    sliders[REAL].value    = data->origin.real *
                                          sliders[REAL].multiplier;
    sliders[IMAG].value    = data->origin.imag *
                                           sliders[IMAG].multiplier;
    sliders[RANGE].value   = data->range *
                                    sliders[RANGE].multiplier;
    sliders[DIST].value    = data->maxDistance *
                                          sliders[DIST].multiplier;
    sliders[NCOLORS].value   = data->ncolors;

   /*
    * Move each scale to the correct position.
    */

```

```
    for ( i = 0; i < XtNumber ( sliders ); i++ )
       XtVaSetValues ( sliders[i].w,
                       XmNvalue, sliders[i].value,
                       NULL );
}
```

The `OkCallback()` function loops through XmScale widgets, retrieving the current value represented by each slider. This value is then assigned to a member of the `ImageData` structure that controls the fractal image. `OkCallback()` calls `CreateImage()` to recompute and redisplay a new image.

```
static void OkCallback ( Widget    w,
                         XtPointer clientData,
                         XtPointer callData )
{
    int        i;
    ImageData *data = ( ImageData * ) clientData;

   /*
    * Retrieve the current values from all sliders and
    * store in the ImageData structure.
    */

    for ( i = 0; i < XtNumber ( sliders ); i++ )
        XtVaGetValues ( sliders[i].w,
                        XmNvalue, &( sliders[i].value ),
                        NULL );

    data->depth       = sliders[DEPTH].value /
                                  sliders[DEPTH].multiplier;
    data->origin.real = sliders[REAL].value  /
                                  sliders[REAL].multiplier;
    data->origin.imag = sliders[IMAG].value  /
                                  sliders[IMAG].multiplier;
    data->range       = sliders[RANGE].value /
                                  sliders[RANGE].multiplier;
    data->maxDistance = sliders[DIST].value /
                                  sliders[DIST].multiplier;
    data->ncolors     =  sliders[NCOLORS].value;

   /*
    * Recompute and redisplay the fractal.
    */

    CreateImage ( data );
}
```

The function `CancelCallback()` simply unmanages the dialog without regard to any changes that have been made to the preference panel.

```
static void CancelCallback ( Widget    w,
                             XtPointer clientData,
                             XtPointer callData )
{
    /*
     * Just unmanage the dialog without updating any values.
     */

     XtUnmanageChild ( w );
}
```

Application Resources

The `fractal` program depends on several resources for correct operation. The fractal program's app-defaults file specifies various labels as well as initial values of the parameters that affect the appearance of the fractal image.

```
!!!!!!!!!!!!!!!!!!!!!!!!!!!!!!!!!!!!!!!!!!!!!!!!!!!!!!
! Fractal: Application resources for fractal program.
!!!!!!!!!!!!!!!!!!!!!!!!!!!!!!!!!!!!!!!!!!!!!!!!!!!!!!
! Set labels for menu items
*Preferences.labelString:                  Preferences...

! Set labels, ranges, and default values for
! all preference controls
*autoUnmanage:                             False
*preferences.dialogTitle:                  Fractal Parameters
*preferences.okLabelString:                Apply
*preferences.cancelLabelString:            Dismiss

! All scales should be horizontal and show the numeric value
*preferences*XmScale.orientation:          horizontal
*preferences*XmScale.showValue:            True

! Ranges, default values, and labels for individual controls
*preferences*depth.titleString:            Maximum Iterations
*preferences*depth.minimum:                   1
*preferences*depth.maximum:                1000
*preferences*depth.decimalPoints:             0
*preferences*depth.value:                   200

*preferences*range.titleString:            Range
*preferences*range.minimum:                   1
*preferences*range.maximum:               10000
```

```
*preferences*range.decimalPoints:          3
*preferences*range.value:               2000

*preferences*distance.titleString:         Escape Distance
*preferences*distance.minimum:             1
*preferences*distance.maximum:            10
*preferences*distance.decimalPoints:       0
*preferences*distance.value:               4

*preferences*realOrigin.titleString:       Real Origin
*preferences*realOrigin.minimum:       -3000
*preferences*realOrigin.maximum:         300
*preferences*realOrigin.decimalPoints:     3
*preferences*realOrigin.value:         -1400

*preferences*imagOrigin.titleString:       Imaginary Origin
*preferences*imagOrigin.minimum:       -1000
*preferences*imagOrigin.maximum:        3000
*preferences*imagOrigin.decimalPoints:     3
*preferences*imagOrigin.value:          1000

*preferences*numColors.titleString:        Number of Colors
*preferences*numColors.minimum:            1
*preferences*numColors.maximum:          256
```

Setting Performance Goals

Before measuring the `fractal` program's performance, it is useful to establish some performance goals. We have already established some goals for program start-up, and ideally, the `fractal` program should meet these goals. The `fractal` program is a bit different from the programs discussed so far, however, and it is tempting to make excuses to increase the targeted time, because we can almost be certain the program is going to be slow. However, goals should be based on the user's needs, not the limitations of the program.

So, sticking to the same goal we have used throughout this book, we would like to be able to start the fractal program in three tenths of a second, with one second being a worst case fallback position. We should also establish a goal for displaying the preference panel in a reasonable length of time. Because a user will post a preference panel in order to make a change to the image, it should appear almost instantly, within three tenths of a second.

With the `fractal` program, start-up times are only part of the story. The `fractal` program allows users to manipulate a fractal image interactively once the program is running. The user can change parameters in the preference dialog, and also select an area of the image to zoom into. To allow the user to explore the fractal image without lengthy delays, these operations should be nearly instantaneous. Of course, all normal user interface operations, such as posting menus, resizing the window, and so on should occur instantly as well.

Figure 11.3 summarizes these key operations and the performance goals we hope to achieve.

Operation	Goal
Program start-up (initial response)	0.3-1.0
Launch preference panel	0.3
response to parameter changes	0.3
Zoom in on selected areas	0.3
Resize window	0.3
Redraw on Expose	< 0.3
Menus, sliders, buttons, rubberbanding	< 0.3

Figure 11.3 Performance goals for `fractal` program.

Some of the operations in Figure 11.3 are a bit ambiguous as stated, and should be clarified. (For example, when is a window considered "resized"?) For purposes of this exercise, we will consider an operation to have been completed when the program is ready for the next user interaction. If it is not possible to complete an operation in the desired amount of time, performance may be considered acceptable if the program can provide consistent and clear response within the desired period of time.

Some initial measurements can be made to see if the `fractal` program meets these performance goals, and if not, what operations need to be improved. To make reliable measurements, we must identify a repeatable, reproducible experiment. If any problems are detected, and performance improvements are attempted, it is important to be able to repeat the same operations to see if the changes were successful.

The most variable factor in the `fractal` program is the size of the image. If a fixed size is used for all tests, the results should be reasonably reproducible. For all experiments in this section, the `fractal` program is run as:

```
fractal -geometry =400x400
```

to produce a window 400 pixels high and 400 pixels wide. This geometry specifies the size of the program's main window. The fractal image will be slightly smaller, to allow room for the menu bar at the top of the window.

Initial Measurements

In most tuning efforts, the first test or tests can be rather coarse, because the purpose is to explore and identify problem areas. Because the most significant issue, at least at first, is user-perceived time, a stopwatch may be the only tool needed for initial tests. To begin examining the `fractal` program's performance, the first step is to gather the data reported by the calls to `ReportTime()` inserted into the program. We may need a stopwatch to measure some of the other performance characteristics.

Figure 11.4 shows the results of running the `fractal` program on System A and posting the preference panel two times.

```
% fractal -geometry =400x400
Starting:
Up:
   Elapsed Time = 15.360
   CPU Time     = 14.15
   System Time  = 0.160
Posting Preference Dialog:
Preference dialog up:
   Elapsed Time = 0.290
   CPU Time     = 0.130
   System Time  = 0.020
Posting Preference Dialog:
Preference dialog up:
   Elapsed Time = 0.110
   CPU Time     = 0.030
   System Time  = 0.010
```

Figure 11.4 Initial performance measurements.

The results show that the program's window first appears 15 seconds after the program is launched. Based on this measurement, the challenge in tuning this program is quite clear. Fifteen seconds is a long way from the goal of start-up in three tenths of a second. Even with an order of magnitude improvement, the program will still take longer than our worst case goal of one second.

Although this program clearly has a serious start-up problem, some aspects of the runtime performance are quite good. Once the fractal window appears, menus pop up quickly, the rubberbanding rectangle used to sweep out an area in the fractal image is smooth and fast, and the image is redrawn instantly when the window is closed and reopened. The preference panel also appears in a reasonable amount of time. As shown in Figure 11.4, the preference panel appears in 0.29 seconds the first time it is used, and in 0.11 seconds for subsequent postings.

However, there are a couple of problems that cannot be measured with our initial placement of calls to `ReportTime()`. Fortunately, as slow as this program is, it is easy to use to a stopwatch to gather data manually. First, when the window is resized, the program begins to regenerate the image. Stopwatch measurements show that it takes 39 seconds to redraw the fractal when the window is resized to 440 by 440 pixels.

The same problem occurs if a parameter on the preference panel is changed. The panel appears quickly, and the sliders move smoothly while the dialog is posted. However, when changes are applied to a 400x400 window, the fractal is regenerated and the program is unable to respond to input for approximately 33 seconds. The time required to make changes in the fractal parameters is a serious problem. The long delay required to see the results of a parameter change discourages the exploration the preference panel was intended to support.

Sweeping out a region of the fractal to be enlarged shows another performance problem. Although the user can select a region quickly and easily, the program is unresponsive for 33 seconds after the selection has been made. This feature was meant to encourage rapid exploration of the fractal image, but the user is likely to be hesitant to use this feature once it becomes clear that it will cause the program to hang for at least 33 seconds each time an area is selected.

On the X terminal, System B, the situation is much worse. Starting with the good news, the preference panel can be displayed in 1.27 seconds initially, and in about 0.96 seconds on subsequent postings. This is consistent with the generally slower response of this system. Given the relative performance of this system, this time seems acceptable. However, the `fractal` program initially requires 39.77 seconds to appear, or more than twice the time required to launch the program on System A. In addition, redrawing the image once the program is displayed takes over 245 seconds on this system.

Figure 11.5 summarizes the results of this first set of performance measurements, compared to the goals set earlier.

Operation	Goal	System A	System B	Meets Goal?
Program start-up (initial response)	0.3-1.0	15.36	39.77	No
Launch preference panel	0.3	0.29	1.27	Yes
Response to parameter changes	0.3	33	245	No
Zoom in on selected areas	0.3	33	245	No
Resize window	0.3	39	295	No
Redraw on Expose	< 0.3	~0	sluggish	Yes
Menus, sliders, buttons, rubberbanding	< 0.3	~0	sluggish	Yes

Figure 11.5 Performance of the initial `fractal` program.

Based on this initial analysis, it appears that the `fractal` program's most significant problem involves the function that computes and renders the fractal. It is particularly curious that generating and displaying the image after the window is visible takes substantially longer than the initial generation. To explore this further, it would be useful to be able to measure the time spent in the `CreateImage()` function without using a stopwatch. Figure 11.6 shows the results of starting the program after adding calls to `ReportTime()` to the beginning and end of that function.

```
% fractal -geometry =400x400
Starting:
Starting Fractal Generation:
Fractal Generation Complete:
   Elapsed Time = 0.18
   CPU Time     = 0.15
   System Time  = 0.00
Starting Fractal Generation:
Fractal Generation Complete:
   Elapsed Time = 15.210
   CPU Time     = 14.02
   System Time  = 0.110
Up:
   Elapsed Time = 0.190
   CPU Time     = 0.000
   System Time  = 0.000
```

Figure 11.6 Performance measurements for `CreateImage()`.

The measurements shown in Figure 11.6 reveal an interesting surprise that we could not have detected with a stopwatch: the fractal is being generated twice! Looking at the code, it seems likely that this is caused by the program's geometry management. The fractal is generated when the XmDrawingArea widget is resized. It appears that the widget changes from its initial size to some intermediate size, before settling into the final size specified on the command line. Fortunately, the initial size is quite small, and the initial image is being created in only 0.18 seconds. Although this issue may become important eventually, this brief time is currently dwarfed by the 15 seconds required to create the larger image before the window appears.

Measuring Server Requests

Any fractal image can be expected to be computationally expensive to generate, but there may be steps we can take to generate the image faster in this program. For example, it is worth exploring how much server traffic this program generates. We know from the code that the program draws two points for each pixel in the image. The program also manipulates graphics contexts and may make other server requests as well.

To measure the server requests made by the `fractal` program, we can run the program though `xmond`. Rather than watching the output of `xmond` as it runs, we can use `xmond`'s ability to report statistics at a later time. Figure 11.7 shows the drawing-related requests reported by `xmond`. Only requests that are directly relevant to the fractal display are shown, for simplicity.

Request	# of Requests
CreatePixmap	5
FreePixmap	1
CreateGC	10
ChangeGC	19751
FreeGC	1
CopyArea	1
PolyPoint	19883
PolySegment	6
PolyFillRectangle	10

Figure 11.7 Summary of server requests, produced by `xmond`.

Most of the requests made by the `fractal` program seem normal. There are a few requests to create windows, some colors are allocated, and so on. However, two figures are large enough to warrant some attention. According to `xmonui/xmond`, the `fractal` program makes 19,751 `ChangeCG` requests and 19883 `PolyPoint` requests. The `ChangeGC` requests are undoubtedly due to the calls to `XSetForeground()` before drawing each point. The `PolyPoint` requests correspond to calls to `XDrawPoint()`. Together, these requests account for nearly 40 thousand requests to the X server, which is certainly enough requests to cause some performance problems.

We should also check the requests made when the program regenerates the fractal image after the window is visible on the screen. Figure 11.8 shows the requests made after a user clicks on the preference panel's Apply button.

Request	# of Requests
ChangeGC	19462
ClearArea	17
PolyPoint	180696
PolySegment	8
PolyFillRectangle	9
PolyText8	2

Figure 11.8 Summary of requests made after window is visible.

The results of this measurement are very interesting. Regenerating the fractal produces nearly the same number of `ChangeGC` requests as the initial image, but the number of `PolyPoint` requests has increased dramatically, to over 180,000. Seeing these numbers raises some interesting questions. We can estimate how many drawing requests this program should make by multiplying the number of pixels in the window by two (for the XmDrawingArea plus the pixmap). Ignoring the size of the menubar, the image should require approximately 400x400x2 = 320,000 requests. Of course, the middle portion of the fractal image is not drawn, so this estimate could be reduced, perhaps by 50%. This means that the initial number of drawing requests is quite low, even at 20,000. The 180,696 figure is undoubtedly the number of times `XDrawPoint()` is actually called.

The question, of course, is "why does the initial rendering use fewer points?" The answer lies in the fact that Xlib buffers requests when possible to reduce the number of requests actually sent to the X server. We can examine this behavior by running the fractal program through `xmond`, set to display full information about `PolyPoint` requests. Figure 11.9 shows a portion of the output of `xmon` when the `fractal` program starts up.

```
............REQUEST: PolyPoint
    coordinate-mode: Origin
           drawable: DWB 05000017
                 gc: GXC 0500000a
             points: (35)
............REQUEST: PolyPoint
    coordinate-mode: Origin
           drawable: DWB 05000017
                 gc: GXC 0500000a
             points: (15)
............REQUEST: PolyPoint
    coordinate-mode: Origin
           drawable: DWB 05000017
                 gc: GXC 0500000a
             points: (18)
............REQUEST: PolyPoint
    coordinate-mode: Origin
           drawable: DWB 05000017
                 gc: GXC 0500000a
             points: (100)
```

Figure 11.9 `PolyPoint` requests made upon start-up.

It appears the Xlib is buffering requests and sending them in groups of various sizes. The most likely explanation is that Xlib buffers each set of requests until the GC used to draw the points is modified. Whenever the GC changes, Xlib must draw all pending points before changing the GC. Notice also that the drawable ID in each request is the same. Either Xlib has noticed that the XmDrawingArea widget's window is not visible and is only processing requests for the pixmap, or the XmDrawingArea widget has not yet been realized at this point.

Now, let's compare this behavior to the requests made after the initial image is displayed. Figure 11.10 shows a portion of the requests made when the fractal is regenerated after the window is visible on the screen.

```
............REQUEST: PolyPoint
       coordinate-mode: Origin
              drawable: DWB 0500001c
                    gc: GXC 0500000a
                points: (1)
   ............REQUEST: PolyPoint
       coordinate-mode: Origin
              drawable: DWB 05000017
                    gc: GXC 0500000a
                points: (1)
   ............REQUEST: PolyPoint
       coordinate-mode: Origin
              drawable: DWB 0500001c
                    gc: GXC 0500000a
                points: (1)
   ............REQUEST: PolyPoint
       coordinate-mode: Origin
              drawable: DWB 05000017
                    gc: GXC 0500000a
                points: (1)
```

Figure 11.10 `PolyPoint` requests made when image is regenerated.

Here, notice that each request draws only a single point. Also notice that the drawables listed in these requests alternate between two IDs. Once the window is visible, Xlib to stop buffering requests because the program alternates between drawing in the window and a pixmap. The larger number of requests undoubtedly explains the increased time required to regenerate an image when the user changes a value in the preference panel.

Clearly, we need to make some changes to reduce the 180,000+ requests produced by this program at runtime. However, even the 20,000 requests made when Xlib is buffering seems excessive. Even if the X server can handle this many requests efficiently, it is best to minimize requests as much as possible, to give the X server a chance to process requests from other applications. In this case, even if the impact on the fractal program itself is not significant, the program may be hurting the performance of other programs running on the system. It seems likely that the reducing the number of requests is particularly important when using the X terminal.

11.2 Reducing Server Requests

The data gathered in the previous section provides some clues that can be used to improve the performance of the `fractal` program. It is clear that the `CreateImage()` function is the bottleneck. Although there may be other problems, the large number of server requests made by this function seems like a potential problem that could be solved without too much effort. This section explores what can be done to reduce the demand on the server.

One way to reduce the number of server requests is to stop drawing each individual point, and to combine these requests into batches. There are several ways this could be done. As a first attempt, we can try using the function `XDrawPoints()`, which draws multiple points with a single server request. All points drawn using `XDrawPoints()` must use the same graphics context, but the points do not have to be contiguous. By not drawing points sequentially, the graphics context will not need to be changed so rapidly. The only part of the `fractal` program that must be changed is `CreateImage()`.

The following implementation buffers points that have the same color, and draws them with a single server request. By buffering the points ourselves, we can effectively change the buffering algorithm used by Xlib. Instead of buffering contiguous points until the GC is changed, we can maintain a separate buffer for each color. A drawing request will only be made when a buffer is full. This implementation retains the calls to `ReportTime()` to allow the performance of the new implementation to be measured. Changes from the previous version are shown in bold.

Start timing

```
void CreateImage ( ImageData *data )
{
    Widget w = data->canvas;
    int  x, y, iteration;

    ReportTime ( "Starting Fractal Generation", FALSE );

   /*
    * If the canvas widget is realized, clear it.
    */

    if ( XtIsRealized ( w ) )
        XClearArea ( XtDisplay ( w ), XtWindow ( w ),
                     0, 0, 0, 0, FALSE );

```

```
    InitBuffer();

   /*
    * Erase the pixmap by filling it with black.
    */

    XSetForeground ( XtDisplay ( w ), data->gc,
                     BlackPixelOfScreen ( XtScreen ( w ) ) );

    XFillRectangle ( XtDisplay ( w ), data->pixmap,
                     data->gc, 0, 0,
                     data->width,  data->height );

   /*
    * For each pixel on the window....
    */

    for ( y = 0; y < data->height; y++ )
    {
        ComplexNumber z, k;

        for ( x = 0; x < data->width; x++ )
        {
           /*
            * Initialize K to the normalized, floating
            * coordinate in the x, y plane.
            * Initialize Z to ( 0.0, 0.0 ).
            */

            z.real = z.imag = 0.0;

            k.real =  data->origin.real +
                 ( double ) x / ( double ) data->width * data->range;

            k.imag =  data->origin.imag -
                 ( double ) y / ( double ) data->height * data->range;

            /*
             * Calculate z =  z * z + k  over and over.
             */

            for ( iteration = 0;
                  iteration < data->depth;
                  iteration++ )
            {
                double   real;
                int      distance;

                real    = z.real;
```

```
                    z.real = z.real * z.real -
                                     z.imag * z.imag + k.real;
                    z.imag = 2 * real * z.imag + k.imag;

                    distance = ( int ) ( z.real * z.real +
                                          z.imag * z.imag );
                   /*
                    * If the z point has moved off the plane,
                    * set the current foreground color to
                    * the distance (cast to an int and modulo
                    * the number of colors available), and
                    * draw a point in the window and the pixmap.
                    */

                    if ( distance  >= data->maxDistance )
                    {
                        Pixel color;

                        color = ( Pixel )iteration % data->ncolors;

                        BufferPoint ( w, data->pixmap, data->gc,
                                          ( int ) color, x, y );
                        break;
                    }
                }
            }
        }

        /*
         * Draw all remaining points.
         */

        FlushBuffer ( w, data->pixmap, data->gc );

        ReportTime ( "Fractal Generation Complete", TRUE );
    }
```

Stop timing

The primary difference between this version of `CreateImage()` and the version shown earlier is that instead of calling `XDrawPoint()` directly, `CreateImage()` calls a new function, `BufferPoint()`. This function stores points until they can be drawn as a group using `XDrawPoints()`. The function `InitBuffer()` must be called before beginning the calculations to initialize the data structures used by the buffer routines. `FlushBuffer()` must also be called to draw any remaining points once `CreateImage()` finishes computing all points in the image.

The buffering routines use a global data structure that contains a two-dimensional array of `XPoint` structures. The array holds `MAXPOINTS` number of points for `MAXCOLOR` possible colors. The `points` structure also contains an array of integers that indicates how many points are stored in each point array.

```
#define MAXPOINTS 500
#define MAXCOLOR  256

typedef struct {
    XPoint  points[MAXCOLOR][MAXPOINTS];
    int     numPoints[MAXCOLOR];
} PointBuffer;

PointBuffer  buffer;
```

The function `InitBuffer()` initializes the number of points of each color to zero.

```
static void InitBuffer()
{
    int i;
    for ( i = 0; i < MAXCOLOR; i++ )
        buffer.numPoints[i] = 0;
}
```

`BufferPoint()` first checks how many points of the given color are already stored in a buffer. If the buffer is full, `BufferPoint()` uses another auxiliary function, `Render()` to draw all points stored in the buffer in both the window and the pixmap. Then, `BufferPoint()` resets the number of points for the given color to zero, and stores the current point in the buffer.

```
static void BufferPoint ( Widget w, Pixmap pix,
                          GC gc, Pixel color,
                          int x, int y )
{
    /*
     * Don't allow more than MAXCOLOR colors.
     */

    color = color % MAXCOLOR;

    if ( buffer.numPoints[color] == MAXPOINTS )
    {
        XSetForeground ( XtDisplay ( w ), gc, color );
```

```
        Render ( w, pix, gc,
                 buffer.points [ color ],
                 buffer.numPoints [ color ] );

       /*
        * Reset the buffer.
        */

        buffer.numPoints[color] = 0;
     }

    /*
     * Store the point in the buffer according to its color.
     */

    buffer.points[color][buffer.numPoints[color]].x = x;
    buffer.points[color][buffer.numPoints[color]].y = y;
    buffer.numPoints[color] += 1;
}
```

The function `Render()` displays the current image in both the XmDrawingArea widget and a pixmap. This function calls `XDrawPoints()` to draw all currently buffered points in the pixmap with one server request. A second call draws the points in the `canvas` window, if the widget is realized.

```
static void Render ( Widget  w, Pixmap pix, GC gc,
                     XPoint *points,
                     int     numPoints )
{
   /*
    * Draw all buffered points into the off-screen pixmap.
    */

    XDrawPoints ( XtDisplay ( w ), pix, gc,
                  points, numPoints,
                  CoordModeOrigin );
    /*
     * If the window exists, also draw the points in the
     * window, so the user can see the progress.
     */

     if ( XtIsRealized ( w ) )
     {
         XDrawPoints ( XtDisplay ( w ), XtWindow ( w ), gc,
                       points, numPoints,
                       CoordModeOrigin );
     }
}
```

The function `FlushBuffer()` must be called when the image calculation is finished to draw any points remaining in the buffer. This function loops through all colors, drawing the remaining points in both the window and the pixmap.

```
static void FlushBuffer ( Widget w, Pixmap pix, GC gc )
{
    int i;

   /*
    * Check each buffer.
    */

    for ( i = 0 ; i < MAXCOLOR; i++ )
    {
        /*
         * If there are any points in this buffer, display them
         * in the window and the pixmap.
         */

        if ( buffer.numPoints [ i ] )
        {
            XSetForeground ( XtDisplay ( w ), gc, i );

            Render ( w, pix, gc, buffer.points[i],
                     buffer.numPoints[i] );

            buffer.numPoints[i] = 0;
        }
    }
}
```

Once these changes have been integrated into the rest of the program, we can run this program again and measure the performance to see if it has improved. Running the program on System A produces the following output:

```
% fractal -geometry =400x400
Starting:
Starting Fractal Generation:
Fractal Generation Complete:
   Elapsed Time = 0.020
   CPU Time     = 0.010
   System Time  = 0.010
Starting Fractal Generation:
Fractal Generation Complete:
   Elapsed Time = 14.780
   CPU Time     = 14.38
   System Time  = 0.070
Up:
   Elapsed Time = 0.190
   CPU Time     = 0.000
   System Time  = 0.000
```

Figure 11.11 Performance measurements for buffered `CreateImage()`.

These figures show that while the program's performance has improved, the improvement is not dramatic. The original program took 15.36 seconds to display the large fractal image. With the buffered drawing requests, this time has been reduced by only 0.58 seconds. This is certainly an improvement in raw time (in earlier examples, we were often happy to shave a half second from the start-up time). Unfortunately, much greater gains will be needed to reach the goals established at the beginning of the chapter.

When we consider the drawing time required for subsequent operations, the effort put into reducing server requests seems more worthwhile. The regeneration of the fractal now takes approximately the amount of time as the initial image creation. Buffering server requests has reduced that time from over 30 seconds to less than 15.

The performance of the modified program on the X terminal is also interesting. Figure 11.12 shows that the latest version runs significantly faster than the original version, on this system.

```
% fractal -geometry =400x400
Starting:
Starting Fractal Generation:
Fractal Generation Complete:
   Elapsed Time = 0.090
   CPU Time     = 0.080
   System Time  = 0.000
Starting Fractal Generation:
Fractal Generation Complete:
   Elapsed Time = 20.570
   CPU Time     = 13.790
   System Time  = 0.070
Fractal Program Ready:
   Elapsed Time = 2.740
   CPU Time     = 0.000
   System Time  = 0.000
```

Figure 11.12 Buffered performance on X terminal.

The reduction in server requests has obviously had an impact when the program is used on the X terminal. The time required to create an initial image has been reduced from 39 seconds, to almost half that figure. The runtime image generation has been improved more dramatically. Figure 11.13 shows the time required to regenerate the image when displayed on the X terminal. The time has been reduced from 245 seconds to only 27 seconds. The program is still quite slow, but the performance is moving in the right direction. For System B, the `fractal` program's performance has been improved by almost an order of magnitude.

```
Starting Fractal Generation:
Fractal Generation Complete:
   Elapsed Time = 27.260
   CPU Time     = 13.800
   System Time  = 0.120
```

Figure 11.13 Runtime image generation on X terminal.

Before going on, it is worthwhile to check the number of server requests made by this new implementation. Figure 11.14 shows the requests produced by the modified program when drawing the initial fractal.

Request	# of Requests
CreatePixmap	5
FreePixmap	1
CreateGC	10
ChangeGC	391
FreeGC	1
CopyArea	1
PolyPoint	393
PolySegment	6
PolyFillRectangle	10

Figure 11.14 Buffered server requests made at start-up.

Figure 11.14 shows that the number of server requests has been drastically reduced. The new version produces mostly the same requests and events, with only two significant changes. The number of `ChangeGC` requests has shrunk to 391, while the number of `PolyPoint` requests has been reduced from nearly 20 thousand to only 393.

Figure 11.15 shows the requests made by the `fractal` program when the fractal is regenerated. Here, we can see an even more dramatic reduction in server traffic. The number of `PolyPoint` requests has been reduced from over 180,000 to just 698 requests.

Request	# of Requests
ChangeGC	347
ClearArea	17
PolyPoint	698
PolySegment	8
PolyFillRectangle	9
PolyText8	2

Figure 11.15 Xmon summary of buffered server requests.

Figure 11.16 shows a portion of the requests traced by xmon while the image is being generated. As expected, all requests are buffered and a large number of points are drawn with each request.

```
............REQUEST: PolyPoint
    coordinate-mode: Origin
           drawable: DWB 04000017
                 gc: GXC 0400000a
             points: (499)
............REQUEST: PolyPoint
    coordinate-mode: Origin
           drawable: DWB 04000017
                 gc: GXC 0400000a
             points: (499)
............REQUEST: PolyPoint
    coordinate-mode: Origin
           drawable: DWB 04000017
                 gc: GXC 0400000a
             points: (499)
............REQUEST: PolyPoint
    coordinate-mode: Origin
           drawable: DWB 04000017
                 gc: GXC 0400000a
             points: (499)
```

Figure 11.16 Buffered requests made by `fractal` program.

There are other techniques that could be used to draw the fractal, which might be more efficient in terms of raw data to be transferred between the client and the server. For example, we could stop drawing to the `canvas` widget and only draw to the pixmap. The contents of the pixmap could then be copied to the window when the image has been completely drawn. Another possibility is to create an `XImage` and just store each point in the `XImage` structure. This approach would eliminate the calls to change the graphics context and reduce server requests, because the image manipulation would be done in the application's address space.

On the other hand, System A is apparently CPU bound, so reducing the number of server requests will very little impact. With the current level of performance and only 761 remaining server requests, any attempt to reduce the traffic between server and client is unlikely to provide any significant benefit to System A.

This theory can be tested easily, of course. Commenting out the body of the `Render()` function and running the program produces the measurements in Figure 11.17.

```
% fractal -geometry =400x400
Starting:
Starting Fractal Generation:
Fractal Generation Complete:
   Elapsed Time = 0.180
   CPU Time     = 0.010
   System Time  = 0.010
Starting Fractal Generation:
Fractal Generation Complete:
   Elapsed Time = 14.560
   CPU Time     = 14.36
   System Time  = 0.070
Up:
   Elapsed Time = 0.190
   CPU Time     = 0.000
   System Time  = 0.000
```

Figure 11.17 Performance with no rendering.

So, even with absolutely no drawing requests to the X server, the time required to generate the fractal only shrinks by less than a quarter of a second. To reach a goal of less than 3/10ths of a second, this quarter second may eventually become relevant. Currently, this figure is lost in the noise, compared to the remaining 14 seconds.

Although we could try to reduce the number of requests even further to improve the performance on the X terminal, the performance of this program on System A is still so poor that additional work in this area does not appear promising. At this point, it should be clear that we must find a way to speed up the fractal computation itself, or start thinking about ways to deal with the user's perception of the performance.

11.3 Tuning the Fractal Computation

The thought of tuning the fractal computation itself is somewhat intimidating. Fractals are known to be inherently expensive, and the computation itself seems clear cut. There is no way to avoid the nested loops, and the repeated iteration in this computation is the key to the fractal. It seems that the only way to produce the fractal faster is to explore the theory of fractal mathematics and produce a better algorithm. While this might be possible, it is outside the scope of this book.

However, there are other things that can be done. First, the fractal computation is in many ways a classic candidate for traditional code tuning techniques. Particularly when the drawing is minimized or eliminated as described in the previous section, the `fractal` program is completely CPU intensive. There is no memory allocated, no system calls, just straight-forward basic computation. In such cases, it is useful to rely on performance tools that can give detailed information about the execution times associated with an application. Depending on your platform, you may be able to use `tcov`, `pixie`, or other similar tools. The UNIX `prof` program would not be much help, however, because it only provides function-level granularity, and we already know which function is using the time.

Because no single tool of this type is widely available, this section does not dwell on how to use these tools, but only reports some very simple results of one such analysis. Analyzing the `CreateImage()` function with a tool that reports the number of instructions required to execute each line of code reveals that the most recent version of `CreateImage()` requires 744,321,479 instructions to compute the full fractal image. This number is highly system-specific, and applies only to the reference platform used for these tests.

The analysis also reveals that each statement in the inner loop of `CreateImage()` is executed 12,133,384 times, which is useful to know. It is easy to predict that this number might be large, because in the worst case, the inner loop is computed width x height x depth, or about 400 x 400 x 200 = 32,000,000 times, ignoring the fact that the fractal is not quite 400 pixels high. However, the loop can be terminated earlier than the maximum number of iterations, so it is hard to estimate how many times the loop is really executed. Because we know that the inner loop is executed 12 million times, there may be opportunities to tune the fractal by examining the implementation carefully. Shaving even one instruction off a line inside the inner loop could save 12 million instructions.

Let's start by looking in detail at the current implementation of `CreateImage()` on page 447. To start with, notice that all relevant parameters are stored in a data structure that must be dereferenced each time the parameter is referenced. The impact of this overhead would be unimportant to most programs. In this case, however, every instruction counts, and each dereference can potentially add 12 million instructions. This problem can be addressed by assigning each value in the `ImageData` structure to a local variable at the beginning of the function. The results of this can be seen in the revised version, below. Lines 332 through 343 declare local variables, which are initialized to the values in the `ImageData` structure.

There are other opportunities as well. For example, consider the code at line 376 on page 448. Although the value `k.real` depends only the value of `x`, it is recomputed with each pass through the `y` loop. While this computation is not in the inner-most loop, moving it out of the loop can provide some savings. To move this computation out of the loop, it is necessary to allocate an array of values, which can be pre-computed outside the loop. The resulting code can be seen in lines 367 through 375, in the modified version below.

Another observation can be made about this computation. The value `data->width * data->range` is a constant for any given fractal computation. Not only is it wasteful to compute this value over and over, but the entire expression on line 376 is written so that a division is required, which is generally an expensive operation. By changing the calculation and pre-computing the constant value, this expression can be reduced to one multiplication each time through the loop. These changes are shown in the following implementation, on lines 347 and 348, where the values are pre-computed and on lines 375 and 382, where the values are used.

A few other similar changes can also be made, producing the following implementation. All changes are shown in bold.

```
330 void CreateImage ( ImageData *data )
331 {
332     Widget w = data->canvas;
333     register int  x, y, iteration;
334     double rangeByWidth, rangeByHeight, *xconstants;
335     int depth            = data->depth;
336     int height           = data->height;
337     int width            = data->width;
338     GC gc                = data->gc;
339     Pixmap pixmap        = data->pixmap;
340     double maxDistance   = data->maxDistance;
341     double origin_imag   = data->origin.imag;
342     double origin_real   = data->origin.real;
343     int ncolors          = data->ncolors;
344
345     ReportTime ( "Starting Fractal Generation", FALSE );
346
347     rangeByWidth = data->range / ( double ) width;
348     rangeByHeight = data->range / ( double ) height;
349
350
```

Start timing

```
    /*
     * If the canvas widget is realized, clear it.
     */

    if ( XtIsRealized ( w ) )
        XClearArea ( XtDisplay ( w ), XtWindow ( w ),
                     0, 0, 0, 0, TRUE );

    InitBuffer();

    XSetForeground ( XtDisplay ( w ), gc,
                     BlackPixelOfScreen ( XtScreen ( w ) ) );

    XFillRectangle ( XtDisplay ( w ), pixmap, gc, 0, 0,
                     width,  height );

    xconstants = ( double* ) XtMalloc ( width *
                                        sizeof ( double ) );

   /*
    * Precompute the constants for each X value.
    */

    for ( x = 0; x < width; x++ )
        xconstants[x] = origin_real +
                                   ( double ) x * rangeByWidth;

    for ( y = 0; y < height; y++ )
    {
        double z_real, z_imag, k_real, k_imag;

        k_imag = origin_imag - ( double ) y * rangeByHeight;

        for ( x = 0; x < width; x++ )
        {
            z_real =  z_imag = 0.0;
            k_real =  xconstants[x];

           /*
            * Calculate z =  z * z + k  over and over.
            */

            for ( iteration = 0;
                  iteration < depth;
                  iteration++ )
            {
                double   real;
                int      distance;

```

```
                    real   = z_real;
                    z_real = z_real * z_real -
                                      z_imag * z_imag + k_real;
                    z_imag = ( real + real ) * z_imag + k_imag;

                    distance = ( int ) ( z_real * z_real +
                                         z_imag * z_imag );

                  /*
                   * If the z point has moved off the plane,
                   * set the current foreground color to
                   * the distance (cast to an int and modulo
                   * the number of colors available), and
                   * draw a point in the window and the pixmap.
                   */

                    if ( distance >= maxDistance )
                    {
                        Pixel color;

                        color = ( Pixel ) iteration % ncolors;

                        BufferPoint ( w, pixmap, gc,
                                      ( int ) color, x, y );
                        break;
                    }
                }
            }
        }

        FlushBuffer ( w, pixmap, gc );
        ReportTime ( "Fractal Generation Complete", TRUE );
}
```

Stop timing

Running this version on System A shows that these changes produce some improvement. Figure 11.18 shows the time required to create the fractal, which has shrunk from its previous 14.78 seconds to 13.44 seconds:

```
% fractal -geometry =400x400
Starting:
Starting Fractal Generation:
Fractal Generation Complete:
   Elapsed Time = 0.010
   CPU Time     = 0.010
   System Time  = 0.000
Starting Fractal Generation:
Fractal Generation Complete:
   Elapsed Time = 13.440
   CPU Time     = 13.15
   System Time  = 0.060
Up:
   Elapsed Time = 0.190
   CPU Time     = 0.000
   System Time  = 0.000
```

Figure 11.18 Performance after manual code tuning.

While performance is better, 13.44 seconds is still a long way from the goal. It is interesting to see how many instructions have actually been saved by reworking the `CreateImage()` function. Using the same tools that previous reported that 744,321,479 instructions were used to create the fractal, shows that the latest version requires 611,174,514. So, even though the new implementation reduces the total number of instructions by over 133 million, the fractal is still slower than desired.

One obvious thing that has been overlooked so far is the optimization[1] level of the compiler. Some of the inefficiencies found in the inner loop might be just as easily fixed by a good optimizing compiler, and there may be further room for improvement as well. Unlike other tests in this book, all the measurements reported so far were for a program compiled with no optimization at all. Although compiling with optimization turned on should be the first step when tuning a program, it is not uncommon to overlook this step. Typically, when developing an application, the program is built with full debugging information, and no optimization to best support debugging. Rebuilding the latest version of the fractal program with the highest level of optimization supported by the compiler on the System A produces the results shown in Figure 11.19.

1 This is not a contrived situation. This chapter presents a genuine case study that reports the process I went through in tuning this program. I truly forgot to compile this example with full optimization. Moral: never assume you haven't overlooked something obvious.

```
% fractal -geometry =400x400
Starting:
Starting Fractal Generation:
Fractal Generation Complete:
   Elapsed Time = 0.020
   CPU Time     = 0.010
   System Time  = 0.000
Starting Fractal Generation:
Fractal Generation Complete:
   Elapsed Time = 9.830
   CPU Time     = 19.58
   System Time  = 0.060
Up:
   Elapsed Time = 0.160
   CPU Time     = 0.000
   System Time  = 0.000
```

Figure 11.19 Performance with full compiler optimization.

The compiler optimization shaves another 3.61 seconds off the fractal creation time, reducing the time required to create the image to 9.83 seconds. Yet another instruction-level analysis shows that the optimized code requires 361,561,406 instructions to create the fractal image. Between the hand-coded optimizations and the compiler, we have reduced the total instruction count to less than half the original figure.

However, at this point, the tuning effort seems to have come to a halt. We have reduced the number of server requests from over 180,000 to less than 800, and cut the number of CPU instructions to less than half. The fractal creation time has been reduced from about 15 seconds at start-up (and 30 seconds thereafter) to just over 9 seconds in each case.

However, the program's performance is still an order of magnitude from the worst case goal of a 1 second start-up time, and further still from the 0.3 second we would ideally like to achieve. With all the tuning we have done so far, it seems highly unlikely that an order of magnitude can be gained by continuing to tune using the approaches taken so far. It is time to consider some more creative approaches.

11.4 Using Work Procedures

By now, it is clear that the fractal is simply going to take a long time to compute, no matter how much tuning is done. The work we have done so far is useful, because we have reduced the demands the program makes on the server and the system as a whole. However, it is easy to get side-tracked when tuning a program and to focus so narrowly on reducing instructions and server requests that the real goal is forgotten. The goal is not necessarily to implement an algorithm that can create the complete fractal image in under 0.3 second. The goal is to get the fractal program up and running, ready to respond to user commands in that period of time. An additional goal is to remain responsive to user input more or less continuously once the program is running. Recall that we defined the goals for this program based on the time required for the program to resume responding to events following a major operation.

One way to achieve such goals is to create and draw the fractal image as a background task, while allowing user input to be handled as the task proceeds. Because the fractal computation is a simple iterative process, the operation can easily be performed in a work procedure, a function that computes a small portion of the image each time it is called. Between calls to the work procedure, the program can handle any pending events, which allows the user to popup menus, manipulate items on the preference panel, or even resize the image.

To compute the fractal in a work procedure, the function `CreateImage()` must be modified to simply install a work procedure when it is called. With this new approach, the computation is actually performed in a new function, `CreateImageWorkProc()`. This function is called repeatedly to draw a small part of the image. The new version of `CreateImage()` is called any time a completely new image needs to be created. This could occur when the program first begins, when the user resizes the window, when the user changes a parameter in the preference panel, or when the user sweeps out an area to be expanded. `CreateImage()` always removes any currently installed work procedures to stop any fractal computation in-progress before a new series of work procedures begins.

This implementation requires one small change to the fractal.h header file. The `ImageData` structure must be modified to include a new member, a Boolean value named `restart`. The modified data structure is defined as:

```
typedef struct {
    Widget          canvas;
    Pixmap          pixmap;
    GC              gc;
    GC              xorGC;
    Dimension       width, height;
    int             depth, ncolors;
    double          range, maxDistance;
    ComplexNumber   origin;
    Boolean         restart;
} ImageData;
```

The new version of `CreateImage()` begins by checking whether there is an existing work procedure and removes it if necessary. Then the `restart` member of the `ImageData` structure is set to indicate that the fractal computation should be restarted and the `CreateImageWorkProc()` function is installed as a work procedure, to be called whenever there are no pending events.

```
extern Boolean CreateImage ( XtPointer clientData );

void CreateImage ( ImageData *data )
{
    static XtWorkProcId id = NULL;
    Widget w = data->canvas;

    if ( id )
        XtRemoveWorkProc ( id );

    data->restart = TRUE;

    id = XtAppAddWorkProc ( XtWidgetToApplicationContext ( w ),
                            CreateImageWorkProc, data );
}
```

The function `CreateImageWorkProc()` is nearly the same as the old `CreateImage()` function, but has several important differences. First, the function takes the form of a work procedure, which takes an `XtPointer` as its only parameter, and returns a Boolean value that indicates whether the function is finished. The variables that were previously initialized to values in the

ImageData structure are still declared at the beginning of the function, but are no longer initialized. Instead, all initialization is performed only if the value of the restart member of the ImageData structure is set to TRUE. Another important change is that nearly all these variables are declared to be static, so that their values are maintained from call to call. This implementation includes calls to ReportTime() so the time required to compute the image can be reported. However, the first call has been moved inside the if statement on line 367, to start measuring each time a new sequence of work procedures begins.

Start timing

```
345 Boolean CreateImageWorkProc ( XtPointer clientData )
346 {
347     ImageData      *data = (ImageData*) clientData;
348     Widget          w = data->canvas;
349     static int      x, y, iteration;
350     static double rangeByWidth, rangeByHeight, *xconstants;
351     static int      depth;
352     static int      height;
353     static int      width;
354     GC gc           = data->gc;
355     Pixmap pixmap = data->pixmap;
356     static double maxDistance;
357     static double origin_imag;
358     static double origin_real;
359     static int      ncolors;
360     int             slice;
361
362    /*
363     * If the restart flag has been set, reset all parameters
364     * so a completely new fractal can be started.
365     */
366
367     if ( data->restart )
368     {
369         ReportTime ( "Starting Fractal", FALSE );
370
371         height         = data->height;
372         width          = data->width;
373         maxDistance    = data->maxDistance;
374         origin_imag    = data->origin.imag;
375         origin_real    = data->origin.real;
376         ncolors        = data->ncolors;
377         depth          = data->depth;
378         rangeByWidth   = data->range / ( double ) width;
379         rangeByHeight = data->range / ( double ) height;
380         y = 0;
381
```

```
382         /*
383          * If the canvas widget is realized, clear it.
384          */
385
386         if ( XtIsRealized ( w ) )
387             XClearArea ( XtDisplay ( w ), XtWindow ( w ),
388                          0, 0, 0, 0, TRUE );
389
390         InitBuffer();
391
392         XSetForeground ( XtDisplay ( w ), gc,
393                          BlackPixelOfScreen ( XtScreen ( w )));
394
395         XFillRectangle ( XtDisplay ( w ), pixmap, gc, 0, 0,
396                          width,  height );
397
398        /*
399         * Pre-compute the constants for each X value.
400         */
401
402         xconstants = (double*) XtMalloc ( width *
403                                           sizeof ( double ) );
404
405         for ( x = 0; x < width; x++ )
406             xconstants[x] = origin_real +
407                                   ( double ) x * rangeByWidth;
408
409         data->restart = FALSE;
410     }
```

The key to converting the fractal computation to a work procedure is the way the outer loop is handled. This version introduces a second variable that determines how many times the loop is executed. The `slice` variable limits the computation to two iterations each time the work procedure is called. In this version, `y` is no longer initialized to zero at the beginning of the outer `for` loop, but is set inside the first `if` statement, on line 380. Because `y` is now a static variable, its current value is maintained between calls to the work procedure, and the fractal computation resumes where it left off in the previous call. The inner two loops are virtually unchanged, except that some variables are now static so they maintain their values between calls to the work procedure.

```
    for ( slice = 0 ; slice < 2 && y < height; y++, slice++ )
    {
        static double z_real, z_imag, k_real, k_imag;

        k_imag =  origin_imag - ( double ) y * rangeByHeight;

        for ( x = 0; x < width; x++ )
        {
            z_real =  z_imag = 0.0;
            k_real =  xconstants[x];

           /*
            * Calculate z =  z * z + k  over and over.
            */

            for ( iteration = 0;
                  iteration < depth;
                  iteration++ )
            {
                static double  real;
                int            distance;

                real   = z_real;
                z_real = z_real * z_real -
                                   z_imag * z_imag + k_real;
                z_imag = ( real + real ) * z_imag + k_imag;

                distance  =  (int) ( z_real * z_real +
                                     z_imag * z_imag );
               /*
                * If the z point has moved off the plane,
                * set the current foreground color to
                * the distance (cast to an int and modulo
                * the number of colors available), and
                * draw a point in the window and the pixmap.
                */

                if ( distance >= maxDistance )
                {
                    Pixel color;

                    color = ( Pixel ) iteration % ncolors;
                    BufferPoint ( w, pixmap, gc,
                                  ( int ) color, x, y );
                    break;
                }
            }
        }
    }
```

Stop timing

```
460
461     /*
462      * See if a complete image has been computed. If so, return
463      * TRUE to cancel the work procedure. Otherwise, return
464      * FALSE so this function can be called again.
465      */
466
467     if ( y == height )
468     {
469         FlushBuffer ( w, pixmap, gc );
470         ReportTime ( "Fractal Generation Complete", TRUE );
471
472         return ( TRUE );
473     }
474     else
475     {
476         return ( FALSE );
477     }
478 }
```

The final section of `CreateImageWorkProc()`, beginning on line 467, determines whether the function should be called again to continue computing the fractal, or whether the work procedure should be removed. If the value of `y` has reached the value of `height`, the fractal image has been completed. In this case, the work procedure calls `FlushBuffer()` to draw any remaining points, and returns `TRUE`. Otherwise the work procedure returns `FALSE`, and Xt will call it again as soon as all pending events are handled. To measure the elapsed time, `CreateImageWorkProc()` calls `ReportTime()` when the fractal is completed.

With these changes, we can once again measure the time required to start the `fractal` program and display the image. Figure 11.20 shows the times reported by running this program on System A:

```
% fractal -geometry =400x400
Starting:
Up:
   Elapsed Time = 0.340
   CPU Time     = 0.110
   System Time  = 0.050
Starting Fractal Generation:
Fractal Generation Complete:
   Elapsed Time = 10.630
   CPU Time     = 10.050
   System Time  =  0.090
```

Figure 11.20 Using a work procedure.

With this change, the `fractal` program appears in 0.34 seconds, and is immediately responsive. The fractal still requires a long time to draw, but the user can interact with the program while the fractal is drawing. There is a slight cost, as it appears that the fractal now takes a bit longer to create. However, this is more than offset by the fact that the program is completely responsive to user input at all times and starts up in just over three tenths of a second.

The measurements for this latest version also show an interesting side-effect of using a work procedure to create the fractal image. Unlike all earlier versions, the image is only created once at start-up. Because the work procedure is not executed until the window is completely ready, the problem caused by intermediate resizing is eliminated. `CreateImage()` may still be called multiple times, but because any pending work procedures are removed each time, the image is only drawn once. The only remaining cost attributable to the program's intermediate geometry management is the cost of registering and removing a work procedure.

Figure 11.21 shows an updated version of the table used to track progress toward the performance goals we established at the beginning of this chapter. These figures include the times measured on the X terminal, which remain less satisfactory than those on System A, but are quite reasonable, for that system.

Operation	Goal	A	B	Meets Goal?
Program start-up (initial response)	0.3-1.0	0.34	3.16	Yes
Launch preference panel	0.3	0.29	1.127	Yes
Response to parameter changes	0.3	~0	0.48	Yes
Zoom in on selected areas	0.3	~0	0.48	Yes
Resize window	0.3	~0	0.48	Yes
Redraw on Expose	< 0.3	~0	sluggish	Yes
Menus, sliders, buttons, rubberbanding	< 0.3	~0	sluggish	Yes

Figure 11.21 Performance goals for `fractal` program.

With the introduction of the work procedure, it appears that the tuning of the `fractal` program could be considered complete. As shown in Figure 11.21, all originally stated goals have been met on System A. (There is no reason to quibble over 0.04 seconds, at this point.) The program's start-up is very close to the desired goal and the user can always interact with the program. Even while a fractal is in mid-computation, the user can resize the window, post the preference dialog, or change various parameters that affect the fractal image.

On the X terminal, the performance does not meet the ideal goals we established, but the program is quite responsive in relation to other programs running on that display. The start-up time has been reduced by an order of magnitude, to a slow, but acceptable 3 seconds. More dramatically, the length of time a user must wait after making a change to the fractal has been reduced from 245 seconds to less than half a second.

Given these measurements, it would be reasonable to declare this program finished.

11.5 Sleight of Hand

According to the data reported in Figure 11.21, all original goals have been reached and the tuning of the `fractal` program has been completed. Unfortunately, with some use, it becomes apparent that this program still has performance-related deficiencies. The problem with establishing performance goals in advance is that it is not always possible to be sure the goals capture the user's perspective of the program's performance. It is easy to pick numbers as performance goals, but not so easy to be sure the numbers are relevant.

The problem with the original performance goals established for this program is that they do not completely capture the nature of the tasks a user might want to perform. We focused on reducing the time required to perform specific mechanical operations, without thinking enough about the reasons a user might perform these tasks. The work we have done so far is good, and the program is far more usable now than it was originally. However, the improvements are not quite enough.

Although the user can always interact with the program, in the sense that the user can push buttons and so on, the user cannot truly manipulate the fractal in real time to explore different areas of the image. Because the image still requires 10 seconds to draw completely, true exploration remains clumsy and slow. Being able to respond to user input before the fractal is fully drawn is of little help. It soon becomes clear that the user cannot really select an area for further exploration until the fractal is fully drawn because significant portions of the fractal do not even appear on the screen. The user can play with the program's user interface, but cannot easily perform a real task.

Figure 11.22 illustrates the dilemma facing a user who wants to explore parts of the image by quickly zooming in on selected regions. Although the program allows the user to draw a bounding box around any area of the window, the user cannot see the portion of the image being selected. The ability to select a portion of the window is useless if there is nothing visible to select.

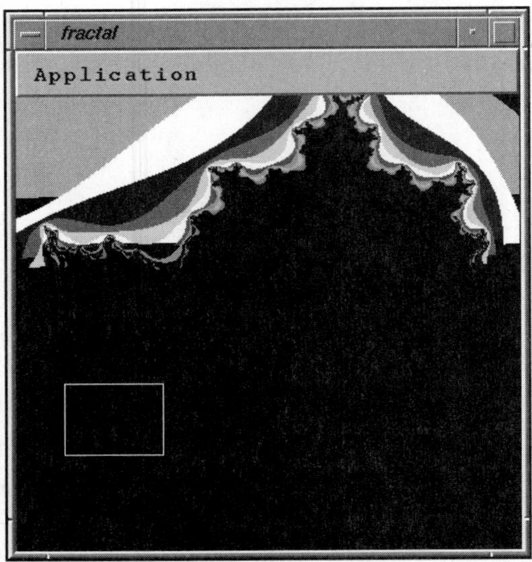

Figure 11.22 Fractal program after 4 seconds of drawing.

It seems that the only way a user could truly explore the fractal image with speed and freedom, is if the fractal could be displayed very quickly. It also seems clear that the only way to create the image more quickly is to reduce the number of computations that have to be performed. Short of inventing a new algorithm, the only remaining way to reduce the computations is to reduce the size of the image, or reduce the depth to which the image is computed. Interestingly, referring back to Figure 11.6 shows that at one time the `fractal` program did create an image *very* quickly, following the first resize. This resize, which appears to have happened when the window was very small, took only a fraction of a second to compute the entire image.

Although an image that is so tiny that it cannot be seen is of little use, the recognition that a smaller image can be drawn more quickly leads to another idea. Each x,y point in the image computation does not necessarily have to correspond directly to a pixel. Even if the window that contains the image is 400 by 400 pixels in size, the fractal computation could assume any size at all. Each "point" in the image does not need to occupy one pixel, but could occupy any rectangular region of the screen. Based on this recognition, it should be possible to display a full sized fractal in a sort of "draft" mode, in which the resolution of the image is less than optimal. We know from the small bug in the early versions of the program, that a low resolution image can be drawn very quickly. The user could interact with the draft mode to identify areas for further exploration, and allow the image to be drawn in full resolution only when the desired spot in the image has been located.

Based on this simple idea, we can create a new implementation of the `fractal` program that computes the fractal multiple times. The image is initially displayed in a very low, but quickly calculable resolution, and progresses to better and better resolutions as time goes on. With this technique, the user should see an image that resembles the final fractal in a fraction of a second, and then watch as the fractal becomes more and more refined. Changing any parameter reveals the general shape of the new image in a flash, and the process of progressive refinement begins again.

Figure 11.23 illustrates this idea with a fractal generated in three steps. The first fractal in the upper left corner is very low resolution, but has an immediately recognizable shape. This fractal is drawn using a height and a width that is 1/16th of the window size, and displays each "point" in the image as a rectangle 16 pixels square. The second refinement, shown in the middle image, is computed based on a width and height that is 1/4th the size of the window, and displays each computed point as a 4x4 rectangle. At this stage, the fractal is quite clear, and many details begin to emerge. A user who wants to explore different regions of the image should have no problem selecting portions of the image at this resolution. The final image, in the lower right, shows the image in the full resolution, in which each point of the image corresponds to one pixel on the screen.

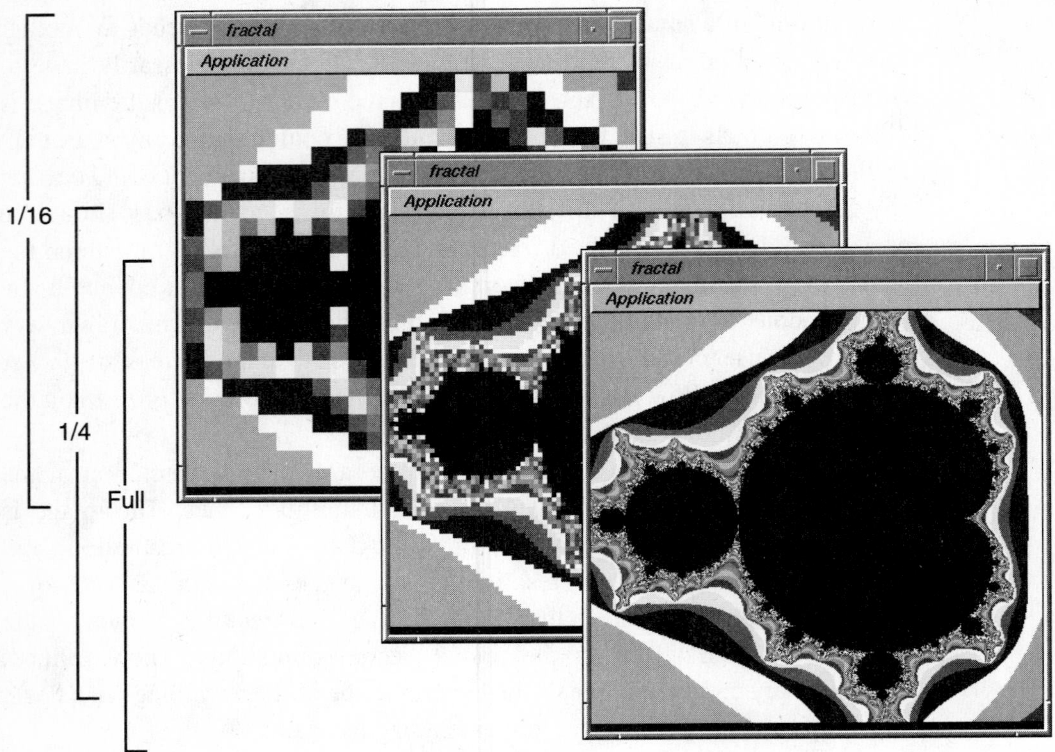

Figure 11.23 A three-stage, progressively refined fractal.

It may seem odd to start with an operation that is inherently slow, and suggest that the way to get better performance is to execute that operation multiple times. Computing the fractal multiple times will certainly require more CPU instructions, and generate more traffic between the program and the X server. However, this is typical of all sleight of hand techniques. The trick is to do more work, while making a task *appear* to proceed more quickly. In this case, we can also improve the usability of the `fractal` program.

To implement these multiple stages of progressive refinement, the `CreateImageWorkProc()` function described in the previous section must be modified substantially. The modified function must be able to create a small amount of the fractal image each time it is called, and must also be able to step through the various stages of image quality. The job is not complete until an image is drawn in the final resolution. The function must also be able to progress between stages quickly. If it takes a long time to generate the first reasonable image, the effect will be lost. The image must reach a usable resolution quickly.

Besides the `restart` member of the `ImageData` structure, this implementation depends on a static variable, `newResolution`, which is used to control when the image is restarted at a new resolution. Some of the data previously initialized at the beginning of each fractal computation must now be reinitialized each time a finer resolution image is started.

The biggest change in this function can be seen on line 376, where the `width` variable is set to the width of the screen divided by a variable named `size`. This assignment is made each time a completely new image is to be generated. The `size` variable is new in this version, and is given an initial value of 16. This variable indicates the size of a single point in the image, and therefore controls the resolution of the image.

Changes from the previous implementation are shown in bold:

```
345 Boolean CreateImageWorkProc ( XtPointer clientData )
346 {
347     ImageData     *data = (ImageData*) clientData;
348     Widget         w = data->canvas;
349     static int     x, y, iteration;
350     static double rangeByWidth, rangeByHeight, *xconstants;
351     static int     depth;
352     static int     height;
353     static int     width;
354     GC             gc     = data->gc;
355     Pixmap         pixmap = data->pixmap;
356     static double maxDistance;
357     static double origin_imag;
358     static double origin_real;
359     static int     ncolors;
360     int            slice;
361     static int     size;
362     static int     newResolution;
363     Pixel          black = BlackPixel ( XtDisplay ( w ), 0 );
364
365     if ( data->restart )
366     {
367        /*
368         * If a completely new fractal image is to be
369         * generated, start from the beginning, with a point
370         * size of 16 by 16 pixels. Reinitialize all local
371         * variables to the correct values.
372         */
373
374         newResolution = TRUE;
```

```
375             size           = 16;
376             height         = data->height / size;
377             width          = data->width  / size;
378             maxDistance    = data->maxDistance;
379             origin_imag    = data->origin.imag;
380             origin_real    = data->origin.real;
381             ncolors        = data->ncolors;
382             depth          = data->depth;
383             data->restart = FALSE;
384         }
385
386         if ( data->restart || newResolution )
387         {
388            /*
389             * If an entire new fractal is being generated, or if
390             * the resolution of the image has changed,
391             * reinitialize those variables that have to change.
392             * Clear the pixmap and reset the point buffers
393             * for the next round of drawing.
394             */
395
```

Start timing

```
396             ReportTime ( "Starting fractal", FALSE );
397
398             rangeByWidth  = data->range / ( double ) width;
399             rangeByHeight = data->range / ( double ) height;
400             y = 0;
401
402             InitBuffer();
403
404             XSetForeground ( XtDisplay ( w ), gc,
405                              BlackPixelOfScreen ( XtScreen ( w ) ) );
406             XFillRectangle ( XtDisplay ( w ), pixmap, gc, 0, 0,
407                              data->width, data->height );
408
409             xconstants = ( double* ) XtMalloc ( width *
410                                                 sizeof ( double ) );
411            /*
412             * Pre-compute the constants for each X value.
413             */
414
415             for ( x = 0; x < width; x++ )
416                 xconstants[x] = origin_real +
417                                      ( double ) x * rangeByWidth;
418         }
```

The inner loop of the fractal computation is mostly unchanged, except for the call to `BufferPoint()` on line 463. This function now takes an additional parameter, the `size` variable, which determines the precision with which the image is drawn. Also, on line 476, `BufferPoint()` is called to draw a point that is inside the Mandelbrot set, if the inner loop has been completed without leaving the complex `z` plane. This is a change from earlier versions, which simply allowed this area to be handled by clearing the window and pixmap. In this implementation, clearing the window before each change in resolution would destroy the entire effect, so each point needs to be drawn explicitly. This will certainly cost more, in terms of server requests, which could be a fatal flaw in this entire approach. Notice that the call to `XClearArea()` has also been removed from the initialization code before the beginning of the loop.

```
419      for ( slice = 0 ; slice < 2 && y < height; y++, slice++ )
420      {
421          static double z_real, z_imag, k_real, k_imag;
422
423          k_imag =  origin_imag - ( double ) y * rangeByHeight;
424
425          for ( x = 0; x < width; x++ )
426          {
427              z_real =  z_imag = 0.0;
428              k_real =  xconstants[x];
429
430              /*
431               * Calculate z =  z * z + k  over and over.
432               */
433
434              for ( iteration = 0;
435                    iteration < depth;
436                    iteration++ )
437              {
438                  static double real;
439                  int           distance;
440
441                  real   = z_real;
442                  z_real = z_real * z_real -
443                                       z_imag * z_imag + k_real;
444                  z_imag = (real + real) * z_imag + k_imag;
445
446                  distance  =  (int) ( z_real * z_real +
447                                         z_imag * z_imag );
448                /*
449                 * If the z point has moved off the plane,
450                 * set the current foreground color to
451                 * the distance (cast to an int and modulo
452                 * the number of colors available), and
453                 * draw a point in the window and the pixmap.
454                 */
```

```
455
456                 if ( distance >= maxDistance )
457                 {
458                     Pixel color;
459
460                     color = ( Pixel ) iteration % ncolors;
461
462                     BufferPoint ( w, pixmap, gc,
463                                   ( int ) color, x, y, size );
464                     break;
465                 }
466             }
467
468             /*
469              * The image is no longer cleared to black because
470              * it would destroy the effect. However, parts of
471              * the area inside the Mandelbrot set will be
472              * drawn incorrectly at previous resolutions, so
473              * we must draw each point inside the set as well.
474              */
475
476             if ( distance < maxDistance )
477                 BufferPoint ( w, pixmap, gc,
478                               ( int ) black, x, y, size );
479         }
480     }
```

The final part of the code, which determines when the work procedure is completed, begins on line 481. The first test checks to see if the value of `y` is equal to the height of the `canvas` widget. In this implementation, the distinction between the `height` variable and the value of `data->height` is exploited. The value of `y` can only be equal to `data->height` if the fractal has been computed to its fullest resolution. In this case, the point buffer is flushed, and `ReportTime()` is called before the work procedure returns `TRUE` to cancel future calls. `ReportTime()` is included only for measurement purposes, of course.

The second test, on line 490, detects the situation in which a complete, lower resolution image has been completed. In this case, `y` must be equal to the height of the low resolution image. The variable `newResolution` is set to `TRUE` to trigger the next higher resolution computation. After drawing all remaining points, this code segment decreases the value of `size`, and recomputes the new width and height of the image. As `size` decreases, the quality of the image increases. Both the initial value of `size` and the rate by which it is changed, have been arbitrarily selected, and other values might be effective as well. This value could even be parameterized so it could be controlled by the user.

As the resolution approaches the final value, we must avoid making an unnecessary additional round of computations. It is possible to compute a nearly full-resolution image (when size reaches a value of one) but not have `width` and `height` come out exactly equal to the size of the canvas window. To avoid this situation, the block of code starting at line 500 sets the image to its fullest resolution if the size of the computed image would be greater than half the final size. It would also be useful to use window manager hints to ensure that the canvas widget has widths and heights that are multiples of 16.

The final case, on line 511, is executed when a portion of a fractal image has been computed, but the image is not complete at any resolution. This code segment just returns a value of `FALSE` so Xt will call the work procedure again, after checking for pending events.

```
481     if ( y == data->height )
482     {
483          newResolution = FALSE;
484          FlushBuffer ( w, pixmap, gc, size );
485
486          ReportTime ( "Fractal Generation Complete", TRUE );
487
488          return ( TRUE );
489     }
490     else if ( y == height )
491     {
492         newResolution = TRUE;
493
494         FlushBuffer ( w, pixmap, gc, size );
495
496         size   /= 4;
497         height  = data->height / size;
498         width   = data->width  / size;
499
500         if ( width > data->width/ 2 || height > data->height / 2)
501         {
502             width  = data->width;
503             height = data->height;
504             size   = 1;
505         }
506
507         ReportTime ( "Round Completed", TRUE );
508
509         return ( FALSE );
510      }
```

```
    else
    {
        newResolution = FALSE;
        return ( FALSE );
    }
}
```

The other function that requires a substantial change is `Render()`. This function must be changed to accept a `size` parameter that determines the size of a single "point" in the fractal image. If the size of the point is equal to one pixel, `Render()` calls `XDrawPoints()` as in the original version. If `size` is larger than one, the function copies the given array of points to an array of `XRectangle` structures and uses `XFillRectangles()` to draw each point as a filled rectangle whose width and height are determined by the value of `size`.

```
static void Render ( Widget  w, Pixmap pix, GC gc,
                     XPoint *points,
                     int     numPoints, int size )
{
    if ( size <= 1 )
    {
       /*
        * If the size of a point is 1 pixel, just use
        * XDrawPoints to draw each point in the given buffer.
        */

        if ( pix )
            XDrawPoints ( XtDisplay ( w ), pix, gc,
                          points, numPoints,
                          CoordModeOrigin );

        if ( XtIsRealized ( w ) )
            XDrawPoints ( XtDisplay ( w ), XtWindow(w), gc,
                          points, numPoints,
                          CoordModeOrigin );
    }
    else
    {
       /*
        * If the size of point is larger than one, convert
        * the buffer to an array of XRectangle structures
        * and draw filled rectangles for each point.
        */

        static XRectangle rect[MAXPOINTS];
        int i;

```

```
        for ( i = 0; i < numPoints; i++ )
        {
            rect[i].x      = points[i].x * size;
            rect[i].y      = points[i].y * size;
            rect[i].width  = size;
            rect[i].height = size;
        }

        if ( pix )
            XFillRectangles ( XtDisplay ( w ), pix, gc,
                              rect, numPoints );

        if ( XtIsRealized ( w ) )
            XFillRectangles ( XtDisplay ( w ), XtWindow(w),
                              gc, rect, numPoints );
    }
}
```

Two other changes are also necessary. The functions `BufferPoint()` and `FlushBuffer()` must be modified to accept the `size` parameter, which is simply passed on to `Render()`. These changes are shown below:

```
static void BufferPoint ( Widget w, Pixmap pix,
                          GC gc,   Pixel color,
                          int x,   int y, int size )
{

   /*
    * Don't allow more than MAXCOLOR colors.
    */

    color = color % MAXCOLOR;

    if ( buffer.numPoints[color] == MAXPOINTS )
    {
        XSetForeground ( XtDisplay (  w ), gc, color );

        Render ( w, pix, gc,
                 buffer.points [ color ],
                 buffer.numPoints [ color ], size );

       /*
        * Reset the buffer.
        */

        buffer.numPoints[color] = 0;
     }

```

```
    /*
     * Store the point in the buffer according to its color.
     */

    buffer.points[color][buffer.numPoints[color]].x = x;
    buffer.points[color][buffer.numPoints[color]].y = y;
    buffer.numPoints[color] += 1;
}

static void FlushBuffer ( Widget w, Pixmap pix, GC gc,
                          int size )
{
    int i;

    /*
     * Check each buffer.
     */

    for ( i=0 ; i < MAXCOLOR; i++ )
    {
        /*
         * If there are any points in this buffer, display them
         * in the window and the pixmap.
         */

         if ( buffer.numPoints [ i ] )
         {
             XSetForeground ( XtDisplay ( w ), gc, i );

             Render ( w, pix, gc, buffer.points[i],
                         buffer.numPoints[i], size );

             buffer.numPoints[i] = 0;
         }
    }
}
```

With these changes, we can once again test the `fractal` program to see if the responsiveness has improved. Running the program on System A produces the sequence of fractal images shown in Figure 11.23, and reports the times shown in Figure 11.24.

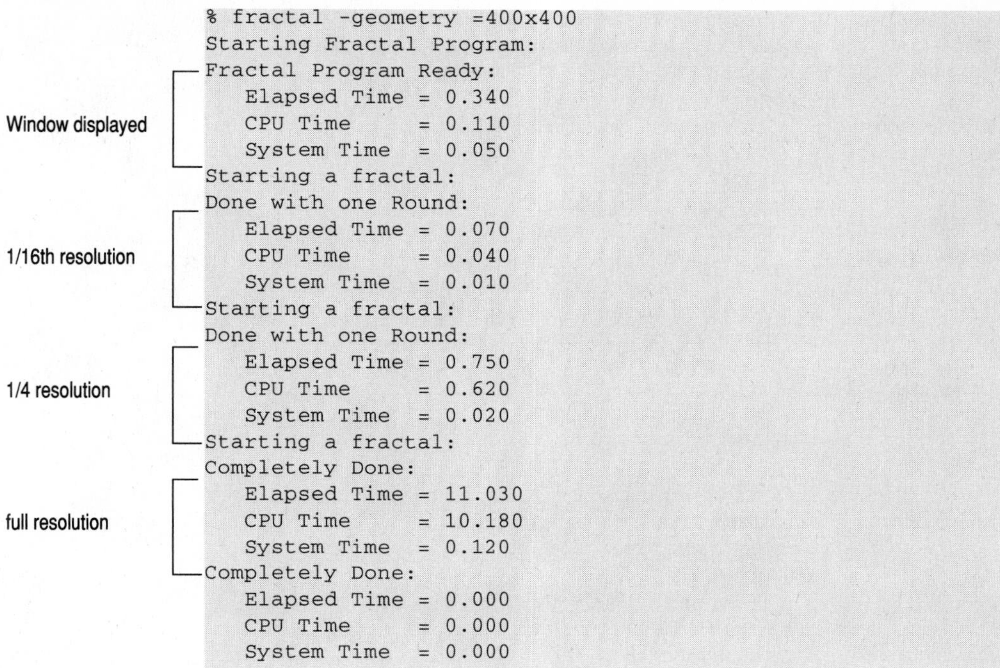


```
% fractal -geometry =400x400
Starting Fractal Program:
Fractal Program Ready:
   Elapsed Time = 0.340
   CPU Time     = 0.110
   System Time  = 0.050
Starting a fractal:
Done with one Round:
   Elapsed Time = 0.070
   CPU Time     = 0.040
   System Time  = 0.010
Starting a fractal:
Done with one Round:
   Elapsed Time = 0.750
   CPU Time     = 0.620
   System Time  = 0.020
Starting a fractal:
Completely Done:
   Elapsed Time = 11.030
   CPU Time     = 10.180
   System Time  = 0.120
Completely Done:
   Elapsed Time = 0.000
   CPU Time     = 0.000
   System Time  = 0.000
```

Figure 11.24 Performance measurements for the iterative fractal generation.

With this technique, the fractal window appears in 0.34 seconds and the first crude, but recognizable fractal image is drawn in 7 hundredths of a second! The second, clearly recognizable image appears after an additional 0.75 seconds. Between these two stages, the program has been started and the user has been presented with a very reasonable image in just over one second. From this point, the image continues to gradually refine itself, as the full resolution image is rendered over top of the lower resolution screen. The full resolution image still requires around 11 seconds. However, for purposes of exploration, the user can now interact with the image immediately.

Figure 11.25 shows the times that can be achieved on the X terminal, using this latest approach.

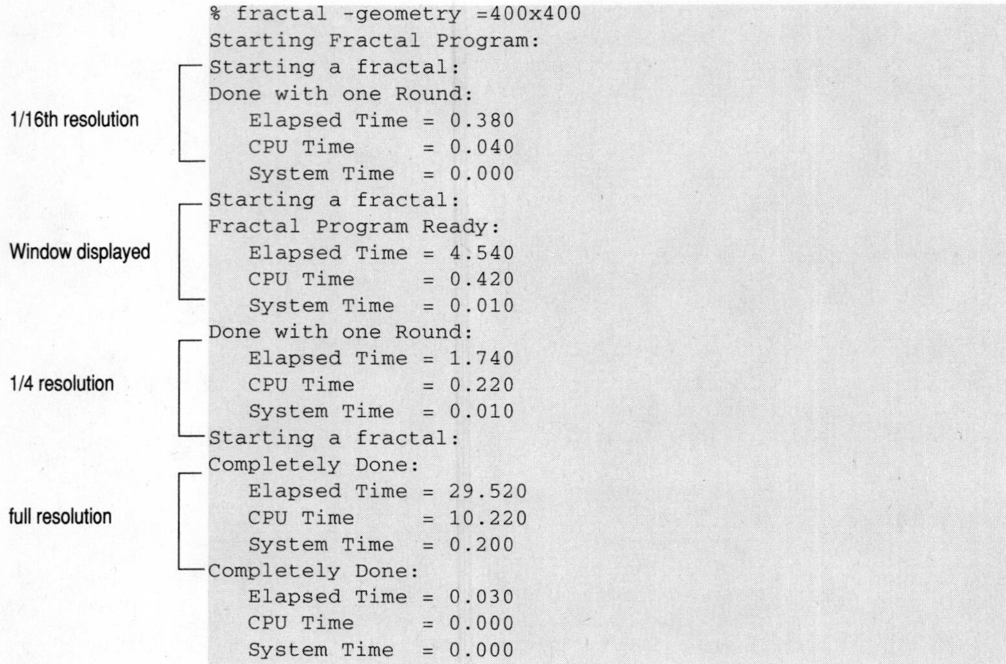


```
% fractal -geometry =400x400
Starting Fractal Program:
Starting a fractal:
Done with one Round:
   Elapsed Time = 0.380
   CPU Time     = 0.040
   System Time  = 0.000
Starting a fractal:
Fractal Program Ready:
   Elapsed Time = 4.540
   CPU Time     = 0.420
   System Time  = 0.010
Done with one Round:
   Elapsed Time = 1.740
   CPU Time     = 0.220
   System Time  = 0.010
Starting a fractal:
Completely Done:
   Elapsed Time = 29.520
   CPU Time     = 10.220
   System Time  = 0.200
Completely Done:
   Elapsed Time = 0.030
   CPU Time     = 0.000
   System Time  = 0.000
```

Figure 11.25 Time for iterative fractal generation on X terminal.

Besides having an acceptable start-up time, at least on System A, this final version is very responsive to changes made by the user. The same process is used for any change made using the preference panel, or by sweeping out an area to be drawn in greater detail. For example, Figure 11.26 shows the stages of the fractal image drawn when the user sweeps out a portion of the original image located in the upper middle of the original image. As with the full image, the first rough shape appears in just 0.07 seconds. The second stage appears in less than a second, while the third gradually replaces the lower resolution version, transforming the image as the user watches.

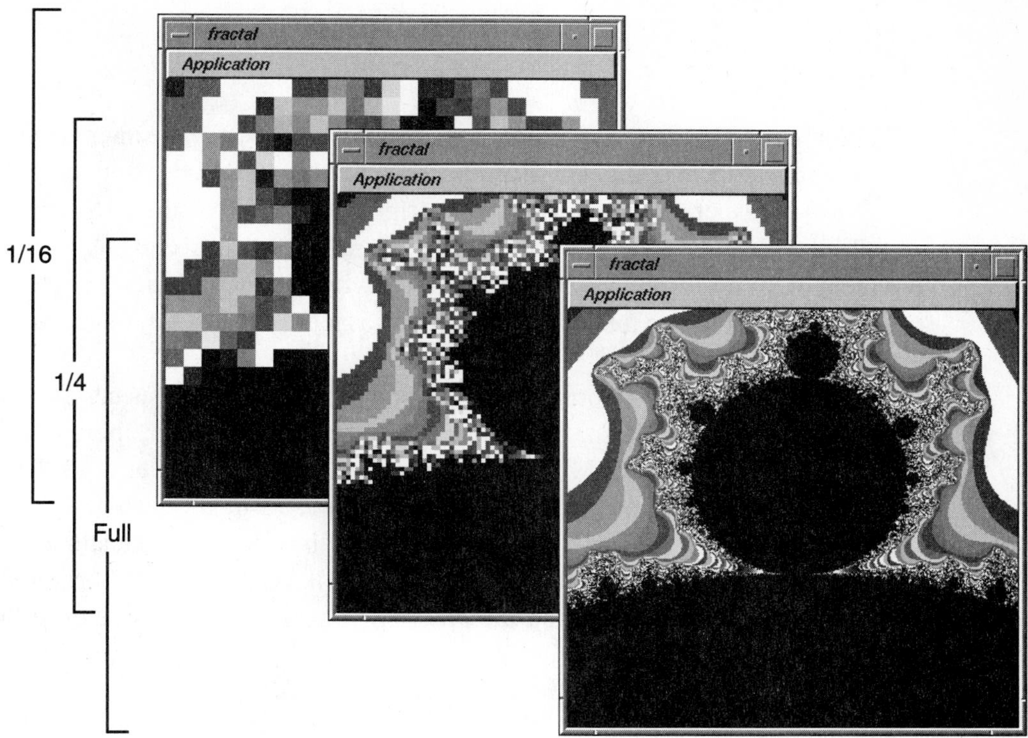

Figure 11.26 A portion of the fractal, displayed in stages.

The exact speed with which the resolution is changed should be subject to some experimentation. More than three phases are certainly possible, and the linearity with which the program converges on the final resolution could also be changed. Also, there may be other variations on this approach. For example, we could leave the size of each point in the image the same, but start by setting the fractal's depth (controlled by the `depth` member of the `ImageData` structure) to a very low value, and increase it with each pass. It might also be interesting to combine the two approaches.

11.6 Conclusion

This case study began with a seemingly impossible task: to take an inherently slow application and tune it to the point that it not only starts up very quickly, but also is responsive at all times. The original program required 15 seconds to display an initial window. While basic operations like selecting an item on a menu were reasonably responsive once the window finally appeared, manipulations that involved the task the program was meant to perform took over 30 seconds.

Initial brute force efforts to tune the program were highly successful, but fell far short of making the program truly interactive. However, these efforts did greatly reduce the load the program placed on both the CPU and the X server. Finally, by focusing on the way in which users might wish to actually use the program, a slight twist led to a truly interactive application. The program's window appears with an initial image, in very close to the originally stated goal of 0.3 seconds, and the program is instantly responsive once the interface has been created.

12

Case Study #2: A Desktop File Browser

This chapter completes the discussion of writing efficient Motif applications by looking at a program that is similar to those found on many desktop environments. The program described in this chapter displays the contents of a directory as icons. The user can open files and directories by clicking on any icon displayed in the browser. Clicking on a text file launches an editor to view that file, while clicking on a directory launches another browser that can be used to view that directory.

The program, known as `dirview`, is not as elaborate as the commercial-quality desktop file managers available on many contemporary systems, but the basic features are similar. In addition, the techniques used in this interface can be applied to other situations as well.

Figure 12.1 shows the interface presented by the `dirview` program. Each file or directory is displayed as an icon. Directories are represented by "file folder" icons, while all other files are represented by "document" icons. Commercial file managers typically distinguish between many types of files, but to keep this case study simple, `dirview` recognizes only directories and files.

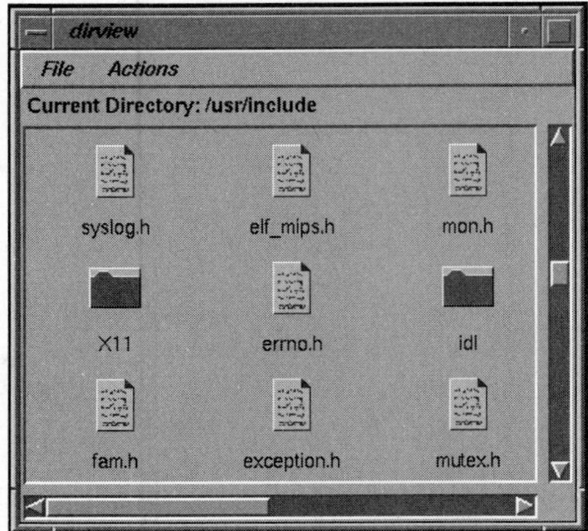

Figure 12.1 A simple desktop file and directory browser.

12.1 Initial Implementation

The following sections examine the initial implementation of the `dirview` program. The program is organized into six source files and two header files. These files are:

- main.c: The file main.c contains a driver that initializes Xt and handles the event loop. It calls the function `CreateBrowser()`, defined in browser.c, to create the main user interface
- globals.h: This file contains some declarations and macros used in the rest of the program.
- browser.c: This file contains the `CreateBrowser()` function, which creates the interface shown in Figure 12.1.
- menus.c: This file contains functions that set up the program's menu bar and the entries in the menu panes.
- icons.h: The icons used to represent files and directories, as shown in Figure 12.1, are created using the Xpm pixmap format. This header file contains the icon descriptions used in this program.
- icons.c: This file contains functions for creating icons for files and directories, and allowing the user to select and double-click on these icons.

- launch.c: This file contains functions for invoking an editor to view a file, or a new `dirview` program to browse a new directory.
- select.c: This file contains functions for setting and accessing the currently selected icon.

The following sections examine the implementation of this program, file by file.

main.c

The body of the program just initializes Xt, calls an external function to create the browser interface, and enters the event loop. Calls to `ReportTime()` are included to measure the time required to display the program's initial window.

Start timing

```
/*****************************************************
 * main.c: main driver for dirview program.
 ****************************************************/
#include <Xm/Xm.h>
#include <stdlib.h>
#include "TimerTools.h"

extern Widget CreateBrowser ( Widget shell, char *dir );

main ( int argc, char **argv )
{
    Widget       shell, browser;
    XtAppContext app ;
    char         *directory = NULL;

    ReportTime ( "Starting", FALSE );

    shell = XtAppInitialize  (  &app, "Dirview",  NULL, 0,
                                &argc, argv, NULL, NULL, 0  );
   /*
    * Retrieve the directory to browse from the
    * optional command-line argument. If directory is NULL,
    * CreateBrowser() opens the current working directory.
    */

    if ( argc > 1 )
        directory = argv[1];

   /*
    * Create the browser window. This function returns NULL
    * if the given directory cannot be opened.
    */
```

```

    if ( ( browser =
                CreateBrowser ( shell, directory ) ) == NULL )
        exit ( 1 );

    XtManageChild ( browser );

    XtRealizeWidget ( shell );

```

End timing

```
    WaitForWindow ( shell );
    HandleEvents ( shell );
    ReportTime ( "Up", TRUE );

    XtAppMainLoop ( app );
}
```

globals.h

Several data structures and macros are used throughout this program. These are defined in a header file, globals.h, which can be included by other files, as needed.

```
/*******************************************************
 * globals.h: Common definitions needed in dirview.
 *******************************************************/
#include <sys/stat.h>
#include <dirent.h>

/*
 * Define symbols for types of files.
 */

typedef enum { REGULAR_FILE, DIRECTORY } FileType;

/*
 * Convenient macros for checking type of a file/directory
 */

static struct stat Statbuf;

#define exists(file) (stat(file,&Statbuf)<0 ?      \
                     0:Statbuf.st_mode)
#define GetType(name)(exists(name) &&              \
                      S_ISDIR(Statbuf.st_mode) ? \
                      DIRECTORY :                \
                      REGULAR_FILE)
```

browser.c

The heart of dirview's interface is implemented in browser.c. This file contains the function CreateBrowser(), which constructs the widgets that form the program's user interface, and also reads a directory and displays its contents as icons. The file starts with some declarations of functions and variables.

```
/*************************************************
 * browser.c: main dirview interface.
 *************************************************/
#include <Xm/Xm.h>
#include <Xm/MainW.h>
#include <Xm/RowColumn.h>
#include <Xm/Label.h>
#include <unistd.h>
#include <stdio.h>
#include "globals.h"
#include "TimerTools.h"

/*
 * Externally-defined functions
 */

extern Widget CreateMenu ( Widget );
extern Widget CreateIcon ( char *, Widget, FileType );

/*
 * label widget that displays current directory.
 */

static Widget currentDirLabel;
```

The function SetCurrentDirectory() displays the name of the current directory in the currentDirLabel widget, which is located near the top of the window, as seen in Figure 12.1.

```
void SetCurrentDirectory ( char *dir )
{
    char buf[300];

   /*
    * Just display the given directory in a label.
    */

    sprintf ( buf, "Current Directory: %s", dir );
```

```

    XtVaSetValues ( currentDirLabel,
                    XtVaTypedArg,
                    XmNlabelString,  XmRString,
                    buf, strlen ( buf ) + 1,
                    NULL );
}
```

`CreateBrowser()` creates an XmMainWindow widget that manages an XmRowColumn widget as its work area. The function reads the contents of the given directory and calls an external function, `CreateIcon()`, to add a file or directory icon to the XmRowColumn widget's children. `CreateBrowser()` also calls the external function `CreateMenu()` to add a menubar to the window.

Show time

```
Widget CreateBrowser ( Widget parent, char *dir )
{
    Widget         mainWindow, rowColumn, commandPanel, menuBar;
    struct dirent *entry;
    DIR           *fd;

    ReportTime ( "Starting Browser", TRUE );

   /*
    * No directory is interpreted as meaning the current
    * directory. Determine the directory to be displayed,
    * and open it.
    */

    if ( !dir )
        dir = getcwd ( NULL, 300 );

    if ( ( fd = opendir ( dir ) ) == NULL )
        return ( NULL );

   /*
    * Create widgets for this window.
    */

    mainWindow = XtVaCreateWidget ( "browser",
                           xmMainWindowWidgetClass,   parent,
                           XmNscrollingPolicy,        XmAUTOMATIC,
                           XmNscrollBarDisplayPolicy, XmSTATIC,
                           XmNcommandWindowLocation,
                                       XmCOMMAND_ABOVE_WORKSPACE,
                           NULL );

```

```
    menuBar = CreateMenu ( mainWindow );

    rowColumn = XtVaCreateManagedWidget  ( "rowColumn",
                                 xmRowColumnWidgetClass,
                                 mainWindow,
                                 XmNpacking,    XmPACK_COLUMN,
                                 XmNnumColumns, 8,
                                 NULL );

    commandPanel = XtVaCreateManagedWidget ( "commandPanel",
                         xmRowColumnWidgetClass, mainWindow,
                         XmNorientation,    XmHORIZONTAL,
                         XmNentryAlignment, XmALIGNMENT_CENTER,
                         XmNpacking,        XmPACK_TIGHT,
                         NULL );

    currentDirLabel = XtVaCreateManagedWidget  ( "label1",
                          xmLabelWidgetClass, commandPanel,
                          XmNalignment,  XmALIGNMENT_BEGINNING,
                          NULL );

    SetCurrentDirectory ( dir );

    XtVaSetValues ( mainWindow,
                    XmNcommandWindow, currentDirLabel,
                    XmNworkWindow,    rowColumn,
                    NULL );
   /*
    * Read each item in the directory, and create an icon
    * for each item according to its type.
    */

    while ( ( entry = readdir ( fd ) ) != NULL )
    {
        Widget icon;

        icon = CreateIcon ( entry->d_name,
                            rowColumn,
                            GetType ( entry->d_name ) );
        XtManageChild ( icon );
    }

    ReportTime ( "Icons Created", TRUE );

    return ( mainWindow );
}
```

menu.c

The menubar and its related functions are implemented in the file main.c. The menubar in this example is very simple. There are two panes, a "File" pane and an "Actions" pane. The File pane contains only a "Quit" item, but could support other entries if the program is expanded. The Actions pane is meant to support various actions to be performed on the currently selected file or directory. The only operation supported in this implementation is "Open." Other possibilities include commands to delete a file, rename a file, and so on.

The file begins by implementing the callbacks to be invoked when each menu item is selected.

```
/*******************************************************
 * menu.c: menu construction and callbacks for dirview
 *******************************************************/
#include <Xm/Xm.h>
#include <Xm/RowColumn.h>
#include <Xm/CascadeB.h>
#include <Xm/PushB.h>
#include <stdlib.h>

extern void  OpenSelected ( void );

/*
 * Callback functions
 */

static void QuitCallback ( Widget    w,
                           XtPointer clientData,
                           XtPointer callData )
{
    exit ( 0 );
}

static void OpenSelectedCallback ( Widget    w,
                                   XtPointer clientData,
                                   XtPointer callData )
{
    OpenSelected();
}
```

Each menu pane is created by a separate function. While it maybe overkill for such a small menu, this approach allows new menu items to be added easily, and creates a structure that can easily support a larger menu. `CreateFilePane()` creates the File pulldown menu and the Quit item in that pane.

`CreateActionsPane()` creates a second pulldown menu that contains the Open menu item.

```
void CreateFilePane ( Widget parent )
{
    Widget cascade, submenu, quit, openNew;
    int    i;

   /*
    * Install a File menu pane. This pane initially
    * contains only a Quit item.
    */

    submenu = XmCreatePulldownMenu ( parent,  "File",
                                     NULL, 0 );

    cascade = XtVaCreateManagedWidget ( "File",
                                   xmCascadeButtonWidgetClass,
                                   parent,
                                   XmNsubMenuId, submenu,
                                   NULL );

    quit = XtCreateManagedWidget ( "Quit",
                                    xmPushButtonWidgetClass,
                                    submenu, NULL, 0 );

    XtAddCallback ( quit, XmNactivateCallback,
                    QuitCallback, NULL );
}

void CreateActionsPane ( Widget parent )
{
    Widget cascade, submenu, openSelected;

   /*
    * Install an "Action" menu pane. This pane initially
    * contains only an "Open" item.
    */

    submenu = XmCreatePulldownMenu ( parent, "Actions",
                                     NULL, 0 );

    cascade = XtVaCreateManagedWidget ( "Actions",
                                  xmCascadeButtonWidgetClass,
                                  parent,
                                  XmNsubMenuId, submenu,
                                  NULL );

```

```
    openSelected = XtCreateManagedWidget ( "Open",
                                           xmPushButtonWidgetClass,
                                           submenu, NULL, 0 );

    XtAddCallback ( openSelected, XmNactivateCallback,
                    OpenSelectedCallback, NULL );
}
```

The function `CreateMenu()` is called from `CreateBrowser()` to add a menubar to the `dirview` window. This function just creates a menu bar and calls `CreateFilePane()` and `CreateActionsPane()` to implement the menu items.

```
Widget CreateMenu ( Widget parent )
{
    Widget menu;
    int i;

   /*
    * Create a menu bar and call convenience functions
    * to create each pane.
    */

    menu = XmCreateMenuBar ( parent, "menuBar", NULL, 0 );

    CreateFilePane ( menu );
    CreateActionsPane ( menu );

    XtManageChild ( menu );

    return ( menu );
}
```

icons.h

The file icons.h contains definitions of the icons to be displayed for directories and files. These images could be defined as bitmaps, or Xpm pixmaps (See [Young94] and "Getting Software Described in this Book," on page 563 for information about Xpm). The window shown in Figure 12.1 uses color icons created by Xpm, whose descriptions are shown below. You can draw any icons you choose, of course. The icons used here represent a 40 by 40 pixel image. Using Xpm's ability to assign symbolic colors, the background of each icon is assigned a name of "background". This can be used to make the icon blend with the widget that contains it.

```
/*************************************************************
 * icons.h: Icon descriptions for file and directory icons.
 ************************************************************/
static char * fileIcon[] = {
"40 40 4 1",
"         c #9f9f9f s background",
".        c white",
"X        c #523600",
"o        c #d2aa77",
"                                        ",
"      .....................X            ",
"      .ooooooooooooooooooooXX           ",
"      .ooooooooooooooooooooXXX          ",
"      .ooooooooooooooooooooXXXX         ",
"      .ooooooooooooooooooooXXXXX        ",
"      .ooooooooooooooooooooXXXXXX       ",
"      .ooooooooooooooooooooXXXXXXX      ",
"      .ooooooooooooooooooooooooooX      ",
"      .ooooooXoooooXooXoXooooooooX      ",
"      .oooXXoXoooXoooXXooXXooooooX      ",
"      .oooooooooXXoooooooooXoooooX      ",
"      .ooooooooooooooooooooooooooX      ",
"      .ooooooooooooooooooooooooooX      ",
"      .ooooooooooooooooooooooooooX      ",
"      .oooXXoooXooXoooXoXXXXoooooX      ",
"      .oooXoooooXooXXoooooXXoooooX      ",
"      .ooooooooooooooooooooXoooooX      ",
"      .ooooooooooooooooooooXoooooX      ",
"      .oooooooooooXooooooooooooooX      ",
"      .oooooooooXXooooooooXXoooooX      ",
"      .oooXoooooXooooooooooooooooX      ",
"      .oooXXoXXXoooXooXXXoXoXooooX      ",
"      .ooooooooooooXooooooooXooooX      ",
"      .ooooooooooooooooXoooooooooX      ",
"      .ooooooooooooooooooooooooooX      ",
"      .ooooooooooooooooooooooooooX      ",
"      .oooXXooooXoXXXXXoooooXooooX      ",
"      .oooooXXooooXoooooXXXoXooooX      ",
"      .ooooooooooooooooooooXoooooX      ",
"      .ooooooooooooooooooooooooooX      ",
"      .oooooooooooXooooooooooooooX      ",
"      .ooooXXXoXXXoXoXXXXXXXoXoooX      ",
"      .oooooooXooXooXXooooXXoXoooX      ",
"      .ooooXoXXooXXXXoXoooXXXooooX      ",
"      .ooooooooooooooooooooooooooX      ",
"      .ooooooooooooooooooooooooooX      ",
"      .ooooooooooooooooooooooooooX      ",
"      .XXXXXXXXXXXXXXXXXXXXXXXXXXX      ",
"                                        "};
```

```
static char * dirIcon[] = {
"40 40 5 1",
"          c #9f9f9f s background",
".         c white",
"X         c #d69b9b",
"o         c black",
"O         c #895454",
"                                        ",
"                                        ",
"                                        ",
"                                        ",
"                                        ",
" .....................................  ",
" .XXXXXXXXXXXXXXXXXXXXXXXXXXXXXXXXXXXXo ",
" .XXXXXX.......XXXXXXXXXXXXXXXXXXXXXXXo ",
" .XXXXX.OOOOOOO.XXXXXXXXXXXXXXXXXXXXXXo ",
" .XXXX.OOOOOOOOO.XXXXXXXXXXXXXXXXXXXXXo ",
" .XXX.OOOOOOOOOOO.XXXXXXXXXXXXXXXXXXXXo ",
" ....OOOOOOOOOOOOO....................o ",
" .OOOOOOOOOOOOOOOOOOOOOOOOOOOOOOOOOOOOo ",
" .OOOOOOOOOOOOOOOOOOOOOOOOOOOOOOOOOOOOo ",
" .OOOOOOOOOOOOOOOOOOOOOOOOOOOOOOOOOOOOo ",
" .OOOOOOOOOOOOOOOOOOOOOOOOOOOOOOOOOOOOo ",
" .OOOOOOOOOOOOOOOOOOOOOOOOOOOOOOOOOOOOo ",
" .OOOOOOOOOOOOOOOOOOOOOOOOOOOOOOOOOOOOo ",
" .OOOOOOOOOOOOOOOOOOOOOOOOOOOOOOOOOOOOo ",
" .OOOOOOOOOOOOOOOOOOOOOOOOOOOOOOOOOOOOo ",
" .OOOOOOOOOOOOOOOOOOOOOOOOOOOOOOOOOOOOo ",
" .OOOOOOOOOOOOOOOOOOOOOOOOOOOOOOOOOOOOo ",
" .OOOOOOOOOOOOOOOOOOOOOOOOOOOOOOOOOOOOo ",
" .OOOOOOOOOOOOOOOOOOOOOOOOOOOOOOOOOOOOo ",
" .OOOOOOOOOOOOOOOOOOOOOOOOOOOOOOOOOOOOo ",
" .OOOOOOOOOOOOOOOOOOOOOOOOOOOOOOOOOOOOo ",
" .OOOOOOOOOOOOOOOOOOOOOOOOOOOOOOOOOOOOo ",
" .OOOOOOOOOOOOOOOOOOOOOOOOOOOOOOOOOOOOo ",
" .OOOOOOOOOOOOOOOOOOOOOOOOOOOOOOOOOOOOo ",
" .OOOOOOOOOOOOOOOOOOOOOOOOOOOOOOOOOOOOo ",
" .OOOOOOOOOOOOOOOOOOOOOOOOOOOOOOOOOOOOo ",
" .OOOOOOOOOOOOOOOOOOOOOOOOOOOOOOOOOOOOo ",
" .OOOOOOOOOOOOOOOOOOOOOOOOOOOOOOOOOOOOo ",
" .OOOOOOOOOOOOOOOOOOOOOOOOOOOOOOOOOOOOo ",
" .ooooooooooooooooooooooooooooooooooooo ",
"                                        ",
"                                        ",
"                                        ",
"                                        ",
"                                        "};
```

icons.c

The file icons.c contains the functions needed to create and manipulate a single icon that represents a directory or a file. Each icon should have an image that indicates the type of the entry, and should also display the icon's name. The user should be able to click on the icon and perform some action, so the icon needs to have a callback for button clicks. There is no single Motif widget that fits this need, in the current version of Motif (Motif 1.2.3, as this book goes to press). However, it is easy to construct such an icon using an XmRowColumn widget that contains a button and a label. The XmPush-Button widget can be configured so that its shadows do not appear and it does not "push" when the user clicks on it, so each collection appears to be a single labeled icon.

The file icon.c also contains a callback function to be invoked when the user clicks or double click on an icon. This function, `SelectCallback()`, calls an external function to record the widget specified in the callback as the currently "selected" widget. The call data structure supported by the XmPush-Button widget also supports double-clicks by indicating the number of mouse button clicks in a `click_count` member of the structure. If the user double clicks on an icon, `SelectCallback()` calls another external function, `OpenSelected()` to browse the item directly.

```
/************************************************************
 * icons.c: Create an icon to represent a file or directory
 ************************************************************/
#include <Xm/Xm.h>
#include <Xm/RowColumn.h>
#include <Xm/Label.h>
#include <Xm/PushB.h>
#include <X11/xpm.h>
#include "icons.h"
#include "globals.h"

extern void SetSelectedWidget ( Widget );
extern void OpenSelected ( void );

static void SelectCallback ( Widget    w,
                             XtPointer clientData,
                             XtPointer callData)
{
    XmPushButtonCallbackStruct *cbs =
                 ( XmPushButtonCallbackStruct * ) callData;

```

```
    /*
     * Always register this icon as the current selected widget.
     */

     SetSelectedWidget ( w );

    /*
     * Open on a double-click
     */

     if ( cbs->click_count > 1 )
         OpenSelected();
}
```

The function `CreateIcon()` creates the XmRowColumn, XmPushButton, and XmLabel widgets used to display a labeled icon. This function creates an Xpm pixmap for each entry, based on the given type. The XmRowColumn widget is returned to the caller.

```
Widget CreateIcon ( char     *name,
                    Widget    parent,
                    FileType type )
{
    Widget          icon, label;
    int             status;
    Pixmap          pix, mask;
    XpmAttributes   attributes;
    XpmColorSymbol  symbols[5];
    Display        *dpy = XtDisplay(parent);
    Pixel           bg;

   /*
    * Create the widgets that make up the icon.
    */

    Widget base = XtVaCreateWidget ( name,
                          xmRowColumnWidgetClass, parent,
                          XmNorientation,    XmVERTICAL,
                          XmNentryAlignment, XmALIGNMENT_CENTER,
                          NULL );

    icon = XtVaCreateManagedWidget ( name,
                                     xmPushButtonWidgetClass,
                                     base,
                                     XmNlabelType, XmPIXMAP,
                                     XmNshadowThickness, 0,
                                     XmNfillOnArm, FALSE,
                                     NULL );
```

```
    XtAddCallback ( icon, XmNactivateCallback,
                    SelectCallback, NULL );

    label = XtCreateManagedWidget ( "label",
                                    xmLabelWidgetClass,
                                    base, NULL, 0 );

   /*
    * Retrieve the depth, colormap, and background used by
    * the icon widget and store the results in the
    * corresponding field of an XpmAttributes structure.
    */

    XtVaGetValues ( icon,
                    XmNdepth,      &attributes.depth,
                    XmNcolormap,   &attributes.colormap,
                    XmNbackground, &bg,
                    NULL );

    symbols[0].name  = "background";
    symbols[0].value = NULL;
    symbols[0].pixel = bg;

    attributes.visual = DefaultVisual ( dpy,
                                        DefaultScreen ( dpy ) );

    attributes.valuemask =  XpmColorSymbols | XpmDepth |
                            XpmColormap | XpmVisual;

    attributes.colorsymbols = symbols;

    attributes.numsymbols   = 1;

   /*
    * Create the pixmap
    */

    status = XpmCreatePixmapFromData ( dpy,
                                       DefaultRootWindow ( dpy ),
                                       type == REGULAR_FILE ?
                                               fileIcon : dirIcon,
                                       &pix, NULL, &attributes );



   /*
    * If the pixmap was created successfully, set the
    * button's  labelPixmap resource.
    */

```

```
    if ( status == XpmSuccess )
        XtVaSetValues ( icon,
                        XmNlabelType,   XmPIXMAP,
                        XmNlabelPixmap, pix,
                        NULL );

    return ( base );
}
```

select.c

The file select.c maintains the currently selected icon. A static variable, `selectedWidget`, indicates an icon. The icon is not accessed directly by the rest of the program, but can be set or retrieved by two convenience functions, `SetSelectedWidget()` and `GetSelectedWidget()`.

```
/**********************************************************
 * select.c: Functions for manging the selected icon
 **********************************************************/
#include <Xm/Xm.h>
#include "globals.h"

extern void LaunchEditor ( Display *dpy, char *file );
extern void LaunchNewBrowser ( Display *dpy, char *file );

static Widget selectedWidget = NULL;

/*
 * Access functions
 */

void SetSelectedWidget ( Widget w )
{
    selectedWidget = w;
}

Widget GetSelectWidget()
{
    return ( selectedWidget );
}
```

The function `OpenSelected()` retrieves the name of the selected widget, and determines the type of the file represented by the widget. Depending on the icon's type, `OpenSelected()` calls `LanchNewBrowser()` or `Launch-NewEditor()` to "Open" the selected item.

```
void OpenSelected()
{
    if ( selectedWidget )
    {
        Widget   parent = XtParent ( selectedWidget );
        Display *dpy = XtDisplay ( parent );
        XmString label;
        char    *text;

       /*
        * Get the label of the selected widget.
        */

        XtVaGetValues ( selectedWidget,
                        XmNlabelString, &label,
                        NULL );
       /*
        * Get the text of the compound string.
        */

        XmStringGetLtoR ( label,
                          XmFONTLIST_DEFAULT_TAG,
                          &text );
       /*
        * Handle the file or directory depending on type.
        */

        if ( GetType ( text ) == DIRECTORY )
            LaunchNewBrowser ( dpy, text );
        else
            LaunchEditor ( dpy, text );

        XtFree ( text );
    }
}
```

launch.c

The file launch.c contains functions for starting new subprocesses to execute an editor to view a file, or to launch a new version of `dirview` to browse a directory.

```
/*********************************************
 * launch.c: launch subprocesses to view a
 *           file or directory
 *********************************************/
#include <stdlib.h>
#include <unistd.h>
```

```
#include <Xm/Xm.h>

void LaunchEditor ( Display *dpy, char *file )
{
    /*
     * Find out what editor the user wants to use.
     */

    char *editor = getenv ( "EDITOR" );

    if ( fork() == 0 ) /* If in the child */
    {
        char *args[3];

       /*
        * Overlay the child process with the editor process
        * before exiting the current process.
        */

        args[0] = editor;
        args[1] = file;
        args[2] = NULL;

        close ( ConnectionNumber ( dpy ) );
        execvp ( editor, args );
        exit ( -1 );
    }
}

void LaunchNewBrowser ( Display *dpy, char *file )
{
    if ( fork() == 0 ) /* If in the child */
    {
        char *args[3];

       /*
        * Overlay the child process with a new dirview
        * process before exiting the current process.
        */

        args[0] = "dirview";
        args[1] = file;
        args[2] = NULL;

        close ( ConnectionNumber ( dpy ) );
        execvp ( "dirview", args );
        exit ( -1 );
    }
}
```

12.2 Performance Goals

Before we begin to measure and evaluate the `dirview` programs' performance, we should set some performance goals. Although this program is fairly simple, there are several distinct operations that should have adequate response time. We can separate the basic category of start-up time, into several steps.

First, the window should appear on the screen as quickly as possible. The second goal involves the time before the user can interact with the program. Ideally, the program would be ready to be used as soon as the window appears. However, users might tolerate a small delay between the time the window appears and the time the icons in the window are displayed and ready for interaction. It seems reasonable to try to display a window in 0.3 second or less, and for any icons the user can see to be visible at that point. The program should also be ready to interact with the user at this point, although it may not be necessary for all icons to be displayed initially. Icons that fit into the visible area of the window should be displayed immediately. The program might be able to construct others in the background. However, the browser should be completely finished in under one second to allow the user to browse files or directories.

There are also several operations that fall under the category of runtime response. Of course, menus should pop up immediately, and we should be able to scroll about the browser window with no lag in response time. In addition, a user should be able to browse to a new directory in no more than the time required to launch a new browser. Browsing a file should require even less time.

Figure 12.2 summarizes these goals and proposes specific numbers.

Operation	Goal
Window visible	0.3
Icons visible	0.3
Ready for interaction	0.3-1.0
Browse file	0.3
Browse directory	0.3-1.0
Scroll to new location	~0

Figure 12.2 Performance goals for `dirview`.

It is somewhat difficult to know how realistic the goals shown in Figure 12.2 really are because there are many variables that can affect performance. For example, different directories contain different numbers of files, and the `dirview` program is likely to take longer to browse a large directory than a small one. When making measurements in the following sections, it would be useful to have a range of realistic directory sizes to measure. As an example of a small directory, we can choose the directory that contains the `dirview` program itself. This directory contains 16 files, 10 source or text files and 6 binary files. As a medium sized directory, we can use the Xt source directory, which contains 138 files, of which 50 are binary files. The Xlib source directory is an example of a large directory. It has 783 files, including 369 binary files.

When setting performance goals for a file and directory browser, it is also useful to consider other ways a user can accomplish the similar tasks. For example, if we consider only the ability to display the contents of a directory, we could compare the performance of `dirview` to the performance of `ls`. Let's see what we are up against, by timing `ls` in each of these directories. Figure 12.3 shows the time required to display the contents of a directory using `ls`.

```
% cd dirview; time ls

real    0m0.08s
user    0m0.00s
sys     0m0.03s

% cd /usr/src/x/mit/lib/Xt; time ls
real    0m0.06s
user    0m0.01s
sys     0m0.03s

% cd /usr/src/x/mit/lib/X; time ls

real    0m0.27s
user    0m0.07s
sys     0m0.09s
```

Figure 12.3 Time required to run `ls` in various directories.

If we consider only the relative time, it will clearly be difficult to match the performance of `ls`. However, a graphical directory browser has other advantages, such as the ability to select a file or directory with the mouse, for further exploration. Ideally, an interactive directory browser allows a user to navigate through the file system easily, while `ls` simply displays the contents of a directory.

12.3 Measuring Initial Performance

With some goals established, and keeping in mind the challenge offered by the performance of `ls`, we can begin to measure the performance characteristics of the `dirview` program. Figure 12.4 shows the times reported by `ReportTime()` when the program is started in the dirview directory. The initialization in the main part of the program takes 0.12 second, creating the icons takes 0.47 second, and the program requires an additional 0.18 seconds before the window appears on the screen. So, the program requires a total of 0.77 seconds to display a small directory. While this performance is not too bad, it is far slower than `ls`, and slower than our goal.

```
% dirview
Starting:
Starting Browser:
   Elapsed Time = 0.120
   CPU Time     = 0.040
   System Time  = 0.040
Icons Created:
   Elapsed Time = 0.470
   CPU Time     = 0.290
   System Time  = 0.050
Up:
   Elapsed Time = 0.180
   CPU Time     = 0.070
   System Time  = 0.020
```

Figure 12.4 Performance of `dirview` displaying the dirview directory.

We also need to consider `dirview`'s performance in larger directories. Figure 12.5 shows the results of using `dirview` to display the files in the Xt source directory. With this larger directory, the time required to create the icons has a definite effect on the program's start-up time. The program requires a total of 3.67 seconds to start-up, of which over 3 seconds is spent creating icons. Three seconds is a long enough time that a user might be annoyed by the start-up time of this program, so it appears we may have some work to do.

```
% dirview
Starting:
Starting Browser:
   Elapsed Time = 0.130
   CPU Time     = 0.050
   System Time  = 0.040
Icons Created:
   Elapsed Time = 3.040
   CPU Time     = 1.980
   System Time  = 0.260
Up:
   Elapsed Time = 0.500
   CPU Time     = 0.250
   System Time  = 0.040
```

Figure 12.5 Performance of `dirview` displaying the Xt directory.

Measuring dirview's performance when browsing the Xlib directory, shows the seriousness of the performance problem. When used to browse the Xlib source directory, `dirview` requires 17.23 seconds to display the initial window. Few users would wait 17 seconds to see the contents of a directory. This is especially true since we know that `ls` can display the files in this directory in 0.27 seconds. A browser that requires 17 seconds to start-up will simply not be used.

```
% dirview
Starting:
Starting Browser:
   Elapsed Time = 0.130
   CPU Time     = 0.040
   System Time  = 0.040
Icons Created:
   Elapsed Time = 14.150
   CPU Time     = 8.590
   System Time  = 1.390
Up:
   Elapsed Time = 2.950
   CPU Time     = 1.300
   System Time  = 0.150
```

Figure 12.6 Performance of `dirview` displaying the Xlib directory.

Figure 12.7 shows how the times measured for this program compare to the goals established earlier. Browsing to a new directory requires launching a new browser, which takes the same times as the start-up time already measured. However, browsing a file produces far better performance: a file can be displayed in an editor almost immediately.

The one performance characteristic that is difficult to measure is the time required to scroll to a new location. Subjectively, `dirview` handles scrolling quite well when used to display a small directory. However, even with a directory the size of Xt, the interactive feel is noticeably slow. When browsing Xlib, the scrolling performance is extremely jerky, with easily noticeable delays.

Operation	Goal		Rev. 1
Window visible	0.3	dirview	0.77
		Xt	3.67
		Xlib	17.23
Icons visible	0.3	dirview	0.77
		Xt	3.67
		Xlib	17.23
Ready for interaction	0.3-1.0	dirview	0.77
		Xt	3.67
		Xlib	17.23
Com-pletely Ready	0.3-1.0	dirview	0.77
		Xt	3.67
		Xlib	17.23
Browse file	0.3		< 0.30
Browse directory	0.3-1.0	dirview	0.77
		Xt	3.67
		Xlib	17.23
Scroll to new location	~0	dirview	~0
		Xt	slow
		Xlib	jerky

Figure 12.7 Comparison of `dirview` and original goals.

To get some idea of how we might proceed, it is useful to gather some more data about `dirview`'s behavior. For example, `xmond` should provide some interesting information about the number of requests and events involved in displaying this program. Figure 12.8 summarizes the most interesting requests made by `dirview` for each of the directories used as a test case. A few numbers stand out, in particular. Notice that when browsing the Xlib directory, the program creates 2373 windows and 791 pixmaps. It also allocates a color 2362 times. Most of these requests seem to be directly related to the number of files in the directory being displayed.

Request	**# of Requests**		
	dirview	**Xt**	**Xlib**
CreateWindow	72	438	2373
MapWindow	5	5	5
MapSubwindows	24	146	791
ConfigureWindow	3	3	3
GetGeometry	18	140	785
CreatePixmap	24	146	791
CreateGC	33	155	800
FreeGC	19	141	786
ClearArea	2	2	2
CopyArea	8	8	8
PolySegment	18	18	18
PolyFillRectangle	24	24	24
PutImage	20	142	787
AllocColor	61	427	2362

Figure 12.8 Requests made by `dirview`.

The events generated by this program are less interesting. There are a few `Expose` events, some `ConfigureNotify` events, and so on. The only event that seems to indicate any potential performance problem is the `MapNotify` event. For the small directory, `dirview` receives 49 `MapNotify` events. For the Xt directory, this number jumps to 293, while for the Xlib directory, this number is 1583. This seems to correspond to the increased number of windows in each case.

It might also be interesting to see how much geometry management is involved in displaying the `dirview` window. We can link the program with the XtGeo library and use `grep` and `wc` to get a measure of how many geometry requests are made, how many times a parent configures a child, and how many `change_managed` requests are made. Figure 12.9 summarizes this information for each of the directories. Again, the numbers are related to the number of files displayed in the browser. While these numbers are not enormous, 1581 geometry requests is a bit high, for example, and could consume a fair amount of CPU time.

Action	dirview	Xt	Xlib
being configured	147	747	3973
geometry request	51	291	1581
change managed	30	150	795

Figure 12.9 Summary of geometry management reported by XtGeo.

Because this program creates so many widgets, it may be interesting to look at the size of the program, as well. Using `ps` to measure the total and resident size shows that `dirview` uses 1109 pages (4,542,464 bytes) when browsing its own directory. Of these, 509 pages (2,084,864 bytes) are resident after the program starts up. When browsing the Xt directory, the size grows to 1173 pages (4,804,608 bytes) total and 564 pages (2,310,144 bytes) resident. Browsing the Xlib directory causes the program to grow to 1483 pages (6,074,368 bytes), of which 882 pages (3,612,672 bytes) are resident. Clearly, this program can use a lot of memory, which could also be the source of performance problems on some systems. As with the other measurements, the size of the program seems to be directly related to the number of files displayed.

12.4 Version Two

Given the information in the previous section, let's see what can be done to improve the performance of this program. One of the first things we might do is to try to display the window before the icons are created. The window is being created quite quickly in all cases, and it seems to be only the number of icons that slows down the start-up. If we can display the window quickly, and perhaps display a busy cursor while the icons are being created, the user's perception of the start-up time may be improved.

The easiest way to create the icons after the window becomes visible is to create the icons in a work procedure. A new function in the file browser.c can be used to create the icons. This function, `ReadDirWorkProc()`, reads each entry in the directory and creates an appropriate icon for each item. `ReadDirWorkProc()` also calls a new function, `DisplayBusyCursor()`, which displays and updates an animated busy cursor. The busy cursor is updated for every fifty files or directories processed. Once all files have been read, the work procedure manages the parent widget, removes the busy cursor, and returns `TRUE` to tell Xt not to call the work procedure again.

First, several declarations must be added to the top of the file browser.c:

```
extern void DisplayBusyCursor ( Widget w);
extern void HideBusyCursor( Widget w);
static char *currentDirectory = NULL;
static DIR *fd;
```

Then, the new function, `ReadDirWorkProc()` can be added to browser.c, as follows:

```
Boolean ReadDirWorkProc ( XtPointer clientData )
{
    struct dirent *entry;
    Widget          icon;
    Widget          parent = ( Widget ) clientData;
    static int      count = 0;

    ReportTime ( "Creating Icons", TRUE );

   /*
    * Display an initial busy cursor while the
    * directory is being read.
    */

    DisplayBusyCursor ( XtParent ( parent ) );

   /*
    * Read each item in the directory.
    */

    while ( ( entry = readdir ( fd ) ) != NULL )
    {
        count++;
       /*
        * Update the busy cursor for every 50 files.
        */
```

```
            if ( ( count % 50 ) == 0)
                DisplayBusyCursor ( XtParent ( parent ) );

            icon = CreateIcon ( entry->d_name,
                                parent,
                                GetType ( entry->d_name) );
            XtManageChild ( icon );
        }

        XtManageChild ( parent );
        HideBusyCursor ( XtParent ( parent ) );
        ReportTime ( "Icons Created", TRUE );
        return ( TRUE );
}
```

The function `CreateBrowser()` is much simpler now that the task of reading the directory has been moved to `ReadDirWorkProc()`. The new version just creates the main interface and registers the work procedure to display the icons after the application returns to the event loop.

```
Widget CreateBrowser ( Widget parent, char *dir )
{
    Widget mainWindow, rowColumn, commandPanel, menuBar;
    XtAppContext app = XtWidgetToApplicationContext ( parent );

    if ( !dir )
        dir = getcwd ( NULL, 300 );
    currentDirectory = XtNewString ( dir );

    if ( ( fd = opendir ( currentDirectory ) ) == NULL )
        return NULL;

    mainWindow = XtVaCreateWidget ( "browser",
                        xmMainWindowWidgetClass,   parent,
                        XmNscrollingPolicy,        XmAUTOMATIC,
                        XmNscrollBarDisplayPolicy, XmSTATIC,
                        XmNcommandWindowLocation,
                                    XmCOMMAND_ABOVE_WORKSPACE,
                        NULL );

    menuBar = CreateMenu ( mainWindow );

    rowColumn = XtVaCreateWidget ( "rowColumn",
                                    xmRowColumnWidgetClass,
                                    mainWindow,
                                    XmNpacking, XmPACK_COLUMN,
                                    XmNnumColumns, 8,
                                    NULL );
```

```
    XtAppAddWorkProc ( app, ReadDirWorkProc,
                       ( XtPointer ) rowColumn );

    commandPanel = XtVaCreateManagedWidget  ( "commandPanel",
                          xmRowColumnWidgetClass, mainWindow,
                          XmNorientation,     XmHORIZONTAL,
                          XmNentryAlignment, XmALIGNMENT_CENTER,
                          XmNpacking,         XmPACK_TIGHT,
                          NULL );

    currentDirLabel = XtVaCreateManagedWidget  ( "label1",
                          xmLabelWidgetClass, commandPanel,
                          XmNalignment, XmALIGNMENT_BEGINNING,
                          NULL );

    SetCurrentDirectory ( dir );

    XtVaSetValues ( mainWindow,
                    XmNcommandWindow, currentDirLabel,
                    XmNworkWindow,    rowColumn,
                    NULL );

    return ( mainWindow );
}
```

The file cursors.c implements the functions `DisplayBusyCursor()` and `HideBusyCursor()`. `DisplayBusyCursor()` creates a simple animated busy cursor, that consists of only two images. The images are defined using an X bitmap format, and then converted to pixmaps, which can then be used to create two cursors. The cursors are created the first time the function is called. After that, `DisplayBusyCursor()` just installs a cursor in the given window, alternating between the two patterns.

```
/****************************************
 * cursors.c: Create busy cursors
 ****************************************/
#include <Xm/Xm.h>

#define cursor_width 16
#define cursor_height 16

static unsigned char cursor_bits[] = {
   0xc0, 0x01, 0xf0, 0x07, 0xfc, 0x1f, 0xfc, 0x1f, 0xf2, 0x27,
   0xe2, 0x23, 0xc1, 0x41, 0x81, 0x40, 0xc1, 0x41, 0xe2, 0x23,
   0xf2, 0x27, 0xfc, 0x1f, 0xfc, 0x1f, 0xf0, 0x07, 0xc0, 0x01,
   0x00, 0x00 };

```

```
static unsigned char cursor2_bits[] = {
   0xc0, 0x01, 0x30, 0x06, 0x0c, 0x18, 0x0c, 0x18, 0x1e, 0x3c,
   0x3e, 0x3e, 0x7f, 0x7f, 0xff, 0x7f, 0x7f, 0x7f, 0x3e, 0x3e,
   0x1e, 0x3c, 0x0c, 0x18, 0x0c, 0x18, 0x30, 0x06, 0xc0, 0x01,
   0x00, 0x00 };

static Cursor cursors[2];
static int currentCursor = -1;

void DisplayBusyCursor ( Widget w )
{
    Display *dpy = XtDisplay ( w );

   /*
    * Create the busy cursors if this is the first call.
    */

    if ( currentCursor < 0 )
    {
        XColor   xcolors[2];
        Pixmap   pm;
        Screen  *scr    = DefaultScreenOfDisplay ( dpy );
        Colormap cmap   = DefaultColormapOfScreen ( scr );
        Window   root   = DefaultRootWindow ( dpy );

        xcolors[0].pixel= BlackPixel ( dpy, 0 );
        xcolors[1].pixel= WhitePixel ( dpy, 0 );

       /*
        * Retrieve XColor structures needed
        * by XCreatePixmapCursor
        */

        XQueryColors ( XtDisplay ( w ), cmap, xcolors, 2 );

       /*
        * Create each cursor by creating a pixmap
        * that can be converted to a cursor.
        */

        pm = XCreateBitmapFromData ( dpy, root,
                                     cursor_bits,
                                     cursor_width,
                                     cursor_height );

        cursors[0] = XCreatePixmapCursor ( dpy, pm, pm,
                                           &xcolors[0],
                                           &xcolors[1],
                                           0, 0 );
```

```
            XFreePixmap ( dpy, pm );

            pm = XCreateBitmapFromData ( dpy, root,
                                         cursor2_bits,
                                         cursor_width,
                                         cursor_height );

            cursors[1] = XCreatePixmapCursor ( dpy, pm, pm,
                                               &xcolors[0],
                                               &xcolors[1],
                                               0, 0 );
            XFreePixmap ( dpy, pm );

            currentCursor = 1;
        }

       /*
        * Once the cursors exist, just call XDefintCursor to
        * display a busy cursor. Toggle between the two cursors
        * to produce an animation effect.
        */

        currentCursor = !currentCursor;

        XDefineCursor ( dpy, XtWindow ( w ),
                        cursors[currentCursor] );
       /*
        * Unless we flush server requests, the cursor may not
        * take effect until we are no longer busy.
        */

        XFlush ( dpy );
}
```

HideBusyCursor() simply calls XUndefineCursor() to restore the default cursor in the given window.

```
void HideBusyCursor ( Widget w )
{
    XUndefineCursor ( XtDisplay ( w ), XtWindow ( w ) );
}
```

Once these changes have been incorporated, we can measure the performance of the dirview program once again. When browsing the dirview directory itself, the behavior of the program is much better. As shown in Figure 12.10, the window appears in 0.35 second, and briefly displays a busy cursor before the icons appear. The total time required to completely display all icons is approximately the same as before, but the window comes up much more quickly.

```
dirview
Starting:
Up:
   Elapsed Time = 0.340
   CPU Time     = 0.160
   System Time  = 0.070
Creating Icons:
   Elapsed Time = 0.000
   CPU Time     = 0.000
   System Time  = 0.000
Icons Created:
   Elapsed Time = 0.530
   CPU Time     = 0.330
   System Time  = 0.050
```

Figure 12.10 Browsing the `dirview` directory.

Browsing the Xt directory provides a better picture of how the new browser is meant to work. In spite of the larger number of files, the program's window appears on the screen as fast as when browsing a smaller directory. The busy icon is displayed, and goes through several stages of animation before the icons appear. The program displays all icons in a total of about 7 seconds, as shown in Figure 12.11. Notice that the icons take almost twice as long to appear as the original version. The longer time is somewhat made up for by the quick appearance of the window and the busy cursor.

```
% dirview
Starting:
Up:
   Elapsed Time = 0.340
   CPU Time     = 0.170
   System Time  = 0.080
Creating Icons:
   Elapsed Time = 0.000
   CPU Time     = 0.000
   System Time  = 0.000
Icons Created:
   Elapsed Time = 6.440
   CPU Time     = 4.850
   System Time  = 0.320
```

Figure 12.11 Browsing the Xt directory.

Unfortunately, when browsing a large directory, the appearance of the window and the busy cursor do not compensate for the much longer time involved. As shown in Figure 12.12, the time required to display the Xlib directory has increased to over a minute and a half, which is far too slow to be useful. Users might tolerate a delay of a few seconds for the advantages of a graphical interface, but a minute and a half cannot be justified when `ls` can display the contents of this directory in a fraction of a second.

```
% dirview
Starting:
Up:
   Elapsed Time = 0.350
   CPU Time     = 0.160
   System Time  = 0.070
Creating Icons:
   Elapsed Time = 0.010
   CPU Time     = 0.000
   System Time  = 0.000
Icons Created:
   Elapsed Time = 93.610
   CPU Time     = 79.460
   System Time  = 1.890
```

Figure 12.12 Browsing the Xlib directory.

The problem, of course, is that by moving the icon creation into a work procedure, we are now creating each icon as a child of a realized parent. Each icon is a widget, which is managed individually. In the case of the Xlib directory, over 700 XmRowColumn widgets are created and managed, one at a time.

Besides the slow start-up time, the consequences of this change can be seen by looking at the requests made by this program. For example, the original version made only three `ConfigureWindow` requests, because all geometry management was completed before windows were created. The new version creates dramatically more `ConfigureWindow` requests, from 95 when browsing the dirview directory, to over 58,000 when browsing the Xlib directory.

12.5 Version Three

The first attempt to improve the performance of the `dirview` program, described in the previous section, succeeds in displaying the window in a very short period of time, but at the cost of a much longer time to display all the icons. The problem occurs because the program manages a large number of widgets as children of a realized parent. In this section, we try to improve `dirview`'s performance by addressing both of the factors that contribute to this problem.

First, we can manage widgets in groups, which we know can provide a significant improvement in performance in some cases. In addition, this program provides an opportunity to introduce a slight variation on the usual approach. Instead of going for the maximum gain in performance, we will give up a small amount of performance in exchange for some improved user perception. The following version of `ReadDirWorkProc()` manages the first 50 widgets as a group, so they can be visible to the user as quickly as possible. Then, any remaining widgets are created and managed as a group.

In many situations there are two ways to improve a program's performance: you can do the task more efficiently, or you can do less work. In this program, we can do both. Besides managing the icons in a group, it is also possible to reduce the number of icons to be displayed. As originally written, this program displays *all* files in a directory. However, not all files are interesting to users. The times measured so far include the time needed to display the binary (.o) files in the various directories. Because these are seldom useful to see in a browser, we can filter these out, and reduce the number of icons that must be created. This change will also help the user by not cluttering the browser with unnecessary files.

To filter the files, we can write a simple function that returns `TRUE` if a file should be excluded from the browser. The following implementation simply excludes any file whose name ends with ".o". This function should be added to browser.c.

```
Boolean exclude ( const char *name )
{
   /*
    * Return TRUE if a file should not be displayed. This
    * simple test excludes files whose names end in ".o"
    */
```

```
    if ( strlen ( name ) > 2 &&
        !strcmp ( &name [ strlen ( name ) - 2 ], ".o" ) )
        return ( TRUE );
    return ( FALSE );
}
```

The new implementation of `ReadDirWorkProc()` reads fifty entries in the directory each time it is called. The first group of fifty (if there are more than fifty) are managed as a group, and the remaining icons are managed when all children have been created.

```
Boolean ReadDirWorkProc ( XtPointer clientData )
{
    struct dirent *entry;
    Widget      parent = ( Widget ) clientData;
    Widget      icon;
    WidgetList children;
    Cardinal   numChildren;
    static int count = 0;

    if ( !count++ )
      ReportTime ( "Creating Icons", TRUE );

    DisplayBusyCursor ( XtParent ( parent ) );

    while ( ( count++ % 50 ) != 0 &&
            ( entry = readdir ( fd ) ) != NULL )
    {
        if ( !exclude ( entry->d_name ) )
           icon = CreateIcon ( entry->d_name,
                               parent,
                               GetType ( entry->d_name ) );
    }

    if ( entry && count <= 51 )
    {
        XtVaGetValues ( parent,
                        XmNchildren, &children,
                        XmNnumChildren, &numChildren,
                        NULL );

        XtManageChildren ( children, numChildren );
        XtManageChild ( parent );
        ReportTime ( "First 50 Done", TRUE );
    }

    if ( entry )
      return ( FALSE );
```

```
    XtVaGetValues ( parent,
                    XmNchildren,    &children,
                    XmNnumChildren, &numChildren,
                    NULL );

    XtManageChildren ( children, numChildren );
    XtManageChild ( parent );
    HideBusyCursor ( XtParent ( parent ) );
    ReportTime ( "Icons Created", TRUE );
    return ( TRUE );
}
```

These changes produce a significant improvement in the program's performance. The dirview directory itself contains less than fifty files, so the time required to browse this directory is nearly the same as the original version. However, the total time required to browse the Xt directory is now slightly less than the original implementation, and much less than the previous version, as shown in Figure 12.13. Furthermore, the user is presented with a window containing the first fifty icons in about 1.6 seconds.

```
Starting:
Up:
   Elapsed Time = 0.340
   CPU Time     = 0.160
   System Time  = 0.070
First 50 Done:
   Elapsed Time = 1.300
   CPU Time     = 0.890
   System Time  = 0.100
Icons Created:
   Elapsed Time = 1.580
   CPU Time     = 1.020
   System Time  = 0.100
```

Figure 12.13 Time required to browse the Xt directory.

The latest version of `dirview` browses the Xlib directory in about 24 seconds, which is slightly slower than the original version, but much better than the version in Section 12.4. As shown in Figure 12.14, `dirview` presents an initial window with the first fifty icons in 1.6 seconds, even though this directory is quite large. Because the remaining icons are created in a work procedure, the user can interact with the browser and browse the initial files while the others are being created.

```
Starting:
Up:
    Elapsed Time = 0.340
    CPU Time     = 0.160
    System Time  = 0.080
First 50 Done:
    Elapsed Time = 1.330
    CPU Time     = 0.900
    System Time  = 0.100
Icons Created:
    Elapsed Time = 22.590
    CPU Time     = 19.000
    System Time  = 0.810
```

Figure 12.14 Time required to browse the Xlib directory.

Figure 12.15 summarizes the progress we have made so far toward the goals set at the beginning of this chapter.

Operation	Goal		Rev. 1	Rev. 2	Rev. 3
Window visible	0.3	dirview	0.77	0.35	0.34
		Xt	3.67	0.35	0.34
		Xlib	17.23	0.35	0.34
Icons visible	0.3	dirview	0.77	0.88	0.64
		Xt	3.67	6.85	1.64
		Xlib	17.23	93.61	1.64
Ready for interaction	0.3-1.0	dirview	0.77	0.88	0.64
		Xt	3.67	6.85	1.64
		Xlib	17.23	93.61	1.64
Com-pletely Ready	0.3-1.0	dirview	0.77	0.88	0.64
		Xt	3.67	6.85	3.22
		Xlib	17.23	93.61	24.26
Browse file	0.3		< 0.30	<0.30	< 0.30
Browse directory	0.3-1.0	dirview	0.77	0.88	0.64
		Xt	3.67	6.85	3.22
		Xlib	17.23	93.61	24.26
Scroll to new location	~0	dirview	~0	~0	~0
		Xt	slow	slow	slow
		Xlib	jerky	jerky	jerky

Figure 12.15 Performance summary of first three `dirview` versions.

The overall start-up time remains rather long, but the time required to display a window has been reduced significantly. Even for large directories, the most recent version of the program displays icons in less than 2 seconds, and supports limited user interaction. However, the total start-up time remains far too slow. In addition, the runtime behavior of this program is not entirely satisfactory. Even scrolling a moderate sized directory is noticeably slow. Scrolling in a large directory is very slow.

The latest version of `dirview` also reduces the number of requests made to the X server. As seen in Figure 12.16, the number of `ConfigureWindow` requests has been greatly reduced from the previous version. Other requests have been reduced as well, largely by reducing the number of icons created. For example, `dirview` now creates only 1266 windows when browsing Xlib, compared to 2373 in the original.

Request	**# of Requests**		
	dirview	**Xt**	**Xlib**
CreateWindow	54	288	1266
MapWindow	18	96	422
MapSubwindows	16	94	420
ConfigureWindow	7	33	87
GetGeometry	12	90	416
CreatePixmap	21	101	428
FreePixmap	3	5	6
CreateGC	29	107	433
FreeGC	15	93	419
ClearArea	13	13	32
CopyArea	12	20	24
PolySegment	24	32	34
PolyFillRectangle	25	27	28
PutImage	16	94	420
PolyText8	9	13	15
AllocColor	43	277	1255

Figure 12.16 Summary of requests made by the `dirview` program.

12.6 Version Four

All previous versions of dirview have several problems that can be seen by examining the requests in Figure 12.16. Xmond reports that the program creates a large number of windows for all but the smallest directories. In addition, the program creates a large number of pixmaps and graphics contexts, and also allocates large numbers of colors.

The reason for the windows is obvious: each icon requires three windows. An easy way to reduce the number of windows is to use gadgets for the button and label of each icon. Each XmRowColumn widget manages only two children, so this situation is not exactly like earlier examples that benefited from replacing widgets with gadgets. Nevertheless, it seems worthwhile to see if gadgets can help, given the large numbers of widgets created by this program.

The pixmaps and colors are another issue. The current design of CreateIcon() has a basic flaw. This function creates a new pixmap for each icon to be displayed. Although each icon requires new widgets, there is no reason to create a new pixmap for each icon. Creating a new pixmap each time adds server requests and uses server memory unnecessarily.

The following version of icons.c separates the process of creating an Xpm pixmap into a separate function. Each type of pixmap is created only once, and the file and directory icons are used over for each new icon.

```
/*******************************************
 * icons.c: Functions for creating icons
 *******************************************/
#include <Xm/Xm.h>
#include <Xm/RowColumn.h>
#include <Xm/LabelG.h>
#include <Xm/PushBG.h>
#include <X11/xpm.h>
#include "icons.h"
#include "globals.h"

extern void SetSelectedWidget ( Widget w );
extern void ShowSelected ( void );

static Pixmap filePixmap = NULL;
static Pixmap dirPixmap = NULL;

```

```
static void SelectCallback ( Widget    w,
                             XtPointer clientData,
                             XtPointer callData)
{
    XmPushButtonCallbackStruct *cbs =
                  ( XmPushButtonCallbackStruct * ) callData;

   /*
    * Always register this icon as the current selected widget.
    */

    SetSelectedWidget ( w );

   /*
    * Open on a double-click
    */

    if ( cbs->click_count > 1 )
        OpenSelected();
}

Pixmap CreatePixmap ( Widget w, FileType type )
{
    int              status;
    Pixmap           pix, mask;
    XpmAttributes    attributes;
    XpmColorSymbol symbols[5];
    Display         *dpy = XtDisplay ( w );
    Pixel            bg;

   /*
    * Retrieve the depth and colormap used by this widget
    * and store the results in the corresponding field
    * of an XpmAttributes structure.
    */

    XtVaGetValues ( w,
                    XmNdepth,    &attributes.depth,
                    XmNcolormap, &attributes.colormap,
                    XmNbackground, &bg,
                    NULL );

    symbols[0].name  = "background";
    symbols[0].value = NULL;
    symbols[0].pixel = bg;

   /*
    * Specify the visual and set the XpmAttributes mask.
    */
```

```

    attributes.visual = DefaultVisual ( dpy,
                                        DefaultScreen ( dpy ) );
    attributes.valuemask =  XpmColorSymbols | XpmDepth |
                            XpmColormap | XpmVisual;

    attributes.colorsymbols = symbols;
    attributes.numsymbols   = 1;

   /*
    * Create the pixmap
    */

    status = XpmCreatePixmapFromData ( dpy,
                        DefaultRootWindow ( dpy ),
                        type == REGULAR_FILE ? fileIcon : dirIcon,
                        &pix, NULL, &attributes );
    return ( pix );
}
```

The functions `GetFilePixmap()` and `GetDirPixmap()` are convenience functions that call `CreatePixmap()` with the required file type if the requested pixmap doesn't already exist. Once a particular pixmap exists, these functions just return the pixmap.

```
Pixmap GetFilePixmap ( Widget w )
{
    if ( !filePixmap )
        filePixmap = CreatePixmap ( w, REGULAR_FILE );

    return ( filePixmap );
}

Pixmap GetDirPixmap ( Widget w )
{
    if ( !dirPixmap )
        dirPixmap = CreatePixmap ( w, DIRECTORY );

    return ( dirPixmap );
}
```

`CreateIcon()` is much simpler now. The function simply creates the XmRowColumn widget used to contain the button and label gadgets. The pixmap returned by `GetFilePixmap()` or `GetDirPixmap()` are installed in the XmPushButton gadget, depending on the file type.

```
Widget CreateIcon ( char    *name,
                    Widget   parent,
                    FileType type )
{
    Widget icon, label;
    Pixmap pix;

   /*
    * Create a row column widget to hold a label and pixmap
    */

    Widget base = XtVaCreateWidget ( name,
                          xmRowColumnWidgetClass,  parent,
                          XmNorientation,    XmVERTICAL,
                          XmNentryAlignment, XmALIGNMENT_CENTER,
                          NULL );
   /*
    * Get a pixmap according to the file type and install it
    * in a pushbutton gadget.
    */

    if ( type == REGULAR_FILE )
        pix = GetFilePixmap ( base );
    else
        pix = GetDirPixmap ( base );

    icon = XtVaCreateManagedWidget ( name,
                                  xmPushButtonGadgetClass,
                                  base,
                                  XmNlabelType,        XmPIXMAP,
                                  XmNlabelPixmap,      pix,
                                  XmNfillOnArm,        FALSE,
                                  XmNshadowThickness, 0,
                                  NULL );

    XtAddCallback ( icon, XmNactivateCallback,
                    SelectCallback, NULL );

    label = XtCreateManagedWidget ( name, xmLabelGadgetClass,
                                 base, NULL, 0 );
    return ( base );
}
```

This change produces some improvement in performance. The most noticeable change can be seen in the requests made by the program. Figure 12.17 shows a summary of the most relevant requests made when browsing each directory. The number of `CreateWindow` requests has been reduced significantly, as have the number of graphics contexts created. The number of pixmaps required for this program has shrunk to about a dozen, and far fewer `AllocColor` requests have been made.

Request	# of Requests		
	dirview	Xt	Xlib
CreateWindow	30	108	434
MapWindow	18	96	422
MapSubwindows	16	94	420
ConfigureWindow	7	33	35
GetGeometry	12	90	416
CreatePixmap	11	13	14
FreePixmap	3	5	6
CreateGC	19	19	19
FreeGC	5	5	5
ClearArea	13	13	68
CopyArea	12	20	24
PolySegment	24	32	34
PolyFillRectangle	34	42	48
PutImage	6	6	6
PolyText8	9	13	15
AllocColor	12	12	12

Figure 12.17 Summary of requests made at start-up.

Unfortunately, the timed performance characteristics of the `dirview` program show less obvious improvement. The worst time, the start-up time for browsing Xlib has been reduced by almost three seconds, but remains unacceptably slow. Even when browsing the Xt directory, the time required before the application is ready for user input exceeds one second. However, the latest `dirview` implementation finally offers reasonable runtime performance. Scrolling is smooth and fast, even with a large collection of icons. We can attribute this to the change to using gadgets, because gadgets produce fewer `Expose` events when a new portion of a scrolling window is exposed.

Figure 12.18 summarizes the progress made in achieving the goals for this program.

Operation	Goal		Rev. 1	Rev. 2	Rev. 3	Rev 4
Window visible	0.3	dirview	0.77	0.35	0.34	0.34
		Xt	3.67	0.35	0.34	0.34
		Xlib	17.23	0.35	0.34	0.34
Icons visible	0.3	dirview	0.77	0.88	0.64	0.54
		Xt	3.67	6.85	1.64	1.23
		Xlib	17.23	93.61	1.64	1.23
Ready for interaction	0.3-1.0	dirview	0.77	0.88	0.64	0.54
		Xt	3.67	6.85	1.64	1.23
		Xlib	17.23	93.61	1.64	1.23
Completely Ready	0.3-1.0	dirview	0.77	0.88	0.64	0.54
		Xt	3.67	6.85	3.22	2.24
		Xlib	17.23	93.61	24.26	21.85
Browse file	0.3		< 0.30	<0.30	< 0.30	< 0.30
Browse directory	0.3-1.0	dirview	0.77	0.88	0.64	0.54
		Xt	3.67	6.85	3.22	2.24
		Xlib	17.23	93.61	24.26	21.85
Scroll to new location	~0	dirview	~0	~0	~0	~0
		Xt	slow	slow	slow	~0
		Xlib	jerky	jerky	jerky	~0

Figure 12.18 Progress toward performance goals.

12.7 Version Five

Figure 12.18 shows that we are making slow but steady progress toward the goals set for this program. The most promising change so far was to switch to using gadgets, because this change improved the run-time performance of the program. We have also had success at improving the time required to display an initial interface with a small set of icons, while continuing to perform additional work in the background.

This section explores each of these ideas further, in an attempt to get more performance out of this program. The first change that seems worth trying is to replace each multi-widget composite icon with a single gadget. The main reason for using the XmRowColumn widget to contain a label and a button is that Motif does not currently include a widget that displays both text and a pixmap at the same time. The approach used so far had the advantage of being straight-forward and easy to implement. However, just because Motif does not provide a ready-made component does not mean that such a component cannot be implemented. There are several other approaches that can be taken. For example, this section examines an implementation of `CreateIcon()` that uses pixmaps and drawing functions to render an icon that can be displayed in a single gadget. The required steps are relatively simple, and the entire operation requires about 100 lines of code. The basic idea is to create a pixmap large enough to hold both a label and the icon pixmap. The icon pixmap is copied to the larger pixmap, and the label is drawn into the pixmap below the icon image. The large pixmap is then installed as the `XmNlabelPixmap` for a button gadget.

This change involves only the function `CreateIcon()`, in the file icons.c. This implementation requires a new graphics context, `inverseGC`, which is used to clear the background of a pixmap. The following declarations must be added to the top of the file:

```
static  GC gc = NULL;
static  GC inverseGc = NULL;
static int depth = 0;
```

Then, `CreateIcon()` can be written like this:

```
Widget CreateIcon ( char     *name,
                    Widget   parent,
                    FileType type )
{
    Widget          icon;
    Pixmap          pix;
    XmString        label;
    XmFontList      fontlist;
    XFontStruct    *fs;
    XmFontType      fontType;
    Dimension       width, height;
    static XGCValues values;
    int             junk;
    Display        *display = XtDisplay ( parent );
    unsigned char   alignment;
    Pixmap          labelPixmap;
    int             totalWidth, totalHeight
```

```
    /*
     * Get the pixmap for the file type.
     */

     if ( type == REGULAR_FILE )
         pix = GetFilePixmap ( parent );
     else
         pix = GetDirPixmap ( parent );

     icon = XtVaCreateWidget ( name,
                               xmPushButtonGadgetClass,
                               parent,
                               XmNlabelType,       XmPIXMAP,
                               XmNfillOnArm,       FALSE,
                               XmNshadowThickness, 0,
                               NULL );

     XtAddCallback ( icon, XmNactivateCallback,
                     SelectCallback, NULL );

     if ( !gc )
     {
         /*
          * Create two GCs, one to draw the text and copy
          * the pixmaps and another that can be used to erase
          * a pixmap by filling it with the background
          * color of the label widget. Because the normal GC
          * is used by XmStringDraw, which modifies the font
          * attribute of the GC, allocate this GC using
          * XtAllocateGC() and specify GCFont as modifiable.
          */

         XtVaGetValues ( parent,
                         XmNdepth,       &depth,
                         XmNforeground,  &values.foreground,
                         XmNbackground,  &values.background,
                         NULL );

         gc = XtAllocateGC ( parent, depth,
                             GCForeground | GCBackground,
                             &values, GCFont, 0 );

         values.foreground = values.background;

         inverseGc = XtGetGC ( parent,
                               GCForeground | GCBackground,
                               &values );
     }

```

```
    /*
     * Get information needed to draw the label.
     */

     XtVaGetValues ( icon,
                     XmNlabelString, &label,
                     XmNfontList,    &fontlist,
                     XmNalignment,   &alignment,
                     NULL );

     fs = ( XFontStruct* ) XmFontListEntryGetFont ( fontlist,
                                                    &fontType );

     XSetFont ( XtDisplay ( parent ), gc, fs->fid );

    /*
     * Compute the size of the label string and the pixmap
     */

     XmStringExtent ( fontlist, label, &width, &height );
     totalWidth = 48 > width ? 48 : width;
     totalHeight = 48 + height + 10;

    /*
     * Create the final pixmap using the combined size and
     * fill the pixmap with the background color of the widget
     */

     labelPixmap = XCreatePixmap ( display,
                     RootWindowOfScreen ( XtScreen ( parent ) ),
                     totalWidth, totalHeight, depth );

     XFillRectangle ( display, labelPixmap,
                      inverseGc, 0, 0,
                      totalWidth, totalHeight );

    /*
     * Copy the Xpm-created pixmap into the larger pixmap and
     * then draw the string below the pixmap.
     */

     XCopyArea ( display, pix, labelPixmap,
                 gc, 0, 0, 48, 48,
                ( totalWidth - 48 ) / 2,
                 0 );

     XmStringDraw ( display, labelPixmap, fontlist, label,
                    gc, 0, 48 + 10, totalWidth,
                    alignment, XmSTRING_DIRECTION_L_TO_R, NULL );
```

```
        /*
         * Install the final pixmap in the widget.
         */

         XtVaSetValues ( icon, XmNlabelPixmap, labelPixmap, NULL );

        /*
         * Free the string retrieved from the label widget.
         */

      XmStringFree ( label );

      return ( icon );
}
```

The other area in which we have had some success is using "sleight of hand" techniques for making the window appear on the screen more quickly. The following implementation of `ReadDirWorkProc()` carries this approach a bit further. We know from Chapter 9 that creating and managing a large collection of widgets can be done more quickly if the parent is unmanaged. Therefore, we might gain some time if the XmRowColumn widget that manages the icons in `dirview` could be left unmanaged while the icons are being created. However, this would destroy the effect of managing the initial group of icons to allow the user to see some files quickly.

Fortunately, there is an interesting technique that allows us to have both of these features. The basic approach is this: start with the XmRowColumn widget unmanaged. Then, create the initial fifty icons, manage them, and manage the parent. Next, call `XSetWindowBackgroundPixmap()` to set the background pixmap of the XmRowColumn widget's parent to `None`, and unmanage the XmRowColumn widget. This step effectively leaves a frozen snapshot of the XmRowColumn widget and its children visible on the screen, even though the widgets are no longer present.

Once the XmRowColumn widget is unmanaged, we can proceed as quickly as possible to create the remaining icons. Once all icons have been created, they can be managed as a group, the XmRowColumn widget can be managed, and its parent's background pixmap can be set to `ParentRelative` to restore the window to its original state.

The following version of `ReadDirWorkProc()` implements this approach.

```
Boolean ReadDirWorkProc ( XtPointer clientData )
{
    struct dirent *entry = NULL;
    Widget         parent = ( Widget ) clientData;
    Display       *dpy = XtDisplay ( parent );
    Widget         icon;
    WidgetList     children;
    Cardinal       numChildren;
    static int     count = 0;

    if ( !count++ )
        ReportTime ( "Creating Icons", TRUE );

    DisplayBusyCursor ( XtParent ( parent )  );

    while ( ( count++ % 50 ) != 0 &&
            ( entry = readdir ( fd ) ) != NULL )
    {
        if ( !exclude ( entry->d_name ) )
            icon = CreateIcon ( entry->d_name,
                                parent,
                                GetType ( entry->d_name ) );
    }
    if ( entry && count <= 51 )
    {
         XtVaGetValues ( parent,
                         XmNchildren, &children,
                         XmNnumChildren, &numChildren,
                         NULL );

         XtManageChildren ( children, numChildren );
         XtManageChild ( parent );

         XmUpdateDisplay ( parent );

         XSetWindowBackgroundPixmap ( dpy,
                             XtWindow ( XtParent ( parent ) ),
                             None );

         XtUnmanageChild ( parent );
         ReportTime ( "First 50 Done", TRUE );
    }

    if ( entry )
        return ( FALSE );

    XtVaGetValues ( parent,  XmNchildren,    &children,
                             XmNnumChildren, &numChildren,
                             NULL );
```

```
    XtManageChildren ( children, numChildren );
    XtManageChild ( parent );

    XSetWindowBackgroundPixmap ( dpy,
                                 XtWindow ( XtParent ( parent ) ),
                                 ParentRelative );

    HideBusyCursor ( XtParent ( parent ) );
    ReportTime ("Icons Created", TRUE );
    closedir ( fd );
    return ( TRUE );
}
```

With these changes, the performance of `dirview` has improved dramatically. When browsing a small directory like the dirview source directory, the start-up time has improved somewhat, from the original 0.77 second to 0.59 second, as shown in Figure 12.19.

```
Starting:
Up:
   Elapsed Time = 0.340
   CPU Time     = 0.160
   System Time  = 0.070
Icons Created:
   Elapsed Time = 0.250
   CPU Time     = 0.150
   System Time  = 0.020
```

Figure 12.19 Measured performance of `dirview` with gadgets.

However, the more significant gains can be seen when browsing larger directories. With gadgets, `dirview` can display the entire Xt directory in 1.25 seconds, down from 3.67 in the original version. More significantly, the program can now display the entire Xlib directory in 3.63 seconds, down from 17 seconds in the original. Most of this gain can be attributed to the change to using gadgets. The trick involving the window pixmap also contributes to the user's perception of smoothness. As shown in Figure 12.20 and Figure 12.21, `dirview` starts very quickly, and displays a window of icons in the same period of time, regardless of the size of the directory.

```
Starting:
Up:
    Elapsed Time = 0.380
    CPU Time     = 0.180
    System Time  = 0.070
First 50 Done:
    Elapsed Time = 0.470
    CPU Time     = 0.290
    System Time  = 0.040
Icons Created:
    Elapsed Time = 0.440
    CPU Time     = 0.250
    System Time  = 0.030
```

Figure 12.20 Browsing Xt with gadget version of `dirview`.

```
Starting:
Up:
    Elapsed Time = 0.430
    CPU Time     = 0.160
    System Time  = 0.080
First 50 Done:
    Elapsed Time = 0.420
    CPU Time     = 0.230
    System Time  = 0.040
Icons Created:
    Elapsed Time = 2.820
    CPU Time     = 1.640
    System Time  = 0.360
```

Figure 12.21 Browsing Xlib with gadget version of `dirview`.

Subjectively, the run time response of this version of the program is better. Scrolling is smooth, even for large directories. Setting the window background pixmap to `None` minimizes visible changes in the window as the program is reading the directory. Launching a new directory browser is also a reasonable operation, now that the time required to start a browser has been reduced.

Figure 12.22 summarizes the performance characteristics of the latest `dirview` implementation.

Operation	Goal		Rev. 1	Rev. 2	Rev. 3	Rev 4	Rev 5
Window visible	0.3	dirview	0.77	0.35	0.34	0.34	0.34
		Xt	3.67	0.35	0.34	0.34	0.34
		Xlib	17.23	0.35	0.34	0.34	0.34
Icons visible	0.3	dirview	0.77	0.88	0.64	0.54	0.59
		Xt	3.67	6.85	1.64	1.23	0.81
		Xlib	17.23	93.61	1.64	1.23	0.81
Ready for interaction	0.3-1.0	dirview	0.77	0.88	0.64	0.54	0.59
		Xt	3.67	6.85	1.64	1.23	0.81
		Xlib	17.23	93.61	1.64	1.23	0.81
Com-pletely Ready	0.3-1.0	dirview	0.77	0.88	0.64	0.54	0.59
		Xt	3.67	6.85	3.22	2.24	1.25
		Xlib	17.23	93.61	24.26	21.85	3.63
Browse file	0.3		< 0.30	<0.30	< 0.30	< 0.30	< 0.30
Browse directory	0.3-1.0	dirview	0.77	0.88	0.64	0.54	0.59
		Xt	3.67	6.85	3.22	2.24	1.25
		Xlib	17.23	93.61	24.26	21.85	3.63
Scroll to new location	~0	dirview	~0	~0	~0	~0	~0
		Xt	slow	slow	slow	~0	~0
		Xlib	jerky	jerky	jerky	~0	~0

Figure 12.22 Summary of `dirview` performance vs. goals.

It is also interesting to examine the server traffic produced by this latest implementation. Switching from widgets to gadgets might substantially change the types of requests and events produced by this program, and we should make sure the changes are really an improvement before going on.

Figure 12.23 summarizes the most relevant requests made by `dirview` while browsing each of the test directories. As expected, the number of windows created has decreased. The remaining 18 windows are created by the basic interface of the program. However, some other requests have increased significantly. Unlike the previous version, this version once again creates a new pixmap for each individual icon, so the number of `CreatePixmap` requests has increased. Also notice the large number of `CopyArea` requests, which are needed to copy the icon pixmap to each individual pixmap.

Strictly from the perspective of server requests, it is clear that this implementation is a step backward. However, remember that elapsed time and user perception is more important than a few extra server requests. Nevertheless, the server traffic may warrant some further investigation.

Request	# of Requests		
	dirview	Xt	Xlib
CreateWindow	18	18	18
MapWindow	6	7	7
MapSubwindows	4	4	4
ConfigureWindow	7	1	1
GetGeometry	30	14	14
CreatePixmap	42	2	2
FreePixmap	4	107	389
CreateGC	21	8	8
ChangeGC	1	21	21
FreeGC	5	1	1
ClearArea	12	5	5
CopyArea	43	358	2050
PolySegment	26	125	407
PolyFillRectangle	65	58	58
PutImage	6	175	457
PolyText8	33	6	6
AllocColor	12	94	376

Figure 12.23 Partial list of requests made by gadget version of `dirview`.

12.8 Version Six

Although `dirview` now runs significantly faster, there are still some small problems with the program's performance. For larger directories, `dirview` still takes several seconds to display a browsable set of files. Also, the system is somewhat awkward to use when rapidly traversing directories. Each time a new directory is browsed, a new `dirview` process is launched. This takes time and requires the user to change focus to manipulate the new window.

Launching a new browser for each directory can also lead to some awkward situations. For example, if the user starts a browser in the dirview directory and browses "`..`" to access the parent directory, a new browser is launched. If the user then double clicks on the dirview icon in that browser, yet another dirview browser is created. Now there are two independent processes that display the dirview directory. If a user tries to use this program to navigate the file system, a large number of windows will be created. While not exactly a machine performance issue, this design issue clearly affects the user's ability to perform useful tasks.

One way to make this program more useful for navigating the file system is to maintain a single window, and to replace the contents of the window in-place when the user browses to a new directory. The user can explicitly launch multiple browsers, but within any one browser, the window is reused as the user navigates the file system. Besides being more manageable, this approach should also improve the time required to change to a new directory.

We only need to make a few small changes to implement this strategy. First, the function `SetCurrentDirectory()` needs to be modified to change the program's current working directory when a new directory is browsed. This allows the browser to continue to use the name of each file relative to the current directory.

```
void SetCurrentDirectory ( char *dir )
{
    char buf[300];

   /*
    * Change the program's sense of the working directory.
    * This allows the program to continue using relative
    * names for files and directories.
    */

    if ( dir )
        chdir ( dir );

   /*
    * The name of the currentDirectory is needed
    * when opening the directory to read entries. To eliminate
    * names like ../../././.., which could result from
    * browsing many directories, set the current directory
    * by calling getcwd().
    */

    if ( currentDirectory )
        XtFree ( currentDirectory );

    currentDirectory = getcwd ( NULL, 300 );

```

```
    /*
     * Display the current directory in the label
     */

    sprintf ( buf, "Current Directory: %s",
              currentDirectory );

    XtVaSetValues ( currentDirLabel,
                    XtVaTypedArg,
                    XmNlabelString,  XmRString,
                    buf, strlen ( buf ) + 1,
                    NULL );
}
```

Next, we need a new function in the file browser.c. This function, `BrowseDirectory()`, calls `SetCurrentDirectory()` to establish a new working directory. It then retrieves the list of icons from the XmRowColumn widget, and calls `XtDestroyWidget()` to remove each icon. Finally, `BrowseDirectory()` calls `XtAppAddWorkProc()` to register the function `ReadDirWorkProc()` so it will be called until the new icons are all displayed. The variable `count` is moved out of the function `ReadDirWorkProc()` and made global to this file. Setting this flag to zero allows the `ReadDirWorkProc()` to be reinitialized and to create icons for the new directory. `BrowseDirectory()` also needs access to the XmRowColumn widget that contains the icons. We can move that declaration out of `CreateBrowser()` and declare it as a global, static to the file browser.c

```
static int count = 0;
static Widget rowColumn = NULL;
```

Next, the function `BrowseDirectory()` can be written as follows:

```
void BrowseDirectory ( char *dir )
{
    WidgetList children;
    Cardinal   numChildren;
    int        i;
    XtAppContext app =
                 XtWidgetToApplicationContext ( rowColumn );

```

Start timing

```
     ReportTime ( "Browsing new directory", FALSE );

    if ( ( fd = opendir ( dir ) ) == NULL )
        return;

```

```
    SetCurrentDirectory ( ( char* ) dir );

   /*
    * Remove the row column from the screen for more speed.
    */

    XtUnmanageChild ( rowColumn );

   /*
    * Get the current list of children.
    */

    XtVaGetValues ( rowColumn,
                    XmNchildren,    &children,
                    XmNnumChildren, &numChildren,
                    NULL );
   /*
    * Destroy current list of children
    */

    for ( i = 0; i < numChildren; i++ )
        XtDestroyWidget ( children[i] );

   /*
    * Reset the work procedure by setting count
    * back to zero, and reinstall the work proc.
    */

    count = 0;

    XtAppAddWorkProc ( app,ReadDirWorkProc,
                       ( XtPointer ) rowColumn );
}
```

The last change is in the file select.c. The function `OpenSelected()` is modified to call `BrowseDirectory()` if the selected item represents a directory.

```
void OpenSelected()
{
    if ( selectedWidget )
    {
        XmString label;
        char     *text;
        Widget   parent = XtParent ( selectedWidget );
       /*
        * Get the name of the selected item.
        */
```

```

            XtVaGetValues ( selectedWidget, XmNlabelString,
                            &label, NULL );

            XmStringGetLtoR ( label,
                              XmFONTLIST_DEFAULT_TAG,
                              &text );

            if ( GetType ( text )  == DIRECTORY )
                BrowseDirectory ( text );
            else
                LaunchEditor ( XtDisplay ( parent ), text );

            XtFree ( text );
        }
}
```

With this change, browsing between directories is very fast and convenient. From a usability standpoint, `dirview` is much easier to use. Because the user can browse to a new directory without creating the main window, and without starting a new process, the program is much faster to use. For example, Figure 12.24 shows the elapsed time required to browse into the dirview directory using this new model. For testing purposes, we can start the program in a directory, and browse to the "." directory, so we always browse to a directory with a known number of files. As shown in Figure 12.24, browsing to the dirview directory requires only 0.17 second, which users should find quite satisfactory.

```
dirview
Starting:
Up:
   Elapsed Time = 0.420
   CPU Time     = 0.170
   System Time  = 0.080
Icons Created:
   Elapsed Time = 0.150
   CPU Time     = 0.090
   System Time  = 0.020
Browsing new directory:
Icons Created:
   Elapsed Time = 0.170
   CPU Time     = 0.110
   System Time  = 0.010
```

Figure 12.24 Browsing into dirview directory within same browser.

We should also see how this new approach works for larger directories. Figure 12.25 shows the elapsed times reported when browsing the "." icon from within the Xt directory.

```
Starting:
Up:
    Elapsed Time = 0.400
    CPU Time     = 0.180
    System Time  = 0.090
First 50 Done:
    Elapsed Time = 0.470
    CPU Time     = 0.290
    System Time  = 0.040
Icons Created:
    Elapsed Time = 0.450
    CPU Time     = 0.270
    System Time  = 0.050
Browsing new directory:
First 50 Done:
    Elapsed Time = 1.860
    CPU Time     = 1.520
    System Time  = 0.050
Icons Created:
    Elapsed Time = 0.430
    CPU Time     = 0.270
    System Time  = 0.030
```

Figure 12.25 Browsing into Xt directory within same browser.

Interestingly, `dirview`'s performance when browsing the Xt directory is less impressive. In fact, the program seems to take over 2 seconds to browse the directory in an existing window, which is longer than it takes to launch a new program.

There could be something wrong with the measurement, but it would be worthwhile to try a much larger directory to see if the same problem exists. Figure 12.26 shows the elapsed time reported when browsing the "." icon for the Xlib directory. We can see from this figure that the initial start-up time remains reasonable, but the time to re-browse the Xlib directory has increased to over one minute!

```
% dirview
Starting:
Up:
   Elapsed Time = 0.380
   CPU Time     = 0.170
   System Time  = 0.080
First 50 Done:
   Elapsed Time = 0.470
   CPU Time     = 0.270
   System Time  = 0.040
Icons Created:
   Elapsed Time = 3.570
   CPU Time     = 2.310
   System Time  = 0.390
Browsing new directory:
First 50 Done:
   Elapsed Time = 57.900
   CPU Time     = 53.790
   System Time  = 0.350
Icons Created:
   Elapsed Time = 4.080
   CPU Time     = 2.520
   System Time  = 0.390
```

Figure 12.26 Browsing into Xlib directory within same browser.

Clearly something has gone wrong with our "optimization". In an effort to understand the problem, we might run the program through `xmond` and examine the requests made when a directory is browsed from within `dirview`. Figure 12.27 shows the requests made by this program. Although many of the requests seem reasonable, an extraordinary number of `ClearArea` requests are being made. With over 165,000 requests, it is not surprising that the program takes a long time to execute.

Request	# of Requests
ChangeWindowAttributes	22
MapWindow	2
UnmapWindow	2
ConfigureWindow	125
GetGeometry	416
GetInputFocus	1
CreatePixmap	424
FreePixmap	8
CreateGC	2
FreeGC	2
ClearArea	165119
CopyArea	460
PolySegment	64
PolyFillRectangle	506
PolyText8	417

Figure 12.27 Requests made while browsing Xlib from an existing browser.

We could investigate further, using tools like the XtGeo library, or even a debugger (to see the callstacks associated with calls to `XClearArea()`), but with some thought, we can make a pretty good guess about the source of the problem because the last set of changes were fairly localized. The function `BrowseDirectory()` calls `XtDestroyWidget()` to destroy each gadget, one at a time. Because each gadget is unmanaged as it is destroyed, the effect is much the same as when each gadget is managed individually while the parent is realized. In addition to the geometry requests that result from unmanaging each icon, manager widgets must erase the area formerly occupied by a gadget when the gadget is no longer displayed.

If this is the source of the problem, we should be able to improve the performance by unmanaging all gadgets at once, before they are destroyed. The following implementation of `BrowseDirectory()` adds a call to `XtUnmanageChildren()` before the widgets are destroyed.

```
void BrowseDirectory ( char *dir )
{
    WidgetList children;
    Cardinal   numChildren;
    int        i;
    XtAppContext app =
                 XtWidgetToApplicationContext ( rowColumn );

    ReportTime ( "Browsing new directory", FALSE );
    currentDirectory = XtNewString ( dir );

    if ( ( fd = opendir ( dir ) ) == NULL )
        return;

    SetCurrentDirectory ( ( char* ) dir );

   /*
    * Remove the row column from the screen for more speed.
    */

    XtUnmanageChild ( rowColumn );

   /*
    * Get the current list of children.
    */

    XtVaGetValues ( rowColumn,
                    XmNchildren,    &children,
                    XmNnumChildren, &numChildren,
                    NULL );
   /*
    * Destroy current list of children after unmanaging
    */

    XtUnmanageChildren ( children, numChilden );

    for ( i = 0; i < numChildren; i++ )
        XtDestroyWidget ( children[i] );

   /*
    * Reset the work procedure by setting count
    * back to zero, and reinstall the work proc.
    */

    count = 0;

    XtAppAddWorkProc ( app,ReadDirWorkProc,
                       ( XtPointer ) rowColumn );
}
```

Figure 12.28 shows the results of this simple change. The program now requires only 4.68 seconds to browse the Xlib directory. This is not much less that the time required to browse this directory in a new `dirview` program, but that is to be expected because the time to create the icons dominates the start-up time for large directories.

```
Starting:
Up:
   Elapsed Time = 0.470
   CPU Time     = 0.160
   System Time  = 0.090
First 50 Done:
   Elapsed Time = 0.460
   CPU Time     = 0.280
   System Time  = 0.040
Icons Created:
   Elapsed Time = 4.170
   CPU Time     = 2.350
   System Time  = 0.310
Browsing new directory:
First 50 Done:
   Elapsed Time = 0.970
   CPU Time     = 0.750
   System Time  = 0.050
Icons Created:
   Elapsed Time = 3.710
   CPU Time     = 2.480
   System Time  = 0.360
```

Figure 12.28 Time to browse "." within Xlib directory.

The price we paid to move to gadgets was that the program once again creates a large number of pixmaps, one for each icon. This does not appear to be a problem for a single browser, but it is worthwhile looking at the impact the pixmaps might have when the user can quickly navigate through the file system in a single window. One quick test we might make is to look at the size of the X server as we browse to various directories.

Figure 12.29 shows the size of the X server, as reported by `ps`, after repeatedly browsing the "." icon in the Xlib directory. Each time we browse into this directory, the X server grows by about 205 pages, or well over 800K bytes!

```
% ps -elf | grep X
30 S   root 459 456 0 26 20 * 1673:817 8829e32c 19:48:59 ? 0:10 /usr/bin/X
% ps -elf | grep X
30 S   root 459 456 2 26 20 * 1878:1023 8829e32c 19:48:59 ? 0:10 /usr/bin/
% ps -elf | grep X
30 S   root 459 456 0 26 20 * 2101:1246 8829e32c 19:48:59 ?  0:11 /usr/bir
```

Figure 12.29 Size of X server after each browse into Xlib directory.

With some thought, it is easy to guess that the reason for the server growth is the pixmaps being created by the program. Although the widgets are destroyed in `BrowseDirectory()`, the pixmaps created for each gadget are not freed. Fortunately, this can be fixed fairly easily. The loop that destroys each gadget can be extended to retrieve the pixmap used by the gadget, and free it, before destroying the gadget. The required code segment would look like this:

```
for ( i = 0; i < numChildren; i++ )
{
    Pixmap pix;

    XtVaGetValues ( children[i], XmNlabelPixmap, &pix, NULL );
    XFreePixmap ( XtDisplay ( rowColumn), pix );
    XtDestroyWidget ( children[i] );
}
```

With this problem fixed, we can once again compare the performance of this implementation with the goals established at the beginning of this chapter. Figure 12.30 compares the performance of the latest implementation with the goals and the performance of the original implementation. It is clear that a lot of progress has been made. With the exception of the larger directories, the performance is quite good. Even with a large directory like Xlib, we have decreased the total start-up time from 17.63 seconds to 3.63 seconds, and the time required to browse a new directory after the program is running has decreased from 17.63 seconds to only 2.63. For smaller directories, the times are much faster.

Operation	Goal		Rev. 1	Rev 6
Window visible	0.3	dirview	0.77	0.34
		Xt	3.67	0.34
		Xlib	17.23	0.34
Icons visible	0.3	dirview	0.77	0.59
		Xt	3.67	0.81
		Xlib	17.23	0.81
Ready for interaction	0.3-1.0	dirview	0.77	0.59
		Xt	3.67	0.81
		Xlib	17.23	0.81
Com-pletely Ready	0.3-1.0	dirview	0.77	0.59
		Xt	3.67	1.25
		Xlib	17.23	3.63
Browse file	0.3		< 0.30	< 0.30
Browse directory	0.3-1.0	dirview	0.77	0.08
		Xt	3.67	0.56
		Xlib	17.23	2.63
Scroll to new location	~0	dirview	~0	~0
		Xt	slow	~0
		Xlib	jerky	~0

Figure 12.30 Performance of latest `dirview` compared to original.

12.9 Version Seven

Although the performance of the program at this point seems fairly reasonable, it still falls short of the goal. Fortunately, there are many other things that can be done to improve the performance even further. For example, it seems like a waste of time and resources to destroy gadgets and pixmaps, only to create new ones each time a directory is browsed. Perhaps it would be faster to reuse these gadgets in some way. We could simply unmanage all gadgets when leaving a directory, and then manage the ones that are needed for the new directory. This can be tricky, because we must deal with varying numbers of items in a directory. With the current approach, we cannot reuse the pixmaps, because the file an icon represents will change, requiring a different pixmap to hold the file name.

However, these are relatively minor details, and can be handled by re-implementing `ReadDirWorkProc()` just slightly. The following version of this function starts by checking for existing children of the XmRowColumn widget. If any children exist, these children are reused by specifying each child as the last argument to `CreateIcon()`. This function, which also must be changed, reuses the given widget instead of creating a new one. If additional widgets are required, they can be created by passing a `NULL` as the last argument to `CreateIcon()`.

The new version of `ReadDirWorkProc()` can be written as follows:

```
Boolean ReadDirWorkProc ( XtPointer clientData )
{
    struct dirent *entry = NULL;
    Widget     parent = ( Widget ) clientData;
    Widget     icon;
    WidgetList children;
    Cardinal   numChildren;

    DisplayBusyCursor ( XtParent ( parent ) );

    if ( !count )
    {
       /*
        * If this is is an initial call, find out how many
        * existing children there are.
        */

        count = 1; /* Avoid confusion in late mod call. */

        XtVaGetValues ( parent,
                        XmNchildren,    &children,
                        XmNnumChildren, &numChildren,
                        NULL );

        if ( numChildren )
        {
           /*
            * Read as many directory entries as we have children,
            * reusing the existing widgets.
            */

            count = 0;
            while ( count < numChildren &&
                    ( entry = readdir ( fd ) ) != NULL )
```

```
            {
                if ( !exclude ( entry->d_name ) )
                {
                    icon = CreateIcon ( entry->d_name,
                                        parent,
                                        GetType ( entry->d_name ),
                                        children[count] );

                    count++;
                }

                if ( ( count %50 ) == 0 )
                    DisplayBusyCursor ( XtParent ( parent ) );
            }

           /*
            * Manage the existing widgets in case some were not.
            */

            XtManageChildren ( children, count );

           /*
            * If entry is NULL, all items have been read. See if
            * there are any existing widgets left, and if so
            * unmanage them.
            */

            if ( !entry )
            {
                int diff = numChildren - count;

                XtUnmanageChildren ( &children[count], diff );

                HideBusyCursor ( XtParent ( parent ) );
                ReportTime ( "Cached Icons Created", TRUE );

                XtManageChild ( parent );

                closedir ( fd );

                return ( TRUE );
            }
        }
    }

   /*
    * If we get here,there must still be items to be displayed,
    * but no existing widgets, so proceed as before.
    */
```

```
    while ( ( count++ % 50 ) != 0 &&
            ( entry = readdir ( fd ) ) != NULL )
    {
        if ( !exclude ( entry->d_name ) )
            icon = CreateIcon ( entry->d_name,
                                parent,
                                GetType ( entry->d_name ),
                                NULL );
    }

    if ( entry && count && count <= 51 )
    {
        XtVaGetValues ( parent,
                        XmNchildren,    &children,
                        XmNnumChildren, &numChildren,
                        NULL );
        XtManageChildren ( children, numChildren );
        XtManageChild ( parent );

        XmUpdateDisplay ( parent );
        ReportTime ( "Initial icons created", TRUE );

        XSetWindowBackgroundPixmap ( XtDisplay ( parent ),
                                     XtWindow ( XtParent ( parent ) ),
                                     None );
        XtUnmanageChild ( parent );
    }

    if ( entry )
        return FALSE;

    XtVaGetValues ( parent,
                    XmNchildren, &children,
                    XmNnumChildren, &numChildren,
                    NULL );

    XSetWindowBackgroundPixmap ( XtDisplay(parent),
                                 XtWindow ( XtParent ( parent ) ),
                                 ParentRelative );
    XtManageChildren ( children, numChildren );
    XtManageChild ( parent );

    HideBusyCursor ( XtParent ( parent ) );
    ReportTime ( "Icons Created", TRUE );

    closedir ( fd );
    return ( TRUE );
}
```

The function `CreateIcon()` must be modified to accept an existing gadget (or widget). If an widget is provided, this function simply installs the pixmap into the existing widget. Otherwise, the function creates a new gadget, as before.

```
Widget CreateIcon ( char *name,
                    Widget parent,
                    FileType type,
                    Widget existing )
{
    Widget           icon;
    Pixmap           pix;
    XmString         label;
    XmFontList       fontlist;
    XFontStruct     *fs;
    XmFontType       fontType;
    Dimension        width, height;
    static XGCValues values;
    int              junk;
    Display         *display = XtDisplay ( parent );
    unsigned char    alignment;
    int              totalWidth, totalHeight;
    Pixmap           labelPixmap;

   /*
    * Get the pixmap for the file type.
    */

    if ( type == REGULAR_FILE )
        pix = GetFilePixmap ( parent );
    else
        pix = GetDirPixmap ( parent );

   /*
    * Change the label string on an existing widget or create
    * a new widget as needed.
    */

    if ( existing )
    {
        icon = existing;

        XtVaSetValues ( icon,
                        XtVaTypedArg, XmNlabelString,
                        XmRString,
                        name, strlen ( name ) + 1,
                        NULL );
  }
```

```
    else
    {
        icon = XtVaCreateWidget ( name,
                                   xmPushButtonGadgetClass,
                                   parent,
                                   XmNlabelType,       XmPIXMAP,
                                   XmNshadowThickness, 0,
                                   XmNfillOnArm,       FALSE,
                                   NULL );

         XtAddCallback ( icon, XmNactivateCallback,
                         SelectCallback, NULL );
     }

      if ( !gc )
      {
          /*
           * Create two GCs, one to draw the text and copy
           * the pixmaps and another that can be used to erase
           * a pixmap by filling it with the background
           * color of the label widget. Because the normal GC
           * is used by XmStringDraw, which modifies the font
           * attribute of the GC, allocate this GC using
           * XtAllocateGC() and specify GCFont as modifiable.
           */

          XtVaGetValues ( parent,
                          XmNforeground,  &values.foreground,
                          XmNbackground,  &values.background,
                          XmNdepth,       &depth,
                          NULL );

          gc = XtAllocateGC ( parent, depth,
                              GCForeground | GCBackground,
                              &values, GCFont, 0 );

          values.foreground = values.background;

          inverseGc = XtGetGC ( parent,
                                GCForeground | GCBackground,
                                &values );
      }

     /*
      * Get information needed to draw the label.
      */

      XtVaGetValues ( icon,
                      XmNlabelString, &label,
```

```
                    XmNfontList,    &fontlist,
                    XmNalignment,   &alignment,
                    NULL );

    fs = ( XFontStruct* ) XmFontListEntryGetFont ( fontlist,
                                                   &fontType );

    XSetFont ( XtDisplay ( parent ), gc, fs->fid );

   /*
    * Compute the size of the label string and the pixmap
    */

    XmStringExtent ( fontlist, label, &width, &height );

    totalWidth = 48 > width ? 48 : width;
    totalHeight = 48 + height + 10;

  /*
   * Create the final pixmap using the combined size and
   * fill the pixmap with the background color of the widget
   */

  labelPixmap = XCreatePixmap ( display,
                   RootWindowOfScreen ( XtScreen ( parent ) ),
                   totalWidth, totalHeight, depth );

  XFillRectangle ( display, labelPixmap,
                  inverseGc, 0, 0,
                  totalWidth, totalHeight );

  /*
   * Copy the Xpm-created pixmap into the larger pixmap and
   * then draw the string below the pixmap.
   */

  XCopyArea ( display, pix, labelPixmap,
             gc, 0, 0, 48, 48,
             ( totalWidth - 48 ) / 2,
             0 );

  XmStringDraw ( display, labelPixmap, fontlist, label,
                gc, 0, 48 + 10, totalWidth,
                alignment, XmSTRING_DIRECTION_L_TO_R, NULL );

  /*
   * Install the final pixmap in the widget.
   */

```

```
    XtVaSetValues ( icon,
                    XmNlabelPixmap, labelPixmap,
                    NULL );


   /*
    * Free the  string retrieved from the label widget.
    */

    XmStringFree ( label );

    return  ( icon );
}
```

The function `BrowseDirectory()` must also be changed to not destroy or unmanage the icons. The new version of `BrowseDirectory()` can be written like this:

```
void BrowseDirectory ( char *dir )
{
    WidgetList children;
    Cardinal   numChildren;
    int        i;
    XtAppContext app =
                 XtWidgetToApplicationContext ( rowColumn );

    ReportTime ( "Browsing new directory", FALSE );
    currentDirectory = XtNewString ( dir );

    if ( ( fd = opendir ( dir ) ) == NULL )
        return;

    SetCurrentDirectory ( ( char* ) dir );

   /*
    * Reset the work procedure by setting count
    * back to zero, and reinstall the work proc.
    */

    count = 0;

    XtAppAddWorkProc ( app,ReadDirWorkProc,
                       ( XtPointer ) rowColumn );
}
```

With these changes, the time required to browse a directory whose size is less than or equal to the largest directory previously browsed is faster than the previous versions. Figure 12.31 shows the time required to browse the "." icon in the dirview directory, a very brief 0.08 second. The same operation in the Xt directory takes 0.56 second, while browsing Xlib requires 2.69 seconds.

```
Starting:
Up:
   Elapsed Time = 0.300
   CPU Time     = 0.140
   System Time  = 0.070
Icons Created:
   Elapsed Time = 0.210
   CPU Time     = 0.060
   System Time  = 0.010
Browsing new directory:
Cached Icons Created:
   Elapsed Time = 0.080
   CPU Time     = 0.040
   System Time  = 0.020
```

Figure 12.31 Browsing into dirview directory.

12.10 Additional Suggestions

The changes described in the previous section produce far better performance than the original implementation of `dirview`. Still more improvements are possible, although they would require substantially more work. For example, the attempt in the previous section to cache gadgets was only moderately successful because while the gadgets can be cached, new pixmaps still have to be created for each gadget. A more dramatic improvement in performance could be made if we had a gadget that could handle a pixmap and label simultaneously. With such a gadget, we could return to the model in which only two pixmaps are needed. A gadget could be reused by simply changing the label string.

Although such a gadget does not exist in the current version of Motif (1.2.3), it may be available in future versions. Furthermore, one need not be limited to using the widgets and gadgets provided by Motif. It is always possible to write custom widgets and gadgets, although such an effort is outside the domain of this book. If writing a new widget or gadget is a possibility, we might also consider writing an icon panel widget that replaces the XmRowColumn widget or XmScrolledWindow in this example. Such a widget could take a list of strings, much like an XmList widget, but also display a pixmap above each label. A widget like this could be written in a general manner, so it would be useful to many people. Although it would require some work, the benefits to others should compensate for the development time required.

We can get some idea of the performance that could be gained by writing custom widgets or gadgets by just using an XmPushButton gadget for each item, without worrying about the label for each item. While a browser implemented in this way would not be very useful, we can get some idea of the performance implications, to decide if it is worthwhile designing and implementing a new widget or gadget.

The following exploratory implementation of `CreateIcon()` is much simpler than previous versions. This function simply installs a label and a pixmap in an existing gadget if provided. Alternately, it creates a gadget, if necessary. Of course, the label will be ignored if the Motif 1.2 XmPushButton gadget is used, but this is only an experiment.

```
Widget CreateIcon ( char * name, Widget parent,
                    FileType type, Widget existing )
{
    Widget icon;
    Pixmap pix;

   /*
    * Get the icon for the file type.
    */

    if ( type == REGULAR_FILE )
       pix = GetFilePixmap ( parent );
    else
       pix = GetDirPixmap(parent);

   /*
    * Change the label string and pixmap on an existing
    * widget or create a new widget as needed.
    */

    if ( existing )
    {
        icon = existing;

        XtVaSetValues ( icon,
                        XtVaTypedArg, XmNlabelString,
                        XmRString,
```

```
                          name, strlen ( name )+1,
                          XmNlabelPixmap, pix,
                          NULL );
    }
    else
    {
        icon = XtVaCreateWidget ( name,
                                  xmPushButtonGadgetClass,
                                  parent,
                                  XmNlabelType, XmPIXMAP,
                                  XmNlabelPixmap, pix,
                                  XmNshadowThickness, 0,
                                  XmNfillOnArm, FALSE,
                                  NULL);

        XtAddCallback ( icon, XmNactivateCallback,
                        SelectCallback, NULL );
    }
    return ( icon );
}
```

With this change, the program starts up more quickly in all cases. Figure 12.32 shows the time required to start the program in the dirview directory, and to browse the "." icon. Start-up time is now only 0.4 seconds and re-browsing the directory now takes only 0.03 seconds! It seems that this version, if completed by writing a custom widget, might be truly competitive with `ls`.

```
dirview
Starting:
Up:
   Elapsed Time = 0.310
   CPU Time     = 0.140
   System Time  = 0.070
Icons Created:
   Elapsed Time = 0.090
   CPU Time     = 0.050
   System Time  = 0.010
Browsing new directory:
Icons Created:
   Elapsed Time = 0.030
   CPU Time     = 0.020
   System Time  = 0.010
```

Figure 12.32 Time to browse `dirview` using a gadget.

Browsing the larger directories is also significantly faster. Figure 12.33 summarizes the times for various actions in each directory. We can see that in the worst case, start-up time in the Xlib directory is less than two and a half seconds, with the icons visible in 0.6 seconds. For more typical directories, the performance is much better, and the directory browser offers a very usable level of performance, even when compared against non-GUI solutions like `ls`.

Operation	Goal		Rev. 1	Rev 8	Icon Gadget
Window visible	0.3	dirview	0.77	0.34	0.34
		Xt	3.67	0.34	0.34
		Xlib	17.23	0.34	0.34
Icons visible	0.3	dirview	0.77	0.59	0.43
		Xt	3.67	0.81	0.63
		Xlib	17.23	0.81	0.63
Ready for interaction	0.3-1.0	dirview	0.77	0.59	0.43
		Xt	3.67	0.81	0.63
		Xlib	17.23	0.81	0.63
Completely Ready	0.3-1.0	dirview	0.77	0.59	0.43
		Xt	3.67	1.25	0.89
		Xlib	17.23	3.63	2.49
Browse file	0.3		< 0.30	< 0.3	< 0.3
Browse directory	0.3-1.0	dirview	0.77	0.08	0.03
		Xt	3.67	0.56	0.16
		Xlib	17.23	2.63	0.78
Scroll to new location	~0	dirview	~0	~0	~0
		Xt	slow	~0	~0
		Xlib	jerky	~0	~0

Figure 12.33 Times for a hypothetical labeled icon gadget.

As shown in Figure 12.33, this approach produces significant better performance, particularly when browsing from within an existing `dirview` window. Browsing the dirview directory, after the initial icons have been created now takes only 0.03 second, an amazingly short amount of time. Even for the Xlib directory, this operation takes only 0.78 second, which should be acceptable to most users.

Of course, exactly as written, this browser is not very useful. The icons are not labeled and all look alike. To benefit from what this experiment has shown, we must write a new gadget, which can be quite difficult if you do not have access to Motif source code. As this book goes to press, future versions of Motif are expected to solve this problem in two ways. First, new widgets should be easier to write, and the process of writing Motif widgets and gadgets will be documented. Second, a future version of Motif is expected to support a standard widget that displays text and a pixmap simultaneously. If your version of Motif supports these features, you should be able to take advantage of them to produce better performance.

12.11 Conclusion

This chapter describes a simple directory browser that has some characteristics common to many Motif programs. The example displays a browsable set of icons in a scrolled window. The program behaves well for small data sets, but like many programs, there is no upper limit on the amount of data a user might attempt to display. As the number of icons increases, both the start-up and runtime performance deteriorate rapidly.

The case study demonstrates a tuning process that ultimately produces a program whose performance is reasonable for even large data sets. Although the performance is always worse for larger amounts of data, the program is able to present the user with an interface within a constant period of time that is independent of the number of icons to be displayed.

We can summarize the stages of the tuning process as follows:

1. The original program was written with only minimal regard for performance. Most implementation choices were based on ease of programming (such as creating labeled icons using an XmRowColumn widget to contain a button and a label). The performance was adequate for small directories, but very slow for even moderate sized directories.

2. The first attempt at tuning moved the process of reading the directory and creating icons into a work procedure, to allow the window to come up quickly. The program also added an animated busy cursor. This effort succeeded in making the window appear immediately, and providing ongoing feedback, but at a cost of an even slower total time.

3. The third version of `dirview` reduced the amount of work to be done

by filtering out files that users should not be interested in browsing. The program also managed an initial set of icons to present the user with a full screen more quickly. In addition, all icons were managed in groups.

4. Next, we reduced the number of pixmaps being created and switched to gadgets within each XmRowColumn widget. This improved start-up and runtime performance and reduced the number of server requests.

5. Because gadgets seemed to help in this situation, the next step was to replace the icon built from multiple widgets with a single gadget. This step greatly improved performance, but created more pixmaps than version four.

6. The next step attacked both performance and usability issues by changing the browser to reuse the existing window rather than creating a new browser for each new directory. By redisplaying new directories in the existing window, the time required to start the process, initialize Xt, and create the basic interface was eliminated. We encountered a few problems along the way, including an unexpected regression in performance and a serious memory leak in the X server. The final version, however was faster and more usable for quickly navigating through the widget hierarchy.

7. The next step explored ways to reuse widgets instead of destroying and re-creating them each time the user changed to a new directory. This step produced some improvement in the program's performance when browsing into new directories.

8. The final step explored the potential benefits of writing a custom widget or gadget for this program. Creating interfaces from existing components is fine, and in most cases produces adequate performance. However, when large numbers of widgets are involved, or a program has special needs, writing a new widget can be the most efficient approach. Of course, writing a new widget or gadget can be a significant challenge, and it is often a good idea to be sure the effort will be worth-while before investing the time. In this case, it appears that a gadget that displays a pixmap and a label at once could provide substantial improvement in performance.

Getting Software Described in this Book

The source code for the examples described in this book is available free of charge to anyone with network access. The example source may be downloaded using the ftp command from ftp.prenhall.com. You may also find the sources at other ftp sites. On ftp.prenhall.com, the examples can be found under in directory pub/software/doug_young, in a compressed tar file named young.debug.tar.Z.

Assuming you have access to the Internet, you can download the software using the following sequence of commands. (Type "ftp" or "anonymous" at the login prompt, provide and your name, email address, or system name as a password, as requested.)

```
% ftp ftp.prenhall.com
> cd pub/software/doug_young
> binary
> get young.debug.tar.Z
> quit
```

Once you have the compressed tar file, you can unpack the files with the commands:

```
% uncompress young.debug.tar.Z
% tar xvf young.debug.tar
```

These commands will create a directory named MotifDebug, which contains subdirectories for each chapter in this book, as well as several other files and directories. Look at the README file for additional information about the software, instructions on how to build the examples, and so on.

Ordering Example Source from Prentice Hall

For those without network access, Prentice Hall can provide copies of the software for a small fee. See the reply card in the back of this book for details. Prentice Hall distributes the software on an IBM disk. This software is expected to run on a UNIX system, and should be copied from your PC to a UNIX system. As distributed by Prentice Hall, the software is packed into a single file, known as a "shell archive". The examples are in an ASCII file named examples.shar. To unpack this file, copy examples.shar from your PC to a UNIX system. Then type the following command in a terminal window:

```
% sh debug.shar
```

This command creates the MotifDebug directory as described above. Check the README file for up-to-date information and instructions for building the software.

The Xpm Library

The Xpm library used by some examples in this book is distributed with X as contributed software. Some vendors may make this package available on their systems, but others may not, because it is not a standard part of the X Window System. If you do not have it, the sources to Xpm can be downloaded from ftp.x.org. The package includes documentation.

Editres

Editres is available as part of the X11R5 distribution.

XtGeo

XtGeo can be downloaded from ftp.prenhall.com in the same directory as the source for this book,. Download the file xtgeo.tar.Z.

Appres

Appres is available as part of the X11R5 distribution.

Xscope

Xscope is available as part of the X11R5 distribution.

Xmon

Xmonui and xmond are available as a contributed part of the X11R5 distribution.

Dbmalloc

The dbmalloc library can be found on various ftp sites as part of volume 32 of the usenet sources. This library is also available from ftp.prenhall.com in the same directory as the sources of this book, as described above. Download the file dbmalloc.tar.Z.

Searching the Internet

Network addresses, and the location of the software described here is subject to change from time to time. Many of these packages may also be available from other locations on the Internet. There are many books that describe how to navigate the Internet and find whatever you are looking for. If you have trouble locating any of this software, one of these books may help you locate the package you need.

Bibliography

Asente90 Asente, Paul, and Ralph Swick, *The X Window System Toolkit*, DEC Press, 1990.

Bently82 Bently, Jon, *Writing Efficient Programs*, Prentice Hall, 1982.

Dowd93 Dowd, Kevin, *High Performance Computing*, O'Reilly & Associates, 1993.

Droms90 Droms, Ralph and A. Wayne Dyksen, "Performance Measurements of the X Window System Protocol", *Software Practice and Experience*, Vol. 20, No. S2, October, 1990.

Foley82 Foley, J.D., and A. Van Dam, *Fundamentals of Interactive Computer Graphics*, Addison-Wesley, 1982.

Georges94 George, Alistair, and Mark Riches, *Advanced Motif Programming*, Prentice Hall, 1994.

Jones89 Jones, Oliver, *Introduction to the X Window System*, Prentice Hall, 1989.

Kobara91 Kobara, Shiz, *Visual Design with OSF/Motif*, Addison-Wesley, 1991.

Lee94 Lee, Ken, "Software Engineering for X Application Performance", *The X Journal*, May/June 1994.

Maguire93 Maguire, Steve, *Writing Solid Code*, Microsoft Press, 1993.

Mansfield93 Mansfield, Niall, *The Joy of X*, Addison Wesley, 1993.

Martin92 Stitt, Martin, *Debugging: Creative Techniques and Tools for Software Repair*, John Wiley, 1992.

McConnell93 McConnell, Steve, *Code Complete*, Microsoft Press, 1993.

McCormack90 McCormack, Joel, "Writing Fast X Servers for Dumb Color Frame Buffers", *Software Practice and Experience*, Vol. 20, No. S2, October, 1990.

McMinds93 McMinds, Donald, Mastering Motif Widgets, Addison-Wesley, 1993

Mulder Mulder, Art, *How To Maximize the Performance of X*, monthly posting to comp.windows.x newsgroup.

OSF94 *OSF/Motif Programmer's Guide*, *OSF/Motif Programmer's Reference*, *OSF/Motif Style Guide*, Prentice Hall, 1994.

Peterson92 Peterson, Chris, and Sharon Chang, "Improving X Application Performance", *The X Resource*, Issue 3, Summer 1992.

Scheifler92 Scheifler, Robert W. and James Gettys, *X Window System*, Second Edition, DEC Press, 1992.

Smith90 Smith, Connie U., *Performance Engineering of Software Systems*, Addison-Wesley 1990.

Thielen92 Thielen, David, *No Bugs*, Addison Wesley, 1992

Ward89 Ward, Robert, *A Programmer's Introduction to Debugging C,* R & D Publications, 1989.

Young94 Young, Douglas, *The X Window System, Programming and Applications with Xt, Second OSF/Motif Edition*, Prentice Hall, 1994.

Young92 Young, Douglas, *Object-Oriented Programming with C++ and OSF/Motif*, Prentice Hall, 1992.

Index

A

B

C

D

E

F

G

H

I

L

M

N

P

R

S

T

U

V

W

X